Published by: Ronald B. Shaheed, Charlotte, NC.

Copyright © 2025 by Ronald B. Shaheed

Library of Congress Control Number: 2025911964.

ISBN: 979-8-9874119-0-2

Book cover design by Zuhairah Shaheed.

Acknowledgements

I extend my heartfelt gratitude to Imam Shaheed Al-Ghani of Racine, Wisconsin—my trusted companion on the road during our many years of travel from Wisconsin to the south suburbs of Chicago to meet with Imam W. Deen Mohammed. I also honor the memory of Khalid Morocco of Chicago (may Allah forgive his shortcomings and grant him Paradise), both of whom were instrumental in helping gather the content shared in this publication. Their presence and participation in our private sessions with Imam W. Deen Mohammed—spanning nearly four years—were invaluable.

I am deeply thankful to Imam Nasir Ahmad for his unwavering dedication in transcribing much of the material I have drawn upon throughout my published works. On numerous occasions, I have expressed to him that his tireless efforts are what have made my work possible. May G_d bless him abundantly in this life and the next. I am also sincerely thankful to my dear brothers in faith, Imam Ibraheem Abdul Malik of Savannah, Georgia, and Imam Qaid Young of Pittsburgh, Pennsylvania, for their encouragement and valuable assistance in proofreading this work. May Allah reward them with the best of this life and the Hereafter.

I also extend my deepest gratitude to my beloved wife, Zuhairah, whose unwavering support and encouragement have been a constant throughout the journey of completing this publication—as they have been in all of my endeavors. In addition to her steadfast emotional support, she contributed her expertise as the graphic designer of this book, as she has for the majority of my published works. May Allah bestow upon her His Mercy and Care in this life and in the Hereafter.

Contents

(On September 19, 2007, Imam Mohammed said to us, Khalid Morocco, Imam Shaheed Al-Ghani, and Imam Ronald B. Shaheed):

"I have told you all about the burden that I have on my heart and any way you can help, help. What you record of me I feel good about it because I don't want everything to die with me and be lost. And what I share with you all, I'll give it to you in writing that it's your responsibility. You have no obligation to anybody, my office, the Ministry, The Mosque Cares, or anything. (If you want to appeal to the people to finance putting some of it in writing or all of it writing for the future, you can do that with my support.

But you have no obligation to give the responsibility to anybody, and that includes the money. If you get money for it, use it for yourself. If you want to give a donation from it, that's up to you all. I'm serious! This is not something I'm just thinking about! I looked at it a long time ago. Yes, this is a project for you all. You don't owe anybody anything, not me, nobody anything. It's a service. It's valuable. This is my way, and I believe G_d is moving me to do this. This is my way of putting it into your charge. And don't think that some of this doesn't have a place on the bookshelves, or libraries of higher institutions of knowledge, higher institutions of learning."

Foreword

The title of this book is both symbolic and literal. It reflects the spiritual and intellectual wealth uncovered during our weekly Thursday visits with Imam W. Deen Mohammed in the final years of his life. These sessions—private, profound, and often deeply personal—offered insights not only into his vast body of knowledge but also into his inner world, where revelation met reflection, and vision met responsibility. I have been a follower and student of Imam W. Deen Mohammed since 1975, and my relationship of active service spanned over eighteen years. I assisted him in the coordination of his university lectures and witnessed his tireless efforts in fostering interfaith relations. But it was in those Thursday conversations— recorded in the quiet of his home—that I encountered the rarest jewel: the unfiltered, evolving, and intimate thoughts of a man entrusted with reshaping the spiritual identity of a people. What you hold in your hands is more than a book. It is a living document, part memoir, part tafsir (commentary on Qur'an), part testimony.

The Treasure Under the Wall: Thursdays with the Imam emerged from the random, private conversations that we had with Imam W. Deen Mohammed for nearly four years, that he passed on to us as a gift and responsibility. He said he hoped we would put some of this "gift" that he gave us into book form and make it available to the world at large, but the responsibility was solely ours.

The publications that emerged from these recordings serve not merely as religious commentary, but as a blueprint for an American Muslim consciousness rooted in Qur'anic guidance, universal human values, and the sacred responsibility of leadership. The implications of this journey are profound. I have become, by the blessing of G_d, one of the custodians of Imam Mohammed's legacy—tasked with carrying forward his voice with authenticity and care. His teachings continue to resonate, not only within the community he nurtured but also across religious, academic, and cultural spheres that still hunger for the clarity and depth he offered. This book invites you to sit with us on those Thursdays, to hear, to reflect, and perhaps, to find your own treasure beneath the wall. We pray it opens for you a door to new understanding, just as it did for us.

In reality, this book is more than just a collection of commentary or reflections. It is a journey, quiet, intimate, and deeply personal. These pages are drawn from moments spent in quiet conversations, listening, learning, and simply being present. Each Thursday held a special rhythm, a sacred pause in the chaos of the week. The Imam's words, always profound and insightful, carried a weight that lingered far beyond the conversations themselves. They were not just teachings, but invitations: to think more deeply, to feel more honestly, and to live more intentionally and responsibly.

This book does not claim to have all the answers. Instead, it offers glimpses of wisdom discovered beneath the surface of ordinary days. Like a hidden treasure under an old wall, forgotten by time, yet glowing with quiet truth, these moments were uncovered not by force, but by presence.

May these reflections serve as gentle reminders of the treasures waiting to be found in your own life. And may you, too, find your Thursdays.

Ronald B. Shaheed, 2025

Introduction

(The most effective way to introduce Imam W. Deen Mohammed is perhaps with the words of Imam W. Deen Mohammed, himself. Consequently, the introduction that follows is the direct words of Imam W. Deen Mohammed wherein he explains the various aspects and factors in his life that led to his becoming the leader of the largest Islamic community in America).

I will begin my story by saying that I was born in 1933 in this new creation in America, and that is exactly what it is, a new creation called, the Nation of Islam. The Nation of Islam started, as it is recorded in our community, in 1930. We have records showing that there was temple activity in early 1931. It started in Detroit, Michigan, in what was called the Black Bottom. I hate to say, slums, because there were really decent, poor people in that area, but they called it the slums of Detroit, poor people both in money or in the pocket, and poor in education. These were the people that the stranger (Mr. Fard) came to. I call him a stranger because he was not native American. He came from outside of America. It is said that he came from Turkey. It is also said that he came from what is called now Lahore, Pakistan, and I tend to believe that he was not Turkish. I think the reason for believing he was Turkish is that our flag or our national symbol was a flag looking exactly like the Turkish flag, except the moon is a new moon and the Turkish flag is an old moon, with the crescent on the left, and our crescent is on the right, the new moon.

At this point, I would like to say that the Honorable Elijah Mohammed made it clear that we were not yet established in Al-Islam popular, or what you would say is true Al-Islam. He would say, "We are a baby nation", when Muslims would come from abroad (whether they came from Egypt, Saudi Arabia, Palestine, Lebanon), and they would come and ask him, "What is the difference?" I remember once being at the house and twenty-one young students from the Muslim Student Association that had recently formed in the United States and Canada, were at table of my father. He had his office in the house. He had a big house at that time. He started off with a little house in a garage on the alley. That is how it started out, not lit by electricity, but by kerosene lamps, candles, and a big, pot belly stove. I remember as a little kid about seven, or eight years old, smelling acorn squash pie. There was only a few of us and they cooked two acorn squash pies, I believe, on top of that stove, and they served them to us. We had a little treat.

"You Have to be Resurrected In the Bible"

Every time we would meet when we were a small group, there would be some treats for us to eat and a very good spirit. We were a happy group when we started out. The visitors would come from overseas and they would ask my father, "Why is there such a difference in your religion? This is not what we know." He said, "Well, brothers, this is a baby nation". That is what he would say to them, and they would buy it. I guess they said, "At least we have hope. He said it is a baby nation. When it gets older, it will perform better, maybe." At that time, we were not taught from the Qur'an. We were taught from the Bible, and the mysterious teacher from abroad said the reason for us being taught from the Bible was because, "You died in the Bible. You have to be resurrected in the Bible." So, the minister would get up and instead of teaching Al-Islam, he's teaching from the Bible, but he is encouraging us to be a separate people, or a separate nation, to separate from the evil, white world. "Come out of the evil, white world!" That was the message. It was a message of separation, given the circumstances that we were experiencing in the 1930's, in the 1940's, in the 1960's up to the last of the 1960's when changes came, and the two laws, one for blacks and one for whites, were struck down. Up until that time, I stood solidly in support of an organization like that.

Respect for Those Who Wanted to Separate

There were many African Americans who thought like that, not all poor either. Paul Robeson was one who disagreed with his citizenship in the United States, and he joined the Communists and was ordered out of the country. He went to China and lived in China for a good while, and he came back before he died. He died in his own homeland here in the United States of America. What I am saying now is to do justice by our people we have to respect those who said, "This land offers me nothing but shame. I want pride and respect as a human person, so let us separate!" I respect those who wanted to separate. They led me. I was a boy. I had no say in the matter. I was a small boy. I could not vote, but if I could have voted, I think I would have told them that your position is justified based upon the treatment of our people in America, and denial of full rights, citizenship rights to us. I would have told them, if I could have spoken or had a chance to speak as an adult or a youngster, "Your position is justified! I hope that we can work this out, so we can have a real future in this country, but for right now I'm agreeing with you to separate! But I hope we can change the country, so we all can live together." With my nature and spirit, I think that is what I would have asked for.

So, we asked for separation and at one point the Honorable Elijah Mohammed asked for separate states. Now, I'm a young man. I am no more than 8 or 9 years old, and I said to myself, "This country went to war. The people of this country went to war with each other. They killed each other. They lost fathers, mothers, sons and daughters, over just that, whether there is going to be a separation, two Americas or one." The Civil war, that is what I was referring to, and I said to myself, "If they fought each other over that and those who wanted to be separated loss, I know blacks are not going to win against all the whites and have separate states of their own". I couldn't believe in it. I didn't accept it. In my heart, I couldn't believe in it. In my heart, I didn't accept that.

The Honorable Elijah Mohammed, our leader at that time, who was leading this effort to separate from America, one day at the table with his big staff, his top leaders in the Nation of Islam, he said, "Brothers, we ask for separate states. We know we are not going to get it. But we just want to be on record for taking that position", and then I felt comfortable. I said, "Okay, I know it is not real for him. It's not reality. This is a strategy."

Three Years of Education In the South

So, I felt very comfortable with my father, our leader at that time, that he knew what he was doing. He was a wise leader, not formally educated. He never was formally educated. He told us he only got three years of education in the South. He said after he got three years he had to come and help his father on the farm. He said, "I taught myself to read. I taught myself to write a decent handwriting". So, he was a self-taught person and very smart, but as you know, he met his teacher from abroad, who was called Fard, spelled F-a-r-d, not F-a-r-a-d but is pronounced Farad. The name Fard, though he wrote it in English, it means a John Doe. It means just a person, so that tells us a lot about him. He came in as a stranger. He didn't give his real name. He called himself Mr. John Doe or Mr. Fard, a person.

Now, I studied him for over thirty years. I studied his mind. How do you study a person's mind? Study their language, study their expressions, study their aspirations, what they want, and you can actually learn their mind. You can learn that person. You can know that person better than those who perhaps lived with the person for thirty years, but didn't study them, did not study their expressions, their mind, etc. So, I feel I know him, and I know him so well I know what he would and would not do.

Blacks Are Outside of the Mind Needed to Establish Community

I know he copied a formula for establishing a people who were outside of human intelligence regarding how they should establish themselves as a community. So, he knew that African Americans were outside of the mind and intelligence that is needed to establish ourselves as a community, and his purpose was to situate us mentally and sentimentally so that we would strive hard to get ourselves established as a community. In my thinking, community means that we ourselves be responsible for our homes and for our neighborhoods. That is what he wanted. He wanted to condition us to go forward and to one day be successful in establishing our home life and also our community life, be responsible for our own neighborhoods, for the businesses in those neighborhoods as well as for the decency in those neighborhoods, to establish decency and also business. He worked hard to contain us in a language environment that was designed to make us decent, righteous, truthful, just by ourselves and just by others. He said, "If you work for a white man", that he called the Devil, "give him an honest day's work." He said, "Don't cheat anybody." There are witnesses that know this teaching like I do.

Mr. Fard's Role and Formula

Lastly, he got his formula and also his Temple model from the Bible, and his role as a savior from the Bible. He came in the role of the savior in the Bible, the New Testament, and that savior is in the Old Testament, if you understand it. And he came also saying that he came to save the stolen property. What he did was charge the white man with stealing the African American or the black people of America but not stealing them physically from the land. We are not talking about bringing them from Africa as slaves. We mean raising them as babies on the plantation without the knowledge of their forefathers' culture, religion, or whatever. So, they were completely cut off from their past life as a people, and you know a people are constituted in a certain way. If you are from the people of France, you are constituted in that way. If you are from any other country, you are constituted in that way. From the Niger river, Ghana or wherever we came from, we were constituted as a people

12

at one time. If it was on no more than a tribal level, we were constituted as a people.

A Whole People Stolen From G_d

So, Mr. Fard said by taking Africans from Africa to America and raising them as babies on plantations and not allowing them to be taught how they should be constituted as a people, they stole a whole people from G_d, and he was coming from the Bible. The Bible says, *"Will a man rob G_d? Yet you have stolen this whole people."* So, he came with all of that. There were certain circumstances already existing in Detroit for him to feed on, too. There was a big black preacher. I say black, African American, but he was also black in color, pigmentation, a big African American preacher who presented himself as Father Divine. He told his congregation (I have read these words myself), "If you want to see Jesus Christ look at me." That tells us that he was dissatisfied, wasn't he? He was in the Church, he was in Christianity, but he was dissatisfied with the way G_d was perceived by his people.

He thought that G_d was presented to his people as a white man, so he presented himself as a black man to counter that. So, Mr. Fard was aware of all that and he was aware of Booker T. Washington, who was in that same time, too. Booker T. Washington was working to establish us to have some sense of industry where we would discipline ourselves. Booker T. Washington established drill the same way the Nation of Islam established drill. He established drill before the Nation of Islam, so Mr. Fard copied him, too. He copied Father Divine, and he copied Booker T. Washington's program for training and instilling discipline in blacks in making them industrious. He copied that, too.

He also copied Noble Drew Ali's connection with Al-Islam. Drew Ali came just a few years before Mr. Fard, also. Noble Drew Ali established an organization he called the Moorish Science Temple. He used the word, temple, first, not Mr. Fard. He didn't have the Qur'an, and likewise Mr. Fard didn't have the Qur'an taught to us, but he gave the Qur'an to my father. I always saw one high on the wall, attached to a little ceiling molding that went around the ceiling. He had it nailed up there on a string, a nice cord, and it was attached to the Qur'an in a green, velvet pouch. That is where the Qur'an was and that is where I saw it. We didn't take it down into our hands.

However, we saw a picture of Mr. Fard holding it in his hands, looking very pious and devoted to what he was reading, showing his face from the side. That is the picture that we had of him. I am going to end with this because I cannot tell it all at this time. He wrote lessons and teachings for his students. He called all of us students. You could not join the Nation of Islam without first passing the student enrollment. Everybody was called student. He said the student who best works out this problem will be rewarded with so much money. I forget the amount of money, but it was a good amount of money, and he said, "A family Qur'an Shareef." Shareef means honorable. We have many names for our holy book, Generous Qur'an, Noble Qur'an, etc. So, he used this name, noble. That tells me that if the highest prize was the Qur'an, then what he wanted most was for his students to qualify to read and devote themselves to the Qur'an, the holy book of the Muslims. He wanted that to come, one day, in the future. He put the Qur'an above all his esoteric teachings, all his secret language teachings, or locked up language teachings.

The Thought of Going On My Own

I grappled with the thought of going on my own. I was put in prison for refusing a Selective Service order as a conscientious objector. This was in 1960. While in prison, I'm alone with my thoughts, so I'm figuring out how am I going to live with this new mind of mine that cannot accept that Mr. Fard is G_d. I love him and appreciate what he did for us, but I can't accept that he is G_d. I wasn't coming from Qur'an. I was coming from my own heart and nature, and I just couldn't accept that he was G_d. I said, "My father told us that Jesus Christ is not G_d, and he is a man, and he gives us another man, and he says, "This is G_d." So, that was bothering me. It was troubling my mind, and I could not live with it any longer. I said, "When I get out of prison, I'm going to have to tell my father I can't live with this any longer". That is when it started, but I did not really start to think as a leader. I was thinking just as my father's son. I did not start to think as a leader until I saw my father's organization in serious trouble. It had begun to be called the Black Mafia in Philadelphia, Kansas City, and in Detroit. Our members were charged with establishing a crime organization called the Black Mafia.

The FBI was aware of that. I did not know that they were aware of that until I reported some real serious things that were sent to me by people who knew me, personally. So, they mailed this evidence to me and left it in my hands. I took it to the FBI because it was very serious. It was at that time that I started thinking as a leader. I wanted to save our community, and I think the seeds were planted in me already. I was named after the man that they called the savior, or G_d in person, in the flesh, incarnate, and I was also told that my parents had to make a promise to this man, this mystic, mysterious man. I do not want to say the mystic because that might carry some other things. He was not a holy man, that is for sure, but he was mysterious. This mysterious man told my parents I was going to help my father. This is what my parents told me, and my sister, next to the oldest sister, she knew that, and she was very serious about it. When she saw me playing outside just as a normal child, she would holler to me and say, "Wallace, stop playing with those boys! You know you're supposed to help your father one day! You have the name of our savior!" She would actually tell me that. This is going to have some effect on a child's mind and spirit, even though I couldn't understand it. As a child, I couldn't understand it. It was too much for me to understand, but it had an effect. My parents told me, "He (Fard) told us to promise him that we would raise you to be a helper to your father, and to him"; not just my father, but to my father and to him. My father told me once, he said, "Our savior told me to promise him that we would let you help us with this work", meaning himself and our savior. So, in some ways I think that was working in me, too, and then I saw the problem in the community, in the Nation of Islam. I saw it headed for destruction, loss of all our credits that we had built up as decent, law-abiding people, not giving ourselves to crime. So, when I saw that, then I started to feel that I should stand, I should work, I should do something to protect the Nation of Islam for the future. That is how it started.

The People Who Walk In Darkness

There was a Muslim who was a slave in America. He was a slave, and he was mentioned in this book I read, *The People Who Walk in Darkness Have Seen a Great Light*, from the Bible, and the writer was a German man. This German man was writing about us, the plight of black people up from slavery and he mentioned Omar Ibn Sayyid. Since I initially mentioned these things, some have done research, and we have books out about Omar Ibn Sayyid by Muslims from our community, the followers of the Honorable Elijah Mohammed and myself. So anyway, he said Omar Ibn Sayyid was put in prison, and they noticed that he wrote a language that was foreign on his prison cell wall. When they finally got somebody to translate it for them, it was the Qur'an, but it was also the Bible. It said he was doing a comparison of Qur'an and Bible. When I read that it went right into me. Naturally, I have my own personal interest, but it was more than that. It was like the spirit was pushing it right into me, and it has influenced me up to this time. It is still influencing me with a desire to write a comparison.

I was already doing a comparison, not doing it as a project, but doing it for my own satisfaction. I took it to Libya, two Bibles, and strangely, both Bibles were gifts to me. One was a regular Bible with a black cover. The other one was white but had a fine, white cover. It looked almost like leather, but it was not. It was something over cardboard that made it look like leather. I was studying out of both of those Bibles and making a comparison. Those were the Bibles I had, and I said I'm going to read it all the way through without stopping to question it or anything, and that is what I did. I started with the black one and I read it all the way. I didn't question a thing, just read it straight through to the end of Revelation. I then took the white one with me to Libya, and I knew I would have plenty of time in the hotels and everything to read it carefully, so I did. I studied the white one carefully. I read the black one straight through like I promised myself. I made a promise to myself that I would not interrupt it to question anything, just read it continuously.

My Mother, Clara Mohammed, Put the Love of Nature In Me

It just happened that I started on the black one reading it and ended up with the white one questioning it. But when I finished the Bible, I was convinced that the Bible was a holy book, not like what Mr. Fard said. You see, I am not exactly his student. I am his student and somebody else's student, my own student and his student. I am my own student and the world's student, the universe's student. I study the universe, and I have a soul, a spirit, that just embraces everything.

I have been that way ever since I was a little boy. I love nature, and I think it must have been my mother, Clara Mohammed, who put it in me, the way she carried herself and everything. She was a very sincere, church woman, and she wanted me to follow my father, "And obey his teachings", she said. But I do not know. It is strange even to me. My mind even as a child did not want to accept anything if it did not make sense. I would not believe it just because you said it. It had to make sense, and I was a person who respected everybody, especially my mother and father. I respected all grown-ups, and I even had respect for everything. Now that is strange, but that is the kind of person I was.

16

She Was Really Devoted

So, that is just my nature, and I have always been like that. My brother, Elijah, he would always say, "His mind, you never know what is on his mind. He would be studying a tree leaf." He would be exaggerating, but I was definitely different. So really, I think prayer is powerful, and I do believe that the best of my parents' nature went into me for this religion, and I think believers were praying for me. Prayer is powerful, and I know Mr. Fard prayed for me. In fact, I believe his whole purpose for coming was not to produce Elijah Mohammed, or the Nation of Islam, but to produce me, because after I was born, he left.

I believe prayers brought G_d's blessings into my mother's womb and made me the person I am, and she was different. She was really serious. She was really devoted. Nothing could make her budge in any way to take her off course or make her think differently, and my father was the same way. I heard her call him stubborn once, behind his back. She said, "He is just stubborn! I told him he should not go out there in that bad weather with that little coat on. He is just stubborn!" But he had gone outside already, and really, she was like, "Can you help me with him?" The boys, we were there in the house. I think she was making a plea, because otherwise she would not even have said that little thing. That is the strongest language I think she ever used around us with reference to him.

She would always be covering for him and justifying what he was doing, but by that time he was up in age, and she was trying to keep him from going out in the rain. He would go out into the rain, and she would say, "You need an umbrella or something!" But he would be in a hurry and would go out in the winter with his collar open. Now he normally would not do that. All his years he was just well-dressed, but he got a little sloppy at the end of the road, and she said, "Look at him going out there in that bad weather (it was wintertime) with his coat and his collar open like that! He is just stubborn!" She had been working on him, telling him, "Do not go out like that!" We don't know. Only G_d knows how to explain everything that happens. We can guess and feel, and I do not know, but I do know that prayer is powerful. I have come to believe it very strongly during the last ten or fifteen years of my life. I started reflecting on what was going on, what was happening over the years, and the main answer is prayer.

I Have Nothing Except What G_d Gave Me

You have to have the right attitude, the right condition of mind, soul, and spirit. You have to be in a good human condition for G_d to bless you with His great blessings. "Are you bragging that G_d blessed you with His great blessings?" No, I am not bragging. Every time I think of how I have been blessed my soul is making sajda (prostration). I am making sajda inside my body. I humble myself completely to G_d, because I know I have nothing except what G_d gave me. I have nothing and I wonder, "Why me?" I am nothing! I came from a man from Georgia. He was nobody. He couldn't stand the depression times. He couldn't come home to see his wife and children with no money, so he stayed out in the streets and drank all the time, so he would not have to be conscious of it, no more than he had to. My mother told me, "Son, I had to go out and find him in the streets and bring him home on my shoulders." She was a strong woman. I saw her carry a hundred pounds of beans up the steps. Yes, my momma carried a hundred pounds of beans. That was during the time when they were rationing food and the Honorable Elijah Mohammed told us to store food away, to put food away. I was too small to carry that hundred-pound bag, but she would carry it.

She told me, "Son, I used to carry your father on my shoulder, take him to the bed and push him off my shoulder onto the bed. He would fall upon the bed and that is where he would stay until he woke up the next day." She was telling me that not to tell me my father was a drunkard. She was telling me that to tell me that what my father received from Mr. Fard, W. F. Muhammad, or W. D. Fard, made such a change in his life that we should be so happy that happened; because, if that hadn't happened, we would have a drunk for a father. That is what my mother was telling me. That is what I came from. I was born from him. I was born to him. That was my father, and I was born to Clara Mohammed, who never received more than seven grades of education. She said, "Son, the highest I was able to go in school was the seventh grade." My father told us the highest he was able to go in school was the third grade, not because they were ignorant, but because they had to work in the fields. Their parents told them to work in the fields, I guess, or their boss told them, "Look, you are not bringing enough in! You had better put those children out there in the field to help you!" So, they had to go to the field with their parents to work.

A Tough Little Woman

My mother (Clara Mohammed) would be ready to take a stick and beat you saying, "You don't come over to my house looking like that! You don't come in here dressed like that! Now, you've got to get out of here!" And she would be showing anger, no love. Many women came from love. She came from anger or hate. She came from hate and decency. She hated indecency! A woman got in an argument with her. I guess I was about eight or nine years old. Suddenly, I'm hearing loud voices outside, on the back porch, in one of our houses that we lived in, on the second level. She said, "I will be beat you, not only your child!" And I heard some foot sounds running up and down. She chased that woman up to the third floor. She was a tough little woman. You would have to kill her. She would fight and Allah protected her, because there's always somebody who will kill you, and it would be the person you least think capable of doing it.

"Am I That Blued-eyed Devil?"

I was given three years and did fifteen months in prison because I followed my father. The judge said, "The boy is dominated by his father. I'm going to give him three years." He was trying to help me, wasn't he? But do you know what he said right behind that? "I will recommend parole." That is what he said immediately, right behind that. I did not make it the first time. The second time I came up they gave me parole. The first time I came up for parole one of the representatives of the parole board was a blued-eyed man. I mean bright, shiny, blue, and he looked at me, put his head toward me and asked, "Am I that blued-eyed devil?" And he was bucking his eyes. I said, "No, you are not the blue-eyed devil, to me!" And it looked like he said, "I was not completely satisfied with that answer!" The look on his face was like, "I'm not completely satisfied with your answer!" But right after that they did not ask me anything else and did nothing else. They said, "We will consider you being given parole, and you will hear from us." I heard from them alright, it was not long, "Denied!"

I went up the second time and they hardly asked me anything. They just asked me how I was doing, "We will recommend parole," that is what they told me. I was paroled in less than a couple of weeks behind that. They gave me my parole date and everything. So actually, I did no more than about fourteen months and maybe a few days in the federal prison. However, I did like two or three weeks at first, in Chicago County Jail and guess what? When they took my blood for the medical to make sure you don't have any contagious disease or something I guess, it was a brother who accused me of being at a dance. I know his name very well, but I can't think of it right now. He accused me and remained my friend, no bad feelings or anything. Captain Shariff said, "Brother Wallace, the Messenger's son, you are accused of going to a dance at night. Is that true?" I said, "No sir!" I had to choose between the sin of lying and the sin of hurting my father and my mother, so I chose, and I said, "No sir!" He said, "We have a witness." I knew who it was because he was there. I saw him. I said, "You have a witness? Well, if he was there, you don't need a witness from me. He was there. He said he was there". So, he (Captain Shariff) couldn't do anything. That stopped him. He did not know what to do with me, so he let me go. "You may have your seat," that is what he told me. So, that brother became more my friend after that than he was before. So, anyway, this is after all of that. I'm going to prison now, maybe a year or so after that, and he's taking my blood. He saw me and I said, "Brother, I'm surprised to see you here doing this". He said, "Yes". He was one of the first persons I saw. After they searched me and took my belongings, next, I was sent to him. We were friends before that time and even became stronger friends after that. Right now, if we would meet, his face would be lit up and mine, too. We would be greeting each other, happy to see each other.

Inspiration From a Variety of Things

G_d has blessed me ever since I stood up as a young man. I don't know how old I was, in Chicago, on 5335 Greenwood. My friend urged me to go up and speak. It was a night where they invited you to come up and express yourself to see if you're qualified to be a minister. That was the practice back there. So, my friend shamed me out of sitting there. I was very shy, and I got up there trembling almost, but when I stood up there it looked like I could feel the audience, what it was thinking, what it was feeling. And as I spoke, I would respond to what I felt from the audience. So, I've always had this and I can feel you. So, I'm just caught up in this thing, you know.

My inspiration came from a great big variety of things. It came mainly from my study of Scripture and mythology, not just the Qur'an. But Qur'an, Bible, mythology, and spiritual thinkers on the search for truth or meaning, that is what I was searching for. So, I found a book that was on the search for meaning and I read that book, and I really liked it a lot. It kind of centered around the Bible, *"In the beginning there was the Word"*, but they did not use Bible. They just went right to the subject without making any reference to where they were coming from. *Logos,* that was the name of the book. And the word, logos, is related to logic and language, the Bible, *"In the beginning there was the word."* It was just a lot of books, but mainly mythology.

I started with Asian mythology, because I knew Mr. Fard was from Asia, but also, I went to African mythology. My mind got interested, so I just started reading mythology, Greek mythology, of course, and world mythology, but mainly Asia and the Mediterranean areas, a little bit of Africa, not too much into Africa. I went into Africa for other reasons, but when I was searching for understanding Mr. Fard's language and to understand Bible myths, I went to these areas: Asia, and the Mediterranean mostly, the Greeks (they are in the Mediterranean area) to understand the logic. But ancient Egypt was very attractive. I went into that much later. It was like maybe twenty-five years or more later in my leadership that I was attracted to go to Egypt to study Egyptian mythology, and do you know what clicked? In the Bible, Mary was told to, *"Flee to Egypt with your child".* That started it. It said, *"Flee to Egypt with your child.* They copied the Egyptian, Pharaoh strategy for governing the masses of the people, his scheme for governing the masses of the people." That is what came to my mind almost immediately, because I remembered reading in a book that to come into Cairo, you couldn't get into it until you answered the questions of the Oracle. And the Oracle would ask you, "What walks on four, then on two and then on one?" And if you answered correctly, "Man", you could come in.

G_d Wants Us to Arrive at Our Spiritual Purpose

So, that attracted me, and by the way, you can see 1, 2, 3. It comes up so often. So, it is spiritual logic, three, but it is also the purpose for your evolving or ascending. Abraham is all the way up in the 7th layer, 7th level, but 3 is not all the way up there. Three is where Joseph is, Yusuf is, and she, Mary, was engaged to Joseph, wasn't she? But she could not reach Joseph, directly, could she? So, the third represents what G_d has created us to arrive at as a purpose, and the purpose He wants us to arrive at is spiritual purpose.

What is the purpose of your soul, your spiritual body, not just your flesh? If that is all you want, then eat with the cows and other animals. But if you want the divine purpose, then it is a purpose for your own soul, and it is a spiritual destiny. It cannot be just a material destiny, and that means you have arrived at your purpose. So, you go from mortal life to mental life, the purpose for that. What is the purpose for this mortal body? What is the purpose for this mind? You find that then you are with Joseph. G_d blessed Joseph to be put over the storehouse, didn't He? He was born with a strong psyche. They put him in jail, and he told people what their dreams meant. He was so impressive the king said, "Bring that man up here! That sounds like the guy I want to solve my problems!"

Now, those men in prison with Joseph that he helped and then they forgot about him when they got out are just like the average follower of mine. They do not have anything important on their minds, so they can witness something important and then it will be overlooked just like it was not important. That is the way it is and that is in the Qur'an repeatedly: *"They forgot Me, so I forgot them"*. You see, the mind that can reflect is the mind that accounts for real progress for any human society, the mind that can think and then reflect. And the natural human being in the Qur'an is not called by any other name except dhakir, and it means to be conscious and then reflect on what appears in the consciousness, what appears in your mind; not to ignore it but look at it again. So, you see and look at it again.

Chewing the Cud

That is chewing the cud, because the cow will chew and then after it has eaten it is still chewing. It is bringing it back up to chew it again for complete and through digestion. So, that is the way it is with the brain of those who are blessed to be true thinkers. They do not just have something in their mind's eye and take it for granted. There are things in their mind's eye that require them to look into it. So, they think and then think again. That is exactly what it means. Isn't that going up the mountain and coming back down? Coming back down allows him to go a little bit further the next time. He might have gone up to the first level. He might have climbed all day and night and did not reach anything but the first level. What he thought he reached was the third level, so he comes back down. He tries to apply it, and he has to go back up again.

A lot of the believers praying the Tarawih Prayer, even for the international Muslim world, I do not believe they understand that actually the last prayer of the Tarawih Prayers, the last one is a single rakat. You actually conclude saying, "As salaam alaikum wa rahmatullah". It is not for Witr that you pray in the evening. It is not one of the obligatory prayers, but in the Ramadan Prayer, the Witr, you're supposed to conclude the two rakats and then you stand and do the single Witr, one. And Allah says, *"And there is going to be one blast of the trumpet and they all will stand."* So, man is evolving to where G_d wants him, but there is going to come a time when you will not have to depend on man evolving. G_d is going to make things so clear and plain that one standing will be enough. One command, "Stand", will be enough, and that is the time of conclusion for the logic.

When the Logic Concludes As to Who Is G_d

When the logic comes to its conclusion as to who is G_d, the logic for man's identity and purpose on this earth, that logic has to be concluded. The time is going to come. It's right now. It is in this time we are living. We are blessed. The time is going to come when the evidence to support the true logic, the real truth of G_d and man's life and purpose, is going to be so evident, so accessible, that everybody is going to see the light. It will not take much. All these other lights will go out, but G_d's Light is going to be so bright. Just like the sun puts out a flashlight, a brush fire, it will put out all other light, make them seem insignificant in the light of the sun. Who will go over a piece of reading to a flashlight or to a big barn fire while the sun is shining bright at midday, and there are no clouds in the sky?

You Can Hardly Bring Me Any Food I Don't Like

You can hardly bring me any food I don't like. I like foods like acorn squash. An old pioneer sister when my father was in prison in 1942, we were having Temple in a house that was on an alley, and when you went up into her house you went in the back way. So, they were probably renting the front out to somebody, because she was by herself, and they were renting the back to her. You would go up the back stairs and that is where we would go for Temple, with no electric lights, only candlelight, oil lamps, and she didn't have a stove like we have now. She had one like down South, an old pot belly, iron stove, and she would bake the pies in that stove. I can't recall just how she did it, whether she had a way of putting it inside, but I don't think so. I believe it was put on top of the stove. You know those stoves.

You pick up the iron part and you stir the coals down there. But that iron part, if you sat water on it, you could boil the water.

That is the kind of stove she had. And she would actually fix acorn squash pies on there. I remember the taste. It tasted like smoke. I was a kid, but I remember the smoke taste. I told it across the rostrum. I was talking about the pioneers, how they supported my family. My father was in jail. Mother could not get welfare or anything. My father told her to refuse it. She couldn't ask for any government assistance. So, the believers knew that, and they would provide for us. We were well taken care of. Every weekend, on Saturday, different ones would come over. Ephram Baha would come over and sometimes he would bring live chickens to my mother, and he would bring fruit. He loved apples. So, this tradition is continued, a very precious tradition. So, this sister, we would have Temple at her house, and it wasn't on Sundays, just Wednesday nights. I remember going there once a week and it was Wednesday night. So, my father must have told them to have it only once a week. There were only about sixty believers, followers of my father, and most of them were old men and women. That wasn't including the children. They didn't count the children. They said it was about sixty adults. Some of the brothers like in their fifties and sixties went to jail because they wouldn't sign the draft card. All they had to do was sign the draft card and they would not have to go to prison. But they refused to sign the draft card because my father refused to sign it.

No Active Duty Permitted

My father permitted us to get draft cards, but not to go into the service, not to accept active duty. I had a real problem with it. I never told him I didn't see anything wrong with going and working in the hospital. I knew I could become a laboratory technician if I went to the hospital. I'm thinking about a way to live. "I am not going to be under you all the time". He never said, "No". He never told us not to, but he said, "If you accept that job and it gets hot on the battle front, they will send you out there and you would be peeling potatoes or doing something out there on the front line for the soldiers." I didn't believe that, but I went along with him, and the judge knew I went along with him. When the judge said, "He's dominated by his father", he was right. I could have brought two thousand there and said, "All of these are dominated by daddy". You just started counting, man! We did what he said. He didn't have to say it. If we knew that was what he wanted, that is what we had to do. There was no question about it, we submitted our judgment to his judgment. I don't regret it a bit, not the time or anything else.

No Spirit to Sacrifice

Nowadays, there seems to be no spirit to sacrifice. They do not have what we had and what we still have. I still have that same spirit to sacrifice. I never lost the spirit to sacrifice. I was talking to them when I first became the leader and I said we do not have to be poor if we would just stop spending so much money, stopped driving these cars, get on a bicycle, do some walking. That is what I told them… and in a number of years, we could be strong financially. My spirit is to sacrifice. I am comfortable with little or nothing, if I know it is for something. Who wants to sacrifice for nothing? That is a fool. He should be sacrificing. I think the main reason is that our expectations were high, way up, and my father told the leaders, but they should have shared it with the followers that, "We are going to lose this! It's not going to stay with us." And then it wouldn't have been such a blow to them that we would be losing all these properties. The IRS, they don't worry about you. They will let you individually go and pile up debt, penalties, and interest. They know they will get you sooner or later, that is, if they know they can get you. Now if they know they can't get you they will hit you right away. But if they know you're piling up property, you have an expensive car, as long as they have something to compensate for what you are not paying, they will let you go. That is their way, because they end up getting more in interest and penalties. Marcus Garvey went down materially. He built up a lot, financially, and he went down to nothing. Noble Drew Ali had built up. Once, they had stores in different cities where they were, just like the Nation of Islam, and trucks to deliver their products. And when he went, they came in there and took everything. We are just one of the many they've done that way, and I'm sure they do their own people like that, too.

We Should Have Been Prepared for Disappointment

So, that disappointment, we should have been prepared for it. They should have been taught all along that we are making a showing. My father said it, but he didn't come out plain enough. He said, "We have to make a material showing." That is what he said when he came out of prison, "or our people won't pay any attention to us". That is why he went into the businesses, but it made money, too. He didn't need money from a restaurant or grocery store, or newspaper. Those believers would give him a hundred dollars, sometimes, on Savior's Day. They used to get stars. I remember a brother getting, I think, eleven stars behind his name. That is $1,100.00. That was one man, one person. He took it and used it for the Nation. Most of the money he (my father) had of his personal money was used to carry the Nation of Islam. Who else had it? He had it. So, he was the one they came to for it. That was the big co-mingling of funds. He's getting money from Savior's Day, from other treasuries. That was his, "Number 2 Poor" members. They were getting money. When I say, "They", not necessarily them. He was over it, but they were getting big money from *Muhammad Speaks Newspaper*. So, sometimes they wouldn't have the money to pay the bills to run some of the businesses. I doubt if there was a week that passed that they didn't have to come to him, and he had to give them money out of his own account to pay those bills. That was the way he kept control over them, too.

I want to have the picture clear. They were told they were going to have big things, and they saw their money was going into businesses and the newspaper, and we had a big printing plant; and to lose all that was just too much of a blow to their faith. Now, they won't trust anybody, and that includes me. You know, very few people donate to me. I doubt if it is one tenth of our following. Maybe two or three percent of our following donate to me on a regular basis, and in the business, it is the same. In the business, which they trust a little more, we have close to a thousand investors, but how many people do we have coming out on Labor Day weekend? About ten thousand. Some say more, because some come in and go back. They don't stay for everything. So, that is one tenth. It is not real because we have much more than ten thousand following me. You have to multiply that at least by ten. We have at least one hundred thousand people following me and if you count their children, it is more than that. I believe it is like two or three percent who donate regularly to WDM Ministry, and we know them by name because we process donations all the time. At least four or five are Christians who donate regularly. Occasionally, a Christian or two will send some money in and we acknowledge theirs just like we do everybody else.

That is one factor. Another factor that may be bigger than that one, is after you work with people a long time, you win their trust, and I think I have won over, again, the faith and trust of most of them that we lost. But what holds them back now is just the condition that is in all the people. We are living in a different time. Back there in the 1940s, 50s and even the 1960s, not only blacks but whites, too, they still had respect for family, G_d, and family values. But for all the people of the United States of America we suffered a great loss of family values and respect for sacred matters. The street mentality living for temporary pleasures, gratification of quick, temporary pleasures and luxuries, showing off what you have, that mentality just killed it. I talk to people in big business, and they say the quality of our work force is gone, destroyed. You can't depend on anybody from the American work force, and that is true. So, who are they hiring? Hispanics, Asians. So, we have to look at many things when we are looking for an explanation as to why we don't get more support from our people.

"The Brother Is a Mirror for His Brother"

I am working to restore the individual person. I've been trying to do that all along. I'm trying to educate them, and I have something that I told you, you will really like. It is going to take me a few months to get it finished, but it is going to help us out a lot. It is a book I'm putting together. It is going to help the mentality; help heal the mentality of our people and anybody who is in the same condition. I'm not just writing it for black folks, but I am writing part of another book that I'm calling, *"Message to the Black Man Volume II"*. You did not get all your message. I have been thinking for years about doing a volume II of my father's book. First, I thought about doing it myself. I was going to say, *"A Letter from Imam W. Deen Mohammed to Black Folks"*, but I said, "My father already gave them a message". So, my mind said, *"Volume II Message to the Black Man*. He spoke to them like a daddy, and he helped us and a lot of our people. I'm not going to speak to them like a daddy, but I'm going to speak to them like a brother." The Prophet said, "The brother is a mirror for his brother".

Just imagine you being a mirror and you tell your brother "Look in the mirror, black brother"? It is a real mirror, so he will see himself, right? If he has a piece of crap on the side of his face, he will see that. You will embarrass him. You will tell him "Turn your head". It means the mirror lied to him, because the mirror can't talk back, but you be his mirror. You can tell him, "You look like you're ready to go on stage and do a great performance, but I'm your true mirror. You are a pile of dung, and you are stinking up the quarters of decent people! You have to overcome that ego or that vanity that is hiding the stink from you!" That is the brother who is the mirror. The mirror can't think and talk, and you go on with what you want to see.

Obviously, the Prophet knew that people's vanity had a lot to do with a mirror that shows them the image they want to see. Vanity is one of the common sins, one of the major sins. We're living in different times. We can't depend on people giving us much charity and we're not going to stoop to methods of getting charity that build people up and deceive them. It is good. I think it is the way Allah wants it, so we become businesspeople because that is what we need. If we become businesspeople, we won't need that much charity. We will be able to give somebody else charity. But still people need to give. Giving has a way of purifying the soul for those who need to earn G_d's Favor. It is a way of helping them purify their soul when they give charity. And charity also brings comfort to the soul of a good person. When they give it comforts their soul. They feel it is what they're supposed to do, and it will earn reward from their G_d. I said that to say I don't like making everything free for our members. They should pay for something.

The Poor Man's Eye Is On Spending

Even the poor should pay for something. They are going to pay for a lot, and they do not know anything to do but spend. A man works to have something to take care of his needs if he is normal, but in this abnormal time we're living in people spend and then look and see what they have left. They are watching their spending not their earnings. They are just spending, buying this and that, and they usually spend beyond their income, and they never catch up because they are spending. Their eye is on spending and not on income. If the eye is on income, they know when they should spend. But the eye is not on income. It is on spending, get this, get that, use this card. I don't know if I used it up or not. Let me use this one. So, you're working and never can catch up, and after a while you're out of a job or something. You get in too much misery, and it hurts your job. The job can't take it because now you are causing problems for your job. After a while they are out of a job. This is the time of blindness. People are just not seeing and living with their eyes closed.

Messianic Leaders No Longer Needed

We have, in the past, depended on messianic leaders. It is because when the world was really oppressive, they put us in slavery and degraded us, but we were not the only ones. There were others treated the same way by their people. They have been pushed down, too. The Polish people have been rejected by the world, most nations, and they treat them like they are not worthy of respect. You go there and the country is in bad shape. They are way behind the rest of the European countries, especially Britain, and they are way behind us. When I went over there Poland looked like the United States when I was in my early teens. Horse drawn wagons, you can still see them on the streets, the people looking like they are on welfare or suffering. I mean by the way they dress and look. This is war time I'm talking about, World War II time. The people are carrying a great load. It is only a very few having a good life.

So, it was the whole world that was in bad shape like that. Now the world has changed, and you do not have strong nationalism anymore, because people have to live with one another. They have to live together. They have to cooperate with and trust each other, benefit from each other, and help each other. That is the attitude now of nations. So, you do not have this sharp national line separating people anymore. When that was the case there was still a justification for messianic leaders. Not only that, but the biggest problem for black people was also that we were rejected socially. Nobody wanted to socialize with us or have us in their social environment. That social rejection has gone. You can go in some of the smallest towns now, East and West, here and everywhere, and you can find blacks all mixed up with whites, all in the same area. So, to make it very short, nationalism and racism is what made it necessary for a messianic leader.

Now that that is not of much consequence at all in our lives, real racism or nationalism, the messianic leader is not necessary. A messianic leader comes to save a people, not all people. This is true of every messianic leader that I know of in the Bible. They are not in the Qur'an. It did away with it. Mujeddid, someone to renew the faith, is different than a messianic leader. A Mujeddid is not necessarily a Moses or a David returning. The role of Mujeddid is reviving religion, and it has nothing to do with people directly. They revise the religion. He is doing it for everybody who needs the religion made right.

A Servant of the Word of G_d

I am a servant, first of all, of the Word of G_d and that has been in me ever since I can remember. I want the Word of G_d. I want to understand it, so I can live it better, and knowing that other people misunderstand it, too, I want to make it available, so they can understand it better. That is number one for me, the Word of G_d. What G_d communicates to mankind I want to serve that and thank Allah He has made a good servant. You have not seen the last of it. I think as long as I live G_d will be teaching me. That is what it is. G_d is continuously teaching me. It has gotten so plain and good now that all I can do is just express amazement, occasionally, to Him, directly. "Oh, Lord, how wonderful You are! It is magnificent what You are doing! Little me, a nobody!"

You're going to see the evidence of it more and more, because it has gotten so good now. I do not want to tell you everything, but the Prophet said something that explains me, too, right now. He said, "A believer, a devotee, can get so close to G_d in obedience that when he speaks, it is as though G_d spoke". If he strikes with his hand, it is as though G_d struck. That is true. I know it is true; it happened to me. He didn't say that person is going to be a Prophet, Messenger, Mujeddid, or Messiah. He said a devotee. But he also said in support of what is happening to me, about the signs in the end of time, that the servant girl will give birth for her mistress. That means the husband is going to have a child by the servant girl and not the mistress, not the lady of the house. It says, "The servant girl will give birth for her mistress." Now if you are thinking about a physical child that is okay, because that happened in the time of Hagar (Hajar). But the Prophet didn't mention Hagar (Hajar) or anybody. He said that is going to happen. But he also mentioned poor people. He said the end of time is going to be where poor people are going to be competing with the rich in building skyscrapers.

So, am I fool-hearted to have these big dreams? If I am then something is wrong with the Prophet, with his imagination. So, it does not mean a physical child. It means the production that guarantees life, the society surviving and having a future. It will not be in their hands, but it will be in the hands of a little child born of a servant woman. That is big, but that is where we're going. I might not see it all, but it is going to go right there, and non-Muslims who see me and know are going to help you get there, and I'm not a Prophet. I just have long-reaching head lights.

Alone With My Love!

Ever since I was little I loved loneliness; that's my nature. I am happiest when I am alone. G_d and the work He's got here for us, because of that I'm never alone. And that's more pleasure for me than being with people, socializing, doing what we're doing now, and alone and with you at the same time. Yes, I'm alone with my love. You see, my love is what we are doing, but even though we are doing it together, I'm still alone with it. So, that's why I say, sometimes, the best of my life is when I am with you all (sharing my thoughts, insights, etc.) … It has amazed me for a long time. I say, "Wow, this is a blessing!" It amazes me. The things that would come to my mind, come to my vision, into my vision, would amaze me and still do. It doesn't shock me like it used to. It just would stop me, you know. I would just wait. I would stop and wait for my mind to get started, again.

Created to Come Alive In Another Dimension

Yes, I had to do that. But now, the world is so big, and the language of revelation is as big as the world, because Allah created the world to reveal. Yes, He created the universe to reveal to man. And so, he needs help along the way. Allah reveals help along the way, but the help comes from himself, his own nature. G_d has already created him to come alive in another dimension, and that other dimension doesn't sound like much, but it's powerful, it's faith. Yes, he comes alive in the dimension of faith and his faith is so strong he waits on G_d. He makes an effort and then waits on G_d, and G_d turns on his superpower, his super perceptive tentacles, and things that he's got in his makeup. G_d turns it on and He's able to extract from the darkness, light, intuitive power. Now, it's deep water, but that light was in the depths of the water, wasn't it, according to Genesis? And he was just climbing on the surface. Why? Because the surface revealed the deep and then he gets in trouble. He could see himself on the surface of the clear water, and it started on the surface and darkness was in the deep, *"And G_d said, 'Let there be light'."*

So, if G_d said, *"Let there be light",* G_d wants the light to be in the deep. He said the darkness was in the deep. If He said darkness was on the surface, then you would expect the light to be on the surface. He could handle the surface. He was looking at himself in the water and the water quivered and changed the way he looked. The water is disturbed, and it changes the way you look. It breaks up the picture. So, he needs what's in the depths and that's the insight, deep insight into the matter that he questions or that he wants to know about. He needs deep insight into it, and the water is only given because it starts within his sensitivity, his concerns.

The True Human's Aim Is As G_d's Aim

There are sensitivities and there are sensibilities. Now, I could tell you that, really, he was on the surface trying to find the truth, but he was positioned upon his sensitivities, his concerns. And straining long enough turned on his sensibilities and then he will be able, he will have light in the depths of his sensitivities. Straining with your sensitivities eventually brings to action or activity your sensibilities. The human being is not just sensitivities. The human being is sensitivities and sensibilities. You sense things, right?

The concern is sensitivities. Like I said, *"And He revealed it upon his heart"*. Why upon his heart? His sensitivities, his concerns. The heart registers all the sensitivities that are in the deepest of oceans. So, He revealed it upon his heart, because his heart would not give up. His heart would not give up working to better the state of mankind, so that life could be better on this planet earth. G_d created him like that, so G_d's Will is right in that. It's like two arrows. So, you become so devoted till your aim is G_d's Aim. G_d brings you to His Aim by creating you to have the human aim and the human aim is the same as G_d's Aim. The true human aim in life is the same as G_d's Aim. Why should it be any different? He's the One Who designed me. He created me. He designed me. He gave you your potential and your hunger and the appetite in you for perfection. So, what more do you need from Him than just to have the light turned on in your house?

Paradise Is Right On This Earth

And that's the beauty of G_d, to me, that He doesn't impose anything upon His creation. He's given the creation everything it needs to come to the state that will please the human soul, in complete satisfaction. So, the return to G_d, according to the Qur'an, is not a return to Him. They say, "Oh, he has returned to G_d and he's sitting down in the company of G_d". He says, "No, return to My Paradise. Enter you among My servants. Return to My paradise. Enter you My paradise". So, we're right in Paradise, now, if you can feel it! You can feel it right here. Yes, when those serving G_d reach liberty, freedom, where they are happy where they are and they don't want to go anywhere else, they're in Paradise. Whether it be on this earth or after this life, they're in Paradise, and the real Paradise is on this earth for the living. Paradise is right on this earth and in this creation, and I'm not saying that that's the only Paradise. No, I believe that there is Paradise after this is gone, all this physical world is gone. But isn't all this physical world gone once you come into the true life? So, I expect to continue on this path. I don't want any other path.

My Father Had Me In Court

My father had me in court, once, like he did on Wednesday nights. Wednesday night was court night because somebody may have done something against the teachings of my father, and they were going to be put on trial. My father had me on trial. Twice he had me on trial. I was reported to have said Mr. Fard is not G_d. The first time he was really emotionally upset. "How can you think like that? How can you say that when you know your father was in the streets, and you know your father was a poor, drunk on the streets, and it was our savior who dignified us and brought me to be the man and leader I am? How can you say that? Ungrateful!" He was really upset.

Now mind you, when he (Mr. Fard) came those were the hard days right at the time of the depression. It was in 1930, 1933. I said, "Daddy, you led me to disagree with that." He looked at me and at least I changed his mood. He didn't say anything more about that. I didn't carry it further. I knew he would know right away what I was referring to, because there were a lot of rational teachings in his teaching, also. So, when he told me to be truthful, don't be a liar, to be righteous, all that teaching was strong enough to make me differ with it.

Faith In Allah and My Own Intelligence

I didn't have any help like you all have, and Allah blessed me to get it. The only help I had was faith in my own intelligence, faith in my rational mind, and faith in Allah, and Allah will not lead anyone astray. Now, Allah is definitely Merciful, and if anyone is led astray that person will be redeemed by His Mercy. Yep, that's all the help I had. And when you are taught to depend upon your own rational mind, you aren't going to be blindly led. You're not going to be led, blindly and you're not going to see that that conflicts with reason and not suspect that there is something wrong with it, either hidden singly, or it's just a lie. The help I'm giving is the help that's in the Qur'an. But I'm giving it plainly and consciously, that you have to connect back with real life and real nature, the nature before man changed it and put his language to it; and that's a good situation to be in to come to the right perception or to get the Qur'anic insights.

Ignorance Heavier On the People of Muhammed's Day

The world is not as dark now as it was back there in Muhammed, the Prophet's day. It was much darker. Ignorance was heavier on the people in his day than it is nowadays, and I was raised in a Christian country, in a Christian environment, in a church environment. I heard preachers preach, you know, and I'm an African American born as the son of a man who had rejected the church, my father, Elijah Mohammed. So, I'm in that Christian environment and I'm hearing them preaching, but I already had been influenced to suspect that something is wrong with what they're saying. So, my situation was much more, I'm favored much more than Prophet Muhammed was. Yes, my circumstances favored me coming into the light much more than Prophet Muhammed's circumstances favored him coming into the light. If he had any advantage over me, it was taken away by Mr. Fard when he said that this whole world is nothing, but a lie and the Bible is a lie. Everything is a lie.

G_d Has Been Protecting Me

When I became leader in 1975, I knew I had a lot of support in his teachings, though it looked like I was just condemning everything, and I should be killed. As a brother would say, "You hypocrite, you should be killed!" Believe me, I had people threaten my life! I got terrible calls. I lived in an apartment, and they would come in between the houses, the building I lived in, and the house next door late at night, hollering "You hypocrite! You're going to get it!" One night a gun was fired just to scare me. In fact, for two nights there was gunfire. One night I was coming home late and was crossing the street to get on the side where I was living, and I saw a car looking suspicious. I could see figures in it, but they had the lights off and as I stepped into the street, I sensed that car was going to try to do something. So, I stepped into the street, and they turned the bright headlights on and headed towards me speeding like they were going to kill me. I didn't believe it. G_d has been protecting me. I didn't know it. So, something in me said, "Don't get afraid and don't run! Just go normally across the street!" So, when they got close to me, they hit their brakes, went around me, and did not hit me. I looked quickly to see if I could see the license plate number. They had the lights off. Quickly, they turned the lights off, so I couldn't see the license plate. I lived on Wabash Avenue, in Chicago. Once, I was coming to my house and a gun was fired a distance away from me, down the street, and I saw sparks on the street, so it must have been pointed downwards. It must have been from the gunfire.

Support From Mr. Fard

Also, when I became the leader, I knew I had a lot of support from Mr. Fard who named me. He said name me after himself. My name, Wallace D, is one of the aliases he used. He was often referred to as W. D. Fard. So, when I was a boy, they didn't call me, Wallace D. They called me W. D., even my mother. That did not last long. I was about 15 or 16 years old, and they started calling me Wallace. So, I'm knowing all this. I know I have support, and the Honorable Elijah Mohammed said a lot of things. He said, "What we have will last for maybe five hundred years, but there will be a change coming one day, and the religion as we know it won't be here anymore. Maybe the next one may not accept any of what we have with us." That is big help, if you are suspicious and curious. He was talking about leaders in the future just for this particular religious group. I just gave you one example. If I would explain all this to you, you would have to be as serious as I am about hearing it.

They will tell you when I first came into the leadership, on a Sunday, I would begin with the sun shining, in the late afternoon, but once, it was sunrise time when I finished. The day was breaking. Imagine that! Mr. Fard said it's a powerful magnetism. He was right. They were still there. I was still holding them in the morning. I felt so sorry when it dawned on me what had happened. I said, "I know these people are hurting and all cramped. There is too much pressure on their brains. I should not have done that!" I regretted it later, but they survived. Some of them have brain damage, but most of them survived.

An Environment Controlled by Language

So, I said "I know how to change this thing. We have been put in a controlled environment that is controlled by language". I said, "What I have to do is form a new language and have it also mystical or rooted in myth." That is what I did. I even created some of my own myths. I added to it. I came from world myth, but I created some myths. I remember I was talking once, and I said there were a people lost in Africa, and they finally got a leader to help them get their mind straight, called the tribe of Shabut. I created these stories, and it helped them. It worked. I created it to wean them off that, to give them a new language environment, and have it point more sensibly towards reality. That is what I did, and it worked. My father gave me a lot of help, but you have to find it in his teachings.

Once, the Honorable Elijah Mohammed's ministers were at the table. Every Sunday he would have the national staff headquartered in Chicago to come to dinner for a table talk, and for him to iron out problems for the Temple believers. One Sunday, I had spoken at the Temple. I was not the head minister, but a minister who was given special privileges, and the Honorable Elijah Mohammed would tell the head minister, "When my son is there don't take up all the time. I want him to speak." My father was like the messenger of G_d of Mr. Fard, who was called G_d, or like Jesus Christ is called G_d in the person, or in the flesh. One of the ministers after I had been the main speaker on this Sunday he said, "Dear holy apostle, your son doesn't teach like we teach." My father said, "Yes, I know, brother. He won't teach the Bible like we do." I know many would have a lot of questions, such as, "Was he teaching the Bible?" He (my father) was coming from the Bible and using it, like most black religions, to support the idea that we are the oppressed people of G_d, like the Hebrews were, and G_d is our Deliverer. So, it fit. It worked out pretty well.

He said, "My son is not going to preach the Bible. He's going to teach the Qur'an." I had a lot of help from my father, from Mr. Fard, who told my father and mother before I born, I was going to be a boy. He was guessing. He said, "When the child is born promise me, you're going to give him my name", the exact words my father and mother told to me and my sisters, and older brothers. They were old enough to witness all this. They would remind me, too, "You know you have the savior's name," when they thought I was straying, not into sin, but just straying from those ideas. They would suspect I was giving too much time to the world or to my Christian friends, but I was a normal boy. My father and his teacher made me very unique in the following of the Honorable Elijah Mohammed by saying that I have the name of our savior, and that the savior asked my father and mother to not only give me his name. He said, "Raise him to help us in this work." It all came to pass, a self-fulfilling prophecy or whatever; it happened.

Highest Position That Human Beings Can Ascend To

When we say Muhammed is the Messenger, we mean he is not the son of G_d, is not a divine being. The real human being, the excellence of the human being, the highest position that human beings can ascend to is not to be an angel, or divine creature. No, it is mortal man who has been created to have that high place in the creation. Marrying, having sex, and doing all these things that are natural for man, the mortal, G_d has blessed him to have all this, not somebody who will deny his nature and become other than man; a man in one half and something else in the other half; no, a mortal man. And that is what Jesus Christ is a sign of, but they misunderstood it. He was a sign of a mortal man, but one not raised by the world. Therefore, the world's teachers cannot claim that they birthed him. Allah birthed him. Allah created him. Allah says, "Whenever I want one, I just create him from the ones I already have. I already have all these. I created all of these, so when I want a special one, I choose him from the ones I already have". It always bothered me as a youngster, a young man studying this religion knowing what others were saying, that Jesus Christ has no father, and to say because he had no father, he is G_d. That didn't set too well with me. He didn't have a father? Well, he had a mother, and every child is formed in the belly of his mother, not in the belly of his father. So, he was born flesh and blood as a mortal, just like all the rest.

And then I came back with the other conclusion. Mary was not born without a father. Mary had a father and a mother. So, if Jesus didn't have a father, he had a grandfather and that, to me, said he had the genes of a man in him. See how it is shattered? G_d shattered that for me when I was nothing but like him, his age, not knowing all these things that I know, now. But G_d shattered it for me. It was over. I said to myself, "I do not want the Bible. This is a book for insane people, an insane book for insane people". My father told me, "I know you do not care for the Bible, son, and our people died and are in the graveyard in this religion, the Bible. So, they have to be resurrected out of it." But he never told me to study the Bible. Do you know what he said in the presence of others in the house, family, and sometimes ministers, big leaders, in the house? He said, "Well, my son, Wallace, he is not meant to teach the Bible. He's going to teach the Qur'an."

At that time, I was young. He said these things when I was 11, 12, or 13 years old. He helped me separate from the Bible or not look to the Bible. I did not look to the Bible but look how G_d works. When he, himself, needed help and I was wondering how I could help him, my mind said, "Go study the Bible and the Qur'an." I studied both. I studied the teachings of Mr. Fard. That is what my mind led me to do. If Shirley was here, right now, the wife I was with at that time, she would tell you that I used to sit at the table where we ate, and I made the table a worktable. I would have papers, books, and stuff, all over that table, and I would be sitting there. One night, she came down and she said, "Are you still down here?" It was daylight and I said, "Yes". She said, "You've been down here all night." That was true. I would be down there all might, sometimes. Do you think I was doing it for money? I did not have to do anything for money but just go along with my father and I knew how to do that, too. I could have done that very well. So, I did not have to do that for money. I was not doing that for money. I was doing that following the spirit of thirst in the soul for understanding and the right way, and G_d rewarded me, tremendously. He rewarded me amply and I would say more than amply. As a Prophet said in the Bible, *"My cup runneth over"*. He filled it beyond its capacity to receive all that He was giving, and it just spilled all over, and every now and then, I'd take a sponge and pick up some of it. It was too much for the cup and I soaked the sponge, because it is good stuff.

I Studied the Bible From Genesis to Revelation

Prophet Jesus, peace be on him, in Qur'an, it says he was to have spoken while he was in the cradle. And it said a question was asked of his mother and they expected the mother to answer, but she did not have any answer for them. She pointed to her child and her child spoke while he was yet in the cradle. I read the Bible, and I have shared this experience on many occasions. I read the Bible all the way through from Genesis to Revelation, just so I would be acquainted with what is on the pages of the Bible, and I promised myself that I wouldn't stop to study it or to question what I would find on those pages. I would just go right straight through it, read it, and I did. Allah blessed me to do that. And I, also, promised myself, it was a strong pledge like an oath, after I finished the Bible, reading it without interruption or stopping to question it, I would read it, again, and I would read it as a student searching it to see, to know what was on those pages, and that is what I did.

I made a lot of notes all through the Bible. I didn't choose to have it that way, but the first Bible was a nice-looking Bible in my house. I always had a lot of books, especially religious books. People would give them to me. When I was a young minister, they would give me books. It started a long time ago. I had a nice Bible, and I had more than one, but this happened to be a black Bible with a black back. That is the Bible that most people have, preachers, too. That is the one I read straight through. The second Bible I read, I didn't look for it, but it just happened to be the one that I picked up the next time when I started to search. It was a nice white leather, like a man-made leather back. I still have it somewhere in some of these places where I lived. I lived in three or four different places.

I Lived In Many Cities and Places

I lived at what we called, the National House, where Minister Farrakhan is. I lived there for a little while. I lived at 8752 Cornell where my wife Shirley still is. She is there now, still living there. And I lived out of the city, in Philadelphia, when I was serving as a minister for the Honorable Elijah Mohammed. I lived in Oakland, California, for about three years. I lived in little Rock, Arkansas, for about three years, and I came back and lived in Calumet City, Illinois, in hotels. I actually did my work in hotels. I have had some kind of life.

I fed ministers, imams, in a little L-shaped efficiency apartment. When you came into it, you saw the whole area. You come into it, you turn left, and you go to the kitchen area. Everything was open, nothing was closed. The bed was in the wall. I had to pull the bed out of the wall when I got ready to go to bed. I sat up there and ran what is now called the WDM Ministry, Mosque Cares. Back then, it was called the MACA Fund, Muslim American Community Assistance Fund. It wasn't spelled Mecca, but we called it the MACA just to have that sound, and that as our interest. Our people are orientated towards Mecca, because that is where the Ka'bah is, etc. We stayed there for a while and some financial relief came. I was asked to work with the Saudi Royal Embassy in Washington, D.C., so I was working with them, and they gave me a place on the Supreme Council of Masaajid. They were paying or giving me an average of Seventy thousand dollars a year, and I was paying taxes on it. It lasted for a few years. So, we moved from where I was in that little place, and we moved to 226 Madison where we are now. We still have that house there, my daughter lived there. After we finished using it for an office, my daughter, Ngina, stayed there. She was already there, so she stayed there and raised a family there. Now, I am back there.

She had gone to another nice house, and I was back there at that office, living temporarily, until they finished my house in Markham, Illinois. Once they completed adding rooms so I would have enough room to live there, I moved back. I didn't want to move out of the neighborhood. I have such wonderful neighbors. One is a real Muslim, who is a real Christian. He goes to church, not to the mosque, but he is a real Muslim who is a real Christian. I just wish we had a lot of Muslims like him, a wonderful man. His name is Isaiah Thompson.

I moved from that apartment I had on Madison to the house on Madison, and from there I moved to Wentworth for a temporary time, again, in Calumet City, at that little L-shaped efficiency apartment. Some ministers asked to visit me, imams, our ministers, all from us, our group association, and I believe there must have been about eight of them there in that little place. It was packed and I bought fish and fried fish in that little oven for all of them, no air conditioning. It was not air conditioned. Water was just running off me. I sweat profusely, if I get hot. Water just starts running off me. I'm just sweating, and water is dripping off me and half of them or more were the same, just wet with sweat. But we had such a good time we were not conscious of the heat or anything. We were just eating fish and enjoying each other's company. It was really nice!

I moved from there, perhaps not immediately, because I stayed, again, in a motel out there in that area. There used to be an *Econo Lodge* on Halsted. It is still there, around 171st street. I stayed there. Everywhere I stayed I took my work with me. I did my work in the place where I stayed. I stayed in the *Red Roof Inn*, also, on

Torrence. And there was an *Econo Lodge* right at the corner of Madison at the expressway, on Sibley. I stayed there for a little while, but I also stayed in the *Red Roof Inn* on Torrence about 171st. I think that is in Lansing, MI. And I stayed at the *Red Roof Inn* on Halsted near the *Econo Lodge*. I saved a lot of money, too. They would give me monthly rates when I was there. I didn't have to buy a house, or anything. I knew it would be temporarily. It would not last forever. Then I got married to that beautiful tall lady, Binah, and lived at her address for some time. Actually, she raised Mohammed. He was like 2 and a half years old when I brought him up from Little Rock, Arkansas, and we married, and Mohammed knows her as mother, although he knows his mother. He is aware of his mother all the time. She wasn't with him. She was not able to take care of him. From there, I moved on the street where we are right now where the house is in Markham. I moved to 16133 Cambridge, and I was fortunate. A Muslim had that place. Sadruddin Ali's wife, Ameena Ali, Khalilah's (who married Muhammed Ali) mother. They had the house as a place where they would just get away from everything, and they would spend time over there just to get away from work and have a place to rest. It so happened that they weren't using it at the time. So, I was able to move there and then I noticed 16416, diagonally across the street at an angle from the house I was in, I saw that house was for sale. I said, "I'm going over there and check out that house". I went over there and checked it out and it was in bad shape.

But I felt it could be put in good shape if the price was low enough. Sure enough, the price was low enough, so we had the office, WDM Ministry, buy the house and repair and fix it up, remodel, or rehab it and I stayed there until now. That is my house. It is our house. Those are some of the places. I skipped around a little bit, but I got the major ones in. Believe me, I guarantee you I can go to at least half of those places and find some of my books. So, once I get enough space, I'm going to go around and get my books and have my library with me. I have a lot of good books, especially in Arabic. We are not reading them now. We're not using them, but they will be left here, and they will be for the future. It will not go to waste. They will be for the future, for our young generation coming up. They will have those books available to them, if they want to check them out and use them. En sha Allah, everything will work out fine.

My Father, the Honorable Elijah Mohammed

I think I should tell you a little something about my father that many don't know about. The first restaurant that the community of the Nation of Islam had the Honorable Elijah Mohammed opened it, and he managed it, and he made it successful; my father, the leader that was admired so much and loved so much. The first grocery store we had was opened, managed, and made successful by the Honorable Elijah Mohammed. The first butcher we had was the Honorable Elijah Mohammed. He told us that he went to the market and told them, "If you will show me how to make the meat cuts, I have a following and we will do big business with you. He said the owner said, "No problem!" The owner put an apron on the Honorable Elijah Mohammed and then he showed him the cuts of the meat of the cow, and showed him on the chart all the meats, and then demonstrated to the Honorable Elijah Mohammed how to make those cuts. He gave the Honorable Elijah Mohammed the chart that he was teaching him from. The Honorable Elijah Mohammed took the chart and hung it up in the facility that he had bought with our money, because it was the community's money. The Honorable Elijah Mohammed was supported by wonderful people. He didn't have an outside job because he didn't have to have any work outside to try to get money from somebody, Arabs, or anybody. He didn't have to do that because the pioneers loved him so much they would give him everything they had and even suffer if they had to. They would not mind suffering only the loss of money and the loss of the convenience to have certain things, but they didn't suffer. They were so happy doing that. That's the kind of followers he was blessed with, and a man that would lead the people the way he led the people deserved those followers.

I Had to Say He Was Wrong to Break His Grip

You say, "Well, why didn't you tell us those things when you were back there, and you were telling us that he was wrong?" Because I first had to tell you he was wrong to break his grip on you, so I could take you where you had to go. It wasn't my pleasure to tell you anything bad about the Honorable Elijah Mohammed. That was never my pleasure. It was what I had to do.

Now that that is over, we should lift him up, because he was much more of a Muslim than he was not. He was a courageous believer. If he had the knowledge that G_d has blessed me to have there would have been no need for me. That man could have done it. I miss him now. I wish he was with me. I would say to the Honorable Elijah Mohammed, "You could whip ass, and I don't like doing it". Now see, don't say, "He used a curse word." I will tell you the picture I had in mind when I said, "ass". It is a dumb, stubborn, donkey that balks on you when you need him most. The Elijah Mohammed didn't tolerate that. He didn't tolerate people disrespecting their post, disrespecting their job, disrespecting our investments, disrespecting what we want as a life. He didn't tolerate it.

I can be patient and pray for you and keep looking at you, and the next day see if you improve a little bit; and even if you go back, you start going backwards, I'd say, "Well, they're going to come forward after a while." Sometimes, I hate that side of myself. I wish the Honorable Elijah Mohammed could be resurrected and whip ass. He was a strong man. Nothing could deter him. Nothing could turn him around. The world, threats of putting him in jail, the F.B.I, nothing could turn that man around; even suffering, imprisonment, suffering the lack of the good of this world, because his followers were extremely poor in the beginning, the 30's and 40's and the 50's, too. The change only came in the middle half, the last half of 1955 and on up. A big change came, but nothing could change him. Big shots were coming from across the waters to question him on what he was teaching, and he would say, "Brother, you just don't understand." Nothing could turn that man around. If he had not been that kind of man, we wouldn't be here today. I wouldn't be here. You wouldn't be here. So, now that we are over the troubled waters and we're on the land where we can see what G_d wants us to do with our lives, I want you to know my father.

A Modern Day Prophet

The earlier thinkers were called seers, then later called thinkers and Prophets, that is, according to history. First, they are identified as seers, meaning that they could see things that others could not see. Then they were identified as thinkers, and then Prophets. Prophets means they got a revelation or something from G_d. You would be surprised to know, some of you, that I meet leaders, very important people, not only in religion but in business, and some of them tell me my father was a modern day Prophet. That is what they tell me. I can understand them seeing him that way, too, because really if I was not his son and saw him as an outsider, I would have to say he was a Prophet, too, especially with my knowledge of Scripture, now. I would have to say he was a Prophet, but not Qur'anic, not in Qur'an. Within the Bible, he is a Prophet. By the Bible's definition the Honorable Elijah Mohammed was a Prophet, but not by the Qur'an's definition.

Qur'anic Scripture Deals Only With G_d's Plan

Now what is the difference? The difference is that the Qur'an deals only with the Plan of G_d. It is on the high level of revelation where you are inspired by G_d, and G_d assists your thinking and your spirit, etc. The Qur'an only deals with that. The Qur'an does not call persons Prophets who do not have that high level or that connection. They are those who simply are psychic and highly spirited, having a strong spirit as psychics where they can perceive what is going to happen tomorrow or perceive some things of the future, and have the Spirit of G_d in them to address those things. So, they have psychic power, but not necessarily revelation on that high level.

So, the Qur'an does not deal with those persons as Prophets. It doesn't even credit them as Prophets. I think it will just credit them as being thinkers or those whom G_d inspired, but on the level beneath the level of revelation that Prophets get. That is what I think. The Honorable Elijah Mohammed could not be called a Prophet in the Qur'an. To be called a Prophet in the Qur'an he has to be like Abraham. He has to be like Moses, Jesus, and Muhammed. He has to be like those persons to be called a Prophet. I know that my father had the ability to see into the future, too, and predict future things, because a lot of his predictions have come true. And I know his teacher did not give him all this. His teacher may perhaps have discovered that he had that in him, and maybe that is why he chose him. That could be. We don't know, but he definitely had it, and he had an exceptional mind, although he was not educated. He received no education, except three years in elementary school in Georgia.

We were doing an algebra problem, my brother and I, this was an occasion at the dinner table in the evening that permitted us to talk. When my father had company, we boys could not talk at the table. We just had to be quiet and listen. But if my father had no company and there were only family members at the table, we could talk. So, this was one of those evenings and we had an algebra problem that we both had been working on, so my brother Herbert, Jabber, we call him now, asked me, "Wallace, did you figure out the problem"? I said "No, I did not go back to it". I said, "Did you"? He said, "No". So, Jabber recalled some parts of the problem, and he was trying to reason how it should be worked out and I, too, was trying to reason how it should be worked on. And my father said, "If this such and such and if that such, such, such, then this is the answer, such, such should be answer." It was correct. We had one of those books that had the answers already in the book, but we were trying to get that answer. We were trying to find the formula or the method to get that answer and my father came up with it in his head while we were talking.

The Honorable Elijah Mohammed Helped Other Black People, Too

When I was questioned by some investigators from the intelligence department here in the United States just before the passing of the Honorable Elijah Mohammed, during the time I was put out of the community, they investigated me and told me, "We know that your father, Elijah Mohammed, does not only help Muslims. We know that he helps other black people, as well. He has even given charity to some black Christians." This is what I was told by them. But I know from my own experience with the Honorable Elijah Mohammed, as his son and a minister preaching for the Nation of Islam under his leadership, he also, had the interest of all black people, not just those who were Muslim. What I mean by that is this. He did not see Muslims, only, benefitting from his teaching. He saw all black people benefitting from his teaching. Al-Islam addresses us as community and asks us to accept responsibility for community life. So, the Honorable Elijah Mohammed was really Islamic in his programs and in his designing of his programs. Al-Islam requires that Muslims establish community life, and that they are about establishing their own identity as a community. So, that has been the direction that I have followed.

An Extraordinary Man

That brings me to the direction that I took as the leader upon the passing of the Honorable Elijah Mohammed, in February of 1975. The Honorable Elijah Mohammed had set up an organization or had been successful at establishing an organization that included religion, preaching, schools, education, and also strong, great emphasis on building business for African American people.

His economic blueprint was called by different names. He had farmland, businesses in the cities that he hoped would be supported by farmland, such as grocery stores selling meats and whatever. So, the Honorable Elijah Mohammed's vision was not small in any way. His vision was community vision, and community vision is what Al-Islam is all about. Al-Islam addresses us as community and asks us to accept responsibility for community life. So, the Honorable Elijah Mohammed was really Islamic in his programs and in his designing of his programs.

You see, a man that can hold people as long as he did and keep them going in the direction as long as he did and keep his position before the world as long as he did and persevere it like that can't be an ordinary person. Ordinary people don't do that. He was extraordinary. The Honorable Elijah Mohammed was an extraordinary man and perhaps the only man we will see like him on this earth. His coming was a one-time event. He's gone. We won't see anything like that again, where a man comes from where he came from and achieved what he achieved against the people that were most feared by everybody, the most feared race in existence. But he stood up to them and challenged them and everything they believed in and none of them wanted to do battle with him, because they knew that even though they came out the winner perhaps with their intellectual buddies, they would cause so much to be exposed to the public mind that ultimately, they would be losers in the battle with the Honorable Elijah Mohammed, and he was a black man from Georgia. That should make us proud, and I would not be the man that I am if it were not for him. I was formed upon what was formed in him. If I did not have anything to form myself upon, I would not even be here. I would be a nobody. It was fortunate circumstances… I see my father as phase one in G_d's Plan, and I am phase two. Who knows, there may be phase three after me. I don't know.

A Good Time for Us In America

For Muslims, we have to realize that this is a good time for us in America. Economic predictions are not good for the next twenty years or more, they say. But they don't predict any serious thing happening that is going to cause a great alarm. We are just going to have to learn how to not splurge and waste so much and be willing to accept that other people live, too, around the globe; Third World people, poor peoples' nations around the globe.

Don't you know America was living high on the hog that belonged to the whole world? That hog that it was living high on belonged to the whole world. It is now a part of the world. Say, "Hey, that is my ham sucker! You don't have this anymore." They started claiming their part of that hog, and now America ends up with nothing but the head. I repeat, we should understand. If a person doesn't realize the situation for themselves, they are in the dark. You can all have faith in your ability, "I know I'm equipped, I'm ready", but ready for what? You've got to know your situation, so you know what to be ready for. The potential is there for advancing you and advancing the world by your own efforts or your own contributions to it, but you can't apply it until there is a situation for it. We have to know the situation, and many of us were so knocked out by the blow of the news of the Honorable Elijah Mohammed's passing that we just became disconcerted. We didn't have any sense of where to go or what to do. It dealt such a terrible blow to our psychological makeup, to our sense of balance and direction, that we have just been lingering, kind of suspended in space.

"One Sun Is Setting and Another One Is Rising"

We have to wake up and realize that the Honorable Elijah Mohammed was not disappointed at death. Death didn't disappoint him. He was prepared for it. He was ready for it. He was expecting it, and he was working hard, like a beaver, to do all he could before the clock ran out on him. So, as the song said, *"He fought a good fight."* So, we don't have to weep. He fought a good fight. He was not disappointed. He said, "One sun is setting, and another one is rising." That is the saying of a man with hope. That is not the saying of a man disappointed, saying, "One sun is setting, and another one is rising." That was one of his last words. Now, you say, "He's talking about himself." No, I am not. The only thing that made me think of myself was when I realized that you all are going to think of me. I wasn't thinking of myself. I am thinking of the life, the life that was in us before the Honorable Elijah Mohammed, the life that he tried to advance, the life that he knew would keep living and would rise up again after a temporary fall. "One sun is setting, but another one is rising."

I witness that today, and if he were here, he would look at us and say, "Son, are these the same people?" I would say, "Yes sir!" He would say, "I can go on and lie down, again!" And I can see my mother standing by him, see her smiling and saying, "I'm going to rest very well, too, honey!" The children are affected more by

46

the hurt of the old ones than the old ones themselves. The old ones have to come to the aid of the children and say, "Honey, no, it is not that bad. Don't cry, it is not that bad!" That is what they would be doing to us if they were here seeing how some of us just won't stop crying. We are going to cry until Judgment Day! If they could come back, they would put their arms around you and say, "Honey, it is not that bad. Don't think that we are weeping, we are happy." If they could communicate with us, they would say, "Don't think that we are weeping. We are happy!"

I'm sure that the Honorable Elijah Mohammed didn't expect this much longevity to be existing this soon. I think he expected a long period of almost total inactivity. In fact, he told us, "All of this is going to be lost." But he also told me, "In modem times, we don't accept predictions of Prophets that weren't authorized." Though he never said he was a Prophet, that is a prediction that I am going to try like hell to beat.

So, I set out to fight against those influences that he predicted would take us away, that would unseat us. I went out right away to fight against them, because he had conditioned me to not shy away from prophecy that I don't like. You prophesy something I don't like, my father sensitized me to go after it, prove it wrong, beat it, defeat it, tell it, "Back up! Go back there and predict again, sucker!" That is the kind of courage we need. We need the courage to say to anybody that says anything negative, anything to dull our spirit to set us back, to say to them, "That isn't in me, sucker! You are appealing to something that is not here. It isn't in me to respond to your negative talk. I'm a forward moving creature, today, tomorrow, and always!" That is how you have to meet the opposition.

Learning From the Uncle Toms of the Past

I learned from the Uncle Toms of the past. I learned how to survive until I can do better, how to do a little bit and lighten a whole lot in the dark. They thought that I was a new thing in Islam. They thought I was the new Islamic spiritualist, holiness, sanctifier, wanting nothing but an angel existence, ready to live permanently and internally in dhikr, deep spiritual meditation, uninterrupted, untouched, and unmoved by worldly matters. That is what they were trying to mold me into. So, since I saw the intention of the heavy boys with the controls in their hand at that time, I went along with their game.

You see, I had a little bit of the gene awareness of how we survived during the white man's cruel domination. I give you what you want in this day and time, and I am going to kick your behind in the latter day. And I lived to do it, didn't I? I can say… I dismantled that machine, and then I got your help to carry it away to its burial place, and we buried it, put the dirt over it, and we put guards out over it to watch it to make sure there is no resurrection. If it does, we are going to kill it, again.

I Don't See Myself Separated From My Father

I don't see myself separated from my father, not as an objector, but as a thinker and as a worker for the good of the people. I see my thinking extending from his thinking in my service to the people, as being an extension of his service to the people, not separated. Should you worry about what you're going to be? Don't ever worry about what you are going to be. I never thought about it. My people told me what I was going to be, but I never thought about it. I just heard it. All I knew was what I was at the time and what I wanted to be. I wanted to be, at one time, a radio and television repair man. I became very excited, and they were saying I was going to be a minister, but I wasn't hearing that. I was not paying attention to it, and I am sure you all have had your parents say something about what you are going to be. You just heard it, but you did not say, "Oh, I'd better think about this!" You just heard it and kept playing. Well, that's how I was. I heard those things, but I just kept going. I could not deal with it. To me, it was above my head at the time, that I would be a minister and that I would follow in my father's footsteps. That is what was done by a lot of seniors who said, "Now remember, Brother W. D., you are supposed to follow in your father's footsteps!" They reminded me of that, and I heard it just like some old person saying, "Hey, boy, you'd better be serious! Don't go too far into play. Don't sit with the rest of those boys." That's all it was to me, a check on me saying, "Watch your behavior," that's all. But to think about being the leader, no, it never entered my mind.

If Allah Wants You Somewhere You Are Going to be There

I was ministering for the Honorable Elijah Mohammed and still the leadership never entered my mind. I was minister in Philadelphia and even then the leadership was not in my mind. Do you know what was on my mind? How to talk better, how to get more people for my father, that's all that was on my mind. You know I'm a welder. I love welding. I'm a good welder. I'm a combination welder. I can take sheets of metal, and I can make practically anything you put on a blueprint. I can take the blueprint and make all those things. I can even go and form the metal. I go to the right equipment in the shop, form the metal, bend the pipe, put threads on the pipe, cut the sheet, whatever. I can do that, and I love that kind of work. But look where I am. So, if Allah wants you somewhere, buddy, you're going to be there! You don't have to worry about it. You don't think about it. Just think about what you like and what you want to do.

W. Fard Muhammad

Now, the Nation of Islam was built by the Honorable Elijah Mohmmed, and its blueprint was given to him from an Arab, or a Muslim from overseas, named W. Fard Muhammad, also called, W. D. Fard. However, it is important for us to know that Mr. Fard was interested in all African Americans, and that he came from a people of India who were, also, under British rule. And many of the Indians who were under the British rule their skin color is black, not black people as we know, but their skin color was definitely black. They range from white to black and I mean the whitest of white and blackest of black. The northern Indians are white-colored, and they have mixed all together, now. The Indians who lived in the hotter zones are black in skin color.

Mr. Fard had dark color. He was not very white-skinned. He was brown-skinned and when he came to America, he experienced some discrimination. I think what he experienced in his own country of India under the British with his people there and what he saw and experienced when he came to America had something to do with him accepting to assist African American people in the ghetto with their lives. He came to Detroit, Michigan, to the Black Bottom, or the poor area of the African American, or black people's community and he began preaching, or teaching of separation from white people and having your own.

He told the Honorable Elijah Mohammed and other African American who he preached to, or spoke with, that the African Americans in America, the blacks, had a great past, that they came from an Islamic past and they should return to their religion. So, that gives you an idea of how it all started. It is important, also, to know that Mr. Fard had all African American's interest at heart. He said that there were approximately, seventeen million of us existing when he came, and that was around 1930 or 1931. And in his esoteric language, or preaching, which is a kind of occult language, a secret language, he said that he had seventeen million keys to unlock, or free black people.

The Temple of Islam Was a Concept

Mr. Fard spoke of a meeting of Muslim saints in 1929: "Twenty-three scientists who met in the root of civilization concerning the Lost Found Nation and they must return to their own. So, they sent a messenger to teach them of their own." Now, who was that? That was Mr. Fard. The Temple of Islam was really a concept, and it became real and alive for us. So, he gave a concept to us that we brought to life, but with him it did not mean anything like that. He did not mean a physical wall. The temple was all inside the mind, training for the soul, to discipline the soul. The marching and everything proved that. You gave the original salute as soon as you came in. You were supposed to salute the flag on that board. The original salute, that is not a salute. Salute is a gesture of respect, isn't it? The original respect for what you originally had in your nature you have to bring it back out. It is beautiful when you understand it. It is all in abstract. The concrete is not to be seen as concrete. It is supposed to be seen in abstract. It is a teaching. Everything is a teaching.

Temple means it is not going to be around here always. When you wake up, you are going to leave this. This is just time, tempo, temporary. Christ Jesus, what did he say? *"Destroy this house and I'll put it back together in three days"*. This is just something that you are going to have to destroy, because when you catch on to what is going on, you are going to do away with it. It is going to be too small for your intellect.

From Royal Families

Mr. Fard couldn't have put all that together by himself. He said that is what happened. I believe it. They met overseas and you know the record says when he first began preaching in Detroit, he first started in homes, and do you know how he got in the homes? He was selling silk, yard goods, on the street, carrying it on his arm and they did that in Detroit. Even now, I think some Arabs still do it. There is a big Arab population in Detroit, especially Yemenites. He would put some yard goods on his arm and the women would ask him questions about the material. So, he said, "This material is the kind of material you wore, what your people wore before you were brought to America. Most of you come from royal families. You wore silk and long dresses." That is how he got their attention. And when he got their attention, he finally asked one of them, "Do you have a home?" If they said, "Yes", he asked, "Would you like to hear more of this?" They said, "Yes". I'm telling the story that was told to me. He asked, "Would you like to hear more of this about your people who came from the holy land?" They said, "Yes, we would like to hear more".

So finally, some Christian sister invited him to come into her home and have meetings, and he had meetings in that home until he collected enough followers and collected enough charity to rent a facility. Nobody would let them in except the Shriners, Masons. So, they rented the Masons, Shriners' facility and they started. And I was told that he would come on himself and he would speak, first. Then after he would speak for a little while, he would introduce a Japanese and the name was told to me, too, by one of the pioneer brothers, Edward Ali. He was a captain way back then in those days. He met Mr. Fard and got his name from Mr. Fard. He said he would introduce that Japanese man, and he would just tell them that they need to get on to their own kind right away because the world is going to change. The end of time is coming. When the Japanese man finished, then he would come on and would preach. After about a year and a half, he started using my father and he would give the main part of the lecture, not him. He started out, himself, following the Japanese man. He would preach for hours. But he started having my father teach for hours and he would just introduce him saying, "Hear Elijah." He would not say, "Here". He said, "Hear Elijah" and he would just greet them and tell them "Hear Elijah". They say the last time he spoke was in Milwaukee and Chicago, and he spoke for a long time, saying you won't be seeing me anymore and when he finished, he said, "Hear Elijah", and left.

W. D. Fard Was Muhammad Abdullah

I know he didn't have the ability to do all that alone by himself, and I'm sure Muhammad Abdullah was that man. And I don't think he had the ability to put all of that together. He had the mind to do it. He most likely was the one presiding over the meeting. He had the mind to do it, but I'm sure he got help from different ones who were headed into esoterical metaphysics. I think they helped him and I'm sure he had others who had other skills, political, psychology, and different things. I really believe they met and planned how they were going to do this. But I think the main idea of setting up a Temple and accusing the white man of being the main trouble for everybody everywhere, the Devil, I think that was him. I believe that was straight from him. He was raised as an Ahmadiyya, but he turned on them and set up his own thing. In the Fiji Islands, he set up a school and he taught his own way. He did not make them Ahmadiyyah. He said, no, and they called him Master Gee like we call him Master Fard, and Gee means honorable, reverential. They are not Ahmadiyya's. They have a different mind.

He Came to Have Us Come Into Independence

But they are his staunch followers. They love that man. They are very strong followers of his. He took me to visit them in the Fiji Islands and introduced me to them and them to me. They are much like the Nation of Islam followers, very devoted to him, like we were to the Honorable Elijah Mohammed. I plan to go back there. I really want to go back there. The men and women, they are big limbed, strong bodied. It is really something. I am sure that he did meet with persons and just like he said, he came to the United States on July the 4th 1930, which is symbolic and 1929, symbolic. It means that he came to give us, have us come into independence. That is all it means, because July 4th is Independence Day; 1929 means one short of thirty. It did not reach purity yet, but he's going to clean us up. That is what he had in mind, saying, "I'm going to clean these people up and they are going to be very valuable. He told the Honorable Elijah Mohammed, "They are like a pearl that is down in the mud. All you have to do is pick it up and wash it off".

W. D. Fard Studied Black Leaders

I am sure that W. D. Fard left Europe and was here for a few years earlier than 1930. And I'm sure that he studied the ghetto in Detroit, and he studied what black leaders were saying. He knew what they were saying, he took it all in and he tried to incorporate some of each of them. He took the ones who were looking at G_d and divinity and that was Father Divine. He looked at him and studied his followers to see what they were and how they were having problems with Jesus Christ as a white man, because he changed it from Jesus Christ is a white man. He said, "If you want to see Jesus look at me". That is what he is recorded to have said. And he was a heavy, strong, black-skinned man. I know he (Fard) studied Dubois, Booker T. Washington and he studied the Jamaican, Marcus Garvey. Those are the main ones he studied, and especially Noble Drew Ali. You see, he put the fez on the Fruit, just like Noble Drew Ali, the same fez. He added the drills of Booker T. Washington, because at Tuskegee he had a drill for all the boys. I think the girls drilled, too. Booker T. Washington explained why he had the drill. It made it easy to discipline them, his students, for work. You know, they did vocational work. They built the facilities and everything of brick.

Asia Means Foundation

Obviously, Muhammad Abdullah, called Master Fard, he studied all of that, and Noble Drew Ali identified with Islam in Asia. He said we were not Africans. We were Asiatics. So, Mr. Fard used the same thing, the Asiatic black man. Let me tell you something about the word, Asia. In Arabic, it means, "Foundation", and a form of the word is in the Qur'an, but it is in there as a word that means foundation, not in there as a country. Asasa is from Asia. Asia is Asiya in Arabic and Asasa, means structure, foundation. But if you want to stretch your mind a little bit more, Asia is the biggest continent, isn't it? It is possible that man, a long time ago, knew Asia as the biggest continent and instead of the planet being called earth (which is from European language), they probably called the ground, Asiyah, which means foundation. The Qur'an says, *"The foundation that was built upon regardfulness"*. That is in the Qur'an. All these things, you know, they are mysteries or just unknown, but G_d has taken me by a route where I know I am right. I do not want you to believe things that I know you have no basis for, no reference, but what I tell you is true.

Mr. Fard Intentionally Attracted Persons From Secret Orders

I am aware of persons in the community who had been in the community since it started in Detroit in 1930, or 1931. I was aware of them still being around, and I am aware, also, that they have passed their knowledge on to their children, or somebody in the community that they trusted. They passed their knowledge on to them. When the Nation of Islam started in Detroit, Mr. Fard attracted them, and he knew it would attract such persons. He attracted masonic, black Masons and he attracted Eastern Stars, females and males who were belonging to secret orders. He attracted them and they understood a lot that the average person did not understand. So, they just kept quiet, because that was their nature, to keep quiet, not to express what they knew, and they are still with us. And perhaps their number, now, is more than it was back then, because they have passed it on to others and others have joined, come in like them since that time.

So, I know they are there, and I know they understand the language. I know they understand more of the language than the rest of the members. So, I'm talking to them. I am talking to the Nation of Islam. I never stopped talking to them. I stopped being their leader, but I never stopped talking to them, therefore, my teachings or my speeches are designed to reach those people, to reach those who are in the secret orders, to reach the Nation of Islam in their darkness, to try to penetrate the darkness for them, and speak to the general audience at the same time. That is what I have been doing over the years, and it has really paid off. Now, it is really paying off.

The Movement From W. D. Fard to W. Deen Mohammed Was a Strategy

This then was not easy to understand, the movement from Mr. Fard and the Honorable Elijah Mohammed to my leadership, if you do not see it as a strategy. Mr. Fard planned to introduce the Qur'an and Al-Islam in America, but he knew blacks were militant, and angry with whites. Consequently, he sought the angry, dissatisfied ones and they were receptive. They received his teachings. But he planted among them the Qur'an, though he did not encourage the Honorable Elijah Mohammed and his ministers, or the leaders to preach it. He told them that it was the pure, holy book, the book without defect or errors. He pointed to that book only in that way. He did not point to his esoteric teachings. He never gave his esoteric teachings the kind of sacred respect as he gave the Qur'an.

So, in time, he prayed and hoped that I would be the one, the one, he said, who would become an assistant to my father and help do the work. This was his hope. At that time, I was just in my mother, as a fetus. He left right after I was born in the early part 1933. I was in my mother's womb. On October 30, 1933, I was delivered, I was born. Mr. Fard was still in touch with the Honorable Elijah Mohammed and my mother and the small community that he started, and he sent my mother a message saying, "Take good care of the new arrival," meaning me, then he was gone.

A Brand-New Organization

We came in with a new policy and with a brand-new organization and they knew the organization under me was going to be safe for America. So, they did what they had to do to support my leadership, the law. The law supported my leadership. The law could not go anyplace. They were waiting on me and they finally got me, and we reversed the things that were going on. Praise be to Allah! The Qur'an said Solomon had jinn in his army. It was not because he commanded the jinn. It was because his image was such that would attract even the jinn to support him.

Allah will support you from directions, as the Christians say, which you cannot perceive and that is Qur'an, too. You just be straight, just be for Him all the way. Do not hold anything back from Him, and He will do the rest for you, and give you support from directions that you can't perceive. Look, my father sent me to No. 12 (Philadelphia) and told me, "Son, I am sending you to No. 12, the city of brotherly love," and he said twelve with an emphasis. That is what he told me. I said, "Yes, daddy!" I was ready to go. It sounded good to me. I felt ready to be responsible for a temple. So, he sent me there and that place where he sent me became the strongest place for undoing his work, corrupting the interest, and undoing his work.

"Get the Money!"

Kansas City was one of the places. That was my brother, Nathaniel. He was trying to get a bunch of money, big money, too, so he's taking money from drug dealers. They're putting money into the charities and he's taking it. Detroit was another one. Those were the three worse places, Philadelphia, Detroit, and Kansas City, in that order. I am sure they had reached others, too, with their influence, but those with the basis for that corruption. Some of the things they did are almost unbelievable, and the FBI came to me and told me about it. They said, "Your father, do you think he condones it?" I said, "No sir". They said, "That was our position." That is what the FBI told me. I said, "No, it looks like stuff has just gotten too big where it is out of his hands, but the teachings that my father gives are against that". But in a way, he gave them something to go on when he said, "We're going to do this job, be successful or get this job done at any cost". Those were his words, and then he also said, "Get the money!" He started using that language. He never used language like that before, but around the end of his life, "Get the money!" I heard him in his house, when his official staff was there from around the country, ministers of other areas there with the local Chicago based staff and he said, "Brothers, get the money!" So, somebody who wanted to encourage unconscious behavior or conduct, or criminal behavior, they have something to go on now, thinking, "Don't ask me what you're supposed to do! Get the money!" Obviously, that is what they were doing, letting Jeremiah and the rest of them say, "We can do it! We've got drugs, whores, prostitutes, in the area. We have enough manpower to take over. "They should be paying Mr. Mohammed!" That is what I heard them say, and I'm sure Abbas Rasul and Raymond Sharrief said, "Well, he said, 'Get the money'!" And my brother, Elijah, all he was interested in was just giving orders to the Fruit. He had a thing with just giving orders to the Fruit. He wanted a big gang. That is all he wanted. So, I can't say they set us up. We set ourselves up to fall. That is what we did. We cannot blame anybody but ourselves.

I Changed My Understanding

Believe me, I never changed. I changed my understanding, that is what gave me a new freedom of mind. I changed my understanding, but I never changed my heart. So, my mother told me, "Don't lie, don't steal, don't break the laws, don't drink wine, smoke cigarettes, don't take narcotics, don't be an indecent person. Be a decent person." That stayed in me. I was born to be that way, I believe. So, this is me and nobody can tell you. I was out for many years. No one can tell you or anybody that this man changed his life when he was put out of the Nation of Islam. In fact, it just tightened up. It got more educated in how to judge what is morally correct. You know what I mean? Ideas became stronger in my nature that my mother raised me in.

Therefore, it was easy for me to come back, and I never would have accepted what the followers of the Honorable Elijah Mohammed had become. I could never accept that, and I knew that there was enough support in his following to support me. I knew that the majority was with righteousness. So, we were winners from the beginning. And even the understanding, I knew that there were others who were not pleased with irrational belief. I knew that. So, when I started talking, I knew I did not have to convert everybody, and that many were already converted. They were those who tolerated, I would say, darkness, but there were people living in the light and wanted more light. Once I got it clearly out to the people, to the believers, what I was all about, I said, "I've got you! You are not too big to deal with anymore. I have been tolerating you, trying to show you that I am your boy.

Time is out for that! I started exposing them before the believers. I knew I did not have to fear them anymore. I knew they were weak, and I was strong. I did not have to fear that anymore and they knew their time was out.

The Kool-Aid Man

Abbas Rasul, I've got to say he supported me as a loyal supporter for the whole time that he was with us. He came to me one day, and he said, "Chief (He called me Chief Minister) I see where you want to go and I don't want to be a problem for you, so I'm just going to go, get away. If you need me for anything, just call me." He left me his number. I admired him as a real man and a true man. But old Shakir, the national secretary, who took his place when he left, do you know what he told me? We're in the office and we're not talking about anything, just regular business, a report here and this problem here, and there was like a pause. I was doing some things, handling some of my personal matters and he just spoke right out in the silence: "Go on and go blind!" That is what he said to me. There was nobody in the office but the two of us. I knew that there was some irritation in him that was getting bigger and bigger, because I was getting farther and farther away from this guy that they had put in their minds that they were going to create. They were going to create a guy, a phony, that would meet with anybody, meet with that guy who committed suicide with his followers, Jim Jones, the Kool-Aid man, meeting with him and a couple of other guys, a bunch of phony stuff!

He Went to the Town Store for Knowledge and I Went Up the Mountain

I went along with them, because I didn't want them to know where I was taking the community, the following. However, at one point, I guess he said, "This guy is just ignoring everything that we've given him". They bought me a big, thick book on signs in religion, and one Russian woman, her ideas about these mystical signs in religion, the cross, and that stuff. I didn't waste my time reading it. It was a very thick book, so I just flipped the pages and everything, and I said to myself, "A waste of time!" They had two big ones. I just flipped the pages. I never sat down to really read one page of it. Do you know what I told them when they asked me about the book? I said, "That is not what we need. That can't help us at all. Those books are nothing but an attempt to understand the Bible. We don't need that!" Abbas Rasul said, "Chief Minster, that is fine with me", but Shakir, he was different. He majored in some classes in school, and some the classes he took had a lot to do with Scriptural mysteries. So, he went to the town store for his knowledge. I went up the mountain.

"Go On and Go Blind!"

He couldn't stand it, because it was giving a new image of what I represented and a new image of the direction for us, and we're going towards the Qur'an and the sunnah of the Prophet, and he didn't accept that. He wouldn't accept that. "Go on and go blind!" That is what he said, and I treated what he said the way I treated, much later, what Edmund Hafez said. He was taking me home at night and I'm getting ready to go out of the car, and he said, "Be careful!" But the way he said it, I know he didn't mean it like we say, "Take care, brother", in a friendly way. It was not that way. He said, "Be careful", in a threatening way, and he came from the streets as a gang banger into the Nation of Islam. Then he looked at me and said, "Tell Rafah to be careful, too." I didn't reply at all. I said to myself, "Sure, that is good advice, 'Be careful'. You will never speak to me, again!" I never saw him again. I just gave the word about what he did, and that he could not come around us anymore.

So, for Shakir, I didn't say a thing, but I said to myself, "Buddy, you say, 'Go blind!' Well, I'm going to go blind. I'm going to close my eyes to your absence and not feel a thing. You will never be here anymore!" I went back to the office and told them he couldn't be here anymore. He got out and it hurt my feelings to hear what he was doing, delivering mail at the post office. Now, here was a man way up there, national secretary for us, going overseas with me, and traveling around the world. We actually went around the world, almost, together once. We saw the ruins down in Mexico, from continent to continent, and came back to the United States on a free ticket from the airlines, because we had done so much business with them. They gave us two free tickets. That guy saw the history of the world and meeting with kings, rulers of governments, high places, and said that foolish thing to me, and now, he's out there a mailman, going door to door. That hurt my feelings, and it hurts me right now to think that man came down from that high place, but he did it to himself. So, he didn't deserve it.

Take the Hurt and Make It a Help

He did not deserve it, so he lost it. So, if we learn from all our experiences, then nothing we experience hurts. You take the hurt and make it some help, instead of a hurt. Instead of loss it becomes a gain, if you study it and benefit from it. That is the way I see life. So, I studied those guys back there, Jeremiah, and all of them, and do you know what he did? He got a bad end. You know he came to a bad end. They found him dead, his body partly decomposed. I think he started drinking and walking in the streets. The same thing happened to Mustafaa. They found him dead, too. He was drinking. He went back to the life that he had in ignorance. So, why do I say that when I think about them? I feel sorry for them, but then the sadness disappears, evaporates instantly when I saw that these guys asked for that. They did it to themselves, and they didn't have any true allegiance, true loyalty, just depending upon their expectation, and it was selfish expectations. They were not for the good of the community.

It was the same thing with Valora Najeeb. She supported Farrakhan for a while, and she and Farrakhan could not get along; then she ended up by herself and was found dead, the same thing, partly decomposed. Her own mother did not even keep in touch with her. Her own mother told me, "Wallace, that girl is something! She is so cold!" And she could be very cold. She was only nine years old, I think, when her mother brought her to see my father. Her mother was so impressed with her intelligence, so she gave a demonstration before my father. The girl could read. You could hand her anything to read, and she would just read it really fast. My father was impressed, and her mother said, "I am just showing her to you. I want her to be a helper for you." So, my father accepted it, and it was not long after that she finished high school. I think that she was working as a secretary in what I call the National House, my father's house and office place. So, as they say, such is life. You cannot have it without some strife. Scripture says, *"Do you think you're going to be accepted saying you believe and others before you have been tried?"* So, we have to believe and then pass the test.

Minister R. T.

There was also Minister R. T. Nobody could forget R.T., if they ever heard him. He was a big guy, not a sloppy-looking guy, but big and heavy. I mean big! He had a style of his own. He was a Christian preacher. He joined the Honorable Elijah Mohammed from his church. He was working in a church. He was a pastor of one of the churches, but not his church. He was not the main pastor. So, he left the church for the teachings of the Honorable Elijah Mohammed he said, because he knew the Bible said that the black man was G_d. I said, "Here is another crazy preacher!" I never bought that, even as a youngster. He came in when I was about 18 or 19 years old. I was very young. I was like a student minister when he came in and it was not long before my father had me as a minister. I used to be up on the platform with him, and we both would be speaking, and when he was speaking, I would not have much to say at all. I just liked to hear him. He was entertaining. He said, "That little skunk, he is a pretty little thing, black and white. It makes you want to take him up in your arms. But if you do that, he might squirt you and you will never get his scent off you!" He was talking about the white man.

The Zebras and Five Percenters

He said, "I know you have a lot of love in your heart, you black people. You just want to take that pretty, little thing there, and you do not know what it is." Minister R.T., do you know what his trademark was? He said, "The Bible says, 'If you can bring three witnesses, you've got a case. Jessie said, 'I am black but comely'." Then he would keep on and get three witnesses. He would start with Jessie, because Solomon was black, and he would end up with his three witnesses. He would say like it was real, "The Bible is telling you brothers, G_d is a black man!" He was really strange when it came to the way he thought. He was extreme! I think he believed it, or he was planted among us to hurt us, because he started the teaching that produced the Zebras of California. They were brothers from the Nation of Islam and belonged to the FOI (Ed. Note: Fruit of Islam, a trained security organization of men in the Nation of Islam) in California. They were not all from California, but some of them were from California, and they started the black zebra group that kidnaped the publisher's daughter (Patty Hearst). You remember that being in the news. They kidnaped her and she turned out to be a believer. She joined them. I think it was all to build a case not so much with the public as with the government to convince the White House and Senate that "This is how you handle these people!"

That is what I think, because another brother (Clarence 13X), he was an FOI, too. He started something called the Five Percenters. We believe or I believe strongly, that R.T. was the influence to get them started, too. And my brother also contributed, but he did not do it intentionally. He contributed to these real extreme groups forming. My brother, Nathaniel, he talked out of the lessons (of Mr. Fard). He was trying to show that he knew something, but he did a lot of teaching out of the lessons, and it is dangerous if you don't know how to handle it. The Honorable Elijah Mohammed knew how to handle it. He didn't ignite any fires that he could not put out, but others took it and went astray. Then at the end of it, the end of my father's life, he had people that were feeding that thing, working right with him, too, but he didn't know. However, I think he did catch on to it, but it was too late. Abbas Rasul, he was giving support to Joe Tex (the singer/entertainer) and making the Honorable Elijah Mohammed think that Joe Tex was really a good supporter of his, and Joe Tex was teaching weird teachings. You know he was working for somebody. Why would he come way over here, the Midwest, etc.? He was teaching strange teachings, i.e., hybrid woman and stuff, a white woman that if she kissed you one time, you're finished.

I have been a thinker or all my life. I do not play with fire. If I do it, I am like Moses. I have a ring around me. I figure that it is a waste. You end up wasting time. If you don't get killed, you have to go to the hospital and all of that. The police are going to come in on it. Why be bothered with all of that? It is a waste of time. It is not worth it. It is like in the Qur'an and the Prophet said, "Peace, and keep going."

Changing the Nation of Islam's Thinking

Also, it might be concluded that I have differed so much with the Honorable Elijah Mohammed's teachings and with his programs that I should be charged as the one who did away with or destroyed his programs. Well, that is not correct. But I am the one who changed the thinking of his following and thank G_d for the help that I received to do that. You may be surprised to know that the biggest help I got to do that came from the Honorable Elijah Mohammed, himself.

The Honorable Elijah Mohammed always encouraged me to be a man of Scripture and not the Bible, but the Qur'an. He always encouraged me to be a free thinker. He did not hold me to the thinking of the Nation of Islam. He told his followers, especially his leaders, "He is not going to preach like the rest of you. He is going to be different. He is going to use the Qur'an." So, the Honorable Elijah Mohammed prepared his leaders to accept me in my different posture that I took. I took a different posture or stand from the Nation of Islam in that I came to establish Islam as given in the Qur'an.

"Sometimes, It May Be Best to Leave the Next Man Alone"

My father told me when I came back, "I need to talk with you. There are some things that I promised our Savior that I would tell you." I'm around the house. I'm not going to bother him. That is not my nature. So, he was going to Phoenix, once, and he said, "I'm getting ready to go back to Phoenix, son. When I'm there, I'm going to call for you, because I promised my Savior." He didn't invite me back. I did not go back. He invited me once, but when I got there, no conversation or anything. Now, he's getting ready to go back, again, a second time, but nothing happened.

He gets sick and they take him from Phoenix to Mexico, where his house was. It is still there, which is good. I'm in the house with him and he is not doing too good. He is in bed most of the time. He got to feeling better and I was getting ready to leave and he said, "Well, son, sometimes, it may be better not to bother the next man. I wanted to tell you some things I promised my savior I would tell you, but sometimes, it may be best to leave the next man alone." That is what he said. Now, that was his judgment.

You know he said a lot to me when he said that? I felt so good. I said, "He is not buying everything Mr. Fard said". It made me feel so good that he was not just following Mr. Fard, blindly, because that could be dangerous. Muhammed Abdullah (who was Mr. Fard) one day said, "I asked you to come and work with me in the garden and we both planted in the garden. I planted string beans, and you planted string beans. Yours came up better than mine and produced more than mine." Now, I know what kind of mind he has, now. He is telling me "Go on your own. You don't need me anymore." So, that is the way that happened.

The Devil Can Be In Anybody

I believe, the Honorable Elijah Mohammed couldn't do what he did by himself. No way he could be that strong and that consistent, that determined and that forceful in delivering what he knew he had to deliver and doing what he knew he had to do. G_d's Spirit had to be with him. He was obeying the Spirit. In the last major address he gave, he was telling us that we have come to where we have to change. We can't see the white man anymore like we have been seeing him, as the Devil, because the Devil can be in anybody. He made that clear, and he made it clear that he wanted us to accept white people. "If they can accept us, we are supposed to accept them. If they can respect us, respect them." That was his message, saying, "See, I told you the white man is a devil, but I'm telling you this white man (sitting on the dais with him) is a Muslim saint."

A Need To Be Called From the Waters

I will never be rested at all until our people have ascended. No, we just can't have some of us. We've got to have our people as a whole uplifted, or in a spirit to ascend, and not give their life to vulgarity and foolishness. And that's where I was coming from when I said, "This time let us liberate ourselves…" That's where I was coming from, these feelings and thoughts I have inside here. This time let us liberate ourselves. Nobody else can liberate us. In the Qur'an, Allah doesn't ask us to seek somebody else for liberation. *"Oh, you who believe, liberate your own souls and your families from the fire"*, and the real fire or passions, flying passions. You know, fires always start where there is no light. So, if it is talking about knowledge and science, it starts in ignorance. That's where it began, right in ignorance. And if it's talking about morality or human decency, it starts, too, where there is no light. And where there is no light, the passion can be a passion for corruption and self-destruction.

We've lost our individuality. We've lost our true individuality and Allah made all of us individuals upon five senses and that's our common bond. That's the first common bond for mankind. And the heavens, what does it say, the heavens have how many doors? Seven, (the mouth, two eyes, two nostrils, and two ears). And all you have to do is put the head under water and there is no light, no ascension. There is nothing. It's all gone, drowned out. Hold it under the water long enough, it's lights out for everything. The leaders in the black church, they are in the water nature, in the water constitution of mind and spirit and everything, and they love it so much they hate you for trying to pull them out of there. Yes, I know, because they love me, but not when they found that I'm trying to pull them out of the water of the Church. Use the water, but don't submerge yourself in it too long, especially your head. Wash in it and sprinkle a little bit of it, that's okay, but good G_d Almighty, you all are living underwater! That's what most of the church leaders are doing. They have their congregations living under the water, so it is only fish that they are fishing for. So, they need to be called from the waters, again.

A Sense of Togetherness Under G_d

But we should not be going to churches and trying to help them. That won't work. If they invite us to go then respect the invitation. If the invitation is to help them understand, then help them understand. But if the invitation is to support their good understanding, then just support their good understanding. So, that's not the way.

The way is what I have been saying. We need to study what happened to the spirituality of our people from the time when we had good leaders, and we were doing well to the time that we lost that, and we lost it just recently with the loss of Dr. King. We were losing it, a lot of us, and lot of us hadn't come to it even when Dr. King was our leader. We hadn't come into it, but the people always had a sense of togetherness as a people under G_d, not just togetherness under black power or love for money or something. No, we had a sense of togetherness under G_d. That's what saved us through slavery and after slavery up to the time when we lost our true leaders. That's what saved us, a sense of togetherness under G_d, not just togetherness, togetherness under G_d. We have to see when that was lost and what transpired to take us from that, to take us out of that; what transpired in the culture and in this environment to do that, because it brought down the Church, brought down the church leadership. And you know in the average church the preacher is just preaching there to keep his job, to keep his money coming in, and to keep his people happy; not to direct the life of his people, but just to keep them happy.

A Champion Inside of Us

I definitely have always had an interest in all African American people, in human beings, period, but mostly in African American people. What should be expected of me other than that? It should be expected of me that I would have the interest of all African American people at heart. We have a spiritual life together, as well as a racial life together. Racially, we know we're tied together, because we all came from Africa, originally, and we're called black people. We have a history coming from slavery to the present time, liberated or a free people who have been included in the American citizenry and in the American society, American life. So, we all share that history, but we should understand that certain events in that history have made very deep impressions upon our soul. Spirit is really an expression of the soul. So African Americans, as I said in New York, at the Apollo Theater, "We have a champion inside of us, and it is the African American soul", referring to the experiences we had as slaves, during the time of lynching and Jim Crow, both in the South and the North, as a subclass people struggling to get full recognition as citizens in America.

These experiences have affected us, along with certain horrible incidents in the North, like lynching, the murder of Emmitt Till in Mississippi, etc. He (Emmitt Till) was from Chicago, and it has affected the North, and we have suffered, even in the North, not only discrimination and depriving of opportunities that are given to whites, but we also have suffered in the North brutal physical treatment. That time has passed, we hope, and will never come back. However, there are insane, deranged haters of whites, Jews, of Catholics, haters of anything that they can find to hate. They just have to hate something and occasionally we will see a demonstration of that hate. Even now it is possible we will see a demonstration of that kind of hate that has lingered and stayed in some of the sick people of our society. But the point is we have experienced this. It has touched our hearts. It has touched our souls. It has gone deep into our soul, and it has influenced the way we feel. It has influenced the way we think. It has influenced what we want to achieve as a people.

We have shared that experience, so we are all tied together, more importantly, by shared experiences. We are tied together by that more than anything else. The black skin, alone, is not enough. You will find black people in Africa divided and fighting each other. The black skin cannot unite them and likewise for us in America. Black skin could never unite us. It has been our shared experiences on the road to progress that has made us a people of one ethos and one and the same ethos, one in the same racial spirit.

Dealing With the Psychology of Our Behavior

My leadership has dealt more with the psychology of our struggle and more with the psychology of our behavior than with the physical needs that we have. And I came to conclusion, years ago, that building the psychology of the individual and building the psychology of the race, building the spiritual life and the mentality of the race and the individual, is the key for putting us into a situation where we will have the spirit, the ambition, the assertiveness to tackle the hard job of changing our physical picture in our neighborhoods. Where our neighborhood depends on outsiders for its business life, that should not be, and that has to stop. That is really the scene that the Honorable Elijah Mohammed was addressing, also, when he said we must build businesses in our own community, in our own neighborhoods and have them to be quality businesses and have them survive and thrive.

So, we are bringing a message of not only spirituality, which is extremely important. It is important that we know how to recognize our own spirituality, so we can be successful in managing our own spirituality, not spiritual life, not religion, but spirituality. In other words, manage our impulses, manage our tendencies to give support to certain things that are no good for us, manage those tendencies. And to manage those tendencies, I call managing my own spirituality. You have to be able to manage your own spirituality. You have to have psychological insights into the nature of your spirituality to manage your spirituality. That is a necessity.

However, what is most critical at this time is for us to address how to qualify for complete inclusion, the inclusion that a community asks for. If we're going to be successful in establishing a community, we have to be successful as businesspeople and as educators, people responsible for the education of our little children, bigger children and our teenagers, people responsible for schools. We are going to have to be planning to be successful as people who know how to grow in the system of these United States, to use the system, to benefit from the system as other ethnic groups do. We are going to have to be able to manage that. We have great, Christian leadership who have brought us a long way and have realized inclusion as people, but now we need inclusion as a community.

Our communities are not thriving, financially, and as a result, they are not strong communities. They are very weak communities. If they are strong financially, it is because of us contributing to the tax base and because of us being a consumer people contributing to the business strength of those who come into our community. Because of our own neglect, we invite them into our own communities. So, they come to our communities and take over a business that was boarded up, deserted and they put a strong business there and bring new life.

The Honorable Elijah Mohammed's Way Must be Continued

One example is Madison Street on the Westside of Chicago. When you travel down Madison Street, it is not the deserted street, business artery that it was some several years ago. Very recently, life has come to Madison Street that separates the North side from the South side of Chicago and runs through the Westside, predominantly African American neighborhoods, or community. It is alive because of Indians from India, Pakistanis from Pakistan, whites, and some Arabs, all doing big business on that artery. But the consumers, or the buyers, are African Americans. We are the ones who are keeping those people in business. This is not to attack them. No, they had the right to go in there and do business. America is a free country, and we believe in free enterprise. But that doesn't excuse us from the shame of neglect on our part that we did not go in there and we didn't bring business life to our own neighborhoods. The Honorable Elijah Mohammed's way must be continued. We must continue his way of addressing the needs of African American people, which is not only a spiritual and moral need that is strong and first, but there is, also, a material or business need.

So, I have followed the excellent life pattern and community life pattern that was established by the teacher of my father, Mr. Fard, as a blueprint. I, also, followed the good works of the Honorable Elijah Mohammed, and I hope that as his son and as the leader of many who followed him, I have continued in the best tradition of the neighborhood concerns of the Honorable Elijah Mohammed; and I hope I am traveling in the best tradition of the universal Prophet, a mercy to all people, Muhammed, the Prophet, the prayers and peace be upon him, of Mecca who was preaching on this earth more than 1,400 years ago.

We are in the Islamic calendar now, more than 1,400 plus years since the migration of Muhammed, the Prophet, and his followers to Madinah, where he set up a model of community that has become an international model for Muslim community life all over the world. We pray that blessings and peace be upon our Prophet and what follows of our traditional salute to the last Prophet.

My Preparation for Leadership of the Nation of Islam

I have been asked when did I know that I had to prepare for this mission for my leadership to continue the work of the Honorable Elijah Mohammed? When did I know? I was told that all my life. I cannot remember a time in my life when I was not told that. My mother would remind me. My sister, Lottie, she would remind me. I have two sisters Ethyl and Lottie, called Riyah. They would remind me, when I was seven or eight years old or younger, saying to me, "You are out there playing with those boys. You have to remember that you're supposed to help your father. Our savior gave you, his name." They called Mr. Fard, savior, and Savior's Day was celebrating his coming. Riyah (Lottie), she would tell me, "I used to have to go over the chalk where he wrote your name on the wall, behind the door. I used to have to go over it with chalk to keep it bright."

My mother would say, "Son, you are not to be like other boys. You're different." She meant I was not to let my spirit go to the streets. I was not to be one of the guys on the street with the street spirit. I heard that all the time. She would say, "Our savior said that you are going to help your father in his work." Now, you're telling a little child 5, 6, 7, 9 years old. I remember myself at five or six years old sitting on the front row in the temple hearing the ministers preach and all I remember is that they said, "Islam is freedom, justice and equality". They said that so much I could not forget it. I was a teenager. I had a moustache, and my father told me, "You have a moustache, so now, you have to join the men." He would take me with him to business meetings, even to meetings where he had to make a serious decision whether to keep a person in position or fire them. So, I was there as a young teenager, hearing that talk and I said to myself, "Daddy, really doesn't want to lose us. He wants to keep his sons with him".

But later, I looked back as I progressed in my own thinking, because more responsibility was given to me, and I accepted it. I said, "That man was wise." He was actually preparing me to assist him in the leadership, letting me see how he ran things; letting me see the kind of things that came at him and how he dealt with those things. The Honorable Elijah Mohammed was very wise, and he prepared us, and it was not at any of those times that I became aware of the heavy decision that I had to make to take on responsibility for leading my father's followers. Never did that come to my mind, even when I was preaching. I was preaching as a minister from about 1951 or 1952 until I went to prison in about 1960 and then came out. I was a minister responsible for Temple No. 12 in Philadelphia and even then, that did not come into my mind. When my father showed sickness and began to be weak, then I started to worry about the future of the Nation of Islam. That was when I started to take it seriously. It was in the early 1970s, maybe even starting around 1968 or 1969. When I was released from prison, I cannot forget it. Freedom is an important thing. You do not forget freedom. I may forget the day they locked me up, but I will never forget the day they let me go. It was January 5, 1963. When I was released, I was released on parole. I was turned down for parole the first time. The second time, I made parole. So, I was a parolee. I was not free to do anything. I had to report to my parole officer. Therefore, the Honorable Elijah Mohammed advised me to be low key and not to speak from the rostrum, etc. He helped me because I couldn't do that, anyway. My parole, my conditions for parole, would not permit me to do that. I was not supposed to go and preach the Nation of Islam's teachings of separation from whites. I was not to do that during my parole. I had to serve my parole time out.

Troubling Activities Happening In the Nation of Islam

It was not even then that I saw myself coming into position to be responsible for the following of the Honorable Elijah Mohammed, carrying his best tradition on. But at that time, I did worry about the future of the Nation of Islam, because certain things had occurred in Philadelphia, Detroit, and some other places that were giving the Muslims' a black eye, or a bad face. There were charges of dope pushers contributing money to the Nation of Islam in Philadelphia, Detroit, in the Kansas City area, and some other charges of a black mafia forming inside the following of the Honorable Elijah Mohammed, which was very serious and very troubling for any of us, if we heard that. Most of the believers, I do not think that they heard that. But the law enforcement knew about it and the top leaders of the Nation of Islam knew about it.

But some of the followers had to know about it, especially in the Detroit, Kansas City and the Philadelphia areas. I did start to worry about the future of the Nation of Islam during that time of the late 1960s. By 1971 or 1972, I was free from my obligation to my parole, but I was also free to start preaching. My father let me back in. As you know, I differed with some things, such as Mr. Fard as being G_d, a man being G_d. I differed with that, not that I did not love and appreciate the man. But I saw that having the religion correct was more important than having the man in a certain picture. I thought we should take him out of that picture of G_d and put him in the picture of a social reform teacher, or something.

Malcolm X Advised to Not Oppose the Honorable Elijah Mohammed

I was making those changes not in opposition to my father and better than that. I told Malcolm, "Nobody can oppose the Honorable Elijah Mohammed and keep his following. If you oppose him you will lose his following". I knew that. I told Malcolm that I would not be opposing the Honorable Elijah Mohammed. I'm not trying to take his place. I even had a foreign Muslim tell me, once, "You don't put two swords in one sheath." I didn't even reply to him. He was saying that "You cannot be boss. The Honorable Elijah Mohammed is the boss". I was wondering what put that in his mind. Maybe he was clever enough to try to plant the seed of division in my mind. But anyway, I did not even respond to him. I rejected him. I didn't like him at all for saying that.

The 1940's and 50's brought changes. The Honorable Elijah Mohammed changed his main message or interest in his message. Malcolm came straight to the Honorable Elijah Mohammed's home. I saw him myself perhaps before his own relatives saw him. He came straight from prison to the Honorable Elijah Mohammed, at his home in Chicago. You could tell he looked like he was straight from prison, in good health, good spirits, but looking like he had been out of the sun for a long time. I think he was sentenced to prison for fourteen years. I don't know how much he served, but he served a good amount of that time in prison. He came to the Honorable Elijah Mohammed, but before he arrived, the Honorable Elijah Mohammed told the family at home, and I was in his presence when he said this. He said, "I've got a young minister coming. He's not going to be like these old ministers, just satisfied to have the Holy Qur'an and the Bible up under their arms. He's coming and he's going to help me progress and build the nation." That is what the Honorable Elijah Mohammed said. The Honorable Elijah Mohammed knew that he (Malcolm) was attracted to Honorable Elijah Mohammed's new viewpoint, new focus for his message. So, he came out and he proved to be just what the Honorable Elijah Mohammed said he would be. He was very productive, hardworking, and had a terrific spirit. That was Malcolm X, who later was called Malcom Shabazz. The time changed. That was the early 1950's. By the 1960's there was a lot of trouble in the public life, in the institutions, in the churches, colleges, of our people manifested or seen in the public life. There were demonstrations by our people and very brutal treatment from law enforcement in the South, and in the North.

All this bad scene pushed a lot of church people to black nationalism and to militancy. SNCC, the Black Panthers, and others became very militant. What do you think influenced them? The teachings of the Honorable Elijah Mohammed, the Nation of Islam. So, don't underestimate the value of the Nation of Islam in the life of our people. Also, it was the Nation of Islam that influenced blacks to give more attention to business and material growth and development. It was the Nation of Islam that had the greatest influence on that. Their leaders will tell you this in private. Some of them will tell you openly in public, "Well, it was the Nation of Islam that influenced me to change and be this way and do these things like that."

Now we are living in a new time and a changed time, a changed focus and a change registering in the mind and in the heart what is important. So, can't you see that the movement of Al-Islam, as started in the African American community by Mr. Fard or Professor Fard, was something formed to go stage by stage, one language to take you to a stopping point I call a way station, where you stay there and get yourself together to go from there to another point? And then the next point is also a way station. You go from weigh station to weigh station until you get home. Home to what? Tell me. Freedom, justice and equality, that is the main point. It is not that you are going to be Muslim, not that you are going to be Arabs. It is that you are going to have what your soul called for, what slavery and mistreatment under white supremacist America took away from and deprived you of.

"He's My Son, Too!"

That is our history. There is no Malcolm in any other history except ours. I'm telling you if he impressed black people, he impressed them while he was speaking for the Honorable Elijah Mohammed and the Nation of Islam. Now that might be a sensitive issue, but one thing is sure, something is wrong with our African America history writers if they will take the Honorable Elijah Mohammed out of our history and try to set up Malcolm. When Malcolm was in prison serving a 14-year sentence for being a pimp and a hustler on the streets of Harlem, New York, it was the Honorable Elijah Mohammed's message that woke him up, stirred his energies, and brought him to come to the Honorable Elijah Mohammed and be taught how to speak to our people.

Credit is due to the person who deserves it and earned it. Don't give one man's earnings that he is due to another man, take the earnings of one man and give it to somebody else who didn't earn it. I'm not knocking Malcolm. I loved the man. My brother, Elijah Mohammed, loved the man. We loved the man. My mother loved the man. He came to my house and what did my mother say to us? She said, "He is like my son, too." She let us know of her respect for him and her appreciation. And that is a real mother and real wife who has her husband's work and interest in her heart, and if she sees you supporting it, you are endeared so much that she will tell her own children, her own boys, "He's my son, too!"

Put Out of the Community

I had friends very close to me. I had relatives very close to me, and they would be asking serious questions, sometimes. In fact, they had difficulty accepting certain things that they were taught, too. So, I'm thinking, "I am among trustworthy friends" and I'm sharing with them: "Really, what is not correct is Mr. Fard. He cannot be G_d. He invited us to Islam. Islam has a book that is the authority of Islam. It is the

Qur'an, and it does not allow that we say any man is G_d. That is the worst crime we can commit, saying G_d is a man, according to our Qur'an."

So, I would tell them that. It got back to the lieutenants and captains, and that is how I got put out. They brought it to the leadership, then the Honorable Elijah Mohammed called me in to question me. He said, "Son, we have some charges against you. You are charged with saying that our savior is not G_d. Who is G_d?" That is exactly the way he spoke to me. I said, "Daddy, you have the Qur'an, and you have more knowledge of the Qur'an than most of us. I won't answer that question". Well, it did not make him comfortable, but at least it kept me out of trouble. I did not have a sword to fight him with. I was not going to pull a sword out and start fighting him. I came to help him, not to fight him. When he put me out and I knew about the drugs and I knew about Malcolm's passing, I said, "It is going to take a lot to keep these people". That is when I started thinking, seriously, about it.

I Went Into Deep Studies

When I was put out, I knew that the following would have to be saved from infighting and saved from the attacks from the outside on us, on what we believed and what we were all about. I knew that. So, I went into deep studies. I said to myself, "Most of the following of the Nation of Islam, they have been taught the Bible, to see themselves as a people like the Jews, persecuted and needing to come out from under the rule of their persecutors into an environment and a society of their own". That is the way I saw it. "So, I am going to have to study the Bible". I was not a Bible minister. I was a Qur'an minister. I said, "I am going to have to study the Bible and get familiar with the Bible". So, I did. I have told the story more than once. I will not go over it, again. It takes too much time. But I studied the Bible, and I came to conclusion as to how I should use the Bible, if I used it at all. I was already familiar with the Qur'an, but I also obligated myself to study the esoteric teachings. I hate to use the language, cult, or secret teachings of Mr. Fard. I knew I had to study that, too, so, I did.

That signaled me to world myths, to the mythologies of the world. So, I traveled out of Illinois. I went to libraries in other states looking for books and I found books on mythology in different places. I read the mythology of the Asian people. I read the mythology of some African tribes, or people, like Egyptian mythology. I read these mythologies, and all this coming together was not my genius, but it was the assistance of G_d. G_d was assisting me and giving me signals from Mr. Fard's teaching, signals from the Qur'an, signals from the Bible, that brought me to do this kind of vast research; and then digesting or extracting from all that research what I thought would be my strategy and a successful strategy for bringing the following of the Honorable Elijah Mohammed out of a language prison to freedom.

Our Life Was Uprooted

We are a people shaped, as all people, by our experience in community environment. We are as the people in the Bible and in Qur'an who were rejected by the society they were in and who were blessed by G_d to make a transition, an exodus, or a cultural and spiritual transition to find a new life. We are a people like that. We were forced almost to seek a new life as a people because of us being separated so completely from any conscious traditions that we had in Africa. We were not following any traditions that our people had in Africa. Slavery had obliterated, erased, done away with all of that, even the roots. That is why they say we were uprooted. Being transported from Africa to the plantations really uprooted our life that we knew.

The Genesis of the African American People

As a result, we had no recognition of or knowledge of where to retreat, no way to go back, to return. Mr. Fard acknowledged that when he said, "They could not swim 9,000 miles to go back home", meaning it is impossible for our minds to go back to Africa and start all over, again. We have to pick up our life here and build the life, here, for ourselves. This will be our new origin, or our new genesis. I gave a lecture once in New York, titled, "The Genesis of the African American People." So, while I was preaching for the Honorable Elijah Mohammed, it just began to vibrate, very strongly, inside of my spirit, that we have to recognize that we are a new people. We are not like any other people in America. All these people follow past traditions. They are tied to past life traditions, past cultures, but we are not. So, we are a new people. We are a new people born on this soil. The first Americans, called the American Indians, they were here before the white man. But history says they came from somewhere else, also. They came to this land. This land was not populated, and they came to this land and populated this land. This is what history says.

Our Home Life Was Slave Life

Now, here we are brought here as slaves, but completely separated from our past, babies taken from their mothers and daddies and raised just to be workers on the plantation with no ties back to home life at all. The home life was slave life. That is all it was. Gradually, we became acquainted with Christianity, and we became Christians. But actually, the movement of the Church did not start until we were freed from the plantation. That is when the big movement of the Church started with the African Methodist Episcopal Church. That is when the black church started. They are a new people. They are Christians. They have a Christian origin that began in the soil of the South, and all of us have our origin beginning in the soil of the South. So, I said we are a new people.

That idea helped me so much, when I accepted that we are a new people. Our history begins in America, in the South and in the North as a new people. If we are new people, then G_d is obligated to help us, to work with us. In the Bible, it asks the question first, *"Will a man rob G_d?"* G_d is speaking. *"Yes, you have robbed Me of this whole people."* I began to see that as being something that we should be concerned with more than even the Jews, because though it is speaking of the Jews in the Bible, that the world had robbed them, they were in Egypt under Pharaoh. The world had taken them, but they were still in touch with their religious life. They were still in touch with their religious history.

The Most Thorough Theft of a People Ever

Now, here the world had robbed G_d of a people, again, but you robbed more than the synagogue. You robbed more than the church, the mosque. You robbed the cradle. You robbed the first place. You went and took the baby out of the cradle and took him away from all that he was familiar with, and started him off in a new environment, new circumstances, where he had no way of being in touch with the religious life that he once had, with the business life that he once had, with the political life that he once had. He had no way to go back to any of it. He had no way to recall any religious connections or anything. So, this is the most thorough theft of a people that ever occurred on the planet earth. So, we are a new people.

If we would just register that and understand that we would go forward. You do not even need the help from G_d. Your own nature will thrust you. Your own nature will push you forward, will urge you to go forward. A baby learns how to walk on its own intelligence, power, and energy. A baby learns how to crawl, to stand up, how to walk. A baby learns our language and how to talk on its own energy. What is that energy? The energy of new life. So, if we accept that we are new people, we will have the energy of new life helping us. Now, if you believe in Scripture like I do you will, also, know that G_d is on your side.

For Christians, Christ asks no less of the followers, of the Christians, and for Muslims, our G_d, Muhammed, our Prophet, ask no less of us, that we have a heart that can have room in it for every person on this earth, for all people. Strong language is in both books, Bible, and Qur'an, urging us to become charitable and open-hearted where our hearts open up to accommodate all people, welcome all people. But I have to say this, also. I'm a product of my African American people's experience, as a people coming from slavery to freedom. I am a product of that road and that experience, and that has worked positively in me to connect me with all human beings, because the issue is not how they treat a certain color. The issue is how they treated human beings, and all people are human. Do you see? So, I am the fruit of Islam, and the fruit of the African American experience at the same time.

The Real Mother That G_d Made

G_d wants us to know that we lose our inheritance when we lose the family connection, when we lose the good parent who bore us, who gave us birth. It is speaking of the mother that G_d created for us. She has love of humanity, love for G_d, and she wants to see her child completely free to be all that child can be, if that child has the desire without anyone blocking that freedom for that child or holding that child back. So, the real mother that G_d made is the mother that wants to see her children have all the good life that they can have that G_d has made possible for human beings. So, if we have mothers like that, then we are in good condition, good shape. But who is expected to defend the rights of the mother and her child to have that life? The husband, the man, and if he loses his respect in the eyes of his fellow man, then the son, and the daughter, the children lose their father.

A Father With No Responsibility

The father can be living, but if the father has no respect, if he is not responsible anymore as a father, it is the same as though he is dead, because he's not there present to support the mother and to defend the rights of the family. This is not suggesting that we men are to defend the rights of our family irrespective of the laws of the land. No, indeed! But there is always a way. Even when the Muslim's life is persecuted Allah does not excuse us from our obligations. The Qur'an says in the Judgment, some will say, "I couldn't live my Muslim life because they persecuted us". Allah will say to them, *"Did not I make my earth spacious? Why didn't you go somewhere else?"* You can migrate, you can leave bad situations, and I don't think it is just for nations or armies that hold us down or hold us back. I think it is saying any bad situation you are in you will not have an excuse when G_d has you to face Him. You won't have an excuse before G_d if you say, "I couldn't do this. The neighborhood was bad, and drugs were everywhere, and we couldn't get any help. I didn't have any money. My mother, my baby, my sister, thirteen years old, had to prostitute herself and I had to sell drugs." No, Allah (Highly Glorified is He) will say, "How come you did not leave those bad circumstances and find better circumstances? Why didn't you go elsewhere?" And there is always the freedom to pull up stakes and go elsewhere. People have done that all through history to have a better condition for themselves. This country was populated firstly by people who were persecuted back in the old country, in the old world, in Europe. They were persecuted there, and they came to this land, so that they could have freedom to live their religion without having their religion and themselves oppressed and persecuted.

So, this is really a place that we should remember when we are reading in the Qur'an where G_d says they will say, *"The people were strong, and they persecuted us"*. And G_d will say, *"Why didn't you go elsewhere?"* You should remember the Pilgrims, those who first came to this country and populated this part of the world, so that they could practice their religion and not be persecuted, blocked, denied, or held back from the life that they believed G_d wanted them to have. We in America today, we have favorable circumstances, and we want the life that G_d wants us to have, and G_d wants us to have a complete life.

Abraham Came Into Religion With His Whole Self

And this again is in the Scriptures of the Bible and Qur'an, that G_d wants us to have the whole life. When Abraham, called Ibraheem, in our Qur'anic Arabic language, when he was mentioned by G_d as a model and as one worthy of being called a leader for all nations or a father of all the nations, as the Christians and Jews say, G_d points to something about him to let us know what earned him that great respect from G_d. G_d says, "He fulfilled his debt to G_d". He completed his debt to G_d. He gave himself completely. His heart was completely firm or sound. He gave his whole life to G_d, not just part of it. Abraham lived a complete life for G_d, and he gave not only his spirit to G_d, but he gave his brain, his intellect, to G_d. He showed the way for the people to come fully into religion, not just spiritually, but come into religion with your brain, with your intelligence and come into religion with your whole social life. Bring your whole community life under G_d. That is Abraham, the one who was worthy of being called leader, *"An imam for all the people or for all the nations",* in our holy book, and in the Christian's language, the father of all the people, or of the many nations.

So, the inheritance we are denied is because people do not respect G_d and His Way. When people don't respect G_d, the Creator, and His Way, then they will see us as prey for them and say, "Oh, we can prey on these people. They are weak, ignorant. They don't have the strength to resist us. So, let us exploit them. Let us make them our resources." So, they will make a whole people their resources to supply and strengthen the life or the society that they want, if you don't take your responsibility in your own hands to spend on your own souls. As Allah says, "Spend on your own soul. Spend for the betterment of your own condition within yourself, within your body, your mind, your heart, etc."

Just Beginning to See Muhammed, the Prophet

You know, Jesus Christ saw himself in Adam, and I see myself in Adam, not in Jesus Christ. I see myself in Adam and I see myself in Muhammed, peace be upon him, because Allah, Highly Glorified is He, created Muhammed. This isn't the Muhammed that was born of flesh and blood from his mother, Amina. This is the Muhammed that Allah created. Allah created Muhammed, and He can create whatever He wills. Whenever He wants a son, He can just go to the men or the women He created for a son.

Some things I tell you all I have no proof for, but to me it's reality. I know that Allah has shown me Muhammed's life, the man in his complete picture, and his complete picture was much too much for those newly converted pagans that he was preaching to when he was on earth. It had to come in time, and it is just coming right now. It is coming, now. The scholars in Islam are coming to see Prophet Muhammed better and a lot of them are stopping this crazy hang up they have with the West, that they have to be in some kind of tug of war with the West or something. A lot of them are giving that up, men and women. More women scholars than men are giving that up and they are starting to free their minds to see the serious fields of work that Allah opened up to us through His Servant, Muhammed, the last Prophet. They are just starting to see him.

So, I see him (Muhammed, the Prophet) in his big dimensions. The old man, Muhammed Abdullah (W. D. Fard), my friend and my father's friend before me, he was very dissatisfied with the way the Ahmadiyyahs perceived Prophet Muhammed. Yes, he was, and the late Mufti, Kuftaro (of Syria), the same thing. He was very, very, alone almost, among the leaders of the world when it came to having a real picture of Prophet Muhammed in his mind. Muhammed was much bigger than the Muhammed that they have given us, the Muslim world has given us, and Mufti Kuftaro and Muhammed Abdullah, I just mention them, but I believe that there are others, too, like them.

Whatever G_d Sees He Can Give It to You

This is a strange side of my life that I am sharing with you right now. I have come to know Muhammed so completely and so clearly that I feel there's nothing in his life that I don't know. Now, it's strange for me to believe this as a rational person, you know what I mean? But that kind of reality is with me, and not only him, Mr. Fard, too. If G_d is with you, whatever G_d can see, He can give it to you. Yes, I mean the language is real. The language I'm giving you, there's logic for it. But now, if your faith is not strong enough, you'll say, "Oh no, that didn't happen!" Well, you all can say, "That didn't happen". You can say, "Ah, that never happened", and I'm not hurt. I'm not made uncomfortable. I won't say, "Ah, they didn't believe me!" That's fine. Whether you believe me or not, I'd like you just as you are. But I'm sharing this with you all because this is my reality. I studied Mr. Fard, and I think I know him better than anybody on earth does. That's right. I think I know his whole life. I know all about him, and the same thing for Muhammed, the Prophet, 1,400 years before Mr. Fard. Yes, the same thing, for Jesus Christ, too.

The Source of My Knowledge and Revelation

For a long time, I was sharing what I felt was happening inside me. I was coming from what was already an activity inside of me that was convincing me that whatever was in that person I was getting it. And I was not getting it to be it, but getting it to know it, so I could go and do what I had to do, and that's the reality. That's my reality. So, when you heard me talking, I'd be saying Scripture is my reference, but not the source of my knowledge or revelation. No, the source of my knowledge and revelation is G_d, Himself, and the activity in me is the activity that is required by the nature of my own being and soul.

I'm a product of our experience as a people, rejected, and then searching for the truth, like that group called, the Essenes, searching for the truth; not just Muslims, but Christians, too, searching for the truth, wanting to know, "Where does G_d want me to take this life?" The Bible says of Jesus' mother that they were pursuing her because they wanted to get rid of her child. So, she was told to, *"Flee to Egypt with your child"*. The woman was told to, *"Flee to Egypt with your child"*. So, by some strange happening, G_d put Mr. Fard in our life, and Mr. Fard took us to Egypt with our life. And questions unanswered (and some appear to be unanswerable for a people of the Essenes' nature who are searching for the destiny that G_d wants for us on this earth) is the worst form of oppression. It's the most powerful form of oppression.

"Flee to Egypt With Your Child"

So, for our minds, we were under great oppression. So, Allah as a Planner, put Mr. Fard in our life, and then Mr. Fard put us in a very difficult religion to understand, to make sense of, and we're under that and that's the new oppressor on us; not on those that just want to be big shots or want to think they're better than other people, black power and all of that, or black supremacy and all that kind of stuff. No, it is for the real serious ones who want understanding and want that understanding to be approved by G_d. That's us in the belly of the whale, or us in Egypt, oppressive Egypt, and the language is confounding us and just defeats every effort of our rational mind to arrive at the answer we want. So, this is the new oppressor. This is the new Egypt. *"Flee to Egypt with your child"*.

"I Come Treading the Wine Press Alone"

Jesus Christ said, *"And I come treading the wine press alone"*. I think that's how it goes, the wine press, alone. The juice of the grape is going to be made into wine and wine tastes good and even makes your insides feel good, makes you just feel so good inside. But that same wine can befog your mind. He says, *"I come treading the wine press alone"*. So, what is the Bible saying, and what am I saying here, now? That that kind of teaching that's so difficult to understand, on your mind can be like wine, and take you out of your mind, take you out of your right mind.

But if you can keep your good mind and work with those ideas and symbols that can take away your good senses and make you dizzy in your head, if you can remain faithful and rational long enough, eventually, you'll be able to see clearly. It will have no effect on you to befog your mind. The effect will be to clear your mind. The same thing that will make one drunk, the average non-believer or misguided person drunk, won't make you drunk. It will clear up your thinking. And Jesus Christ said, *"I come treading the wine press alone"*. That means, "The innocence that I have is what is needed to bring truth out of these cloudy matters, and if you don't have this innocence, you can't do it. Leave it only to my innocence. Nobody else can do it." And that's the truth.

Look at these coffee drinkers we had, black coffee drinkers, brothers in the Nation of Islam trying to get the knowledge; my brother going to Egypt for Arabic and coming back home, but doesn't have anything for us, nothing to help us. But Wallace D. Mohammed, the one that was named after Mr. Fard, was the only one that was able to drink the wine and clear up his head. Praise be to Allah!

A New Life and New Beginning for All Muslims

When Muhammed came into his mission, the answer for all the world was given. But Muhammed said that darkness was going to come on his own following, and as it began the first time, that's how it will be defeated when it comes again. He said it would be on the poor, and the poor in Scripture is not just the poor in materials. It is the poor in knowledge of Scripture. They are also the poor. So, those who think they know, they can't get it. They're off track and can't get it, because they already think they know. They can't get it, but the poor person in a time of mental agony and strain for religious thinking in the world and in his following, in that time of darkness and poverty, the spirit shall move on the face of the waters and G_d is going to say, *"Let there be light!"* And the world is regenerated. Praise be to Allah! I know it's a regeneration for us, and for us it's the first time we're coming into the clear knowledge of the world. But I do suspect that what has happened to us is the opportunity for new life and a new beginning on this earth for all the Muslims in the world. I do.

Better Off Without Them

In response to the question as to whether or not other Muslims in America and worldwide will eventually come around to accepting my understanding and what

Allah has blessed me with, I would say, "Well, you know what the spirit is moving me to give you as a reply? The spirit is moving me right now to give you as a reply, 'No comment! They are not worth it! They are not worth us even wondering if they're going to come, go north or south, or east or west, stay where they are, find a deliverer among themselves, or look at us and get direction. They're not worth it! They are not worth us worrying about their circumstances, or whether they are going to support us or not'." So, that tells me that G_d doesn't want us to waste our time even thinking about that. I have no desire. I am not moved in any way... We should just do what we have to do, and Allah will take care of the rest. And I think it's because really the shape they are in right now, we are better off without them.

I believe the future is going to be better for all of us. Yes, we will have bigger and better opportunities to make contributions to our own life, where we see our own life free from all these falsehoods and misconceptions in our life, but also, we will be able to make great contributions to the world of mankind. Yes, it is going to come. It is coming, guaranteed. You know, different people at different times, I'm talking about the people who search for G_d, for a way for man on this earth, they look at the same thing that others before them looked at, and they come up with a compatible language. The language is compatible, but not exactly the same. So, the Scripture will have what these people saw for this time and what people saw at a later time, and even a projection, sometimes, of what people imagined was going to come, was going to be the reality. This is the nature of Scripture.

The Meaning of Desert

I was talking about the understanding of dhikr starting in your original nature. The Bible says that babes give perfect praise. Out of the mouth of babes comes perfect praise. And aren't you glorifying G_d and praising Him when you are doing dhikr? And it starts with the babe, the baby finger. It's the baby finger, the first finger, the original, innocent, nature inside us that comes with every baby born. They're born innocent. They are not guilty of anything. So anyway, you start down in the nature or in the roots of your life and you come up to that which is above the surface. The roots, they're under the earth, right? And then the part that comes up is called the stem, but the movement is going straight up, standing straight up, perpendicular. Lastly, it comes to a circle. I told you what it represents, but it also represents, in the Gospel, the palm tree, and in the Qur'an, the fig tree. These trees, they usually grow up straight, very straight, and they don't give their fruit until they are high up. It's high up and they don't give fruit until the growth stops going straight and goes out, outward, reaching outward as far as it can reach all around.

Jesus Christ Riding the Donkey

So, when your vision grows like that, fixed strictly to what is right, at some point in the heights G_d is going to open your vision to see that you need to branch out and give more than just yourself, and give to more than just yourself. And when you branch out and give to more than just yourself, when your branches go out to give to others, then the fruit appears! And it clusters and is so nice and sweet! The people saw Jesus Christ. They had been doing just that and when they saw Jesus Christ, they recognized that Jesus Christ was the one that would call them to that nature, to the original nature and to the straight path, the siratal mustaqeem, just like that tree growing up. And he would be a sign, himself, of that generosity that G_d wants in man. When they saw that he was the leader, they threw out their palm branches and made a path for him and his donkey. "Ride your donkey here over our palm trees". What they were saying was, "We submit our knowledge to you! You are our leader!"

It's beautiful! That's a great picture, a beautiful picture, Jesus Christ riding the donkey. That's what he was riding. But Baal was riding a donkey, wasn't he? And when the donkey saw the angel in his pathway with a flaming sword he rebelled against his master and questioned his master, *"Why have you struck me these three times?"* The donkey spoke with a man's voice. It only means the people that have been carrying the burden of the world finally found a just rider.

G_d Has Liberated Our Souls

Now, Jesus Christ was on the back of this donkey. But actually, who was really on the back of that donkey? On the back of that donkey is the donkey's soul! But now his soul has been liberated. G_d has liberated his soul and now the same soul that used to punish him and made him a pack animal for the world has now been liberated and is on his back riding him as his guide. Yes, and now he's transformed! He's no more a donkey! He's a man! That's what has happened! G_d has liberated our soul and put our soul on our back, new, fresh, and free. It isn't that slave soul anymore. It isn't the soul of our people anymore. No, their soul is riding them down, most of them. Is that true or not? Yes, it's riding them down. But G_d has revealed to our soul and put it on our back as our rider and khalifah, meaning one who is orientated from the back, from the rear. Yes, it was a great sign, and I said all of that to say that we have been freed. We have been freed, and we have become our own khalifah. And the same soul that wouldn't let us rise above the status of a donkey in the world is leading us. Now, mind you, this is in the world. This is not off in some separate place. No, this is in the sight of the world. We're the donkey.

"They Always Put Us Last"

A good picture of this is in the Bible. It says Rachel was going to the place where they were to have their life re-established. She was riding a camel, and she had the treasure chest with her on the camel, and with her were some other camels. She was the boss lady riding the head camel, the camel at the head of the train. Behind the camels were horses, and behind the horses, donkeys. So, you know we always said, "They always make us last!" That was the complaint of our people. "They always put us last!" That is the donkey, the position of the donkey. And they also did not open possibilities for us to get equal knowledge, or to have equal access to higher knowledge. They kept us out of their best schools and everything. So, the picture in the Bible, don't think about the world. Think about the people struggling for G_d and their circumstances.

The Whole World Is a Desert

In the lead is the camel. Why a camel? Why not an elephant? Why not some other big, strong animal? It is a camel because a camel is known to take people safely across the desert, and the people of G_d, they are a people who thirst for understanding. The camel takes them across the barren world, because you can have oak trees and cedars, everything, and you can have farms, grazing land, and everything. But for what I want in this world, your whole world is nothing but a desert. So, don't think about a real desert. Think about a place that doesn't offer something for the thirst of a devoted servant of G_d who's trying to find his way to establish what G_d wants for man as a life on this planet earth. Yes, so the whole world is a desert! The whole world is a desert, and the camel is the one that takes you through the desert.

The camel knows where the water is. You can't see it, but the camel knows by instinct where the water is, and the camel will take you there and stop. The one who knows camels, they know that if you don't see water, take a stick or something and dig in that spot. The water is down there. The camels know that the water is there, and that is how an oasis forms. The camel takes them there and they can't see any water, but they start digging the sand out, and a little well forms there in a puddle. Eventually, if they continue to work it, it becomes a fertile spot and there's life and it becomes an oasis. Many Arabs, they are migrants, and they go from oasis to oasis. So, the camel not only knows to take you to an oasis where something is already growing there around the water, but they know how to find water where nothing is growing. They take you there, you dig, you find water, and you come there and start making routine trips there to get water. Pretty soon, things start growing around that spot. I guess that's because they eat and drop seeds there, and eventually something catches on there. After a while they have a beautiful little area, a small area. They are small, but an oasis is like a little garden in the desert.

The Camel a Picture of the Intuitive Nature

The camel is not in that physical picture. The camel is inside the human person. So, G_d has blessed man with the brain and the vision to deal with this material reality, but G_d has also given man intuitive power whereby intuition can take him to something that he's seeking. By intuition he can be guided or be taken to something that he needs or is seeking for his benefit. So, this is the camel inside the man. The camel inside our makeup is that intuitive power and the camel has strong instinct or intuitive power for taking his master to where his master can find some help in desperate times. This is the camel. So, Rachel is depending on, more than anything else, the intuitive power. Rachel has reference to the feathers on the bird, on a flying creature, feathers of a creature that flies that is conditioned by habit to fly. If you take the feathers off him, he can't fly. So, those who were looking at these pictures of reality, they came to a picture for the intuitive nature or power in man, and they gave the camel as a picture of that power.

And this particular Rachel, she is the hope of this favored people of G_d. She is their hope. She is their hope, and she is depending upon intuition and obedience to G_d, not just intuition for any person. So, that's what she is riding upon, herself, and behind her are horses, creatures that were just naturally made to follow in the spirit until they drop dead. Very committed, that's what it means, spiritually committed. They will drop dead before they stop obeying their master. That's the racehorse, isn't it?

The Donkey Is Human

And behind the horse is a donkey. It's beautiful, because it shows that she didn't forsake them. The ignorant, rebellious masses, she didn't forsake them. She had them in the rear, bringing them up. But the Bible says that that donkey is going to be transformed a man, and it gave the picture of Baal riding the donkey. And all the time we thought that was a man riding the donkey, that was the donkey's soul. The donkey was never a donkey to start with. The donkey was always a human being, a man, but the world made him a donkey, and the world made him a donkey by leaving him out, or not including him with the educated people, setting him out, separating him from the educated people and restricting his freedom to the status of a donkey, or the life of a donkey, and putting him in the rear. But really the main problem, or the main cause of him being formed a donkey when really G_d created him a man is that he did not respond to believe in his own soul for his elevation and progress. He didn't respond to it.

So, it says he saw an angel with a flaming sword. He saw the Word of G_d that can defend life and also take life. The sword defends life but also takes life. So, he saw the Word of G_d having the power to defend life and also take life. He saw the Word of G_d as a liberator, and as a destroyer. When he saw it, he repented and he realized that he had oppressed himself, as Abraham said, *"Surely, I have oppressed my own self. I have wronged or oppressed my own self."*

Question Your Own Nature

Abraham then was a sign of how everybody comes to reality, face to face with their own reality, and repent their own part in their own bad life or bad faith. This is what the donkey does. He sees G_d's Word and His Justice, and he feels condemned, and he repents his wrong that he's done himself and he comes to liberate his own soul. When he liberates his own soul, then the ignorant soul that he had before is not riding him. It's the liberator, the new soul, the liberator that's riding him, and then he asks Baal, *"Why have you struck me these three times?"* The language makes it seem as though he's really having a complaint against Baal. He is, but Baal is his own soul. He is, but that Baal is his own soul that he's now liberated from and he's asking his own soul, *"Why did you strike these three times?* You defeated me in my nature. You defeated me in my mind, and you defeated me in my urge to find my destiny to come home."

In baseball, you have three bases. If you can get past those three, you can go home. But if he's caught on either one of those three, he's out. So, he said, *"Why have you struck me these three times"*, meaning in my nature, in my mind, and in my purpose or my destiny you defeated me. He was questioning his own soul. Allah says, "You question G_d. Why don't you question your own soul?" Question your own nature, your own beginning. That's the way to come to reality.

Question Our Own Spiritual Trials

What did I say all of that for? We are now liberated. We're liberated, but we should be, especially the educated ones among us that are sincere and faithful, questioning our own spiritual trials and tribulations from slavery to where we are now. If we do that, we will come up with literature that can help all our people. We were situated to free ourselves and we did bring the white world to accept us, that we be free. Why is it that we are not enjoying freedom, but still complaining? So, let us research our trip or our travel up from slavery as a spiritual people under G_d, under the Church, in the Church, and under G_d. Let us see what turns we made, what attracted us to get off the path and what brought our religious leaders to be devoted in the Church but not devoted to the liberation of the African American, or the black people in America? Why did Dr. King have to be our last leader?

The Problem Is In the Group Soul

There's a new kind of slavery. It's not one imposed upon us by segregation, by two laws in the United States, or a strange law for us in the South and one for white folks. That's gone. We don't have that anymore. So, it's obvious that we need a new kind of struggle or liberation. We need, really, the knowledge of our own spirituality and what has happened in our own spirituality or in our soul to take us off course, divide our energies, and disperse our productive sources so that they are not united anymore, and not serving the people anymore, the African American people anymore; but just working here and there in little places and satisfied. So, what we need to discover is that the problem is in the group soul. Every people that has experienced life over generations they have a group soul, collective soul. We have lost that group soul, and we need to see what happened over these generations. With Dr. King and after him, what happened that he goes away and there are no more leaders? We can find the answer. The answer is in our experiences in this real world, and these neighborhoods, in this cultural environment. The answer is in our experiences up from that time till now, and insha Allah (G_d willing), this can be documented. It can be put on paper, and it can give us insight into what the real problem is that we stopped progressing as a people with the loss of Dr. King.

If we are progressing as a people, it's just because the world is progressing, or because of good opportunities for us in the world, like in the corporate world. We rise, make progress in there. It's not black and white anymore. It's open, open to diversity. All these good opportunities are here, so individuals are progressing and that affects the status of the many or the masses, but there is no movement.

A Need for Community Liberation

There is no leadership for all our people anymore. There is not. If there are they are so small that they're not seen, like me. My leadership is always for that, but we are small. We're not seen. So, we're not reaching the many and the, for want of a better word, Devil, himself, Shaitan, is in the life of the people in the culture and making it very difficult for any of them to pull away from the strong magnetism of this bad life to even recognize a person that's working in the place like I am and a few others. It's not just me. There are some Christians working hard, but they, too, are not seen. Nobody recognizes them. If they're working hard on what we want, we're the same. We shouldn't separate ourselves from them, but we should realize that they're comrades in arms, and we should be seeing ourselves as one force. However, we need to liberate the souls of our people, and if we cannot liberate the souls of our people, they will never come again into that collective soul or that group soul and realize the great power or spirit and power for better changes in their life. And they realized that under the people they believed in, the leaders that they believed in, like Dr. King, and for us the Honorable Elijah Mohammed, and that time passed. We had that sense of soul force, and it was the soul force or the spirituality of the whole group. We shared one spirituality, one soul force.

We still should be there, but the constitution for that soul now is different from the constitution that was needed in the souls of the past, even Dr. King, though he was a Christian and a peacemaker. But it's different. The constitution for that time of the soul of the African American people, who still have not reached the destiny (we have not reached our destiny), the constitution is quite different. The constitution now is enlightenment for community liberation and really that's what it always was. That's what it always has been, a need for community liberation. In

87

the South, as servants for the white man, or his white world, the white South, plantation slavery or whatever you want to call it, even after slavery the life in the South, it was a people who couldn't advance as a community. If the white slave master liked you well enough, you could advance as an individual. Some of them would say, "Really, that boy there, he takes care of everything for me. If I didn't have that boy, I couldn't do a thing!" Yes, some of them would even acknowledge that the slave that was helping them was really the factor for their surviving.

We Don't Think Community

So, it wasn't the individual. The situation wasn't the need for any individual liberation. There was a need for the liberation of the people in their community life or in their neighborhood life. That was the need. As obvious as it is that we can't manage our neighborhoods, can't even manage our own neighborhoods, as obvious as that is, I don't hear any leaders saying we have to liberate our neighborhoods from drugs, etc. The drugs wouldn't have come in, wouldn't have gotten in, if we were liberated as a community. Because we were not liberated as a community, that's why the drugs got in. If you get the drugs out, you're going to have the same problems. We just don't think community. We don't think responsibility for our neighborhood or for our community life.

Now, we're in a better situation to turn these things around than any other people existing on this planet earth, or in any of these United States, why? It is because this is what we were denied as slaves, and this is what we did not receive when we were freed. The knowledge that this is really what we were deprived of that other people had, a sense of community responsibility, will be motivation in us to make us succeed in a marvelous way. We just can't start where we are. We didn't just begin to be crippled or deficient when it comes to taking charge of our community life. This thing was denied us as slaves. So, when we bring it back to where it started and bring it up to where we are now, we have the power to change it, and we have the power that is not given to any other people in the United States or on the planet earth, because none of them were denied the right or the responsibility for their own community like we were as slaves and as freed slaves.

Conditioned to Depend Upon Ourselves

So, that's what is on my mind. That's what G_d has got working in me and if we can study that, we're better situated to do that. How are we situated better? This is divine intervention, I call it, a people who were dissatisfied with their life under the white man taken and gathered in a new reality for them called, the Nation of Islam, that didn't depend on outsiders for anything; that thought they, themselves, could deliver themselves and the rest of our people, if they would follow or join. So, we were a people who had an appreciation for self-independence, for a big measure of self-independence. That's what you can't find out there among black people. They think they need outsiders, that they cannot do it by themselves and need outsiders. They don't have a lot of faith in doing things alone. They have to have the white man with them or over them, most likely over them or backing them, for them to really have the courage to go forward with their plans. But we have been conditioned, as followers of the Honorable Elijah Mohammed or members of the Nation of Islam, to depend upon ourselves, and to have faith that we can do it ourselves more than any other people out there I know. So, we have this working for us.

Mr. Fard Says He Came on July 4th

When Mr. Fard came here, he said he came on the 4th of July 1930. That's what the lessons say, and they are all symbolic. He might have come in 1930 or 1931, but I know it's all symbolic. July is the seventh month and that's the soul of man, seven, that's created as one soul to have seven elevations, to ascend seven steps to universality, seven. So, here is the seventh month. Don't think about July anymore. Think about seven and the soul with the power to ascend to the seventh heaven, and the fourth. The fourth represents the four directions, east, west, north, and south, which really means the whole of the universe, universality.

"Forty Acres and a Mule"

So, here is a man coming on the fourth day of July. It means he's coming on a day to work and influence the people, so that they'll be moved into their nature that is ascendant, where they will have a spirit to free themselves and free their souls. This is not freeing themselves from the white man. It's freeing themselves, freeing their souls, and they want to free to their souls so they can have their independence. But to have their independence they must be able to manage the environment that G_d created and it's north, south, east, and west. Now, the white man down South I think he was too ignorant to say what he said. I think somebody up North or somewhere else put it in his mind. He said, "Ah yeah, you're free and we're going give you forty acres and a mule!" Forty "achers", that are going to make you ache, hurt, pain, forty acres. Isn't that something, how man puts his hates into his language? Say, "Yeah, you think… if you want to follow me as a farmer you've got to be willing to ache a lot. You're going to really ache trying to develop these acres. It's going to bring you a lot of pain and suffering." And it will, especially the old ways, the way that they had to do it. It was hard work. That's what it means, hard work. That's what that old cracker meant. "Yeah, we'll give you a piece of land, but it's going to be hard work and we're going to give you a mule, because that's all you've got! That's all you've got up here (a mule head)." So, that was his opinion of us, and he knew the condition that he had left us in.

Meet G_d by Conforming to His Purpose

So, Mr. Fard, he didn't want us to just become Muslims. He wanted us to free our souls and ascend with our spirit and our soul to higher levels of vision and understanding where we will become universal in our vision and understanding and better qualified to establish ourselves in equal respect, form, and respect with other people who have established themselves on this planet earth. That's what he wanted for us. As Marcus Garvey said before Fard, that one day he believed we would "rise up and take our place in the constellation of the heavens".

Allah says in Qur'an Adam did sin, or he fell victim to the suggestions of the evil one, but he repented. It says he met a Word from his Lord, and he repented. Then G_d says that those who keep their faith and strive, persevere, and also those who are just heedless, they all must one day meet their Lord. If Adam met a Word from his Lord, he met his Lord. Stop thinking that you have to meet G_d like you meet the Honorable Elijah Mohammad or his son, Imam W. Deen Mohammed, or Chiara Lubich or somebody like that. That is not the way you meet G_d. You meet G_d by conforming to the purpose for which He created you. When you conform to the purpose for which He created you, then you meet your Lord, you have met your Lord. That is your return and that is your meeting with your G_d. And the Word, G_d has made it to live with us and help us to come to that meeting where we are conforming to the purpose that Allah created us for. So, let's take the mystery out of these things and be free and not burdened. We can do much more and much greater work in the world when we become free for G_d's Purpose.

A Drink Called "Kafurah"

When the spirit of truth has come, it shall lead you into all truth, make you free. So, what was the people under before? They were under the spirit of falsehood and thinking they were under the spirit of truth. It says in the hereafter they will be given a drink called, "Kafurah". It sounds like kafir, doesn't it? That is what it is suggesting, that in the hereafter they will be given a drink, and a drink is for people who thirst. They will be given a drink called, Kafurah, and they say it is camphor. Camphor has the letter, "M", in it. Kafurah has no, "M", in it, and that is one of the basic letters that should be in it, if kafurah is camphor.

What it is alluding to is just what it says. You shall come to reject things that you believed in. That is what G_d is going to bless you with in the hereafter. In the hereafter, He will bless you with the comfort in your heart, spirit, and soul, of rejecting things that you firmly believed in before, things that you held sacred. G_d loves us to be so faithful we believe it just as He gives it to us. The angels were somewhere in the big council in the heavens and Satan was up there with them, disguised. And when G_d brought out His Purpose, that He was going to create a man and give him power that Satan would be jealous of, Satan manifested himself. He was no longer appearing as an angel. Now, he shows himself as a jinn. He rejects G_d's Plan, and the angels become worried. This is a great theater in the sky. I undo that theater, and I put it down here in man, in the human world, so that it is a drink of kafurah, and I thank Allah for it. I like it. It is a good thing!

A Stirring In Your Soul

All the mysteries G_d created me to understand, not to be burdened with mysteries. G_d is not a mystery, and His Will, Purpose, and Work are no mysteries. They are mysteries only to those who are ignorant, don't know and have no will and nature to see them as they are. When G_d changes and gives you a new nature, a new form that does respect to the human intelligence that He created you with, then you will be able to accept it, see it and understand it, and you will be most comfortable with the new life and new understanding. That is what has been stirring in your soul ever since you have been created. The human soul has not been created to live in the dark. The human being wants to live in the light. If we have any purpose stronger than any other purpose in our life force itself that purpose is to understand. What can torment a lover more than anything is that he is losing his love, and he can't understand why. Now, if he could just understand, he could walk away and wipe his tears off somewhere down the road. But if he cares, that is the worse burden to live with, not understanding. It is too much burden.

Concentration In the Interest G_d Wills for You

As you are aware, Zakariya is the one who was assigned to Mary, the mother of Jesus Christ, and she was in the mehrab, according to the Bible and according to the Qur'an, and he left her there and didn't disturb her. But occasionally, he would go to check on her to see how she was doing. And whenever he checked, she needed nothing from him, although they assigned him to her to take care of her needs. However, when he would check, she wouldn't need anything. There is nowhere in the Bible where he did any service for her or that he attended her needs. He was just assigned that position. However, he did nothing but check on her. But to actually help or assist her, he didn't have to help her in anything. That is very important for us as Muslims, to believe in Christ Jesus and his mother, and to say what we say of Prophets, peace be on them. What is that saying and what is the mehrab? The mehrab means like the womb. For the woman's body, a child is going to be born, so the life is in the mother in the womb. It is formed in the womb and delivered from the womb of the mother. The mehrab means concentration when you're completely absorbed in the interest that G_d has willed that you have.

Many Persons, One Delivery

Her being left like that means though we want to assist that life and help it to have what it needs, there is nothing we can do but just have an interest and watch. It is all in the Hands of G_d. Just like the forming of our baby in the womb, male or female, all we can do is just wait. We check on the mother, do the best we can, but there is not much we can do but just wait for delivery. So, that is all Zakariya could do, just wait for delivery. It means that even the mother of Jesus Christ, though she wasn't a Prophet, she was completely in the Hands of G_d, and what was being done to form her for Jesus' birth was all in the Hands of G_d.

I don't want to tell you this, but I have to say it. The Honorable Elijah Mohammed, his works, you who sat there and listened to it and stayed with it, you couldn't help it. There was no way you could have changed. G_d's Will was working. He was going to hold you there and watch over your formation and make sure you formed and reformed until you got where He wanted you to go. That is what happens to the germ in the womb. It forms and reforms. He is going to do it until you're delivered. Can you believe this? Every one of you who stayed with it and you're sincere and truthful, you are delivered as Imam Warithu Deen Mohammed, many persons, one delivery, and Allah was in charge of the mehrab, and nobody else could do anything in that situation.

"W. D.!"

So, you have to give them what is rational. And without telling the community or telling me, that influence from Mr. Fard and my father and mother and others that supported them in what they were trying to raise me for was there. Like John Hassan, the investigator and a cousin of Supreme Captain Raymond Sharrief, he had his way of just smiling and treating me differently, without talking, like a Zakariya. So, whenever he spoke to me, I don't care who was around, he never said, "Minister Wallace, or Wallace D." He said, "W. D.!" And he said it like that, like it was something really mysterious about this "W. D." I had. He was going to make sure that I tied it to Mr. Fard without telling me that, without telling me to do that. It didn't work for a long time, but when I started to open my eyes to want to see in the dark of Mr. Fard's world that he created for us, then his face came to my mind, and his voice saying, "W. D!"

Actors On the Stage

So, it all has worked out as planned and we're nothing but pieces in the puzzle, actors on the stage given a role to play. We're not our own creator. We didn't make ourselves and if it's for you, you can't escape it. You'll be going down a road that is not even in the world that fate has designed for you. But when it's time for you to come out, you're going to come out of that world and you're going to get on the road you're supposed to be on in the other world. Every human being has got a role. There's a role prepared for them and sometimes it's not major at all, very minor. It has no real meaning in man's world. It has no presence, no meaning in man's world. But what G_d has designed for one of us, He designed for all of us. If He designed that servant's life to be what He wants his life to be in His Plan before they're born or come into reality, if He designed it for one, it's designed for all of them. Yes, you had to be what you are. You couldn't be anything different.

No Name Without It Being In G_d's Plan

It's the same for all of us. It's in G_d's Plan, and I don't believe anybody receives a name without it being in G_d's Plan that they be named that. If his name is, "Dog", or "Hyena", I don't care what his name is, that name had to be approved by Allah, by G_d, the Creator, before that name could be accepted in his life. If that name wasn't to be his, it is not going to be his, no matter what it is. And there is more to names than we think, much more. I've done it, studied for many years now, at least, for longer than my life as a leader. I have studied for more than half of my life as the leader how names influence the outcome of the person that has that name. Now, sometimes the person can defeat the influence of the name and become the opposite of it, whether good or bad, become the opposite of that name, but that name was the cause of that's person making the change.

No, we can't name anything, and I guess I always knew that. I never wanted the power to name. Whatever the wife wanted I let her do, even though I didn't agree with it. I wouldn't name unless she asked me to give names. If my wife asked me, "Can you give me some names", I would never give her just one name. I would give her several for her to select one from. That was just my nature. It had nothing to do with me fearing to do this, that Allah wouldn't approve of it, or something like that. Allah didn't come into the picture at all. It was just my spirit, just my nature and spirit that I didn't want to name a human being. I thought the mother should be the one to do it, or I'd give her help to assist her in selecting a name.

"Gardens Underneath Which Rivers Flow"

"Gardens underneath where rivers flow" is referring to the psychic urges. Now these rivers flow underneath our feet because underneath is that that we stand upon, the ground. Our feet touch the ground. So, it is saying underneath your feet, and where is the most sensitive part of your feet? You are standing on it. The most sensitive part of the feet, underneath, is the sole of your feet. From underneath is where rivers flow. So, the spiritual sensitivity in the Church, when they get real worked up, what starts moving first? The feet, and they say, "Oh, Lordy!" So, the feet received it before the head did, and it made the feet have to express that, "Something is happening in my soul", and after a while the whole body gets it. They have to stand up and start jumping around, but it started way down there. That water

starts rising way down there. *"Gardens underneath which rivers flow"*. Praise be to Allah!

The psyche is not the rational mind. You're not thinking how to work this out. What the preacher is saying you are responding to it with your spirit. You are responding with your human sensitivities. You are responding to what he is saying and through that particular medium you're taken over, you are overcome with joy. So, that nature is in all of us. Even in the coldest of us the nature is there. You just have to bring it out. Sometimes it is not a communication of joy that brings it out. It is a communication of pain. You put enough pain on that hard guy that never responds emotionally, and he will break down emotionally, saying, "That is enough! My G_d, leave me alone! Leave me alone! Stop, if you have any sense! You have no mercy! Stop please! I told you to stop!" He panics, too. He gets hysterical, too. You just have to find a way to reach him.

"Gardens underneath which rivers flow", is speaking of the spiritual urges that appear below in the construction of the human form before it comes up to the rational mind. These rivers are two and in the Qur'an, Allah tells us about the rivers, that one is a river of honey. Now, didn't the Christian world tell us that in the heaven or paradise we're going to have milk and honey? Yes, Allah mentions the rivers of honey. Honey is sweet, isn't it? … You know there is a chapter in the Qur'an for the bee. Some of these animals are so important Allah devoted long passages to them, and it became a whole chapter.

G_d Has Done It Again

Zakariya is very important. It is a play on two things, on two meanings, purity and charity. You can almost hear, "Zakat", in, "Zakariya". It is a compound word, zakat and riya. Pure, and then riya suggests light, but light for seeing, pure light for the eye, that is close to the meaning of Zakariya. Scripture says, *"And every eye shall see."* That man they selected, wouldn't that fit the logic, that they would select the one who had pure light for his eye to take care of Mary? But she didn't need any help from him. All she needed was to be left alone, because G_d was going to work on her, Himself. We should not look for these things in the past now that G_d has repeated His work for us in the present, and that is no exaggeration, the great wonders in the creation of G_d, the Creator, in the life of man. It doesn't say anything when you say G_d created mankind. It doesn't mean that He created something flesh and blood, physical things. When He created the earth, He did that. He created the earth to bear all kinds of life. Do you think man needed a special act of G_d or something to create man, when G_d didn't need any special act to create the whole universe? So, why do you think He needed a special act to create you when you're flesh just like monkeys, like other animals? Your heart beats and ticks just like theirs do. You holler and scream and sound like an animal when you get in trouble, like they do, so why does G_d need some special, divine power, and special divine act to create that? It is what G_d is going to put inside of that which is the great wonder.

Take it from me, He has done that, again, in the belly of black people and He created a human being, again, not the physical human being, the spiritual human being, the same way He created the first one. The Qur'an says the likeness of Jesus is the likeness of Adam and He created him from dust. He didn't say it was more difficult, creating Adam was more difficult than creating Jesus. He already had human life but G_d created human life when there was no human life. There was nothing but dust and He created human life, called Adam. So, don't make a big wonder over G_d creating Jesus Christ without a man. He created the first human being without a man or a woman, from dust. Does the Bible say the same thing? Yes, it says the genealogy of Jesus Christ, meaning how he came forth from parents to be the child he was at that time, they say it goes back to Joseph. But how is it that Joseph didn't touch his mother, Mary, to create his birth, but nevertheless, he had to go back through those people? They trace him all the way back to Adam, and it says Adam, who was created by G_d. He was born of this one and that one, then Adam, who was created by G_d. Allah blessed Muhammed, the Prophet, to see this and it was revealed to him that the likeness of Jesus Christ, his creation or his being born is the likeness of Adam, and Adam was created from dust. G_d, His Will is only to say, *"Kun faya kun. Be and it is"*. It means to express His Will, and it comes about. It exists.

G_d Is Creating a New Everything

The creation of man in the Qur'an is given plainly in the Qur'an. It is not the creation of mortal flesh and blood. It is flesh and blood, but only by interpretation, the blood meaning something else and the flesh meaning something else. It all has to do with the hunger in your mind, the need in your mind to have the knowledge and guidance to establish your life to your soul's satisfaction. That is what G_d's Work is about in creating man. So, He creates a new mind, a new person with a new spirit, a new everything. The old makes everything new. This is in the Bible. He creates that person, and he is to be seen in a relationship with the need to be educated, to know, to have knowledge, and to know how to establish the human life that G_d wants established. So, it is all about man learning and being prepared to build the world that G_d wants him to build for his life, having that life and building the world for that life. If you look at the world, even the Muslim world, it has lost that. So, Allah has caused the same act of creation to come about, again, and I know it! I see it! I witnessed it! I'm living it!

We Are All Connected

We're connected though we see ourselves not connected. We are connected as life. There are spiritual orders or spiritual, devotional societies, that meet together just for that purpose. They have it as the main function of their spiritual organization or spiritual group, to meet together. Even Muslims do this, meet together just for that purpose, so that we will learn how to have patience and how to believe in the Will and Spirit of G_d, and how to sit and have patience, reflect on G_d, reflect on His wonderful names, His purity, and reflect on His Peace; to come more into His Peace, so that we become peaceful; that the things that normally trouble us are not reaching us at that particular time. You have separated yourself from all trouble and you are just dwelling in G_d's Peace. I'm using these terms for want of other terms that you would perhaps understand better to be in G_d's peace and to have patience and wait on Him, not to ask for cake and ice cream, or for a drink of water. Ask for nothing, just be patient and wait on Him. And while you're waiting patiently, you're doing this in conjunction with other members in your immediate environment and circumstances. And if you do that, G_d brings great relief to your soul and spirit and sometimes G_d enriches your mind and understanding. You should wait on G_d to manifest in one of you His Mercy and His Blessing for that effort. So, these spiritual orders believe that one person will speak. Sometimes, one will speak, and another will follow, and different ones will speak who are witnessing this. They believe that when they speak, it is G_d they are hearing and not themselves.

Listen a Lot, Talk a Little

I said all that to point to people who have faith. First, we must have serious faith, like those people who practice that kind of spiritual obedience and silence where their silence, their own interests are for the sake of knowing G_d. We have to have faith. We have to have patience, and we have to have that degree of seriousness to have what we need to listen to each other. They are the wisest of people. You can have a room full of Ph. D.'s and they will have trouble listening to each other. It is not a lot of knowledge that is needed to have us listen to each other. It is just a certain condition of the spirit, and soul we need to be able to listen to each other.

We put G_d first and foremost, and we realize that what we have to offer is absolutely nothing when it is seen in the light of what G_d has to offer us. We don't think of ourselves as so important, then we can shut our mouths for a while and listen to each other. The proof of real intelligence is that you will listen to others. That is one of the greatest signs and the greatest evidence of a person being intelligent. They will listen to others. Anybody who must talk all the time and is uncomfortable listening to another person, even though that person may be under you in knowledge or formal education, if you have no willing spirit to listen to them, your intellect is flawed badly. You have a listener, here. I love to listen to others, and I encourage to all of you to listen more than you talk. Listen a lot, talk a little.

Giving Birth to Imam Warithu Deen Mohammed

Actually, if we don't understand it, if we could just accept what I said, that Allah is working on us as a collective group of people to give birth to a particular mind and spirit for His work that He wants to do through us and with us; and all of your births was the birth of Imam Warithu Deen Mohammed. To say that, whether you know it or not, your desire to stay with it, your patience, your endurance, your perseverance, your sacrifices, what was behind all of that? Giving birth to Imam Warithu Deen Mohammed, and when my mind is born, you are born. It is in your nature, your natural life, to wait for Imam Warithu Deen Mohammed to be completed. And as he grows, you take him into your mind, your heart, your life, and G_d forces me to share with you. I said I'm not comfortable doing these things. He forces me to share with you things that He has given me that the world would say, "That man is crazy, out of his mind!" G_d forces me to give that to you, because you and me, we should be like one human body. We should be like one human body, because what G_d is doing with me is for you, with you and for you. So, it is just one thing. G_d is making one life come forth and that life is for you and for me. I can't have mine without you and you can't have yours without me. Mine is not just for my body. It is for the collective people. Therefore, what I hold in my body will burst the whole body if I don't give it up.

The More Important Thing Is to Have the Life

I have to give it to you! The sunlight doesn't shine on just some of the planets. It shines on all of them. The sunlight has to reach all of the life. I'm not the sun of man. I don't want you to associate me with that, but I'm giving you a picture, a parable. If I am the sun with the light that G_d is bringing into this world, if I'm the sun and you are a plant, the light has to come to you and come into you. The sun can't say, "I have to restrain some of this light". The sun has no power to take some of its light and give it to this plant and not others. It has no such power. Its light has to go out and shine the complete light. It can't take something away from the light, because it is meant to give life to those things that it is created to give life to. Really, it is the life that is the result. The life is the goal, not to have light, but to have life. So, though light is necessary to have life, the more important thing is to have the life. I have no meaning, and I have no value if I don't give you what I receive. My mind is not comfortable giving you a lot of what I give, but suppose I die without giving you all these things? Wouldn't that be a waste? Am I to say who will understand and who will not? Am I to judge you and say, "There is not a person in this room who will understand what you're trying to say? Don't say it to them"? I don't know that, and we don't know each other. We have people among us advanced spiritually, very advanced in religious understanding, but we don't know each other, because persons like that don't show off. They are not interested in you seeing them, so we won't even know them. But Allah knows who is among us. So, I feel uncomfortable saying a lot of things to you, and I hope that you will be able to handle it and not change the way you look at me. I'm nothing but a sane, old person.

"Live As Though You Are Going to Die Tomorrow"

What we have been needing all the time, even when we were slaves, was to free our own souls and then if the man told us we were free, we would have gone on and made a beautiful world. A lot of men have come to grips with the problems of their own soul and liberated themselves while they were convicted prisoners and came out of prison and did marvelous things in the world. They became thinkers. That's what I want to say to you all, that you know that you are free, and I want you to go on and do the best that you can with whatever you see of benefit in me and in my leadership, because I feel that I'm going to be around here. I feel good, really. I feel I'm going to go for a good while, but who knows? Prophet Muhammed said, "Work, live, in the world as though you're going to die tomorrow." That means try to hurry up and get your life in the best shape you can get it in to please your Lord, and that means the whole life, life in community, the whole life. He said, "And again, live as though you're going to live forever, as if you're not going to die." That means invest in the future. Hurry and get your own life in the best shape you can get it in, but invest in the future, the long distance. Yes, that's the way to live. So, we're trying to do that, prepare now and prepare for the future.

I Wanted to Write Books

I wanted to write books, and I still do. In fact, I am putting things together right now for publication, and a long time ago, I had just gotten out of prison. That was in 1963. That's a long time ago. I went and bought some books. I said, "Well, I don't want to go to school for all of this. A lot of this I can get on my own." So, I went and bought books and a few of the books I bought, two or three of them, were on composition and what to do to become an effective writer. So, I got those books and one of those books I read, because I was writing stuff and looking back at it saying, "Ah, I don't want this. This isn't what I want". And the book said, "Good writers, they're throwing more of their writings in the trash basket than they are saving". So, after I read that I said, "Well, I sure was one of those writers." When you have a special interest, until you find a way to really communicate that special interest to your satisfaction, all that you write is trash for the trash basket. And I have been doing two things, attending the needs of our souls, and at the same time planning publications that I think will help. And the first one I had in mind that I told my father I felt we needed is, *Prayer in Islam*. I'm working on it now. It's not what Jabbir did. He went and got a mufti and everything from outside us, an African American Ph. D. in English, got all that money to put out the prayer book, and he came up with one. It's a beautiful job as research material or as expensive writing on prayer and Islam. But the average person, they don't need all of that. In fact, even with all the prayers included you could put it in a small pocketbook, a book that could go in your pocket. So, I never was pleased with the big project he made, only that it was good research material, very good research material for library people who want to know what prayer in Islam is. But for practical use it's too much, you know.

So, I told my father while he was living, no more than three years before he passed, I said, "Daddy, I would like to write two books for you and the Nation of

Islam". I said, "One is *Muslim Prayer,* and the other is *Introduction to Islam for New Converts*". I didn't do those, and an introduction to Islam for new converts I don't think we really have to have that. Any imam can do that themselves, locally, especially those who are educated. However, I still see a need for a book on prayer to come from me. One reason that is stronger than any other reason is it would be a book on prayer for Muslims, not prayer for other people of the world. Prayer for other people of the world, as I know and as I am understanding it, is dua'. That's what they call prayer. When they say prayer, it means holding the hands up to the sky and begging G_d. That's making dua'. That's not salat. There's a great difference, big difference.

Now Is the Time to Establish Our Community Life

So really, I'm always innovating things, thinking up something new, but I'm going to do it, again. Salat should not be translated, "Prayer". Salat should be translated, "Worship, devotional worship." The meaning of salat for Muslims is worship. Now, they call worship, ibaadah. Ibaadah or ibaadat, that's the word they use for worship. Salat is not only individual, the devotions for the individual for the life of the individual, but it's devotion for the life of the community; and no community ever was destroyed or lost until they left off prayer, and it means salat, not dua'. In the time of our Prophet, to the man who was going with his hands raised to the heavens complaining to G_d that, "I don't have this, I don't have that", the reply was, "Your whole life is a life of haram!" So, he hadn't left off dua' prayer, had he? So, insha Allah, G_d-Willing, we have a lot of work to do. I feel Allah has freed us to do great work. Now is the time that we should be doing great works. Yes, it wasn't back there in the depression time and exodus time, coming out of Egypt… Now is the time to establish our community life.

Spooked Up About Thursday

For some reason I have always been a little superstitious, a little spooked up about Thursday. I don't know why. I guess all of us as individuals are like that. The Prophet was born on a Monday. I have been a little superstitious about Thursday since I was a child. I will share this with you. If I really was attracted to a young girl and I'm talking about when I was younger than 14 years old, I think when I was 10 or 11 years of age, if I was really attracted to her and I had a chance to see her on a Thursday, I knew everything was going to be alright; and it stayed with me until now. If something happens to me on a Thursday, everything is going to be alright, and I know I have been "Thirsting" all my life. That's been my life, thirsting and trying to find the right drink.

Imam W. Deen Mohammed

Chapter 1

What Is Islam?

In the time of Muhammed, the Prophet (peace be upon him), the desert Arabs were ignorant of Scripture. They did not know Scripture. They did not have any knowledge of Scripture before Prophet Muhammed. Like the people of Moses, they were very skeptical, always doubting, and had no knowledge to judge, just like most with me today. Most of us do not have the knowledge to judge with, because we are not students of Scripture, and we have not inherited knowledge or knowledge has not been passed down to us from religious leadership who know Scripture, like the Catholic Church, Protestant Church, Jewish people, and many others. So, the Arabs were told to question the people of the book or people who received revelation. All those centuries have passed and still most of them need to ask the people of the book. I do not say all of them, but most of them do not have knowledge. They just go by simple tradition, mostly rituals, and they are still doing that, following what their fathers followed without knowledge. I do not pay any attention to it. They do not bother me. None of them bother me.

What Is the Qur'an?

What is the Qur'an? Let us not give our own answers before using what we're taught. What is the Qur'an? *"This is the book wherein is no doubt, guidance for the G_d-fearing."* So, what is the Qur'an? It is guidance for the G_d-fearing, guidance for those who put G_d above everything else. It is guidance, *"Hudan lil mutaqeen",* for those who reverence G_d or have taqwa, meaning they put nothing, no authority above G_d.

What else is the Qur'an? The Qur'an is clear guidance or clarity that serves to make clear what is guidance and what is the criterion on that that enables us to distinguish true guidance from false guidance, and not only to distinguish truth from falsehood, it enables us to also distinguish the features of the guidance, for the guidance has different features. Again, what is the Qur'an? The Qur'an is plain language, language that we all can understand, and metaphorical language. Allah says in the Qur'an while making this known to us that the Qur'an has these features, it is plain language and it is metaphorical language, shubaha. Shubaha means what is given is a resemblance, not the real thing. It resembles the real thing, but it is not the real thing. That's what shubaha is.

That Which Makes It Easy to Follow the Logic

Muhkamaat is that that makes it easy for you to follow logic, to follow it logically. You can follow it logically. It has been made plain and very rational, so that you can easily follow it logically... Allah wants to give everybody, an opportunity to choose Islam, if they want Islam. So, what does Allah say in Qur'an regarding these two features of the Qur'an? Allah says, "They", the Qur'an, or the Revelation, the verses are, "Shubahat and Muhkamaat". They are allegorical, as one translator puts it... it's the basis of the book. So, if I want to know Islam and practice Islam in my life, should I be more interested in the basis of the book, or in the pictures, the picture language of the book? The Word gives us a picture language, too. The Word gives us a picture language, and it gives us a rational language. So, should I be more interested in the picture language or in the logic, the rational language that forms the basis of the book?

You know the answer, now, what Allah says of those who prefer the picture language to plain rational language. *"In their hearts is a corruption, a defect"*, that's what G_d says. Those who prefer the shubahat, that that resembles something that G_d is trying to get you to understand, they prefer that over the rational, clear teachings of the Qur'an. They have a defect in their hearts. They're perverted. So, remember that.

A Reality Behind the Reading

I can read the Qur'an and understand it, its Arabic and everything now. That's because I see the reality behind the reading. There's a reality behind the reading that's in the reading. The reading is addressing a reality. If you know nothing but the reading and you don't know the reality that the reading is addressing, then you are feeling your way, and you don't know. All you can do is follow print. But I can test print and make sure the print is right, because I know the reality that the print is addressing.

Allah says it, firstly: *"None can touch it but the purified ones"*. That means you can't even touch the meaning. You can't even sense it with your feelings, with your heart, and your spirit. They can't even touch what G_d is saying, not your brain, because it hasn't even come to your brain, yet. You can't even suspect. You can't even anticipate. You can't even feel what G_d is saying if you're not purified. G_d says that, and now I know it. I know what He means. I know what Allah means when He says that. No, you can't touch it!

The Mother of the Book

It (Qur'an) speaks of the mother of the book. You know the scholars, they understand Al-Fatiha to be the mother of the book, because it's the essence of the book. Some of them also say it's the mother of the book, ummul kitab, that it's referring to Al-Fatiha, and the mother of the book. And umm, mother, is used in a lot of different references, like "umma qurra, mother of the village or the town". That's referring to the area called Hijaz in ancient times, or a long time ago. It's not the exact borders of Mecca, but very close to it.

It's close to the borders of Mecca or the holy precincts, the sacred precincts. When you come in by plane or whatever, when you get to that border, you're supposed to put on or have on the ikhram. So, it's referring to that area. Qurra means like a village. But if you listen to qurra you have qara'a, to read, Qur'an, all related to umma qurra, the mother of the town, or the mother of the village.

The Qur'an Is Jesus Personified

I believe the Qur'an is Jesus personified, the Word of G_d. That's Scripture. You know it says that the Qur'an is a healing for what is in the breast. So, the Word, itself, is Elijah's power. Qur'an says He would raise up from their brethren one like unto Moses. So, Muhammed came to establish government, but not a government like most people think. Why do we have thirty sections for the Qur'an? The Qur'an is a book that if we follow it, it will take us to or develop us into that spiritual model that G_d wants for mankind. It will eventually develop you into that spiritual model that G_d wants to be leader for mankind, all people.

They Created a Puritanical Order

Jesus Christ was betrayed for thirty pieces of silver. It means they sold his worth as a leader leading people to give their life, their spirit into G_d's charge as servants of His. They sold it for puritanism, thirty pieces of silver. So, they got the puritanical society. They sold his effort to bring the people into the spirit of obedience to G_d to bring about a puritanical society. So, they created a puritanical order to enforce purity on the people. They didn't have Jesus Christ's faith in people, so they enforced the law, and that is what he came to break. He came to bring people out from under the law, so that they would trust their own good nature and connect with G_d so that good nature would get its proper support and food.

If you study the history of the Church, that is exactly what happened. After Jesus Christ went away, they became puritanical, puritans. They were hiding their human weaknesses. They weren't angels. They weren't protected or safe from error, morally, sexually, or whatever, but they hid it all. They would not let the public know that they were falling victim to the laws that they were enforcing upon people. So, if you couldn't stand up under the law, you were treated like an animal. You were not respected as a human being. They would beat you like an animal, holler at you like you were an animal, kill you as though you were an animal. You would not have to be a police officer to kill somebody. Any man of standing in their eyes, could kill one of the common people, and would not go to jail or anything. Believe me, it is almost like that in some countries right now. A common citizen, I can be a police officer and kill you and someone could say, "What happened?" The response would be, "Oh, this loudmouth, troublemaker, lazy, resisted me and I had to kill him!" They would take his body away and that would be all. That goes on in the world right now. Don't think every country is like this country where you are protected by law. No.

Prophet Muhammed said, "Matters are judged by intentions." So, actually, Jesus Christ was governed by intent. He said, *"Don't you see I have to be about my father's business?"* So, his intention was always to serve G_d, to do what G_d put him in the world for. If you keep the intent right, pure, it will become automatic obedience for you. When it becomes automatic obedience, now you've come into the spirit to obey. Al-Islam is designed to do that. The Qur'an is our salvation. Al-Islam is designed to bring us into that obedience to G_d and to develop us to have pure intentions, all clean, innocent intentions. And if we have that, then the human spirit is free, meaning you can give your spirit to whatever you want to give it to. But the human spirit is also, by nature, hungry for the best possible condition. It wants the best possible condition for itself.

Whatever You Follow Will Take Over Your Spirit

So, people will choose a moral life because they know that enables them to have more comfort for their spirit. They can live with a more comfortable mind and spirit, if they choose to follow G_d's Guidance and follow it very determined about that. If nothing else is more important to them than that, then eventually, their spirit will be the spirit of G_d's Guidance. If you follow something your spirit will become that. If you follow the rappers, your spirit becomes the spirit of rap music. Whatever you give your spirit to, whatever you follow, that is what you will become.

First, it is the intent. You have to have the intent, first. You have to intend to be right. If you don't intend to be right, then anything can take your spirit, the rappers, or whatever. But if you intend to be right, even if you don't know G_d, He will eventually come to your aide. Prophet Muhammed didn't know G_d. If you intend to be right and you're so set upon that, you won't take anything from the world to give that up. They can't pay you to give that up. If your intention is to be right like Prophet Muhammed was and like other servants of G_d, then that intent will eventually bring you to seek G_d. Your mind won't be satisfied with the world. Things in the world will disappoint you one behind the other and you will be lost for something to support your good nature and your good intent. You will be crying out to the void, to the darkness, for light and G_d will come in there and speak to you. G_d will guide you. That is what happened to Prophet Muhammed. That is what happened to those before him. G_d will speak to you and guide you.

That is the way it happens when you don't have guidance, but now we have guidance from men who experienced those things. Now, wouldn't we be fools to put aside this guidance and follow just our good intent? In that case, G_d is not with us, because you're asking Him to help you, personally, and He already helped everybody. You want personal help. You won't follow what He revealed to Prophet Muhammed, so He is not going to help you. You will never get help. You have to recognize the good that is already here and support yourself with that good that is already here, then G_d will give you additional support, too. This is the way of G_d.

No Man Has Control Over the Spiritual Dimension

This is not a small thing we're talking about. The spiritual dimension is never solely in our control. Nobody can control the spiritual dimension, alone. You can only control it with G_d and when He begins to guide you by way of inspiration, or intuition you can't say, "I'm going to use my intuition to figure this out." It does not work that way. It comes, but you do not know when it is coming. You can just hunger for it, and Jesus Christ said, "Knock. Don't be impatient. Knock and someone will answer." The door will be opened if you just continue to knock. Don't give up. Have faith and keep trying to receive help for you good intent in your mind. You want to develop your mind for a particular purpose. You want to serve a particular cause, and you need more help. You need more light on the subject matter. Don't give up. He said keep knocking. You're knocking on the door for help. You want somebody to answer it. We do it with dua', with salat. We also do it with our conscious mind. We talk directly to G_d as though He is there before us, like a person, and eventually, you will get the answer if you keep the purity of intention.

The Spirit Always a Future Thing

It is a future thing. The spirit is always a future thing. It still has somewhere to go after the world is made right, because you're going to die. If G_d made me to want to obey Him and serve Him, forever, why did He make me like this if I can't do that? This is wrong for Him to make me like this, if I can't do that. I don't want to serve Him ten more years, or twenty more years, or a thousand more years. I want to serve Him forever, so why can't I do that? The will is in me to serve Him forever, so why can't I do that? I can and you can, too, and that is what faith is all about. It is about believing that there is something beyond this world that we know now.

The Book to Be Read

The Qur'an is the book to be read. This is what Prophet Muhammed gave to all the believers. What should be in the hands of all the believers is the Qur'an, not hadith! Prophet Muhammed said, "I leave two things with you, the Qur'an and my sunnah". Where was his sunnah then? Was it in a whole lot of volumes of what he said? His sunnah was in what they had witnessed. They had witnessed his actions and his deeds. Sunnah doesn't mean everything somebody reports that Joe said he said. No, sunnah refers more to Prophet Muhammed's way of doing things, not to every word that came out of his mouth, because that can be reported falsely, sometimes by mistake. It doesn't have to be because of bad intentions. By mistake they can give a false report on what Muhammed, the Prophet, said. Allah didn't say He would protect the sunnah. Allah said that there are guards on the book, the Qur'an, protecting the Qur'an against anyone who would tamper with it. He didn't say the sunnah of Prophet Muhammed has this protection, too.

Muhammed's Sunnah Is to Free Every Human Soul

Someone may ask, "What happens in the sunnah of Muhammed?" As for the effect, the destiny of the global community, I know everything was revealed to Muhammed, the prayers and peace be on him. The sunnah of Muhammed is for us to live and grow in. That is why Allah established both. He established the fard, the Qur'an, and the sunnah. As for as the Qur'an, it is complete and says everything that needs to be said about the global community, its nature, and how it is going to be concluded. It is so vividly clear in the Qur'an. But as for our human interactions and how we are to advance our life as human beings in the world, but also in the cause of G_d affecting the world and in the soul of man for man's pleasures, and for his enlightenment or understanding, that continues after the Prophet. That continues to grow after the Prophet, and that is his sunnah. His sunnah is to free every human being to have the best and biggest life possible for the human soul. That is why women are obligated to carry out his sunnah, just like men are. It is the continued life of the human soul in the material world G_d made for it, to feed it and support it.

Command by the Best Standards

The Qur'an, its revelation reveals G_d's Plan for the world and warns us against Iblis' plan for the world; and it tells us how it is going to be concluded, because G_d saw the end of Iblis, how far he could go. So, it also reveals how this world is going to be concluded, and it is clear teachings. And the revelation of Qur'an that is applying to this present time that we are living in, right now, describing it, I cannot describe it better. We want to get back to the best traditions that the natural life of humans asked for and supported. Allah says, in the Qur'an, *"Wa ya'muruna bil ma'ruuf"*, *and order or command by that which is 'ma'ruuf'."* The translator says, *"By the best standards, by the known and tested"*, or *"by the best traditions"*. That is exactly what it is referring to. It means those who lead, they should be aware of the history of society, the history of the developmental world of man, and they should know what things have lived while innovations have died and passed away, while guesswork has died and failed man. They should know what traditions have stayed and accounted for man's endurance and long-lasting life and establishments, and what has contributed longevity to man's good works? It has been the best traditions. We follow the sunnah of Muhammed. We say the traditions of Muhammed. What is his sunnah? His sunnah reflects the best traditions of life in human society going back to all the life of nations in times before him.

All Born to Have Commonsense

All human beings were born to have five senses or commonsense, and all of them were born to have a fishing mind, a searching mind. In the Bible, it says Jesus Christ took care of all of them. He didn't have anything except two fish, and the mind fishes for something to digest, something to take in. Once it takes it in, then it wants to reflect on it saying, "Wasn't that good?" The same mind that was attracted to it also wants to study it to see, "Maybe I want to keep this, or maybe I want to build on this, or maybe this is something I shouldn't take in my mouth, again". Thought and reflection that is the two, and that is what dhakir means. It doesn't only mean thought.

The Male Is Not Like the Female

Dhakir is from the verb, dhakara. When you use it by itself as a noun it means a male person, not a female. In the Qur'an, it says *"The male is not like the female"*. In what respect? As a thinker. Most females, they observe and enjoy what they observe. But the characteristic of the male is to observe and see how he can use it down the road. So, he reflects on it and associates it in a situation that can help him benefit from it.

Women have that nature, but it's not popular among them. So, that is why it says that, but in the Qur'an, it also says *"The males who think and the females who think"*, and that comes up in connection with Mary being pregnant and having a male child, and they announced that she had given birth to a male child. Qur'anically, it is no big deal. The male is not to be confused with the female. So, the exact language, if you study it in the environment or in the text, as the preacher would say, or in the context as the public student would say, you get a more complete meaning for that word that is being expressed. If you just look at it as a word, you miss its ramifications. You miss what it's touching upon, and what it is influencing in that word environment. So, the word is male, but the way it comes in the context of Jesus being born and it's in a male child, it doesn't only point to its own meaning, but it influences the meaning of the word in its environment. It influences those meanings. So now, the dhakir taking this special meaning in the Qur'an influences the meaning of untha.

Woman Is a Type of Community

It is not a female anymore. It is talking about one who makes it history, saves history, records it and makes it history, and another one who just makes rituals of it and forgets. Actually, nisaa, is women and untha is female. Both of those words allude to the tendency to lose things in history. So, the woman is a type of community, a plural body. She's a type of the plural body in its social orientation, or social nature, and performance; whereas the male represents the concern with making it better, working it, so that it lives in the future, and recording it. That is the male nature.

Actually, the way that masculine or male identity is treated in the Qur'an, it gives us also a richer meaning of what is female, and it is in Scripture. Jesus Christ and his mother are for a sign. There was a wedding feast and which of the Mary's was working with Jesus to prepare for the guest? His mother. She sets the table for the feast. She arranges things as they are supposed to be at the table. She arranges or sets the table. She pours water in the glasses, and they are still doing that. You go in the restaurant, and they pour water in the glass. The Bible said Jesus turned the water into wine. Now, that is unacceptable with my homies. It is not accepted for us to put our hands in our food, but when you go over there with our homies on the desert, it's acceptable.

Cultural Taste Changes With the Environment

Cultural taste changes with environment, the location. Where are you? If you're in another country, it changes. The woman, she knows by habit how to perform her duties. It's customary that you do this. So, she knew what was customary. She set the table, and she poured the water, then Jesus comes with that which is uncommon. It hasn't been introduced yet, but once he introduced it, over the years it becomes habit, too. So, he changed the water, which represents natural relief that comes to the spiritual nature, the spiritual body, naturally. The physical body, if it is thirsting ii is like the spiritual body wanting to be lifted up, wanting to be satisfied, set to rest, wanting to rest. "Make me feel comfortable, at rest, make me feel at ease." Isn't that what the soul wants? That is the spiritual side, so that is the water. Sensitivities are a feel for needs that will make your soul rest, and don't forget, water is associated with delivery, childbirth.

The Home With All People

This is something original inside the person. This is a need originally inside the person. Water breaking means the life is no more supported by the soul. The soul, sensory body or sensitive body and the water are a picture, or symbolic picture representing that. The world is going to engage the mind now. So, what you've been resting on for nine months with mama, you're losing it. The water comes out first. It says this was the original state of this life. The original state of this life was spirituality symbolized as water. And if you think of your spirituality, it wants to rest, doesn't it? That is the nature of the spirituality, to want to be at rest. Water wants to be at rest. That is the nature of water, speaking in terms of physics, not necessarily in religious terms. It will keep moving until it can be at rest. So, do you see the picture of the soul? But it also, in the right conditions, will serve as a mirror. It will show you your picture only when it is at rest, because if you disturb it, the picture is distorted, or maybe completely lost. Water finds its place of rest. It comes from the mountain. The river runs looking for its place of rest. Rest is in the ocean. It runs out to the ocean and there it finds rest. Now, if it rests in a little puddle, a little mud hole, it's going to be terminated. The sun comes out and dries it up. But as long as it can keep moving, eventually, it will find a body big enough to accommodate its need to rest. That is when it merges in with the universal soul, the human soul. It is no more Wallace's soul. It's no more the Poole family's soul. It's no more Chicago's soul. It's no more the United States' soul. It's the universal soul. Its home is with all people. It is beautiful these meanings.

"I Left You Eating and Drinking"

So, Jesus was blessed to know how to take the Scriptural language addressing the human soul and sensitivities, or as they say, sensitivities and sensibilities, to address that in a way to excite the interest, that is, turning it into wine, making it tastier, giving it more flavor and making it stimulate the mind. Wine is a stimulant. So, the people became enthusiastic after hearing his teaching, Christ Jesus. They were excited and the old teaching lost to the new teachings, because the old teaching was flat. It wasn't exciting. People were tired of it. If you keep giving me water soon,

I'm going to get up and go somewhere else. I want more than water. My thirst for water is going to run out soon, and that is the way it is with the world. You get on something, and you don't know when you've done enough of it, and you wonder why people are not interested and don't find you exciting anymore. What makes the religious teaching attractive and exciting for long periods of time? Jesus left. He said, *"I'm going, but I'll be with you, always"*. So, he's gone and still present at the same time. "I'm going as a performer of my task or my work or mission, but I left my work with you, and my work satisfies your soul's need to have life and to have it more abundantly".

So, "I'm gone, but I left you eating and drinking, and it's a supper to remember. It's the last one as a performance from me, but it is something that I don't want you to forget. So, repeat this over and over again in remembrance of me". Isn't that beautiful, especially, when you know that "Me" means the Will of G_d for the people, the Word and the Spirit? So, when we see these meanings, terms, in their context, the meanings become richer, bigger, and they touch on other things and spread their influence in the word environment. They are touching other words with their influence and making those words have bigger meanings, giving the old terms more expression.

The Whole World Is Nothing But a Reflector

What I am doing here is addressing Scriptural reasoning, not just a communication. But what is the reasoning supporting this communication and giving it a new reality and sending it to its destiny that G_d wants it to go to? What is doing that? It is the line of logic that started with the need for man to get help from G_d, and then it represents that logic (as Allah says in the Qur'an) for us all the way to its conclusion. The logic has a conclusion, a destiny, an aim. It has a purpose. It is to stop somewhere. So, it's scriptural reasoning, and just like that water that comes from the mountain and makes a river, and it is not satisfied until it gets into a big, big body, it wants to be in the biggest body where it will be represented, universally, and it will be in the universal nature; not in your concept of what is the soul and what is the human spirituality and sensitivities, but in that definition that everybody will recognize right away and say, "That's what I feel! That is me!" All that we see in the world with our physical eyes is deception. It is "ghurur", and it means deception, and why is it deception? Because the soul is transparent, invisible. Human spiritual life is transparent, invisible, but that's its essential life. That is our essential life. We are in these environments so that we can support and express that life. We are not in this environment to become this environment. The environment is a means for us finding ourselves and our true nature and expressing it in language that will come to the mind and leave a picture or an imprint, a concept. How are you going to leave a concept, and you do not have a concept? So, the world is a reflector, not just the water. The whole world is nothing but a reflector. It reflects what I am. It reflects my life. It reflects what I want to do with my life. It reflects the conclusion of my life, because He put everything in a universal scheme, and these things evolved and evolved, and they weren't satisfied to be at rest until they connected with each other, and they all could rest.

Religion and Science Are Coming Together

Do we think the solar system was always with these other systems going along in a universal system? No, that is not how they started, according to Scripture and according to science. They started in chaos. That's mythology, and the scriptural language is, *"They were in violent commotion,"* they were restless. The material body was restless in different forms. Smoke, fire, winds, storms, all that was part of the beginning as imagined by scientist and by the thinker in Qur'an, or in Scripture. And it says the heavens were *"dukhan, as smoke"*. Smoke is restless, isn't it? It churns, but its nature is to be at rest. It's going to smoke out. It can't stay that way, always.

So, the whole universe began for us in religion, and they say religion and science are coming together, and when you understand it, science says the same thing. Mythology, myths, say the same thing, that the creation started from restlessness and separation, then it started to connect with that which it could connect with, and more and more matter connected bodies, and systems holding bodies in a discipline formed, like our solar system.

Where G_d, Himself, Will Be In the Leader

The Qur'an has thirty parts, and it is to bring us to that spiritual leadership where G_d, Himself, will be in our leader moving our leader where he should go, and we follow him where we should go. So, Jesus Christ is just a sign that that type of leadership is for the whole world. The spiritual leader who has the Spirit of G_d in him is the leader we want for the whole world, for every human being, exactly. It is definitely for the leader, because if it is not in the leader, then the ones who do not have that spirit in them will be leading the people astray.

The word, "Nas", do you think it is related to the word, "Ansar"? Yes, it is. So, "nasrullah", is the victory that G_d gave Prophet Muhammed and the believers with him, and "ansar" means those who help achieve victory. They are helpers, but not just helpers for anything. They are helpers who help until they get victory. This is very important. They are helpers who help until victory is won. These were also the disciples of Jesus Christ, according to G_d, in the Qur'an. He (Jesus Christ) wanted help, and they told him, *"We will be your helpers for G_d, to get the victory for G_d"*. When the victory comes, what victory is it talking about? If it came, what was the victory? When the help of Allah comes and you see people coming in crowds or great numbers, in groups of large numbers, they're coming as Muslims in the religion of G_d. That means they are coming as believers. These are groups of big numbers. What is meaning of the word, fath? It is from the verb, fatiha, that means to open. In ancient and medieval times mostly, they used the expression meaning to conquer the city. They said, "Open the city". That is how it is expressed in English. "The troops opened the city", means they conquered the city. This word, "fath", means the opening of what? The opening of the city, the stronghold that the disbelievers were holding. So, this is talking about the conquest of Mecca. The opening of Mecca is the conquest of Mecca.

So, look at Al Fatiha. It is translated, "The Opening", but do you think you could prove me wrong if I translated Al Fatiha as, "The Victory"? You could not prove me wrong. It means, "The Opening", but it means, "The Victory", also. It is the victory not of a city. It is the victory over confusion in revelation. G_d cleared it all up. He opened it all up, and the prophecy is that a little lamb took the book and opened it and broke the seals. Seals means the understanding was secret and he broke the secrets and got the understanding.

An Innocent Person

The little lamb, they say, is Jesus Christ on Easter. "The Lamb of G_d", that expression is in Christian religion. Lamb can not only be referred to as Jesus. It was also Isma'il (Ishmael), Abraham's son. In fact, the lamb we use for many, but Jesus is also seen as the lamb of G_d. Lamb means a nice, innocent, person with no bad in his nature. It is a peaceful or peace-loving person. Lambs are very peaceful. They don't attack anything, and they are very social, very gregarious. They are socially bonded very tightly as members in a group. This is talking about the servants of G_d. They want peace and want to be close to one another.

The victory of the lamb, this is Christianity. It is the opening, the disclosing of the secrets in Scripture, and the Christian report says the lamb took the book from his hand. The Qur'an does not like the way it is expressed, so it puts it differently. It just alludes to it rather than say that with Al Fatiha. How many seals were there to be opened? Seven. And in the Qur'an, Al Fatiha has seven verses, but they are seven verses, "methana", which means seven verses that are mated. So, really there are fourteen complete expressions, but in seven verses. They say the seven oft-repeated verses. It is saying, *"Bismillahir Rahmaanir Raheem."* That is verse one. It is saying two things, that G_d is "Ar Rahmaan and Ar Raheem". It is very important in religious understanding, these two expressions of G_d. Taken from the history of the theology of G_d by these major religions Christianity and Judaism, they mean little or nothing. It is nothing to say G_d is kind and loving. Everybody knows that. Ignorant people know that. But it is something to identify that which has been hidden and misused in Scripture and address it with these two attributes. That is exactly what is happening.

Qur'an Is Showing Something That Was Not Seen

The Qur'an is revelation, not just talk. Revelation means showing something that was not seen. If it was already seen then why is it revelation? *"Bismillahir Rahmaanir Raheem. Al hamdu lil laahe rabbil alameen"*, that is another complete verse. *"The thanks are to G_d"*, that is one statement. *"Rabbil 'alameen, the Lord of the worlds"*, that is another statement. One day we will take Al Fatiha, and we will see the repetition, how two expressions come with each verse for a total of 14 that is unlocked, not just seven. There are seven seals and seven verses, but each verse has double or two keys. In the Qur'an, it says, *"With G_d are all the keys to the heavens and the earth."*

The Qur'an is a book to be read, that means read, but when you read in the Qur'an what Allah is saying about revelation, about Qur'an, you know that you are not only to read the book, but it is a book to be studied. It is a book to be recited. It is a book to be understood. All these terms are in Qur'an. That tells us this about the Qur'an. The greatest fear that the religious leaders have is the fear that what they keep secret will be told openly. Allah did that when He gave the message of Qur'an to Muhammed, the Prophet. He exposed all their secrets. I can't expose their secrets. They are already exposed. G_d has already exposed them. I just read what G_d has done. But if you cannot make the right connections, you will not even know that G_d is exposing the secrets, because you do not make the right connections. The leaders have taught the masses, most people in religion that they are not taking in as their private, little, secret students, they have taught them all in a way, so they'll never make the connections.

You will think this is all just talk. You need to know that it has reference to something. You cannot make the connections with the references, so you cannot learn the Qur'an. You cannot see the superiority of the Qur'an. If you do not know what it is talking about in the history of religion, Christianity, Judaism, etc., then you do not know the superiority of the Qur'an. It is impossible for you to know the superiority of the Qur'an.

The Dawning

Fujura is to be understood by knowing what man is observing when G_d speaks through him, or when He says fujura. Fajr means the dawning. It is the first sign of light coming. It is still dark, but fajr appears, the first appearance of light on the horizon going horizontal, not up and down. That is the light that spreads to everything in man's soul. All it is talking about is the occurrences in man's soul that want to be in accord with his G_d. He wants to be satisfied that he is not going against the law in creation that points to the one G_d. Fujur is taken from that, and it means the awakening of that light of fajr in the soul of man. And fujur is spiritual before it is rational. Man has not depended on alarm clocks to get up. His nature wakes him up.

Scripture addresses history and it must be related to history to understand it. So, this is dawning. Though it is a dawning that takes place, and every individual has the nature, it occurs for everyone. It is a product that belongs to every individual, this fujur. We should relate it to history, and it tells us that man's civilization no man knows when it started, but we know when the history started, maybe. So, this is the dawning of history, man in history, and how the soul then goes so far, runs out of energy, and has to start all over again. And when it starts over again, it starts the same way it started the first time. It must have a dawning inside the soul.

Man Will Be Shown His Whole Life Within a Flash

You'll see everything in a flash, almost. Mankind will be shown his whole life within a flash, almost, from the earliest time when he was a baby until the end of it, and that applies both to the individual and to the society. So, the society has a history. We have a life span. So, man will see his history almost like it's given to him in a flash, instantly almost. Now, what man is that? That is the man that has been leading the world and is responsible for the mess that was made. So, when the right time comes for a change, like another Noah's flood, when that time comes the history will come in the mind of these people that have been running the world for us, and it will be like a flash. He will see his wrongdoing almost in an instance.

G_d Will Teach You, Himself

The Qur'an says, *"It is Allah who teaches you"*, plural, not singular. It can't be speaking to the Prophet. It is obvious that He spoke to the Prophet. Allah communicated to us through the Prophet, but He says, *"It is Allah who teaches you"*. So, that means, yes, the Prophet teaches you, but if you deserve it, G_d will teach you, Himself, if the time deserves it. And all the time it is G_d who is teaching you, because the Qur'an is His Word to all of us, and if you study sincerely, you are going to be educated in the Qur'an without a teacher. All of us get guidance, all of us get better educated in Al-Islam by reading and studying the Qur'an.

Qur'an Revealed to Us to Be Our Imam

So, the Qur'an is also called Imam. Based upon what G_d says of Moses and his people, its role is also to serve as our Imam. It says He (G_d) revealed the book as an Imam to the people of Moses. That is to tell us in our book, too, he is a man like unto Moses. So, our Qur'an, too, is revealed to us to be our Imam. You see, the movement of Al-Islam in the Prophet is the liberation of mankind, all people, and what has prevented the people from being awakened to their best nature and the course they should take to freedom? Religious leaders who keep the whole pot and give the people a little broth. So, that has been the problem. Therefore, the Qur'an and Muhammed, the Prophet, come to make it available to everybody and they don't have to come through anybody, no intercessor, mediator, one who mediates between G_d and you, and no priesthood. That means our religion doesn't depend on religious, or spiritual leaders to keep it in the public. Men and women are obligated to follow the sunnah of our Prophet where no one leads the other. Perform it independently, on your own. All that points to the order that we need for mankind on earth to get rid of all forms of slavery and all that. So, Prophet Muhammed is to be seen as a liberator, a teacher, who teaches universality, universals, and situates us to get the maximum benefit from academic studies or interests, education.

Most People Do Not Understand Their Religion

They are worried about Muslims becoming Christians. Many Muslims have become Christians who were born in Muslim lands. Many of them come over here, go to church and become Christians. But have they really converted a learned Muslim? No, they converted somebody who is just as ignorant as anybody. In fact, a Christian may know his religion better than he knows it. We're living in a time when most people do not understand their religion. If I wanted to, I could teach the Bible better than I think almost ninety percent of the preachers who are preaching, maybe more than that. It may be a higher percentage than that. I could teach the Bible much better than they could teach it. They do not know it. They do not know what they are talking about. They do not know what they are reading. These books are from G_d, and He is not talking about simple stuff. G_d is addressing grave matters in the history of religious people, very serious matters in the history of religious people. Jesus Christ, he said, *"I come not of water only, but of water and blood"*. So, his mission or role is to reconcile spirituality with social nature. Blood is social nature. Blood means my brother born of my mother and father. It is referring to my natural life. He came to reconcile spiritual life and community or social life, to bring those two together so that they agree. However, they misunderstood him. They didn't see the mystical signs and read them correctly. They misread them.

"I Know What You Know Not"

So, it is not a picture of Jesus Christ as a person. It is a picture of the evolution of human life from primitive nature up to what they call divine nature, but up to khalifah of G_d, and they rejected him. They said, "This thing You're making is just going to cause trouble, bloodshed. This is an animal You're talking about." That is what the angels said. G_d didn't deal with it at that point. He just said, *"I know what you know not"*. Then He challenged them. After He made the man, He said, *"You angels, tell Me your names"*, and they couldn't even tell G_d their own names, and finally, they admitted they had no knowledge, except what G_d had given them.

This is the realm, sphere of revelation, G_d's communication. These people who thought they understood G_d's Purpose for man on this earth, they had gone astray. They didn't know G_d's Purpose. There was a jinn among them, leading them, the angels. So, the angels were not responsible for themselves. The jinn was their leader. The jinn, he refused to accept Allah's Plan for man. But the angels, when they understood, when G_d showed them themselves and they understood their limitation, and that they shouldn't question G_d (their nature was to obey G_d) they did, and that is when the trouble started for man.

World Constructed Against Your Good Nature and Future

This is the jinn who had become the rebel that is now Shaytan, the Devil, and now he is going to set out to defeat man in his purpose that G_d assigned. If you believe that, then you should believe that this world has been constructed against your good future. That is what it is saying. That is not me saying it, that is G_d saying that, and the same thing is told in the Genesis in the Christian Bible, how the serpent came up and blocked the way and led the man and the woman to fall from their high place that G_d had given them in the garden. So, don't take this lightly! This is very serious! The world has been constructed against your good nature and your good future!

The Devil Thinks He Is Right

I'm perhaps the only person who could tell you this. Nobody else will tell people this. The Devil thinks he is right. He never thought he was wrong, and the Devil doesn't realize that he is talking to G_d and G_d talks to him. The Devil never heard G_d say, *"This is what you have done? You are cast out!"* The Devil never heard that, only man hears that. The Devil never hears anything from G_d, except what he wants to hear. So, he continues on thinking he's innocent and under his rule. They do not know they are under Satan's rule. They think they are under the rule of their great wisdom. Under Satan's rule the inciteful ones, the real scientists among them, they have kept up with everything that has happened in man's world from Abraham and Moses all the way down. So, by deceit he brought about their fall. "When they tasted of the tree their shame became manifest to them and they began to sew together the leaves of the garden over their bodies, and their Lord called unto them: *"Did I not forbid you that tree and tell you that Satan was an avowed enemy unto you?"* Every important event, they kept up with it.

Allah tells us in the Qur'an, He gave Adam the ability to name things, but Adam was deceived by Satan, and we're not told what happened. He was deceived, and until he corrected himself what was he doing? Shaytan's biddings. Shaytan came to him to use him as an instrument to carry out Shaytan's wishes for man's life, for the world. Adam is a man of the earth. It means he is a rational man, he is a scientific thinker, and he is a cultivator of the world, but Shaytan got him. If Shaytan got the developers, he still has them. The Adam who repented, he was a spiritual man. He left the world of material excitement. He took the road of spirituality, so who is left? The Adam that Shaytan got, and he has his language everywhere. It is in all the sciences, but they are not all the same. Allah says there was a party of the jinn who heard the recital of the Qur'an, and they marveled over it and said it is a wonderful recital. They praised it, the jinn. This is in the Qur'an saying, *"Neither man nor jinn should find any fault with this".*

So, they are not all the same, science and industry, science and technology. They are not all the same. Some care nothing for religion, but there are others who reverence G_d and care a lot for religion, and they are the ones who want to see the two come together. Their language is everywhere, language that tells me clearly that they know more about the sciences of Scripture, the real light of Qur'an and the Bible, than these preachers you find in these churches. They are the dumb ones. They know nothing. The average preacher is nothing but a dumb man carrying something he knows nothing about. I am telling you the truth. They gloat over some little interpretation, some little light they have. They hold it tight and keep it secret.

Satan Is No Mystery

If you have a secret work in your neighborhood, black preacher, what you can do is a fifth of what the white man can do in his neighborhood, if you really have something. I say the same thing for the white preacher in his church. They do not have anything. If they did, they would have influenced more than they have. Who was able to succeed in this world materially? The Catholics, shrouded in mystery, just moved right into the material business, got a big hold in it, and have their people in all areas of business. The Shaytan wants to defeat the Catholics, so they have been influencing the Catholics, and the Catholics are waking up now to the influences of the Shaytan among them.

Satan is bigger than we think. He is no mystery. Allah says to us, *"Hell fire is reality."* He is also saying the Devil is reality. If you believe hell fire is real, it is not a mystery, it is not a superstition, it is reality, then G_d is situating you to find out also, that the Devil, himself, is reality. He is real, too. Where is he? In Qur'anic Arabic, it says, *"Minal jinnati wan naas. Among the jinn, and the people".* This is as clear as day. Something can be so clear, and you cannot I see it, because if you have not been conditioned to see it, you have been conditioned not to see it. So, if you are conditioned not to see something, it is like hypnosis. You see only what the hypnotizer conditioned you to see. You'll be looking right at the truth and cannot see it.

What Is Islam?

We have our Prophet being asked, "What is the best Islam?" Someone asked him that question. We have him also giving us what is Islam. Someone asked him that question, and we have him giving us, in his own words, what Al-Islam is. When he answered the question, "What is Islam?" he said, "Al-Islam is built upon five"; and we take this to mean five pillars, five principles, five essentials. It is translated different ways by different translators. He named them saying, "It is to believe in G_d, to fast the month of Ramadan during the daylight hours. It is the month in which the Qur'an was revealed in the later part of the month, after twenty days. That is why we devote ourselves intensively to reading the Qur'an, and the Night of Power comes within that last ten days. He said, "It is to visit the house." He made it very simple to make pilgrimage to the house built by Prophet Abraham and his son, who was also a Prophet, upon them be peace.

The Five Essentials

We know these five essentials have very strong reference to the essential life of every human being. The Qur'an emphasizes five. Prophet Muhammed emphasized five. Jesus Christ emphasized five. The Prophet, Jesus, said there was a woman washing at the well and he said, *"You have had five husbands and the one you have now it not yours."* Again, he fed the multitude with two fish and five loaves of bread. There five is, again. David picked up five smooth stones from the water and he used just one to take down the great threat to his people, the mighty Goliath. So, we have this five in common. There are many things that we cannot explain. So, why should we always ask for explanations for little, simple matters in life? We want you to stop using drugs. You say, "Why should I? I like it!" We want you to stop living a life of violence, and your reply is, "I say this is my world." Well, it did not start right there. You did not start being dumb right there. You started being dumb way back there in your life, and it was not all your fault. Our leaders, today, they are too busy trying to impress us so we will support them. They are too busy trying to march to our beat. They are too busy to rethink life and rethink this behavior that we have in the public. They are too busy for that. They are too busy trying to win us over, thinking that "I am your man." In this time, we don't need anybody to be our man. We need a man who can be his own man, who manages his own life, first, and then he can manage to help us with our life. This is a very difficult time we are living in.

Satan Deceived Adam

It all begins in the story of man being made and put in a garden, a garden of paradise, a garden of beauty, a garden of health, a garden of peace and security, and he lost that. In the major religions we call the heavenly religions, the religions of Abraham, the story goes like this: He found himself in the garden and a deceiver came up to him and told him how he could have much more than he had then. Now mind you, he was in Paradise. He had peace. He had security. He had his life, and he had his woman. Nobody had taken his woman. But now he is listening to a deceiver and he's about to lose his mind and his woman. That was an environment that was in space. That is not what happened. G_d revealed that to tell us what He wants to happen. He wants you to take your life and be sincere with it, and be decent, be honorable, upright, and you will have heaven. You will have paradise. And He wants you to not listen to anybody who wants to use you, your mind tools, your mental tools of rationalization, to deceive you into following your own reasoning to the point where you rationalize anything into the form that you want it in. So, the filth is not filthy anymore. You rationalize it to be clean. The act that will ruin your family and cause you to lose your life and ruin your family, you rationalize it. It is not dangerous anymore. It is not threatening a family anymore. You rationalize it, saying, "I'm entitled to a little bit on the side. After all, I work hard, and she doesn't have to want for anything, and I have all the boys and girls doing well. I am entitled to some pleasure of my own, now. So, I'm going to have this little sweet young thing, right here, and I am not going to let her know. What she doesn't know is not going to hurt her!" That is rationalizing. You are not keeping the important things before you. You are not respecting truth and reality. You are going off from truth and reality and forming your reasoning, false rationalization, to support your act. But in your mind, it is not false rationalization. In your mind it's justified. That is what happened in the garden, when the deceiver came up and said, "Don't worry about that tree. You are not going to die if you eat from that. I know G_d told you that you will die if you eat from it. But you're not going to die. Your eyes are going to come open." And that is what gets us into a lot of trouble. We just want to see everything.

The Need to Manage Our Own Space

We're talking about space, the need to manage space. If you give a child a bedroom or if you only have one room and you give that child a space in that one room, and that child sleeps in his or her space, you should raise that child to respect its own life and not want its own life to be hurt by what that child does, if it does not keep a clean room. The room is going to pretty soon hurt the life of that child. If it doesn't keep its shoes where they are supposed to go, and its clothes where they are supposed to go, etc., it is going to hurt that child. You are going to wonder, and that child is going to wonder, why it just likes to hurt things. G_d made the human soul to live in peace, to live in clean space and to have order, not a bunch of confusion all around it. So, the child won't know why it is behaving badly, or wanting to be violent, and you will not know. You will say, "I'm going to have that boy see a psychiatrist!" Before you do that, let the psychiatrist come and see the space the boy lives in, and you might save yourself some money.

In Another Dark Place

Space is very important. A little small germ that we can't see with our physical eyes becomes a full human person in the environment we call the body of mama, and then it is delivered out into our world. Somebody gave us a lot of help, but it seems that we can't get to benefit from the help anymore when you come out here in what they called this space, Mother Earth, another mother. You were living on the body of mama, getting all your needs from her body. Now you are out here with the family, and you are living on Mother Earth, and she is supporting your life just as your mother's body supported your life when you were confined in her.

Something should come to your mind if you make these connections. Here I am in my mama, existing as nothing. Nobody could see me with their physical eye, but there formed a complete human being in that confinement, in that dark place. And then I'm delivered out into the world, and they tell me I'm living now on Mother Earth, and I need her, too, for all my life needs such as food, clothing, shelter, transportation, whatever; and it seems I have light out here. The sun is shining. I have light, but for most of us we are in a dark place just as you were when you were in your mother. We are in another dark place. The light is on, but you cannot see how to direct yourself. But if you would just rest like that baby did in its mother and accept help from all the directions that are coming, you would do something with your life out here in what you call daylight, or sunlight. Your life would be helped because the good people they will give you what you need. The good teachers, they would love your peace, not your "piece" that shoots and kills. Your P.E.A.C.E, your quiet, your peace of mind, your faith in the new environment, it can support you like the one that supported you when you were a germ and could not make yourself, Mother Earth. It is important for students of the Qur'an to know the difference between saying, "Islam" and "Al-Islam. When you say, "Islam", you are talking about how I perceive as a person, individually, Islam, and how Islam is in my mind, personally, and G_d addresses that in the Qur'an. He says, "Islamukum", and it means, "Your Islam". This is, really exposing those who have their own ideas about what Islam is. But when G_d says, *"I have preferred for you the religion of Islam"*, it is not Islam. In the Qur'an, it is "Al-Islam". "House" and "The House", have different meanings. "Islam" and "The Islam", have different meanings.

Islam Is the Religion of Origin

In the Qur'an, our religion is clearly presented as a religion of human origin. Is this something different from what the Bible is saying? No, it is only making clearer what the Bible is saying. The revelation, Qur'an, comes to extend further the message of revelation that was already existing in the world, to make it clearer and to extend it further. So, it addressed the future of man in a way that leaves no need for any further revelation. It comes to a conclusion.

The Qur'an comes to a conclusion. The Bible attempts to come to a conclusion. Why do I say attempt? Because in Revelation, it is not G_d, but it is the Prophet, a man, who receives revelation who is saying, "It is sealed!" And John, the Revelator, says, *"Let no man alter it, influence it, or change it, but it is sealed"*. That means final. John, the Revelator, he makes it final. It could be final, I don't know. But when you study the history of the compilation of the Bible, they had to search for lost pages, lost books, and they had to salvage pages. This is the history of the Bible, how it was collected. I read where there were fires. Some pages they found burned and flooding, some damaged by water. But finally, they were able to go and search in different places and come up to their satisfaction that they had a complete Bible, Old Testament and New Testament.

But as you have been told and if you study and do research, you know for yourself from your research that it took centuries before they settled the matter of the identity of Jesus Christ, whether he should be identified as a mortal or as a god, a divine, or whether he should be identified as both mortal and divine. They spent centuries discussing, debating, arguing it, before a conclusion was reached. When the conclusion was reached, everyone was not in agreement and that is why we have the Eastern Church and the Western Church. We have an Eastern Pope and the well-known Pope in the West that we all know. They did not all agree and back then there were no Protestants. There were only Christians. Later, they came to be called Catholics, and they were the Eastern Church of priests and the Western Church of Rome. We have a Bible, but the Bible is not as defendable as the Qur'an, because the Qur'an is in history, and it has not been changed. The pages were never lost.

Chapter 2
Muhammed, The Prophet

Mohammed went to the mountain. He did not wait for the mountain to come to him. But he did not favor the mountain, because it is said G_d offered him two ways, the route through the mountains and He offered him the route through the plains, and he chose the route through the plains. However, he had no problems going to the mountain. He got rebuked for it. *"He frowned and turned aside"*, away from the blind man, because he was going to see the big shots. He did not want to be disturbed or held up, so he treated him, the blind man, with disrespect. The Arabic word, "tawalla", means he did this, looked away, gestured and kept going, then G_d corrected him. But isn't that a wonderful Prophet? He didn't have to tell us everything that G_d told him, and if he had bad intentions, G_d would have stopped revealing to him. But He kept giving him revelation. So, his own soul was bothering him, and he put it out there for everybody to see.

Muhammed was an upright, honorable, person before he knew anything about religion. He didn't know anything about religion as we know it. He knew human nature and he was among those people of Saudi Arabia who believed that they should be the best in their human makeup, that they should live the best that is possible for them in their own human makeup. That is called hanif, and he was of the hunafaa, the plural form of the word. The hunafaa were people who prided themselves in being the best of their human make up. That is the kind of person he was, and G_d chose him to be the last Prophet, His Servant and Messenger, and a mercy to all of the worlds. G_d is talking about him when He says, *"Ar rahmaan al-lamal qur-an, the Merciful G_d taught the Qur'an; khalaqal ensaana and created the human person"*. This is the second creation. I can give you plenty of evidence for this, so much evidence that nobody can argue with me. I'm saying you will make yourself crazy, look stupid, trying to argue with it, because I can bring the whole Qur'an and Muhammed's life to support what I say.

A Mighty Foundation of Character

Muhammed, the Prophet, is the one who is singled out in the Qur'an by G_d for having the mighty foundation of character. His uswa, his model, was given to us as a model G_d approved for human beings, because He said, *"For any who believe in*

G_d and the Last Day." It did not say, "for Muslims". That means believing in G_d and believing in being accountable to G_d, that you have to answer to G_d one day. You fear G_d rejecting you, so that is working in you, in your soul, and your nature is to appreciate human excellence, or excellence period. That is working in your soul, and if you have those two working in your soul, then you should recognize that Muhammed is the ideal model of that for mankind.

When G_d spoke to Muhammed, the Prophet, He did not say, "Muhammed, you speak Arabic and not English. They say, 'G_d', but you speak Arabic. My name is Allah. You speak Arabic. My name is Allah. This is Allah talking to you. Allah has a mission for you." No, G_d did not give him the name, Allah, and He did not give him the name, G_d, because G_d in English means something you worship, that is all. It means a deity, something you worship. G_d did not give him that. G_d said, *"Muhammed, read in the name of your Lord Who created".* So, he told Muhammed who He was. He did not tell Muhammed what He exists for. He exists for man and man should worship Him, but Muhammed did not need that. He could go to any church or synagogue and get that. Muhammed needed understanding. So, G_d said, *"Read in the name of the Lord Who created; created man when he was nothing but a little liquid drop. Read and your Lord is Most Generous".* He is talking to Muhammed. Muhammed needs some help and G_d is saying, "I have plenty of help and I am Generous, not stingy. I give a lot!"

G_d Has Inscribed Upon It Its Nature

I like the idea that's out now about science and religion coming together. Darwin and other thinkers in science, they had their theories, and they came from religious communities, and I think they just wanted to avoid trouble. But I think a lot of those ideas that are truly good for the world are in science but were found in religion before they were given to us in science; because, actually, it's clear in the Qur'an that G_d created everything to evolve from simple to complex, from corrupt to pure, or from corruption to purity. The Prophet said, "Everything that exists G_d has inscribed upon it its nature excellence". G_d has inscribed into the nature excellence. And in science, every living thing is selected, and the species have evolved because of selecting the better and rejecting the worse, environmental situations, but also the choice of climate in eating, and everything. And because of the creatures being selective, they have evolved, including human beings. This is science now. I love science, religiously. And I think that's why the Muslims made so much progress under Muhammed, the Prophet, not spiritual progress, community progress. It was because they understood the connection with nature and the natural environment.

The Son of Elijah Mohammed Starts a New Life

The Qur'an says, *"The One Who taught how to use the writing pen"*. G_d is telling Muhammed, "I am the One Who educated man, all people. I taught him what he did not know before meeting with Me." So, here is a man who had no formal education and no help from the people who were managing the world for everybody. He came into a knowledge that interrupted man's history and brought in a new history, a new light, a new understanding, and a new and superior education. And history bears witness, today, that the scholars and the educated from all the known world, at that time, came to Muhammed's teachings for guidance; as a result, there was a reawakening for the intellectuals.

And as a result, there was a reawakening for the scholars, a reawakening for academic interest, and that initiative has been responsible for the progress of mankind ever since. Even what progress we have now in education, it is because of that great enlightening period. Now you might say, "He's trying to convert us to Al-Islam." No, I am not! You might say, "He is trying to get us to see Muhammed, that we should follow Muhammed." No, I am not. I'm trying to get you to see that when the world makes their time piece, makes a clock for everybody else, sets seasons for everybody else, even sets the time for you to live and die morally, when the world does all of that and the architects of that world are fascinated by their own creation, they think that they have life and death in their own hands. And the son of Elijah Mohammed rises up with no knowledge from their institutions, breaks the spell, and starts a new life.

Prophet Muhammed Comes In the Progression of the Revelation

Prophet Muhammed comes in the progression of the revelation. He comes in the sequence of Prophets who came one after another, succeeding each other, and the Qur'an is a book that is composed of books that came before. That simply means there is no big deal. Don't be telling me, "Your head is hurting, and this is deep!" If that is true of you, you should not want to hear me. In fact, you should just watch

TV and listen to the radio and music and forget about serious matters. You are not conditioned for it. Your mind is not conditioned for it. Something is wrong!

Do you know, sometimes, you open your mouth, and you say, "I'm a hypocrite, I'm a disbeliever", and you are not saying anything but "Man, he was heavy. I couldn't get it. Did he give you a headache, brother?" But when believers hear you, they hear the voice of a hypocrite, a disbeliever. I'm talking about the true believers among us. They know you. You can't hide from them. They know each other. If you are not one of the believers they know you right away, and we knew that under the Honorable Elijah Mohammed. We could tell a phony when we looked at him or when he appeared.

Muhammed's Mind Wouldn't Go Along With What Was Wrong

Prophet Muhammed came to answer the mystery where Jesus Christ comes into the world and he leads the people, and he doesn't trust the world. He doesn't even trust the Scripture that came before him. He didn't follow the Jews. He trusted what was in him by nature, and what G_d had added to that as the spirit and guidance from G_d, Himself. So, that is what he trusted. He spoke to them in parables. His job wasn't to lead them all the way, but he said, *"If I go away the father will send him unto you."* They understood that to be the Holy Spirit, the Holy Ghost. Yes, but still, it is a mystery. We really want to understand this as Muslims, i.e., the urge in man to obey the Holy Spirit and wait on the Holy Spirit to indicate where I am to take this, where I am to go, or how I am to get further in the road. That is Jesus Christ. Here we have a child born (Jesus), and his spirit won't go along with anything but what G_d wants. The next stage is not in the spirit; it is in the rational mind. Jesus was born of a spiritual nature. He was born of a spiritual order. He comes from a religious order, so he was a spiritual formation in the mind, or in the nature. Prophet Muhammed was born in a rational society that was astray as far as religion. It was backwards and very much astray, pagan, idol worshipers, but he never went along with that. His mind would never go along with them.

Struggling for Understanding Generates a Spirit

Here we have a child born (Jesus) and his spirit won't go along with anything but what G_d wants. Now, we have another child born, Muhammed, and his mind won't go along with anything. So now, just as the spirit protects us and guides us aright and will not disappoint us, never betray us, so will the spirit develop in support of the mind that devotes itself to strict obedience to what is rational, but also, to what is correct and decent for human beings, or for a human order, or human society. That mind is a rational mind, struggling to make things come clear in his own rational mind so that he can see it logically, and express it to people who have a common language of logic and reasoning. He struggles for that, and his struggling also generates a spirit. After he has done that for a long time, it generates a spirit. Now, his spirit has come into obedience to the mind that wants to go right, the thinking that wants to be correct. His spirit now conforms to it. He doesn't even have a spirit to disobey that direction in his mind, and what happens? There is an intuitive burst of light, and he starts to see things that were never seen before by himself, or anybody else. That is G_d revealing to him, and he will then speak to the people, and it won't be in parables. It will be in plain language.

Jesus Was the Fig Tree

Now, somebody will say, "Jesus Christ condemned the fig tree". Jesus Christ was the fig tree! That is why he said, "This tree that you Jews have offered me gives no fruit, so cursed be this tree that it bears fruit no more. I will feed. I am the fruit. Eat of my fruit. I am the fig tree. Your fig tree is finished." It did not mean what we thought it meant, that he cursed a fig tree. That would be insane! The tree didn't do any wrong, why curse it? It is made so extremely ridiculous to force the rational person to put it down, or to see a different meaning. It was made, intentionally, very stupid and irrational. Here comes a holy man and he sees the tree. He is hungry and he has his disciples with him now. Picture how this is given in the New Testament. They are out, and they don't work. They are holy men, and they expect for somebody to just give them something. The neighbors see them, and you have some bread, "May we share with you your bread? We are travelers, and we are holy men serving G_d." So, he comes to this tree. "This is a fig tree, why does it not have any figs? Well, I'm the good shepherd. I'm the Lord. I'm this, I'm that, and it doesn't have any fruit for me? Cursed be this tree! I curse it, so it will bear fruit no more, dry up." That is pure insanity to treat a little, innocent tree like that. You have the power of G_d to make this tree not bear fruit anymore and you are going to do it because it didn't have fruit for you? Take him straight to the funny farm!

THE TREASURE UNDER THE WALL: Thursdays with the Imam

"Have You Seen Lat and Uzza?"

It doesn't mean that at all. It means that G_d created Jesus Christ to trust his nature that was pure, and to trust his own human spirit, because his human spirit would not disobey G_d. So, when it says, in the Qur'an, the rejecters of Muhammed and his religion, they said, *"Have you seen this G_d?"* That is what they asked Prophet Muhammed, like they asked Moses. Muhammed was told by G_d to ask them, *"Have you seen Lat and Uzza?"* Those were the names of their gods. If they had said, "Yes, he's on 59th street", they would say, "Can he speak to you? Can he move from 59th street? You are talking about something dead that you made with your own hands." So, they were wise. They knew where he was going to take it. They weren't fools. So, they didn't say anything like some of you when I speak. You won't challenge me because you know you're going to be wiped out, so you just keep quiet, and won't say anything. So, they didn't say anything.

Two Arrows Shot by One Bow

In explaining Muhammed's spirit and the Holy Spirit, the Qur'an says, *"They were as two arrows fired, or shot by one bow, and they went and didn't deviate, and met on the far horizon"*. They went as two arrows shot by one bow. It means they went parallel. I know you see it, but I want to make sure. Here is the bow. The string is pulled. Here are the two arrows. One is the Holy Spirit, that is, G_d's Will, the Spirit of G_d's Will in the person, and the other is the human spirit. One is the human spirit. One is the Holy Spirit.

Muhammed's spirit is coming from his original nature, the nature that G_d gives all of us when we're born. A baby, his nature is to obey his G_d. There are two spirits. One is Allah's Spirit, and one is man's spirit represented in Muhammed, the Prophet. If your spirit will be 100 percent in agreement with G_d's Purpose for you and mankind, G_d will bless you with the additional support of His Own Spirit, and you will be one person, a human being, but you will be motivated by your human spirit and by G_d's Spirit. Both will be in you, your human spirit that wants to be perfectly in accord with what G_d wants and wants to be a perfect human being.

His Own Soul Pleasing to Him

It says, in the Surah 89 of Qur'an, *"Yaa ay-yuhan nasul mut-ma'innah"*, translated, *"Oh soul, in (complete) rest and satisfaction"*. This is the disposition in the soul to want to have complete satisfaction.*"Irje-e ilaa rab-bika raadeeyatam mar-deeyah, return to your Lord pleasing and pleased"*; two conditions. How is the human spirit able to go parallel in perfect agreement with G_d's Spirit? With obedience. Now, once he achieves this, he is pleased with himself. His own soul becomes pleasing to him, and G_d says to him, "Now, I am pleased with you. You are pleased with yourself, that you have conformed in perfect obedience to My Will, My Purpose for you and mankind, and you are pleased with yourself. Your soul pleases you." And G_d says, *"You have also pleased Me. Therefore, enter you, now, among My servants, the workers, pleased and pleasing; pleased with yourself and pleasing your G_d. Enter you My Paradise"*.

Pointing of the Fingers

In some of the prayers, the saintly people point two of their fingers at the end of the prayer, in jalsah (sitting position). It is connected to the arrows, and they are saying the arrows are going in perfect agreement with each other, parallel, agreeing with each other in the purpose and in the direction. One is the Spirit of G_d, and the other is the spirit of man. Which one is the Spirit of G_d, and which one is the spirit of man? The pointing (index) finger is man, and the middle finger is the spirit of man that G_d comes into. Once He comes into that spirit that man can't control by himself, then that spirit becomes the Spirit of G_d. And what do they say with the middle finger? It is saying, "F-you", to show you what this world thinks about it, that is, Satan's influence in the culture. The same generator who generates the writing of God backwards and it spells, "dog", he generated this vulgar, middle finger meaning. So, what is it saying? The human life and human spirit are created good by G_d and our own thinking corrupts it following misguidance, following the world, following somebody that is wrong, or following ourselves giving into our weaknesses. But if you can keep it from being corrupted, keep it pure, eventually, G_d's Spirit will come into the human spirit, because the human spirit is right. It is right for G_d, right for mankind. If it stays pure, G_d's Spirit will come into the human spirit.

The Spirit Is Always More Far-Reaching

The spirit is always more far-reaching than our rational mind. The spirit goes out ahead of our minds. I have a spirit to get up from here and do something useful, then my mind works it out for me. The spirit is always ahead of the mind, and even if the mind jumps the gun and goes out first, if the spirit is not with it, the mind is in trouble. Stop looking for something big and unreal, something that doesn't look like this world of reality. G_d says when we wake up in the new creation, we're going to say, *"This resembles what we saw before"*. So, don't look for something strange. G_d says even after death you will be resurrected. You will see the world of reality that will exist beyond this world, material things. He says you're going to look at it and say, "This looks like what we saw before." What I want to say is that guidance in Muhammed's teachings, in the Qur'an, should protect us from making an unnecessary mess for ourselves, struggling unnecessarily. If it doesn't look like what's rational and what's decent in this world, you should reject it, because He said it's going to look just like what you have seen before.

Trying to Frighten People Into Obedience

You saw in your human life what was moral decency, human, and what was not human. You saw what was beautiful, what made sense and what didn't make sense. So, in the next, look for the same thing. Look for what makes sense. Look for what is clean. Look for what is decent. Don't look for something way out, like somebody died and was put in a grave with fifty snakes and serpents and seventy raving bulls came into the grave with him. So, you are trying to figure how big that grave was to get all those fifty and seventy creatures in it. How did they get into that little grave he was put in? You are wasting your time! That doesn't resemble what is sensible in this world. That doesn't resemble what is fair and decent in this world. Why would G_d do that? All he had was a little poontang and he wasn't married and now he's going to have serpents coming at him, a bunch of bulls charging at him, and at the same time fire is leaping all up. "Why go to that extreme, Lord? Why do something that extreme? You need a psychiatrist! You have a strange way of getting Your pleasure!" These guys are trying to frighten people into obedience. They are dealing with ignorant publics, and they are trying to frighten them into obeying G_d. So, they tell all these outrageous stories and say it came from Prophet Muhammed's hadith. If the Prophet were here, it would be too bad. I'm sure he would announce that all of them are shirk. They're false and shouldn't be associated with Al-Islam.

Now, you know, if they tried to do it in his lifetime, certainly, after he died they would try to give the people something in his name. The Prophet was living, and this man asked Prophet Muhammed if he could do it. He said, "You're the Messenger of G_d, but I'm also the messenger of G_d". And he asked Prophet Muhammed to accept that there is a second messenger, along with him, while Prophet Muhammed was living. Prophet Muhammed, naturally, rejected him and the people who followed Muhammed rejected him. If they did that in his lifetime, what would they do after? Much worse. I know one thing. I don't love confusion. I hate confusion. I don't like disrespect, and you disrespect my intelligence when you tell me stupid stuff and tell me I'm supposed to believe it. You are disrespecting the intelligence that G_d gave us. He gave me human intelligence, and you're giving me this crazy stuff and telling me I'm supposed to believe that blindly. So, you're not respecting my intelligence. You're telling me that G_d did certain things, and my estimation of G_d is so high that down there on that level that you have put my G_d, I can't accept that. You have disrespected my intelligence. You have disrespected my estimation of G_d's Greatness, so I can't follow it.

Muhammed Never Worshiped Idols

The Arabs didn't believe in religion like we believe in religion, or as the world understands religion now. But there was a special group of them who prided themselves in being conscious of the excellence of human life, and I'm sure that they are the ones who are called, hunafaa, in the Qur'an, after haneef. Prophet Abraham, peace be on him, he was haneef. It is in the Qur'an. They translate it, *"the one who was upright in his nature"*. I'm sure he (Muhammed) was of the hunafaa, and it is believed by a number of scholars in Al-Islam, and of the few I have met at least two believe that Muhammed, the Prophet, was one of them. Allah said of him that he was already in the most excellent human character. His character was excellent before G_d chose him. He was not a leader of anything. He didn't belong to any school, or anything. They didn't have any school organizing anything, but they were just like certain people. They gravitated towards each other because of their similarities. They were similar in aspects that were important for them, so they associated with each other, and I believe that Muhammed, the Prophet, his companions, they were all hunafaa, except 'Umar. 'Umar was converted from idol worship, but there is no evidence that any of the rest of them worshiped idols, i.e., Abu Bakr, Uthman, Ali, may G_d be pleased with them. There is no evidence that

I know of that they worshiped idols, and Muhammed, the Prophet, the history says that he never worshiped any idols.

Only East comes with Jesus Christ. He is a way to get to the West. He comes as the new life, new birth, new creation in its original nature created by G_d. He (G_d) says when He wants a servant, He creates one from among those He already created. And then the explanation comes in Surah Rahmaan that Allah taught the Qur'an and created humanity. It says in Qur'anic Arabic, *"Al-lamal Qur'an, khalaqal ensaan,"* translated, *"He taught the Qur'an and created the human person from those who were already existing".* Muhammed, the Prophet, is the one who it is referring to directly. He didn't know revelation, Scripture, but G_d revealed it to him and then taught him. It says, *"We shall teach you, make you know and understand revelation by teaching."* There are many references, not just one, that say Allah is going to teach him. Allah is going to ease his way, ease his difficulty, take the burden off him, and teach him.

G_d's Plan Only For the Ideal Human Being

Scripture (Bible) speaks of Jesus Christ as a word, and it says he was existing before the foundations of the world. That is to be understood in several ways, but one clear way is that G_d is saying that the world of mankind, the world we live in, it should conform to the Plan of G_d, and G_d's Plan is for the ideal human being. It is not for every human being. It is only for the ideal human being. The ideal human being is man in his created excellence, the best moral life, and the best rational life, with all the talents and possibilities for him in a real world. Jesus Christ is a sign of that, and Muhammed, the Prophet, is the proof of that, not just a sign. Jesus Christ points to that in his creation. Muhammed is the fulfillment of that. It was achieved in the life of Muhammed, the Prophet. An excellent society, a just society, an enlightened society, compassionate society, humane society, all of that was achieved by Muhammed, the Prophet, in his lifetime; not something to point to, something manifest under his leadership. It was produced by him leading the people to the way, and as a result it fed the whole world, not just those immediate people.

The language of Jesus Christ and Muhammed belong together. That is why Muhammed said in the end you shall see them together. Allah says, in the Qur'an, *"You will find the nearest people to you are those who call themselves Nasara, the Christians."* The Jews are closer to us in the expression of the concept of G_d, monotheism, one deity, but obviously, that was not important enough to be a problem for our relationship with Christians. This is in the Qur'an (not the hadith), from G_d speaking, *"You will find the nearest people to you are those who call themselves, Nasara"*, the Christians, people from Nazareth.

"Seek Knowledge From the Cradle to the Grave"

In reference to Easter, you should be aware of the closeness of Prophet Jesus and Prophet Muhammed, peace be on them, and you should not be burdened with mysteries but know that Jesus Christ came to personify. If you don't know these words, go to the English dictionary. Do not be the kind of student who hears a word and do not understand it, and do not make a note. When I was in school, I stayed in school. After I left the walls of the schools, I continued. I kept myself in school. Wherever I was that was my school. I kept studying. I still do that. I live the life of a student always studying. Muhammed said, "Get knowledge from the cradle to the grave." There is no time to retire from being a student. I have a spirit to do that. I don't have to make myself do that. I can't stop myself from doing that. It is just my spirit and that's life. That is what makes your life so pleasant and enjoyable, when you're constantly growing as an intellect. You stop growing as a biological flesh and blood person, but you continue to grow as an intellect. Some people get old, and they can't think. They can't use their minds so well and it is probably because they haven't kept up the mind by feeding it and giving it the right treatment. Just like an old car or wagon, if you don't put a little oil on the wheel, the axle, every now and then, it might get rust and break off, and you will lose the wheel. I don't see any difference in my mind now than I saw when I was twenty years old. My mind is just like it was when I was in high school. I don't see any difference. In fact, it is better. I think better. I think faster. I think clearer. It operates better now than it did when I was a young man or teenager.

The Ascension of the Prophet

The Prophets on the different levels in the Miraj, it is like a ladder, Jacob's Ladder. Adam was the first level, and Jesus and John were on the second level. *"Nafsin Wahidah, one soul, then He made of them two"*. So, the next level is two. That is the spiritual, and the social. Christ is the spiritual, John is the social… He came blasting people. Jesus came sharing his heart and love, feeding them love. John was telling them, "You'd better get straight, or hell is going to break loose! Repent now, the wrath of G_d is coming!" But then Christ Jesus came. They were separate, but together at the same time, like two sides of one coin, two sides of the same coin, heads and tails. Christ Jesus was the head and John was the tail. That is why he said, "How can I baptize you? I'm not superior to you." The reason why John baptized Jesus Christ is because Jesus could not do his mission unless he was baptized by John, and John is the one who addressed problems in society. Jesus is the one who looked for healing. But he wouldn't be qualified, if he didn't recognize problems and then accept that "this man is a legitimate Messenger of G_d, like I am". That was not his goal. What that picture is saying, both in the Bible and Qur'an, is, it is not the role of Jesus to be negative, or to condemn people. His nature is not that. His nature is to find reason to compliment, embrace, and love. That's his nature, but they both are on the same level of emotionality. In the Genesis, the Spirit moved along the face of the waters. *"Darkness was upon the deep, and a voice came and said, 'Let there be light' and there was light'."* And G_d hung a lamp in the heavens, a lesser lamp and then He hung a greater lamp. But it all came about because of the Spirit moving on face of the water. That is what set it all off.

So, the two lamps are the sun, and the moon. The moon was first, according to the spiritual generation, the generation of spiritual life. But according to the world no, the sun was first. So, here is Jesus and John, both born of the same condition and circumstances which produced both, but the lesser one came ahead of the greater one. That is John. John was the moon. He took a little moonshine, too. He was a little tipsy, too. Christ Jesus was level all the time, just cool, and level-headed all the time. But one had to come to prepare the way for the second. The kind guy doesn't come along until they have a warning, "You have to stop this crap", preparing the way for the other guy saying, "You have to be calm. You have to listen to him, and you have to repent to appreciate this man". Doesn't it make sense?

The Bible says of Jesus Christ, *"Behold, I come quick!"* It means it is so urgent it is like a woman having labor pains. She can't wait. She has to deliver that child, now, and that is in the ninth month. So, it says, *"Behold, I come quick!"* Now, that is of Jesus Christ. But it didn't say it of John, but it was observed that both of them were alive and active in the womb, both of them. They were born separately, but both of them were alive and active in the womb, and in different mothers. But while one was in one mother being born, he stirred in the womb, he affected the other in another mother. The other one, Jesus Christ, had another mother, but his quickening affected the one in the other mother, and caused him to quicken, too. He responded to it. One child kicking, and the other child responded and kicked, too, meaning they are so closely connected spiritually that whatever happened to one psychically or spiritually, it affected the other one even before they were delivered from the womb, Jesus Christ and John. You know they must have been pretty close together because, otherwise, he would not have been grown and on his job baptizing to receive Jesus Christ. Jesus Christ represents passions for healing and comforting, and John, the Baptist, represents fear.

A New Set of Circumstances For the Same Human Type

The moon is cold; the sun is hot. The heart is warm. On your back it is cool there. The spinal cord, it goes up like a snake. That is cool. The brain is hot, but it wants to be cool. So, therefore, you get hot, you sweat, you cool off, and even when you're hot, you feel your head up here and it is not hot. It is cool. If it is hot, something is wrong with you. You are sick. John the Baptist, he is the cool side, but he is a wild man, too. He is the one who can be excited. He is fear, becomes very fearful, so he warns the people. He baptizes before it is too late. "Repent before it is too late!" That is John, the same type in the Revelation, the same John, just appearing in different circumstances. A new set of circumstances for the same human type for G_d appears, again, in Revelation, and he is alarming the world, too, telling them doom is here, and he describes how it is going to happen. The same human type, not the same person. That is why he is called, John, the Revelator. The other one is, John, the Baptist, because he baptizes, but they both represent fear.

Man is fear and appetite. Which is the strongest, fear or appetite? Appetite will get you killed, and you are looking at death. You are looking at death knowing, most likely, you're going to get killed, but your appetite is so strong you have to go on and take the risk. You have never heard of John standing on the water, have you? Fear can't stand on water. Faith stands on water. It is beautiful, and it is all about human life. You have to give your life to the One Who designed it, that is, G_d. He designed your life, and He is telling you how He designed it, and the wise who awaken to it, they stay with G_d.

Clouds Represent Man's Confusion On Earth

Now, we know that there is trouble up there, but you do not hear it. What you hear is trouble down here. The mist goes up and meets the cold currents. The lightning flashes and the thunder roars, and all of that was started by us down here. It was our vapor that went up, clouded up the heavens, and caused negative and positive charges, lightning, and thunder. That is the lower heavens. That is our heaven. It came from down here and went up there. Trouble starts down here and goes up. It starts down and goes up. That is why the Bible talks a lot about the clouds and the noise in the heavens, to let you know that it is not a good thing all the time. The Bible says, G_d says, *"You are clouds in My Feet.* My Feet are to clear up. You are at peace with Me because I cleared the matter up. Now, you are bringing those clouds to My Feet, bringing your confusion and your problems to My Feet." Man repents and when he repents, water comes from his eyes, and that is what we need to grow our life down here. We need man's repentance and his love. His repentance comes in the form of teardrops and for the environment, it is rain.

The Universe a Reflection of What Is In the Soul

So really, rain is not talking about rain that comes naturally to the ground. It is talking about repentance, and the tears of love falling from the eyes of human beings that is what is needed to feed and grow life. Hardness won't do it. Like the rocky desert, you can't get much life from there. Where the rain falls there is life. So, it is a beautiful sign and none of it is just to be taken literally. It is not literal. The tree, sky and everything are in our soul. Everything in the sky is in our soul. It is not literal. Everything in the sky is in our soul. The cosmos is in the soul, and they call it the microcosm, and that is the macrocosm out there. But you have to see all that in here (the soul), then it has reality for you; otherwise, it is nothing but what Allah says in the Qur'an, "ghurur", which means signs that will send you off in your mind, signs that will make you subject to have delusions. If you take them for granted, you will be deluded, or what you think is real will be nothing but illusion, allurement, not reality. That idea was long before these Prophets we know of by name. Long before the Prophets there were seers and others, and they saw that the universe was really a reflection of what is in the soul. That is why it is called, "ghurur", it is not real. It is real out there, but it is not real for the person who wants to understand that language and apply that language. You cannot do it. You are not supposed to apply it out there. You are supposed to apply it, here, inside.

The One Who Comes to Finish Building the House

So, there were seers. It meant that they were able to see into the nature or soul of man and see that the language out there is really expressing the life inside. G_d made that to speak the language of the soul. Prophet Muhammed said of himself that Prophets had been sent, one behind another, and each one came and put a block in the house, and there was one block yet to be put in the house, so G_d sent him. So, he is the last Prophet, and it means the one who comes to finish building the house. There is one stone missing, and he has to place that stone. That was the black stone, and the stone that was missing was establishing the society of G_d, the society that G_d wants, or the kingdom of G_d, as it says in the Bible establishing the kingdom of G_d. Moses did not get to the kingdom of G_d. Jesus Christ prayed for it. It was left to Muhammed. They knew the way of life, but they didn't know how to accomplish it in this world, how we are going to establish this order in this world. Prophet Muhammed was given the wisdom and the guidance to establish it in this world, and he did. Actually, Muhammed is more than just a spiritual leader. He is the leader for all levels, and he is a political leader, also.

The Society of G_d's Servants On This Earth

The Prophets before Muhammed, their vision was limited. They were so involved, committed to establishing the life that they couldn't give themselves to establishing the order within the order of the world. So, they never achieved it, because it was not that strong in their spirit to do that, but they knew it had to be done one day. They all pointed to it, and really the Prophets Abraham, Jesus Christ, these are multiple figures. They are one type but having many figures, one type, but plural figures. Muhammed, the Prophet, he had to go back to the base. He had to go back to Adam and that is why he kissed the black stone, because he was so happy that G_d reconciled him with his father, Adam. He understood Adam in his makeup, his type. He knew the type he was. So, he had to start there and go upwards. Why did he have to go upwards? Because he wanted to establish the society of G_d's servants on this earth.

Man Is the Human Being In His Best Nature

So, he needed to know, "How am I going to establish this ruling order? It is an order. It has rules over it. It is a government, but it is a government under G_d, not under man. Now, how am I going to establish it? I have to establish first, man, and when I establish man, I will have the foundation." So, he established man. Man is not the Jew. Man is not the Muslim. Man is the man, the human being in his best nature. He said, "That is where I have to go!"

The United States understood, saying, "We hold these truths to be self-evident that all men are created equal and endowed by their Creator with certain inalienable rights, among these, life, liberty, and the pursuit of happiness". I'm giving it in the first language. They saw what Muhammed did. They saw what he was saying, and they understood Jesus Christ, because Muhammed came to point to Jesus Christ. Jesus Christ pointed to Muhammed, and Muhammed points back to Jesus Christ. That is why it says he has come back. Even the Ahmadiyyah say he's coming back. He is already here! He's back! He is just the common black man. He is black over all the planet earth; I don't care what color his skin is. The original man knows nothing. He is the man who lives upon faith, not upon light.

Moses Was the Mountain

His type is representative of the plural body. That means all the people. Moses went up to see G_d. He couldn't see G_d, so G_d told him how he could see Him. He said *"Look at that mountain. If it remains as it is, you will see Me."* But when he looked at it to see G_d, his mind went off. His mind just was blown. It blew his mind. It was too much for him to digest or to fathom. So, he fainted trying to see G_d, and when he woke up the mountain was still there, but he crumbled to dust. His senses crumbled to dust, but the mountain did not change. It was still there as it was, which means this: That when he was looking at the mountain, he was looking at himself. He was only looking at his intelligence and his mind. So, he looked at it and it got to be too much for him. He could not see G_d through that, so he fainted. And when he fainted, with G_d, it was as the mountain, because G_d sees his self (Moses) and the mountain as one. He climbed up the mountain to see G_d. G_d sees him climbing up in his own self to see G_d, not up a mountain out there. "You are climbing up in your own self to see Me, and the head of the mountain is your head. The foot of the mountain is your feet. So, when you didn't see Me, you crumbled to dust, but the physical world that I made wasn't moved. When you woke up, you saw the mountain is still standing, but you lost your footing. You cannot see Me, directly!" That is what He said. In Qur'anic Arabic, it is, *"Laa tudrikuhul absaar"*.

That means no vision, whether it is an animal, eagle, a man, or anything, can reach Him. You can't catch Him with your vision. It says, *"You can't catch G_d with your vision".* It did not say, "See Me there." He said, *"The vision can't catch Me".* G_d defies all vision, if they want to reach Him, but He told Moses to look at the mountain. What was He telling Moses? "You can only see Me by reference. I created this world to refer you back to Me." The Prophet said, *"I know by Your handiworks that You exist".*

Sajdah Made to the Pattern For Your Existence

Your sajdah is made to the pattern, your pattern, the pattern for your existence, your creation in the material universe. That is what you are submitting to. Since Adam represents the first man, then you are submitting to the original pattern that G_d established all people upon. So, if we submit and we follow that pattern in everything that we do, we will ascend and ascend and become completed and perfect as G_d wants us, which is the perfect human, not an angel. So, this understanding wouldn't be here if it wasn't something we could use and grow with. I know that.

Chapter 3

Jesus, the Christ

Muhammed, the Prophet, peace be upon him, put emphasis, first, on literacy, learning to read. He obligated every follower of his to write down what he would give them and then teach it to another person who could not read. So, he made really, teachers of all his followers. He said, "If you only can remember one line, teach that one line to another person". In the Qur'an, he is mentioned as a liberator. It also says of him that he is the unlettered, meaning not formally educated. He received no formal education from anybody. He was not belonging to any rabbinical school, or any order that would educate him. No, he was not formally educated by anybody. He belonged to no body, had no teachers, and belonged to no school. G_d says of him, *"He is the unlettered Messenger, Prophet, mentioned in the Torah and in the Injeel."*

We're told that we are to believe in the Prophets, all of them, and we're told not only are we to believe in Jesus Christ as a Prophet. We're told that we are to believe in him as Christ, also. How many of Muslims are aware of that? If they are, they don't show it in their language. We are to believe in Jesus Christ as a Prophet, and believe me, the Bible says he's a Prophet. The Bible says he's a Prophet, and we're to believe in him also as a Christ. The Bible says he's the Christ. We're to believe in him as the Christ, and even further than that, because Christ only means the anointed, and David was anointed by them putting special oil on his head and wiping his head with the oil.

The Immaculate Conception

So, he's more than just that. He is, also, the child, man of the immaculate conception. Do Muslims believe in the immaculate conception? Yes, but how do we explain that, I would say, great sign? Allah said he and his mother are signs. How do we explain it in Islam? In Christianity, we know how it is explained. I don't need to go over that. In Islam, we say G_d is the Creator and has power to create whatever He wills, and Jesus' creation, peace be upon him, is as the creation of Adam, the first man, Adam. That's what we are told to say. "Oh, but I want to know more". You've got your mind on sex too much. You will never learn the religion if you're just going to be sexy through and through. Get your mind off sex. This is not about that thing that you do. It's not that small. It is a big thing. This is a big, big conception.

We believe that G_d has the power to create whatever He wills and as He created the first life, He can create the second and repeat it. It says, *"And as He created a man from the dead earth, He can certainly create a man from a living woman"*. This is G_d. We're supposed to believe in the power of G_d to create whatever He Wills. And again G_d says, to make it very simple for us, "If I want a son, I can get a son from those that I've already created, thank you". And He created Adam. Didn't He create Adam? Was that not the first man He created, Adam? And He said, "If I want a son, I can get a son from those I've already created".

The Second Adam

I read the Gospel, the New Testament, one of the books of the New Testament that's giving us the genealogy of Jesus Christ, peace be upon him. The genealogy of Jesus Christ is traced from his mother back to Adam. It says, "Who was created by G_d". Need I say more? In Christianity, in Christian theology, Jesus Christ, peace be upon him, is also called the second Adam. That's why the Bible, New Testament, has to trace his genealogy back to the first Adam. Was Adam a man? Adam was a man, wasn't he? That explains why Jesus Christ is called both the son of man and the son of G_d. When Jesus Christ wanted his followers to know him better, he said, *"Who do you say I am? Who do you say, I, the son man am?"* He didn't say, "I'm not the son of a man", but he let it be known, to keep his disciples from missing the point, *"Who do you say, I, the son of man am?"* And one of those disciples said, *"You are the son of the living G_d"*, and he let it be like that.

Light Upon Light

Again, we look at the Bible. I won't go to the Old Testament, but it's there, too. What you're more familiar with is the Gospel, as it is presently. The Word of G_d personified as Christ Jesus, peace be upon him, comes into the world not of water only, but of water and blood. So, the water of science, or the science formed of water is in the heavens and the heavens and the earth were separated, and the heavens were confused as churning smoke. And Allah directed Himself to the heavens, and He said to the heavens and to the earth, *"Come ye together willingly or unwillingly"*. And Allah, highly Glorified is He, also says, *"Can't you see that this creation was once one continuous whole?"* It wasn't always just smoky heaven and an earth needing to be reconciled with a heaven that was in bad shape. Our knowledge then is one. Creation is one. Knowledge is one. It is expressed in so many different forms, but it is one. It is light upon light, *"The Light of a blessed tree, an olive."* Its oil appears to be lit before there is fire. It gives off a light before there is fire, and the fire does not touch it. Doesn't this sound like empiricism, objectivity, where you're not forming anything until the essence tells you to form it, and you're not forming it in any way that the essence is not saying form it? You see, our discipline and our knowledge are the same as the jinn's discipline and his knowledge, but our result is different. His result is different. His obedience is to matter. Our obedience is to the Creator of the matter.

Jesus and Muhammed Together

There are scholarly persons in Islam that have searched the language of the Gospel before it was translated into English, and they say that the word, Paracletes, in the Gospel, is the same as, Ahmed, in the Qur'an... There is a change in his mission, and he sends his disciples out, according to the Gospel as it is now, in English, in the West, on a mission to give the Gospel to all the worlds, to everybody, to the whole world. Our Prophet, peace be on him, it is reported that he said: "The day will come when they see the Prophet Jesus and myself together", peace be upon the Prophets. Now, you know the ready meaning that any one of us would get is that it appears to the Christian world that the Prophet Jesus, the Prophet of G_d, and the Prophet Muhammed, the Prophet of G_d, are at odds with each other. So, the obvious message in that to us is that one day they will see that the two are not at odds with each other.

But how will they come to arrive at that conclusion? That's more important than that first level reading of what those words from Muhammed, the Prophet, are saying to us in the world. I strongly believe that what the Prophet is saying to us is told in Scripture, but most of us can't see it. The world hasn't seen it, that Jesus Christ depicts the Word. He is a personification of the Word. The Word of G_d is the same yesterday as it is today, and it will be the same tomorrow. We believe the Qur'an to be the Word of G_d. And if Jesus came, firstly, addressing his own people, the Jewish people, but then later sent his disciples out on a mission to give this to all the world, then Jesus was not only a depiction of the Word of G_d in Israel but the Word of G_d in the earth, to all people, and that had to be told. Muhammed, the Prophet, peace be upon him, is described by his wife, 'Aisha, may G_d be pleased with her, as the Word in the world living, demonstrating, communicating, teaching. Now, can't you see the two coming together?

Jesus and Muhammed Were Both the Word of G_d

One is personifying something that is enshrouded in the time of Muhammed. How do they differ? They are alike and they're different. How do they differ? Jesus, the Prophet, peace be upon him, he represents the Word in the soul of man trying to light the intellect of man and be perceived by the intellect of man. That is an inherent urge that G_d has created us with. Jesus represents that, and he says, *"I go away. I have to go away, for if I don't go away, the Comforter will not come unto you"*. That's the Word in Muhammed. It is going to come in Muhammed. "If you continue to trust this automatic nature, you will never trust the neighboring intellect. So, I'm going to pull myself out of the world. I do this because that's the purpose for which I was sent into the world. If I do this not the Comforter will not be sent to you", or "will not come unto you". Can't you see how they come together? The two come together in humanity and also come together in the bigger stage or on the bigger stage, the stage of knowledge, the stage of true, revealed knowledge, the Qur'an. Both were the Word of G_d but established or brought into the world by two different means, by two different facets or properties of human nature, but they agree, and they are necessarily connected in man and in Scripture.

The Death of the Word

Let's go back to the mystery of the Gospel, and this is not something to be talked about publicly. We should be like the Christians. Their mysteries they talk about among themselves. When the Roman soldiers came to see if Jesus, reportedly Jesus, had died, it said that they had to break his arms down, which means that rigor mortis had set in. Now, after they had done that, it looks like we've seen enough. That was a conclusive piece that he was dead. A body that rigor mortis has set into is dead, no doubt about it. But that wasn't enough. They took the spear and speared him under the rib, and it says, *"Out came water and blood"*, separate. That's the proof of the death of the Word in the form that G_d wants it in. It's not the proof of Jesus' death, but the proof of the death of the Word. The Word has become a cliché. It was meant to be the light, but it has become a cliché. And it says, *"Out came water and blood",* showing that the water and the blood had separated. This happens with wounds. The wound, after the blood stops pumping out, you'll see, sometimes, water separate from the blood. This is told in the Bible, in the New Testament. The same thing that is told here is told in the New Testament. The water here is the spiritual order. The blood is the social order. So, the death of the Word depicted, or personified here says this: The world will be given religion on the one hand, on the one side, and society or government, social order on the other side, and they will be separate. It is telling us long before it's established, that the world is going to be spiritual and secular. The loss of tauheed is the death of the Word, and Jesus is sent as a sign to depict that. That's one of the mysteries. He not only depicts one thing. He also depicts the resurrection, the life and the death, and perhaps some other things..

The Golden Fleece and the Lost Sheep

You know the Bible, I can't say the Qur'an, but I do know that the Bible carries an influence of ancient Egyptian religion, and the sciences of ancient Greece. In the myths of ancient Greece there is the expression, "Golden fleece". So, there's a golden fleece, and then there's a white fleece, ordinary fleece, golden fleece and ordinary fleece. The lost sheep means the lost social knowledge, the lost social science. Sheep is symbolic of man's social bonding, or his gregarious nature, his need to group with others, to be with others. It's depicted as a sheep to say that the best of the social people are the victims of the wolves of the world. That's what it's depicted to say.

Invisible Man Disconnected From His Social Commitment

It doesn't mean that that group of people are sheepish in the negative sense. It means that they are just strongly social, and isn't our community a brotherhood? It's a brotherhood, and brotherhood is another way of saying strongly social. My brother is the closet relative, even closer to me than my father or my mother, because my brother has both my father and mother in him like I do. So, it's a stronger word for social bonding than even parents and children. So, the lost sheep is told by Ralph Ellison (in the book, *Invisible Man*) explaining his whole plight as he had suffered. He said, "Somewhere behind me I got disassociated, disconnected from my social commitment." So, the bond of the sheep in explanation or in interpretation is the social commitment, and the lost sheep is Ralph Ellison that has gotten separated from his social contract or his social commitment. Now why did we think of ourselves as the lost sheep? It was for that same reason that we were all spiritual in religion but were not established upon blood (social). Oh, it's wonderful to stand on water (spiritual), but even more wonderful to be erected in blood! Praise be to Allah!

Rigor Mortis Has a Bad Meaning and a Good One

Blood is where you find water and material reconciled and when you destroy that agreement by separating water from blood you end up with asceticism, and then, eventually, spiritualism and secularism, like we have in the world right now. The cross depicts rigor mortis. The cross is a sign of rigor mortis and rigor mortis has two meanings, a bad one and a good one. Rigor mortis is death of the Word in man's life or in man's world. That's why it said he (Jesus) did not die, but G_d lifted him up to himself. In man's world he was dead. In man's perception he was dead. But G_d lifted him up, meaning G_d lifted him up out of the world (not him, a man), and brought him again to G_d. What does that mean "brought him to G_d"? In the mind of the saints, he didn't leave them. He never left them. They saw him with G_d. They say, "Well, there's no place for him in the world now. The world has rejected him, but he's with G_d. The Word is with G_d".

So, rigor mortis, now, is to be read in a positive way and in a negative way. Rigor mortis in a negative sense means that the social life of those people that were the victims of that misperception of the Word, the rigor mortis on them is that their blood has stopped flowing and has lost its life and become dead and stiff in the body, no expression in the body. So, it stiffens the life of the body and causes the life of the body to not have any expression or flexibility, just stiff and rigid. That's the bad sign. That's the sign in its bad consequences, in its bad perception, in its bad understanding. Now, where is the good one? *"Die not, except the death of a Muslim!"* So, now, how can we bring this balance? This sign (cross) in ancient Greece sciences is a sign of balance. It's a sign of balance. You can balance really well when you stick your arms out. The tight rope walkers they use the extended arms to walk a tightrope. So, it's a sign of balance. Perpendicular and horizontal, that's what G_d wants. He wants us on the siraatal mustaqeem, perpendicular, but on the sabeelillah, horizontal. It's a sign of, *"Die not accept the death of a Muslim."* Therefore, see the cross as something that has a bad meaning, and the cross as something that has good meaning. And when the Prophet I says, "See that you not destroy even a cross", do not break the cross, because it has a good meaning.

The Unconscious Social Animal In the Secular World

I don't believe the hadith about Jesus coming back with a great sword to slay pigs is authentic hadith. I believe it's a hadith that was put there by others after the Prophet, but it can be accepted. Though it's not authentic hadith, it can be accepted. When the truth of Jesus comes, the Word will slay pigs, but not the physical pigs. That unconscious social animal in the secular world responsible for the secular world's deviation, that's the pig it will slay. You know the pig appears to be nude even when he's covered. Yes, and he's intelligent. They say, science says, he's very intelligent, but his behavior is not, no morals, no ethics. He doesn't only eat slop. He likes it on him. Yes, he wallows in it. He likes it on his body. So, the Word destroys that, doesn't it? And it breaks that false, I would say, wrong attempt of people to associate with the wrong meaning of the cross, or to read the wrong meaning in the cross. It breaks that false cross.

"I Thirst!"

Now, I could give you so much proof of that. I said a lot of these things before, and some have probably forgotten it. Some, maybe they didn't get it. In the Bible, what actually happened to let them know there was death? As I said above, the spearing says in a quiet, revealing way, "not dead". The spearing of him, the blood coming out and the water is saying he was not dead. But what happened the day that he died? He was suspended on the cross and obviously, it was hot out in the sun, again, like Jonah. Isn't that Jonah on the bank of the river, him up in the air, suspended up in the air in a similar situation like Jonah was on the bank? But he (Jonah) wasn't suspended. He was standing upon sand, and the sun was punishing his head. Jesus said, "I thirst!" Did they give him water? No! They had him there to punish him. They had rejected him. They brought vinegar, and in Latin vinegar is aceta, a play on ascetic. That's what killed the Word in the followers of Jesus, asceticism. It said as soon as they applied the vinegar to his nose, to his spirit (nose is symbolic of the ghost, the soul taking in the breath of life), when they put it to his nose, he readily gave up the ghost, so, says the New Testament. They are saying by that depiction or by that picture story that what really brought the Word to be dead in the followers of Jesus was asceticism. And we know from the history of their struggle that to find themselves, to get themselves in accord with the life and teachings of Jesus, peace be upon him, they became Gnostics and later ascetics, i.e., the Roman Catholic Church.

What is ascetic? Look it up in the dictionary. Most Roman Catholic priests are still ascetics. Ascetic means separate yourself from the world. You don't marry and have children. You separate yourself from the world. That's why the Prophet, prayers and peace be on him, he said, "Whoever does not marry is not of me". You're not of him. You're of the monks or the ascetics, or somebody else, certainly not him. Now, to understand this vinegar, or this asceticism as to how it came about, we have to understand the meaning of wine in the Gospel.

"Don't Pour New Wine Into Old Bottles"

Wine is blood, according to the Gospel, and blood is the doctrine, according to the Gospel. And he said, *"Take this to commemorate or to remember me!"* It is talking about the science, the knowledge that he was guiding them for their social life. And since they had been denied that freedom, before his coming, the coming of the Word, they were really thirsting for religion that would respect their social life and their social needs. When Christ was able to, symbolically speaking, take the water that they would ordinarily drink and turn it into wine, it became wine to them, not to say that it was intoxicating to them, but to say that it was exciting to them.

He made something that was flat, like water, exciting when he showed them that G_d didn't intend for you to have this water right here like this. He intended for you to have social science. When he did that, he made them enthusiastic, and it was like the description of it is given in the difference between them and the old order, or the religious people as told in water and wine. You drink water and nothing happens. You drink wine and people start talking more. "Hey, what's happening man!" So, this is not in a bad sense, it's in a good sense, and the Qur'an addresses that. It says you shall be given a wine that will not leave you heavy headed. It won't burn your head, no hangovers. It's going to be a pure drink. So, now that we understand that let's look at the vinegar, aceta. The Bible says, *"Don't pour new wine into old bottles."* That's too much for an old bottle. It may break it. All of this is symbolic, picture language, picture stories, a story told in picture language. Vinegar is dead wine. Can't you see the connection? Can't you see everything agreeing perfectly? *"Al-hamdu lillahi rabbil 'alameen."*

The Christ Nature Is In Everybody

Muhammed, the Prophet, said that a time will come when they see he and Christ Jesus together, meaning the two of them are the same, in origin. He was born in the purity of his original nature, and Jesus was born in the purity of his original nature. So, for Muhammed, that is what supported him for forty years until revelation came to him from G_d. G_d chose him because he was in his original nature and established as G_d wanted. G_d never said that, "Now, we're going purify you and establish you on good morals". He said, *"We beheld you already established upon the most powerful foundational morals, or morality"*. Christ Jesus said, *"I in you and you in me*. You are members of my body, but I am also in you". What is he saying? The Christ nature is in everybody, but some people just do not awaken to their Christ nature. The world pulls them out of that nature, can cause them to live a life of sin, but everyone is born of that nature. They say they crucified him, but he said, "You don't take my life. I give it to you". So, what is he saying? "You can't check me". The cross means, a check is going to hold you here. He said, "You can't check me. I check myself. G_d created me to check myself. You are not checking me; I am checking myself. This is my purpose for being in the world".

You Cannot Crucify the Word of G_d

So, that is why the Qur'an came saying, *"No, they did not kill him or crucify him; neither did they kill him, nor crucify him, but it appeared that way to them"*. They are looking at him and seeing him being crucified, but the real understanding, they do not have it. He cannot be crucified. For the unbelievers, it is a sign that they are going to check his work. His mission is not going to be able to get out of their check and balance. The cross is balance, too. You are not going to be able to get out of that check. But in reality, they never crucified him, because he was in the original nature and he is just a sign, really. He is not the reality. He is a sign pointing to the reality. So, how could they crucify him, and he is the Word of G_d? You cannot crucify the Word of G_d, and the Word has influence and Spirit. You can't crucify the Spirit, Allahu Akbar! It is beautiful when you understand it. Jesus said, "You cannot check me. I check myself. I came into the world for that purpose, to check myself under G_d, to remain obedient to Him in my nature."

The Original Man Is Your Original Nature

That is our original nature, as Mr. Fard said, the original man. When he said the original man, he meant your original nature. I believe that what is described as him speaking in the cradle, Jesus Christ (not that I am Jesus Christ), what describes him is this that I have experienced as the wise before me experienced it, and they called it, "speaking." He spoke while he was yet in the cradle, and Mary, whenever she was asked a question, she could not answer, and she pointed to the child in the cradle. That is the virgin, Mother Nature. It is part of my existence, but it cannot speak for me. I have to speak with my own human intelligence and voice. It is wonderful! It takes the mystery out of it, and that is what G_d wants to do. G_d never wanted to burden us. The intelligence, He made it to see, and if we keep it in the dark, that is not G_d's Will. The first time, He puts it in the dark, Himself. He brings the mind under the matter, matter births the mind, and then mind rules the matter, later. What we should remember is not to ever see ourselves as big and important in life. We are nothing in the light of G_d. What we should remember is that none of this could happen without G_d preparing us for it or creating us for it. So, whenever we realize that, we have the power or capacity for something supernatural, or above normal. That is what I mean by supernatural, above the norm. We should always be very submissive. As soon as your "self" comes into the picture say, "I am nothing but a speck of dust! My Lord has brought me up!" And He will continue to, as the Bible says, *"Dwell with you!"*

Jesus' Body Is His Teaching

The Qur'an was put in thirty parts to let us know that this is the Word of G_d that Jesus represents. Jesus represents a Spirit and a Word from G_d. He is a Word and a Spirit from G_d. So, the Word is revelation, not flesh, and it is in the Gospel. He said, *"Do this in remembrance of me"*. He gave them unleavened bread. They ate the bread, and he said, *"This is my flesh."* In the Gospel, it says the bread is the doctrine. That is the teaching of the New Testament. So, the Bible doesn't leave us in the dark as to what bread is. It did not say the bread is in the grave, or the bread was embalmed. That would be his flesh. It did not say the bread died, or the bread is in the tomb. It says the bread is the doctrine of the New Testament. Doctrine means teachings. Isn't that what the Qur'an says that he is a Word from G_d? So, if he said the bread represents his flesh, and the Bible says bread is the teaching of the New Testament, then what does his body represent? His body represents the message of revelation that he was given. It represents his teaching that was his body. I can prove that in any court of intelligent people. Before any judge, I can prove that to him. Some of you are messed up. Satan messed you up. I can't reach you, but I can go to any sane court and a sane judge will say, "The man is correct." I don't care what you say, preacher. The Pope might say, "No, that's not the way!" The judge will say, "No, Pope, the man is correct! He's not talking about something that is invisible. He is talking about what is written in your Bible and it is right here. It says, Jesus Christ told them to, 'Do this in remembrance of him, and he said that the bread was his flesh. And this man has shown us that in the Gospel, the same teachings of Jesus Christ that you have says the bread is the doctrine of the New Testament and doctrine means teaching." The judge will be on my side. Now, go back to what the Bible says, and the Qur'an says, that he was a word, himself.

Language Taking On Flesh

Everybody high up in religion they know what bread is. It is the doctrine. It is the teachings. *"In the beginning was the Word and the Word took on flesh"*. In the beginning, G_d's Will was with G_d, then He put it into a human being, and it took on construction. First, it is just spirit. It is just a will to do and obey, but it is not a communication. Language is coming and the language takes construction. You make an expression. You make a sentence. You make a paragraph. You make a chapter, and it is taking on construction, and it is giving you a picture of the message. That is the language taking on flesh.

The Flesh Speaks

Flesh means feeling, expression. This is my flesh. I feel it and it communicates to my mind. I pinch it, and it says, "That hurts!" It is a pinch. I rub it and it says it feels good. My flesh tells me that. The flesh speaks, doesn't it? *"In the beginning, there was the Word, and the Word took on flesh"*. The Word came into flesh and flesh yielded to the Word of G_d, just like a baby's flesh is obedient to goodness, not to evil, when it first comes here. The flesh yields to G_d. The mind, now, looks at that and the mind likes that. Now, the mind is engaging flesh, seeing how obedient flesh is to a higher purpose.

Now, the mind takes over and revelation is coming to the mind. Help now comes to the mind from G_d, because you have connected with the Will of G_d in your flesh, to obey Him, to appreciate beauty, righteousness, and goodness. You have embraced that. You have connected with that, so you are now in tune with that. Now, your mind has become like your flesh. It does not want ugly stuff. It does not want pain. It wants pleasure. It doesn't want filth. Baby flesh doesn't want filth. When you get old you might like filth better than you like cleanliness, but every baby cries when filth is on it. They don't like filth.

The Second Development Is In Your Mind

Now, the mind is becoming like the flesh in its originality. In its originality it (flesh) is good. The mind becomes like that, then the mind, now, is rational, so the mind starts like the flesh. It is put together in an orderly way. It is in the Qur'an. It is constructed from a clot of blood, then a morsel of flesh, and then bones come in and give structure to it. It is then covered with flesh, and then it is completed, a whole creation. And it says, *"Then comes another creation."* The Spirit comes into it. The Spirit of G_d comes into the flesh and makes another creation, and the development starts all over, again. Where is its development? It's not physical. This second development is in your mind. It is the Spirit moving your mind and having your mind obey the Spirit, and the Guidance of G_d.

The Rational Construction of the Word of G_d

Here your mind begins to form in obedience to G_d, and you now can express to somebody else what has happened. What you experienced you communicate that to somebody else, and they will be so impressed they write it down. Now, it is written down. They are writing it, but it came through you. Now we have the rational construction of the Word of G_d. It is taking, conforming, to sentence structure, paragraphs, into a written scroll or book. It is forming and they use the human body, because everything started with the human body. So, they are not talking about flesh, but they are talking about a new body, and we say, "a body of knowledge," don't we? There is a church that calls itself, "The Body of Christ". The members are all called the body of Christ, and the Bible speaks of them as members in Christ, people who follow him as members in him, members in Christ.

If you can follow what I have been saying to you, it should be perfectly clear to you that the Bible is not talking about Jesus' meat on his bones, on his body that came from his flesh mother. Instead, it is talking about his mind, how his mind is formed into another body, a mental body. His mind takes the shape of a mental body and in his mind, there is order, just like it is in his body. In his mind, there is a heartbeat, in his mind, there is a brain, in his mind, there is a moral pulse or a social pulse. In his mind, are all the things we have. You touch with your hands. He also touches with his mind, or you feel with your hands, you see with your eyes. He also sees with his mind. You hear with your ears. He also hears with his mind. So, since the body is such a perfect metaphor, figure, symbol, concept, or picture of whatever reaches you, that is why speaking of these is associated with what takes place in the construction of the mind in its obedience to G_d, like all flesh forms in obedience to its Maker, the G_d Who created it.

G_d Is In Him

Every baby comes here just as the G_d Who created it wants it. You come here crying. You come here laughing. You come here wanting to be happy or be relieved from misery. You come here wanting to learn. You come here wanting to socialize with people and be loved by people. G_d makes all of us the same; likewise for the man who wants to become obedient to his G_d as his body was when he was born, and G_d recreates him. G_d creates him anew. G_d puts his Spirit into that man and that man's mind, heart, and everything, forms anew, and he becomes a higher creature, a human but a higher order, a human being of a higher order. G_d is in him. That is how we should understand that.

The Leader In the Leadership That G_d Wants for the World

"Matters are judged by intentions", Muhammed, the Prophet said. We only need three to perform Jumah Prayer. You know, we hope to have many more than three people, but if we have three people, we can do Jumah Prayer. If we have three people, we can do any prayer, including Jumah and 'Eid Prayers. There is three again, i.e., body, mind, and spirit. So, if there is three of us, one stands to the left, one stands to the right, and the third one goes out in front. The third one is the leader. It represents the leader in the leadership that G_d wants for the world. He wants the third one. He is in the front. That is the Spirit. We want the Spirit of G_d to be in our leader. He stands out in front.

Now, if we don't have him, i.e., a man inspired, or a man who knows how to follow the Spirit that G_d wants in us, we just have two. The one on the left leads the prayer, not the one on the right. The one on the left is the leader, so who is the one on the right? The one on the right is the one who trusts his mind. Who is the one on the left? The one on the left is the one who follows his moral nature G_d created for him. He obeys the moral nature G_d created. He is like Joseph. He is supposed to be in the form like Joseph is in. So, we pick the moral man, the clean and upright, moral man and he leads us, though we know more in the world than he knows. However, if we have the third one, the one inspired by G_d, the one who has G_d's Spirit in him, then he is our leader. He steps out in front.

"Behold Your Mother!"

In the Bible, where the angel, Jibril, shows up to influence Mary, the single person, and the plural person, Jesus is the Church and she is the Church, also. He is the Church while he is alive among them. She is the Church when he goes away. He's on the cross and dying and he said, *"Behold your mother!* That means, "I will not be with you anymore, but the congregation is with you, and the congregation has its leadership. You are going to now be in the body of the congregation, and not directly in my body, or in my message, in my mission", which is his body.

Jesus Born of a Congregation

So, here are two situations, one while he is living, and one after he is gone. The one that is in the Qur'an is the one after he is gone, but it is used why? It is because that is how he came to be anyway. He didn't come to be from nowhere. He came to be from a woman, from a congregation. The original Jesus came out of a congregation, and he was their leader. Now, the Qur'an wants us to see how he really came about, so it starts off with his mother, not with him. That's really the one who is first. The mother is before the child. So, it starts off with her story. She's told by G_d, by the means of an angel, that she is going to have a child, and she is surprised, saying *"How can I have a child?"* Like Sarah, she laughed when G_d said she was going to have a child. Mary didn't laugh, but she said, *"How am I going to have a child? I'm a virgin? I can't have a child!"* And the Holy Ghost overshadowed her. It meant she was influenced with a concept bigger than her reality. It covered her up and blackened her whole existence. It was so much bigger than she was. The concept was so much bigger than she was until her whole existence was overshadowed, and when she had nothing to feed her but the Holy Spirit, she became pregnant with child.

Three Lights In One

The concept of the Holy Ghost was so much bigger than she was and so much more powerful than she was until it took over, influenced her existence from that point on, and she became pregnant with child. She became pregnant with another concept, a smaller concept, and it is an immaculate conception. Praise be to Allah! Isn't this wonderful? I have been entertaining this for some time and every time I think, "That is too much!" When Jesus wanted to show his disciples himself, they had been with him, why could they not see him? He goes up in the mountain and shows them the configuration, or transfiguration, and there he showed himself as light, not as flesh. He shows three lights, the light of Moses, Elijah, and himself, but they were three lights in one. Now, where did they get three gods in one? Jesus did not show them three gods in one. He showed them three lights in one, the light of the cultural leader, Moses, and the cultural leader is a political leader in the world. So, it shows the light of Moses, who was a cultural leader, to bring them into a new culture. They were into a culture that was oppressive in Egypt, so he had to take them out of the culture of oppression and bring them into the culture of life, enlightenment, and freedom. So, Moses is that figure. He is that light, then Elijah, he is a healer. So, what heals? Obedience to G_d, and the courage to defy authority that is in the way of G_d. That was Elijah, and that heals. The Bible says Elijah healed the widow's son. She does not have a husband, no man. He heals her son, and then his life is compatible with those lights. That is why they can become one. They are one light.

"I Come Not Only of Water"

Jesus came to establish new world leadership, to take the people out from under the oppressors and to reconcile the spiritual life with the social life. That heals, too. It all means a healing for people who are not having that. Do you see? So, what it is saying is that Jesus comes with a light like that of Moses, a light that frees and liberates the people, and he comes with a light like that of Elijah, that heals those suffering because they don't have the light that G_d created them for. That is the widow's son. He healed the widow's son. Elijah had the power to bring down from heaven both water and fire. He prayed at the altar and the fire came down and consumed the offering, and then the water came down and put out the fire. So, Elijah had the power to pray for water and fire and to have both of those agencies serve him for the purpose that he was put in the world for.

Jesus said, *"I come not only of water, but I come of water and blood"*. In Scripture, blood and fire are the same. It says, *"And blood shall come up to the horse's bridle"*. It is a sign of a great time of killing, suffering, and great tragedy. The war is going to be so terrible, and blood is going to flow up to the horse's bridle. That is in the Bible. It is called blood in the New Testament, but in the old days, the Old Testament, the old time, it was fire. So, that which was fire before Jesus Christ becomes blood in the time of Jesus Christ.

The Spiritual Life Turned Into Social Passions

You don't read about any fire getting anybody in the New Testament, do you? It just speaks of what the Old Testament said, warning them of the consequences, why? Because blood has become the term, now, that holds the meaning and not fire, but both are still true. The Bible, Old Testament, talks about the world being destroyed by fire, but it says blood is the life of the body. Now, blood is the life of the body and plagues came upon the people in the Old Testament and one of the plagues was that the water was turned to blood. In the New Testament, that is not a plague. That is a blessing. In the Old Testament, turning the water into blood was a curse, why? Because they were seeing fire as wisdom and seeing blood as human passions. Fire was wisdom, blood was human passion. So, you turn the spiritual life into social passions. That is a punishment for the people, because now, they are going to be on their own social life and not on the spirituality that G_d revealed. Everything begins from water in the Bible. It says the water turned red, just plain water, and the light appeared in the water and the world was generated, in the Old Testament, water as light and blood as passions.

The New Testament kind of reverses all of that, whereas blood is not passion. What is the New Testament doing? Deceiving the dictatorships of the world, saying, "Now you think you understand what is going on here? You don't! The fire has become blood, and the water has become stagnant spirituality. This man is going to change this dead water into living wine". This is the beauty of it. They tricked the savage rulers. So, when they looked at it and saw it, they said, "This is good!" They said, "He wants to take care of our tired and worn-out people. We need help. Let him give this to them. It is not going to hurt us." That is what they thought. But the following who became the leaders got the insight from the teacher. Jesus taught them how to look at that.

Rulers Gave Their Masses to Christianity

The world could not see it, so they let them work, then they got the people with them; like Jacob, he made a deal with Laban. He said, "All the cattle that comes out reign-streaked will be mine" and Laban agreed to it. So, the Christians said, "This man only wants your tired and worn-out people who cannot do you any good anyway. They are donkeys! He can ride this donkey for you." So, they bought it. They gave their masses to Christianity. That took a lot of trouble out of their hands, and what the Christians were doing was selecting them, very carefully, to educate them, as many as they could educate. Finally, their leaders ascended to the throne. They were better qualified and the whole, so-called heathen nations of that area, converted to Christianity. Once they learned what was happening it was too late, already. Their best minds were Christians, but by secrecy. They were hiding what they were teaching, and they came into power.

So, in the New Testament blood is both fire and education, fire and teaching, wisdom. It is fire because it is wisdom in the social life, nature, and social passions of mankind. That is where its wisdom comes from. So, it is fire that enlightens, too. It is a light, and it warms you. Social teachings will warm you up like fire, passions. They warm you up. They make you spirited, and the more you put air into fire the bigger and more powerful it gets. So, they put G_d's Spirit into the passions, and the more excited the passions became, it warmed up the world. That is Jesus Christ. He was blessed to have that. He was blessed with the Holy Spirit, and it was not given to go out on the waters. That is the way the world started on the water. The Holy Spirit, here, is to be fired into the social life and passions of the people. So, he is not only of water. He is of water and blood!

Chapter 4
Ibraheem (Abraham)

What Abraham was studying was the world and how it operates, the universe, the world and how it operates. He was studying it to see, "What it suggests to me." It suggested to him the unity of matter, the universal system of matter, and that suggested to him that there was one Plan and One G_d. So, he is the father of faith for us, whereas Adam is the father of nature for us. Abraham is the father of faith for us, and it is a rationally based faith. Abraham had both a powerful, rational mind, and very powerful faith. Prophet Muhammed was born among people who had irrational faith. Their religion was irrational. They worshipped idols, but he was not of them. He was of a special class and that class was the intellectuals of his day in his tribe, the Quraish, who believed in the excellence of nature. They already believed that, and they were called the hunafaa, the plural of haneef.

When Muhammed was shown the path, and he knew Abraham in the Scripture was shown favor as a father, leader, for all the people, he identified their belief, the hunafaa, as the belief of Abraham. The only thing that was missing in the hunafaa was that they didn't have revelation. So, when he got revelation, then he understood that revelation complemented the Hunafaa's identity as a creation, human creation, that it complemented it. So, then he saw that to purify that nature, we need revelation. Though we are striving for excellence to purify it, we need G_d to reveal to us. So, G_d gave him revelation to show him how to purify his nature, but he already believed in the excellence of his nature.

Islam Came to Complement the Hunafaa Nature

However, revelation showed him that the way to continue the life of the excellence of his nature he needed revelation. He needed G_d to open up the whole world to him. So, when Allah says, in the Qur'an, that it is the deen of origin, deen al-fitrah, His religion of origin, the originality or the origin that this human society is fashioned upon, then Muhammed understood that it was the hunafaa, that nature that Islam came to complement; and that the pattern that Allah had designed the Qur'an to fit is really the hunafaa, the excellence of man's nature.

I believe that our Prophet, Muhammed, peace be on him (pbuh), was in a situation that didn't permit him to disclose what is the real, I would say, theme, overriding theme for the Qur'an and for his own mission, because he was talking to persons who had been idol worshippers, and few who had been nature lovers; and those nature lovers were in his immediate circle. They were his companions. They are called in the Qur'an, in common language, those who were upright in their nature.

Muhammed and Christ Together

When Muhammed, the Prophet, got revelation and got connected with Scripture, he was told by G_d, by revelation, that Abraham was the first of the hunafaa, those upright in their nature. So, what I have come to see and very clearly is that that hunafaa nature, and the Prophet's main focus on humanity, helping humanity, is in the Bible. It's in the Gospel. It comes to light in the Gospel. And when he said, "The world or the people will come to see myself and Christ together", I think that's what he was addressing, that he was all about uprightness, the inherent goodness in human nature that G_d put there. I think when Christians say, "Christ within", they are saying the same thing we're saying when we say, "the uswaa of Muhammed within", meaning his model, his human model. We are to emulate his human model. It is talking about discovering the purity of human nature that G_d put in us, that purity, and living it to the best of our ability. Jesus Christ is put in the nativity scene, with animals. So, it is something he had in common even with animals. That's what we're talking about, what G_d preserved in human beings, in nature, and in all creatures.

Creation Has An Overriding Aim

They are called hunafaa, from the word, haneef. Abraham is called haneef, and the Arabic speaking people approve of the translation meaning upright in his human nature. That simply means those people were companions associated with each other, because they had like minds, and like spirit, like character, like values, and principles. Their belief was that a human should live out the best of his life, and he should build upon the best of his life. He should never follow weakness and something that brings down his life. He should only follow strength and that which makes his life more excellent. It is said by G_d in the Qur'an that this was the nature and the position of Abraham, the upright in his nature.

Abraham is the father. He's the father because he was before Muhammed, and the first one to question the external reality, looking for G_d. He concluded that G_d is none of this, that G_d is the One that designed it. How did he come by that? He was hunafaa. He was haneefa, the plural of hunafaa. He believed that his creation had an overriding aim. Maybe it would commit an offense here, or maybe it would disgrace its value here or there, but it has an overriding aim, and it is going to come out in somebody. So, it came out in the hunafaa, that group that he gravitated towards, or they gravitated towards each other. He believed it originated in nature, that it was nature, and it was the dominant nature. He believed that everything created had that same nature, but it's not called by that name. For humans it is called haneefa, or hunafaa.

Prophet Muhammed, when asked about his life and how he succeeded without being overcome by sin, he said it was because of the Mercy of Allah. The same goes for everybody else, because of the Mercy of Allah. Now, why does the Mercy of Allah work for him, but it doesn't work for so many others? Because his spirit was always to do the best, to do the correct thing, and to be the best in his character and conduct. He was always truthful and trustworthy, so he earned Allah's Mercy, and that Mercy was to free all people, *"rahmatan lil 'alameen, a mercy for all the people"*, because of one person. Didn't the Bible say if there was just one righteous person in the city, He wouldn't destroy it? It says, *"Surely your life and your death are as one soul"*, in the Qur'an. Because there was one, all of humanity got mercy. So, how is all of humanity going to get mercy without revelation? That's why G_d revealed to him.

The Mercy of Allah

Now, that's not the end of this logic, because he said, when they asked him, "What accounts for you being saved from that", he said, "The Mercy of Allah"; the same as for everybody else, the Mercy of Allah. So, what do I see in that? Because he was truthful and trustworthy, that in his nature was also mercy from Allah. Allah knew that this creature that has formed from his mother and his father, this creature wants no evil, wants no wrong. G_d knows in the beginning. G_d says, "Here's a soul that wants nothing but Me. He wants Me. He wants to serve Me. He wants to find Me, and serve Me. So, I'm going to make it easy for him. I'm going to be the Protector of his purity." Allah protected his purity and put him in circumstances that would aid that. So, Allah was working with him as his Lord and Creator, right beside him

163

from the day he was conceived in his mother, to the time he died, like two arrows shot out of one bow.

We Don't Need Everybody to Save Mankind

So, you know, G_d knows. Therefore, none of us, no one can be without sin. *"They all* (I'm talking from the Bible) *are sinners"*. Was Jesus Christ a sinner? But it says all are sinners. Did it say Jesus Christ was a sinner? No, it's speaking of him, that all other than him were sinners. And why was he not a sinner? In the language of the Bible, it was because he was the son of G_d, a Spirit and a Word from G_d. How could he sin?

Now, for Muhammed, I already explained to you how he couldn't sin. So, we all are human with these human limitations, and without the intervention of G_d, Himself, we all would be lost. Yes, we don't need everybody to save society. All we need is one soul. One soul started it, and one soul can redeem it, or bring about redemption, earn redemption.

Abraham Is a Community

Abraham found the Black Stone, and the way the story went it is like he saw the Black Stone fall. Now understand that this is the story of a scientific thinker who is looking for scientific support for what he wants to introduce to people to order the society. He was a community thinking man. He thought community. How do we know that? Because Prophet Muhammed said "the ummah of Abraham" and "the millah of Abraham". This is the millah of Abraham. It means the hope of Abraham and it is a community after the order of Abraham haneefa, the upright in nature. So, we know that Abraham is a community.

I was in Saudi Arabia as a member of the Supreme Council of Masaajid (Masjids). As I was leaving, the president of Rabita Al-Islami, the Islamic World League, he said, "You know Imam, Abraham is a community!" He said that because he wanted to leave that on my mind. He was one of those learned people that if he likes you, he likes to share something with you. I said, "Yes", and he said, "And Muhammed is a community." I had to think on that. I did not say, "Yes". I didn't say anything. I remained quiet and just went out. I greeted him and left. I was getting ready to leave and come back home.

But that is true. I don't know a Prophet who is not a single figure and a plural figure at the same time, especially Jesus Christ, Adam, Abraham, and Muhammed, peace be on them. Those for sure, are single and plural figures at the same time. That means when we think of that person, that picture, or that figure, we should understand that it is a man, a single person, but also, he is a picture of the whole people that he leads or is sent to lead. So, he is a community picture as well as a personal or individual picture. It is very clear, and in the Christian world, the church uses the expression, "The Body Christ", and they are not talking about Jesus, personally. They are talking about the Church, the whole congregation, the following.

Abraham thought where the Black Stone fell the message to him was, "Build My House, here". So, that is where he built the house, he and his son. And they put the Black Stone in the corner of that house. Too many tend to just take these things and don't try to find out what it is all about. If you would follow the guidance of Qur'an, and follow the guidance of Muhammed, the Prophet that he gave us, too, with his teachings and comments on things, you wouldn't be lost like that.

A Simple House Representing the Home of All Mankind

So, this same thing has to take place in man's evolution. His evolution for the community life that will support him and make him comfortable, he can rest there. "I can settle here. I can establish my life here, not only for me, but for my children, too". In order to have that destiny he has to connect. He's an individual and he has to connect with other individuals. He's a family and the family has to connect with other families. He's a nation. Nations have to connect with other nations. That is where we are right now, and it is symbolized in the term, "Ka'bah".

You go there and it's a simple house representing the home of all mankind. It is the home that gives us a focus for the fifth pillar of Al-Islam, for the whole community of human beings, mankind. That is the house that represents all people. Why does it represent all people? Because it is a house under G_d, built by a man, Abraham and his son, Abraham, the father, Ismail the son, Abraham, the leader and Ismail, the follower. The man, Abraham, is called the leader for the nations, or father of all people. So, he symbolizes, like Adam, the unity or community of people not under nationality, not under race or anything else, but people, period. So, it says, *"The first of the houses built for all people."*

165

You Have to Form Connections

So, the concept of a house that was built to house everybody is the understanding that we should have when we're looking at the house, praying towards that house, or going to visit that house during pilgrimage. That is what we should be aware of, that G_d wants us to see that He wants us to come to a perception of a home that is the home of everybody, not one people. And to reach that destination you have to form connections, and that is what Ka'bah means, making, forming connections, and starting in the foot. The first connection is the ankle that connects the foot to the leg. That's the first connection in your structure. It says, "buniyal", which means making a construction. So, the first connection in that construction in the ankle that connects the foot to the leg, the bottom of the leg. Some people say the leg is the foot and everything, but when you lose your foot, you don't say you lost your leg or a piece of your leg. You say you lost your foot. It all goes together, but the foot, in itself, is a distinct construction. It does not have the same parts and same construction the legs have. So, there is one pattern in the construction that is the foot, and the leg is supported by it, but it needs the ankle. It needs that round bone, universal logic. Universal logic makes it possible for us to connect one logic to another.

Now you can go only up so high. You're coming up to the thigh and it is different from the leg below the knee. The leg below the knee is all about bone structure and the thigh is all about bone and muscle, although down below the knee has muscle, too, but that is not what is predominant. What is predominate below the knee is a powerful tibia bone. In fact, it is, I would say, constructed that really the front part of it says, "bone, shin". When you feel that, right away, you don't think meat, muscle, or even skin. You think bone and it goes straight up from the foot in its performance supported by the ankle, a round bone. When it gets to its limit, it needs to connect to the thigh in the upper quarters, and it has plenty of muscles, because actually you need the thigh to bring the structure up so it can rest upon the leg bone.

Now, we said Ka'bah, and ankle is ka'bain. It means like two ka'bahs; and when I get to the knee, you don't say, ka'bah, but the knees, again, is another connection of another ka'bah. But you don't have to talk about it because the basic, the foundation, has already been established, that whatever connects above the ankle is supported by the ankle. We make other connections going up, but they all are supported by the ankle. So, that's the Ka'bah, that is the connection that makes possible for us to graduate this connecting to support bigger and even more important things in the structure, and the last thing to support is the head.

Now, the head doesn't have a round bone supporting it, except in the base. In the back, in the base, it has a swivel. When you get sleepy, it drops. Not all the time, but most of the time you're nodding, it drops because it's on a swivel. It's on a round bone. And it is the last of the connections, because the head has no more connections. After the head there is not anything to connect with unless it is mystery, fiction and lies. You go above the head, you have hair, but that is a head, too; like you go above the surface of the earth, you have trees, wind, all these other things. But science says all these are in the environment of the earth. They can't escape the environment of the earth.

Man's Evolution Is to Establish Authority

So, my hair is of my head. It belongs to my head. This tells me something about the possibilities for my head. This is not possibilities for some new entity or imagined thing. After the head nothing else is in the structure. So, what is the purpose of the edifying or the construction of this body in this pattern going up from the foot and finishing in the head? Man's evolution is to establish authority not just in a body, but to have an authority over that body. So, man needs government, and his evolving is to find that government that has responded to the whole body and has been set upon the whole body and accepted by the whole body in the position of authority. The foot and every other part of the body needs a crown.

"I Hear and I Obey"

So, man's destiny is government, but government that will please the whole body, representative of all the people. *"And you are members in my body"*, that is what the Scripture says of Jesus Christ. So, it wants to establish authority that will be supported by the whole body. The temple is another way of saying, the body. And when he has that kind of authority that is supported by the whole body, the body says, "I hear, and I obey". Isn't that what the body says? If the body had to have shuraa (consultation) for me to drink this and do all the other things, wouldn't we be in trouble? So, what is G_d telling us with this guidance? He's telling us, if we put the right head on the body, the body will perform without sitting down nit picking and arguing little points, and this and that, little petty problems. It won't do that. When the body needs to move and the head says it's time, all parts of the body say, "To hear is to obey". But when we establish authority pleasing to G_d, it is going to be pleasing to our self, because He leads us to the best conditions for ourselves. He knows what conditions will satisfy the soul in all of us.

Pleasing G_d, striving to get where He wants us to go, once we're there we find out that really this is where we had to go for our own pleasure, our own comfort, for our own fulfillment. So really, it's small. The scholars or thinkers, it is small of them, of us, to think that my destiny is all about pleasing G_d. It is all about establishing myself in my best condition. That is my destiny, and that is what it is all about, establishing myself in my best condition, but I can't do it without G_d. Because they were able to do both, feel and think, they thought themselves in situations high above the common masses. Consequently, they rule you from distances that you cannot reach, and G_d has made the physical mass to reflect the beauty of the spiritual mass, the human soul. So, you look up there and see it bedecked with jewels, sparkling like diamonds in the night. And He says on that day He's going to gather, also, those in the heavens. You know that is in the Qur'an. Why? "I thought only the people on earth were going to be gathered for judgment". No, there is more of them up there, and they are the big actors, so they have more sins up there in one thread than you have down here in all the garments you made. You see, down here you have fish running around in the water. Up there you have big, heavy, material masses. They are in water, too. They think they are on solid ground, but they are not. They are swimming, too. Isn't that reality?

Blood Is the Life of the Body

Something is missing that is extremely important. The sacrificing of the sheep or the lamb, it involves steps, not just cutting… Well, let's start with the first part of the process that brings it to the table and brings it to be ready for the guests to start eating. The first process is your handling of the animal to kill or slaughter it. You handle it with as much gentle care as possible. According to the way of the Prophet Muhammed's sunnah, you make the knife very sharp, so that the pain is not prolonged. It is very quick, cutting to have the least pain come to the victim. You sacrifice the sacrificial lamb and then the blood comes out. You want to drain as much of the blood as you possibly can, and this is the blood of the lamb. Scripture says the blood is the life of that lamb. So, you're draining that creature of its life. Its life is not going to be in it anymore. So, you rejected its life. You don't want its life. You can't eat the blood. It is not halal. So, you rejected the life of the lamb, now you're eating its meat. Meat represents its teachings, or doctrine, as the Bible says, and the blood was not fit to be taken directly. So, you don't take the blood itself. You drink wine, representing the blood. The wine is not the biological life of that creature, but it's talking about a human community, or human congregation. The wine is their spirit, and the spirit of the sheep is sweet. The wine is sweet, and the wine will lift your spirits and make your soul feel so good.

So, you now have transferred the reality from a sheep to a sheepish people, and they are sheep-like because they think they're supposed to be that way. They think to please G_d they're supposed to be against violence, not have a rebellious spirit. They're supposed to be peaceful and accommodating. "We'll tolerate you until the Lord brings us better". So, really, what this is all about is not sacrificing people who are sheepish, but educating people who are sheepish, educating them in the knowledge of their own nature, so they will remain peace loving people, but will know when to stand up.

Your Student Is Your Son

You have to bring light into the dead matter. Abraham was destined to be a teacher for mankind, and what was a problem for him was being a leader for the spiritual people who were sheepish. So, G_d showed him how it doesn't mean you sacrifice your son. "Do not sacrifice these people. They are your students, and your student is your son. Don't sacrifice people, physically. No, don't reject them and throw them away, but use their own nature as the way of educating them so that they will not just give themselves to pressures and other communities that will use them. Educate them." And that is what we have to do. We have a lot of them, but we're trying to educate them. Jesus Christ, peace be on him, he is the sheep, himself, but he is the enlightened sheep. So, he speaks out in defense of the rest of the sheep. Jesus said, *"As you have done to the least of them you have done it to me."* It is beautiful!

Only Allah Can Give Them Faith

It takes the burden off us when we understand that Allah only wants us to accept responsibility for extending the help to the people that He has revealed for their good, and our good. If they reject it, don't respond to it. That is not ours. Allah says that burden is not on you. He has not given you power to give faith to them, if they don't want it. You cannot give them faith. Only Allah can give them faith. We can't give them faith. We can only give them the help that G_d has revealed, and they have to make the choice. Even their respect for it is their choice, etc. They can become too much of a burden on us. Allah says, *"Don't fret, torture yourself, and grieve over them and don't force them. Say, 'Peace' and part. For you your way and for me my way'."* Separate yourself from them. Even if you have to live side by side, sleep in the same bed with them, separate from them as a person responsible for them, and separate from them spiritually. I don't live in your spirit, and you don't live in mine.

Getting Close to Allah

Now, what is the necessary situation for getting close to Allah? Qur'an says, *"And you shall be made to return to Him bare and alone, as He created you the first time"*. It means from all that pretentious life that the world gives you. You have to strip it all off, get down to the bare nitty gritty, to the nature Allah gave you at birth, the nature of a newborn baby. That is Scripture, and when you have the baby, the baby always comes here naked. It does not come with any clothes on. The animals, a lot of them come clothed, but not the human. The human comes naked. He's a creature of flesh, feelings, and sentiments. That is his first life until the world spoils it for him, or until he spoils it by giving himself to the bad influences of the world. So, that is how you have to come back to G_d.

You Crucified Your True Destiny

Feeling, force, and intelligence, that will save us. Feeling is first. We're talking about the naked baby, nothing but the human wrapped in love. His skin is love. There is no hate in the baby until the world puts it in, and then after it is formed in the mother by expedience, it has to come out, be forced out. It was too heavenly inside. Many don't want to be moved. They want to stay comfortable. We've got that bad. When we get in a situation, we're comfortable and we don't want any change. No matter how intelligent it is to change or move, we want to stay right there where we are comfortable. So, it is forced out, and it is usually nine months. That is the hour that they hung Jesus Christ, according to the Bible. So, it is time of the urge for life. It was time for it in his people, but instead of them responding to it, they hung him, crucified him. It does not mean him, himself. That is why Allah says in Qur'an, *"It appeared like that to you, but you didn't really crucify him"*. You're crucifying your own life urge. Instead of allowing the social community to be born, you went up to asceticism, up in the sky somewhere, and crucified your true destiny".

The first step is feeling, and the second step is force. So, if you respond to feeling correctly you will be alive and in good shape to accept the force; and if you accept the force, you're going to be given intelligence. Jonah, after he was thrown out on the shore free of the fish and the water as containment for his life, he said, *"I have a three-day journey*. I have to get above feelings and accept what I'm compelled to do by virtue of my nature and G_d's calling; and if I can accept that, G_d is going to enter me into the garden of intelligence among His Servants, and I'll be free at last". And this is the time, isn't it? It is a beautiful time and a beautiful world despite the trouble that is in it. It has overcome racism. The world has overcome racism. The people haven't, but the world has. The leadership rejects it. All intelligent leadership rejects it, even the old cracker down South, he is not going to defend it. It is a wonderful time for us!

Live the Whole Life

Abraham thought of the spiritual community at that time, that maybe they'd be better off dead. It didn't mean sacrificing them outright. But it means just don't help them and let them die. "But Isma'il, here, he isn't like these priests. This is my son! He's devoted to the spiritual life, but that's my son. He came to the spiritual life because he saw knowledge. He saw light. I know they need to be left behind, but I can't sacrifice my son! This is too harsh for me!" So, G_d told him to sacrifice a sheep, that order that separates from the world and take all the abuses from the world for the sake of being at peace, spiritually, inside.

No, that's not what the G_d that created all these things wants. He didn't create you to neglect this world. You've got to get into the world. You've got to be involved in the world. So, sacrifice the sheep and then feed it, kill it, sacrifice it and slaughter it; then prepare a feast and feed it to those who have and those who don't have. So, give them the science in this life that they have. Let them digest the science that's in this life they have chosen, and they'll see how to balance it and how to live not just as sheep. That's just one part of the life. That's a facet of the human soul. Live the whole life.

Pass Knowledge to the Next Generation

For the future generations, you have to do just what the people did before us, and what they do now. Those who really have that kind of knowledge, they make sure that they pass it on to the next generation. But they don't share anything with any individual until that individual has proven themselves, and they know that their devotion is to G_d and service to humanity. When you know that and you're sure of that, then you give them like my mother was told by Mr. Fard. You give them milk and don't even let them eat a piece of fruit, the whole fruit. No, you make it kind of like apple sauce. She would take a spoon. She told me this. She would take a spoon, and she would grate it. Fard showed her how to grate it, and she would take a whole delicious apple, and she would scrape it and feed it to me, and I couldn't eat the regular food. Even when I got old enough to eat cooked food, I didn't eat cooked food, right away. She gave me grated apples and milk and then later, she started giving me bread.

"If a Child Asks for Bread, Would You Give Him a Stone?"

Christ Jesus said, *"If your child asks for bread would you give him a stone?"* No, you give them bread. That means you educate them. You don't give them some logic that they can't handle. It'll break their teeth up. The intelligence that they use to break down difficult things for their mind is their teeth, and if you give the baby that very difficult logic, then the intelligent tools up here that's made to be teeth to break this down before they put it in their system won't be able to handle it. They'll break just like teeth break when you're trying to chew rocks.

Starting Your Own Culture Just Like Going to the Desert

I'll bet you when mail came to Abraham's house when he was living with Sarah, when Hagar got it, it was neglected. And that is one reason why she (Sarah) said, "No, you can't have that child, not in this house! Take her somewhere else! You are not going to have her children inheriting this house! Inherit that desert!" It is real, and not just a story. Inheriting the desert, the reference for Hagar and her children is, "We're not going to have any uneducated, servant people inheriting our culture. Go make your own!" So, starting your own culture is just like going to a desert. There's nothing born there yet. The desert has been used as a symbol for the absence of cultural development. In our dictionary culture is more than just entertainment, a beautiful environment with flowers and stuff. The strongest element of culture is its true educational sciences, because it is usually the sciences and education based in reality that improve the culture of a people to take on new growth. You go up in the North with its little sunlight, and there is not much life up there. You do not go there to find all the beautiful flowers and the luscious farmland that you find in the warmer zones. Up there at the pole you expect to find the absence of that, and it is because of the sun. They get very little sunlight up there, long periods of night, short periods of sunlight.

Sunrise Like the Birth of the Sciences

So, the birth of the sciences is like a sunrise, and in time the sunlight favoring that area produces many different kinds of growth. Allah says in Qur'an, *"beautiful pairs in beautiful relationships"*; not just with each other, but a relationship in the context of community life for human beings, and relationships in other beautiful growth, politics included. Don't they all support each other? The beauty in the physical environment supports the soul, the spirit and nature of the human soul, and it gives beauty to the landscape. The rich and poor like it and the high ups and the low people on the ground, grass roots, like it. It just forms relationships, and all of these contribute to our good social life as citizens.

So, the water that G_d addresses when He tells us how He started growth everything had its beginning in water. And Genesis says, *"In the beginning there was darkness, and the spirit moved along the face of the waters",* and things started to happen. What Allah gave Muhammed behind that, a few centuries afterwards, was tied right into that, but instead of saying *"In the beginning there was darkness"*, and giving that same story, it says everything living had its beginning in water. And then it gives seven levels of light in the Qur'an, and it says the water is darkness. Water is darkness and land is light. It doesn't say that. I'm just carrying it further. You don't set a fire in the water. You set it on the land. Some fire is too big for it to put out though, it just keeps turning to steam. We say, "He is just blowing off steam". When the water man and the fire man, fire producer, and water producer, when they get together in a clash or in a debate, if that fire is built and that fire man is big enough, every time that water man throws something at him, it turns into steam, like a puff of moisture in the air and it is gone, it disappears. You know, the expression in the Bible is, *"In the beginning there was the Word, and the Word took on flesh and dwelled in the life of men."* That is not exactly the wording, but that's it, the message.

Books In Their Upright Position

The Qur'an is a book of previous books in their corrected form. That is the way it is translated, but the Word in the Qur'an is not "corrected", not exactly. However, you can arrive at that understanding from the language of the Qur'an. What is the exact word? "Qayyimah", and it comes from the word whose root is, to stand up. So, the meaning is standing up correctly or reaching the standing position in its highest evolution, or in its highest progression. That is what the word, "qayyimah", suggests to me, the books in their corrected form, or the books progressed to their intended progression. They were not meant to stay there. It was meant for the Holy Spirit to inspire those people and guide them into further progressions of understanding.

So, what G_d gives in the Qur'an, Highly Glorified is He, is language to start that interest again, so it will continue its progression until it reaches the progressed state that Allah intended for the understanding of that language, *"In the beginning there was the Word"*, and you know the rest of it. I gave it just now, but you know it. We know it all by heart. So, the Qur'an comes back with the language, *"Kun fa yakun."* This expression, like all the expressions in Scripture, is addressing the human mind, human intelligence. What that word is saying is when the human mind gives itself or its attention to the language in that expression, "Kun", with philosophical insight and reasoning, you can follow that language to where Allah is going with it.

From Exist to Establishment

So, He said, "Exist". "Kun" means exist. "Be" means the same thing, "Exist". So, it starts with the focus on existence. *"Be and it is"*, but not immediately. It (Qur'an) says, *"Kun faya kun, be and thereafter it is,"* not immediately, but there is more in that because this expression is in the language called Arabic. Now you start with just existence. What is existing? Follow the verb "Be". That verb has evolved in the Arabic language from exist to establishment. What they call establishment is the conclusion for that progression that I'm alluding to. My establishment is called my "makan" from the word "kaana" also from the word "kun." I have an establishment, I have a makan. So, the Qur'an is saying G_d ordered the existence, and existence of its own nature will eventually increase and progress by stages until man has his human establishment.

Allah Is Knocking On the Door of Our Human Intelligence

They will eventually be successful and accomplish what is intended in the Plan of G_d. Also, the word, makan, establishment, order, the command form of the verb, to be, is kun. So, the "kun" says it was ordered, whether you believe in G_d, or not. If he's a materialist, if he is an atheist, it is his understanding from material life, material dynamics or whatever. He doesn't have to believe in a G_d like we believe in G_d. He still should follow that language that from existence the same existence progresses, and for man, the destiny for his existence is established community life. In the Arabic language you have *"kun, yakun, kaana."* You have all these derivatives, and finally for your establishment you allude back to the verb, to be, and it is called "masaakin". G_d promised them beautiful or excellent establishments, and the word, in the Qur'an, is "masaakin", derived from the verb, to be. So, the language sounds like Allah is asking us to believe in magic, *"Kun faya kun, order it to be, and it comes to exist"*.

But He (Allah) is knocking on the door of our human intelligence: "Can't you see by observing My world that is always growing and developing in some phase or another, that I simply created you and brought you into existence, and the process automatically started to bring you to your establishment?" All these comments are on, *"In the beginning was the Word, and the Word took on flesh and dwelled among men"*.

The Khalifah Kissed the Black Stone

It is said that one of the great khalifahs kissed the black stone. This is after the passing of the Prophet. He said, "If I hadn't seen the Messenger of G_d doing this, I would not do this." Understand that the persons in the immediate association of Muhammed, the Prophet, were men who were called the Hunafaa. They did not believe in superstitions. They only believed in what they could understand with their normal, rational minds. But they also believed that the human being's creation (they did not call it creation but the human's form among living things) was the most excellent of forms. Any thinking person can come to that conclusion. We can do more with our minds than any other living thing, so we are the best and the highest of all living things on the earth. So, that was their belief, and the logic for their discipline was just that. Since I am the best then I should respect my form over all other living forms. I shouldn't behave like a dog. I am a higher creation than a dog, or a higher form than a dog. So, these were the Hunafaa.

Abraham Was Inclined Towards the Rational

We were called the children of Hagar, and Abraham's son, Isma'il is a picture of a spiritual balance. Abraham needed his son to help him structure the house, because Abraham tended to be inclined towards the rational more than the spiritual. He was so much inclined towards the rational because he saw the great future production for people who devote themselves to reason and to the rational for the material construction of the world. He knew how important that was. So, it really bothered him that, "Now, I have a son, and this son is devoted to the spiritual nature, and I know G_d wants me to do what I'm doing. G_d wants me to build a society under Him, a world under Him, and I am rational. We have to deal with the rational and material reality, and this son of mine, he may cause a problem. If he gets too many people into his spiritual mode, we will have difficulty building a material society, an industrial world. G_d, this is my son, and my thinking is telling me You want me to sacrifice him! I love him. This is my child. Lord, this is my child! Please, what am I going to do?" Allah would not speak to him.

So, he went and got the knife. I believe it was a shining sword, illuminated sword. He got this illuminated sword, and he was getting ready to kill his child, and G_d said, "Do it not. You have already completed your commitment to Me. Your willingness to sacrifice him for My pleasure is enough. Instead of sacrificing him, get that little, innocent lamb, that sheep, and slaughter him with that knife, sword blade you have. When you kill it, take all the stinky stuff out of it. Wash it up really good and then put it on the fire and cook it and let a sweet savor as steam and smoke go up to the heavens. Then serve it to the poor, and you to eat from it, Abraham." So, we have that ritual every 10th day of the Hajj, where we make our slaughter, our halal of our sacrificial animal. The best animal to have for the occasion is a lamb. You can have a cow, or camel. They eat different kinds of meats, and they sacrifice them, too, over there. But the best is the lamb, because it is the most peaceful of all of them. What a beautiful story, I'm telling you, the scene where he is tormented in anguish, in agony, and G_d relieves him by showing him what to do. So, G_d removes from Abraham's vision his son and by some kind of activity in his mind, there is an illusion, and the son is replaced by the sight of a lamb. And by him seeing that in a day vision, he reasoned that G_d is saying, "No, don't kill your son, kill a lamb!"

Don't Let Your Life Become the Life of Sheep

So, don't kill him. Kill a lamb. "Kill this tendency in your house, or in your following, to tolerate abuses and be eaten by other animals, and hunted by other animals, slaughtered by other animals. Get that out of your people. It's an innocence this passive way of theirs. It is innocent, but Abraham you are right! It is a problem for the work of establishing the new world under G_d. So, tell them that this nature in them is to be digested by their minds and protected by their intelligence and their faith. Don't let your life become the life of sheep but benefit from the life of the sheep by digesting the knowledge and wisdom. The sheep are peaceful, and you are to be peaceful, in accord with your best nature, your Muslim nature. The sheep like to be with each other, and you should be close to each other, like the sheep. And the sheep does not like to engage in arguments and fighting. I want you to be like that, too. But if I command you to kill, I want you to stop being a sheep and be a man on the battlefront! So, Abraham, teach them My Signs that I put in the sheep and from the sheep you get wool, and you can take the wool and protect yourself from the cold of night or winter. So, you be like that. You produce that which will help the people and keep them warm on cold nights or in the winter." You see all the beautiful signs? The sheep is well-balanced, like Isma'il. "So, tell them that not only your son, but they, too, should all be well-balanced, spiritually. Don't be too heavy on the left. Don't be too heavy on the right. Don't be too heavy forward. Don't be too heavy backward but find the just mean for balance. Be haneefa, upright, erect, not inclined to go off from the balance, spiritually balanced."

A person who is spiritually balanced will stay rational. It is only the person who goes to spiritual extremes in one direction, not respecting the whole situation, not circumspect, not respecting the whole situation all-around, that is imbalanced. So, they are going off on a tangent from the mean, from the balance, or from the plummet line. You preachers out there, you're leaving the plummet line and going to extremes, and wasn't it G_d, according to the Bible Who ordered the plummet, and the plummet line?

The Bible Has a Continuous Stream of Purity

Somebody may say, "When he starts saying that the Bible has a continuous stream of purity in it from Genesis to Revelation, he lost me! That is the poison book!" With all this that G_d has shown me in the Bible, I cannot disrespect that book. I would be a sinner to disrespect it, and an ignorant person to disrespect it. If there comes a storm and it blows trash and dirt and the water rises so high that that dirty, muddy, water comes into the masjid under the masjid door, are you going to throw the masjid away? You should clean the masjid up and make your salat. That is what Prophet Muhammed was guided to do by G_d, not to go and destroy churches, condemn the Christian people and prevent them from practicing their religion under his order or in the land. He did not prevent them. He saw the corruption. He saw the filth, and there is filth in the Bible that is very embarrassing. But that was produced for the pagans who were a people who were vulgar. Many of them were educated, but at the same time, their fun was vulgarity, sexual indecency, and vulgar display of their sexual interest. They were a people who prided themselves in being powerful as an army. That instinct and that spirit in them to fight and kill was so strong, and they took such pride in it that their sport was to put fighters against each other to actually fight to the death. There is much I have to say on that, but we do not want to waste time.

Keeping the Spiritual People Separate

Abraham kept them separate. He kept science separate from religion, and he didn't feel that he was responsible for religion. He was a rational man, teacher, educator.

But then his mind led him to believe that in order to go further, keep moving forward with true knowledge, it was going to mean the death of the spiritual community. He didn't want to see them left so far behind that they would become of no importance for the future of the real life on earth. So, he thought that G_d was opening his eyes to tell him, "You can't carry them, and as much as you cherish this and have this sentimental attachment to the spiritual people, they just can't make it into the future. So, you should make a sacrifice". He thought he had to sacrifice them.

This is addressing what happened before in society. The social people were sacrificed to have the spiritual people advance. And Abraham was of the mind that the spiritual life has to be sacrificed, so we can have the social life the way it should be. When the figure was rejected or transformed as a sheep that was the answer. The sheep are peaceful like a typical priestly society. The sheep are typical of someone who wants the life of peace, and they like to be to themselves. They are close to each other, you know. So, the picture I have in mind of that spiritual order back there is a kind of order that existed before Prophet Muhammed came and led the people into community life and whatever and guided them to be responsible for the needs of community life.

As we stated before, the unity of matter (tauheed), we associate with Abraham. He concluded that it was one system with one universal law. Abraham was not just rational, but a scientific thinker. He came to the conclusion that he must not let his mind interfere with his search for understanding. His orientation or discipline in his search was scientific. He wasn't testing the physical sun, and neither did the ancient people. They weren't seeing those things except as metaphors or symbols of something in their own life. More importantly, and truthful to the language of man and history, he was saying that "This consciousness that rises up out of you to light the world, your ideology, was not G_d. I have tested it, and it has limitations. It dies and is like everything else in the material world, it comes and goes. All these things are signs of what happens to man and man's ideas".

Abraham is the true educator, because he is not guessing and is following reasoning, and arrives at the gate of science, and does it for all mankind. So, the one that comes to know that all life can be studied and you can discover laws and nature, and behavior of matter can be discovered, he opened the door to a treasure that covers the span of the universe. The Qur'an says the throne used to be over the water but now extends over all land and water. Its expanse is over the width of the heavens and the earth. Abraham was a man of faith, devoted to rational concerns, and known for digging wells. In digging wells, you have to get down deep into the earth and you discover water, and you need an apparatus to go down and bring it up. Even if you make a hole square, water is going to round it out. The hole represents perception, a way of seeing. Allah made all human eyeballs round. So, your seeing of things should be universal, like your round eyeballs, and your vision should seek to complete itself, and should have one vision in common with mankind and all things.

Trying to Make the Mortal Too Big

Trying to make a mortal too big is what confused the culture and made the culture oppressive, an oppressor. That's what the culture is. It's an oppressor, and the culture is just like the sun. It rises up. It goes away and we're under darkness. It comes up in the morning and it wakes us up, and it goes to its height, and it starts descending and it goes out, again. In the Egyptian's mythology, the culture is one science, represents science, one science that governs the people, mankind, one science that governs human beings, and it rises as though it's coming out of the earth. If we don't know by rational inquiry or science, then we look at it and it looks like it's coming up out of the earth. That's exactly what it looks like it's doing, coming up out of the earth. If it comes up where there is a large body of water, it really looks like it's coming out of the water, because it seems to drop golden drops back into the ocean or water as it pulls out of it. It appears that way. You know that isn't happening, but that's the way it appears, and Allah made it to appear that way.

The Potential for Enlightenment

So, it looks like it's coming out of the earth itself, and it is! We should understand that it is coming out of the earth itself. As a part of the physical universe the earth is turning toward it, and it makes it appear to be rising up, but the meaning for the common man is not that. The meaning for the common man is that it's coming up out of the earth or coming up out of the ocean, if there's water. That's the way he sees it. So, the Egyptians had it that the sun is like a living thing, and it comes up out of the earth and lights the world so we can have our life. It goes back into the earth on the Western side. It goes back down into the earth, and it doesn't stop traveling. Now, the Egyptians were no stupid people. It doesn't stop traveling. The arc below the earth, the dark side, it travels through that. That's called the land of the dead. The land of the dead is up under the earth. It travels through the land of the dead and comes back up to the land of the living.

Therefore, it represents the potential for enlightenment. The potential for our enlightenment is first in the earth and it rises out of the earth, seemingly, meaning up out of our own body. We are the earth. So, it's in our body as dormant power. It's in our body as dormant power, but it eventually rises from this dormant power, or from sleep, this deep sleep or death. It rises and it shows itself and it lights our world, that potential. But that potential rests. It doesn't stay up. That potential rests and we're under darkness, again. It goes its route, and it comes up again. So, it's over and over, again, like a Mujeddid.

So, a hundred years is the time it takes to set and come up again. Now, it isn't a hundred years. In the Bible, it's a thousand years. No, it's more than that, because it says a thousand years with man is as a day with the Lord, with G_d. A thousand years reckoned by man is as one day with G_d. I believe I have it right. I believe that's the way it is, a thousand years. So, what is this day? This day is your survival as an intelligent, enlightened people, and the survival is the survival of your social nature that G_d gave you to hold you together.

The Arabs have that language, a thousand years... the surah called, Quraish... *"Ilaafihim rihlatash shita'i was saif, their protection is given to them for winter and summer, through winter and summer"*, the two extreme seasons, through winter and summer, ilaafihim. You know, ilaafihim, means binding together, holding together. So, that's the social order. They hold together. They don't separate. Their social order keeps them together, keeps them bonded together through winter and summer, through the two extremes that can break the social bonds. The extreme of warmth can break the social bonds, and the extreme of passions can break the social bonds. Our people lost their social bonds to the extreme of passions. So, these extremes are working against that. If the bonding is not powerful enough these extremes work against staying bonded.

Now, a thousand years, do you know how you say a thousand? Alf, from the same word. So, this is the thousand years of the Lord. There is no thousand in calendar years. Don't think about counting days or years or anything like that. The thousand is just to say when you lose your social bonding you become a people no more, as the Bible says, *"Let us go down and cast their bands asunder, so they won't be banded anymore together. Let us go down and cast their bands asunder so that they be a people no more"*. That's the Bible.

Your Real Life Is Social Life

G_d created us to be socially bonded together, so that we be a people and remain a people until we achieve what we're to achieve in the capacity He gave us for our destiny as a people. So, that's the day in the language of the Lord, or in the presence of the Lord. That's the day, one day. A thousand years is as one day. What is Allah saying, or what is G_d saying to us in the Bible and Qur'an, too, if we understand it? He's saying that your real life is social life, and the Muslims are a brotherhood. That's what the Prophet told us. Your life is seen by G_d as a community life, or social life. Community life is the same thing as saying social life in Islam, because the community is a community of brothers and sisters. It's a family. That's social bonding.

A day… so, that's life, that's referring to life. Day is when our life comes on for the average one. We know we have night work and everything now, and for the night worker, the night is his day. If he's sleeping in the daytime, the day is his night. It's still the same. The language is still the same, it doesn't change. We just have to identify it in that that has broken away from the norm.

The Conclusion for the Destiny of Man

Muhammed, the Prophet, saw the conclusion for the destiny of man. He saw the conclusion. He knew what was going to be the end of the social order of man on this planet earth, or the communities of people on this planet earth. He saw the end. He knew exactly what the end would establish. He knew that G_d had revealed it to men before him, and to him. He was the one that presented the conclusions to us, the exact conclusions, all of them, the conclusions for man's spiritual disposition.

They Wrestled With G_d

Man takes three main dispositions towards himself and the external reality. They are given in the three nafs. One is he tends to make decisions arbitrarily and moves on impulse rather than on sound reasoning. That's one tendency in him. Another tendency in him is that as he knows more, he tends to be more critical of everything. So, he's critical of everything, and that's really the Zionist Jew, very critical. This disposition is very strong in them, very critical of everything. They even criticize G_d and brag. I've had rabbis brag to me, "You know we wrestled with G_d!" One told me that. He probably knew I'd heard it from the Bible. He said, "We". He said, "You know we wrestled with G_d". He said, "Actually, we wrestled with the angel, but we were wrestling with G_d". That's what he told me. They brag that they question G_d, and many of them became atheist long before we knew the word atheist in English. Long before the English dictionary gave us the word, atheist, they were already atheist, called Sadducees. They didn't believe in any hereafter, no spiritual life, except for the one that's in you now, no hereafter. They believed you're the product of a material world and enlightened man is the highest form in the material world, therefore, he is G_d. They didn't say that, but they don't accept any G_d. They didn't accept Jesus. They rejected Jesus Christ, and they didn't talk about G_d, not the Sadducees. So, they were the atheists of the ancient world or of the olden days, Medieval times, and before. They were the atheists, then they came up with this term, atheist.

And would you say Karl Marx was an atheist? I would say so. He dismissed G_d from man's mind. He said man should plan his mind based upon dialectic materialism. That's the Sadducees coming into power. But they sent one Sadducee to Communism, and the other Sadducee is sitting in the colleges and universities as professors trying to take our students, our young, bright minds from believing in G_d. Yes, they aren't satisfied until they break your religion, tear down your religion, or make you think that your religion is in the way of you becoming really educated, and they are right. Religion as they planned it for us is in the way of us becoming really educated.

The Impulse Is Also the Fig Tree

The impulse is also called the fig tree and after Jesus Christ comes, he said, "You didn't have any food for me, because G_d has formed my impulsive nature. So, the fig tree of your world let it bear figs no more." Isn't that what it said? He cursed it to bear figs no more. Now, we don't see any fig tree that's cursed, not bearing figs. So, that has nothing to do with those material things out there. It's all right in here, in the soul. So, there's a tendency in the soul to dawn in the mind or intellect, and when it dawns upon impulse, suddenly, intuition just brings so many things to your mind, fills your mind up with lights like the many seeds in a fig. Now, that's different than a figment. A figment means that this is off by itself. Figment in the heaven of our mind is like an asteroid or something going through space…

From Love of Purity to Enlightenment

But the light, the bright order of stars, are so many, like the seeds in a fig. Scripture says of Abraham, *"And your seeds shall be like the stars in the heavens"*, also, *"Like the grains of sand on the seashore"*; but they're going to rise up from there. Once you purify that material, clean it up and purify it, the next stage is going to shoot you up to the sky, the night sky. They are going to show you so many lights that you're not going to be able to count them! So, from a love for purity, you rise to enlightenment. That's what it's saying. *"Your seeds shall be as the sand on the seashore"*. You won't be able to count the grains of sand like your seeds.

Again, who is it talking to? It's talking to Abraham, and Abraham is the man of rational faith. "By you being the leader for all people on the earth of rational faith you're going to first bring those who are pure at heart to you, and your following shall be like the grains of sand on the seashore, so many you are not going to be able to count them".

The Urge in Abraham's Intellect

But then the next progression is going to be for the intellect, because G_d is going to bring them to the intellect. If they become pure at heart, they won't have to bring themselves into the intellect. G_d is going to bring their reasoning to burst into a bright galaxy and it's going to be in the rational mind. It's going to come from purity to the rational mind, and your rational thoughts shall fill the heavens and shall be so pure, we're going to call it, "The saints"!

Yes, it's really beautiful! So, it's talking about the urge in Abraham's intellect, that his urge stems from the purity of his heart, and he was a man of great faith, great, unshakable faith. But he respected logic, and he respected reasoning, supported logic so strongly that he never would separate his rational from his spiritual. He kept the two together until they became reconciled. So, he understood that one is not against the other. Both are given to man to carry man to the destiny, and he became a father, or leader for all mankind.

Letting Them Stay In the Womb

He tended to think that for the end, for the goal that the community of people seek on the earth the spiritual was in the way. The spiritual was holding them back. But it was holding them back because it had not reconciled itself with the rational. So, when G_d told him to kill his son, it pained him that he had to kill his son. That's the ignorant, spiritual masses. So, it pained him that he had to kill him. He was a man, a good man. He was a father to everybody. He loved everybody and he cared for the poor. But how was he caring for them? He was caring for them by letting them stay in the womb. That's how he was caring for them, by letting them stay in the womb. As long as you're in the womb, you can be at peace. But G_d said, "No, they can't stay in the womb. I want them all to come forth to My Destiny I planned for them." And when he understood that, then he said, "I've got to kill my own child?" It pained him. Then Allah said, "No, you don't have to kill him. Just kill that sheepish nature in him and feed that sheepish nature to the people. Let them be educated regarding this sheepish nature, that you don't take it to the extreme and you don't defend yourself and let the wolves keep coming in and other things keep taking advantage of you."

Feeding Is Teaching

So, he stood the sheep up in a man's clothing, in a warrior's clothing. Yes, feeding is taken to the New Testament, and Jesus Christ. The feeding is not really killing something and feeding it to something. No, the feeding is teaching. *"Take this bread"*, symbolic of my body, the doctrine of the New Testament, the teachings of the New Testament. So, how do you "feed my sheep"? You teach them of my knowledge that G_d gave me as my body. Isn't that something, that a man sees his body as his knowledge, not as his physical flesh? So, "body of knowledge", yes siree! The blood is the life of the flesh, the life of the body, and he said it's the spirit of the New Testament. That's what his blood is, his blood, or wine, that he gave out. He gave the wine as a reminder, something to remind them of his blood. The wine is only a resemblance of blood. Blood is sweet tasting, and wine is sweet tasting, and the alcohol is the life in the wine. If it has no alcohol, it has no life, and then it isn't wine anymore. His (Jesus Christ) exciting teaching that lifted the people's spirit was the alcohol in his blood, and the blood is the spirit of the New Testament.

They had that attitude towards Scripture before Christ Jesus came, because it says in the Old Testament, *"If the salt has lost its savor"*, meaning it doesn't excite you anymore. If the salt has lost its savor, meaning they don't savor it anymore, "what good is it but to be thrown back into the earth?" So, then the enthusiastic doctrine of Jesus Christ comes and replaces the Old Testament, and finally the salt is thrown back into the earth. So, something pointed to in the Old Testament is fulfilled in the New Testament. That's the way Scripture is.

"Surely I Have Oppressed My Own Self"

Now, still working in the same vein, Prophet Abraham, when he got the understanding and when his mind was turned on and he understood for the first time what his purpose should be, he said *"Surely, I have oppressed myself. Surely, I have wronged, I have oppressed my own self"*. There he is speaking for humanity. He's not speaking for just himself as a single person. Abraham is speaking for humanity. Abraham is speaking in the history of human denial, human mistreatment, the oppression of humanity, the mistreatment of humans, the oppression of the humanity of all people. He's speaking for all of us, and He's saying to all of us that we have wronged our own self. We have been our own oppressors. Now, how was he the oppressor? How was he his own oppressor? He was trying to find G_d. He was trying to find G_d, so he would know the truth, so he would understand what this world means, this big scheme of things, what it means; what it should mean to him; how he should understand it in his own mind, and where should he be in it. What should be his place and role in it, he wanted to know that. So, he was searching the creation to find where the G_d is. And after he decided that none of these created things are G_d, but there is a Designer, there's a Will, there's a Cause behind this or before this that produced all this, He called that One, Allah, and He said He's the Lord of the worlds. He is the Lord of all the worlds means the One Who brought all the worlds into existence stage by stage, from nothing to something, and then developed them, or brought them to completion, finished the products, step by step, stage by stage. That's what Rabb means. So, he said He's the Rabb, Lord of all the worlds.

Fear of the Mortal Life Enslaved Humanity

How did he oppress himself? He oppressed himself not as a person, not as an individual. He oppressed himself as a human being in a certain human state, or in a certain condition. What was that state? What was that human condition? Fear. Fear of the unknown had caused him and humanity (he's the father of this new humanity) to wrong themselves and to oppress themselves. It was fear of the unknown, not knowing the Real G_d, looking for the Real G_d in things that are not G_d, in places where G_d is not, not as the G_d, you see.

So, that's what oppressed him, the tendency to find a god and put that god over yourself. So, men looked in the world and they were frightened by thunder, by lightening, by wind, and different things, by water, or other things, and they made those things their god. They were frightened by their rulers, and they made their rulers their god. Men made other men their god. So, this fear, mortal fear, fear for my own mortal life, enslaved humanity, enslaved us, and it was the Prophet Abraham that was put in that role, as the one who discovered what had caused all the problems.

Abraham and Man's Search for the Real G_d In History

And G_d doesn't include Abraham, but G_d says, *"And the worst form of oppression is shirk."* Now, we may say Abraham was never guilty of shirk (idolatry, polytheism, or the association of G_d with other deities). It appears that way. It appears that Abraham was never guilty of shirk, but he was looking for G_d, wasn't he? He also thought things were G_d that were not G_d. Now, Abraham is not doing this himself. Abraham is putting himself in the position of humanity, in the history of time, in the history of humanity, and he looks at the thing and he says, "This is G_d". And then he says, "No, it can't be G_d, because of this or because of that". And he looks at something else and he says when it appears, "Oh, that must be G_d. No, it can't be G_d, because of this, because of that." And he, finally, stayed all night searching the heavens, the skies, for the G_d, and the sun came up in beautiful, wonderful, marvelous, splendor, bright, overpowering sunlight. And he said, "This must be G_d!" Abraham said, "This must be the G_d." So, Abraham is speaking for man in his search for the truth, in his search for the Real G_d through the history of time, over the long trail of time.   So, he sees the sun, and he says, "This must be

G_d", and he watches the sun. Now this man, he was a 24-hour searcher. He spent the night and then he saw the sun set. Then he said of that one (the sun) that had really roused him, "Oh no, my G_d can't be one that sets." So, that's when he turned. After he had seen the glory of the night and the glory of the day in this world, he said, "Nothing of this world can be G_d", and he turned and he said, "The One behind this, the Cause that produced all of this, that's the G_d." Praise be to Allah! And he said to G_d, *"Surely I have oppressed my own self."*

"They Ask So Many Questions of G_d"

Now, man looked outside of himself for G_d. If he would only listen to his own soul, if he would only look into his own nature, into his own life, then he would know that "All of this outside could not have been produced by me, and I can't trust my faculties. I can't trust my eyes. My eyes are too small to see the great reality of G_d." He would know his own excellence, his own greatness, and he would know his own smallness, his own limitations, if he would only study himself, and search into himself, not the outer world. It is the search into the self that brings man, quickly, to know that "There is a Being of a different nature, a Being of no limited power, a Being that cannot be described in physical terms that is responsible for my being." He would know that, but not only that. If he would turn to himself and examine himself, it says, *"They ask so many questions of G_d, why don't they ask some questions of their own creation?"* This is the answer. You should ask questions of your own creation. This is Allah in Qur'an.

G_d Will Say, "Here I Am!"

Yes, if we would turn the search light towards our own selves, into our own souls, and look into our own souls, into our own natures, look into the workings of our own creation, we would come into the understanding that we are not G_d, and that the G_d must be something bigger than us. We would also come to understand that we're bigger than the world in terms of what the world can do, and what we can do. The world does things, the world is bigger than us in its creation and in its power, but we're bigger than the world in terms of free mobility, free action on our part. The world can't act on its own part freely. Only man can do this. Only human beings can do this, therefore, if we would turn and look into ourselves, we would see ourselves. We will come to know that we are not G_d, and if we're not G_d, then I can't trust my own judgment. So, we won't even look at something and say, "Is that G_d?" We will say, "G_d, You are beyond my grasp!" And when we say that G_d will speak to us. That's all G_d wants the human being to say, "I can't find You on my own! I can't reach You on my own! I don't have an arm long enough, a sight long enough, or a scope big enough to capture You, G_d!" And G_d will say, "Here I am!" Praise be to Allah! Yes, so now, we wrong ourselves by fearing the unknown and trusting our logic, our own reason, to find something bigger than us, too big for us to manage. That's how we wrong ourselves.

The Issue of the Value of the Human Being

We made false gods on the strength of our own knowledge, or intelligence. We trusted our own intelligence to find G_d and we made mistake after mistake and oppressed our own selves and humanity with false gods. So, Abraham is making the repentance to G_d, not for himself, only, but for the whole of humanity, and he puts it in the first person because he's the father, he's the teacher. He represents the freedom of the intellect, the first freedom, the first time the human being's intellect was completely freed, and he's speaking for all the enslaved and all the oppressed. He says, *"Surely I have wronged, or oppressed, my own self and I confess my faults."* He goes on to say G_d is the only Forgiver of wrongdoing. He said, *"Forgive me my faults, for none can forgive faults but You"*. He goes on with the prayer. We know it. It is the prayer of Abraham. Yes, a wonderful, wonderful, story with the human being, the issue of the human being's value in the center, right in the center. That's where the focus should be the issue of the value of the human being.

Now, isn't this a wonderful creature, even though he goes wrong, eventually, in his search? He trusted his own material. He should trust G_d. But how should he trust a G_d he doesn't know, yet? You understand? So, G_d created him above this, but created him to grow to that point where he can manage that. So, in his (Abraham's) inferiority, G_d didn't say, G_d never told Abraham, "You have sinned", did He? It was Abraham that thought he had sinned. G_d knew what he was going to do. That's why He told the angels, "Wait, I know he's going to do these things. I know he's human, and I know he's going to make all these mistakes." They said, "This thing You're creating is going to cause bloodshed." G_d did not say, "No, he isn't going to cause bloodshed!" G_d didn't even respond to it; and he did. He went crazy, and he oppressed, he killed, and he murdered his own brothers and sisters. He shed the blood, much blood. He spilled blood all over the world. But finally, he came to himself, and he confessed his sins to G_d, and he pledged himself to serve G_d's Will and to liberate humanity, liberate mankind. Isn't that wonderful? Yes, he said, *"Surely, I have wronged my own self. Surely, I have oppressed my own self."*

The Human Excellence That G_d Deposited Into Human Beings

So, the human soul is the human excellence that is your humanity, your true humanity, the human excellence that G_d deposited into the human being. When He made us, He inscribed excellence. He put it into the very nature, the very growth nature, the growth nature, the nature of the cells to grow, the nature of the abstract body to grow. He put it in that very growth nature. He put it in there that that nature should want better and better, more excellence, more quality, more intelligence, and he's a growing thing, as a plant. G_d says he's a growing thing, growing from stage to stage until he reaches his completion. So, G_d has put that in him. And when he goes to the false thing, trusting his own limited mind and intelligence, and chooses things as a god, he oppresses that. He stops that. He puts a stop on that excellence. And we know the oppressors of man, oppressors of humanity, they kept the society of man, stale, dull, stagnant, no growth, no progress for the human potential for excellence. This is what we're talking about, that he's speaking for the whole of humanity, that we have wronged our own self.

Human Means Prone to Make Mistakes

G_d says, "Don't blame Me. Blame yourself!" G_d gave you what you needed inside, but you trusted your intelligence, and you should have trusted your spirit. You should have trusted your good spirit, and your good spirit would have reconciled you with the best of your intelligence, and you would have benefited from your intelligence. So, G_d didn't create you wrong. G_d created you human, and human means prone to make mistakes. So, you are going to make those mistakes, but eventually, you're going to realize that position you took was wrong. It's doing nothing but getting you into more and more trouble, and you're going to come away from that position and do as Abraham did.

Abraham's Night and Day

He (Abraham) started in the dark. What does that mean, he started in the dark? Dark night means he separated himself from his own judgment. He put his own judgment of things aside, and he started to search with a mind trusting that "The truth will come to me, if I'm not prejudiced by my own judgment, or my own opinion". So, he was free out there searching the heavens at night. And when the day came, now, he becomes rational. Now, he goes to his rational faculties. He puts his rational aside for all the night, and after he saw all those things in the night were not G_d, then he accepted the rational. And when he became rational and looked at the rational, he said, "No, not even that is G_d. The only G_d is the One Who created all of this, Who caused all of this to be!"

Chapter 5
Moses and Other Prophets of Scripture

When Moses perceived a fire in the mountain, the mountain is the important thing in this picture, and it is symbolic of rule, authority and government, but why? Because it represents how the intellect, or the mind must develop in order to be at the top and rule, and it has to start from a base that everybody can touch. Everybody can't climb to the mountain top. Everybody does not even have the desire to do it. They don't even have an interest to do it, but the base of the mountain is available, reachable for everybody. So, it represents general thinking, the general mind of the masses, or the people. I do not mean masses like communism or something, but masses meaning the majority of the common people. It starts there and as it goes up its logic unfolds, the logic for governing unfolds. You start with the common people and the common life, and then you have to go up from what is general to reach what is specific. Now, whether it is the people themselves, their graduation as Allah says in the Qur'an is that of the believers. He has made ranks in grades, not all the same level. So, they think it's the same. The people at the base have their common thinking, but as you go up, the logic for being able to govern that society increases. So, the more it increases, the more mass it eliminates, like a mountain getting narrower and narrower. When you get to the apex maybe only one person can stand up there, or very few can stand up, gather at the top and be supported.

Moses Was Searching for the Logic of Community

So, it is eliminating numbers as the logic graduates, and that is the same way the rule of logic works. You start with a problem or a purpose that you want to reach, or a problem you want to solve. You start with it, and you go step by step until you finalize the logic, until you reach the finality, the final point of the logic. In other words, you reach the conclusion for that logic, for that step-by-step development in that logic. Once you reach the conclusion in it you come back to the base, and you apply what you acquired at the top. Isn't that what Moses did? He got there and he met G_d. G_d gave him the Ten Commandments, and he came back down with it and applied it to the base. So, it is a search for a logic that is consistent, and you follow it from its generalities to a specific, from generality to specific, and once you get the language for the specific need, then you come back down. But coming down you have to apply it, again. Going up you are searching for the conclusion of it, but when you're coming back down, if you do not have the right conclusion, you're going to make trouble at the base. Sometimes, it is more difficult to come down a mountain than it is to go up. Now, you have to test that logic, make sure that it stands up at the base of the mountain. So, when he saw the fire, G_d was teaching him, and he was searching. Even though he was traveling, he came to visit with those people at that place. I think that is where he got his wife, at that very place near Mount Sinai. He was searching for the community logic that would serve, organize, and establish his people, so that they would be a community, a nation or a people. That is what he was looking for.

So, we came to the mountain, and he said, *"I think I perceive a fire"*, and the fire was at the base of the mountain. It was not at the top. So, when he went there, he said, *"Perchance I will get a brand."* Now, a brand means a burning stick, or something burning. He could go and put a tree branch or something in the fire and light it and bring it back to his people. So, the brand is like a branding iron. You heat it up and put your brand on the cattle. He meant, "We do not have any fire here. There is a fire there. We do not have any fire like that, and perhaps I can take one of our branches or something or my stick, put in there, and get a light and bring it back to you, and we can use the light to light fires for us".

"Take Off Your Shoes"

When he got there, he heard a voice saying, "Oh, Moses, take off that spirit that Egypt gave you", but it is disguised. It said, *"Take off your shoes"*. It means, "Take off that spirit you are standing upon that you got from Egypt! You are standing in a spirit that won't work here!" So, he took off his shoes. You need something on your feet if you're going to climb a mountain. They will be bleeding all the way up, so the logic does not fit unless you translate the language. I think it means it was a group of religious people. Even the mountain, itself, was not material. It was people, and the mountain is a mountain of wisdom. He saw people at the base of it, and he came to a group of these religious people. When he got there, they did not tell him with their mouths, but he knew that those people, he should not come to them with his spirit he got from Egypt.

"Shoo Those Flies Away!"

Shu is one of the mythological gods of the ancient Egyptians. Shu is the god of spirit. That is what it means. Our people used to shoo flies. See how language survives saying, "Shoo those flies away from the table"? So, that shows you language survives in some form. Even though they hide it, it survives to be an expression among the people. You'll still find traces of it somewhere; that is, for most strong beliefs or strong ideas, they survive. Even though the people have consciously lost contact with the knowledge they used to have, it survived in their language. I would not be surprised if that expression, "Shoo flies away" came out of our people who came from an Islamic past, knew that language, and had that wisdom. It could have survived in them. They could say it subconsciously and not even know what they were saying. The soul has not lost that. Your mind lost it, your conscious lost it, but your soul didn't, so it comes up as an expression, and you do not even know where it is from. I kind of believe that "shoo" came from them, or wise persons said it around us, and we picked it up. That is a strong possibility, also.

Moses and the Holy People Dressed In White

I think they was a group of people, and they were holy people dressed in garments all white. Moses saw them, and he was attracted to go to them. When he went to them his own nature told him, "These are special people, and I should get rid of this base that I have". Shoe is on the base. "I should get rid of the spiritual base that I have from Egypt", because obviously Moses was learned. He was in the house of Pharaoh, and he knew that Egyptians had the god, Shu. Moses had to dismiss or take off the spirit that he got in Egypt, and with these people he was going to get another spirit. It means that if you disposition yourself incorrectly you cannot go up G_d's mountain of logic, because that was G_d's Knowledge. That was not a philosopher's knowledge. That mountain was G_d's Mountain. You cannot ascend G_d's Mountain of logic for the leader until you first prove yourself independent of the spirit that the world gave you. So, that is what he had to do, and he had such confidence in those people that he met there, in their righteousness. He saw light that just caused him, right away, to question himself, to question what he was standing upon.

The Description of Moses Suits Our Situation

So, the description of Moses, the mountain, etc., I think it applies or suits the situation for us. It fits our situation. After the Honorable Elijah Mohammed's leadership, we had to undo before we started constructing again. We had to undo a construction that was there before we started constructing a new way of thinking. Yes, I furnished a base that I was trying to make available to all, to the masses of our people that were with me, the mass of those who were following me. So, I was trying to provide a base that would be a commonsense base for all of us. It worked, but it had some mystery in it, and the mystery is to say we never know everything, so we leave some mystery in it, intentionally.

The mystery will make some unsatisfied to just stay in the generalities or in the commonsense thinking of the new base. So, you had a good one and I saw a brand. I saw a fire and I said, "Maybe I'll go there and get a brand, and we could light our own fires, so I kept going up, building logic upon logic. As Paul said, *"If you do not edify, you do not have anything to impress me"*. So, we kept putting construction upon construction, drawing to a conclusion, the need to have a conclusion, and that is to reconcile our language with the language of the Qur'an that is at the top of the mountain, and Muhammed is at the top of the mountain. Mr. Fard said, "Your reward will be a free trip to the holy city of Mecca to see Brother Muhammed". We said "Muk Mud" back then. We were not going to see Brother Muk Mud. We were leaving Brother Muk Mud to see Brother Nur, Brother light!

Yes, it fit us, too. We were attracted to something that was general or something that can be understood by the people in the bottom of the construction. Our faith in that, that there was light there is what enabled us to go up the mountain, to ascend to higher levels to get more understanding, in fact, to get a conclusion. We want to have this thing concluded, so we'll know what we have. We have to know what we've got to eliminate darkness and mysteries. That is what you're going up for, to get away from darkness and mysteries. The mountain, going up is symbolic of going to defined light in a dark world. Christ, what did he say? He said, *"The light of this world is darkness"*, so we are in the dark. And when night falls and everybody is in the dark, if the clouds are not up, there is a lot of light. The Arabs said the night has a thousand eyes.

195

THE TREASURE UNDER THE WALL: Thursdays with the Imamegment>

The Mountain of Enlightenment

So, the mountain that Prophet Muhammed ascended, they call it Mount Hira. That was in the old, pagan time. It means mountain of a cat. I guess nothing but a cat went up there. Hira means cat, but it is also from Greek. After Prophet Muhammed went up there it was not called Mount Hira anymore, and we should never call it by that name, because that is what the enemies of Al-Islam call it. They want to keep it like it was in pagan times, that he went up Mount Hira. But once he received guidance from G_d, which was light for us down here, it is called Jabl Nur, the Mountain of Enlightenment. And that is why he went up there, to call on a Higher Authority and hope that he would be enlightened and could come back down and guide his people to success. His people were all people on the earth. He never thought narrowly. He was always thinking of mankind or humanity, not of a particular people, or his people as a nation. It is important that we know this. He put them down as a nation. He did not have admiration for his people as Arabs, although they once had a great civilization and great social leaders at one time in their lives. This is all part of Arab history. But their tendency was to rebel against the best leadership, just like Jews, and selfishly take for themselves what they want from the past and pride themselves in it; but not be unified, not having any desire to become unified. So, they existed as tribes threatening each other, claiming their rights and stuff. That was the Arab people in the time of Prophet Muhammed. You had to pay a toll. You actually had to pay the chief to cross his territory. If you wanted to go to Syria or somewhere and came across his territory, you had to pay a toll.

The Real Mountain In Your Thinking

Jabl Nur, the Mountain of Enlightenment, is not called Mount Sinai, but it is the same. The idea is the same, that Moses had to go up in the mountain and get the light from G_d and bring it down to the people. But when he got it, he got it in the form of commandments that had to be applied on earth. Allah just does not give His Revelation, because if He just wanted to give revelation, He could just give revelation to all of us. He could reach all of us, but He gives revelation and then He qualifies a person to apply the light when he goes back among his people. The same thing that happened for Moses happened for Muhammed; peace be upon the Prophets. But you know Muhammed first had an encounter, because he did not know G_d. He was just seeking answers. He felt that there was a Higher Authority

196

to give him those answers. It was just his nature that was moving him to do what he did. He did not read the Bible, or any Scripture. So, Muhammed, the Prophet, had one encounter on the mountain, and to my knowledge he never had another one on the mountain. What does that tell us? That really the mountain is not necessary, not a physical mountain. The real mountain is the mountain in your thinking. He went up there one time. That was his nature sending him way up there.

Allah says, *"And if My servants ask about Me, tell them I am near*. Why did you leave your people and go way up there on that mountain thinking you were going to get close to Me?"* So, Muhammed did not need anything except one lesson. He knew he did not have to go up there. Sometimes, he would be back down on the ground doing business, and suddenly, he had to cut off business and listen to his Lord. I think you get more when you are on a low-level than you do when you are physically on a high level. The Lord knows I have not climbed up any level. I used to like to climb trees. I have no desire to even climb a tree. My desire is to put my forehead and nose on the ground in sajdah.

A Big-Headed Snake

The serpent appears in the Qur'an, but not in the garden. He appears in the story of Moses, where he is told to cast his rod, and he casts his rod and his rod appears in every respect to be a snake, moving. So, getting back to the snake, if you look at the human body, at the anatomy, you'll see the brain connecting to the ganglia and down the spine, all the way to the end, looks like it had a tail once. The end of it looks like a little tail. So, really, what approached him in the garden was a heartless intelligence that didn't have anything to work with but the brain, the nerve center that goes down, that's all, and it looks like a snake with a big head. So, that's really where their information is coming from. The information is coming from the brain going down. You take the brain and the nerve line that goes all the way down to the end and it looks like a snake, a big-headed snake. That's exactly what it looks like. So, that's the picture they're giving of the Devil, Satan, the intelligence with no human feelings, no heart, no human heart. He does only what his intelligence bids him to do with no regard for human sentiments, or heart, or anything. But he can't see his evil, because he has nothing to register anything else but intelligence. He prides himself in his intelligence. He despises humans, typical humans, because the typical human lets his heart interfere with his intelligence. It's the heart that feeds the whole body, including the brain. A snake is a cold-blooded creature.

The Snake Got Into the Science of the Culture

The snake in the Qur'an doesn't appear again till much later, not like in Genesis. It doesn't appear like in Genesis. It doesn't appear in the beginning. In the Qur'an, when G_d said, *"Get you down from here"*, there's no mention of any snake. That was in the beginning, the Genesis. But it appears in the life of Moses, and he's in the staff that the people use. He got into the staff, and we understand the staff by how Allah, or G_d, brings Moses to realize what his staff is. But Allah is speaking even when Moses is speaking. Allah asks a question and then Moses speaks for Allah to tell Allah what Allah wants to bring out. He says, *"What is that that you have in your hand? Oh, this is my staff. What do you use it for? Oh, I use it to beat back the brush when I'm making a path through the brush."* So, his staff opens a path up through the brush in the woods. That's what he is doing with it, opening a path, so he can go his way through the brush, through the woods. That's the science of culture and the Devil has gotten into it. That snake of the Genesis has gotten into the science of the culture and is regulating the people's life through the science of the culture. So, who's making that path for him? The Devil. Who shows him how to go through the woods? The Devil. I hope it's clear!

The World's Knowledge Established the Way We See Things

He is totally unaware of what he's using, because when he saw it, he was frightened. He got back from it. He thought it was Satan. And when G_d said, *"Throw it away from yourself"*, He's saying, "Look at it objectively, Moses. You've got your feelings involved. You've got your teachings involved that you got in Egypt, from your parents in the land of Goshen. Throw it away from you! Throw it away from everything that you know. Look at it with a free mind." And when he looked at it with a free mind, he saw what it was. So, we're conditioned to see things the way we see things. The world's knowledge has established the way we see things. What we're trying to do, and I think we're succeeding, is to free the mind, condition the mind to connect with the Qur'an, the language of the Qur'an; connect with it, so they'll read not only the literary text, but they'll connect with the insights, and I think it's coming. Yes, it's coming!

All Names Have Significance

Muhammed said his mission shall return to the people who supported his work, and we know his companions were all with him, but they did not know. None of them knew. G_d did not reveal to any of them, except Muhammed, so they were new and hearing everything for the first time, too. Abu Bakr and the rest of them, may G_d be pleased with them, they all were just like the most distant people from the Prophet in terms of their knowledge. They were hearing it for the first time, too. Some of them were opposed to it without knowledge. Umar, he was ready to even beat the followers for listening to him, when we came looking for his daughter to give her a whipping for joining Muhammed or listening to him. The Qur'an was recited, and he was hearing it, and he got touched by it and he changed his mind. It turned him around. What he heard turned him around. One thing for sure is he spoke Arabic, and he heard it in Arabic, in his own language, and he knew that was something above their ability, that the Arabs had no ability to get that. So, he was converted.

But he had to be taught. It was in something totally and entirely new to him. That was all of them, Abu Bakr and all of them. That tells you something about the names they had. Abu Bakr means father of a young camel. Muhammed, the Prophet, was named Muhammed and Ahmad. He was called both, and his name we understand. The scholars know it has great significance in previous Scripture. Would he have companions so close to him, and their names have no meaning, no significance? Names have significance. Again, Abu Bakr means father of a young camel. It is one who protects and cares for something, right? So, he is protecting and caring for a young camel. What is that young camel? It is the dawning of light and understanding in the intellect while it has not yet begun to read. It is intuitive, that is the camel. A camel finds the water. He does not have to see it. By instinct he finds it. His full name was Abu Bakr As-Siddiq. As-Saddiq, the truthful one. So, what is that saying? That says when Allah blesses you with the spirit of understanding, to seek understanding and the intuitive light bursts forth, you cannot lie. If it is ordinary human intuition, yes, that will not change you from a liar, not necessarily. But if Allah causes the dawning of light in you, that intuitive spark is G_d's gift to you, and you cannot lie.

The Qur'an says they both went as two arrows for the target, and they did not separate. They went together accompanied by the Spirit of G_d. You see, the spirit of man is accompanied by the Spirit of G_d, and they are going for the target to achieve what G_d wants man to achieve, and they cannot lie. It is impossible for man to lie because he is going parallel with G_d, in perfect agreement with G_d. Now, willingly or unwillingly is what we see that happens in ordinary situations. But in this extraordinary situation where G_d, Himself, is present with the subject, and He has given the subject His Own Spirit and Will, that is different, much different. So, it is not a question of obeying or disobeying. There is no question.

Moses Is a Dual Figure

Two arrows fired from one bow going parallel to the target is given also in the Qur'an in the search of Moses and the wise man where the wise man said, *"We have to part ways. It went away, sped away as though in a channel, and it is behind us now. We missed it"*. That is to say Moses did not experience this. Moses had not experienced this. His will had not come into perfect harmony in agreement with G_d's Will and Purpose, not yet. He did not know the Purpose. That is why the wise man was taking him on a journey to teach him wisdom. He did not know the Purpose.

If I would tell you that there is no Aaron, Prophet Aaron, our brother, outside of Moses' own soul and existence, would you believe it? I just told you! Moses is a dual figure. Would he be stupid, and Pharaoh had him building for him? He was a builder, a professional, So, I ask you, do you think Prophet Muhammed couldn't read and he is doing business, going to Syria and other countries? Now they are on two different levels, not like John and Jesus. Prophet John and Prophet Jesus, they are on the same level in the Ascension, but Moses and Aaron are on two different levels in the Ascension (or Miraj) of Prophet Muhammed. Aaron is on the fifth level and Moses is on the sixth. So, Moses' mission is six, the sixth level, the social mission, and his brother is on the fifth level, meaning he is on the rational level, and the Jews are strongly rational. They question spiritual things, and they were slow to accept spiritual knowledge. They wanted only the rational. They wanted the rational basis. "Show me the rational side of this". Therefore, Aaron was their leader. Moses was up in the mountain. They did not want him anyway, so they said, "Aaron, make a golden calf. You know how to put this wisdom together for them, make that golden calf. He said, "Give me your golden earrings". He said,

"Let us do this thing. Give me your golden earrings. I will be your leader. I will put it all together for you". So, he got their wives' earrings and put it all together and formed the golden calf. When Moses came down, he snatched him by his beard for that.

Moses Asked G_d to Untie the Knot In His Tongue

Your beard is your mature knowledge, your wisdom, what you get in older years, and it is the knowledge that communicates. It communicates to the listener. The beard goes up and down. The mustache is not going up and down. It looks like the mouth is opening and closing, but it is nothing but the lower jaw going up and down. The upper one is standing still in the heavens. The Signs of G_d are everywhere in the world, as well as in man. This is the Qur'an, the Scripture. So, the beard is symbolic of wisdom, and the wisdom that comes to man, most of the time, it is in his late years, and he communicates it to others. So, Aaron pleaded, *"Do not seize me by my beard!"* Moses asked G_d to untie the knot in his tongue, didn't He? That is the same as saying, "Give me a brother as a helper, which means that he, himself, was not able to use the rational in the spiritual mission. It was too strange for him. So, he is asking for a brother to do that, and what it is saying is that this spiritual counterpart is in his own nature, in his own body, in his own spirituality, in himself, but as his brother.

The Transfiguration

Now, this language that shows more than one person in a person is all through Scripture. When Jesus took his disciples up on the mountain to show them himself, it is called to the Transfiguration. He showed them Moses and Elijah together in one light, and I am saying that he was showing them himself, Jesus Christ. So, what is he saying about himself? He is saying that "I am two in one. I am the light of Moses, and I am the light of Elijah. Both have come together in me". So, Moses and Aaron in the Ascension should be seen in the same way, and he did not say that Moses was the same type as Elijah. So, Moses and Aaron were not the same height, either. One was five feet, and the other was six. But they both were in the same Ascension, the same light beam going up to G_d, a proof that I am right. There are many proofs. I've given some proofs, already.

Moses and Aaron Threw the Rod

In the Bible, Aaron throws the rod for Moses in the contest with the high priests. In the Qur'an, it's the same; but read the whole Qur'an. In another place, Moses throws the rod by himself, no Aaron is with him. The Holy Qur'an also has Moses throwing the rod, not somebody else, not Aaron. So, how is he able to throw the rod at this point? It is because Aaron has now become Moses. It is no more two. It is only Moses. The light of Aaron has merged and disappeared in the light of Moses and come into one beam in him. The man is much wiser now. What it is saying is that, yes, he needed help in the early stages of his life, but eventually, G_d educated Moses. He did not need Aaron. He threw the rod by himself.

Now, it seems like it is one occasion, one big occasion where they meet. No, this challenge is all the time. It's all through the life of Moses. Pharaoh and his witchcraft producers they are following him, so he has to keep throwing the rod. He has to keep manifesting his superior knowledge of their own culture. That is what the rod is. G_d asked him, "What is that? What do you do with that?" He said, *"Oh, I use it to support me when I am walking, and I use it to beat back the bush from the path",* which shows he had knowledge of the culture. Like Moses, we have to meet the challenge all the time. We have to meet the challenge of darkness, superstition, and witchcraft all the time. We have to beat back the darkness.

Everything Is An Expression of the Soul

In the Qur'an, in the story of Moses and the wise man at the junction of the two seas, the wise man is also in Moses. However, Moses could not keep company with his own light of wisdom. He could only go so far, and he would lose it. He would lose the ability to keep up with it. Before he knew anything he would have to say, "I missed something." Really, the place for clarity is the soul. G_d created the soul, nobody else did, the original soul. So, it seems as though we are in the world when we are reading Qur'an and reading history. That is true, but the real focus for what is going on, all the history, wars, and everything, is the human soul. It is as a looking glass in which you see all these things. I don't know if it is called a looking glass... Crystal ball, it is as a crystal ball in which we see the whole world in its stages and what is going on. And really, you cannot see it until you first see the order of the soul for the nature of the soul. When you see the nature of the human soul, then you can understand what is going on in the world. This is philosophy, but everything we have in this world, the buildings and everything, I don't care how big or how small, the station, mission, or program going out in space looking for possible life out there, everything is an expression of the soul.

Nature of the Soul Personified by the Woman

The soul asked for that and if man had not mated with woman and had children by her, he would be still sitting up under a tree singing, *Dixie,* or smoking in the wilderness, nothing created. But when they mate, then the woman reproduces for the man, and reproducing for him makes him more serious, gives him something to work for, a future. It gives him a future to work for and gives him a bigger interest. So now, he needs more, so he begins to seek more, and she is like a metaphor or a sign of the original soul. From one soul He made two and what is the grammatical gender for the soul? It is feminine, not masculine. From one He made two, which means the order and nature of the soul is personified by the woman more than by the man. But when he engages her to produce or have his future with her, then her nature covers his nature, though his nature still leads her nature. He is the leader, but her nature covers his nature. When I say cover, I mean influence. And he becomes like her in his soul. He was not even aware of his soul before, but now she has made him aware of his soul, and she has made him have a sensitive soul. So, that is feminine. She has made him as a sensitive soul. So, they become two, and then G_d reproduces from them all the men and women on earth.

The Soul Wants Peace

So, it is the soul that begins the building of man's world. The soul, itself, begins expressing itself. "I want a building! I want a road!" That is the soul asking for that before the mind asks for it. So, when He says, *"To have comfort in her or in it"* that is the soul. The soul is what is going to comfort it. It wants peace. It wants comfort, and we think it stops. It never stops. It keeps requesting, it keeps making requisitions, "Put me up a road, put me up a city." That is that woman, isn't it? Now when trouble comes in, she looks to you. "Put out those fires, man! Put out those fires! What is wrong with you? You're going to let everything burn up! You are going to let our whole investment, all of it, burn up!" So, He made the man, and he was lonesome, alone, and G_d did not like that the man should be lonesome, or alone. So, He made for him a mate. Now, before He made for him a mate what had he done? Nothing. He was not asleep either, unless he was sleepwalking. G_d decided to put him in a deep sleep.

Every Soul Shall Taste of Death

In Scripture, having a taste of death means you shall experience death without dying. You did not swallow it; you just tasted it. In the Bible, it asks, *"Oh Death, where is thy sting?"* So, the death that had come to the soul is the sting. Taste is not a permanent experience, or permanent condition. It is just a taste, and it is gone. A sting usually comes from something poisonous. When you get a mosquito on you, a bee, or a snake, they leave a sting, the poison. *"Oh, death where is thy sting?* I have overcome your poison. I have built up a resistance to your poison". Praise be to Allah! *"You shall have a taste of death"*. Every soul shall have a taste of death, and Allah gives death. So, what is the death that Allah gives? If Allah gives death, why does He want us to die? As the serpent told Adam in the garden, *"You won't really die, your eyes will come open"*. So, why does G_d create us, and then leave us in a world that is going to bring death to us, eventually? So, our eyes will come open. Experience death means you're going to become conscious of this death, taste it. You are going to know its flavor. It is a bitter pill. I believe it has hemlock in it to lock up my social movement in my system.

Religion, Scripture, Reflect the Wisdom of Myth

You see myth and religion go together. Religion, Scripture, reflect the wisdom of myth. So, did the Greek philosopher, Socrates, really get locked up in prison, physically, and did they really give him hemlock, and he died? No more than Jesus was put on the cross and they gave him aceta, or vinegar, and he died. So, the Qur'an answers it. It says, *"No, you shall have a taste of death"*. So, if a person tastes something, they are still living. It did not say it was going to kill you. It said you are going to have a taste of death. It did not say death was going to kill you. *"Death where is thy sting?"* So, we have to die to the mind the world gives us and come into the mind G_d created us for.

Mud: The Rational Life and the Spiritual Life Together

Jesus put mud on the blind man's eye. The blind man wanted to see, and Jesus put more darkness in the way of his vision, in the way of his sight. But that is what made him see. So actually, that man was not blind. He was blind to certain things, but he was not blind in the usual way. No, he could see, but he could not see the Way of G_d for man. He was blind as to the Way of G_d for man, so Jesus put mud in the way of his vision. What is mud? It is a beginning of creation going in the direction of life. If water and earth does not come together there can be no life. So, he put the water and earth together, meaning he put the rational life and the spiritual life together. It is mud. You put them together and then put them on the man's vision, meaning "See this water and earth that I have formed as a mud and put on your eyes? You see by it and if your faith is strong enough, you'll see through water and mud. You will come to truth and truth is this: that man's spiritual life is to be reconciled with his rational life."

The Earth is symbolic of the rational life. Water is symbolic of the spiritual, which is natural, too. Both are natural, but one is sensitive and the other is not. When he put them together, in time, the blind man's vision, he came back to it. So really, he was not a person who never had vision. He was a person who had been dead to his vision or unconscious of the vision that he should have. However, when Jesus brought into focus the natural order, the natural world, its spiritual counterpart and its rational counterpart and he put them together, made the two dwell together, the blind man came to see. Vision came to the blind man. Allah says, in the Qur'an, that the Iblis caused the angels to disagree with G_d and G_d said, *"Get you all down from here into the earth where you will live, die, and be resurrected again, and where you will find all you need, or aspire to"*. He did not say, "Well, there are some mysterious aspirations you have that you can find no way of fulfilling, reaching, or realizing on earth. You have to go to heaven to get that!" No, "Take everything that you have. Everything that you desire will be found there, in the earth." So, if you desire resurrection from the dead, He already told you *"There you will live, die, and be resurrected."*

Heaven Now and Later

In the Bible, we read where it says, *"No one has ascended to heaven who was not already in heaven"*. So, even going to heaven must be experienced, realized, on this earth, in these natural circumstances. And if you do not achieve it in these natural circumstances, you will never achieve it. That is the Bible. Man is deprived of his complete evolution, for lack of a better word, right now. He is deprived of his complete vision and perception is limited. He is held back from realizing his complete, his full possibility for perception, vision, and understanding in this world, and what holds him back is incorrect delivery of G_d's Word. They do not deliver it correctly. So, by not delivering it correctly man loses the way that G_d created for him. I said, "created".

Eden: Man's First Conception of His Existence As a Thinking Being

So, then to bring him back, he has to go back to origin, or back to Eden. What is Eden? Eden is his first conception, or his first awareness of his existence as a thinking being in creation, before man made anything. There was nothing man-made. There was nothing he could point to as his own work. That is going back in his thinking to the origin. So, that is what you have to do. You have to go back to the religion of origin, the origin upon which He structured man or fashioned mankind, society, and everything, men and women, too.

Christ Jesus As Perceived In Christianity Is Our Enemy

But without G_d's Guidance man cannot find his way, and G_d is always close. In the Qur'an, it says, *"If my servant asks about Me tell him I am near."* As close as your creation, that is where His Guidance is. Abraham said, *"The one who created me shall guide me."* Abraham said, *"All of these other gods are my enemies except the one Who is the Lord of all of the world's"*; the one Who has evolved all mankind, not just one nation, one people, all of them, not only Israel, but all worlds. So, that means Christ Jesus as perceived in Christianity is our enemy. The enemy of Abraham, my father, is my enemy, too. And he (Christ Jesus as perceived in Christianity) did more damage to black people than anybody else, because they have used Jesus on us more than they have used him on anybody, i.e., during slavery, "Remember Jesus loves you", during the Ku Klux Klan era, "Remember Jesus loves you."

Now we have the terror of moral corruption besetting all of us, but nobody is saying, "Look at this serious problem, and remember Jesus loves you." So, we are not making it too well through this terror. The black man is not making it too well, not through this terror. In the terror of moral corruption, moral death, etc., no one is pointing to Jesus to tell us, Jesus loves us. If they would do it, it would save a lot of us. They would say, "Look how we're giving ourselves to a life absent of moral sense, or moral interest to get the girl". The young people and the old people who are joining them in vulgar display, you see this test on us, and if you look at it and really register the whole thing, it will bring tears to your eyes. But remember, while you are looking at it, Jesus loves you. It is not what he wants for you. And who is the Jesus? It is the Muslim in us. It is the Christ in the Christians, that original nature, that original innocence, that will save us, that can save us all the time, always. G_d says, *"He does not change the condition of the people until they change what is bothering their souls."*

The Soul Has the Savior In It

So, they mystify the power of our own souls to deliver us from the world's problems, free us from the world's problems. They mystify it so much that you think it is not possible for you, that you are hopeless. Christ is salvation, meaning that Christ was in you, your savior is in you. You are created with your savior inside of you. That is what Christ said. *"I in the father and the father in me and I in you."* Allah tells Muhammed, *"Say to them, I am a mortal just like you".* Whatever is in my soul is in your soul, that is what it means. Whatever my true nature is it is also your true nature. This is a language of deliverance and salvation, and it can save us and any other people who are under the world's darkness. It can save all of us, but the mystifying does not help at all. When they arrested Jesus what did he say? *"Why do you arrest me in the night when everything that I've done was in the day?"* So, the Qur'an comes. What is the Qur'an? It is the clear understanding for the clear report given. The Arabic word, "Mubeen," means, "very clear, perfectly clear, openly expressed, not secretly expressed".

No Problem Too Big to Solve

So, the answers are all clear and no problem is too complicated, or too big. It says He shall level the mountains. The mountain is symbolic of a lot of things, and one thing it is symbolic of is mystery. The wise man is on top of the mountain. The Wizard of Oz must be up there, too. G_d said He is going to level the mountains. And they say now, "Level the playing field. Do not rig it against anybody". Be fair, that is what it means. In a very strong hadith, taken to be very authentic, Muhammed, the Prophet, said G_d offered him the way to carry out his mission to go through the mountains or through the plains and he chose to go through the plains. This tells us that Muhammed is one of those figures who levels the playing field, or levels the mountains. But then it was necessary, because G_d said if He had not placed mountains on the earth the area would have not been stable, and it would have brought down society structures, or left man's world in ruins. That is what it means.

So, there is more than one picture of the mountain. Some mountains are high but have no snow. They are in hot regions, and they ascend very high, and they are luxurious. They have abundance of beauty and value exposed, whereas some mountains, they are just rocky, stony. They are not supporting vegetation, life, or whatever, and all of them as they ascend so high their tops are very cold. If they ascend high enough no matter where, in Africa, anywhere, their tops are very cold. But look at the mercy in them being cold like that. The collected water turns to ice. They collect, they store clean, good water, and when they experience warm times, the water melts and runs down the mountain and becomes rivers with a mission to relive misery in suffering society.

The Ocean Symbolic of the Collective Soul

John baptized people in the river, and where are these rivers headed? They are headed for the ocean, the lowest spots on earth. So, all that on high shall yield, in time, and let its purity go down to the lowest of the low and is going to end up depositing itself in the ocean. The ocean is symbolic of the collective soul. The biggest body of water, the biggest spirituality that you can find is the ocean. And what is that? It is man's common soul. That is where all people come together, all spiritual instances come together.

Our Aim Should Be to Become Oceanic

So, our aim should be to become oceanic, not little, small lakes, and rivers. The oceans do not exist without salt, and salt is a bad taste in your mouth. If you get too much, you want to rinse it out. When mankind comes together with us not discriminating against people because of race, national origin or anything, what are we doing? We're registering the burden on the human soul, and we get a bit salty, don't we? We say we must organize and change things! Allah loves that, too, in man's soul. That is why G_d, in the Qur'an, says, *"From the sweet water, and the salty water is delicious meat."*

Narrow Thinking

So, this language is so beautiful when we free ourselves. As long as we are in the prisons of our own narrow thinking, we cannot see the full beauty of G_d's Revelation. But if we meet in the ocean of the souls of mankind, we can see it there and those creatures, they move about in a serious fashion. You do not see fish and whatever in an ocean moving about like they are going to a carnival, or to the playground or something. They move around like serious business, like they are seeking serious business. Those little playful fish, sweet water fish, they are just flipping around and about. However, in that big ocean, the creatures are moving with cautious precision. You have seen them, haven't you? If you have not, go to the aquarium and you will see the difference and how they move.

Some fish, say salmon, when they go to spawn, they are headed in a definite direction, and they continue in that direction until they get there. So, what it is saying to us is that there must be a higher purpose in the intellect of man to keep or to hold his intellectual vision where he does not lose it and have things distracting him, and to bring unity to his life. Purpose brings unity to our life. When you give yourself to a higher purpose it serves to unify your intellect where your intellect is not going this way and that way, and every way.

The Intent In Religion and Scripture

So, a definite aim or purpose serves the unity, or a better word in this expression would be integrity. It serves to bring about integrity for man when he has a higher purpose, integrity of conscience where his mind has something to protect and advance his vision going forward, and his thoughts for his vision going, advancing forward, and in harmony. So, it serves to unify or bring about integrity for man's intellect and consciousness. Integrity means wholeness, but it also means, harmony, agreement, and a workable unity, and that is very important for a reproductive mind. It has to achieve a higher purpose, something that appeals to the mind's need for peace, harmony, and integrity. It means agreement in a definite focus. A person of integrity is a very strong person, because something higher has formed, ordered, and has contributed to their mind coming to order, and having a vision, a definite plan, and a commitment to not violate the principle for the plan. Stay moral, stay rational, stay focused, stay obedient to a higher cause. That is what makes great people. That is the intent in religion and Scripture. It is not always respected in religion as expressed by preachers or leaders, but that is what Scripture wants in man. He finds the higher cause that can brings about the best order for his intellect, for his mind. It situates him as a thinker or a visionary, to accomplish all that G_d created man to accomplish on the planet earth.

"Meet Me at the Water Pool"

Muhammed, the Prophet, wanted to see all of us reach that. When he said to his followers, "Meet me at the water pool", the language used is like a big bathtub. So, that says that his mission was to bring us all together for a refreshing bath. In the Qur'an, it pictures him as the unlettered Prophet mentioned in the books that came before, really mentioned in the Torah and the Gospel. And what is his mission? To purify you and to free you from every yoke and bond of slavery. All that enslaves the mind he came to free us from it, and a yoke is what they put on cows. So, taking the yokes off us means to free the intellect of the scholar, because false religion persecutes the scholars.

I mentioned hemlock before. The philosopher (Socrates) was imprisoned and then they gave him hemlock to execute him, to kill him. It does not really mean they killed him, but they locked his "hem" that causes rigor mortis in his blood that feeds his brain and his whole body. That is hemlock. Hemoglobin has reference to blood, and a woman who was a sinner on the ground, she didn't feel clean enough to even stand up before Jesus. She just stayed stretched out on the ground. She touched the hem of his garment and was healed. The hem of his garment forms a wide circle, doesn't it? But that wide circle is down there, low, at the feet with the common man, and she touched it and was healed. She understood his social mission, that it was for the common people. It came all the way down to her. A sinner was healed, and as that song says, "How sweet it is!"

Muhammed Is the Only Prophet In History of the World

Muhammed is the only Prophet that is in history, not just in the history of his people, but in the history of the world; and he came into the history of world not just with

210

his life, but with his birth and with his works. He came into the history of the world, not just in the history of Arabia, whereas the others they are found only in the history of the people who claim those Prophets, and they came into the history of the world from their history. We know Muhammed, the Prophet, lived on this earth. We know his family members still survive. Where are the members of Jesus' family? They are trying to find James, the brother of Jesus Christ. They thought they found him. But just recently, in the newspaper, they said, "No". It turned out to be bogus, false! So, they don't have it. There is no record of it. I believe and I'm not asking you to believe as I believe. Believe what you're comfortable with. I believe that these other Prophets are types, only, and the type was not in a single human being, only. The type was in their people.

Jesus Christ Was Not An Individual Person

So, I believe the real Moses was this spirit and this condition for the human being in a few of the people called Jews. I believe that he is a plural body, not a single body; the same for Jesus, who said that he was a plural body, and said that he is for a sign. And Allah says (in Qur'an) that he is a Spirit and a Word from G_d. So, I believe all those figures were plural bodies, not one. Now, you want to know what is real? Look at what happened to the followers of Jesus Christ. Now, this is in history what happened to the Christians. What happened to him (Jesus)? Nothing. But they do have a record of what happened to his followers. They were persecuted. They were crucified, made to suffer, great suffering.

So, the crucifixion of Jesus, in my sense, is the treatment that the followers got. And what forced the Church to go up in the sky and not attend to matters down here on earth is all given in the Bible, in the language called, the crucifixion of Jesus Christ. That is what I believe. So, I see Jesus Christ, not as an individual person. I don't think he ever was a single human being, or person, but he was that type, that spirit, that life, that protest, and that determination to serve G_d for the good of mankind, in a group of people, not just one person.

Jesus Christ Was the Result of An Effort

Now, most likely, all groups have one leader, don't they? Yes, but I don't think that one leader was his own leader.   He was that group's leader, a representative of his group. In other words, he didn't have to inspire or educate a group of followers. They all were inspired. They all were educated, and they all were protesting, and most likely, they had a representative. But that is not the Jesus Christ I see in Scripture. That representative would not be that Jesus Christ. That representative is the Word of G_d. The Word of G_d goes into anybody who will receive it, and the representative is the Spirit of G_d. And the Spirit of G_d goes into anybody who will receive it, not an individual person. But in Muhammed's case, yes, an individual person. None of his people were inspired like him. He had to reveal himself and the mission to all of them, not in the case of Jesus Christ. And when you think about Jesus Christ, wasn't there people working for his birth, planning his birth? That is what the Bible tells us. So, he was their effort, wasn't he? He was the result of their effort.

Abraham Represents a Movement In People That G_d Inspired

And in the case of Moses, wasn't it the same? People were working for his birth. People were planning his birth. That is why they both are plural bodies. Even Abraham is a plural body, not a single man. He represents a movement in people that G_d inspired. Now, I told you I'm not asking you to believe what I say. Believe what you feel comfortable with. I know some of you from church life, you can't believe the savior didn't exist exactly as they told you. I love you, my Christian brothers and sisters!

I think they would call all the disciples of Jesus, Prophets, but they call them minor Prophets. And the word, Apostle, is used, instead of Prophet. You know, we used to call the Honorable Elijah Mohammed, Apostle, Dear Holy Apostle. They were disciples of Jesus Christ, his close people. Like the companions of the Prophet, they were disciples, too. They were his close associates, his disciples. In Western language, disciple would be what they were.

Now, the question is asked, was Paul a real person? Paul was real. He was a real human being, a real leader. But you know, whoever the Pope is, he's the pope, but he just can't come in his own name, can he? It is because they have a role for him that he has to play. He can't be left to be his own person. They give him a role and that's the role he has to play. So, Saul (Paul) was a person, a real person, but Saul, in the Scripture, is a role. It's more important to see him as a role, a role for a leader, not a person. That's all of them, all the human figures in the Scripture, including Muhammed. Would you believe that? That's including Prophet Muhammed, peace be on him. That's why the emphasis is on his sunnah and his uswa, because it is more important to see him in that nature than to see him as a person named, Muhammed ibn Abdullah, at birth. He said they (the Prophets) all had come to build a house, and one brick was left. What he was to be and do was already told in the design of the house, wasn't it?

Scripture says, *"Never was there a nation that He didn't send a warner to"*. It didn't say, "But in the future it has changed". No, we don't have a Prophet, but you'll have angels and Messengers coming to take care of the business whenever it's needed. That's why the Honorable Elijah Mohammed insisted that he wasn't a Prophet, but he was a messenger. However, the way he gave it, he left it confused, but he tried to clear it up. He said, "I'm like the mail man". He said, "I was given a message, and I've got to give it to you. It's your letter, not mine!" He said, "I have delivered the message, like a mail man". That's what he said, and I'm sure that Mr. Fard told him how to handle that, and I don't think he really knew, himself, how to handle it. But he did his best to defend it. He did his best, but I don't think he understood how to handle it, because if he understood how to handle it, he should have used Christ and the New Testament, not the Old Testament. Christ Jesus, peace be on him, he should have used him as an example, because Mr. Fard, obviously, was identifying himself with the role of the son of man in the Gospel, in the New Testament. The people, they called him the apostle, but he chose to say messenger and that was to say that "You don't look for the Muhammed of the past, or the Muhammed that's in the Qur'an, don't look for him".

My understanding is that none of them (Prophets) before him (Muhammed) were flesh and blood men... The history of the world, does it really have a record of Jesus Christ here on this earth? It doesn't, not for Moses either, none of them except Prophet Muhammed.

Job In the Human Design of All People

The Bible story of Job, that's talking about a whole people, not an individual person. It's talking about Job in the human design of all people, and it's pronounced, Jobe, but it's spelled j-o-b. The "Job" for mankind is to fight the temptations and remain faithful to his Lord. Even your own friends will turn against you. Your wife will say, "Why don't you curse that G_d you worship and die! If he's going to kill you, die! You'd be better off dead!" Whatever Allah has designed in His creation for a person you can't change that no matter what. There is nothing you can do to change that. Just have faith and patience and wait and see what Allah has coming for that design that hasn't manifested yet. Maybe it will be something I can live better with.

No Such Persons As Jesus Christ or Adam

There was no such person as Jesus. I don't think so, only as a type. There was no such person as Adam. They are single and plural figures, both of them. The first Adam, the second Adam, and there could have been a leading person during that time, leading that movement, but I'm sure there were others with him, and I'm sure, they said it was Jesus Christ. But they weren't talking about a single person. They were talking about the leadership, a changed leadership, change for the leadership of the Jews that were definitely inspired to see into things that they didn't understand at that time, about the conclusion of things, the end of the world and how the lifeline of mankind, all people, begins in ignorance and darkness, primitive life, and evolves out of that; and it takes a definite direction and different societies, different areas, go their own way.

Jesus Christ As a White Person Was the Worst Thing Done

Now, if we just look at religion as it has presented itself in the history of man, religion is where you find the Devil, the Satan, the oppressor. In the material world, or in that realm for the interest of man is the bigger Satan. You see, Satan comes in sizes, according to Al-Islam. There is the little Satan, the middle-sized Satan, then there is the big Satan. So, the big Satan is the one that aspires to get up to the seat of G_d and sit on that seat and present himself as though he is the G_d.

Now the figure of Jesus Christ as a white person, if that is not the worst thing that the world has done, tell me what is. To put G_d in the image of the race that works for dominance and uses racism to suppress people or to oppress and hold back one people and to free and advance another, the white and black people, white and black races, if that is not the biggest crime and the worst crime against G_d in religion tell me what is. They don't want you to talk about that, but if you saw those

Jews talking, they have no respect for Jesus Christ at all. Why? Because they know that they have influenced the Gentiles, who were pagans before, to believe in physical pictures more than they believe in pure knowledge. They convinced them to accept an image of a man as G_d, and they call him Jesus.

Jews Do Not Believe Jesus Existed

So, they really laugh to themselves about Jesus saying, "Jesus does not exist! He never did exist! Jesus is not real! That is what we gave them, because that is what will satisfy them. They were used to seeing G_d in their own image, so we gave them a god in their own image. But that is not something we recognize. That is not for us. That is for them. As far as we are concerned, he never lived. He never existed!" That is what they say. That is what is in their mind, not all Jews, but the great majority. They don't have to be orthodox. They can be modern Jews. All of them, the great majority, have no belief in Jesus Christ. You haven't even heard them acknowledge his existence, even less acknowledge of him as a Prophet. They don't even acknowledge he existed.

David a Picture of a Movement In Jewish Religious Thinking

David was a messiah. If you understand the Scripture, G_d says He anointed him (his head) with oil. So, David is the first of the messiahs for the Jews. But what is David, really? Is he a real person, or a person who has a real place in the history of civilization and mankind? No, there is no David. David is a picture of a movement in the Jewish religious, spiritual, and Scriptural thinking. That is all he is, a movement. And they say, "Well, we can't accept any messiah, unless he comes from the house of David! You made this person real! We can't accept him! He is supposed to represent a movement in the religious thinking of the Jewish people, G_d's only begotten!" They say, "If you can't show us that, we are not accepting it!"

Bringing Human Life to Its Best Condition

But what is G_d interested in? G_d is interested in bringing the human life to the best condition possible for them on the planet earth. So, obviously, they all had inspired persons that saw that and said, "This is what we have to hold on to, and we

215

have gotten away from that". So, it brought them back to it. Jesus Christ, as a figure, is representing a certain leadership, a change in the leadership, and was born in the religious community that had its traditions going way back. They had always treasured the sacredness of the human life, the human spirit, and human life in community. They always treasured that. The Qur'an says Mary is a sister of Aaron, talking about the mother of Jesus Christ, peace be on her. Now, you know she's too far away from Aaron to be his sister.

I don't teach this though. I don't teach this because it's too different from what most believe. Even the Muslims, you know, it would cause a bad stir among them. We shouldn't do it, but somebody is going to do it one day, though. Yes, the world is changing fast, especially, how we see things in religion, with religious reasoning, or understanding. You know, the leaders know these things, but they can't tell them, not all of them, not these regular leaders. They ordained themselves, so the others aren't responsible for them. They don't feel they're responsible for them. They let them just remain dumb.

Fard's Fiction

The Honorable Elijah Mohammed said the authorities accused Yakub of causing trouble, a troublemaker. They said, "You can't do that here" So, they exiled him and his followers to the Island of Pelan, also called Patmos, in the Aegan Sea. Yes, that's Fard's fiction that he created for us to see as reality and loaded it with insights. And once you get the belief that there's something hidden under here (and the Honorable Elijah Mohammed always would tell us that) and pursue it and pursue it, Allah may bless you with the insight. And when you see the insight, you're going to connect it with the Bible, with mythology. You'll connect it with world myths, Bible myths, too. And when you connect it all together, it helps you to come where you wouldn't have gone if he hadn't put that attraction there.

Mother Nature Is G_d's Time Piece

Christ Jesus and Muhammed, peace be upon the Prophets, they are not signs for you to look at them and say, "Son of G_d, great Prophet." No, they are signs for you to look at yourself and say, "The same possibility is in me to break the spell of this world, to get out of this cultural maze, and find the true light." What is the new time piece? The new time piece is the time of Mother Nature and no matter how much advancement this world has in science, industry, technology, whatever, it cannot change Mother Nature's time. It may think it is doing it, but it cannot change Mother Nature's time. Mother Nature is G_d's time piece. His time piece is bigger than yours and your seasons are going to be wiped out by His seasons. He is going to bring summer into your winter, and you are going to wonder what in the hell is happening!

Muhammed a Thinker Reflecting On Man's Condition

Wasn't Muhammed a thinker when he was looking at his people and began to bear on his heart the burden of their ignorance and their condition? Wasn't he a thinker when he went up in the mountain for seclusion and went into the mouth of the cave and stayed there in that cave, called Jabal Nur, now named for his concentration, meditation, up there on the mountain of the light? He was thinking and reflecting. That's the thinker. The thinker thinks and reflects, duality. Man thinks and reflects. He thinks on the creation or any single concern or focus on matter, on creation, human life, human misery, whatever. He thinks and then he reflects, like walking with the right foot and the left, or the left foot and the right. Think and reflect, this is the process that goes on in the mind of the philosopher, and it takes him closer and closer to the truth he's seeking.

Schools of Thought

Allah says, *"They did not fall into disputes or disagree until after the guidance came"*. So, when truth comes serious differences that people have manifest, and become private and public issues, and the truth gives support and helps that that they didn't have before. So, you have even Muslims, as the truth reaches them, they manifest their differences of opinion more. They stand out more.

So, in Al-Islam, we have all these differences of thought. We have the four old schools, or major schools of thought. There is the school of Maliki, which is in Africa, the one that most Africans have, and most of the Africans are influenced by big Sufis, mystics. This is not to criticize them. I'm just talking now. I am not putting down or anything. And we have the Hanafi School and the Hanbali school. Most know these major schools. The Shafi school is the fourth. Most of the learned leaders in Al-Islam, they accept all these schools. In fact, I do not know any who reject any one of the schools. Those are not the only ones. Those are just four major schools. In Saudi Arabia, there is the Wahhabi School of Thought, and the name is given because it was Abdul Wahhab, who taught them, and he developed that school. He was the partner with King Abdul Aziz As-Saud, the father, of all the successors to his rule, his sons, who became kings of Saudi Arabia after him. He is the father of all of them. He is one for whom the land was named, after being called just Arabia. He is the one for whom the country was named. So, we have Saudi Arabia. I don't think this was existing before 1918. This is kind of recent.

The Wahhabi School of Thought is not the only one. There are many schools of thought, though they don't make a big show or deal of it. They are closer to these more recent scholars and teachers, pious people, who devoted themselves to obedience to G_d and showing the society how to bring the society to conform to what G_d has revealed, and to what G_d has ordered. These persons are men, mostly. I don't know of any woman, right now. But I'm sure, in time, there will be females, too, who will contribute so much that there will be persons, students, scholars, belonging to the schools of thought perhaps developed, or headed by females. I can't see that not happening one day. Because of sensitivities and attitudes right now, we don't have that, but I believe that will happen one day. It has to happen. It is natural that it has to happen, because the men are not the only ones that G_d has created for this role. Women are also thinkers. The Qur'an says, *"The thinking men and the thinking women"*, to let us know that this is not the property of males, only. Thinking means that they (women) can be philosophers, too. In the world, we don't think of women being philosophers, but G_d showed Muhammed. He was the kind of man that would recognize that these women had intelligence like men. And as they become interested and give thoughts to these things, they are going to be philosophers, too.

We call them scholars, those who head schools of thought, but they are Islamic philosophers, Muslim philosophers, devoting themselves to the study of the understanding of Al-Islam. Philosopher in the world, the term may mean something that we don't accept for our thinkers. It could mean we don't accept it for our thinkers because their orientation may not be G_d. It might not be G_d focused. Christianity has given birth to many great thinkers, philosophers, so has Judaism, and so has all the other religions. Even the non-religious ideas, or non-spiritual ideas have given birth to so many wonderful thinkers who were beautiful humans, and who had an interest in the world and not just in part of the world. They had an interest in humanity, not just in a section of humanity.

Those Not Mentioned

So, we have to regard those people. And I believe when the Qur'an tells us of the Prophets that are mentioned in the book, *"And there are those who are not mentioned"*, that there are some of these people with this description that I'm giving you right now, that if we were to study their life and everything, we would have to say that these were inspired men. These were messengers to their people.

I wouldn't dare point to any philosopher I know of in history and say that he was a Messenger of G_d. I wouldn't dare do that. But I'm saying that among the thinkers that have served the betterment of human society worldwide, I'm sure that there were some of those that were inspired by Almighty G_d, by Allah, and they fit in with those thinkers that are called Prophets and Messengers of G_d.

G_d Initiated An Evolution

The Prophets taught science, but they don't give them credit for teaching science. Only in religion will you find the adherents and authorities in those religions referring to what the Prophets got as not only a message, but also science. This world called the thinkers, philosophers. The Qur'an's language that it established to identify a man as a thinker, a human male as a thinker, it also acknowledges that females are thinkers, too, even though the females were not among those great leaders in philosophy, that led the world in the study of human nature looking for truth. Philosophers are looking for truth. Their knowledge came to them because they were truth seekers, and their activity was as a thinker. They used their minds. They were thinkers. They are called seekers. Seekers with what? Seekers with intelligence, thinkers. The Qur'an makes it very plain. Evolved means you grew in knowledge as a thinker, and all the great communities we have on earth, today, they trace their civilization, or their knowledge back to thinkers. Whether you call them idealists, or whatever, among them were those who were guided by G_d, or who believed they received the religion, revelation, but as thinkers.

The Qur'an brings us home, back to the original meanings, to whoever identified religion with human nature, that actually, G_d initiated an evolution that was going on in the soul and mind of man and then completed that evolution by establishing Al-Islam. Al-Islam is described in Qur'an as a completion and a perfection. Perfection means getting rid of the things that were incorrect in it, and completion means to fulfill that which had not been fulfilled.

Great Wealth Is a Big Fish

"As Jonah was in the big fish three days, so shall the son of man be in the heart of the earth three days". *"In the heart of the earth"*, what is this saying? Jonah was in the belly of a whale. A whale is the biggest fish. He is the master of the water for the fish. He swallows the little ones up with no effort at all, except to open up his mouth. The current that he creates just sends them all down his throat. He's the big fish of the water. *"The heart of the earth"* means desire for the earth. Now, the earth has a good reading and bad reading, too, because Allah speaks of those who can't go heavily. They're heavily pulled down to the earth because of their love, greed, and desire for the earthly things. They're pulled down. They're heavily drawn to the earth. The earth gives us our sustenance, food, clothing, shelter, and many other things. So, *"In the heart of the earth"*, means because of worldliness, worldly appetites, he will be confined, imprisoned, like Jonah was in the whale. Now, wasn't that the same thing? Wasn't that material greed? But not material greed in the material world. It was material greed in the spiritual world. The big fish there, is a sign of great wealth. Great wealth is a big fish.

Greedy for the Sciences of the Earth

What does it mean when you say a man is a "big fish"? The big fish means the wealthy in the spiritual life. So, Jonah was a captive of the wealthy world in the spiritual life, the wealthy people of the spiritual life, and the predicament for the Word of G_d would be that it would be the captive of the people who were greedy for the material, who are greedy in the material world. They're in the material life. They're in the social life. They're in the community life, but they're greedy, too! What are they greedy for? *"In the heart of the earth!"* They're greedy for the sciences of the earth! *"In the heart of the earth!"* They're greedy for the sciences of the earth, not just the material. They're greedy for the sciences, because the sciences will put them in a better position than the man who just has the material wealth. The sciences will give him control over the ones with material wealth. The sciences will give him the material wealth and also control, dominance. So, he'd be the victim of the secular world. Don't think the secular world just came into existence. It's been coming for a long time. He would be the captive of the secular world, the world that wants to reorder the world upon exact sciences.

Jonah and the Whale

It was the big whale that swallowed up Jonah. Let me tell you something about that whale now, what most people wouldn't get from that story. That whale was better than Jonah, that is why it puked him out. Something bad on your stomach you throw up. First, the ship was better than Jonah, so the captain said, "Throw this man off into the water. He's the problem!" And then the big fish got him and held him until he prayed to G_d. When he prayed to G_d, the fish could not stomach him. The one who prays to G_d in bad circumstances, is that one put in a good light in the Qur'an, or in a bad light? In the Qur'an, Jonah and all the Prophets, peace be on them, are put in a good light. Is Jonah in a bad light like that in the Qur'an? It just says a big fish swallowed him, but did it say that he prayed in the big fish? That is in the Bible. And does it mention (in Qur'an) that he was on the ship, first, on the cargo? No, it just mentions that he met with a bad fate out at sea, and the big fish swallowed him and took him to land, which is all positive. But then sleeping on the cargo is negative, so he deserved being thrown out by the captain of the ship.

Jonah's Story Is the Picture of His People

The waters are raging because there was a storm and that put the ship in bad trouble. However, the cause of the storm was Jonah, because of Jonah being thrown off the ship. The reason for the whale swallowing Jonah up was Jonah. But the whale did not even like the mission that G_d gave it. It swallowed him up but could not stomach him. It headed straight for the shore with him and puked him out on the shore. That is all a negative picture. So, what the Qur'an is saying by not having those negative scenes is that this is not the description of the behavior or the spirit of a Prophet. This is the picture of his negligent, rebellious people, and this is the fate that they got into and the consequences for them was bad. You know it is the Bible that says, *"I have a three-day journey"*, not the Qur'an. The Qur'an says he was puked out upon the seashore and G_d had mercy on him and caused a gourd plant to grow up over his body and shade him from the burning sun.

So, he was not left to trial. What the Qur'an gives is the positive picture, because it is only the positive picture that is acceptable to be given the name of

Prophet. As I was saying, even the mentioning of a 3-day journey after he was saved from the raging waters and the belly of the whale says, "My troubles are not over yet. My destiny is a three-day journey and really, I set it back myself, and I am just free now to get back on the mission that I ignored and got myself into all that trouble."

One Day We Are Going to Arrive at the Destiny

In the Qur'an, it situates the Prophet Jonah on the seashore in a picture where he was rescued by G_d, and His Mercy was with him when he was puked up upon the shore, because G_d caused the gourd plant to grow over his body and shade his head from the burning sun. So, it is all positive. I think I have clearly explained it now... It is a bad fate, if you look at the consequences for a people who were rebellious. But if you look at the consequences for a Prophet who was thrown off course, then it is not a bad fate. It was a good fate that the whale swallowed him up, and it does not even charge him with being infested with commercial greed where his comfort is just being with the wealth and resting on it. That means depending on it. His comfort is sleeping on a pile of money he has.

What the Qur'an is saying is not in the description of a Prophet. This is a description of a greedy people that the Prophet was trying to lead the right way. So, the whale now, it can't make it outside of water. So, you have certain sensitivities that you share together and you're in the same boat, so to speak, but this time it is not man made. It is G_d made. The whale is G_d made. The boat was man made, and it went from a man made to G_d made vehicle. So, the people on the boat have a destiny. It is three days long, and not necessarily a journey for each, individually, but it is a journey for their purpose, all of them. And just like the whale (or boat) arrives at a destiny, one day, if you will stay with me, we're going to arrive at the destiny, and it is going to be much bigger than we can imagine.

Spiritual Establishment Ignored the Destiny of Jonah

America is a spiritual public. You know that. We are a people based in faith. We are spiritual and the spiritual establishment, they could not stomach Jonah. They ignored his destiny, and you know that is the reality today. Really, the establishment, they accept that we give up our future and let the commercial world feed on us. They accept that, but do you think they like it? Do you think they are happy with that? No, they don't like that at all. They don't appreciate our people who go after the perishable things in the world and don't make a real serious effort to elevate their souls, their inherent worth. So, when they see Obama and people like us, who meet the challenge of this world, and hold on to the mission to elevate the human worth, to lift the human person up as G_d wanted us to be lifted, when they see us struggling to do that and not giving up, they appreciate and value us so much. We are a big source of happiness and joy in their private lives. And I'm sure a lot of them are making it public knowledge or conversation when they meet each other, and I think that is what the Scripture is saying.

The biggest life in the water does not really like that people give up their destiny and care nothing about their purpose on earth or their purpose in life, and just live for those things that are transitory, perishing, all the time going away. That is what keeps a lot of our people down. They think, "Oh, the world is against us. It is not ever going to be for us. The establishment they do not care about us". But the reality is that they are hurt that you care nothing about your own life in humanity and give yourself away so cheaply. If you would just change the way you treat your own self, you'll find that they will be happy to welcome you in their situation, in their system. So, to me that is the message of Jonah being swallowed up by the whale, and the whale could not even stomach him. "This guy is ignoring his mission. I do not want him in me". He started repenting inside the whale and the whale said, "Hell, is that what you were guilty of? I can't stomach you! You've got to get your own! This is no free ride!"

So, Jonah's mental progression that is needed for the improvement of his life and the deliverance eventually of his life before G_d, Himself, is in the beginning, starting out in its first stage where he is completely ignorant. And you know when you come suddenly out of darkness into light, it hurts your eyes. You have to cover your eyes, sometimes, because you have been for too long in the dark and in such thick, dense, darkness that the light hurts your eyes, and when it says, "to cover his (Jonah's) head", it means burning his mind. Now this is not the eyes out here, it is the mind's eye. It is under so much heat from the light of day, and heat means, sometimes, pressure. Under a lot of heat means pressure coming from something. Here is this uneducated mind in the knowledge of the world system and how it exists and works. It is too much for him, so G_d had to cause a gourd plant to grow up. Now a gourd plant is a plant that has a lot of seeds, but a lot of emptiness. It does not have much meat. You can take the meat out. It is loose and hollow. It is light and there are mostly seeds in it. You take the meat out, and you do not have much left, a big hole.

An Ignorant Mind Is Like An Empty Gourd

Well, that is how an ignorant mind is. It is like a big, empty gourd, and it was once full of seeds before you emptied it. It was full of thought and ideas undeveloped, so many undeveloped seeds, so many undeveloped thoughts and ideas, so you are more curious than anything else. Take the curiosity out, and the head is empty. It has not put together much at all. But from that state of emptiness and ignorance, meaning empty-headed and full of curiosities, from that state G_d causes life to grow. And the life that grows from that gourd seed, it gives you shade that relieves your mind, gives it some relief while it is bombarded by so much knowledge and understanding that is in the light of the world. Do you know that song, "I wake up and the light hurts my eyes, and then I think of you, and the world is alright with me" (*Lovely Day*)?

The gourd is a protection, too. It means you're just beginning to try to survive the light of the world, and your head is empty, or you're ignorant in the knowledge of the world, but your head is filled with ideas that want to be developed, filled with thoughts that are curious. Curious thoughts, though that is your beginning, that alone will work to give you some understanding of what your circumstances are, and how you are situated in this world filled with light or knowledge; a whole world filled with light and knowledge and a great system that challenges you so much until it just puts you at a standstill to go forward in it. But your effort is there, even though you are in that situation where your head is empty except for curiosities, undeveloped seeds that don't help, except for curiosity. Your effort to survive in those circumstances will produce, start some kind of logic to grow inside of your life to support your life.

So, this gourd plant, it gives some kind of logic, and its logic is to pull up on something, because it is too flimsy. It does not have enough strength by itself, so it pulls up on your body that G_d created. You did not design your body, so that which comes out of the earth weak, empty, and not showing much promise, except as a lot of questions unanswered. However, if you will let that life live in you and let it form a logic growing out of the earth, taking root in the earth and then growing up and using your own life as its support, isn't that what we did when we didn't have any knowledge of the world? Didn't we use our own life as our support? We said, "I know this body is just like his. I know I'm a man just like he is. He called me a boy!" Now that is that gourd plant. That logic is growing up on that body.

For Dhikr the Lines Go Straight Up

I was doing dhikr with my fingers, and I know Scripture, believe me. I know the Qur'an. I was doing dhikr and the lines on the fingers go straight up, for the two lower parts, the lines go straight. The first one goes straight up. The second one goes straight. The third one goes in a circle. That's the universe. So, in Islamic dhikr, if you just start at the base, in the nature, and if you can just stay straight after the nature… Allah will eventually put you in the universe… You can be reborn and free. That's free! In the Bible, it's free. It says, *"And on the 5th day G_d created the creatures that fly freely in the heavens",* the birds, on the 5th day it says. According to Islam, it is on the 3rd day. We say the 3rd progression, only two progressions that take you into the heavens. Yes, they call it two progressions. The third situation is heaven. It's in the Bible, too.

Everything Starts With the Human Being

That's with Jonah, too, when he said, *"I have a three-day journey"*, and his being released by the big fish is symbolic of being born out of the womb of your mother, being delivered from your mother. And that isn't the end of it. You should ask questions. You're not supposed to think that that's the end. That's the end of that particular situation, but there's another situation to follow. So, it starts with our birth. Everything starts with the human being, the human body, and the human body as a sign, but it doesn't stop there. It goes from there to the signs that are in G_d's universe, the earth, and the heavens. And the big fish, if I say to somebody, "The big fish is the womb of your mother and the delivery of Jonah from the whale is the same as your delivery, or your birth from your mother", somebody might say, "Ahh, he doesn't know that!" Why don't I know, because I didn't say the rest of it? Why should I anyway? If I want to make that point, that's the point that I'm making.

"You Don't Belong In the Water"

Again, the big fish is the religious order. The Church or the spiritual world is the big fish, and the big fish swallows you up. But if you are rational, you can't be peaceful in the big fish. Once you get rational the big fish has no more taste for you. The big fish spits you out on land. "No, you don't belong in the water!" And that's what happened to Jonah, but both in himself and in the spiritual world. It has reference to both, not just one. And when he was spat out, he was spat out on a desert. The seashore is very seldom furnished with greenery. If it is, it is high up. It will be high up, if there is any greenery. The water is low, running very low. But if it is on the same level, the water will come up there and wash everything away and kill everything near the sea or the water. So, he was thrown out on something like that, and then the gourd plant tells you that there was not much growing there. It was like a barren land. The Qur'an says a little gourd plant grew over him as a mercy from G_d and covered his head from the sunlight, gave him some shade, and in that situation, he said, *"I have a three-day journey"*.

The gourd plant, it represents scarcity of food. The gourd doesn't give you much except a lot of seeds. It doesn't give you much. The gourd plant is like squash, pumpkin. It gives you a lot, but not much. It gives you a lot of seeds but not much meat that you like. You would take the seed part out and throw that away, and eat the outer part, the rind, the hull, and it isn't much. It's not much to like. So, that was Jonah's first situation.

All Life From Water

Now, you know the gourd plant is big, isn't it? And it's given in the Bible again, when it mentions the fig. Jesus came to the fig tree, and the Bible, the Gospel, says he cursed it because it didn't have any fruit on it. So, since it didn't have any fruit on it, he cursed it not to bear fruit anymore. I used to look at that and I'd say, "That's cruel, man! That pure, innocent tree, why would he want to hurt the tree?" Well, when I came to understand it, it is very beautiful. There's an English expression, "That's a figment of your imagination." So, the knowledge is still in the world. Evidence of it is this expression in the West, "That's a figment of your imagination", and "It's a figment". It's spelled f-i-g, fig, and it's "ment". It's a figment of your imagination. If you look at fig, you can see where the word "figure" came from, too. Nothing but figures, no problem solved, just figures.

All life is from water. What it means is the condition that you need to have life is water. If there's no water, life cannot have a beginning. That's what it means, that your beginning is in water. Now, we're not talking about the physical body, but it's true for the physical body. That's why they're saying that science and religion are coming together. It's true for the physical body, but it's not talking about the physical body. It's talking about the mind. The thinking process that brings you, eventually, to understand this universe, that's what it's talking about, and the beginning of that thinking process has to be in your sentiments. It doesn't form in your rational mind, first. It forms in your sentiments, in your feelings. You have to be concerned for life and the future of life and thinking starts there. That's the beginning of that thinking, in the water.

Inherent Perception

In the picture of Jesus Christ, in the New Testament, the woman is crying and using her tears, her water, to clean his feet, his foundation, what he stands upon. Actually, she uses her hair, her inherent perception, her strong perception. Like I've said, a gnat can touch your hair, and you know it hit, because it's as though the hair's roots go beneath the surface of the skin. So, hair is always a mystery and symbolic of the spiritual sense or the inner sense, the inherent sense, and it's in all animals. A rooster, when he is afraid for his life in a fight, his feathers come up. A bull or a dog, when he's in danger, his hair comes up. So, noticing this over a long period of time, man got the idea that this is the inner sense, and it's more powerful than seeing, feeling with the hands.

Phases of Moon Symbolize Thinking Process

Now, on the Hajj, when we complete the rites, we cut the hair. Its benefits are not enough to depend on. It becomes instinct, something that stinks on the inside. When the real thing comes, that's stinking inside. So, when you finish sa'iy (running between the hills Safa and Marwa), then you cut your hair. Running between two hills, that's all instinct, or all that inner sense can do is to go between one extreme and the other. It can never be free. It has to run between one extreme and another, like the moon. The moon starts with the crescent, and it goes out till it's black, and then it starts all over, again, and that just keeps going on forever. It can never complete itself! Every time it completes itself it has to die, die to what it thought was straight. That's all the moon is symbolic of your thinking process trying to find reality. Your thinking process, it goes from, in appearance, oppression, and it is trying to complete itself, and every time it completes itself it's not satisfied. It's not satisfied with its conclusion. So, then it starts throwing off what it has gathered until it gets back to nothing, again. It just keeps repeating that, like Sisyphus trying to get that big round rock up on the side of the hill. Every time he lets it go; it starts rolling back down the hill.

Man's Life As a Worker Under G_d Never Finished

So really, it's a process that takes us from innocent nature, straining. You're straining. It is the path of uprightness, and you are straining your nature. If you're straining your conscious, you can preserve the innocence of your nature and become that life in conscious, and you're still striving for reality, striving for the whole truth. Eventually, G_d is going to reveal to you, and you're going to come into the freedom of the universe! Man's life as a worker under G_d is never finished. There is too much left for us to be idle or retired. So, as soon as we complete something, no matter how important it was, we should, right away, devote ourselves to another task.

The World Has No Control Over the Word of G_d

It says, in the Bible, or Gospel, *"If they say he's on a mountain top"*, or something like that, or *"If they say he's in the sacred chamber, don't believe it"*. It goes on to say, *"As the light shineth out of the East even unto the West..."* to give an explanation, meaning that really, he won't be in the heart of the earth. Really, he won't be in the heart of the earth! The world has put him there, but what they will put there is what they have control over. They don't have control over the Word of G_d. Allah has control over that. Now, you'll think, *"They put him in the heart of the earth"* is saying the same thing, meaning he would be a victim. The people of the ascetic life, that order of the Christians, weren't they the captors of the world of material sciences and government and everything, Rome, and others? And it didn't just start with the cross being like it is given. The cross is a sign of the world, the earth. That's what it's a sign of, and it's no new thing. That's the way the Qur'an traces the origin of the cross, back to Egypt, traces it back to Egypt and when Isis crossed Osiris' path, she formed a cross in the sky. She formed a cross in the sky of herself, her path, and Osiris' path. The path of the two formed a cross in the heavens, and you can go see it right now in the museum like I have seen it. They have something they call a heavenly cow, sky cow, and it's got crosses all in it, crosses all over the body of the cow. It will take too long, if I tell all of it. In that connection there's so much more, but it will take too long.

The Fish That Traveled Straight As In a Channel

Sensitivity is the fish that has the typical behavior in water, random movement, no definite movement. Whatever attracts it that's where he goes. The fish that the wise man wanted to show Moses escaped them, and the Qur'an said it was the fish that traveled straight as though in a channel. So, that is sensibility. That is not sensitivity. Those who go like they are wandering, that is sensitivity, and that is our public. They left their leaders who were leading them in a channel, who had channeled the way to heaven, leading them in a straight line or in a definite direction for a purpose and a conclusion. They left their African American leaders up from slavery and they are all going out on their own, and now we are nothing but a bunch of fish, little sun perches, blue gill, or whatever, in a fishbowl, and the commercial man is giving us a treat every now and then.

This reality is beautiful, and to show you our people were not small-minded Marcus Garvey said that "One day his people would rise up and take their place among the galaxies of stars in the heavens." So, that man had insight. He was on the money! He knew that this world had something over our heads and that heaven wasn't all about this thing that we are falling out in the church over. He knew that for the common people it's an exercise in emotions. But for the knowledgeable people, it is just a higher reality for us in the reality that we're in already.

So, those big controllers of wealth and big planners of the futures of these different human groups down here on this earth, they are the ones who have mansions in the skies, and they travel with the stars. They have their organizations, but they are so big in comparison to ours, light years away from our perception of reality. A light year could be two inches by our calculation down here, but I have to travel eons of time to get from here to two inches away from the reality I'm trying to reach. See how the dimensions change for the mental state? And to describe it you can't describe it like it's across the street. No, it is not across the street. You have to travel for light years to reach this conclusion, light years, not dark years, and look at year. Just take the "y" off, "light ears", ears that light has come into. Light comes into the hearing. So, no matter what man does with the physical reality that G_d gave us, he can't do anything but keep complimenting the pattern, keep complimenting and glorifying the G_d Who did it. Even though he rejects the G_d, what he does still glorifies G_d. The original that G_d did, glorifies G_d. You can try to do anything you want to with it. You can take it backwards, forward, sideways, whatever you want to do, cook it, but everything you do is going to glorify the same G_d, because all your possibilities are within His Scheme.

Two Fish and Five Loaves of Bread

In the New Testament, it is said that Jesus Christ fed the multitude with two fish and five loaves of bread. There is five, again. The word, "multitudes", gives to our minds the picture of a lot of people. This was not a regular gathering of people. This was a great gathering of people. It is really a future picture. It is not talking about the one back then. It is giving to the mind the picture that he had gathered a great number of people around him back in that time, but it is a projection. It is talking about the future, that there will be people from different nations, multitudes of people, and they will be fed by five loaves of bread.

Now, Prophet Abraham, in his true picture as an intelligent human being called hanif, stood upon two feet; two fish and five senses, five loaves of bread. What is bread? How do you make bread? You take what looks like dust, called flour. It looks like dust, and you begin preparing it, add water, and to suit it to your taste, milk, or whatever. You put something in it that breathes into the bread, called yeast. You put yeast into it and the yeast breathes into the bread. And the breath of the yeast causes the bread to swell. It becomes lighter. It won't be flat bread. It will be dinner rolls, loaves of bread. You put it in the heat after you cause it to rise, and the heat cooks it. The heat makes it rise more. Heat expands things, right? It rises and becomes a beautiful piece of bread.

A Seed Is a Promise

The smooth skin on the top looks like the skin of a newborn baby. Then you say we have bread. You eat the bread. The bread comes from a seed of plant life, called wheat, and the wheat grass grows very tall. It stands up very straight. It stands upright, straight. This is all symbolic, metaphorical. That is what the language is. Why do you need heat? Heat can be love, but heat can also be passions that have gone to the extreme. When you submit the life that exists now only in a promise, you can hardly see it. It's like a seed. A seed is a promise that you're going to have wheat grass, or you're going to have corn stalks with ears of corn. So, it is for human life that G_d creates before it evolves, or blossoms into what Allah wants to bring out of it. It is like a promise, and the promise is small, unattractive. It is not exciting, like the seed of something that is going to become a beautiful picture. In its seed, it is not attractive. It does not excite anybody.

Bread Symbolic of Your Intelligent Potential

The human seed, if you the subject it to passions of love, and fire those passions up, make them very hot, whether they become passions, destructive or not, that fire that is cooking this bread, if you put it on you, it is going to kill you. It will burn you up. Put you in the oven with the bread and you will die. Put some life you have with the oven, with the bread, it is going to kill it, destroy it. But the bread survives it, doesn't it? It is because the bread is symbolic of your intelligence and your intelligent potential, those five senses, five loaves of bread. Subject it to extreme heat, subject it to an environment of extreme passions where it is unbearable for life to exist there, and you may die. Your whole generation may die, but eventually, the essence, the intelligence, will survive in others, and just their experiencing the burning furnace, or the burning oven is going to inspire in them new hopes in the intelligence, a new straining of one part of the human intelligence to overcome these difficulties and do things.

Wheat Grass As Human Urges In Our Intelligence

We look back at the history of how the five senses survive, and how they bring intelligence in new opportunities for us, we look back at it as something that started with an unattractive thing, like a grain of wheat seed, of grass. But it stood its life up straight, and it attracted mankind to want to taste it and want to eat it and want to feed his own life with it. Now, we're not talking about the wheat grass as wheat grass. We're talking about wheat grass as human urges in our intelligence that want to stand us up straight, and then we're going to feed on righteousness, on uprightness. And as a people in the history of the world, we're going to struggle much. We're going to come through much heat. We're going to even have animal essence in our bread. But the animal essence is going to be influenced by the heat and come under the effect or influence of the heat, and in the environment of our bread, the uprightness, even the animal is going to contribute to enlarging the mass.

"Let Us Break Bread"

It's going to become bigger, but lighter and more chewable, not so tough to chew with your mental teeth. All of this is talking about human intelligence, the mind. Then you're going to look back on it. One day you're going to look back on that history of how you came from a little unattractive life just wanting to be upright, and how that life, under the influences of society straining and tormenting it, turned out to be a beautiful loaf of bread. Here is man reviewing the history of his rise from an unattractive life, but wanting to be upright, and turning out to be a civilized, blooming society, a blossoming and blooming world. And he sees it as something coming from a wheat grain, and now it's a beautiful loaf of bread. When they sit down and say, "Let us break bread," they have much more on their mind, if they know what they're doing than what we think when we see somebody saying, "Let us break bread." Praise be to Allah! Those who break bread with this knowledge, they are qualified to protect civilization for the future. Praise be to Allah!

Moral Thinking and Moral Life In the Water

So, what are the two fish? The two fish are the ability of your mind to see left and right, to see ahead and behind, to see down and up, to see truth and falsehood, to see decency and indecency. Isn't that how the moral mind works? So, the two fish are moral thinking and moral life in the water. The two fish represent the moral life in the water of intelligence or in the soul, that has intelligence to look and make distinctions, to distinguish between truth and falsehood, to distinguish between darkness and light, to distinguish between indecency and what is decent. This is an important, fundamental life activity in the human intelligence. The Qur'an says He began all life in water.

The man had been formed in the earth, but he couldn't progress until G_d caused it to rain upon the earth, and then he fashioned the man. He was already there, but he had not been fashioned. Then Allah calls the heavens to rain and wet the dry ground, and then He formed him and breathed into him of His Spirit, or His Will and he became a living soul. Know these things in their more appreciated language. Get the language that is more appreciated. Language as an old mythology says, "Eat the food of the gods, ambrosia." We are not of them, and we don't have their position. We do not take their position. Their position brought the world down, but what it points to is good. Their selfishness is what was bad, but the higher knowledge is good. This is not higher knowledge in the secular world. This is higher knowledge in the spiritual world. That is the knowledge that brought the world into existence, the higher knowledge in the spiritual world.

Joseph Sold for Twenty Pieces of Silver

They sold Joseph for twenty pieces of silver. This is better than Arabic. If you have this in Yiddish, it is better than Arabic. They sold Joseph for twenty pieces of silver. They betrayed Jesus for thirty pieces of silver. This is the Bible. This is for imams and students who study the religion to understand the things that are not explained or are not obvious.

They betrayed Jesus Christ for thirty pieces of silver. So, here is Joseph representing one orientation in the mind, or in the mental make-up of the person who is serving or striving for something. For Joseph, it represents moral nature. His rational mind was moral. He did not have a rational mind that was secular. He was a perfect man in his moral nature; Jesus Christ, too, but Joseph typifies or represents that, whereas Jesus Christ represents a spirit.

Spirit Is the Third

The spirit has three. My rational mind has two, essentially, thought and reflection, or thought and memory, thought and questioning, thought and examining, thought and re-thinking. That is the mind. That is the nature of everybody's mind, thought and re-call. Joseph was not like the average person who just thinks for whatever situation. Whatever the Prophet Joseph did or thought, it was governed by righteousness, or moral conscience. He refused to do wrong, even when it would help him a lot, personally, to do wrong.

If he had satisfied the big lady, the wife of the ruler, who wanted him for her man, he could have gotten a lot, because she was the big boss's wife. He could have gotten a lot from her, but he refused her, and he refused those ladies under her who wanted him, too. He was accused by the lady of being forward with her and he was saved by his shirt that was torn from behind. It showed that the lady who wanted him was holding him, so that was the proof that he was innocent.

Jesus Christ Is Three

Jesus Christ is spirit, and spirit comes naturally. Before it reaches the conscious its nature for us is just to be good, to be innocent, to not to want to do wrong. So, the spirit is in our body, and the spirit is good in the body. Then the spirit comes to the mind. Flesh, mind these are the stages. The baby is born flesh. The baby becomes conscious and now his spirit is in his mind or expressed from his mind, not only from his body. That is two, and you know we said body, mind, and we just mentioned Joseph, Yusuf, in Arabic, being typical of the mind, thought and reflection. That is the second.

The Third Dimension Is Purpose

Why twenty? Why not one, two or three? All of these are conscious dispositions. Joseph's conscious disposition, what he was in mind, that is the second part, i.e., body, mind. So, here is the twenty. Jesus Christ, his was by G_d, Who had put the spirit in him. So, he was not conscious of all these things that were working in him. The only thing he was conscious of was his spiritual life, but it is not manifested for him. He is being motivated by G_d. He doesn't know where he will go tomorrow or what he must do. He is guided by the Spirit of G_d or the Will of G_d, so this third dimension, for want of a better expression right now, is purpose. How do we know this? He said, *"I have to be about my father's business."* This is the Gospel, the New Testament. That means he has to do what G_d ordered him to do. That is exactly what he meant, saying "G_d has given me a job. I must do what G_d gave me to do." This is what he said.

Jesus: A Word and Spirit from G_d

So, he was saying that his purpose in the world was to do what G_d ordered him to do or what G_d had assigned him to do, that his purpose was to do that when G_d moves us or when G_d inspires us. He, himself, represents now not the rational life. Jesus Christ, himself, represents the spiritual life. We know this from Scripture also, from the New Testament, and also from the Qur'an. Jesus Christ represents the spiritual life, not the brain with its intuitive powers, like Joseph, Yusuf. He represents the spirit and the spirit in him is the spirit to take him to his purpose. Where does that spirit come from? It comes from him struggling to obey G_d, so his spirit becomes the spirit of obedience to G_d, and G_d will protect that spirit. If you give your spirit to G_d in obedience to Him, G_d, Himself, protects that spirit. He assists that spirit. G_d, Himself, will assist that spirit. You don't know all the time how you will handle a situation. If you are in that disposition, if that is your makeup, you trust G_d. Another way of seeing this is to look at what Jesus told his disciples. He said, "Don't prepare any notes. Don't prepare any speeches." He said,

"Just go and when you get there the spirit will speak through you". According to the Gospel, this is what he told his disciples.

He represents not only that, but he was a teacher who was promoting that kind of trust in people. "Trust G_d. You don't know, we don't know". He was their teacher saying, "I can't tell you everything" and he said that. He said, *"I speak to you now in parables (proverbs) meaning I can't explain all of this to you, but nevertheless I will return and speak to you in plain language."*

"Now you are speaking to me in parables. You're my teacher, what am I going to do? You are telling me to go to this country and speak to the people there. What am I going to do?" Trust the spirit, that is what he told them. Don't prepare anything. Just go there and G_d will speak through you. The Holy Spirit will speak through you, that is what he told them. That is how he taught. What does that have to do with thirty? He is conscious of obedience to G_d. He's conscious of giving his spirit in obedience to G_d. The spirit represents the third, body, mind and spirit. Someone may ask, "Is that for we children, also?" Yes, when you were a baby, you were careful to listen to your mama and you daddy. You get up a little older and you start giving them the deaf ear, and soon you're acting on spirit. So, the flesh was born innocent. Your mind was the second dimension. Your mind was turned on and your mind was at first obedient, then you gave up the conscious effort to follow your mama and daddy, or whoever you should be following. You gave up the conscious effort, and you gave your behavior to the world, to your friends, and to the world. Now, you're not thinking about the right and wrong of things, or whether you should go home now or stay out a little later. You're following your spirit. You have a spirit to stay out all night.

Everybody Moves In Three Dimensions

So, everybody moves in those three dimensions. In your flesh, you act according to what your body wants, like when you are hungry you eat. When you have to go to the washroom, you have to go to the washroom. That is your body. Then you act in your mind. Your mind says, "Well, I have to eat, but it is more important for me to stay here and listen to what the Imam says. I'll eat later. I have to go to the washroom, but I think I can hold it." So now, your mind is ruling over your body. The first one that ruled is not ruling anymore. When you were a little infant, it's gone! The diaper is ruined, and you start crying. You're hungry, you're thirsty, you start crying, and the body says, "Give it to me right now!" It does not say, "Well, mama is busy!" A little infant can't think like that: "Mama is busy, I have to hold this."

Man Created to Be Dominated by Spirit

That is how they go. Your first dimension is your body, the rule of your body, then the rule of your mind. And then your mind, if you don't discipline your mind for G_d's sake, your spirit takes over, and if your spirit is not under G_d, the Spirit of G_d, you go astray. You become self-destructive, destructive to others and other things. Eventually, your spirit destroys you. So, man (the human being) is created to be dominated by spirit, because none of us can guarantee the society that our body will never do wrong. And none of us can guarantee the society that our mind will never do wrong; none of us, no matter how much you are educated. There are Ph. D.'s who go to jail for petty crimes, for shop lifting. There are Ph. D.'s who can't live a decent life, because they have become alcoholics or drug addicts.

So, there is no guarantee that you're going to be saved by your body or by your mind. And there is no guarantee that you're going to be saved by your spirit, unless you give your spirit to G_d, like Jesus Christ did and like Muhammed did, and like all of G_d's Servants did. If you give your spirit to G_d in obedience to Him, now you're really saved. You're saved from the limits of your own mind or the weaknesses of your own mind. You're saved from your body, your mind and your spirit that would be loose on their own, if you bring your spirit under G_d.

Superman In This World

Actually, it is the spiritual dimension that is the most important. A man who has become mature in his spirituality or in his spirit, he is superman in this world that we know now. If he has become mature in his spirit, and he gives his spirit in obedience to what is correct, proper, right, and just, that is what we want. We all are trying to get there. Jesus Christ is a Word and Spirit from his Lord. So, he typifies or represents in his type of man the spiritual life, how the spiritual life must be disciplined, and has to stand up to tests, because the world will try to take you out of that spirit. The Satan will come at you, himself, and this is written in the Scripture about Jesus Christ.

In the Nation of Islam's teaching, I found things that I couldn't accept. But long before that, the Honorable Elijah Mohammed had me as a minister for him and I was dealing with the Bible, and I saw so many things in there that I couldn't accept. I said, "Look, the G_d in this Bible is psychotic! He is suicidal!" I preached it from the rostrum, and believe me, I got young men to stand up and accept their own, many of them. I don't think anybody heard me and went out of there the same. Once they heard me, they were better. If they didn't accept the Nation of Islam, they were better off themselves, and better off for other decent human beings, once they heard me talk, because I dealt with nothing but what is reasonable, what is rational, what is logical, what is good and decent for human beings, what should be decent to G_d. The first time I was afraid. I was afraid of the wrath of G_d, but I said (I actually said this in my mind), "Well, if this is you G_d, if I'm wrong, and this is really you G_d, doing these things, if you have a court, I'm going to defend myself in Your court. I'm going to charge You in Your court!" And I meant it. I was a boy, and I meant that. "If this is You, G_d, then you're wrong. And I'm so convinced you're wrong, I'm going to prove you're wrong! Maybe we'll do away with G_d. There won't be any more G_d, because if you're the only G_d, I'm going to do away with you!"

The Bible a Book of Pure Intent

I'm serious. That is the way I felt, and G_d was with me. G_d helped my mind develop more and more, travel more and more, see more and more, until I came to really know the Qur'an as a perfect and clear book. And I came to know the Bible as a book of perfect and pure intent. The intent is pure and perfect, but it takes you on a nightmare trip to the destination, and the last book is the worst nightmare of all, John, the Revelator, the book of Revelation. Now, you talk about a trip, I had a hard time getting through that book. I made up my mind to get through it. I read the Bible from cover from cover, every word. I didn't miss a word. I got through Revelation and there is really some way-out stuff in there, like a man on an LSD trip. But after I got through it and reflected on it, I could see it all. It is powerful and beautiful! I can now preach the Bible from Genesis to Revelation and bring out the beauty, point to the purity, and show that there is a consistent vein or line of purity going from Genesis to the last word in Revelation. It is not broken. It is continuous. No matter how crazy and confusing it looks to you, it is a holy book. It is a sacred book, and the intent and purpose are pure and not lost.

Think about Muhammed, the Prophet. This is supposed to be hadith. It might be legitimate. I believe it is legitimate, but it doesn't have to be, because they wrote so many hadiths and claimed the Prophet gave it. They say he saw his cousin, Ali, may G_d be pleased with Ali, with a Bible and he was reading it. So, they said he said to Ali, "Oh, Ali". That is the way he spoke to everybody. He wasn't like these new Muslims saying, "Brother Warithudeen, Imam, Dr. So and So". He didn't call anybody doctor, or imam, nobody, mister, etc. He called everybody by their first name, by the name they were known by. That is how he addressed the people. He said, "Oh Ali, is not my Qur'an that G_d sent me with enough for you?" And that is all that was said, and Ali didn't reply. He said nothing, meaning he felt shame, and he did not say anything.

They Don't Want You to Know What Is In the Bible

I don't believe this hadith is correctly reported, even if it happened, because for one thing, the Prophet wouldn't have stopped there. He would not have left the impression that Ali should not read the Bible, when the Qur'an mentions the revelation that came before to Jesus, over and over again. It even says to the pagan Arabs who were doubting Muhammed, the Prophet, that they should consult the Christians, the people of the book, to have them give them certain knowledge that they never had or had never been exposed to. They were told to consult the people of the book to give them that knowledge, so they could understand where Prophet Muhammed was coming from with a lot of things he was saying, because they had no knowledge of the Jews and the Christians.

I can't believe that he would do that without explaining that to him (Ali). The hadith should have said, "I see you frequently reading this book", then I could understand it. But just that he was seen with the book (Bible) in his hand that wouldn't be a reason for him to believe that Ali was preferring the Bible over the Qur'an. However, the leadership in the so-called Islamic world, they don't want you to go to the Bible. They don't want you to know what is in the Bible. Once you become a Muslim, they want you to stay away from the Bible, why? Because they know that the Qur'an and the Bible go together, that the Qur'an is a reference to the Bible, and the Bible is a reference to the Qur'an, if you understand it, and if you make the connections for those two references, you're going to become as wise as they are, or wiser than they are.

You Have to Be Freed

They are afraid that you will become as wise as they are or perhaps wiser than they are, because they have blocked their own minds out of certain things that they can't even get, because they are so narrow minded. Maybe you'll be a little more open minded or freer to think, and maybe you'll become their leader. That is why they don't want you to make connections. But thank Allah we came from the Church. My father and my mother came from church. We had Bibles in the house, and Mr. Fard said, "Look in your poison book". He called it poison, but he said look in it. He didn't say, "Stay away from it" and he told the ministers to, "Use the Bible, because this is what your people are used to. Use the Bible to get their attention and pull them out of the world of sin". That is what Mr. Fard told my father, not only my father, others, too.

These things are very easily understood, but you have to be freed. You can't be a slave to a way of thinking that won't take you to light or take you to the river. You have to be free of those things. Thank Allah, I was freed of them. I had no problem with anything. I wasn't hung up on anything. I wasn't hung up on anything wrong, no matter how holy it looked, or no matter how much they said it was from G_d. If my mind says it looks wrong, it is wrong, and if it is right, prove it to me. If it is ridiculous, I don't have any patience. You take it yourself. It is not for me. My G_d is not ridiculous, so I'm not going to accept anything that you say that is ridiculous about Him. The human beings that I know are not ridiculous. So, I'm not going to accept anything ridiculous that you say about him. I don't care if you're the Holy Ghost, the Holy Spirit, or the holy Pope. I don't care what you are. If you bring something foolish to my mind, you're dropped! You're no more holy and perfect to me. Your image dropped in my eyes, and I don't have to listen to you, don't have to respect you at all. If you don't like me, you go your way, and I'll go my way. I am not going to bother you, and I don't want you bothering me. That is the way I've lived, and that is the way I'm going to live, until I'm dead, unless G_d, Himself, changes me and I don't think He'll do that.

Muhammed Established a Consultative Order

Jesus Christ is one who had to be taught. He had to be baptized. Not that he had to be baptized, but he was baptized, according to the New Testament, and he was taught, according to the New Testament. Muhammed, the Prophet, was also one who had to be taught. But who taught him? Nobody but G_d. G_d was his Teacher, and what he didn't know that he had to know in order to do his job or his mission, only G_d was his Teacher. Now, you know, Muhammed, the Prophet, was a person who established a consultative order, where the leaders, rulers, made decisions after consulting one another, consulting the best qualified in character and in knowledge. They met together and consulted one another, and then addressed the problem, discussed it, and came up with a decision.

That is what you call the democratic process. Muhammed, the Prophet, established that long before there was any republic, or democracy in this part of the world, before America, before Britain, or the United Kingdom. But you can't find anywhere in the Qur'an or in hadith where the Prophet went to anybody, except his wife, upon the first experience he had with G_d. He came to his wife, and she was unaware of what was going on in his life, and he told her about his condition, what he had experienced. He was in fear, and she calmed him and told him she had an uncle who was a Christian, and perhaps he could help him understand his experience. So, she did have her uncle talk to him, and he told him, "What is happening to you is good, and you shouldn't be afraid of it". There was a Prophet mentioned in the Scripture", and the uncle said, "I believe you are that Prophet". The uncle had complete faith in him and everybody else did, too, because he was established for being truthful and was of the best human character, already. Before he met G_d, he was established as such a person.

G_d Taught Muhammed and Jesus Christ Himself

Jesus wasn't made a Prophet until he was in his early 30's, but there he is speaking in the cradle a long time before G_d called him to make him a Prophet. G_d had revealed to his mother, not to him. It was many years. It had to be at least close to thirty years between him speaking in the cradle and him really receiving revelation from G_d to guide him and his people. We must understand then that Jesus Christ was already in the Muslim nature, the upright nature. He was upright in life from his birth and never lost that uprightness, that innocence, that human purity that Allah gives every child at birth, or while they are in the womb or bodies of their mothers, Muhammed, the same for him. He had lived an upright life for forty years, never worshiping idols, never doing wrong, or giving himself to bad behavior, or exhibiting any flawed or bad character, and G_d called him at forty years and then he began to speak the Words of G_d to the people after forty years. Jesus Christ spoke in the cradle. Muhammed, the Prophet, when he had to make a decision that was going to affect others, especially his following, or the community of Muslims with him, he would ask for certain ones that he knew had knowledge and experience that might benefit the effort of trying to arrive at a conclusion or decision, if they were invited to participate. He would call them by name and have them come, and they would look at the situation and make a decision.

But I repeat, when it came to revelation, he never ever went to anybody and said, "Can you help me understand what G_d meant by this?" G_d taught him, Himself, as He taught Jesus Christ. G_d gave Muhammed everything of revelation, and he didn't get help from anybody. Jesus Christ couldn't get help from his mother. His mother refused to help. She pointed to him, and the child spoke while he was in the cradle. That is important to know. Some of you will understand more than others.

Jacob Wanted Insight In Religion

Benjamin and Yusuf were half-brothers. I'm pretty sure they were half-brothers. Rachael was the one he, Jacob, really, wanted to marry. The old man wouldn't give him Rachael. He had to marry Leah, first, and work seven years for Leah. Then after he worked for seven years, he thought he was going to get Rachael, but the old man told him, no, that was for Leah. He had to work seven more for Rachael. I like to study names. I believe Rachael means "I saw or see with the eye" and also the feathers of the bird. The feathers of the bird enable the bird to fly. Any bird that is naked can't fly. So, Rachael is the one who knows Scripture and Jacob wanted to get that knowledge, insight, into inside knowledge, into the religious order. He wanted that inside knowledge, scriptural science. Spiritual science, that is what he wanted. The old man, Laban, gave him Leah, and it means the natural world, dunyaa. Now, you can see how hurt he was. He was saying, "I'll give you this world, that's all I'm going to give you". So, he had to work seven more years. All these figures are just symbolic. They are mythical or symbolic figures. So, he had to work seven more years for Laban, and Laban means, milk, cheese, or it can mean both. Laban is usually a thick milk, like yogurt. He was the head of what we call, now, the secular society, not the spiritual, but his daughter was head of the spiritual society, Rachael. The other daughter was head of what you call secular society, or the dunyaa. So, one represents the dunyaa and the other represents the spiritual life.

Jacob wrestled with his brother Esau and won; he was victorious. Now what it means is that he was successful in outwitting the social order, or the social society,

Esau. The workers, the industrial people, that is Esau, who was taking care of the family. Who does the family depend on? Industry. You have to have jobs, money. So, he was over the family, and he was over the workers. If he was over the workers, he was over the family. If he has the jobs, he is over the family and the workers. You may say, "Does this man know all this?" Believe me I do. I know it well.

Jacob Became Israel

Jacob was called Jacob when he was doing those things, but now that he's going to look for a wife, he is not Jacob anymore. He is Israel, and Israel is Isra'il. He is the one who managed to get way up. Do you know Jacob's ladder that ascended and came back down, that he saw angels going up and coming back down? Well, Isra'il means that he, himself, went up. He ascended and what brought him to ascend was his knowledge to outwit the social order, or what you would say would be the society.

Now, he outwits them. What does he need next? He needs the spiritual order, it's high. He wants Rachael, she flies. So, he goes to get Rachael, and to get Rachael, look at the tricks he pulls. Laban, he's the protector of the social life like a mother protects her children. That is why they call them his daughters. He is like the high priest, and he is protecting the society, but he doesn't have the knowledge. He is kind of dumb. His daughter, Rachael, has the knowledge, not him. He knew that she was much more valuable than Leah. That is why he would not let Jacob have her. He knew that she was much more valuable to him and to the society than Leah, who was the dunya, the worldly order.

The Mother of Civilization Is the Moral Nature

So, Laban is not a bad guy. He has to be moral and ethical in his makeup because he is preserving the moral life for the people, and they call them his daughters, both the spiritual world and the material world (dunya), because the mother of civilization is the moral nature. It gives birth to civilization. The first stages of the growth or development of society are moral, industrial, but when rule comes it is moral just like it is for a family. The authority of the mother is moral authority. She wants all the family members to be right by each other and if they are not, she will enforce it. That is Laban, too.

Scholars Pictured As Cows

What happens is Jacob, he wants to know how to outwit Laban. Laban is a goodie, goodie, but he is not out there with him, so he gets deceived, and Jacob is successful in taking over the education of the people. The scholars are pictured as cows. He had the cows drink from the water, but behind the water was plant life; so, he stripped the bark off the plants and showed them as white and green. So, the cows are drinking the water, but in the reflection of the plants on the water, they see it as white and green. So, he educated them and taught them that morality and development are all in nature. That is what he is teaching the scholars, that it doesn't come from high up revelation, or anything like that. It is all in nature.

So, when the scholars bought that from him, they stopped following Laban, who was using Racheal and Leah to keep the mind divided. One is the material rule or authority, logic, and the other one is the spiritual rule and spiritual logic. So, he has to separate them, and he had control over his daughters. Therefore, both the world and the spiritual order were catering to him, and he was keeping the mind divided, separated, just like it is now in this world. Jacob told them, "Let's make a deal". He said, "All the cattle that are born reign-streaked will be mine, and the rest will be yours". He set it up so he (Laban) wouldn't get anything. All of them were his. All of them came out reign-streaked, because he had them drinking from the water and set something up to influence their thinking and change their beliefs. He made a deal with Laban saying, "Give me the freedom to teach the scholars and if they buy my logic, they will come under me. Those who don't buy my logic, they stay under you". Laban agreed to it, and he agreed to have him marry, be the husband of Leah. That means he let him run the material world for him, but that is not what Jacob wanted.

Benjamin Did Not Want to Stop at a Storehouse

Those are the schemers. You see, in Egypt, Joseph goes to Egypt, and he is put over the storehouse, the distribution of material goods, then he could help his brothers. But he wasn't satisfied just to help his brothers. He wanted Benjamin, the right hand. He said, *"How is my brother?"* He was asking about his brother, the one he was really interested in and who he wanted to help. He wanted Benjamin to join him, because Benjamin does not want to stop at a storehouse. He is going all the way to the top to become the supreme ruler. Scripture (the Bible) says, *"Sit down on my right hand and run the affairs down on earth"*. That is those who are scheming and telling how they are going to do it.

Seven Is the Spiritual Potential In Man

Seven is the spiritual potential in man and working seven years for it, the spiritual potential, also serves the material world. So, before you can become truly enlightened, with no mysteries of the spiritual life, you are striving not for the material life, you are striving for the spiritual life. But striving for the spiritual life is going to first bring your rational mind to see the material life. You will see that first. Once you see the material life, then you are qualified to ascend spiritually and get the spiritual insight, ascend in knowledge to get the spiritual insight.

So, it seems like he was tricked. He wasn't tricked. That is how it has to happen. But Jacob was disappointed, because the ruling order, which was Laban, would not let him go straight to the spiritual and become the ruler there. Just like once a Jew told me, "They said we couldn't go to Miami Beach. We bought Miami beach!" So, that is Jacob. Laban said, "You can't have it". When he says, "You have to work seven years for it", that is saying, "No, you cannot have this". Seven years means G_d has to help you. "If you are not going to get it by me, you have to get it by G_d". So, he worked on himself, really, and elevated himself so high that he was able then to get Leah, the daughter, the material world. He ascended in knowledge to the extent that he could actually govern the material order.

What Is Planned for the World

Laban, he is a mystery rule. He doesn't mind, if you're qualified. As long as you get these things going, he doesn't mind. He has things going well. So, Laban, when he had to sit in counsel with somebody, other leaders, he would say, "Look, what Jacob is doing for us. He has this material thing really blooming." Once Jacob came into the material knowledge, that is where the sciences are hidden. It is hidden in the material world. The sciences for the spiritual world are hidden in the material world. So, when he got to rule that, then he saw how to get Rachael. He (Laban) died a man, twenty-one. He was a man before and he died the man. It means he was not defeated. He just allowed things to happen that benefitted him. He was still a natural man, and he was still following the natural sciences. He was a natural man following the natural sciences, the hidden sciences, but in the natural world. But he, Laban, didn't believe in giving the general world anything but milk. Jacob outwitted him and made, forced him, to have to reckon with Jacob. So, when Jacob became Leah's husband, then the world got more than milk. He started giving them the sciences for the material world. So really, the Jew is telling what they planned for the world, not what they did. That is not past tense. That is the future tense, saying "This is how we're going to get it!"

If You Get Enough Money Rachael Is Ready

Jacob wanted Rachael, and Reuben, one of his sons, was out in the yard and there was a mandrake there. According to the Bible, the mandrake was like an aphrodisiac, so it helped get Rachael ready for him, because when he brought the mandrake back and he gave it to Rachael, she conceived. When you look at the mandrake it is like the ginger root. It is strong, solid. That was Jacob's son that he sent to the field, Reuben, by Leah. Leah is Rachael's older sister, because Joseph and Benjamin are not born, yet. The mandrake is just what it looks to be, stout, strong, and in the earth. He wants to be strong in the material world, but the man of the field has to help him do that. It can't be a domesticated man. It has to be a man out there in the work field who knows how to root into the establishment, into the ground, into the material reality. So, the industrial establishment is strong and solidly rooted. That is what that is saying. If you get enough money, Rachael is ready to go to bed. It is like an aphrodisiac that turns them on, and the spiritual world is like that right now. If you have enough money, they will go your way.

Bible Written In a Way to Protect From Heathen Rule

The ones who rigged the Scripture, they did that, first, to protect themselves from heathen rule, to hide the knowledge from the heathen rule and not let the heathen rule know exactly what they were all about, because the heathen rule would try to wipe them out. So, they deceived them to make them think it was sensual, sexual, and materialistic, like they were. If you look at Scripture and do not see into it, you are not looking for the moral excellence, beauty, and wisdom; if you are not looking for those things, you are just reading it as literature. If you are materialistic, you will be comfortable. If you are lascivious, you will be comfortable.

They deceived the ruling order. The ruling order said, "They are alright! This Jesus is like Bacchus! These people are serious! They are not just saying these things, they are serious. If they can get the masses serious like that, we won't have to worry about them anymore!" Bacchus was a wine god. So, they deceived the ruling order. There is a saying, "Give me your tired and your weary." That's to win over the ruling order, thinking, "They are going to take this burden off us. These hard to discipline, troubling masses we have, they are going to take this trouble away from us! Let them have them!"

The World Is On a Blueprint

According to the Bible, Samson defeated the Philistines with the jawbone of an ass. So, that is the same thing as, "Give me your troubled from these masses. Give me these unruly masses." He came riding in on a donkey, telling the ruling order, "See how I control these boys? They don't give me any problem!" The ruling order says, "Okay, let him have them". They didn't know Jacob wasn't just working for Leah. Jacob was going to get Rachael. He is going to get the highest, and he's going to conquer them. He is going to conquer their highest people in the spiritual order. He's going to get them. When he gets them, then he is the boss. So, it is not something that happened long ago. It is a blueprint! The world is on that blueprint.

He Is Not Going to Worship His Teachers

I think they thought that the Nation of Islam would eventually have a leader that could understand the hidden knowledge, but they did not see, like they always miss, that when he gets that knowledge, he is not going to worship his teachers. He is going to be on his own, on the job! They thought it was going to be me. They thought I was going to be the leader, and they thought that when I became the leader that I would follow the rational over the spiritual, and then they could come in and finish teaching me. They actually thought the leader, in those circumstances, would come out favoring rational and material. He would be moral, but favoring rational and material, and not be so devoted to Scripture; that he would refuse to be influenced by anybody else, they did not anticipate that!

Man, and the Universe as Mates Created for Each Other

"Man, and the universe as mates created for each other: It is timeless relevancy." That is an excellent topic. So, that is what time it is. Religion and science are coming together. That is what they're saying, that is, man and his mate coming together. He's going to get his wife back. Everything has to be seen connected, if it is Scripture, G_d's Revelation. If it is G_d's Revelation or communication to mankind, it is connected. If it is not connected, then somebody has misread it.

"If You Had Not Plowed My Heifer"

The Bible talks about Samson, who said, *"If you had not plowed my heifer, you would not have broken my riddle, my secret"*. His heifer pulls the plow. It is a cow, like a bull, oxen, pulling the plow, but he said it's his heifer. Why did he say his heifer? Because this is a young woman. You didn't get an old woman. You got a young woman. But that is all he had to do, get a young woman, and she put his eyes out. They cut his hair, and then they put his eyes out. They fired up the fire, put it close to his eyes and blinded him. So, getting back to the point, what is it talking about saying, *"Plowed my heifer"*? Plowed, that is, a garden, farmland. Well, Adam was put in a garden and given the responsibility for it.

So, when you plow it, you're making it productive. You are accepting your responsibility for it. When Allah tells us through Muhammed, in the Qur'an, that the garden, the space of it is as the width of the heavens and the earth, and He is going to give you a garden that you will inherit, that means it is your natural right. It is your nature to have it. It didn't say you will get it as a gift. You will inherit the garden. So, that means it is naturally yours. It is yours by nature, your natural property by virtue of your nature. So, the whole universe becomes the garden.

The Real Help Meet Is the Universe

So, what is it telling us? It is telling us that the garden in Genesis is not talking about a physical spot on the earth. It is not even talking about the whole earth. It is talking about the creation, all of it, because in the Qur'an, it says *"The width of it is as the heavens and the earth"*. So, the real help meet, the mate, your wife, is not only the earth, but also the universe. And it is not just the mate of your biological body, which it is, too, because we are one, material creation. It is one, consistent whole, the material creation. So, it is true, literally, but what it is really talking about needs interpretation, and that is man's mind was created to digest the universe. That is exactly what man has been trying to do, and he has made a lot of progress. You know digest does not only mean with your mouth, but you have *Reader's Digest*. They say, "Food for thought". That will let you know this world is not crazy. It's not ignorant. It is not backwards, we are. That is why they have the world, and they have the light. *Reader's Digest*, that is where we want to be, not cannibals. Kindergarten is the innocent garden. Shaytan made the garden G_d gave us not innocent anymore. But the way G_d brings the children here you're working with that light. You're working with the kinder garden. Praise be to Allah!

247

Turn Us Back to the Age of Sixteen

Mr. Fard said he was going to turn us back to the age of sixteen, and some of us were really hoping to be sixteen again. I was a boy and heard that. I doubt if I was more than twelve or thirteen years old, and I never thought that I would actually be physically like sixteen again. Allah protected me. It was nothing spooky. I did not take it that way. I am looking for what you mean. I know you're not talking about being sixteen. I am twelve years old now, and when I get to be fifty years old, you are going to turn me back to sixteen years old? I know that is not true, so what are you talking about? It is saying that you will get a spirit to understand the life and the environment with your intelligence, and you will be a supporter of correct education. *"Thy kingdom come, and Thy will be done on earth as it is in heaven"*. When that time comes, the believers are going to feel like they are sixteen years old. So, Allah says in the Qur'an, *"He feeds us from the earth and from the skies"*, and He says, *"He gives us, every living thing, its needs, provisions, in four measures."*

So, four from the earth and four from the sky, and when they are reconciled, *"Thy kingdom come."* The language is consistent all through the Scripture. Ezekiel said he saw four living creatures go up, ascending to the heavens, with the faces of a man, human creatures, a wheel within a wheel. Now you take one circle and put it on top of another, what do you have, what does it look like? A circle on top of a circle is, 8. It is an 8. You take one square and put it on top of the other square and what is that? Eight. And after you have been fed, what do you say? You say, "I ate (eight)". There is no accident that those sounds are harmonious, they are homonyms.

Delilah Is Samson's Choice Students

The Qur'an mentions four heads of cattle in pairs. That will be eight. As we said earlier, the cow is nothing but a scholar. So, when Samson said to those who captured him and put his eyes out, *"You would not have solved my riddle if you had not plowed my heifer*, he was saying, "You got my secrets from my students, my scholars that I made". So, the woman who was there with Samson, Delilah, that is his helper, and she was very attractive. It means his scholars (students) that received divine guidance and wisdom from him. In the eyes of the world, they were so attractive. They were put into one figure called, Delilah, and he prepared Delilah, his own student, prepared her for the takeover. She cut his seven locks off.

They used her. Those are his students. Those were his choice students, and they were the ones who gave the secret of his power to his enemies through themselves. They are put into one figure, but those are his students, and how do I know this? Because he told his enemy, *"You would not have broken my riddles if you had not plowed d my heifer,"* and his heifer was Delilah. Delilah cut off his seven locks and locks imply secrets, l-o-c-k-s. So, it was hair, but the hair represents his secrets, and how is the hair secret? Because the hair is a metaphor. It is not real, either. The woman is not a real woman. The hair is not real hair, but the hair is a metaphor, and if you see the metaphor, then the metaphor refers you to, or suggests the language that you need to really understand what it is saying.

Now your skin is for touch into you, but hair makes it more sensitive. It makes the sensation stronger. If a little gnat flies onto your hair, you know it. It is like communication lines that go to the skin and a little bit under the surface of the skin to the very nerve endings. So, you just do that, and you feel it. Just touch it lightly and you feel it in your skin. Well, the more penetrating sensation or the stronger sensation, stronger than the natural, the ordinary, is what you get naturally at birth. These are feelings that become worldly. You use them so much in interacting with each other that the skin becomes the feeling that the world gives you. But the hair is the inherent ability to sense what is going on. You know it is funny, around the world, even among the American Indians, they thought the hair, if you take the hair, you steal the soul. So, they scalped the white man and thought that they took his soul. It is superstition, but originally it had science in it, and they lost it. There are people who had it. I guess they went astray. They just lost the connection and became just superstitious.

It is obvious that the hair represents a deeper sensation or a deeper awareness. Animals, dogs, bigger animals, when they do not know what to do and they are in danger, the hair raises up on their backs, on the back of the neck, mostly. That is that deep sense that is telling them, "Don't run up to this! You might regret the consequences, and it will be too late!" So, it is a deeper caution. A deep-rooted caution, or your inherent intelligence. That is what it is.

Some People Will Just Sell You Out

So, he (Samson) was sharing that with his students. The senses that we get that we work with in the world, they are not as beneficial as what G_d works with. G_d works with our inherent nature and our inherent intelligence, and when He wakes it up, then you have a special man in the leader. This is your spiritual sense (hair), and this (hairless skin) is a social sense, or social sensitivities and sensibilities. So, the hair is spiritual sensitivities and sensibilities, always the two go together. It might be asked, "Did Delilah willingly betray her leader, Samson?" Well, did Judas willingly do that to Jesus? Some people will sell you out, that is all. They see something bigger than you, much bigger. They are impressed by it, and they do not have the insight that the leader has.

No Veil Between Allah and His Servant

Allah says, "Nothing is between Me and My servant, not even a thin veil", and in Al-Islam there is no priesthood, because Allah said that nothing, no mediator, is necessary. "You want to help My servants? Good, I will reward you for being a good servant. But if you don't help them, they are still going to get My Communication, eventually, because there's nothing between Me and My servant, not even a thin veil". That is referring to Moses. He spoke to G_d, but behind a veil, and in his ascent up the mountain he spoke to Him by reference. G_d spoke to him and gave him a reference, but not directly. In Judaism, Moses spoke to G_d behind a partition like a veil, and when the Pope, priests, take your confession there is a little veil between you and them, and that is from the same thing: "You can't see My face. Don't talk to me directly," because he is supposed to be representing G_d. Higher governments leaders they are all the same, most of them. Even if he doesn't speak to you, he has someone for you to speak to, not directly to him.

The New World Is Enlightenment and Justice

I was in Saudi Arabia once and this king, I knew he spoke English. He goes to the United States talking to the president speaking excellent English, but I have to speak to his interpreter. I said, "I don't speak Arabic, I speak English", and I wanted to tell him, "You do, too! You speak better English than I do, and you have me speaking to this guy." I turned to him directly and I saw his face a couple of times, and he was offended that I spoke directly to him. And they call them samor sheik, his highness. With the king it is his majesty, but all his brothers, all the princes are his highness. That is the way the world is, but it is going out. The new world is coming in all the time, getting bigger and bigger and growing for thousands of years, getting bigger and bigger.

Religions Obligated to Give Equal Access to All

The new world is enlightenment and justice where people get what Allah created them to have, access to whatever any other human has access to. If you don't want it, you don't have to have it. If you don't qualify, it is not anybody's fault to find you and qualify you. We have an obligation as people answering what we believe to be G_d's design for man on this planet earth. We have an obligation to at least not treat anybody unfairly, but equal access to all, that is not the situation, not even for religion. If we wait on Saudi Arabia, Egypt, and those places to give us what we need in Al-Islam we will never get it. Waiting on these visitors who come over here preaching to give it to, you will not get it. They will never give you something that they think may open the door for you to rise equal to them, or maybe above them. So, they are protecting their superiority. That's it in reality, and I wish that our community would accept it, at least the leaders, so the people are influenced by leaders who have their eyes wide open, and not having closed ones, like Popeye, one at a time. So, en sha Allah (G_d Willing), everything is going to be fine.

Chapter 6

The Reality of G_d

I have come to understand G_d's Presence in the material world, and I don't preach this, because it will border on some other religious teaching more than on ours from the first appearance of it. But I'm convinced of what Allah says of Himself. He says the whole sky, He controls it. He has it in one Hand, and the earth in the other Hand. That means the works of man's life in one Hand and the works of the natural creation in the other, that He has both of these in His Hands. It means in His control. So, that means to me, especially now that I have seen more evidence… but even before I received this kind of evidence that I receive now in my life every day. I said to myself, my thinking, "This is my body. My body is my body, and my body is influenced by my life, my intelligence inside of it. Even when I'm asleep, my body won't roll off the bed. It stays on the bed. And if I've got something pressing on me, my body wakes me up, lets me know it is time to get up. 'You got enough rest! I got enough rest! You get up and go on and take care of your business'." That is my body.

He Is the Apparent and the Hidden

And if a little gnat crawls on the tip of my toe, and the shoe and sock are off, I know it. And it is no big thing for me to take care of that little gnat, saying, "Oh, a little gnat is on my toe. I can continue to write my speech. He is not worth me giving my attention to. He is not harming me." So, I said to myself, "Now, how much more is G_d in control of the universe that He made with his Two Hands? And He is present everywhere". This is the teachings. If He is present everywhere, it doesn't mean He is present outside of everything. *"He is the Hidden and the Exposed"*. In English, it means He is the Apparent and the Hidden. He is what shows. He is what appears before your eyes, and what does not appear before your eyes. Baatin, means that which is inside. What is another word for stomach? In Arabic, it is, "butnun", and it comes from, baatin, and it is inside of your body. That is the interior. This is your stomach. What is in there is the interior. So, it is about center the whole structure. So, for the inside, in Arabic, it comes from the word, stomach. He is the Hidden, but it also means He is the Exterior and the Interior. So, it (Qur'an) says, *"Whichever way you turn, there you will find the Face of G_d"*. It says don't worry about East and West. In case you are out and can't find the direction, you have no compass, pray to G_d. Don't say, "I don't know which way to turn. Pray to Him, for whichever way you turn, there you will find the Face of G_d". It means you're facing Him no matter which way you're looking, and He is the Exterior and the Interior.

See G_d As Existing Within His Creation

So, that brought me to see G_d as really existing within His creation, all of it, no matter how far it extends into space, or no matter how far space extends. We don't even know that concept. That is a mystery. Space is a mystery. Do you know that? It is a mystery because you can't come to the end of it. You cannot even imagine the end of it. There is nothing in the human imagination to imagine the end of space, because whatever he imagines, that is space. It is occupying space. Allah says, *"Think not that your creation is a bigger thing than this creation of Mine."* So, I know just like we use our body (and more so because we are limited), and like we are conscious of our body, G_d uses the whole creation, universe, all this space, and it is no burden on Him at all. Our body is a little burden on us. To know what is happening, to take care of it and everything, it is little burden, maybe a big burden for some people if they get some trouble in their body. But just for ordinary functioning the body is such a small burden that it is serving you, and you are not even conscious that it is serving you, like many things my hand does I am not conscious of that. It is doing that automatically. My eyes are batting, my breathing is automatic, and everything is no burden. It says Allah manages the heavens and the earth and it causes Him no fatigue, and He does not need to rest from anything. It says, *"He neither slumbers nor sleeps"*. So, it says, *"No just estimate have they made of G_d"*, in their effort to try to perceive Him in His totality.

Allah Hovers Between Man's Heart and His Mortal Life

They translate, "qaadirun," to mean, "Allah is overpowering". He is overpowering and overpowers everything. That's one, but there could be several other expressions that are there, I am not sure. But the one (in Qur'an) that says, *"He hovers like a bird"*, gives you a picture that it's like a bird. It doesn't say bird, but it gives you a picture like it's a bird, gives you the picture like He's as a bird. He's inside of your own being, and He's between your vertebrae, the backbone, and the spinal column. He's between the spinal column all the way from where it starts to the top of your head, and the ribs. Now, you know the ribs are in the front and the spinal column is in the back. So, He is between that. That's where the heart is. It says He hovers between that, between those two extremes, the ribs, and the backbone, or the spinal column. A bird is symbolic of spirit, and it puts in your mind a Spirit, that He is fluttering like a bird, standing still in that place, fluttering. You know some birds stand still in the air, not going forward or backwards (i.e., a hummingbird). They just pause right in the air.

So, that's the picture you get in your mind. So, it says Allah is between the ribs and the spinal column. Now, you know the ribs respond to spirit, a metaphor for the air. Every time you breathe, the ribs respond to the air, respond to the breathing. This is the spiritual logic, and the one that goes up to your head is the rational logic. So, He is the One that preserves your life, your spiritual logic, and your rational logic, because they are not the same. The spiritual logic and the rational logic are not the same. But the spiritual logic is supported by the Unseen and the rational logic is supported by the Seen.

Your Intelligence Is a Plow

And in the Qur'an, Allah says, *"And there is a plot, a piece of land, that He forbids that anybody plow in that area"*. It means you are not to go in there to discover what's in there with your brain. That's the plow. Your intelligence is the plow. You are digging to see what's there, to see what you can do, how you can work with it. Well, you don't bring your intelligence into that one area! You respect the Gardener. That's His sacred spot and He, only, should plow in that area. So, I can't tell you anything else about that bird, hovering!!!

G_d Is Everywhere

But it's beautiful! And what is this to tell us? That G_d is everywhere. You know Mr. Fard even said that? He said Allah is an All-Seeing Eye in the heavens and the earth. Isn't that what he said? So, if He is an All-Seeing Eye in the heavens and the earth, Mr. Fard even said He's everywhere. And He's seeing everything and no matter where it is, He's there to look at it. You know, the animal world, that's for man. *"Sakarah ladhi samaawaati wa maa fil aard, He has reduced everything that's in the skies and in the earth to service for man"*.

We Are G_d's Sanctuary

So, animals, the trees, etc., that's for us. It is not for G_d. So, what is for G_d? Our obedience. Our souls and our obedience, that's for G_d. So, He is more in us than He is in anything else. He is more active in our souls, in our hearts, and minds than He is in anything else. So, we are His Sanctuary. Yes! It's wonderful! And when you know this, oh, it brings you such peace! It brings you such peace of mind and faith, great faith, and it protects you from foolishness, from your own foolishness, because a man can trip up from his own ignorance, can't he? When he knows anything, he has busted his head.

They Were In Bondage to the Secret Knowledge

The Egyptians have a cross. If you take the head off that cross, it is the one without the circle on top, and what they put that cross on is the cow. The secret cow in Judaism, the Egyptians had that long before the Jews had that knowledge. The Jews are just responding to what was already in existence. They say they were in bondage to those people. I don't believe that. They were in bondage to the secret knowledge, and they are saying, "We were slaves of this, but G_d gave us a liberator and educated him into the sciences of the Egyptians, and gave him superior science", because Moses had to do battle with the leaders of religion under Pharaoh, and he was victorious. The proof that they couldn't defeat him is in the parting of the seas. There was no parting of the seas. In reality, it is the science of psychology. He and his people were able to walk across the sea to leave Egypt on dry land, and Pharaoh's army pursued him. When they came to the same area that he crossed successfully, safely, they couldn't cross it. The sea waters came in and drowned them. That tells us, beyond a shadow of a doubt… when I say, "us", I mean those who G_d blessed with insight. It doesn't tell the average person anything, except a story. I laugh at it, because it is ridiculous, and I thank G_d that we never were influenced to believe such under the Honorable Elijah Mohammed.

Mr. Fard saved us from being open to that kind of stuff. We didn't believe it. It is common sense not to believe it. When we see a great wind coming, I guess a tornado could do it, and for as long as that tornado is raging no one can cross on that dry land. They would be sucked up by the tornado. A tornado could cross a river and take all the water out of there and when it passes, the waters could come back together. Maybe that is what Moses was, a tornado in the life of the Egyptians.

That was for fun, but it is good. My story is more real than theirs. It has more logic. It is easy to believe than the way they give it.

Mr. Fard Had the Secret Sciences

After Moses and his people crossed the river, the army came behind them and the waters converged and drowned the army of Pharaoh. In the human psyche, all these things can happen and Mr. Fard, I am not saying he was the best Muslim. I don't know. He was the most courageous and the most selfless, giving of himself and expecting nothing for it. He definitely had these secret sciences. That is evident for me. He said, "Islam is mathematics, and mathematics is Islam, and it could be proven in no limit of time". What is he talking about? Secret science. If you study the philosophers of Islamic sciences, they have discussed the number one as a concept and as a reality and they have talked about the number one in connection with G_d as One, and they have used it to say things of G_d. You can't start mathematics, or arithmetic, without one, and every number after one is nothing but one, repeated. Two is one, repeated twice. Ten thousand is one repeated ten thousand times. So, you never can get away from the one. They say G_d is everything... For Him are all the most beautiful names. Once you reduce the whole you have a fraction and when you reduce to a fraction, you still have to have the one, because you're still working on part of a one, less of one. How far can you go reducing one? Forever. And how far can you go multiplying one? Forever, backwards and forwards, but with one. First, you have to have a concept in your mind. Was Mr. Fard wrong, when he said, "Islam is mathematics and mathematics is Islam"? No, because he studied and knew the great philosophers of Islamic sciences used mathematics, the figure one, to help themselves. The scholars and others did this to understand the reality of G_d.

Everything Speaks a Message From G_d

If Allah is G_d and He says everything that He has done speaks His message that He wants to reach man, then mathematics is a science, and it must also speak a message from G_d. Everything speaks a message from G_d. Muslims aren't the only ones. The Jews and all people before had this same idea; not only them, but the American Indian also has the same idea. I think several tribes, embraced this idea, saying everything in the earth and everything that you can visualize or see in the environment or surroundings, has a message. So, it is natural for man to come into that kind of belief, or understanding, that all these things have a message for the human mind in their concept.

You see animated films and they are doing a great job. They are so entertaining. They are better than watching people on film. Anything that has motion in appearance has life. What was that one movie that had tools? It was, *Robots*. They were nothing but metal gadgets, tools, but they gave them life that animated them. That goes back to primitive man in his religion. People in religion believe everything has a soul, even the things you make have a soul, or if you find it naturally, like a stone or a tree, it has a soul.

Everything Has a Soul

Someone might say, "He shouldn't be discussing that superstition of people". Allah is the Creator of everything. It did not say, everything, but man-made things, because G_d works through man and man thinks he is doing it on his own. But G_d created him to do those things and G_d willed that he does those things. So, whatever he makes, still, G_d is continuously creating through His creation, both the human and inhuman things. G_d says, *"He has given everything something of His Ruh, His Spirit"*. So, is the African, or other people wrong to say these things have a soul, or these things have spirit? I say they are right. Everything has a soul, even what you make. A table, once it is made complete, even if you don't complete it, it has a soul, it has a spirit. It has its matter. It has energy. Don't get spooky and crazy! I don't mean it has your soul. You're thinking about your soul and spirit.

G_d's Intent and Will Is In Everything He Made

Your soul and spirit are something from Allah for your life to have you living, and everything that exists has something from Allah, something of Allah's Nafs, or Spirit. What does it mean when Allah says that He has given everything something of His Ruh? What is He saying to us? He's saying that His Intent, His Will, is in everything He made. Nothing can exist, except it comes from something that He already put into existence. It can't really come forth, unless it comes forth upon the laws that He already put in the matter. How can it escape His design on it? How can it escape His Intent for it? How can it escape His Will? That's the answer for everything that exists.

One Day the Earth Is Going to Punish You

Allah made the earth, nobody else. He gave it its nature, and He made it to yield benefits to human beings, animals, creatures, but more so to human beings. If you abuse that earth, one day it is going to punish you as though it is a living thing. Science is starting to use language like that, referring to dead things as having a soul and as being an organism, or organ, though we know it is not an organ or plant life. Why? Because they want to bring people closer to the language of revelation, so that they won't stay in kindergarten, Sunday school, or the life of fairy tales anymore. Just like my stomach is fed up with that kind of stuff, the leaders of science know that the public is getting too educated to have them exist in fairy tales, lies. So, they are, gradually, trying to reconcile the logic and language of science with the logic and language of religion, and they are doing a good job. Thank Allah! It is time for it.

Peace Is G_d's Warrior

Peace is G_d's warrior. Allah does not war for any reason except peace. Can you buy that? The only reason why G_d will accept war is that it is for peace. So, it is peace that wars. Peace is making the war because peace is denied. Peace is making the war, because peace is not respected. So, if it is denied, or not respected, then Allah's Will in the matter will prevail. G_d's Will is also the design for that matter. G_d's Will is not only the will in the matter, but it is, also, the design in the matter. It is because of Allah's Will that this creation has this beautiful and orderly picture. That is Allah's Will being expressed in the matter, and we learn from the matter how to see Allah. We can't learn by looking at Allah. He escapes all attempts to see Him. The Qur'an did not say one vision, but in Qur'anic Arabic it says, *"Laa tudrikuhul absaaru"*, translated, *"No vision can catch Him."* But we can see Him, as He told Moses, indirectly. He told Moses, *"If you want to see Me, look at the mountain"*. When the Prophets and seers in the Bible are all having the same makeup, they are like the philosopher, who has good intentions to better society, to better the human family. They are all seers and Prophets. Even the philosopher, he is a seer, and if he is well-meaning, Allah approves of his effort, rewards his labor, and he is able to make great contributions to the betterment and advancement of human society.

Allah says they did not fall into disputes or disagree until after the guidance came. So, when truth comes serious differences that people have manifest, and become private and public issues, and the truth gives support and helps that that they didn't have before. So, you have even Muslims, as the truth reaches them, they manifest their differences of opinion more. They stand out more.

The Original Man Is Transparent

The original man is transparent. In the dark, you can't see him, and in the light the white man says you can't see him. He pretends you can't see him. "We're not visible". Now, it's not all white people. The racist crackers, they pretend saying, "I didn't see anybody." The original man is our soul. Our color is the color of faith, and faith does not need light. That is the original meaning of black in Scripture, not just the Bible. I found it in Buddhism, in Hinduism. It is in other major religions. They identify the choicest of colors as black and out of black comes white. You see Yakub's history about grafting the white out of black, that's madness. But the truth is that people, "They are like a pearl that is down in the mud, before they are governed by science, knowledge, or leaders. The child, the baby that comes to the mother, it came from that mother, therefore, its nature is to trust what it came from. So, its life begins in faith. It doesn't know who that woman is. It doesn't know that woman's name, but it has faith in what it came from. And that really describes the whole idea, or the whole concept I have in mind when I tell you that human life starts in faith, not in the light of the sun or in the light of knowledge.

That child comes here trusting its mother and its mother takes care of its needs, so that strengthens the bond of faith and love, doesn't it? It is dependent on her, trusts her and loves her, so that is the beginning of the growth of his soul and his spirituality. Now, his soul is growing, taking form. It's becoming bigger and more dimensional because he is feeding on his mother who he trusts and loves. And if you think about the child, he grows up and he follows what he trusts and loves, doesn't he, if he is normal? That's right in the world, too. He gravitates towards those things that he can trust and love. He ends up marrying some girl, woman, he trusts and love. And if he becomes a real leader, he is going to bring the people together in trusting each other, believing in each other, not just believing in him, and loving one another, hence the Prophet said, "You'll never enter the paradise until you have faith, and you will never have faith until you practice loving one another".

"The Stone That the Builders Rejected"

These are the same two circumstances or conditions that exist for that baby to have life and grow and join the men one day. Jesus Christ said, *"Before the foundations of the world I am."* His foundation is the foundation of life that G_d created for human beings. It existed before this world was built, or before they conceived the idea of building the world, it was already in the creation of G_d. The stone that the builders rejected, they reject that stone, but one day they are going to have to come back and pick it up and put it in the corner where the right angle is, so everything will be on the square. All you need is one right angle, and you can get the other three. Just put a straight line from each side of the right angle and you end up with two walls and do the same thing on the other, and because the angles are equal, you have a perfect square. Now, you can build a perfect building. I like that the Masons say, *"The stone that the builders rejected has become the corner"*. That is referring to the Ka'bah, and the original man. It means man in his original nature that G_d gave him. That is acknowledged in the Constitution: "We hold these truths to be self-evident that all men are created equal." They have one creation from their Creator, but they didn't say Creator in the beginning. They said that "All men are created equal and are endowed with inalienable rights, among these, life, liberty, and the pursuit of happiness", and they should have left it just like that. They don't have to say who did it. We know we didn't do it. Leave it for each man to say it. Those who want to say matter evolved, then let them say that, if they want to. We know the Designer did it. Now, they are coming up with this idea and they call it universal intelligence. It has been in the news, this expression, and what they are trying to communicate is that the whole of matter extending throughout endless space is a body that embodies an intelligence, and that all matter has its innate intelligence, or its innate property of intelligence. So, this is the new idea they are trying to give to people, rather than accept Scripture. They are trying to get around accepting Scripture, and they are doing nothing but upgrading pantheism, that the whole world is G_d, everything is G_d. The gods are features of nature or features of the material reality, and that all these gods together are a pantheon of gods, pantheism. So now, they have it as intelligence.

Whole World of Gross Matter Is Going to Be Made Light

You know, I had a dream many years ago, and I know where it came from. My dream came from the Bible reading where John, the Revelator, says he saw the throne and one sitting upon the throne, and light went out from the throne, and it filled the whole area. And it went outside of the sanctuary, holy place, and filled the whole world with light. So, one day I had a dream, and it was just a flash, almost, and I saw light emanating, moving out in all directions from one place and it went outside and everything outside such as trees, became light. It was illuminated. Grass was illuminated. Animals were illuminated. Everything was illuminated, and I told someone, and asked them, "Do you know what I think it means?" He didn't say a thing. I said, "I think that dream means G_d is going to show me revelation, and the whole world of gross matter is going to be made light for me. That is what I told him. That is what I felt, and that is what has happened.

Everything That Exists Is the Voice of G_d

The macrocosm has gone, disappeared, and I see the whole universe right in the soul of man, and that is where it is supposed to be seen. Allah made that out there for this in here (the soul). So, all of that has words and language because of this nature here, and G_d speaks to us through that dead reality. He speaks to our soul, the living reality. That is nothing but His Language out there, and that is what the Prophet said G_d revealed (in the Qur'an): *"There are signs in the heavens and signs in the earth and as well as signs in yourself"*. So, it says everything that exists is the Voice of G_d speaking, and nothing we can make will not speak the Will of G_d, or the Voice of G_d. You can't think of anything, nothing. The couch we sit on, it speaks for G_d. He's the Existent. He's the Reality behind all this, so it speaks His Language. Whatever you do speaks His Language. Whatever you make speaks His Language.

Look how wonderful the computer is as a witness for G_d. "Man, you don't believe that I'm G_d, and that I made this universe and you to do what you do, and for it to do what it does? Okay, I'm going to have you make a computer. You are on the way. Soon, you are going to have your computer, and you're going to put what you want into your computer, and it is going to give you what you put into it and no more. Now, why is it that you can't see Me?"

Understanding G_d's Way In the World

So, it is powerful, and it is beyond reach of the average mind. But if you open yourself, if you are open and are faithful, you can get it, and when you get it, you realize a relief that is better than any charge you can get from a woman, female, sex, drugs, or anything else. Nothing can give you the satisfaction that you get from understanding G_d's Way in the world when you see it, think about it, and just reflect on it. Now, He is so powerful to communicate His Will through all that He makes. The tree cannot do anything but communicate His Will. You put the seed in the ground, and it can't do anything but communicate His Will. And "Man, you think you're free and have free will, but you are nothing but a tree! Put a seed in you, and you can't get any more out of it than what I put in it!"

Misguidance From Religion and Culture

My life is so filled with signs until if I would do a rehearsal of my life and put it in print, people wouldn't believe that G_d has singled me out as His friend that He's going to raise up in the world with our people. When I say our people, all people who have suffered our misfortune in the world. It can't just be us. We are the ones who are focused and put on the stage for the benefit of all who have suffered our misfortune. That is what I believe. My heart goes out to whites who are poor, suffering, and crazy. Once, I passed by a white church, and it made my heart go out to them. They were in there acting crazy and carrying on just like we do, holy ghost screaming, hollering, and carrying on. They were all white. I can't forget that!

We're the biggest group they targeted, but they hurt everyone. This misguidance we have from religion and culture has hurt everybody they didn't care about or didn't need. Now, they want to repent, so they're ready now to make sure we have a comfortable road to where we have to go. I'm talking about big people in this government, and in this society, in religion, and in government. They appreciate us, love what they see that has happened in their midst to people that they didn't think would ever come into knowledge, spirit, and concern not only for themselves, but for others, too. They never dreamed that it would come out of Elijah Mohammed, or somebody of his history and circumstance. So, when they read and find out, they're ready to do whatever they can to see that we have room and help us to get where we have to go. I do believe that with all my heart and soul. This town is not too big for me. When we start growing in here that's going to pull other people back. Other people are going to start coming in here, and I'll tell you who is going to start coming in first, immigrant Muslims.

He Is With Us All the Time

My experience made me understand where the Christians are really coming from when they say, "Christ is my personal savior." I know both the way I see it, and the way they see it, now. But the way I see it is that Allah is ever present and He's with everything He created, and He is with humans more than He is with anything else He created, because He created humans to extend His creation. So, He is with us, personally, all the time, and the more we get in accord with His Will for us the more He manifests His Presence inside of us. But He was there all the time. In the Qur'an is says, *"When My servants ask about Me, tell them I'm near!"* That means, "I have always been nearby. Let them know they are screaming out thinking I'm eons away in the sky somewhere. Let them know I'm right where they are. You don't have to scream so loud. So, if it's inside their hearts, I'll hear it, not with their mouths. Whisper inside their hearts and I'll hear it!". Praise be to G_d!

You Have Found the Greatest Friend

So, really, when you come to know G_d, Allah, the real G_d, Creator of the heavens and the earth that everybody believes in, they call Him other names, but really it's the Real One they really believe in; when you come to really know Him, then you understand that when you really connect with Him in the way He intended for us to connect with Him, you have found the Biggest, the Greatest Love. You have found the Greatest Friend. You have found the greatest wealth in knowledge, and in material things. You have just found the greatest of everything possible that you can think of good, or of use. Really, you can get there by indirect routes, but if you love Him and you have always been moving in that direction since you were aware of yourself, when you find Him, you know that route was the route that satisfied or brought you nearer and nearer to everything worthwhile that you were seeking. The people of faith, they know Him. You can tell the way they sing. They sing about Him, and you know they know Him. David, he really knew G_d, because that was his love. G_d was his Love always, so, they say Jesus Christ is Messiah. Was he from the house of David, and what is David? Love. Isn't that what we should look at if a guy is coming telling us he is a messiah, a revivalist, or something, he is our sheik? Shouldn't we ask, "Are you from the house of love?"

I'm sure the word, "Bethlehem", means, "house of light". They may translate it differently, but I'm pretty certain it means, "house of light". David and Bethlehem are very important. Bethlehem is a place, and David is a human figure of a human leader, and that he was formed of love. His son was the Prophet Solomon, and Solomon means peace. The hadith says, "You'll never enter paradise until you have faith, and you'll not really have faith until you practice loving one another." So, paradise is the abode of peace, isn't it? See how all these things come together and make perfect sense?

A Logic Supporting the World

When you see the theme in Scripture from Genesis to Revelation, or from Al Fatiha to An Nas, when you see the theme in a logic that's growing upon G_d's creation with man as the agent, his human intelligence as the agent, then you really can see what Scripture is all about. So, the world being without form or void I understand it, and the spirit moving on the face of the water and G_d rewarding that effort saying, *"Let there be light"*, and wouldn't accept that darkness be on the deep any longer, I understand it. So, the moon and the sun manifested themselves, and man began to perceive, for the first time, the logic that supports the world, not just moving, having the world influence him, but now he's influencing the world. He's perceiving a logic that supports all of this, and it is so good he has to share it with his fellow man, "G_d sent me to tell you this". He sure did! That's right! He couldn't even put his thoughts together until he loved his brother. He started to feel for others, then he could put his thoughts together. Prophet Muhammed said, "Satan has despaired. He's given up all hopes of ever taking you away from your religion. Now, you have to watch out for him in small things"; and he's not going to be coming at you through Scripture. He's going to try to get you in small things, make you jealous and envious of one another. He sets you up for self-importance. He knows he can bring you down, if you go for it.

Qur'an's Focus Is the Whole Universe

The Qur'an is a universal book, and its focus is the whole universe, but mainly to bring the universe as a message to man's mind to the community of people on earth. That is Jesus Christ, too, and that is a lot of other cultures. They have in the Indian culture this group that I read about. I'd never met them. I thought they were just a group that had, at one time, existed and time just eliminated them, or they just, in time, gave up; but that is not so. The Jains, they still exist. Their idea of the microcosm and macrocosm, if I were to write on comparative religion, and I am a student of comparative religion, I would put them in there. I would say that their concept of microcosm and macrocosm is the people of the book's concept of the heavens and the earth. Allah says, in the Qur'an, they once were one until they were separated, the sky and earth, and scientifically speaking, sky and earth are one. We are nothing but a solar system that belongs to the outer creation and we belong to the Milky Way. But there are more galaxies and look how small the earth has become. It is nothing but one of them in the sky. We are in the sky, too, but we do not know it because we are here. We are small creatures. We're down here on the earth like little ants, so we think the earth is separate from the sky, but it is not. Scientific thinking brings them together. It shows you that it is all one, and that is what these religions did before science did it. They understood that this creation is one whole.

Better Off If Religion Had Never Been Brought to Us

In Greek mythology Prometheus stole the heavenly fire. He got it from up there and Allah says in Qur'an to the jinn and men, *"If you can come up here after the Qur'an, come, but you're going to find fiery shooting missiles."* That is the sky of man's vision and understanding. It is not talking about the sky of the material creation at all. But the average person is left to think it is talking about that sky, and we remain in that thinking. In fact, we would be better if they had left us alone. We would be better off if they had never brought religion to us. The common man's mind is already created by G_d to deal with reality. So, once they give you religion there seems to be something being presented contrary to reality, and it is in the name of G_d.

Consequently, you impose it upon yourself and once you do that then the masses stay ignorant and never want to tackle big responsibility. So, they can stay on the block, live and die on one block like a lot of them do, never go outside; just go to the liquor store, grocery store, and a friend's house, stay, live, and die in just about a one block radius. And the Lord created them just like He created the people who gave them religion, created them with a free mind to engage the universe. So, that is not justice. I cannot accept that, but I respect what men much greater than me respect, and especially Prophet Muhammed, peace be upon him.

So, that is why I mentioned that I had a vision. I did. It was just like it was real and I was with the followers of Prophet Muhammed under the tree when they made an oath to him. The first one put his hand on his hand and then they kept putting hands over hands, and in the dream I came in and I put my hand there. It was a big pile of hands way up there and I put my hand in there, and they just kept on piling them up. The last Hand is G_d's Hand. Allah gives it in the Qur'an that His Hand is above your hands.

Prophet Muhammed Could Have Destroyed Other Religions

They were pledging allegiance to the Prophet, so that says even Allah approves it. After they piled their hands up then G_d put His Hand on top of theirs, meaning that their pledging allegiance to the Prophet was approved by G_d. That is all that it is saying, and it was under a tree. The Prophet was a merciful man, a very kind-hearted person, and he didn't want to be in opposition to the Scheme of G_d that existed before him and had been carried out by Prophets, one after another. So, he spared revealing what he knew would wreck Christianity, wreck Judaism. He could have destroyed all of it if he wanted to, at least expose them so badly until a lot of people would have just turned against not only Jews and Christians, but they would have turned against religion. He did not want that, and Allah did not want him to do that. So, Allah revealed to him because he was, at certain points in his life, really fed up with a lot of things that they were doing. It is evident in his life work and evident in Qur'an, too, that he was really burdened terribly by a lot of things that were going on that he had no nature for. But G_d would not let them hurt G_d's Plan for his life as the last Prophet and a mercy to all the worlds. G_d would give him understanding that gave him relief.

The Prophet Was Also Straying

We think the Prophet was always on the right path. No, the Qur'an says, *"We found you straying, weighed down with burdens on your back, and guided you."* So, he also was straying. In the Bible of Jesus, it says, *"Is there good in it? No not a one"*, not a single one. Everybody has erred or sinned, even the Prophet, the best of the people. Even the most perfect of human beings they erred, only G_d saves humanity. We can do our best, but our best falls short, even the Prophet's best falls short. If his uswa could have been enough for us without G_d's revelation, he wouldn't have gone up on the mountain. He would have just taken care of the problems on earth. But he went up on that mountain because he knew he was not tall enough to take care of humanity. So, he went up seeking the higher voice on high, and if you strain, you'll get an answer sooner or later. The Bible is right. Jesus said just knock, keep knocking, and the door will open up to you. Just don't give up. So, this world is very oppressive, but Allah says He also oppresses, thulumaat. Thulman is oppression. *"He created the darkness and the light"*, and the word He uses for darkness is, lail, night. But in this expression He uses for darkness a word that means, oppression, and it is also darkness. And Jesus said, *"I come treading the wine press alone."* So, he is coming to bring pressure, that is what it means. The grape vine is symbolic of the little weak people in material. They don't have much material, but they know how to climb up on material. The grape vines climb up the fence or the pole and even go up the side of a building.

Weak In Material and Weak In Knowledge

So, these vine-moving things get their support from the big, heavy, structures that they go up on. That is the weak people in material, but also weak in knowledge. The small people who are weak in knowledge they depend on the big people who are great in knowledge to support them and give them a situation where they can mature or grow. So, it is the same for intelligence, and also the same for money. They do the same for money. They want money. They have to pull up on the big people. Some of us don't want to get any higher than their pockets. We don't learn anything. We will never get up there. There is a little kid who will come and grab your pocket and ask "What is that in your pocket? You know you have some money. Let me see!" They won't take, "No", sometimes. You will say, "I don't have anything. I told you I don't have anything." They will say, "Let me see", and all the time they are trying to pull your wallet out of your pocket with their little hands. That is that grapevine crawling up. Jesus Christ, who was he talking to? Big people don't need help to get up. They have knowledge and money. So, the liberator is always coming, because there is injustice done to the little person, Moses, too, the same thing. Even Abraham, he rejected his father, and he wanted to see people treated more justly, so he became a roaming ambassador for G_d.

Chapter 7

Adam, the Man G_d Is Making

Adam, in the minds of most people is the beginning of the human race, and that is true. But what is a human? In revelation, the first human is the human being who was created in his best nature, his good human nature, that is, he was born innocent, like a newborn baby. He hadn't committed any sin. He didn't even have any desire to sin, and G_d communicated His Will to that person. What I'm saying is once that was done, then we had society under G_d, and we had a beautiful life come from that Adam. We had, also, peace, happiness, and love, all the things that we want in us, or in a society that we belong to. That was the Garden of Paradise.

That figure, as I said, is a plural body, not a single, individual in flesh. That didn't come until late in the history of people who we all call human. If we want to see the followers of Adam, we have to see the followers, the people, who believed in revealed Scripture, that G_d revealed man's life and G_d revealed the plan for man's life to. That is the beginning of Adam. That is why it is said, by scholars and learned leaders in the Islamic world, that Adam, also, is the first Prophet.

I heard one imam of the immigrant Muslims (those who came here from overseas) who had been here a long time. I think he came from overseas when he was very young. He was speaking to a group, an audience, and I was in the audience. In fact, I was actually with him. I came to that occasion with him. He said, "Allah made a man from the ground without mother, or father, and that was Adam. Then He made a man from a woman without a father, and that is Christ." That stuck in my mind, and I said to myself, "G_d was obligated to do that, if He says He made man from the ground, the material reality and we see we come from mother, male and female." We come from a woman. So, if G_d said He made man from the ground, out of due respect to the woman, He has to make man from a woman. We know we do not see any men made from the ground. We see all men coming from woman. Every other human being comes from a woman. So, to give respect to woman, the reality of our history is just that, that man is establishing his life. I'm talking in the plural, not just one individual. He established the life for himself and others. He established that life firstly, and in the history of the progress for human society it is addressing, directly, the abundant resources in the ground. That is why I used the expression "from dust to industry". He starts, first, in the ground. That is Scripture and that is reality. After a while, the public life becomes such a big life with comforts, and everything built into it, that it becomes a life separate from the material efforts of man. It becomes education, schools, churches, religious places of worship, cultural places, etc. It becomes government, political owners, all these developments. Now we have a new reality that is not the original ground that man survived upon. Now, man's work has brought in another world.

Society Is Giving Birth to Us

Man's work has given us man's world. For want of a better expression I say, "man's world". It is not the ground producing the thinking. The human sensitivities, the spirit and all that makes my soul, or my life is not the ground anymore. Feeding that directly is a new order. A new, man-made order is feeding that. So, the ground is not producing us directly anymore. It is the city life or the community life that is producing us. We're getting our new minds and our new leaders, our new careers, our new occupations, and whatever we are getting, it is all from this new reality. It has now become the mother. It is the mother now, not the mother earth. It is society that is giving birth to us. So, we should see the real progress for industrious man is coming from agricultural life, the simple life of the farm, or something from the life of city builders. If you notice in Scripture, especially Bible, it is the big cities, the big populations, that are given all-female names, Nineveh, Babylon, all these names. The cities are called women in the Bible because those circumstances are now producing people, producing their thinking and interests.

Look at how the woman changes from spirituality. Her perception, firstly, is spirituality. Now she is a big mama. She's accommodating all these things. So, to say that woman is spirituality is not enough. Woman is spirituality and woman is environment. The environment produces us. The environment changes. With man's progress the environment changes. The environment becomes more complex and much more productive, in time. Get the sex thing out of the study of knowledge and religion. It is not about sex as we understand sex.

"The Sun of Man"

Look at how the Bible starts off with Eve. Why? Because those men back there at that time when they were writing Scripture or Scripture was being inspired and conceived, those men were bothered already by big populations that were giving themselves to sin and corruption. So, the allusion here to the name, Eve, is that we begin in ignorance, and not only that. We also began in spirituality. There was no light. There was darkness and in time we were born out of the darkness into the light, and the light is the sun. Light is symbolized as the sun. So, when Jesus Christ asked, *"Who do you say, I, the son of man, am?"* he was speaking of himself in the same sense as Scripture spoke of man, both as a flesh and blood person, but also as enlightenment, the "sun" of man, the enlightenment for man, but also of man. Man's enlightenment came out of man. Knowledge is in the head of somebody, and they share it with us. Knowledge is light, then it comes to us out of the head of somebody. So, the son (sun) of man is the one who gives light to mankind, or becomes the light for mankind, the one who comes to light for mankind. Jesus Christ was alluding to that: *"Who do you say, I, the son of man am?"* Son is an allusion on or to the light of man, or the enlightenment of man. So, we should think of Adam, too, as an illumined body, not just as a body or a spirit, inspired and made conscious, knowledgeable, and wise by G_d. He represents a body of light, and this kind of reasoning is not just limited to people of the book. It is all around the world. All the myths in the world have started just like that.

"My Mother Is Black!"

I was studying about Buddha, in Buddhism, and he says of himself "My mother is black." This is Buddha talking in that religious, spiritual language. He pursued his destiny or his calling. Something was driving him to search the darkness. His mother was black, and he was driven or motivated to search the darkness. So, that mother is not a biological flesh and blood mother. He is talking about his mother as his country, his environment that he was in that was in ignorance. He saw it in ignorance like Muhammed, the Prophet, saw the Arabs of the land that he was born in. He saw it in ignorance, darkness. Buddha saw his people, the way they were living in darkness, and he says, "My mother is black." He goes on to the road of enlightenment. As he progresses in that road, he comes to see the nature of his society as his mother.

So, the first mother he saw was the land that gave birth to him, or the land that supported him. That was his first mother, the society that he was a member of. Later, he sees the nature. He gets wisdom and insight, and he sees the nature explaining their behavior. When you see nature, you see what explains how it manifests. The "how" is shown, the outer picture. Nature is referring to the inside, the inner picture, the necessary workings of things within a body that gives it character, or gives it design. That is nature. So, he finally gets insight into the nature of his society, and he was still seeing his mother as black.

The Absence of Education Is the First Darkness

The first black is the darkness that is the absence of education, or absence of knowledge. Darkness that is the absence of education, or absence of knowledge, that is the first darkness. The next darkness is the nature itself, those things that operate to make things what they are and to make them perform as they perform, and his mother is black. He said he finally was illuminated, he reached illumination, and he became a body of light. That meant G_d. I know they don't say, G_d, in Buddhism, but I'm saying, G_d. I believe in G_d. He illumined him, made him see and understand things, and he became the light for his society, the illumined one they call him, shining bright with light. Is that any different from Adam? No, it is the same subject. Here is Adam, the man of the ground, man working the earth. G_d blessed him to see inside things, to know the nature of things, and to give them their names. So actually, he was an illuminated body, too, wasn't he? Yes, he was the first light for man, father for mankind. The Bible says the female counterpart was Eve, meaning that was darkness. Buddha, in saying, "My mother was black", is saying the same thing. The most ancient of these spiritual movements, perhaps we can't go any further back, I don't think, than Egypt, and their god, Osiris, the sun, is light. That was their god in ancient Egypt. Osiris is the sun. He's the light, and he was eclipsed by his wife, and in some stories, it is his mother, Isis. She eclipsed him.

Night a Big Shadow of the Earth

What brings darkness? It is a material body in the way of the light. This is world science. This is not spookism. The material body blocks the sunlight and that is how we get night. So, what is night but a big shadow of the earth? That is all it is. The sun is on the other side casting a big shadow of the earth on us, and that brings nighttime. It gets very dark. If they taught our children that in elementary school, it would be easy to teach them. You can reach any child with that. All you have to do is give them a demonstration. Put a flashlight over there, and there is a shadow, darkness. You can show them how the object blocks the light and makes the shadow, the darkness. And if the shadow is big enough, as big as the earth, then there is going to be a lot of darkness, at least for those people in the eye of the darkness, like in the eye of the hurricane. The eye of the darkness is going to be very dark for them. This is a kind of teaching that will make you feel good inside, that will make you feel that you are free and at peace, and consequently, it will make you much more productive. The creation of the human being needs what first? Peace and quiet. G_d says the life germ, sperm of man is placed in the female, and it is put in a situation where it is safe and at peace, protected from noise and trouble, safe and at peace. And because G_d has created a situation like that for the life germ, that life germ completes itself, and gives us a whole person physically, male and female. What a great production! And Allah says that production is made possible because it is placed in a situation where it is at peace and protected from harm and trouble. And we are told the story that we all began our existence in paradise. We were conceived and then put in the world to produce; conceived in paradise and then put into the world to produce, and we were able to produce because we were conceived in heaven. Allah brought us from a peaceful state free of burden, not hurting or in pain, and then He put us in the work field to work, and we are able to produce because we were formed in heaven.

The Devil Is Trying to Build the World of the Ungodly

These people who are being formed in the hells of the street can't see that they are not productive, why they cannot contribute to the establishments, to the structures in their neighborhoods. They offer nothing because they are created in hell. But if we remain devoted to our religion, we will create an environment like this. We are being formed in heaven right now, those who are sensitive to what is happening. We are being formed in heaven right now, and we can go in the world and be productive and they won't cripple us with their sins. Our souls will be sensitive to the needs of human life and each one will go his own way to his own interest and we all will contribute to the building of a new world, and it is happening all the time. It is not to come.

So, when we look at the objective world, we see two worlds and not just one. Shouldn't we see our world, the world of the righteous trying to obey G_d, and the world of those who don't care? Don't let the world of those who don't care dampen our spirit or hurt us in any way. Keep our own world in our eye, so our own world feeds our life. It says don't even gaze upon the wicked world, because if you turn your eyes and look in that focus, you are going to be fed by the wrong thing. You will have the wrong spirits coming into your life. So, keep your vision, eyes, focused on your life and your world, and that will keep you strong to survive all the harm from the things that are happening in the world of the ungodly. The Devil is constantly trying to build the world of the ungodly, so that it will choke out our life and we will have no place to live, but he is going to fail. He is failing, and he is going to continue to fail.

The Devil's Downfall Is Now

This is his big downfall, now, the Devil, himself, he is in for a big defeat! Allah has readied the world for the life He wants in us, and Satan has readied the world for the life he wants. The climax of all of this is here, now. The conclusion of it all is right on us now, and the Devil looks really big, doesn't he? And he thinks of himself as really big, but he's losing faith in this round. He never gives up. He says, "I might lose this round. I'll go back to the drawing board", and he starts the thing all over again. He thought he was going to win this round, but I think now he's wondering, doubting, that he is going to win this one.

Serpent's Root Means He Began In Materialism

They work hard and they are united. Look at what Scripture said, the Bible. I can give you what the Qur'an says. This is very short, brief, and very clear. But to understand what is happening in the West, it is not living by the Qur'an. America is not living by the Qur'an, just some of us, a few of us. The Bible says in one place, *"Rejoice not, oh, Palestine, for out of the serpent's root shall come a flying cockatrice."* A cockatrice is a mythical creature that began as a snake. The snake's egg is put into a bird's nest. The bird hatches the snake's egg, and the bird is not a snake only, but a flying snake with three heads. This is what G_d inspired the saintly people to foresee in Scripture. They saw whatever was wrong with their society, at that time called Palestine. It doesn't necessarily mean Palestine. It could have been Palestine, because whatever the popular nation was that is what they called the whole world. Whatever one is more popular it became the name or the figure for the whole world. So, when Egypt was great the whole world was Egypt. It said, *"Rejoice not, oh, Palestine, for out of the serpent's root shall come a flying cockatrice."* The root means its beginning, from the serpents beginning. How did he begin? In materialism, like man. He began in the material world, the material reality, but now he's going to become a flyer. It means he's going to become spiritual; not materially oriented, but spiritually oriented. He will be a flying serpent.

Again, it says the beast in the last days will be in the waters, and finally, will become the flying cockatrice. They say the same corrupt natured creature we identify as the Devil or Satan, is going to become prince of the air. This is the Bible. That means he will be over the governing forces in the air.

No Material Progress Without the Spiritual

If dust is to make progress it has to have water, get moisture. Without the spiritual component all your interest in material growth is nothing. You can't produce anything. Dust can't produce anything until water comes into it. Here we have land, water, air. He starts in the land and as the Qur'an says, he was cast down. The Bible says he was cast down, too, to bite the dust, to live in the dust, struggle in the dust, but he rises from the dust, or from the material basis. He rises from the dust, though dead, unevolved, un-progressed. He is not progressed. He is poor. Dust means very poor materially. So, here he comes made of the dust. He survived to progress in the dust, in the material reality.

Then it says he shall grow in the water. He shall dominate the water. He will get into the water and rule in the water, the same creature. It means, in the spirituality of the people. Why does it say man in water? Because when a woman's water breaks, it is a sign the baby is ready to come, ready to be delivered from the mother's body when the water breaks. And the crying Mary, who is washing the feet of her master with her tears, in the Gospel, all of that is associated with water. The woman is associated with water. The same water is also used to destroy her and her child. It says a flood went out to destroy the woman and her child, a flood went out from the beast.

He Gives Them Language

We have now land, water, then air. So, where are we in the history of this progression for human life leading society, this essential life that we need in men and women to lead the society? Where are we now in time? Air, we are in air. The air is the last place for the battle. And what does the air have reference to? Communication. You think of air waves, radio, TV that is true, that is the big thing, but something more vital and more critical or crucial for us, for our life and our future is air for us, meaning that which is necessary to bring communication from one person to another. Can you speak to me in a vacuum, and I hear you? If you know science, you know you cannot. Sound will not travel in a vacuum where there is no air. You can't speak without air. Every time you speak, if you put your hand up there you know what is happening. Just put your hand close to your mouth while you're talking, and you know what's happening. So, if you can't hear and you want to know if a person is talking, just put your hand close to his mouth and you will feel his breath hitting your hand, because everything you say needs breath, the movement of the air. More important than being on the TV, the beast is going to be in your communication, your language, and influence how you communicate to one another. Now he has taken over your mind. He is controlling the reality for your own mind to exist and progress in. Your own mind cannot exist and progress in anything except the reality he creates for it. Do you see what makes it so difficult for us to reach people? He gives them language, and even the way they are supposed to respond to language. So, he competes with G_d, that is what you have to realize. For man's life Satan is competing with G_d, and it didn't just start in this part of the world.

When Prophet Abraham said he seeks his guidance from G_d, Who gives life and death, what did Pharaoh say? *"I give life, and I give death"*, boasting that he had formed man's world, his language, and everything, and man could not help but be born as he wanted him to be born, and he gives death, too. He meant, "The same way I have given them life I can give them death. The same world I created to give life; it also gives them death." A man was interviewing me on TV, and I did not please him. I waited until we went off the air, and I said something to him, and he said to me, "The sword that lifts them up will cut them down!" Thank G_d, he had opened my eyes to words, to language. Look the word, "Sword". Why is that word spelled so unusually with the letters s-w-o-r-d? Spell the word, "swear", like you curse, and you can hear the "sw". Why is this "sor" and all the other words with the letters, sw, in it are sw, but this is sor? The letter "s" stands for secret word and the serpent, the beast, he hisses like a snake. He makes an "s" sound. That is for them. It is not for us. It is so they will know, "Our masters are in control! We see the sign that our masters are in control in the language". He can come here from Jupiter, if there are people on Jupiter, and if they are of the same mind, when he gets here and he sees the word, sword, he will say "Our folks are down here." We know he can't come from Jupiter, but he can come from any isolated place in the world, come here and see the language of his master, and he knows that his master is in control.

This is the Devil. It is his work to give the spelling like that. The Satan took the language from Adam, so that he would control the life of the people. Adam was giving the names to things. All that happened in heaven and the spirit that would become the Satan rebelled against G_d giving Adam this authority. If G_d said to the angels, *"Tell Me your names"*, that tells me with my common, good senses, the most important thing for Adam in his role that justified him being given the authority and the position that G_d was going to give him, was his ability to give things names.

"So, They Will Not Be a People Anymore"

If the rebel rejected that, where would he attack Adam? In his ability to form language. So, he would take over the language. To defeat Adam, he's going to have to take over that. What does the Bible say? *"Let us go down and confound their tongues so that they speak no more and babble"*. That is the story of the Tower of Babel. So, if that was achieved, and they came down and confounded the language of the people on earth, so that they only babble, then all that we are doing down here on earth is only babbling. We are not communicating, really, as G_d created us to communicate. In the eyes of those who know we are just babbling.

Believe me, that is what we're doing, because when we are separated from our original nature and the Plan of G_d and our life that we got from our Creator in our own nature and natural makeup, if we are not connected with that, if we are not connected with our relationship that G_d established for us with the objective world, then all of our language is nothing but babble, because there is no real light from Allah in it. There is no real connection with our original purpose in it. Allah made us to speak His Truth, and the reality that He created. If we are not connected with it, we are babbling. In another place it says, *"Let us cast their bands asunder so they will not be a people anymore"*. This is all in the Bible.

Their Language Has Been Confounded

In the Qur'an, a people are called in the Arabic, "qom". From the same root that means "people", you also get the word, "standing." So, to be a people you have to have establishment. The same word gives us the meaning, standing, establishment. So, a people sitting idle are they really a people in the true meaning of Scripture? No, they are not people. Those who are planning to undo everybody else and succeed and be the masters, they say, *"Let us cast their bands asunder…"* That is what has happened to most of the people of the world, their language has been confounded, and their bands have been cast asunder. They are not productive societies anymore. Look how the world is all messed up. We think of just Africa, but Europe is dying. It is struggling for its life. Somebody set us up to see black and white and that is the way we were seeing things for a long time while they were working on us to make us non-productive. Now, we find black people, African Americans, shameful and do not have much to be happy about when we look at the whole of us. I am not talking about these isolated cases.

You look at Africa, it is in bad, bad shape. Look at Europe, bad shape. They are trying to form a union like the United States, at least for economic purposes, if not for other purposes, and they are succeeding with it, but still nothing has happened yet to turn their countries around. They are still in bad shape. They are not the leaders of the world. They are far from it. That is the European nations. So, the influences of Satan that have turned black and white against each other, used black against white and white against black for all these generations, now, have killed productivity in the white people, and killed productivity in the black people. They have succeeded in that, except for a few. We know Scripture says there will always be a remnant, a small number will be saved, but we are looking at the big picture. When you look at the big picture, you will see non-productive whites and blacks, as no people. If I had a business, to tell you the truth, it would not make me happy to see a black or a white person come for a job. It would make me happy to see an Asian or a Spanish person come, not a black or a white. They both have been made unemployable by the influences of the Satan. Satan will lose; he won't succeed. Don't be afraid of that. In fact, he is losing big.

Only a Few Need to Wake Up to Save the Future

It only takes a few to wake up and save the future for the many. There are strong ones among the whites and strong ones among the blacks who are holding their life and waking up to just what is going on. In time, we will have a great, new leadership, and we will recover, but in the meantime, the new reality, this new world situation we're in demands that those who know don't just know for relief. Relief is to free you to have more energy, more faith to work. We should be working hard, giving all our energy to work hard on the life we're building. Don't put all your energy outside of the work field. Know the field of work that we're in and work hard to build on our grounds, not spread it all out and go everywhere with it, and you just have a good feeling that "My heart has been relieved. I think I understand this world". No, you are freed up to work more.

The Temple Is Not a Building

Christ Jesus is the temple. He is a sign of the congregation and the order, and to understand the physical temple you must first understand him, or you do not have any knowledge of the physical, temple because he is the temple. He is the death and the resurrection. He said, *"Destroy this temple and I will rebuild it."* He was talking about himself. It is not a structure. What does the structure offer? It is just another building. It does not speak, it cannot heal. Take the people out of the walls, it is dead. It is nothing but dead stone, or dead wood, whatever you made it from. So, to understand the concept you must understand the concept of Christ Jesus as the temple.

To understand the concept as Muslims in the Nation of Islam we must understand the concept of Mr. Fard as the temple. He has to attract you to something that you can understand, on your level of understanding, but that is not intended to stay always. That has to come down for you to really understand what is behind it. The real body is inside, by interpretation, or translation. People are attracted to the outer body, right? That is the first attraction; like when you marry a woman, perhaps what attracted you to her was the way she appeared to you physically. But if you are blessed, you will have another awakening. You awake to the value of her inside that outer body and that is the real relationship.

So, the Bible says, *"In the beginning was the Word and the Word took on flesh"*. So, the Word existed before flesh. The concept existed before the materialization of the concept, and to understand the concept, you have to know the language. Mr. Fard said, "Learn the language, so that you speak well. You will not speak well unless you learn the language." And he was saying more than what could meet the eye, because the people did not have that kind of insight. One thing, the Honorable Elijah Mohammed, he knew what we had as understanding was not final. There was something deeper to be learned or understood. He knew that. He was never satisfied with the understanding that we had, and the ministers, they would come to the table, and they would express their understanding. "Dear Apostle, what does this mean?" My father would listen to them and say, "Brother, you have to dig deeper." I felt so bad for them, because they would be thinking they have something really powerful. They would bring it up to the Honorable Elijah Mohammed, their insight, their knowledge, their light, and he would say, "Well, brother you have to dig deeper."

Brother Isaiah was a Minister in Baltimore. The Honorable Elijah Mohammed was teaching of himself at the table, himself, in the Bible, saying, "I am that David". Minister Isaiah, said, "Dear Holy Apostle, every time I read Jeremiah, I can feel it. Dear Holy Apostle, am I Jeremiah?" He said "Brother, I come in the volume of the books", which means, "You cannot claim any of them. They are for me to claim". I felt sorry for him (Brother Isaiah) thinking, "Can't you let him have one little piece of the book? All he is asking for is Jeremiah!" Mr. Fard knew all of that. Not only did he know that, but he also knew the counterpart in the Qur'an. It is obvious to me that he knew Jesus Christ as a sign in the Bible, and also, in the Qur'an. In my lectures I have addressed it, but not always directly. I addressed it without saying I was talking about it, in hopes that some would catch on to it in knowing exactly where to locate what I was talking about.

Lectures Designed to Penetrate the Darkness

I am aware of persons in the community, who have been in the community since it started in Detroit in 1931 or 1930. I'm aware of them still being around. Some of them are not dead. And I am aware also, that they have passed their knowledge on to their children, or somebody in the community that they trusted. They passed their knowledge on to them. When the Nation of Islam started, in Detroit, Mr. Fard attracted, and he knew it would attract such persons. He attracted masonic, black Masons and he attracted Eastern Stars, females and males, who were belonging to secret orders. He attracted them and they understood a lot that the average person did not understand. So, they just kept quiet, because their nature was to keep quiet, not to express what they knew, and they are still with us. And perhaps their number, now, is more than it was back then, because they have passed it on to others and others have joined, come in, like them since that time.

So, I know they are there, and I know they understand the language. I know they understand more the language than the rest of the members. So, I'm talking to them. I am talking to the Nation of Islam. I never stopped talking to them. I stopped being their leader, but I never stopped talking to them. So, teachings, or my lectures, are designed to reach those people, to reach those who are in the secret orders, to reach the Nation of Islam, in their darkness, to try to penetrate the darkness for them and speak to the general audience at the same time. That is what I have been doing over the years, and it has really paid off. Now, it is really paying off.

Adam, the Man G_d Is Making

Now, we read in the Qur'an of Adam, the man that G_d is making. G_d says to the angels, *"I'm making a khalifah in the earth"*, and the angels got upset, got disturbed. They didn't have faith in the man, in the role that G_d was creating for him, that he would be successful, that he would be able to be responsible for that role that G_d was giving him, creating him for. They didn't believe it. They didn't have faith in it, so they were disturbed. And G_d knew that state of mind or that position that they had taken to be too rigid, and He didn't want to be wasting time on it, it seems. He told them, "Just wait". He told the angels to, *"Wait until I have inspired him of My Own Spirit"*. That's what G_d said, so what is this saying? Now learned people, learned people in religion, Christianity, Judaism, Islam, many of them don't know what this is saying.

The Natural Capacity to Obey G_d's Will

Now, what is this saying? Some of them think that it is saying exactly what the ancient oppressors believed that the human being is deficient and worthless in his natural makeup, in his human completion, and G_d has to put divine essence into that human vessel in order for that human vessel to be worthy of respect from the leadership, from the power structures of the world. Yes, that's what they think it is saying, but it is not saying that. It is saying that "This human being I have created has the natural capacity to obey My Will and register My Intention. He is created to, in time, register My Will and My Intention and open up to My Will and Intention".

So, in other words, G_d is saying to them, "My man is not complete"; and that's why He didn't say, "I made", or "have made a khalifah". He said, "I am making a khalifah. I'm not through making my man." So, it could be put in other words. G_d could have said to them, "Wait until I have completed the creation of My man". He hadn't completed the creation of His man. He was making His man. He was creating His man. He's forming His man. He is not complete, yet. He's making him. So, this is a very delicate point here, a very delicate point. It takes very sharp-sighted persons and free persons to see this and understand it.

A Misconception of the Value of the Human Person

If you are oppressed by your own intellectual or spiritual arrogance, you'll never see the truth in this matter. You will never see it, because you always see that this human is not fit in his own state. He's not fit in his own creation. Only if G_d puts Himself in the human, then he's fit. So, divine human beings must rule the world, and we know we had a lot of "divine rulers". The emperor of Japan was a divine ruler. I think they learned their lesson and that's kind of recent in history. That's not medieval. That's modern. So, we had a lot of these divine rulers.

G_d says of Muhammed, *"He is a mortal just like you"*. He's not of divine. He's not divine. He is in your nature, your human nature. He is in his human nature, the same human nature you have. The only difference is Muhammed has been inspired. That is to his credit. If I'm here and I can hear the teacher and understand what the teacher is saying, or understand the teacher's instruction, that's to my credit, isn't it? I didn't know what the teacher was instructing me, the end, before he started instructing me. But it is to my credit that I have the capacity to receive an instruction. So, it doesn't mean he's divine. No, he's still human. He's still in human form and only human, but he has the capacity G_d has created him with, a great human capacity, with a great intellectual capacity, with a great spiritual capacity to receive divine inspiration. Even the energy or the Urge of G_d can come into him, and then he begins to express the Urge of G_d. That speaks well of him. It doesn't say he was nothing before. He must have been a great thing before, because for an instrument to pick up something, it has to be tuned for that.

So, the first thing in the dawah is for us to understand that Islam is calling the whole world, and it's an invitation from G_d, the Most High. After that, then we should understand that the major issue for religion is the misconception of the value of the human person. That's what made slavery during the ancient times, and medieval times, and even now. There are a lot of our Muslim leaders in the world who don't know that they have a slave master's attitude. They have a slave master's attitude because they're reading this knowledge, incorrectly, and they're seeing themselves as the illuminated bodies, and we are the creatures of darkness.

Genetic Memory

My Father, he said, "After I came into the knowledge, your mother carried you while she was also following the teaching of Islam". He said, "So, you are different". I believe in genetic life and genetic memory. I believe in it strongly. I'm not spooky. I'm not superstitious. I'm scientific. Believe it or not, I'm scientific, but I believe in genetic life. I believe in the continuation of life through the genes, genetic life, and the world of science that we live in right now, this great world of science and technology, etc. This world, too, believes in genetic life, that much of your life comes to you from the body. From the physical, biological cells of your mother and father you get your life, and that life finds expression that reaches its consciousness in your own body.

So, if that's true, then I am a living Elijah Mohammed and I am a living, Clara Mohammed. Though they're dead, their life lives in me. That's science, not superstitious. So, if that's true, then I have to be like my father and mother. I'm like my father and mother in some ways, or in many ways. Now understand that it's not only them that you inherit. You inherit everybody that was before them and, sometimes, a grandparent, or great, great, great, great grandparent may come into your genes stronger than your mama, stronger than even your father, because you have a new chance at the life that went into them.

So, the life that went into them had a chance, too. Now, the same life that went into them had a chance to express itself. That life can come into another and express itself through different ones, not just those two. And believe me, Clara Mohammed and Elijah Mohammed were not just the products of their two immediate parents. They were the products of those who went before them, too. But because Elijah was so strong in his life germ, Elijah is obviously the strongest in his son, Wallace, and Clara Mohammed was very strong in her life germ and it went into me. So, obviously, I am, myself, much like Clara Mohammed and Elijah Mohammed. Now, if they had been wasters of life, perhaps, another person in the genetic line would have influenced my composition more than they did, if they had been wasters of life. What do I mean by that? Sleepers just sleeping their time away, those genes, they don't reach the goal, or destructive people just living a life of self-destruction or hurting other people, they don't have a chance. Those genes don't have a chance for life.

The Body Has Inherited the Past

I think it is called the ganglia, that comes from the spine to the brain and goes back down, back into the system, the whole body. It comes into the conscious, sometimes, maybe no time. But if it comes into the conscious, then the brain sees what it couldn't see before. You might call it intuitive insight, from the ganglia to the forebrain, the forefront. I forget what that is called up there, the one in the front. Most of the time it comes there, but it doesn't register in the conscious. It goes back and forth. It comes from the ganglia. It goes back from the forebrain, the lobe in the front, back to the back brain, the hemisphere in the back, and then down to the ganglia. I don't think they know where it comes from. But I think insight brought Muhammed, the Prophet, and his followers, and many people over the world to understand what it comes from. It's rested in the body and the body has inherited the past. Every person that lived before a person, i.e., the genetic line, everybody in the genetic line of that person, all that information can come to that person.

Man Is Going to Come Back to G_d

It is in the body. It's in the genes. It's in the body, and the ganglia is the nerve line connecting to the brain. So, it can come from there up into brain and the brain can release it to the conscious, if the person is conditioned to bring it out. And you know, that's what khalifah is, what khalifah means, literally. Khalfan means behind you. If I say, "Huwa khalfan, or khalfani, he is behind me". So, khalifah means that that is behind you, behind you in time, your genetic line, and G_d made the khalifah and G_d made Adam a khalifah. It means that He made man to register his past in his conscious, and if he registers his past, eventually, he's going to come back to G_d. He is going to realize that in his past there was nothing that was under his control. "All of this is under the control of my Creator". He gives the credit to G_d, and then he becomes khalifah if he has the desire to release that, to share that with people, like Imam Warithu Deen Mohammed. But if he has no interest to give to people, he'll never register it in his conscious. It will never register on his conscious. And even if he has the desire, it's still the Will of G_d. The right things have to happen to bring it to the conscious and don't think you can do it without G_d's Personal Help. You have to prove yourself, first. When you prove yourself, then G_d's Personal Help will come to you.

Khalifah a Common Possession of All People

So, khalifah is a common possession of all people, Adam. Adam is a part of all people, so khalifah is a common possession of all people. He (Allah) said He made you khulifah in the earth. That's the plural of khalifah. He made you khalifahs in the earth, and then He says He also made you inheritors in the earth. So, you have the khalifah property, the khalifah property in your nature, in your creation, but He also made you inheritors. You can inherit that property. You are the inheritor of that property. So, it's a common nature and common property. All people have it, and that's the Christ nature, too. However, the Christ nature is above this possession, or form. What I'm talking about is a property, or form, a property of the human form, but Jesus Christ is on a level above that in the Ascension (Miraj). He is on a level above that with John, and that's to say that on his level, the urge is to express it, whereas on the Adam level, the urge is just to benefit from it, unconsciously.

And Prophet John, peace be on all of them, he's on the same level with Jesus Christ (in the Ascension), because his urge, too, was to express it. Jesus Christ was raised in a religious environment. John, the Baptist, was a desert man, so he couldn't speak well, but he was expressing it. "You'd better get right! You'd better get right! The time is at hand!" He knew that much. It's beautiful and it's saying what is the life and possibilities of the common people, for the common people, everybody. However, only a few manage to have it expressed in their nature, or for them.

Dr. C. Eric Lincoln and Islamic Genetic Memory

Dr. C. Eric Lincoln, a great African American theologian, he studied us. In fact, he made us popular when he wrote the book titled, *The Black Muslims in America*. So, he introduced us to many people, and many Christians that we perhaps wouldn't have been able to reach for a long, long time, for generations to come, maybe. He described the Nation of Islam's Islam as pseudo-Islam, and what he meant by that you'd have to ask him. But I have my own idea about what he meant. I believe he meant a protoplasm Islam, the beginning of, the making of a Muslim man, but what we were given was just protoplasm, just germs that would eventually become a man, a Muslim man, a Muslim mind, etc.

Dr. Lincoln mentioned that he had come to believe that those who came or who were brought from Africa, from Muslim life and tradition, who were separated from that life and tradition, and eventually were lost completely from that life and that tradition, have a genetic memory. That's difficult to understand unless you are students of genetics or biology, the genetic life of man. That's difficult to understand for many, perhaps, but not for me. I understand genetic memory. I believe that all people have a genetic memory. So, Dr. Lincoln said the reason why we are attracted to Islam and so many of us are so happy to be Muslims is that we came from Islam, from parents who were Muslims long ago, and that we have a genetic memory. But I would like to add that we have even another genetic memory, and we share this with all human beings. We have a genetic memory of once being at peace with G_d and once being in a heaven of our own souls. Every human being wants to get back to that happiness, that satisfaction, that peaceful state with G_d, and with his own soul. There's a beautiful chapter in the Qur'an that tells us how all men and women are struggling to get back to that heaven that we came from, and there is a genetic memory. Adam was there, our first father.

Muslim Should Be Man's Identity

The identity that is given to us as Muslims, according to Prophet Muhammed, that identity belongs to everybody, because he said everybody is born a Muslim. So, it is not just our identity because we claim it by faith. It is everybody's nature and everybody's identity. I believe it is introduced in the Qur'an to be introduced to mankind, because after all, he (Muhammed) is a mercy to mankind, not just to Muslims.

I believe what it is saying is this. Here you call yourself bashar, which means mortal human being. Bashar does not say that your nature is in accord with the Will of G_d. However, if you are a peacemaker and that is your inherent nature to want peace and to make peace, now, you are in accord with the Will of G_d. Bashar just refers to skin, that human beings are sensitive creatures. They have feelings of love, rejection, hate, and whatever. They register pain, pleasure, kindness, and cruelty. That is all bashar says. But nevertheless, that is the good news bringer. He is a bashir, why? Because if you do not register anything, you are finished. If you are not alive, you are not human.

The Humanly Sensitive Person

Bashar means a member in humanity, a mortal person that registers pleasure, pain, cruelty, goodness. It means he is a humanly sensitive person. That is how we would say it. And there are different names, but G_d, when He gave us our distinctions,

He said, "ins". *"He neither created the jinn, nor ins, except for His worship"*. "Ins" is another Arabic term for, human. "Insaan", means a human being, a human person, and that word is akin to, "nas", people plural, and the human beings' sociability, or tendency to want to congregate and be with each other, have activities together, and share the burden of society together. It is a very important term for man. The language of the Qur'an refers to the "ins" and the "jinn". They are called a group, and it says, if all the jinn could get together, and the men could get together as two separate groups that identifies them as sociable creatures, or gregarious creatures, creatures who want to congregate, want to be with one another, that group together. You know, that is the nature, the tendency. It is identifying the tendency in the nature to want to group together.

A Tendency to Socialize and Group Together

So, it describes both jinn and men, humans, as being of that nature, having a tendency to want to socialize or group together, and G_d says He did not create that creature for any purpose other than His worship. That means service to His Will and Plan for human life. I understand that to be a projection, not just a statement. It means this tendency in you that G_d created you with is going to eventually, bring you together and is going to be stronger than any other tendency in your life. G_d had a plan for it to bring you to your judgment, and it is going to eliminate these weaker tendencies that you have that take you away from G_d. That is the way I understand it.

When the word, "Muslim", is used, it should relieve the Muslim who accepts that identity, who feels comfortable with that identity as his own inheritance, or as his own true self or true nature. Mr. Fard asked, "Who is your own self? Your own self is a righteous Muslim." He did not say a black man. He did not say a member of the human race. He said, "And what is my own self? My own self is a righteous Muslim." So, obviously, he had insight. To me, he must have had that insight.

A Man of the Soil

Science gave us the term, "human". But science had no real belief in educating the public, mankind, or the publics of nations, until they saw what Scripture was saying. So, everything they have that is really important for establishing and progressing society, if you want to understand it, they got that direction from Scripture. I am convinced of the that. So, human, is a man of the soil. Scripture says, *"G_d made Adam from the earth.* "Man, of the ground that is what a human is, a man of the earth, and that is Adam. They are therefore saying the same thing Scripture says. You see, the little people come out, then the big people get afraid asking, "Where are they going to take this? We must prepare the world to protect itself against these newcomers, these young boys taking things out of order, or causing problems for the order that we have established".

So, then they come out and they might like you, but they fear you, too, because they do not know where you may go. They then come out with the light that they did not show before, and if you notice that language that I have used, it is not long before they come out and turn the light on. They see me talking about nature. They hear me, in my language, saying that our schools should include the support we get from the natural creation for education, etc. So, they came out, not so long ago, and said that science and religion are coming together.

Chapter 8

The Angels

Now, you know the Holy Ghost that appeared over Mary, the concept itself, it is the microcosm. They don't want to tie themselves to any language that would tie the people up in another language, so they dropped those concepts. The Muslims have, in the hadith, that people witnessed Gabriel, Jibril. He came through their town and his shadow was so big, it darkened the whole area, but it was the shadow of a man. So, the macro is symbolized as a huge man as big as the whole reality, the sky, and everything white and black, heaven and earth. That is what he was wearing when he was detected in the audience, white and black distinct from the other, like the thread of the Fajr light is the light of the heavens, and the darkness is the darkness of the shadow of the earth. So, it is heaven and earth and all that is in existence, that is the macro. How did that help her and start the concept? It helped her because you cannot arrive at your own reality until you know the reality that you are in. Her child was born having all that knowledge, so he was the new leader.

Allah Made Us To Be of One Spirit

Good Christians, when you are around them, they have the same nature, the same spirit, and you feel this connection, this relationship of a heart to heart, the believer's heart. When a person is right in their faith, believing there is a Superior over them that they can't bribe, but loves them, and they know loves them like any other loves, with Divine love, G_d's Love for us, when you're with them, you forget they are not Muslim. You will be talking and socializing with them, and you forget that they are not Muslim. That shows you that when we are in our innocence and in our purity that G_d created in the beginning, there is only one identity and that is the person of faith. I've experienced that with Jews and Christians. I have experienced that even with some people who are not even named in the holy book. That spiritual bonding is the best, not money, not sexual. Allah made us to be of one spirit. That's what it means when it says, He created the man and then He gave man of His Own Spirit, and then we have that spirit of our first father, called Adam, that G_d gave. He didn't have any children before he got that spirit. In fact, he was not even Adam until he got that spirit. He was in the process of becoming a complete creature.

When G_d put the spirit into him, then he was the man that G_d selected. And I guess that is why G_d told the angels to, *"Wait until I have given him of My Spirit, and then you make sajdah to him"*. That is only to tell us that when we are in the form and spirit that Allah wants us in, His angels are at our service. Their existence is to support our life that G_d wants for us on this earth. One of the principles, articles of the faith or belief, is that we believe in angels. Your faith or belief is not complete until you believe in angels. It does not mean that you accept that principle in Al-Islam, or an article of faith in Islam. It means more than that. It means that you accept that it is real.

You Can't See What You Don't Have a Mind to See

G_d also has angels in His creation, and those angels work for His Plan, His Will and they will be working in your personal, private life. I experienced it myself. I am talking from knowledge, not only from faith. In fact, there is not a day in my life I do not have one or more angels making their presence known to me. When you are sensitive to these things, then you recognize it. You can't see what you don't have a mind to see. If you do not have a mind to see it, it will be right in your presence, touching your eyeballs, and you won't know it.

We have faith in G_d, faith in the life hereafter. We have faith in angels. I have strong faith in angels. I have strong proof in my life that there are angels. We believe in all these things and don't forget the belief in the Qadr, because Jesus Christ is the Qadr. Don't tell everybody everything I'm telling you. You will be giving them too much of an advantage over you, and they don't deserve it. They have cheated the world, so why should we give them what we have? They cheated the whole world, all of us, cheated the church leaders. They cheat everybody.

Angels Cannot Resist Innocence

G_d spoke directly to the angels. You see, he (Iblis) was their leader, so they were not getting any communication from G_d. They were just following Iblis, and G_d had created them to follow the worker, the worker in man's world, in the real world. As long as they think the worker is doing something right, they give the worker their support, but they did not know until G_d exposed the situation to them in the presence of Iblis. It only means that G_d reaches the innocent from man and angels. Angels, they cannot turn down anything that is innocent. They cannot resist innocence. They only resist what G_d does not approve of.

Now, these are not angels in the material system. Angels are in the material system. They work for G_d, holding up the order of the universe. But they are not rational. They are not human. Those things, everything, is given like life, or animated. Practically everything is animated. It does not mean that its real form is what you are looking at. So, angels are pictured as people, human beings, but they are not always human beings. Even the non-animate, not to speak of man, the non-animate forces or the non-animate operatives in the creation, itself, are also angels.

Angels Work to Keep the Order of G_d's Creation

So, what science is explaining as properties of the matter, etc., that accounts for how this thing, how this system works, the sky, the lightning and everything or whatever, they do not call these things that are responsible for keeping the logic or the order, the system, angels. The key things that are operating in the systemic order to keep it, they are angels. Allah created them. So, they are angels, both in the inanimate world, and in the animate world. In all the animals, there are angels. The angels work to keep the order of G_d's creation, all of it, and everywhere. So, some of these explanations are not going to at all show us the human picture or a picture of human society, or human community, not at all. That is why Jibril is described as the figure of a man.

The Angel Jibril (Gabriel) An Operative Inside the Nature of Man

Jibril is described in a figure of a man, because he is an operative inside the nature of man. So, to describe him they say, "Oh, he was so tall, huge", so tall that he darkened the whole area that he came in. His shadow darkened the area he came in. That is there only to say that he is so much bigger than the human form, that the human form is dwarfed by his form. Even their whole neighborhood falls under his shadow when he comes into it. So, he comes with the Ruh of G_d. Jibril and the Ruh of G_d they come together.

The month of Ramadan in which descends the Ruh and the angels, right? The angels, they descend therein. It did not say Jibril descended, but we know Jibril is the one (angel) through whom the communication reached Muhammed from G_d. Now, why did they not say he descended? Because he is already down here with us. He is in us. He is in the common people as well as in the high ups. He is in every human being high and low. He is in all of us. He is a part of our very human constitution, and he is that part that supports reasoning, rational thinking in us, and also excellence, the desire to perform upon excellence, or to perform in excellence.

The Hidden Source of Our Productive Life

So, Jibril is all of that. He is the hidden source of our productive life, the rational and also the moral. He was seen in the audience, bearing witness to Muhammed, and he was not casting any shadow there. So, he does not have to do that, does he? Obviously, he doesn't have to darken the town when he comes in. He could just appear as a normal person, and nobody would recognize him. But he is put into a picture. You know, they did not actually see him. They couldn't see him physically, but he is put into a physical picture to better the communication, to ease the burden on communicating what we're talking about. So, it says the clothing he was wearing was the whitest of the white, and the black was the blackest of the black. So, he represents the black, the material, the mortal life, and the white is the enlightenment, the purity. That is why it says the whitest of the white, to say this enlightenment is pure, it is perfectly pure.

Rational Mind Created to Deal With the Material World

So, that is the purity of man's intellect, and the purity of man's rational mind, because his rational mind wants to stay in accord with material reality. It was created to deal with this material world. That is the main purpose of the rational mind. We live in a material universe and in a material environment. The rational mind was created, so that we can manage it. Is that clear? It is perfectly clear. So, these things have been animated. I like to use the word, animated, so that they work as metaphors. It is very effective. If a speaker talks and he cannot speak from concepts, pictures, and help his audience visualize, he's not yet a good speaker.

A Piece of the Garden That No One Is to Plow

So, he received the communication through Jibril. All human beings get help. I do not care, if they are doing serious thinking and work, they get help from their creation in the form of visions, dreams, or intuition. They get help from their creation. Nobody can turn the stream of intuition on for themselves. And G_d says there is a piece of the garden that is only for G_d. No one is to plow in it. That is this side I am talking about now. We don't have access to it. We have to wait for

G_d to bring it to us. You can't plow in it, and it is productive, too. But you have to wait until G_d brings it to you. He has to bring that garden to you.

In Surah Ar-Rahman, He did say there are two gardens. Those who earn it, they are going to get two gardens, not one. One is the garden that Adam was put in, and the other one is the garden that is in the sky where these big developers are. And G_d says, "You can come up here men and jinn. *Oh, company of men and jinn conspire, work hard. When you come up here you are going to find stars that are shooting missiles that will knock you out of the sky*". Lucifer, himself, was up there, but he fell, didn't he?

Jinn Move From Pure Reasoning

We know the germ, itself, that affects man's intelligence, his reasoning, his spirituality, and has the moral nature, is an invisible agent, but where is it? It is invisible like all other germs that bother human beings. So, where is it coming from? Jinn and people. Who are the jinn in people? Jinn they are those people who are rational like human beings. I am going on nothing but what is taught in Al-Islam. They are beings who are rational like human beings, but they don't move from human nature. They move from pure reasoning. That is why the Satan boasted, *"You made him of mud and made me of fire that gives off no smoke"*. It means, "I do not repent anything. I do not make mistakes with my intelligence, so what do I have to repent for? I followed strictly my intelligence, and he followed his sentimental nature".

Adam Is Not Everybody

This thing is much more than you think it is. The language has been in the hands of Adam since time began. Adam is not just everybody. He is the learned person that G_d chose to be responsible for the environment and to be responsible for man's future under G_d. Satan seduced him out of his nature and got him to be his tool and used him to make the world for Satan. The world was beautiful and safe for human life. This is the saying of the Prophet, peace be upon him, giving us the picture of the beginning of the world of mankind taken over where G_d left off. G_d made the world beautiful and safe for everybody, and then Satan comes in and puts his influence in the world, and then the world becomes unsafe for everybody. It becomes almost impossible for a person to keep their righteousness in such a world. This from the Prophet's hadith.

Satan Breathes His Message To the People

He (Satan) comes in and he fills the world with his messages; whereas the world was to breathe the message of G_d to the people, he comes and decorates it with his thing and breathes his message to the people, and he even shapes the language. He has Adam, so he gets the language. He takes over the languages. That is why you have to say, *"I seek refuge with Allah"*, before you read the Qur'an, because he (Satan) has already given you language. You are reading what the Qur'an says of G_d, but you already have a meaning for G_d in your mind that the world has given you. You already have a meaning for heaven in your mind that the world has given you, and the Devil has inspired these meanings. If you don't ask Allah's protection, you will follow the mind that the world gave you, and you will be reading and not reaching what G_d wants you to reach. But if you ask Allah's protection from the Satan and you really, sincerely, want the protection, He will give it to you, and you will read, and Allah will teach you who Allah is. He will teach you what heaven is. Praise be to Allah!

The Knowledge Has Come Into Our Hands

Jesus Christ, as a sign, points to Muhammed. One, as a sign, points to the original life that we need in order to prosper on this earth, the plan for life from G_d, from the Creator, that is in us when we're born. Jesus is a sign of that pointing to the Ka'bah, because that's a symbol, that is a sign of what I'm talking about. The Ka'bah is nothing but a symbol or a sign of what we're talking about, the original life and the original life pattern. Muhammed is not a sign pointing to that. He is the teacher leading us to that. Christ Jesus is the sign, Muhammed, the guide, the leader, guiding us to that. And he, himself, like Jesus Christ, already was constituted in that as perfectly as Adam was constituted when G_d first made him. Praise be to Allah! Muhammed, the Prophet, said there will come a time when the people, the world, will see he and Jesus together, agreeing in their purpose, not disagreeing. I thank G_d, the son of Elijah Mohammed has found it and seen it, understands it clearly, and knows that the knowledge has come into our hands, now. What comes into my hands comes into your hands. You can't say that, if it comes into another people's hands. Can you say that? If that had come into a people other than you, can you say,

"It came into their hands, and now it's our hand." No, I am a product of your woman. You see how we can talk, now? I am a child of your woman. Your mother and my mother are the same. It came into my hands, and it is now in your hands.

The Angels Harut and Marut

In the Qur'an, angels are mentioned by the names of Harut and Marut in the book of the people of the book, before the time of Jesus Christ, peace be upon the servant of G_d. This is before the time of Jesus, during the time of the great, glorious days for the Jewish people, in the time of Solomon, the wise, the great king, on him be peace. It is said, in the Qur'an, that they were taught certain magic by the two angels, Harut and Marut. And with this magic, which means this mysterious science… There is no word and really there is no word, there, that says, "magic". The translator was trying to convey the idea to the reader in English. I don't have problem with that. That is why we need to discuss these things. That is why we need commentary. Allah revealed to Muhammed that the angels showed them how to affect the relationship of husband and wife with the knowledge. But Allah revealed to Muhammed that they never shared that knowledge with those special leaders before telling them, "This is a trial, and do not become disbelievers", that such knowledge is dangerous in the hands of fools. They were warned, that's what Allah says in Qur'an, before they were given the knowledge.

Your Sexual Act Should Be Devotion to Community Life

Going back to the word, Ka'bah, it wants us to see it is a sign, a symbol that wants us to gravitate to see with our vision, let our sight gravitate to the origin of family, community life. And understand that this symbol or sign called Ka'bah, or the first house built for mankind, is a house that can only be erected, and it can only stand if certain connections are respected, certain relationships are held sacred, respected, and supported.

The relationship of man to wife or husband to wife, is not sexual but sex is a necessary element, that's all. That relationship should never be based upon sex. Even the lower animals do not base their relationship upon sexual pleasure. They have that pleasure and realize that the product of that action is now in the female, and she changes her behavior and becomes serious about being a mother before even the baby comes. This is an animal. And when the baby comes, already, she is devoted to the life of that baby. So, the purpose of mating is to extend life, to keep life existing and to care for life, so after the present ones are gone the life continues in its best form. This is devotion to community life, isn't it?

Your sexual act should be devotion to community life. This is naturally in men before the world of commercialism spoils them. They see a wife as a future, the natural man in his original nature. The wife sees the husband as a future. They look to family, to having babies and having more company than just one or two people. They look to a growing future of family and an organization of people loving one another, working with one another, supporting each other's life, and extending the productivity in the interest of life. That's what they see, and that's what community should be.

When you take sex for nothing but sex, you're less than animal. If that is what your wife is to you, your sex thing, you are less than an animal. I never had it in my spirit to see sex as just sex and a dirty thing. You know what sex was to me? A beautiful flower with pollen. It looks nice and smells nice, and it mixes with something from another, the opposite life, and it reproduces fruit. Here, the plant has been transformed. It's no more just a plant bearing leaves and flowers. Now it is a plant bearing fruit.

Our Original Focus Taken Away by the Attractions of the World

The Qur'an is addressing something that is the main cause for the corruption of society and the world. We have people who have gotten science from the revelation of G_d, and they are using that science to corrupt the relationship of man and wife and to corrupt family life. And they know that if they can corrupt family life, they can corrupt the whole society, and eventually the whole world. That is what has happened, and the prediction is in the Scripture that says, *"Corruption has spread over the land and sea"*. It is in the Qur'an, too.

So, how do they manage that? By giving you a different way to see human life. If they give you a way to see human life and that way to see human life is not in accord with the way G_d made human life, to develop upon definite natural designed plans, then what they give you will undo the life. The vital connections that G_d made for life that are signified in the term, Ka'bah, these vital connections will be lost. Don't think everything in the Bible is coming from the righteousness that is said by a people who are in the position of those who are protecting the way of G_d. For example, it says, *"Let us go down and confound their language, so they babble and speak no more".* That means speak intelligently. And another verse says, *"Let us cast their bands asunder, so they be a people no more."* That is in the Bible. "Separate their bands. Throw them away from each other, so they can't come together and be banded, again". Don't you see all that happening in world? Don't you see what has happened to us as a people? We have had our original focus taken away from us by the attractions of the world, and we don't focus on family life like we used to in the South, when we were fearing G_d. We don't focus on family life, like we did when we were in the South, fearing Allah, fearing G_d. If you called him Jesus, or whatever you called Him, He was a Superior, a Supernatural.

G_d's Preference For You

G_d doesn't blame you for your ignorance. You call Him in the name of Moda Waja, and that is not His Name. He knows the whispering of your heart before it even becomes a word in your mind. He is not going to blame you for saying, "Moda Waja". He is going to answer you just like you called the name, Allah. He is going to respond to you as though you said, "Allah". I said that because a lot of you join the theater of life. That is your expression. You say it so much you think something is wrong with my religion, or faith, because I don't say it as much as you. My heart, every time it beats, it says, "Subhana wa tala, Highly Gloried is He". Praise be to Allah! We know the life. It is not in the show. It is in the heart. So, they break the ties of life connections for human life. They confuse them, and cause you to depart from them, and that puts you in position to be made all over, again, by the wicked world, then the wicked world makes you. And when they make you, they make you for their ends. And what is that end? Money and power.

What I want to emphasize to you, at this time, is that Allah does not offer us something strange when He offers us the Qur'an, and He offers us Al-Islam. He says, *"Count not your Islam as a favor to G_d. It is a favor to you."* And then He says, *"This day, I have perfected for you your religion and completed My favor on you and have preferred for you Al-Islam as religion".* What a wonderful G_d He is! He said, "Preferred." It means, "I'm not dismissing those others. I know there are some other beautiful religions around. But this is My preference for you. Al-Islam is My preference for you!" It means that He didn't eliminate the others. He just pointed to His preference.

I have studied as a student for better than forty years, as a devoted student, as an obedient student for my Lord, Who created the heavens and the earth and me, and I have come to conclusion that it (Al-Islam) is my preference. I studied the communist doctrine. I studied Marx and Engels. I studied all those communist thinkers, because Mr. Fard left something in his teaching that made me think I should study them. What did he say? He said, "Social means to advocate a society of men, or a group of men for one common cause". He said that was the meaning of social. I could hear the ring of Karl Marx when he said that, because I was aware of what was in the air about Karl Marx. Now, understand that the communists were rising ahead of Mr. Fard. He said he came in 1930. We know from the records he was here in 1931. We have proof he was here working among us in 1931. But he said he came July 4th, 1930. That is what he left with my father in the lessons for us. The communist party started earlier than that. In the early 1920's they started. So, they were ahead of him, and some other ideas came into our world ahead of him, too, that he borrowed. I am not going into all of them, but he borrowed their ideas that were already in the world. He just took what he thought would work, and he put it all together and it worked.

Life is born out of the ground, isn't it? What is the dirt that grows our life but stuff that was? Dead leaves became dirt. Dead animals became dirt. Dead insects became dirt. Germs that were rejected became dirt. A lot of things became dirt. So, the dirt is a form of things that were. So, here Mr. Fard, he collected these things and then he put them in a special graveyard for us, and he said, "I'm going to leave them here and they will be resurrected". Thank G_d, it worked. I bear witness. I was dead and now I'm alive forevermore. I bear witness myself. I don't need anybody else. I know myself, and I was dead, but I'm alive forevermore.

Only G_d's Intervention Could Make Such Things Happen

As I mentioned earlier in this publication, the Qur'an says the angels, Harut and Marut, were given the powers to work miracles on man's life and they said, *"Don't charge us, now. We did not bid you to do these evil things that you do"*. And I bear witness that Mr. Fard never bade us to do any evil. He bade us, always to do good, to be righteous, upright, clean, decent, G_d-fearing, and work to be upright as Muslims; and do not say that you are Muslim, but when you are asked to say, "I'm trying to be upright". That is what we were taught. Praise be to Allah! There is more in that than most of us can see. Don't think the learned and wise leaders of great religious orders on this planet earth haven't heard about us and inquired and looked into our history as to what happened and created the Honorable Elijah Mohammed? What created the Nation of Islam? They have looked into all of that, and they are convinced that only G_d's intervention could make such things happen. Allahu Akbar!

Chapter 9

Relieving the Burden of Myth and Culture

Yakub was born in the year 8,400. It is all in the Jain religion, 8,400, 84,000,000. It is all in the Jain's teachings, and the Jains say, "Don't eat beans in the dark. Eat beans in the daytime," because a bean is a composite whole that is unseen. It won't be seen until the bean is placed in the right circumstances, and then a whole life and whole form is going to come out of there. So, don't eat beans in the dark until you're in the light. He's not talking about the real beans. The bean is only a sign of what they are talking about, the Jains.

"Eight Holds Up the Throne"

So, 8,400 is all in the Jains' teachings. But why 8,400? Eight, if you look at it, there is a ball on top of a ball, or eight is a square, because printers put a square on top of a square and a square has 360 degrees, and a circle has 360 degrees. Multiplying ninety by four how much do you get? You see, if my mind is not crowded, I can stay with it. If I tell you something that doesn't make sense, it is because something on my mind is snatching me away from my line of thought. Eight means the whole of reality. The whole created world and reality is the external reality. There is no reality here (inside of us) unless we are connected by G_d to this nature, with the external world in its nature, then this (body) becomes real. But until then it is nothing but guess work, superstitions, and whatever. So, the reality is out there, and the eight is reality. The eight is the real existence, the real world in its reality, in its truth. And (Qur'an says) *"Eight holds up the throne"*. It is the sciences, universal truths, that hold up the throne.

Thousand Is the Social Life

So, in 8,400, the eight means the world. The thousand means social life. So, when you establish that universal logic in the social life, you can then educate the people, properly. The Scripture is all about enlightenment and it does not stop with spiritual inquiries, because He said, *"Get ye down from here into the earth where you will find all of your aspirations in the social environment"*. So, you will be in a social environment where you will find all the goals you aspire to. The thousand is the social scene and the eight the sciences. Coming into the social scene means you're going to have education for the social community. You come with scientific insight and your knowledge is universal. It is not localized. What I teach here stands up in India, Paris, or wherever. Don't you know if I talked to the people of any community on this earth the way I talk to you, they would have no difficulty following me, because it is universal, and it is supported by G_d's real creation, not the one we imagine, come up with from our own imaginations, or take from somebody else who formed it in their imagination and think it is real.

Now, four hundred. When you look at eight, it is four plus four. So, if you reconcile four in the heavens, where the spiritual lies came to our mind to confuse reality for us, if you reconcile four in the earth with the four that is in the heavens that they have misrepresented in our understanding, you have given us the wrong understanding of what is heaven. But when you reconcile that, they are not at odds with each other, and as Allah says, *"Can't they see that the earth and the sky were once one continuous logic?"* They are all a part of the one system. So, when you reconcile the bottom eight with the eight, then you're ready to take care of the social needs. But as long as that conflict is between soul and practical life, or between spirituality and material reality, you can't make progress. You can't do that. But once it's reconciled, then you can teach the people and progress, advance the social community. And when you do that, you'll be doing it on your level, and it won't be a thousand, but you can teach the individual this. Thousand is the plural body. Hundred is the single body. A man lives on the average, a hundred years. Some die before, some live over a hundred.

Four hundred means you can take the individual and then teach him universality. It will be formed so that it will be appealing to any man or person of commonsense. So, here we are down here in our bodies. We each have our hundred, our individual life, and we have four directions, East, West, North, South, and those four directions mean the whole thing. So, the 8,400 brings it all the way to the individual person of commonsense. It means they don't have to die in the four. They don't have to die in the forty, or they don't have to be dead in the four hundred. Now you can communicate to them what G_d wants them to have through their commonsense abilities.

"The Kingdom Shall Be On His Shoulders"

"Eight holds up the throne", but there are also eight cattle, and when they prostrate, they don't put eight prints on the ground. So, there are a lot of hints, and some come from the sajdah. Some come from four heads of cattle in pairs, and some will come

from other sources; like the Prophet, he is the eighth in the Ascension, and he didn't have to go any higher than seven, but he became eight. Seven guided him back down to the earth to take care of the business of the eighth leader, and that is to bring heaven and earth, sky and earth, into agreement. He's not the kind of man who would point to himself. He would not say, "I have been given a mission, and I can hold up the throne".

In myth, Atlas holds up the throne, the world, on his back. He carries the world on his back, and it doesn't mean really, a man carrying the world on his back. It means a man with this intelligence can carry the world for us. The world is not too heavy for him, and from myth it comes into Scripture, and it says, *"The kingdom shall be on his shoulders."* That makes it a little easier to understand, doesn't it? Here a man has the whole earth on his shoulder. That's really some difficult stuff to understand. But in truth, the real leader that is guided right and inspired by G_d to understand His creation and how to establish community life in that creation, he is carrying the whole world. The whole world is not too big or too heavy for him to carry. But it makes it easier to teach it if you don't say the whole earth, but you say the kingdom, the order that G_d wants us to establish for man's life on earth.

The Black Man Was Crucified

The saying, *"It shall be upon his shoulders"*, that is Christ Jesus. Now how is he going to be able to carry this upon his shoulder? You know he bore a cross, too, didn't he? And they made him carry that cross upon his shoulders. The way they put it in myth or the movies it was a big, huge, cross, and they put it on his shoulders and made him drag it to the place of his crucifixion. But look how the black man comes in. It was so heavy for him and who felt sorry for him? It was a black man. This is what they say. The black man had compassion on him and went and got it and helped him carry it. The black man helped Jesus Christ carry the cross to the place of crucifixion, so who was crucified? The black man was crucified, not Jesus. Jesus can't be crucified. Jesus is the Word of G_d, and the spirit or influence of that Word. How can you crucify that? So, we don't accept, the Qur'an won't permit us to say Jesus died or was killed on the cross or was crucified. It says, "No, he was not killed, and rigor mortis didn't set in". That is what crucifixion is, rigor mortis. To get him to stay like that, they first put him in that position, and then they say he was dead. So, rigor mortis sets in because the blood became stiff, and they had to break his arms down. This is what they say. The soldiers came to take him down and they had to break his arms, because they had set that way because of rigor mortis. It might be a slight exaggeration, but rigor mortis fixes you. Whatever position you're in that's the position you would be found in, though they take you away from wherever you were that formed you like that.

Hollywood Made Frankenstein

The Qur'an says they didn't kill him. They didn't crucify him. But the word in the Qur'an for crucify means leave him for his body to stiffen, rigor mortis to set in, and they know all of this. Hollywood, they made Frankenstein, and Frankenstein was formed of dead bodies. He was not taken from the living but taken from the dead. He was formed of dead bodies and then the parts of the dead bodies were put together to complete his body, and to present him in the form of a man in every respect. Then he was put on a slab and raised up high in the sky during a storm, so the lightening would strike him directly, and bolts were put on his neck to take the electricity coming into his dead body, and his body was brought to life by the lightening. But when they brought him down and took him off the slab, he still remembered the position he was supposed to have (arms outstretched and stiff). This is the position he had in the sky. So now, he's walking down here and if he wants to speed up a little bit, the old groove (arms outstretched and stiff) takes over because he wants to speed. He's not thinking too carefully. So, Hollywood has given us a meaning of the cross. You have been fed a lot of dead knowledge from the world that died, and you have been given jolts of electricity. You go and listen to a sermon, and you get jolts of electricity or power, and you'll be quiet and almost about to go to sleep, and the preacher says something and jolts you. "Yes, thank you Lord! Thank you, Jesus!"

You go out of church and all you can do when you have to speed up is form a cross. You can't go anywhere. Your life is checked. You can't get out of the position they put you in, fixed. And the preacher is not satisfied until he has your mind fixated. When he thinks he really has you locked up by what he's giving you, then he's ready to give you direction. He's ready to tell you, "Put something in the offering". But he's not going to give you instructions until he knows you have become fixated, and he jolts you into a cross.

The woman who wrote the book, *"Frankenstein"*, obviously, had insight into Scripture, and she saw the average convert as Frankenstein. But look, frank, means open. Frankenstein, that is Jewish, there is no doubt about it. Frankenstein is a Jewish name. So, she is saying the Jews crucified the Christians. We know they didn't crucify Jesus Christ, so there is nobody left but his followers who were ignorant. And it turns out he was a good guy, right? Because they made a Frankenstein to show he really was a psychotic criminal. He had a good nature and in that movie a girl lost her balloon. It escaped her, and he got it and took it back to the girl. The little girl was afraid of him, but after he showed that kindness to her, she wasn't afraid of him. And then they showed him with a wife, too, and she was screwed up more than he was. She was really out of it.

Slang (Sling) Language

David went to the water, and he pulled out five stones. Doesn't that support what I have been telling you? And then he took one of those stones and he put it in his sling. It was not a sling. You know that. He put it in "slang" language and fired one into the head of Goliath. He only needed one. He did not need five. The one that did that he's smart. He was guided to take over the language of his enemies by working with the common, low people, and giving the common, low people cultural life. He gives them a cultural life, and he knows that the cultural life is going to eventually affect the rulers.

He has one rock in there that is going to knock the brain out of his adversary, Goliath. The big giant is going to be brought down by one. What is that one? That one is feeling, or emotionality. It said five. See how feeling and emotionality have come from the people on the ground, and culture has risen and just knocked the senses out of all the people on top of the world? And some of them, they just can't handle it. No matter how much education they have, they can't help it. They are under the same spirit the rapper is under, or his following is under. You pass by them and you're shocked when the speakers are up and vibrating your car. You turn and look, and it is a white man all dressed up in business clothes listening to that crap!

They have just gone wrong, that is the answer. G_d protects us. We are under G_d. Now he has all the education, is a successful businessman and he listens to that noise and has it up loud. Through feeling you can bring everybody down, and that is what that part of the Bible is saying, that he took one smooth stone out of the water. The key is he took it out of the water, so it is the science, or the logic of the water. It says a smooth stone. It has been rounded by the movement of the water. So, it is a logic that has been refined by the water, and that is the logic or science of how to defeat people through their senses or how to win them through their senses. The same science is for winning them over to righteousness, too.

The Fifth Column

The way to defeat the people is to come in through their five senses without them detecting it. You come through their subconscious. There was a wooden horse, the Trojan Horse. You know, "Wuud", is a name of a god and they knew it. We say, in Arabic, "Wuud", but in English, "Wood". How do you spell wood? You just spell what is pronounced as "Wuud", not, "Wood". Yeah, but that word is like when you woo somebody. Yes, to woo somebody, but without the letter, "d", but "Wuud", is the name of a false god. It is one of the gods of the Arab people, and it means god of love, or love. You know we saw one (Trojan horse) … in our travel. We saw a big Trojan Horse, wood. They put it on wheels, so they could roll it, and a horse or men could pull it. Now, it is all wood, but what is wood? A dead tree. When wood is like that, stripped, uprooted, and stripped of its bark and everything, all the leaves are gone, you're using nothing but the solid mass of it inside. The tree bark is like skin on us. For the tree it is a protection for the wood. When all the bark is gone off there is no more protection. So, it is dead wood. What does it mean? Dead culture, culture that can't speak anymore. It has no life of its own anymore, and they call it the Fifth Column.

So, this is saying, "This is the way we're going to penetrate your defenses and get into your society, get into your culture, or your country and defeat you and your people". When they knew anything, the door on the horse was opened up. It was supposed to be a gift, too, wasn't it? The gift of Jesus Christ. He gave His son to the world. So now, what comes out of this gift are people who are going to defeat you. They are coming to take over you and your land, the Fifth Column. Now, the picture is small when you look at it just with your eyes and try to imagine it with your mind without interpretation. But that wood is huge. It is talking about the whole culture of the people.

Entertainment Culture Takes Most People Away From G_d

And those five persons, human soldiers, who were in there, who came out of there (the wooden Trojan Horse), it might have been a different number, but they are not five. They might be 5,000, or 50,000, or 5 million. It is much bigger than what it is saying to us. But the main thing is to see what it is saying. It's saying that "You're going to be defeated by our plan that we're going to put in your dead culture. We're planning a defeat for you, and we'll put it in your dead culture." That is true. Entertainment culture has taken most of our people away from worshiping G_d and trying to make their life better. And that is what it is talking about, entertainment culture, not the general culture.

The Wolf Man

So, when that woman wrote the story of Frankenstein, the book about the creation of him, she was addressing the same thing that the Trojan Horse addresses, and it is said in so many ways. Her Frankenstein wasn't enough. They had to bring out a Wolf Man. Here is a man, but when the moon gets full, he becomes a wolf. In other words, when his mind tries to perfect itself, he can't do anything but go back to the Roman savage who started their history, they say, from suckling the she-wolf. Two boys were nursed by a she-wolf, and one was killed by the other because he was so stupid his brother killed him. He couldn't make it into the Promised Land. So, who is trying to perfect the mind? It's the religious leadership. They are the ones who want to perfect the mind. They want to perfect the mind. They can't be satisfied with just a human mind. They say, "No, we're more than human! We're human and divine!" There he goes back to the savage!

Now, we want to understand the mentality behind the world stage, because that is what it is. Who said the whole world is a stage? Shakespeare. So, if we want to know who is behind the stage, the orchestrator who originated, created it, go to the Qur'an where Satan says, *"Now that You have embarrassed me, I'm going at them from their left, right, behind them, and from before them. And when I have finished with them, You will not find many worthy, or thankful for this favor You're doing for them, making them the khalifah, making them the ruler in the earth."*

Satan Comes From Behind Us and Writes Our History

So, he said, "I'm going from the right, the left. I'm going from their conscious, from their memory, or we say, subconscious, and from behind them. I'm going from their past life. I'm going to attack them through their past life, and then I'm going to come right in their face and deal with them with what they can see and understand presently". How is he going to be able to put himself in my face, in front of me and I'm not going to be able to deal with him? He's going to escape my ability to perceive what I'm dealing with. How is he going to do that? By coming from behind me and writing history for me, so when I look back, I look at what he told me. Now, he has gotten me totally, and he can put his scheme and everything right in my face. I can't recognize it, and I can't perceive it.

"He Refused and Was Haughty"

So, what does Allah say about him now, before this is brought up? When he was told to submit, he became puffed up with pride, and exaggerated his own power and value before G_d. He became bigoted, in Arabic, "istakbara", which is from the Arabic verb root, "kabara", meaning, "big". He imagined himself big, an exaggeration of his own reality and worth, and he refused to obey G_d. So, how big was his exaggeration? It was as big as he imagined G_d to be, and the Bible said he aspired to rise on the breath of the air, up to the very throne of G_d and put himself in G_d's stead. Isn't that the Bible? So, the Qur'an addresses that in just a few words, *"Abaa wastakbara, He refused and was proud, haughty"*. And isn't that the way of those who just won't accept reality, or truth? The first thing they do is build an argument, and when they think their argument is really convincing, then they become so proud, so exalted in their falsehood. And he became one of the ungrateful ones, but it means he became one of the rejecters of faith. He doesn't go on faith. He doesn't trust faith.

Satan Never Existed In One Individual Body

So, you know that is the Satan, or the Shaytan, but he is plural, as well as singular. That describes the single disposition in minds that become satanic, or Shaytan. This is anyone who takes pride in his own power to find reality in the power of his intellect to serve him. He doesn't need any help, "I don't need faith to help me. I don't need religion to help me." So, those who take that position, they have taken the position that identifies Satan in their makeup.

We shouldn't look to a person, or one individual body for Satan. He never existed in one individual body. But that disposition took place in bodies at different times and not one. It had to be more than one body that took that disposition. More than one life in the body took that disposition. So, you look for that disposition and you see it, sometimes, in different people. It is not only in Jews. The disposition will be in black, white, red, any color. That disposition can be in any person's body, but who started it? Who got into Scripture and planned against man on this planet earth?

Frankenstein, and he made a monster. Mr. Fard would say Yakub, Jacob, made his grafted devil.

Now, just look at the situation for those who were idol worshipers. They weren't stupid, they were scientific. Among their leaders were scientists, great people, doctors, lawyers, everybody. But they had a religion for the masses of people, for the common people, that exploited their uneducated minds. So, they never had any desire to educate the public. Education was not for the public back then in their time, in the reign of the emperors and the people who were idol worshipers. They didn't have a plan to educate the masses. They were workers. They were looked upon as workers, and only those who were related to the rulers were chosen to rule.

Gog and Magog

Gog and Magog are a big subject, Juj wa Majuj, in Qur'an. So, who were they? The anarchists and the law-abiding people. The Gog are law-abiding people. Magog, they do not abide by laws. They are anarchists, and that nature is in people. The world is going to disappoint people so much until a lot of them are going to become anarchists against government, against law, and according to the Qur'an, Dhul Qarnain (Constantine) with insight saw a way to keep them apart. So, he had his men melted iron and then poured it into a groove to make a separation to separate Gog and Magog, or Juj and Majuj. Then he had them put lead over the top of that. When the iron cooled, they poured lead over the top of it to make it very slick. Lead is an impure metal, but it shines like it should be silver or something. So, it is deceitful, in Scripture. As a word in Scripture, it is very deceitful. That is in Christianity, and as I said, the one who did that was the one who came in 325 A. D., the Roman emperor, Constantine. He had a vision. He is in the Qur'an under another name, but that is who it is. He is the one who established Christianity in the way that it is now and made it very slick. It attracts those people who would be anarchists. They are not slick enough to crawl over the separation.

"He Sent Down Iron"

Allah says, *"He sent down iron"* or *"He revealed iron for mighty war"*, and it has reference, directly, to the title of the chapter, Al-Hadid, The Iron. We speak of weightlifting, sometimes, as they're pumping iron. Now, that reference to iron is power. The reference to iron in the Qur'an is a much greater power and that is the social nature of man. If it is used it is very powerful, and when men go to war to defend themselves or their country, they depend heavily on what? Social nature saying, "Brothers, comrades in arms, don't forget your families! We have to defend our families!" So, the social nature is usually what government leaders call on. They try to appeal to that social nature to get the men they need and the supplies, equipment, arms, whatever, for war. We have come to a time when the social nature has been ignored, the family life, so they just impose what they want on you. They don't ask you for anything, just for some more money to finance it.

So, Dhul Qarnain built something to keep Gog and Magog from being at each other. He built a wall of iron and then he poured over the iron molten lead. So, the iron was not showing the lead, and the lead was obviously a protection for the iron, because lead does not rust quickly, like iron. It holds longer. So, the lead is over the iron to protect it.

Lead is a poisonous metal and iron is not. It (iron) is an element we need, and we even need to consume it. It represents the social life. So, he built a great wall, meaning a protection and he built it, firstly, appealing to the social interest of the people and got their interest heated up so hot they were passionate in support of what he was doing. Then he let it cool or set. Then he poured molten lead over it. The iron is the science of the social nature of man in society and the lead is religion, but more, specifically, church religion (the Trinity). It is slick. You can't get over that. You can't climb up on that, buddy!

Lead is in the present or pointing to the future. Led (lead) is always pointing to the past. You put all those past lies together, and it is lead. Put all those ancient lies together and add lies to it, it is lead. That is what it is, poison smelt, very slick. And if rain falls on it, it does not change it, because it is impervious to human sentimental nature, cold. Leave lead outside and put a piece of iron in the same temperature, and when it starts to get cold feel the lead, it is colder. The lead will be cooler than the iron, though they are in the same temperature environment. The temperature is cooling the same. Put them side by side and when you touch the iron, it will not feel as cold as the lead. To me, this is a sign of G_d's presence, that everything in His creation speaks to what is happening to man's nature and life. It says He created the universe so that mankind would have His Mercy. He created the world expressly for His Mercy, a mercy to mankind.

The Scientist Is Ahead of the Imam

And then when He sends His last Messenger, that is what He sends, a mercy to all the worlds. So, that will be revealed and communicated through a human being to all human beings, that G_d created His world for mercy. So, when He says, *"Wasi'at kulla shayen rahmatan wa ilman,"* translated, *"He communicates, or broadcasts knowledge in everything that exists"*, i.e., a gnat, a grain of sand, etc., look what they were able to get out of the sand, microchips, something they took for granted, thought it had no value except at the seashore. That is all.

So, really those two descriptions of matter, how everything in matter broadcasts knowledge and mercy, they can easily be understood when you look at where science has gone. Science has studied everything. They don't eliminate anything, and they study it because they think it has a use to be put into service for mankind. The scientist is ahead of the imam. The imam, he is dumb. In the Qur'an, the scientist is wise. He says, "They think this is nothing but a hullabaloo and get so happy and faint. This is wisdom, science!" And that is what happened in the days of the Prophet. The bright-minded ones, they immediately saw and said, "This is speaking and addressing the real objective, the material world, and it's giving us hints to go to that world and study it, explore it, to utilize what G_d has put in it for human community life." And they did it and got so far ahead of everybody. But what has happened, now, is they are lagging when it comes to real faith and practice of their faith, and they are lagging in moral life. They are behind in their moral life and Allah is getting ready to turn it over to a new generation of thinkers, Obama, and the future; and believe me, he (Obama) captures the whites just like he captures us, no difference. He captures everybody.

They Can't Tell Anybody

So, they designed the world of reality so that the common people would be held by superstition, suspense, mysticism, anything other than reason and logic. So, they lived in a make-believe world, and that is how they were kept in check, i.e., deny them reality, cut them off from reality. Now, the leaders of those pagan cultures, nations, and governments… it was a different one who did it. He was powerful enough that he brought all Rome under Christianity, and that was Constantine, the Great. He made it the state religion, for the whole nation. Now, they later discovered that Frankenstein sent us up in the clouds during electric storms and charged us up with Bible teachings, and when we came back down, we were Frankenstein's monster.

Now, here it is more than 1,400 years later. Muhammed opened their eyes, and they said, "Now, you know this Islam, they've got something! Now, you know we've been suspecting that we were hoodwinked and misled. Now, we know who did it. But if we tell it, look how embarrassed we will be before the whole world. Let's keep quiet. We can't tell anybody. Never reveal this! All those who are not a part of our order will laugh at us. We will be laughed at and scorned, laughed to death!" So, they can't tell anybody. Isn't that something?

Satan Conspired to Change the Way People See Reality

Nobody would suspect that an intelligence in man's world would conspire to do a job on a universal scale to really change the way people see reality, so that they serve the creator of that artificial reality, and not the Creator of the true reality. Nobody would think that kind of intelligence would be in mortals. And really, it's not in mortals, because once you perceive yourself in such role, you're not a mortal anymore. No, you're demon. You're not mortal. A mortal senses pain and hurt. They don't sense pain and hurt. They don't operate from that reality. They operate from pure knowledge. That is why in Qur'an it says he said, *"You made us of fire that gives up no smoke."* He doesn't repent anything. "We're not in the dark as to anything. Why should we give up smoke"? Smoke means something was not consumed and it is dark. So, He says, *"You made us of a fire that gives up no smoke. We repent nothing"*. Isn't that the arrogance of these so-called intellectuals? "The United States, we know what you're giving us. We know what you have done for us. Now, you want us to bow down to you? No, we bend our knees for nobody!" That is what Ariel Sharon said on the radio, boasting. I heard it in Chicago. So, the Qur'an described them perfectly and the Bible, too, if we understand it. "Your light is so blinding that you can't see your own reality and what you're looking at, you can't see it in the true figure. Your light blinds you. You're fascinated by your own light. Your light is everything to you. Nothing exists, except your light. So, you don't respect anything".

They Have Reached the End of the Road

The greatest impediment I see to a possibility for harmony and peace in the world today, is world powers imposing what they believe is good for the world on others.

There are some hardcore Zionists in Israel, and they will not even let the Israeli public, the citizens of Israel, have a free voice. They work with whoever will work with them around the world, and they are trying to impose what they believe should be the order for mankind on this planet. We differ with that, and I think that is the greatest impediment to peace. I wish our country would not be so loyal to the wrong people and to a small people, while disrespecting what the world wants. We should not impose our democracy on anybody. We should invite people to copy the best that we have, if they choose to. But we should not impose upon them. We should let them work out their own future and have their own form of government.

So, now they have reached the end of the road. This plan to take over the world and have the world bow to them, make sajda to them and say, "You are our creator! You're our lord! We know you are G_d's only begotten. We accept you. The United States is at your service. Great Britain is at your service. Saudi Arabia is at your service", that is what they're thinking they're going to get. That is what they have worked for. Now, they're at the end of the road and (President) Bush can't be depended on for anything. You thought you had Frankenstein's monster in Mr. Bush and "He is wild on his own liquor. He is not drinking the one you gave to him, and now all these sober boys are coming up to get rid of him, because we're being set back for another thousand or two thousand years". That is what the hidden Jews, Zionists, hidden bosses are saying in Israel, and in other parts of the world.

They Are Going Back to Ritualism

"You think we're going to be set back for another thousand or two thousand years?" And they say, "Yes, we think so. Tell our boys to go back to ritualism!" Yes, the Pope in the Church, Evangelicals, they're all going back to ritualism. It came out in *Time Magazine*, I believe it was. So, they're turning out all the oil lamps, turning them off, dousing the flames. Everybody is in the dark, and you can see whatever you want to see. Just look at Jesus on the cross. Whatever you see, that is good. Just look at pictures and signs and just express what you feel. You can't talk anymore! The world is too smart, they're listening!

Going to Hell In Droves

For those people who are not living their religion in America, what we're looking at is a public majority that is actually in hell. They're actually in hell! Read the description of hell in both the Bible and the Qur'an, if you can understand the

311

language. It's not difficult. It can almost be taken literally. But with a little interpretation, hell is just as clear. It says hell shall present itself to you, and you shall see it with sure vision, for certain, and that is this time we're living in. The Bible says the people will be going to hell in droves, big crowds, and the Qur'an says this, too, in different ways, almost the same language. The believers will be able to view them from a distance going to hell, but the believers will be going to heaven. How is it going to be that people are going to hell in droves and believers are going to heaven in droves, too, and they are going to be distant from each other, and be able to view each other? At least the believers will be able to view the disbelievers. That means they are in the same circumstances, only one survived it and the other one didn't, and that is the world right now. Some people are hell bent, and you can't turn them around.

"Hell Fire Is Reality!"

In the Qur'an, it says, in hell, every time one skin is finished, burned away, right away it will be replaced with another skin. As soon as one skin is burned away, it will be replaced with another skin. So, the torment is continuous, because when a skin is burned, it becomes dead if it is burned enough. The skin, itself, becomes dead and it doesn't feel. But if you were burned deep, you're still hurting, in pain. But now, here comes another skin to start the pain anew and fresh, or full of sensitivities, again. So, the person experiences the maximum punishment of hell.

Now, what is the interpretation? Skin is what you feel with and the Bible from Genesis to Revelation is all about people becoming hardened to conscience, to feelings, where they don't feel anything. They don't feel what they should feel. So, replacing the skin means, as soon as the people become dead to the punishment, a new sensitivity will be given to them, so they can feel it again and go through the same thing again, over and over again; and that is the way the culture is. It gives those corrupt people one excitement behind another. As soon as one excitement wears off, or becomes dull, not impressing them anymore, they get a new excitement: sensationalism, people living for maximum pleasure, orgiastic nature. They've got to get a high climax. As soon as that one is over, they need another charge, another excitement to bring them to a climax. That is their skin being replaced. The Holy Qur'an is very clear. It doesn't leave you in the dark. But the picture book story of reality is so powerful that you can't show people reality. Their mind is fascinated, fastened to that picture. They think that is real. They think their picture is real. It says in the Qur'an as plain as day, *"An naarul haqq, hell fire is* reality". It is not myth and superstition. It is reality, and it is no new thing. The people of the book, they just copied the old, ancient, oppressors of mankind. The Greeks had a town they called Heliopolis, and Helen was the ruler over there, too, a wonderful queen, and they gave it her name, because under her hell did not even smoke. All the fires were contained so well not even smoke came out.

An Obsession for Acquiring Knowledge

You've heard the expression, "Let me know when we are off the air." Why does it have to be air for this system of communication? Because the Bible and Scripture says the beast was sent down and confined to the earth, was told to dwell in the earth, crawl on his belly and bite the dust for his disobedience, but he was free to challenge the human being and the human purpose if he wanted to. G_d gave him that freedom, so he went to work. The Bible says, *"Rejoice not, oh Palestine, for out of the serpent's root shall come a flying cockatrice".*

He is going to mount the air. Isn't that what the Scripture says? He mounted the air. Why does he have to mount the air? Because the air is above you, and those creatures that manage to mount the air, we are off the air, and we are in the air. We're into it. Those creatures that mount the air have vision stronger than those that can't mount the air. They just walk around on the ground. Those that mount the air their vision is stronger and bigger. They can see more at one time than the creatures can that just stay on the surface of the earth. The message that you should get from him being able to mount the air is that his perception became so much bigger. His vision and perception of reality became so much bigger, for he was all about acquiring knowledge. That was his fascination, his obsession.

He was able to acquire so much knowledge that he was able to mount the air, fly in the higher regions of the space, not physically, mentally. It is talking about human intelligence, human acumen, human ability to grow in mind to master or manage the earth and what it provides. So, he managed to mount the air. In the Qur'an, not only is the possibility of mounting the air addressed, but the possibility of going to outer space is addressed. It says that they desired to get a hearing to hear what is going on up there among the stars. It says you cannot do that unless you have great knowledge and power. G_d did not say that he could not do it, but G_d said, "Where you are situated, now, you cannot do that. *You cannot do it without great knowledge and power!"* In Qur'anic Arabic, it is, *"Illa bisultaani."*

They pursued it and kept pursuing it, and they managed to build a transportation or a rocket to go to the moon and land. I remember when that happened. The Honorable Elijah Mohammed had been for years telling his people that you cannot go out there. You cannot survive out there. He was talking about going to the moon. "If he goes to the moon his blood will boil, his eyes will pop out of his head". My father didn't know anything about space suits that contained oxygen or air in that space suit for him to breathe while he is away from the earth. He did the best he could. He went on what he knew, and I am sure that he wanted to understand. He was not a fool. He was a very intelligent man. He would not tell you, "I made a mistake". That was not his way. He said, "A man who puts himself up high like me, son, he cannot acknowledge a mistake, because if he did the people would say that he was lying all the time".

He could not explain it in his time, but I am him in my genes. Do you understand that? This is not spooky. I am not talking about any superstition. I am the genes of the Honorable Elijah Mohammed. I am the flesh and blood of Elijah Mohammed and Clara Mohammed, and many who went before them. Many that their parents came from, I came from that same lifeline and their life is in me, and Elijah in me is going to explain using my voice.

The Moon In Ancient Egyptian Myth

It was never meant for us to think that the moon in our esoteric, secret language that came from Mr. Fard, was the physical moon that you saw last night, tonight, or see in the daytime, if it appears. It is not that moon at all. What is the moon? It is the moon in ancient Egyptian myth. It is Isis. She was the moon, and she eclipsed her father, the sun. His name in myth is Osiris. She found a way to eclipse him, and eclipse up there means one thing in astronomy, but he eclipsed in government means one rule eclipsed another. It means one rule overpowered the other and a new rule came into its place. This is the way we understand Isis and Osiris. Isis represents the ancient, high science called spiritual science that has embodied within its deep psychology. Isis represents that body of knowledge. She is a human personification of that knowledge. So, they are not talking about two humans, and they certainly are not talking about the moon and the sun up there in the sky.

Psychology Started With the Spirit of the Sciences

They are talking about a knowledge that takes care of their society like the sun takes care of earth. It warms it up. It gives it guidance. It opens darkness, so life can see how to move about, and it grows your food. It grows things, so that you can have more production. It drives the clouds with the wind, and it sends you rain. It sends you darkness, the fire, the sun, and the heat that is associated with the sun. Heat is not associated with the moon. It is associated with the sun. That is high science in the social side of life, the social community, the social sciences, Osiris. Isis is the spiritual sciences that I said also embodied psychology. Psychology started with the spirit of the sciences. When the spiritual sciences are made so attractive and interrupt the flow of the social sciences, and the spiritual sciences become very attractive, so attractive that the social sciences are not in focus anymore like it be used to be, not in the conscious, the spiritual sciences have now eclipsed the social sciences. Isis is the moon, and the Honorable Elijah Mohammed was saying that the spiritual sciences that are with G_d that was given to His Prophets, this white man does not have it. I would agree with the Honorable Elijah Mohammed. How could you have that and be such a fool on this earth, thinking yourself superior because your skin is white, and your eyes are blue, and you can find animals with white skin and blue eyes, and they are not superior to a black man? So, what makes you think your blue eyes, and your white skin makes you superior, when I see a blue-eyed animal and a black man cutting its throat, dressing it to barbecue it? White skin, blue eyes, and straight hair, too, a black man has skinned it and now is barbecuing it.

Talked to by a Snake

That is why I say a man who comes up with that kind of a conclusion must be a fool. He has been talked to by a snake. The snake must have come and talked to him and sent him on a rationalization trip, and he rationalized himself right out of reality and truth. I said I was going to explain to you what the Honorable Elijah Mohammed could not explain to you back then. The moon is a body of science that the white man was not supposed to have been able to reach, and the Honorable Elijah Mohammed said he did not believe he would be able to reach it. "Daddy, if you could hear me, now! He couldn't reach it then, and he can't reach it now! They think they've got it, but they do not have it until G_d gives it to them. If G_d does not give it to them, they will never have it! I will give it to them. I am very generous, and I am nothing but a little, small instrument. G_d is the Big Matter!"

"Son" a Play On the Word, "Sun"

We talked about the three veils of darkness in the Bible, and mind you, it says, *"As it was in the days of Noah, so shall it be in the time of the coming of the son of man..."* It is spelled, s-o-n of man. Son is a play on the word, s-u-n of man, the social sciences that support the life created by G_d, the human community life created by G_d. How are you going to get the social sciences? Do you think man sits down and writes social sciences? No, it is a long process. Man studies nature, the natural happenings in the life of people. He studies how nature moves life in communities and then comes up with an accurate report of what he observed in nature having as its inner workings and connecting workings those that connect man and man, woman and woman, interest and interest, etc., until he has a society or community that is thriving. Man observes that. He studies that, and then he writes what he observes or studies. Then he tests it under different circumstances, and he comes up with conclusions. He writes that. He then gives it to your sons or daughters in college as science.

Science Is the Direct Communication of Mother Nature

Science is the direct communication of Mother Nature, the direct, true science. True, factual science is a direct communication of Mother Nature. Allah, G_d, says in our book there is coming a time when the world is going to be so confused that the earth, itself, is going to start behaving as though G_d revealed something to it, as though she received a revelation. Here is another metaphor, another personification, like a mythical picture of what is happening, but it is accurate and true.

When you abuse yourself eating the wrong foods your own body rejects what you are doing. You vomit, get sick, and you break out in a fever. Your own body is rejecting what you are doing. The whole earth will come to do that when we keep feeding our life that came from Mother Nature insanity, filth, etc. The public life is going to spit up, too. The public life is going to vomit all over the place. We look at the trouble and say, "It is really bad! Look how they are killing each other! Look how they are just going after sex with no intelligence!"

Nowhere to Go Except Back to the Normal Human Being

When a person gets sick with a disease, sometimes the disease is something that builds toxins up in the blood, in the system. The subject or the victim of this breaks out in all kinds of ugly sores. You think it is the end. The doctor comes and looks at him and says, "It is in its terminal state. He is going to be alright after this." That is the way I look at our public killing each other over nothing, ready to kill and be killed for nothing, liking filth, working hard to defy intelligence, etc. They do not live by intelligence. I see this as a terminal state. The poisons are all coming out, and they are going to be well, pretty soon. This is the end of it. What we are seeing is the end of it. There is nowhere to go, except back to the normal human being.

"One Day We Will Rise Up and Take Our Place"

The idea that's really subtle in these movies and what's happening is they're saying it's black people's time and black people, such as Marcus Garvey, said, "One day we will rise up and take our place in the constellation of the stars!" Well, that is what is happening. Hollywood, the cultural world, they all are recognizing that the African Americans have made it.

"WD 40", that is the motor oil from the motor city, Detroit, Michigan. That is where it started, and if the two influences were not here together, I don't think we would ever wake up. I'm talking about the influences from the liberation movement of our people supported by the Church, the Bible, the Nation of Islam, or the Temple of Islam, and the history of the nationalist movement that Mr. Fard was able to just take all the important influences and put them together into one. If that had not happened, I think we would still be sleeping, or one thing is we would not have our own direction. We might be well off just following the way of world. The better of us would be doing well but following the way of the world, like Oprah Winfrey, and many others. They are doing very well managing in the society, but when the Hollywood general culture put black people in those roles showing that they are leaders now, and not just followers, that had nothing to do with Oprah. She did not make it there. She made it with the money, but she didn't make it with the culture.

America Is Modern Egypt

What it is saying is that our people have come into knowledge of this culture and how to make it through that culture and succeed in America with their lives. Independence, that is what it is all about, if you are in a system. You see, this is modern Egypt. Culture-wise, that is exactly what it is. This is no mythological connection I'm making. This is reality. They planned it that way, for America to be modern Egypt. They say, the Promised Land. They acknowledge that, so we can reason then that this is modern Jerusalem, because Jerusalem is supposed to be the Promised Land. But it is not modern Jerusalem. The Jews were in Jerusalem and the Bible says, *"Take your child and flee to Egypt"*. So, it is not Jerusalem, it is modern Egypt. And if you look at the Catholic Church, you see that their hierarchy looks like the ancient hierarchy of the priests under Pharaoh, the way they dress and everything.

Cairo Means It Overwhelms You

You know, the construction in these modern cities, the high skyscrapers, etc., it just overwhelms the poor man. The first time I went to New York City and passed by those tall ones and looked up, I got dizzy. It overwhelms you and that is what Cairo means. It means it overwhelms you. You know the attribute of G_d, The Subduer, Cairo is taken from that name. Cairo is Qahera, and The Subduer is, Al Qaaher and it is no accident that the name, Cairo, is taken from that attribute of G_d. That is to say the mightiest subduers you have in the history of mankind was the Pharaohs of Egypt, but G_d is the real Subduer, because He made Pharaoh, and all of his efforts are nothing, but a sign left for you to remember what happened. The word in English I'm looking for, the Arabic word is, nikal. It has a lot to do with nickel.

Nickel and Kryptonite

Nickel is metal and it is five cents. So, the Arabs use the word, nikal, and it came into our language as, nickel, and it is a very hard metal that looks to be pure. It looks to be silver, but it is not pure, and that is what the culture of ancient Egypt was. It was very difficult to decipher. So, nickel was in their language, but now we say kryptonite. That is made up. There is no kryptonite. You can't get it out there in the metal field. It is made up to say it is very difficult and very hard to manage, and it came from the crib (krib-to-nite). They have the secrets of your life in the crib. That is what they managed Superman with, the evil ones. It is supposed to have come from the planet he came from up there in outer space somewhere.

From Sounding Clay

You know that language has subtle hints, and Allah says they believe that man was made from clay, and Allah said says, *"Yes, from sounding clay,"* potters' clay, that makes a sound, or rings. So, the wisdom of the guidance there, I understand it to be that man has to have an ear for the sound of words, how they sound. So, you have dawn, the break of day, and you have darn, to repair the socks for the feet. You can darn anything. Actually, when you think of darn, if the psychiatrist ever asks you (hope you don't have to go), if you ever have to go to the psychiatrist, and he asks you, "The dawn of day, what comes to your mind?" If you say the darn, like you darn socks, like you darn a piece of material, he says, "What piece of material?" If you say, "Jacket", he is not going to come to conclusion that you don't need his help yet. But he is going to make a little note, because that's the automatic expression, right? "Darn the sock..." You see, I just gave you that example. This generation, they don't know that expression. They not darning anything. They don't know anything anymore. But our generation, some know that women used to darn socks. My mother did.

"And He Taught Adam the Names of Things"

So, it says, *"And He taught Adam the names of things"* and then Adam hid it in the sound, made him of clay, but potters' clay. What is the difference between potter's clay and the clay? Clay means fresh clay. Clay, without the description given in Qur'an, means fresh clay. Fresh clay as a meaning tells us that G_d made man a baby, that's all, the behavior of a new baby, and a new baby is like fresh clay. It is ready for you to shape its mind, personality, whatever you want. He takes his shape from his mother, father, environment, from whoever will groom it, whoever will shape it. So, that's what the clay is by itself. But the sounding clay, that's the expression in the Qur'an, and it means, now, that behavior is fixed. It won't allow any shaping. You have to break that pot. You can't shape it anymore. It's fixed. The clay becomes fixed when you bake it, so sounding clay.

Now, that doesn't only bring to me the message that man's behavior is originally pliable or agreeable to whoever will groom it, or shape it, and then becomes fixed. We also become fixed in our behavior. I get more out of that because the word for potter's clay that is used, it has a sound, and the sound of the word suggests to us the sound that is made when you strike clay with something hard. That's why the translator is right, i.e., sounding clay, potters' clay. Some say sounding clay. His insight is correct, in my opinion.

Adam Left to His Descendants In the Form of Words

This takes us to language. We have to leave clay and come to language, and what fixes us in our behavior? What gives me this conviction that I have, the behavior I want, and this is the right behavior and will not accept that you will influence my behavior, change my behavior? It is after we have gotten some knowledge. We know children are stubborn like that. That's not the fixing we're talking about. The fixing under that kind of fire, it goes away soon. It's a temporary fix. He's stubborn in this situation and he's back to fresh clay, again, after that, so not that. The fire we're talking about is the fire of knowledge. Once the fire of knowledge bakes your clay, it's fixed until somebody brings a greater knowledge. And when they bring a greater knowledge, they don't reshape your clay. They destroy your clay. New knowledge destroys the old vessel, and a new vessel must be made.

This is to tell us in order to understand Adam, we must first understand Adam as an intellect. But we're to understand Adam as language. *"In the beginning there was the Word"*. Adam was the intellect, but what was its purpose? To leave his intellect with his descendants, and to do that he must communicate it. So, he was left to his descendants in the form of words.

The Nature of Language Is Expressed and Covered

We originally see Adam as flesh and blood, but later after he dies, we have to see Adam as language. Words, teachings, knowledge, are given to us in language. Now, over the period of time, because of Adam's intellect, we have to give Adam the credit for it. This language becomes, itself, a revealing thing. It reveals and to say, "reveal", it means something was hidden or something is hidden. So, this is the nature of language. The nature of language is expressed, and language is covered. The same word I use to say something to you that everybody hears, I can use that word to say something to you that nobody will hear but you that I'm speaking to, especially, if I put the right sound to it. Nobody will get the message, but you will, and we do that, sometimes, because we don't want to tell everybody what we're talking about. So, we put emphasis on the sound of this word, and we'll keep talking knowing that we communicated a special message to the ones we communicated it to. *"And He taught Adam the names of things"*.

The Universe Is Speaking Two Languages

He taught Adam the names of things. G_d taught Adam the names of things, and the method of speaking in two languages came from G_d, because G_d is the One that revealed to man, originally, that this universe is speaking two languages. There's sun in the ordinary language and sun in another language... and when He taught Adam the names of things, when He told Adam *"Tell them their names"*, they all submitted. Why? Because angels don't get that. That's the language of man. Believe me, it's in the sciences. The higher you get in knowledge, the more powerful this language is. So, that's why, in the world of literature, it has different terminology for the challenges in the language for the intellect. One of the terms that's used to express great difficulty, great challenges for the intellect is, "kryptonite", and there are other terms to let us know that this is very difficult for the intellect to penetrate. The material is so hard. And if there is "kryptonite", it's in the highest sciences.

It's "Crystal Clear"

So, they come up with a material that you can't find on earth, not granite, not steel, kryptonite, and they have other terms, too. Superman, he brought kryptonite from another planet. He came with it in his hand, in the movie. He brought a piece with him and that's how the crook got it from him, otherwise, the crook couldn't have gotten it. "Cryptic", is from the same word, all are from the same word, "cryptology". Used in one way, it means, grave, death, or dead things, dead matter, study of the dead. The kryptonite (that Superman had) was crystal, and they have the expression, now, "It's crystal clear". That's the language of Adam, but don't be lured by it, because it can take you right into the spider's web.

A Plan by the Zionist Devils

In the Bible, the rich man that Jesus spoke to, he asked how he could be received, accepted, or have the kingdom, and Jesus told him, *"You have to be born again."* He asked Jesus Christ, *"How can I go back into my mother?"* Jesus didn't answer because he knew better. He knew better but pretended like he didn't understand. "What you're saying is impossible! If you don't talk plainly to me, I'm going to treat you just like you're treating me! You're talking to me indirectly, so I'm going to speak to you in the same way. I'm going to pretend like I don't know what the hell you're talking about! How can I go back into my mother?" Jesus said, not dignifying his question, *"Nevertheless, you have to be born again!"*

I studied all this. I searched the book, and searching for what I wanted I came upon all these things. There was a plan by the Zionist devils. They don't see themselves as devils. They see themselves as angels. Iblis thought himself an angel, didn't he? That's why he was up there leading the angels. There was a plan to capture the world for themselves, and one of the strategies for getting the world, or the secret, covert, hidden plan, whatever you want to call it, was to manage and progress the nature, manage the human nature, and progress the human nature. So, whoever can be successful in achieving that they will have the world, won't they? So, G_d revealed His Word to them, to mankind, so that man will be able to be responsible for his own nature, and for advancing that nature in the rich world that G_d put that nature in to get benefits from it. There is no Satan in Judaism. There is no language, Satan, no Devil in Judaism. They say that plainly. You have never heard the Jews preach and say Devil, Shaytan, or Satan. And believe me, Shaytan is the way they would pronounce it because the "sh" is for Arabic, a Semitic language, the same as it is for Hebrew, a Semitic language. So, they won't say Satan as the Christians say. They would say, "Shaytan" as we say. So, it would be Shaytan for them, and sometimes our "s" becomes not "s" with them. It is "sh", like we say, "Salaam", they say, "Shalom". So, if they were to say, "Devil, they probably wouldn't say, "Satan". They would say "Shaytan", even though our "Salaam" for them is "Shalom". Satan would most likely be "sh". But Aramaic is a little different, it's Satan.

How Are They Going to Get the World?

How are they going to get the world, with the nature of the human being under their management, so that they manage it and advance it? They get it by exploiting the nature of the human soul, and what is the appetite in the soul that is there as a need and necessity for the human soul? It is there in the earliest manifestation of the soul and its appetite for things. It is there firstly. What it is? It is given in Qur'anic and Islamic knowledge. The soul and its regardfulness, taqwa and its fujur, appetite. So, there are two originally in the soul, two activities. One is based in the fear of consequences, so the soul is activated by fear of consequences as taqwa, and the fear of the consequences of wrongdoing. So, the first nature in the soul must be described as moral nature. It is that life that wants to be correct. It doesn't want to be wrong. It fears the consequences of behaving incorrectly, so that is the taqwa.

Allah Deposited In the Soul Its Taqwa and Its Fujur

So, Allah deposited in the soul that He made its taqwa and its fujur, its moral orientation and its rational orientation. Fujur is its appetite, its hunger for knowledge and understanding. The flesh hungers for MacDonald's. I had a hard time getting past it when I got my salad. It's the flesh hungering for that, but that is not the first hunger in the soul, because when the baby comes here it doesn't come here hungry. It's been feeding in the womb, the stomach, the system of its mother, so when it comes to us it is not hungry. It's not hungering for that kind of food. It is hungering for understanding. So, the hunger in Scripture is not about the hunger for these material things, except as the material things represent bodies of enlightenment, or understanding wherein its locked up in that body, and you want to decode or break into the nature of that physical thing, so you can see how it operates, what holds it together, what has brought it together, what is its inner nature or behavior.

The Appetite Is for Knowledge

This is the appetite we have. The appetite is for knowledge. So, the Satan wants to get management of our life and wants to be responsible for advancing our life if he can do that, then he becomes leader of the world. Scripture says He aspires to rise up upon the air. This is Scripture. He has already gotten on, started work on the land, and he has already gotten into the waters even before he got on the land. But he is not finished. He wants to get on the air. So, on the land means in our rational minds. But before he got into our rational mind where did he set up his station? In the water. And in myth, they give it as Neptune. But the Zionist devil he got the sciences from the so-called idolaters with the help of heavenly light, where Prometheus, I believe it is, he stole the light from heaven, in myth.

So, the Zionist come behind them and say, "These pagans, they don't know what to do with this world they have". So, he got ahead of even the pagans who were very advanced in their knowledge of the human soul, its nature and how to master it. They had that, too. So, the Zionists get it from them and then they're now saying, the ones who aspire to become the masters, rulers of mankind on the planet so that the world will be exclusively theirs, they say, "The sensitivities of the people we can master them. We can capture them through their sensitivities, or through the door of their sensitivity we can reach their sanctuaries and capture their sanctuaries", which is my private possession of my own soul. Our soul is the sanctuary. "We can capture their very sanctuaries, and the way we do it is to feed them sweetness until they get hooked on it." Now those before us they exploited their waters and they were able to get control over their publics by exploiting their waters, their human sensitivities. We're going to be more powerful than our predecessors. Those who came before us, we're going to be more powerful than them, because we're not only going to exploit their waters. We're going to change the nature of their waters. We're going to sweeten their waters."

Sweet and Salty Water

It is in the Bible that they had a plan to sweeten our waters, and they did sweeten our waters. Now when they sweeten our waters, in time, we're going to be abnormally sweet. We're going to be taken to the extremes of desire for sweet waters. The flower children were really an example of that in the 1960s. They became so sentimental that they were out there saying, "Peace and love", greeting you as a stranger. They didn't know if you were a rapist or who you were. And what did that bring on? The age of Aquarius where the people are just too water dominated. But it just wasn't only water, it was sweet water. Their appetite, their thirst was for sweet water.

So, the manifestation of the extreme of that is what was called, the flower children. It identified that new generation, the new movement in the young. Here is this new generation of sentimental youth who protested the ugly looks of the world. They hated the ugly looks of the world, wars, mistreatment, injustice, and all that. They hated all of that, so they went and got into a groove where they could be happy, and the groove they got into was peace and love. They did not create themselves. They didn't bring themselves to be that. Those who conspired to get the world, the human soul, under their management so they can themselves be the leaders of progress for the human soul in the world, they did that. How are they going to get it? They're going to get it by sweetening it up. *"A certain one put a stick into the waters* (This is Scripture, Bible) *and the waters were made sweet"*.

Now you know the Qur'an talks about sweet water and salty water. It's more than just drinkable water and salt water. It's beyond that. Even the Qur'an is not limited to that, what scientists think. The Qur'an is talking about the two bodies of water. The sweet water is drinkable and the salty waters you can't drink, but no, this is the movement in Scripture. The leaders kept putting salt into the water until all the waters became salty and it was no more desirable. People didn't want salty water. They can't drink it, and they can't enjoy it. So, then they went to the other extreme. The New Testament is the book of sweet water. The Old Testament is the book of salty water.

Sugar Problems

The New Testament was made necessary because the waters had become too salty and all the waters were salty, no natural or sweet water left. So, then they go to the other extreme and they put sugar cane in the water. The stick is the sugar cane. It's symbolic. You know you can't stick a sugar cane stick into the water, lakes, etc., and make them all sweet. So, it's only symbolic. They put the sugar cane in the water or put sweetness in the water that was naturally acceptable and would quench thirst. But now this water they're going to give them will do more than quench thirst. They will want it even after their thirst has been quenched. They will become addicted to its sweetness and in time they will become sick. They will have sugar problems, and they will be like the rich man who has been just so comfortable and so freed, he is just taking too much of the good things, or delectable things. This is in the menu of the world. So, now he has eaten too much dessert, deserting what was natural and normal for him for the extreme life of comforts and pleasures. Now, he eats just desserts. The word has a message in it. The word, dessert, that is what the message has. Now deserting what was normal and natural for you and sufficient for your life gives you an appetite for the extremes of pleasures, extremes of the sweetness of life, and you become diabetic.

Now, you're diabetic, and what's this new habit you have that made you diabetic? What is it going to do? It's going to dry up your productivity and your life is going to become again a desert, not dessert. Your cultural life now becomes a desert. The things that G_d created you to have in the garden are lost. So, the Satan was ahead of us and now our sensitivities are diabetic, first. So, those who have been led to those extremes, though they have wealth, they are diabetic. So, Dives (the rich man/Nicodemus)), he doesn't want a natural drink of water, and he asked Christ Jesus, *"How can I get into the kingdom?"* You have to be born again, because what got you into, the condition you are in is your departure from your original creation. He needs a natural drink of water, because more sugar won't quench his thirst. It just makes him thirstier. So, he asked Abraham, *"Drop down some of that water you have up there."* He said, *"It is too late. I can't reach you with help. It is too late. Hell has closed the door on you, no connection with heaven for you."* When you go to the extreme of disobedience in the world there is no chance for you to reach G_d. You don't have a mind, heart, or nature to reach G_d. It's too late. It is shut out. Your own condition that you accepted and let grow on you has cut you off from heaven.

Dives, diabetes, is really descriptive, now. Back then it was, too, referring to what has taken over the society, their extreme passions for the life of this world that takes them from normal to abnormal, takes them from wanting to have natural life to wanting to have cosmetic, artificial life, artificial pleasures, exaggerated pleasures. So, this is the extreme of sugar in the water, in thirst of the people, the extreme of sugar in the thirst, and Satan planned it.

Masters of Human Psychology

But I also mentioned earlier, before we went back to this diabetes, he (Satan) aspired to rise up on the air and become prince of the air. Prince of the air means he's going to rule the air. His scheme was to first rule the waters, and he used the science of the ancient nations to get that. The name, Poseidon, that figure in myth, and the figure Neptune, these are figures from the ancient nations of their sciences that they had that enabled them to get in the world of man's water and rule him. So, Professor Fard called him Yakub. Here he's coming and grafting the world of the ancient knowledge into a new thing. He's creating a new people with what he's using. He's grafting it from the original man, out of the original man. He's grafting his Devil out of the original man.

Now those pagans, they were not devils. They were just masters of the human psychology, or the soul of the people, and they were able to dominate and rule and keep the people pleased with their rule. Now here comes a new visionary. He has gotten some help from G_d's revelation to His Prophets. Now, he's using the insight that he gets from G_d's revelation to His Prophets, or the nature of the original man, the science of how to rule the original man, how to master and kill the original man. That's Fard's teaching, how to rule and kill the original man. So, he gets this knowledge and is aided or supported by the knowledge of the ancients, who were idolaters, idol worshipers, but not in reality idol worshipers.

Their Idols Represented Their Wisdom

Their idols represented their wisdom, their psychology for mastering the soul of people. And it was only their general population, or their citizenry that were conditioned to accept those idols as having power. The learned of the ancients they are brought into focus by the Qur'an: *"We know these things can't speak, but they are means for communicating or reaching our objectives",* which is to rule and dominate the masses or the general population. We rulers don't buy it. We know they can't speak, but they are a means for us to capture the ignorant or the uninformed in this science or knowledge, and master them, so they don't become a problem for our rule or our leadership."

Those are the ancients, so that tells me we have underestimated the ancient world. It was not a bunch of stupid people worshiping idols. No, they were scientific, and those idols represent only facets of human nature and where these dispositions or forms in the formation of human sensitivities and sensibilities, if we understand, can take society if you manage that. If you manage it, then you can ride upon the constitution of human nature. If you know how it is constituted, then you can ride upon that. It can become your donkey. It can become your horse. It can become your camel. It can become your Mercedes Benz. It can become your 747. If you study and know it, then you can make it your transport to carry you, as the leader of the world, to where you want it to take you. So, this is what they learned.

Mr. Fard Encrypted Us

Mr. Fard, Professor or Master Fard, he was a master in his sciences called, "Yakub's grafted devil". Here comes a world that is formed by conspirators among the Zionists. Here comes a world that will be a demonic, satanic world. Isn't that what we have here? So, you see the intention was that we come to know how to read what Mr. Fard was trying to give us in hopes that one day we would see it in a different light, and would not take it literally, but learn to decode it. I think the word is, encrypt, and it means to take something and influence it, take a body of language, and influence it so that the real communication is so difficult to reach, it is like kryptonite, like trying to decipher kryptonite. But if you look at encrypt, it's from cryptic, which means very hard to understand, almost impossible to understand. When you look at that word, encrypt, you can pronounce it "in crib". You can pronounce the letter "P" as a "B". So, that is what it is a play on, to take you back into the crib where you cannot perceive reality. You're a baby. You cannot perceive reality, and then it puts you on a road towards understanding. That is language of a different nature. It is not a language of simple reality. It is a language that really seems or appears to be, on the surface, in direct conflict with reality.

So, they put you on that road of mystery, and really satire. For Mr. Fard, it is more satire than myth. They put you on that road from a baby, innocent in the head. So, Mr. Fard said, "This world is the white man's world. It is false. His knowledge is false. Your knowledge is different. When you were in your original life and world you wrote history. You didn't depend on the white man's history, and you wrote history to last for 25,000 years, and you renewed your history every 25,000 years." Now we buy that because we trust the teacher. So, he's encrypting us by conditioning us to reject everything we have learned, and as far as progress for the human intelligence, he has put us back in the crib.

The Sleeper In the Church

So really, when the language of the so-called learned says, kryptonite, it's a play on crib, back into infancy and capturing you in infancy, in your innocence, and giving you their language that guides you to follow them in the dark. You take an innocent mind, and you can give it darkness, and tell it that it is light, and it is not light. It is worse than darkness. It has become so intensely dark that it is worse than natural darkness. Here is the natural sleeper. He is not as far from reality as the spiritual sleeper in their new language, in their Church. I hate to put it like that, but in the Church, the sleeper in the Church is sleeping deeper than the man that never met the Word of G_d. He's in a deeper sleep. He is farther from reality than the man who never met the Word of G_d. What you have to do is take him out of the language environment that he has been shaped and formed in, from out of his original nature, and create a new language environment for him that will bring him back to have faith, like a baby. "I'm trusting you. I don't know anything. This world that I've got it is just false. It's wrong for me. Now, please, the Honorable Elijah Mohammed, give us a look at this world that you want us in.

"He Has Risen"

So, even after the Honorable Elijah Mohammed's teaching we needed another transformation. How are we going to get that transformation if we're not taken or weaned off one language dependency and put on another language dependency? That is what we had to do, and it worked. Once we are put into a world of a new language environment, and we have faith in that language environment, if its direction is arrival at the Qur'an and Muhammed s leadership, then once you get there, you're truly free; and you have dropped all the wrappings of the old reality, so that you come bare and alone, like a baby straight from the womb of its mother into a new world of the Qur'an and Muhammed's leadership. You know the world that we have to come out of is nothing but a world of wrappings. So, they say, *"He has risen*. The one who was captured, crucified, and put away and was thought to be dead, he has risen, and a proof that he has risen is he's not dead in there. Here are the wrappings." He is not wearing them anymore. He left the wrappings that were on his head. That is proof that he has risen.

A Climax That Can't Reach the Womb

Now, behind Mr. Fard, the Honorable Elijah Mohammed and Malcolm X, an articulate spokesperson for the Honorable Elijah Mohammed, what they were bringing to the black man and the world? How do you destroy that influence on the new black man? You have to wrap him up, again. So, let us create a generation of rappers, so they can wrap the blacks up again. And we like what we see in them, what they're hungering for. Let's free it, so they can become popular leaders, reach the public, like Malcolm was doing for the Honorable Elijah Mohammed. Let these new generation of rappers reach the public. And as far as their intellectual potential, it is not going to be able to express itself except through a wrapper. So, the womb for the delivery of their life anew will never be touched, because what we're putting on their brain is just like a wrapper on their joint. So, when they screw their public, they will not produce any babies. This new mindset is a wrapper. Isn't that what we're seeing? They can't carry the intelligence of the black people forward. All they can do is give you a climax that can't reach the womb. They're wearing wrappers. See how the Satan gets into our culture?

"Our Hearts Are the Wrappings"

We have had preachers who call themselves rappers replace the old leadership of the church and temple under the Honorable Elijah Mohammed. So, who got the young, the following? Who got the new generation? Not the temple, not the church, the rappers. Satan has learned how to put wrappings on their minds that affect the power or the freedom of their minds to impregnate the intelligence of the masses, just like a wrapper that you wear. A rubber, called a wrapper, also keeps your life germ from reaching your female mate to reproduce you, your life, you and her. So, the mind is no more reproductive. My father used to say, "Brother, are you shooting blank bullets? What is the matter? You and the sister have been married all this time" This rapping is a big conspiracy against black leadership. They are going to make sure they don't get another one who can captivate the young like Malcolm X did. "Make sure that doesn't happen again! Just put wrappers on their intelligence, so when they express themselves, it can't go beyond the wrappers. All they can produce is another rapper!"

This knowledge comes from the secret Jew, the Zionist Jew, conspirators in the world of opportunity for mankind. They say in the Qur'an, *"We're not impressed."* I'm putting it in my own words. *"You can't reach us. You can't influence us. You can't penetrate our hearts. Our hearts are the wrappings"* They are saying, "You're trying to reach us, no, it is deeper than our minds. You can't change our minds. It is the nature of our own hearts. Our hearts have become the wrappings that seal everything out, close out everything else! No influence can reach us!"

The Rising On the Air

So, the rising on the air, I can't give it to you any better than I gave it to you many years ago. The Bible says, *"Rejoice not, whole Palestine; for from the serpent's roots shall come a flying cockatrice."* And the cockatrice is a three-form creature. He's formed as a water animal, land animal, and now he's an air animal. And it says, *"That old conspirator, Satan, he aspired to rise upon the breath of the earth".* So, here the air of the earth is called breath of the earth, and what it means is the consciousness. He's going to rise up upon the consciousness of the people. He's going to find a way to manage, travel, upon their consciousness, from the very breath of their intelligence, because we don't become conscious as a thinker or as a brain until the baby breathes the breath of the air. And this air is what ignites the mind, so the mind starts thinking and it becomes conscious. It doesn't happen until then.

This air is more important than we think, so that is why they just don't call it air. It is the air of the earth really, but in this particular reference that I gave you, it says he shall rise upon the breath of the air, breath of the earth, and he shall become prince of the air. That means ruler. Prince, the word goes back in Arabic and in

Semitic language for the Jews, too. It goes back to a ruler. A prince is a ruler, and he is the one who gives orders and rules the world, because the word for prince, in Arabic, amir, it comes from, amara, which means to give a command, or an order. So, if a king is ruling, usually he doesn't communicate, directly. How does he communicate? Through the prince. So, the real king with us is G_d, and whoever He chooses to communicate His Will through is a prince. The Bible says of Jesus, *"Come and sit down on My right hand".* So, G_d is the Boss. He is the King, but now He has a prince who will be serving as His Right Hand. That means doing the work of ruling and controlling things and sending orders and everything. It is not the left hand that does that. It's the right hand that does that, normally, in the world. It is the right hand that is carrying out the work of authority, the work of rule. I do not care if you are right-handed or left-handed, you go before that judge and he is not going to accept it if you say, "I'm left-handed, judge." He says, "Raise your right hand". We're talking about the general rule, not your exception.

Satan Reforms the Sensibilities

So, he shall become prince of the air. That was his hope, his aspiration, his dream, his destiny, that he becomes prince of the air. So, if he becomes, first, a deceiver on the land, that's the serpent in the garden. But now he runs into trouble. He can't get to where he wants to go fast enough, so he puts the gear in reverse and "Let me go back to the water". He goes back to the water and becomes a ruler in the water, and he sweetens the water, so that the nature of the people will change. They want extremes in pleasure, and life calls for extremes in pleasure. We don't just want to have sex with our wife. We want a continuous orgasm that will last us for an hour. Therefore, he provides all kinds of enticements and gadgets and everything to keep us excited for an hour. So, he leads you to the extremes. This is how he catches us through our sensitivities and then he now has your sensitivities. So, now he reforms your sensibilities where your sensibility is not calling for just the normal and natural understanding that you need for your life. Now, you have abnormal sensibilities and you're looking for fantasies and artificial reality when your nature was not fantasy, but reality and truth. That's what you wanted by nature, but now you want just fascinations.

"And the Devil Deceived Adam and His Wife"

The Qur'an says, *"And the Devil deceived Adam and his wife",* which means the original forms and dispositions in the intellect, the intelligence that is Adam, and the perception of the environment that must feed that intelligence so that it grows and becomes more and more efficient in a real environment, in a real, natural world.

That is Eve feeding. What do you feed is Eve? You have to feed it that which you have from the outer, external world. The Satan caught on to that and he deceived Adam out of his nature, both of them. The Bible gives the picture that Satan gave it to the woman, and she fed it to the man, but the Qur'an corrects that and says, "No, he gave it to both of them". It did not reach the man from the woman. Satan reached both the man and the woman, so he deceived both. The intelligence, nature and the perception, the ability to perceive the world of reality, that is the woman. She is the concept, and in her we are formed. So really, the mother, our physical or biological mother, in Scripture is first environment, and it is to point us to another birth in the external environment. Just like we are put into our mother as a germ to develop and mature into a complete physical form of a human being, and then she delivers us, we're delivered from her body, which means from that world.

Flesh Doesn't Mean We're Human

Actually, she is like a replica, or a picture of how we are born naturally. So, we shouldn't think of her as a flesh body only. The mother is extended when we come out of her, out of the physical person, into the natural environment. Before man put his imprints on the natural environment or redid the natural environment, we were born out of a natural body into a natural environment; and just as that natural body held us and contained us until we came into a complete picture or concept of a person, the external world that we come into takes us and it does the same thing. It contains us until we can become or grow mentally into a complete concept of a human being. Just because we came out a flesh, it doesn't mean that we're going to be a human being. We could be put in an environment that makes us a savage, and we run around on our hands like a monkey, a dog, or wild animal, like a savage man. But if we stay in the pure, pristine world that G_d made, eventually, it produces the complete person. The external world will produce the complete person.

G_d Is Still the Only One Who Can Make a Woman

So, we are the child of the original nature that G_d made. That is who we are. The real, complete, person, the true, human person is a child of the real world that G_d made, and man cannot make the woman for him to engage or have sex with and reproduce himself. G_d still makes that woman. G_d is the only One Who can make us a woman that we can go into and reproduce ourselves. Still, that is left to G_d! So, no matter what man does with this external world, he cannot change the machinery or the factories that produced the first human being. Therefore, we still can come out innocent and just like G_d made us, and we can be inspired by G_d to want the world as it was before man corrupted it, before he made it unnatural for us.

G_d's Word Written Through Heavens and Earth

So, in the process of coming from mother flesh into mother nature and the natural environment to be shaped into a complete person mentally, because she produces us physically and spiritually, G_d produces us in her. But we come here spiritual and physical. We come here even emotional, but rational. That depends on G_d's Word, and if we are attracted to want to know G_d's Word, we don't just have to have the Qur'an and the Bible, for G_d's Word is written through the heavens and the earth as well as in ourselves. And if we ever get that strong spirit to be connected to G_d's Communication, Satan can't block us out. And will I tell you a truth about myself, a fact about myself. I have never been having in my mind and nature a desire for anything other than truth and reality. So, that desire has been in me from birth, I guess, or from as far as I can recall in my life. Even listening to the teachings of the Nation of Islam I didn't have an interest in things that didn't register and give comfort or support to my power to think real, to think reality, and to think truth. I have always been in that nature. No matter what was given to me I kept that appetite for the real truth, and the real nature, and that is why I was able to look into Mr. Fard's teachings and find a direction to reality, commonsense, and rational insight, and the same was in me. When I read the Bible, the same was working. When I read the Qur'an, the same was working. So, when I got help from Mr. Fard's teachings and the Bible, it took me to world myths.

The Soul Needs Sweetness

Then I read world myths with the same mind, not to see myth. I wanted to see where reality is, where the naked truth is, as some people would say. So, I had to unmask myths, take the mask off myth, and get to the nitty gritty, or to the goodies. Here I'm going to the essence of myth, so in everything I was attracted to find the essence. I wanted the essence of Mr. Fard's teachings. I want the essence of the Bible. I want the essence of the Qur'an, so I'm having difficulty. I want the essence of world myth, so after feeding like a bee... the bee wants the juice. He wants the essence, the pollen. He gets the pollen, but he makes the juice. The juice is honey, and it satisfies the soul's need for sweetness, and the occupation of the bee satisfies the soul's need for beauty. The bee is looking for beauty. That is where he is going to be. He feasts on beauty, flowers and the essence. That nature is in all of us. I was situated mentally by things that were said about me, and it so happened it was in the nature of my soul to reject that which is a problem for true human life and nature. It's fulfilling for the soul when you arrive at that which G_d prepared for you to eat. He didn't prepare secularism for us to eat. The deceiver prepared that for us to eat. So, when we arrive at what G_d prepared for us to eat, it is so satisfying.

Following the Inborn Nature to Seek G_d's Purpose for Human Life

The same spirit that all thinkers had that protected them from the darkness of the world, it is something that you have by nature. It is inherent. In the Qur'an, the wise man took Moses on a trip. He said, *"Somewhere back there we lost our fish"*. And he said the fish they were looking for was a fish that swam in the water, not zigzagging, looking for this interest and that interest, looking for food, etc., but it was the one that went straight. That means the one that follows the inborn nature to seek G_d's Purpose for human life…

See Satan Under the Flood Light

Allah is with us without a doubt. There is no way we can get this without Allah being with us. To know what is going on, to know the conspiracy against the human being gives us stronger faith in our ability to do the job that Allah has put us here to do. We don't let Satan take up our time, because he wants to overly occupy us in things that will take us from things that we should be doing and what we're all about. We will only give him a very little time, just time enough to see him under the flood light G_d gives us, so we can move with more confidence on this earth and in this world towards the things that Allah wants us to do.

Everyone Has to Come Back to Where Allah Intended Us to Be

As for family members on the wrong course, the only way we can help them is to call them to get on the Ark with us, and if they won't get on the Ark with us, we can't hold up the sailing. We've got to load up and keep moving and realize we don't have the power to save them all. We don't have the power to save any of them. Those who are to be saved will join us and come with us, and those who are not will be left in the waters. Don't think they are totally lost in the water. They'll drown, but there is coming a time when even those who drowned will have a chance to be resuscitated, if they hold on to G_d. They might not follow us, but they can have a new life, again. Nothing is lost. It just appears that way. Eventually, one day, everyone has to come back to where Allah intended for all of us to be.

Bananas Associated With Your Fingers and Senses

They have a reason for saying banana means crazy. You went bananas. You have gone bananas. The banana, it turns sweeter and sweeter the longer it stays off the tree. It ripens quickly. It turns sweeter and sweeter and the sweeter it gets the less attractive it is for somebody who wants to eat it. But a lot of other fruits the sweeter they get, the more attractive they are to you. That banana, when it gets sweet like syrup on the vine, who wants it? So, I guess that is what that means. And a lot of them associate bananas with your hand, the fingers. They associate the bananas hanging off, coming off, with your fingers and the fingers are connected with your senses. So, if you are a banana, then it means your senses get too sweet and have no more attractiveness, no more value. They lose their value and attractiveness, and that is the silly people out there. They just want to play and want nothing but fun. They just enjoy nothing but fun. Their whole life is nothing but fun. They are bananas. They have gone bananas.

The old man whose name was, Emory, he came to teach us Arabic. He could hardly speak English at all. So, he did not want to waste our time anymore. He just told us he could not speak English and that we would have to get another teacher. He had a lot of difficulty just telling us that he could not speak English well enough, and that we would have to get another teacher. That was not quick like I am giving it to you. It took him a lot of time trying to get us to understand what he wanted to say, and he would finish it with "joz, loz," and it never left my mind. It rhymes. I know what he meant; joz, walnuts, like a brain. Doesn't it look like a brain? A walnut looks like a brain, especially half of it, half of the walnut. Almonds (loz), they associate it with solid intelligence in culture as a hidden metaphor. Loz is a word associated with it, and it means illuminate, that sounds much like loz.

Fig Represents the Ability to Imagine

Figs are another fruit that if you do not get it at the right time, it is not good. They get mushy and too sweet and are not tasty, attractive to your mouth anymore. It is a metaphor representing just what it says, fig, a figment of your imagination. It represents the ability to imagine, to imagine an image, the imagination, to find something by imaging, to learn by imagination, which is very important to intelligence, to compare and imagine with things that you know. So, it is a process in the brain that is important to the brain, but it is not as good as reasoning. So far, we do not have reasoning yet. Brain just means brain. It does not mean you have a brain, now. Where is the brain going to go? Joz, loz, the brain is going to go to intelligence, illumination, and it is going to radiate intelligence.

Every baby born was born with a brain, and every baby born is born with intelligence. So, joz, loz, and teen (fig), now you're on your own. You are using your own imagination. You have great imagination, but instead of imaging correctly you went bananas. Joz, loz, teen (fig), moz (banana), you went bananas… quick deterioration, and they turn black, too, which is symbolic of death in this kind of language, but also symbolic of the original state of nature, life, that is black.

Buddha said, "My mother was black". He doesn't mean a mother like we think in common language. He meant what mothered his intelligence, and that was original nature. And you know, in some parts of the world, the Mother Mary they called the Black Madonna. So, this language is something else. That old man said, "Joz, loz teen, moz". He had us repeat it. He was trying to tell us, "I know enough about this Nation of Islam of yours to know that you all have gone bananas!" He said, "What in the hell is this that they are calling Islam?" He was trying to help the children.

They Exploit Sexuality for Business

You know, they say Adam was walking around among the trees in the garden, and he had taken a fig leaf and put it over his private parts to hide it. It means he protected his nature, and his mind was drawn to his sex, the power of reproduction. He just focused there and thought he was right, and he built an ideology that would explain his life and forces of his life, that the forces of his life start with his reproductive organs, and he put a fig leaf over it. It does not mean that he was ashamed, but that is true, too, that G_d made human beings with shyness. The most important thing it means is that he sought to explain his existence, and he saw his sex organs as a source of his energy, and energy for reproduction or the life for reproduction. He made that more important than anything else, and it was a figment of his own imagination. It was not science. It was not revelation, and that is true. If you look at most of the deities of ancient nations, ancient people, you will find sex worship more than you will find anything else, even in the plant life fertility worship, and for man's life fertility worship. When you look at how they exploit sexuality for business, you see that sex is still the most important focus for exploiting and getting the most out of human society.

The Devil Thought He Was Innocent

So, this world when you understand it, they think they are innocent. The Devil thought he was innocent. That is what most of the students of Scripture do not see. The Devil never thought he was guilty. Satan never thought he was guilty. He thought he was innocent. So, this world that is against the way G_d wants it to go, it is exploited. It takes advantage of human weakness in all forms, ignorance, and whatever, and it makes the innocent, weak, human being the sheep for slaughter, and who eats the sheep? The business world, the big people. The other things, too, but they made the sheep to feed production. They made the sheep to even open up opportunities for the strong and the rich.

They Want the Common Man to Be a Consumer

The battering ram, that is the sheep. "Have the poor, innocent, people go first and open up the society for us, and once the society is open, then all of us are going to feed on the sheep!" That is this world, and they do not think they are doing wrong. They say, "Those ignorant people, they do not know what to do with their life, so we have to incorporate their life as a factor for motoring the economy, or production." Right now, America is the strongest nation, economically, and it is the nation that uses its masses economically. Most other nations do not use their masses. They use them for common labor. America, this democracy we live in, they do not want to use us just for common labor. No, they do not use us, the common man, for labor only. No, they want the common man to be a consumer, and he is ignorant, so consumption will be very big with him participating. So, he is used for consumption, and that is not the government. That is the businesspeople, and who started it? The Jews taught America how to make big money and have a powerful economy.

But when you know these things, what is the benefit? Change your life! Do not conform to their strategy to get wealthy off the ignorant and weak people, to build their markets on consumer appetite, a whole race of people characterized as consumers and not just us; ignorant whites, ignorant Mexicans, everybody, as many as they can get, but we were the battering ram. We opened the world for everybody else.

Build Your Future In the Light

They say, "Jesus". I say, "Yes, 'Jes us'." It is time for us to come down off the cross and get up out of the grave, and everything else. Mr. Fard, he really had knowledge of things, because he said Jesus means justice. If they crucified justice, that says a lot, doesn't it? So, my way is to keep it to yourself but realize you have more light than the average person; then build your future in the light, with respect for the light. I fear nothing! I am not afraid of the future. I am not afraid to plan my life, because I believe Allah is with me all the time. Allah has blessed me to get where I am, and He did not bless me to get where I am to leave me where I am, and I believe in the unseen. When you see how bad, how bleak our future looked, and how burdened I was, but look how He opened up everything. Look at how the darkness has vanished, and He permitted the light to come in.

Help Those Who Are Struggling In Business

I believe we are people who should not go to the big man. We should go to the small man. Our people are poor. Charity starts at home and spreads abroad. All poor suffer a terrible disadvantage in this world of the rich people. So, if we can help somebody, why don't we go and help those struggling people in business who are poor, no matter who they are. So, first take your care of your own. Do not step over our people to help somebody else to manage, but when you run into the other people help them, too. And I do believe that if we concentrate on nothing but the small businessman and businesswoman and bring them the good bargains that we have they would be foolish not to accept it. So, what I am saying is that we should not risk frightening the rich people, because the rich people are not even organized for sell to the poor. They are organized to run a system that is for real, big, rich people. They are organized to keep a system that exploits the poor, but they do not run the poor, individual businesses, not at all.

So, we can get a great percentage of a small businesses to buy from us, and believe me, I think the market or the opportunity there is all we need now and in the future. You cannot compete with the big, big, man, because if he finds out what you are doing, he is going to find a way to beat you at it. And he is already real big, so it is easy for him to get the advantage over you. He has the advantage already, so it is easy for him to execute his powers over you. So, we're not going to compete with him.

And you know, they do have a sense of right and wrong. They do have a sense of justice, and a big, powerful, rich people, they admire poor people when they really get it together. I spoke about my meeting with the big capitalists, the Forbes people. Forbes, the family, they told me, "Mr. Mohammed, we will not get in your way. If we see a way to help you, we will." And he tried to get me to invest in gold. That is their main commodity. They invest in gold. We do not have enough money to invest in gold, but we have gold now. The opportunity we have right now is in gold, but it is not a bad investment. They expect gold to go up real soon. It looks bright for the future. So, if you see an opportunity to invest in gold, do it. The United States is selling gold, too. You know that? They have a big thing going on. It is a good time for gold, and everything works together. What is happening in the field of economics or money, finance, it has a lot to do with what is happening in the cultural life.

Gold As a Metaphor

Now, wisdom is popular. Wisdom is growing more and more popular. They expect the culture to be changed in the future, and what do they say is going to change it? Wisdom is coming as culture and is going to become stronger in the culture for reforming the culture in a good way. So, you see how they have got it, gold, this wisdom symbolically as a metaphor? The Prophet said, "Men, don't you wear gold. Let your women wear gold". That means do not show off your wisdom. For the man with his head on right there is nothing wrong with him wearing gold. It is not for those who can't handle it. Those who cannot drink strong drink and stand on their feet, they should not touch strong drink or handle it. I am talking about spiritually strong drinks. That other physical stuff is poison. If you cannot drink strong drink and stand on your feet, then you should not drink strong drink. And the man who cannot handle wisdom without it messing up his character, or inflating his ego, he should stay away from it. But the man who can manage it, there is nothing wrong with him having it.

We are living in a time of science. This is an age of great science and technology. The secrets, there are no more secrets. Science has come full fledge and the whole world is shining with wisdom. So, where are we supposed to wear gold? When can we wear gold? Muhammed, the Prophet, said in the hereafter. In the hereafter, it is okay to do so. We will wear our gold in the hereafter, that is what the Prophet said. Men should not wear gold. Leave the women to wear gold. We will wear it. We will have our gold in the hereafter. This is the hereafter!

The Golden Age

They speak of this age as the golden age. The golden age is behind us. There is no age behind man in history as bright as this golden age that we are in right now. So, what is the big deal now that tells man, "Brother, you should not wear that gold." It is stupid in this day and time to tell a man that. Gold is everywhere you look. Turn the TV on, gold is putting your eyes out. So, why can't I wear some? This is the hereafter. Those people were ignorant back there. They were not scientific, and they were ignorant. The Prophet, peace be upon him, knew that what he was given would eventually bring the world to appreciate science, industry, and production. He knew it was coming. The only thing that held it up for the old world was the leadership that went off track and thought they were supposed to have theocracies, and dominate the common people, and cheat everybody else out of whatever they could cheat them out of. They thought G_d authorized them to do that, because the world was of animals, beasts, and savages.

The Destiny for the Mission of Prophet Muhammed

But that was changed, and they got back on track. Prophet Muhammed brought the religion back on track, that is what I am saying. When Prophet Muhammed came and changed things, it was just a matter of time before the world opened up to become rational, scientific, and industrious, like what has happened. So, this is the destiny for the mission of Prophet Muhammed. It is to bring the world to science and production, but upon respect for human nature, not exploitation. The one who promotes exploitation is the Satan, the Shaytan. And the true Prophets, peace be upon them, they promoted liberation, refinement, and justice. The bringing of the human being into the best human condition favors the world. I am sure you understand that. The best of our philosophers and liberators, they knew that and promoted that. They promoted the society supporting spending and working for the best human condition environmentally, and internally.

Culture As An Expression of Man's Life

I was feeling really bad when they stopped using blackboards, but I really like the white board. Black cannot hold anything anymore, so they have to put it on other colors. Now, you think I am joking, but that is where they are coming from. They are not talking about black people. They're talking about original nature. It is not recordable or doesn't hold anything anymore. We lost it. This world has destroyed our original nature. Most people do not have their original nature. I am talking about the nature of your brain, and your intelligence has been just about destroyed by this world of corrupt culture. That is what we're talking about. That is what I am pointing to. The world of corrupt culture has just about destroyed the original intelligence in the people, so the board is not black, now.

When Allah tells us there are signs in the heavens, the earth, and as well there are signs, also, in the human being, in the people, it just does not mean in the physical people. It means in the life and works of the people. There are signs in man's industry, man's language, and everything. So, his world is like G_d's original world, the universe. Man's world expresses his life and his spirit, intelligence, and everything. Man has expressed everything of his life in his culture. I am using culture, now, as a complete word. I am not talking about entertainment, only. Culture is everything that comes from man as expression of his life.

So, education, is it not culture? The academic world is part of the culture of the people of the West, or America, whatever. So, culture is also a word that includes all the expressions of man's life as a thinking, intelligent being. Someone may be

339

thinking, "What is the Imam teaching us? I came here to learn Arabic." You came to the wrong place! My students should know they don't just come to me to learn Arabic. They come to learn life, and I didn't just start being this way. I can't remember a time when I was not this way. Whenever I talk, I talk the same way. Have I changed the way I talk? The logic is still the same. My interest is still the same, i.e., life, human nature, intelligence, correcting how we think and reason.

Question it. First, you have to question things. Mr. Fard said, "Ask questions and learn all about yourself". Isn't that something? He didn't say learn about the Qur'an, mathematics. No, "Ask questions and learn all about yourself." So, this man was interested in us knowing ourselves, studying ourselves, and that was and still is our greatest need. We just let the world shape us. We do not question our own creation, our own nature and how we are made. That is the beginning of philosophy. Study your own creation. Study your own self in the role of a living creature born by creation, or supported by matter, the material world. So, when you start thinking that way lights start coming on.

Chapter 10

The Call to Life

The call to worship in Al-Islam is the call to life. It says "Hayy, come alive, come into life, become, yourself, living." It means become, yourself, a living thing upon the pattern revealed by G_d. Salat is the pattern revealed by G_d for our reality. Come trusting prayer, but the deeper meaning is, come conforming to the pattern created for you in the beginning of reality, in the beginning of creation. Come conforming to that pattern.

"Everything Knows Its Mode of Prayer"

G_d says, *"Everything knows its mode of prayer"*. That is in the Qur'an. So, seeing that as we see it, for the believers that is the first step and that is good. We have to hold on to that. This is a call to prayer, to worship, in Al-Islam. But then we have to be able to read deeper and see much farther. Everything knows its mode of prayer, and the word for it is, "Salat", that same word that we use. So, why are we praying? We're praying because we believe that if we conform to G_d's Will for us, we will survive the world, Satan, and all trouble that may be thrown at us. We keep this ritual, or this practice because we believe that we will be able to survive, hearing His Word and responding to it. Every time we make a sajda we're not making a sajda only to the Ka'bah. We're making a sajda to the Word of G_d. That is what we're reciting. And that is what gives us our indication when it's time for ruku, or time to get down on your knees and put your head to the floor. It is His Word demanding that of us.

Allah's Creation Stood Man Up Before Revelation

So actually, we're conforming to the Will and instructions of G_d, and where do His instructions take us? It finds us already upright. You don't come to prayer or start on your knees. You don't come to prayer crawling, and you don't say, "Allahu Akbar", and begin your prayer on your knees. You begin your prayers in an upright position, standing up straight. That is to say, "My natural creation stood you up like that. Don't you come to Me acting like I did not give you some help before I spoke to you! So, come like I raised you up in matter, standing erect with your head on your shoulders, and glorify me there, first. Don't go backwards. I already brought you this far before I spoke to you. You didn't know of My existence. I made My creation to lift you up and stand you up like that. So, come to Me showing you appreciate Me. Show Me what I did for you. I stood you up!"

The Prophets and Seers in the Bible said, the One that they discovered, the G_d behind all things, He even dressed that old, poor, raven bird, stood him up on his two feet, put feathers on him, a dressy coat of feathers, too, and gave him skills to fly the air in the open firmament. And the Seers said "The One Who did that, He can lift me up out of the trouble I'm in. He can dress me up and make it possible for me to rise upon the air, or the breath of the earth".

Those That Say G_d Spoke to Them Are Lying

So, our prayer is really pointing to that which evolved by nature. It is a behavior that is universal for all people and that behavior evolved upon natural creation; and those who say G_d spoke to them, they are just lying! G_d did not speak to you. "You just followed the best urges in your own soul and nature, responding to the challenges in your environment, and it brought you to make progress to this position you have reached where you have intelligent social order, and you have law and order. You have managed all that upon My creation. So therefore, I speak to you, and I say, 'Come to the original state, *Deen al fitraa, fataran naasa alaiyha, the religion of the original pattern upon which I patterned all people upon'.*"

So, just like I said, once you accept that you are homo erectus, you are not bending over like a four-legged walker. No, you are standing upon two feet, and there are not many that stand up like that with you. Of the ones that hold that position the best are birds. Not even the ape holds that position as easily as the birds. "So, now I stood you up, and I want you not to shame Me, and show Me that you don't appreciate what I did for you by getting down on your knees saying, 'Oh, Lord!' No, stand on your two feet in a dignified posture, representing your achievement as a life within My matter that I created for you, and then glorify Me! Are you ready to go farther? Are you ready for Me to lift you up higher? Then glorify Me in that position, 'Allahu Akbar!' Now, recite My Words, not yours!"

G_d Has Already Heard Those Who Praise Him

So, you start reciting the Words of G_d and after you finish Al Fatiha, you do not have to do a small chapter from Qur'an with Al Fatiha. In fact, "You do not even have to do the whole of Al Fatiha, if you would just say, 'In My Name and recognize that I gave you your first comforts, Ar Rahmaan, and I gave you your second comforts, life redeemed, Ar Raheem; and then if you praise Me, give Me perfect praise, and recognize that, 'You are worthy of praise' and you have been earning some praise. But put 'Al' before it and say, 'Al Hamdu, the Praise', which includes,

'All that I have earned is due to You, my Lord, the Lord of all the worlds'. Then once you finish that, you can say, 'Allahu Akbar', and go down to ruku."

This is the fard of Al Fatiha, salat for Al Fatiha. Then you come up saying, "Sami Allahu liman hamidah". You did not say, "I hope G_d will hear me, or hear my praise". No, you say "He already heard it!" It does not say "G_d hears", though they translate it like that. It says "G_d has heard whoever praised Him already". That is what it means, not just me in this prayer, at this moment. It means "Whoever has praised Him since the creation of the earth, He has already heard them." If He hadn't heard them, I wouldn't be here to call on Him. It would have been finished a long time ago. I would not even be here. So, G_d hears whoever has praised Him at any time in the history of man, or in the period of time. He hears them all, going back to the first until now. David praised Him, yes, but before David, too. So, isn't that the strength for our faith and confidence? And I'm not hoping that G_d hears my prayer or heard me praise him. I know that He has heard everyone before me in time, going back to the beginning of time. He has heard everyone who praised Him, and I am just another one. There is no big deal for Him to hear me. He has heard every soul who cried out to him, especially, when they came up honorable and innocent, and recognized Him and was not coming with selfish motives to promote their own interests.

Worshipping G_d to Promote Your Own Interest

The average person worships G_d to promote their own interest, and He accepts their prayers. Isn't that wonderful? Look how wonderful He is. He knows they're liars, hypocrites, and they are self-deluded. They don't even know they are praying lies. They don't know they're reciting lies. He receives them and blesses them for their good intentions and helps them, because they need help and cannot find help inside themselves. It has to come from without. So, He helps, blesses them and strengthens them, so they can grow and prosper, and one day reach that stage where they say, "I have to repent!"

They don't know that they are takers and not givers. Abraham, he is the perfect man as a leader, a picture of the type that G_d wants to lead all people, and he said, *"I have turned my whole self to You."* And the self is the face, because the face is what registers what is inside. It registers the whole person. If you're sad, happy, if you're deceitful, it registers all in the face, although other parts of the body can show it, sometimes, but not like the face. The face is the mirror, or reflector for all that is in the person.

So, he says, *"I have turned my face"*, meaning I have turned my whole self. That is why they translate it that way, sometimes. It says, "My face". That is what it literally says, *"Surely, I have turned my face to You"*. But they translate it, *"Surely, I have turned myself to You"*. And some translations are, *"Surely, I have turned my whole self to You"*, and that is true. That is exactly what it means, and what is that to say? That the true achievement or accomplishment for the soul on its path to its perfection, or on its path to its destiny is to discover its hidden interests, and recognize that "I thought I was doing this for G_d. I was doing that for myself!"

Turning My Whole Face to G_d

But now that I really correctly understand the reality of G_d and know the reality that G_d has established for me as a human person, I don't come that way anymore. I don't have one face for this prayer, and another face for my interest in the world. My face for this prayer is the same face that I have when people see me in the world. I have subjugated or subjected myself and all that is of use and benefit, and all that represents my life in my want for my life I have reduced that or subjugated all that to G_d's Purpose for my existence. So, I have turned my whole face to G_d. I have given my whole self to G_d in obedience to His Will and Purpose that He established for me as His creation. That is what it is.

So, when he did that G_d accepted him and made or called Abraham His friend. That means there are a lot of holy, well-meaning people who are so beautiful in creation and so selfless and are sacrificing so much. "But did you efface yourself, really, for Me, or did you efface yourself to impress your fellow man?" Who knows? Saintly people live a saintly life, and they enjoy the satisfaction of knowing that people see them as souls who have made an extraordinary sacrifice and by so doing, they have lifted themselves up above mortals. "You live on fifty dollars a week. You don't eat too much. You don't go out on Friday nights. Now, here you are knocking on the door of My Jannah, and your own nature is saying it is closed against you. You cannot come in. Now, stand out there and search yourself. If you search yourself long enough maybe you will pray like Abraham did and the gates will open."

That is what we want. It is not easy, and it does not come without Allah's Mercy. I don't want to be guilty, not before my Lord. I don't want to be guilty of anything. But if we strain to be innocent, if you strain to be accepted by your Lord, to not be guilty, or if you strain, strain, and you fall down, you get back up. You leave the path, and you wake up and find something missing and you start searching, and pretty soon you're back on the path. You do that over and over again, and the

Prophet said in inspired hadith that G_d has a servant, that every time he falls by the wayside or sins, he remembers to ask his Lord for forgiveness. He does this over such a long period of time, repeating it, that G_d says, "Go on, My servant! You are on your own recognizance! I trust you with yourself! You are a good manager, a good custodian, caretaker. I'm trusting you with yourself! I don't have to worry about you! You are on your own!"

Allah Trusts Us With Our Own Authority

Have you stopped sinning? No, but you have established a pattern that speaks for your intent to never forget your Lord, and for that He trusts you to your own nature, and to your own judgment, because your judgment is that you should repent if you ever see or recognize that you have done something that you need to repent for. So, Allah trusts us with our own authority. Isn't that beautiful? And the judge will say, "You're released on your own recognizance." Now, you know they got that from the Qur'an. They got that from the teachings of Prophet Muhammed. I bet you if you search the history of the saying, you won't find it in there before Muhammed, the Prophet, came. You won't find it among any judges to tell a person that he's giving him a break. "Go on your own recognizance. I'm trusting you with yourself", that is what it means.

The Head Is Symbolic of the Mountain

When they do wudu', the language in Islam, when they make ablution, or wudu', the ones who don't have knowledge they follow, but they don't know what they are doing. They take their hand, take the water, and they bring it forward (from the back of the head to the front) and then they bring it back. Actually, this is the mountain. The head is symbolic of the mountain. Really, the mountain is just speaking of the human body. So, back there at the base of the skull it is called the ganglia, I think they call it, and this is where thoughts form that have a direction and a conclusion. They start there (at the base of the skull), and they go up to the conscious. The front of the face is consciousness.

So, they come out and struggle for development and they reach consciousness, and then when you go back there, you're applying it to the ganglia, to the ignorant people. You have to bring it forward and pull it back where it started. It started in the darkness, now you're going to bring light to the darkness. Yes, it's now concluded. You start from the base generalities, and they have a direction to become fruitful. They want to get to the top, because at the top is where they become fruitful. Now they're bearing fruit. So now, they take the fruit and bring the fruit down to earth where people can benefit from it, and for the straining in the mind to understand they call it cognition. Once the cognition reaches the top, now you have fruition and it's going to bear fruit; now take it down back down to the people. Jesus said, *"Unless they bear fruit"*, and they think it means out there fishing people in and doing things, etc. No, it means for your own mind, the straining of your mind to understand G_d's world that He created, so you can establish yourself in it and be successful and lead mankind the way Allah wants them to be led on this planet earth. That's the big picture.

The Sunnah of G_d

Every man, technically, every male is imam if he is a Muslim. But is he qualified to even be called an imam at home to his family? He is supposed to lead his family in prayer, so he is an imam, but is he qualified? If he is not doing that and is not qualified to do that, you should not call him imam.

Sunnah, simply means the established way for G_d. What way is established for G_d? If you say G_d performs to advance justice, how? Give me an example of how G_d performs to advance justice. Men have already identified G_d performing justice in the life of man, in the life of the world, in the life of society. Men have already recorded it and left it with us. That is the Sunnah of G_d. G_d's Sunnah is to be seen in everything that has formed, the creation itself, because after all we're talking about people, so never divorce people from what you're talking about. If we're talking about trees that is different. G_d's Sunnah is everything G_d has done with His creation. We know He created creation to bear trees, but we're not talking about trees, we're talking about human beings. So, everything G_d did with His creation to communicate to man's mind and spirit, that is the Sunnah of G_d. Everything that G_d has done with His Prophets, or Messengers, to bring man closer to what G_d wants him to be as a life on this earth, that is G_d's Sunnah. We know G_d advances human life by natural forces, by trouble, etc., so this is the Sunnah of G_d. Really, the great works of G_d in the life of man, what does it begin with? Creation, and then natural life in its innocence and purity, like Jesus Christ, peace be on him, he represents natural life in its innocence, and its purity. We can see the Sunnah of G_d, but also, when we read Scripture, when you read the Bible, when you read the Qur'an, now we're reading a script that presents to us the ways of G_d, how He performs. So, that is the Sunnah of G_d.

346

It Is a Group Project

So, we group to grow in the environment, to grow into the plan that G_d has made for our life. The plan is bigger than we are when we are made, or created, a big plan. We have to fill the capacity, the rooms that Allah has made for our life, and the rooms are so many and so big, and the environment is big. So, the job or the work, the responsibility to develop and grow so that our life occupies all the rooms that G_d created for that life to live in and occupy is a group responsibility. It's not an individual responsibility. We can't do it with just an individual. No one leader can do it. No one human being, no one leader can do it. It takes the whole group. It's a group project. So, it is impossible for Allah to reveal to any one man the plan for our social destiny and that one man lead us into that destiny by himself, not even with revelation, not even with his sunnah can he do it! He has to invite the participation of the excellent men, or people, in his environment and together they work. That's shuraa. Shuraa is binding, even on the Prophet. So, the most important elements for establishing the Islamic community are Qur'an, sunnah, and shuraa, and you can't have it without shuraa. You can have the Qur'an and have the sunnah, but you still can't have it without shuraa. In fact, it is Qur'an and sunnah to have shuraa. So, we have to have that third dimension there, or third element working in our lives for us, that is, the shuraa.

"Where Is It In the Sunnah?"

It is only haram if you're coming from that which is haram and you're communicating something that is haram, but the culture, itself, is not haram. They say dancing is haram. Go to their countries and turn on the TV. You don't even have to do that. Turn on the ethnic channel, right here in the United States and see what comes on the Pakistani station, or some of the other groups that they have on television. See what they are doing. See if they are dancing. See if they are not singing. This is stupid to me, for you to see people, how they behave, and then you are ready to do whatever they say or do. You're ready to run to us, not to me, necessarily. Most know they are going to get fire when they come to me. If they come to me wrong, there is some fire waiting on them. So, they don't like to come to me, because they know they cannot handle me. But they go to those who follow me who they think you can influence. "The Imam said it is okay!" But where is it in the Qur'an? Where is it in the sunnah? Where is this okay? "Imam such as such, he says that this is haram!" And if you are weak, you will join that person, and that person just told you that your Imam is not qualified to lead you. So, you join that person, and you'll continue to say that I am your Imam. But you are following that person who said that, and criticize what I'm doing, my leadership. They just told you that your Imam is not qualified to lead us. So, see yourself. Look at your own self.

Men and Women Must Know How to Follow the Sunnah

Women can never be imam. That title is not for women. They can never be called imam, in a masjid. They can only perform in the role of imam and lead the prayer if they're leading sisters and there are no brothers. Women have to lead the sisters because there is no brother. If we were going to have prayer and it was only women, I wouldn't want to lead. I would ask one of the women to appoint a woman or ask one of them to lead the prayer. If I was the only male, I would not feel comfortable leading a prayer of all women and I am the only man. I would not want to do that. Al-Islam obligates males and females to know how to follow the sunnah of Muhammed, the Prophet. So, sisters should know prayer, should know how to lead prayer, just like brothers, and that should tell you something. That tells you women are responsible for leadership in the society, just like men. If they were not, they would not have to do the fard prayers and the sunnah prayers. Everybody, male and female, has to do fard prayers, the obligatory prayers, and also, the traditional prayers of our Prophet.

We have to do the sunnah. The sunnah is two rakats after the evening prayer. For the sunset prayer, we do three ordered, obligatory, fard, and we do two rakats sunnah, after and no sister is excused from that. The responsibility falls equally on brothers and sisters to do these prayers. Sisters do them mostly, privately, in their homes. That is the tradition, but the obligation is on all of us. So, that means, if a brother is not around and if he does not have good senses, he is not around. So, if there's no brother around, the sisters are a supposed to take the lead. I hope you understand what I am saying.

A Lot of the Hadith Should Be Buried

I have brothers saying that "The Imam is trying to overthrow all the imams! He is trying to discredit all the imams!" That is what they say when they meet with each other, out of my hearing. No, I'm not trying to overthrow any but a bad imam. A lot of the hadith should be burned up, buried, thrown away. They are against Al-Islam. The authentic hadith that most Muslims respect, by Bukhari and Muslim, and many of the other hadith, need someone with understanding to teach those hadiths. Do you think the hadith was made to be placed in the hands of all the believers? If you do, you're wrong.

The Real Message of Prophet Muhammed's Sunnah

Religious freedom is still what you should be seeking. You are Muslim, but the message of freedom is subtle. However, it is stronger in this religion than it is in any other religion. When we pray, we cannot even leave it to the imam to pray for us. We have to know our own prayers. We have to know how to do it by ourselves. We have to keep the sunnah of the Prophet. After the imam leads the prayer, you have to be able to stand by yourself and pray. So, what is the real meaning of the Prophet's sunnah? True democracy, where the individual is capable of leadership for himself. That is the real message of his sunnah, that the individual must share in the responsibility for carrying the burden of society. He must be able to carry out the functions alone. The knowledge for how to live and carry the burden or the weight in government and society must not be on one man's shoulder, but on the shoulders of all of them.

Surah 'Asr Is Not Dua' Prayer

We know it is not a salat, but the time of 'Asr Prayer is a salat at a certain time, and that is between sunset and Thuhr Prayer. So, it is at a certain time. I don't think it (Surah 'Asr) has a direct reference to the 'Asr Prayer, but indirectly. When it says, *"Surely man is lost, except for he who believes, has faith and good deeds, and strives in the support of truth and patience or perseverance,"* that is the end of that surah. So, it is just telling us the virtues we need to be successful in life, and how to keep the life as G_d wants it. And you know human essence is seen in four, and the Qur'an addresses that essence over and over again; and that, indirectly, addresses human essence, because when we lose our essence that is when we lose our life. We lose everything. So, it is addressing human essence, and it is addressing history, because it says, *"Wal 'Asr"* translated, *"By the token of time",* and some of them add, *"Down through the ages".* So, this is talking about difficult time. It is not appropriate because you are not praying, you are speaking. G_d is speaking, and when you say that you're speaking, too. So, you should say at the end of that not, "Ameen", but "Sadaqa Allahu atheem."

Calling On G_d For Help

The immigrant Muslims, they are bringing all this confusion into our country, America, into the Muslim community, and they don't know. Do you think they know the religion? These guys just came from poverty, or struggling to get rich over in their country, and they didn't make it too well over there. They see opportunity over here. They come over here and suddenly, he thinks he can be an imam, because he thinks we do not know anything about the religion. They say, "They're new people. They don't know the religion. I can be an imam there. There is a dua' in the Qur'an and the people are praying to Allah". Prayer, in this sense, is dua, because if we say this and say, "Ameen", that is not salat. That is dua'. So, that is a dua'. Dua', the word comes from the Arabic word, "da'a, which means, "to call, asking for something, call on G_d for help". So, if there is nothing in there calling on G_d for help that is no dua'. Why is Al Fatiha a surah but also a dua'? It asks, *"Oh Allah, guide us on the right way."* So, the Qur'an opens with a chapter that is a dua' and it is a standard dua' for all occasions. It opens up the Qur'an.

So, we have different opinions, and I don't discourage that. I encourage it, even if you're wrong. If you have something to say, say it. Who knows? Maybe we're wrong. Maybe you're right and if we can't agree, now, just let it rest. See if it has a power to come back.

144,000 Saints Will Be Saved

You know, I read the Surah (Chapter) 44 of the Qur'an. I've read the Holy Qur'an, you know, more than once, but I read that surah, and do you know the feeling I got... That that surah was based upon or at least revolving about or around the statement of the Christians in the Bible about 144,00 saints. So, I am sure the number 44, Chapter 44, it has reference to that saying in the Bible of the Christians that 144,000 will be saved and that will be the saints, and 12 times 12 is what? 144. A hundred and forty-four thousand, is universal. That is what it is saying. The righteous are going to be universal, that is what 144,000 says. They're going to be universal. They are not going to be local-minded, but global-minded, because they are the saints. They are working with their brothers and sisters to make the world better. One hundred and forty-four thousand will be the saints, or the stars. It means the saints, too.

Conscious of the Right

You know how G_d has made me so conscious of the right? I say He has made me so conscious of the right that things I used to give no notice to, defects in myself that I used to give no notice to, now I can't stand them. I will give you an example. I'm going out tonight and I just want to be alone. I am not inviting Khadijah (my wife) to come with me, and it came to my mind to tell her, "I am just going out. I might see a friend or something, talk over some business, or something. I'll be back about 11 or 12 o'clock p.m." I cannot do that anymore. That is deceit, almost like an outright lie. Now, I am going out to see a friend. I will see a friend, go to the movies. I am not telling the truth. I am going to a movie, and I know I am going to a movie. I cannot stand that anymore in myself. It has to be the whole truth, hiding nothing, not deceiving anybody in the least. So, I used to pass that by, especially if it was a little something, an innocent, unimportant situation like that. I thought it was innocent, but it is not.

I know most of us do that. They still are good people and still have credit with G_d in heaven, but when the Bible asks, *"Are there any who are good? No not one"*, I say, "Man, only G_d". We all have defects, and we are human. We are blessed to have G_d and His angels to help us overcome our defects. That is special blessings. G_d is so Merciful. He sees you struggling and He won't ask you to take more burden. He just helps you in your struggle, and He wants you to ask for more burden. And a lot of times He will turn you down: "That is too much for you. You're asking too much", a Merciful G_d. He does not want to put anymore burden on you. It is in the Qur'an. *"It is not that I want you to be burdened, but that you should be purified"*. He dislikes burdening His creation. It is wonderful!

The Life of Man Like the Life of a Plant

Whatever G_d shows us of ourselves that He approves of He put it in you in the first place. It just needs the circumstances for it to come out. He already put it in you. That is why it says the life of man is as the life of a plant. If that seed is in the wrong place nothing is going to happen good for it. But if it falls into the right place, it is going to have its life released and come into its form that G_d created for it, the same for human life. If you get in the right environment and the seed has not become defected, the seed can become effective. If the seed has not become defective, then that seed is going to produce the form that G_d intended for that life. Praise be to Allah! So, that is why He says, *"This is the religion of origin, "Deen al fitraa, upon which G_d patterned mankind"*. The origin is the seed, and the seed has the design or the plan that G_d put into it, and it is no mystery. "Just look how civilization has grown from My seed that I put in mankind." So, this religion is not something outside of your nature, and what you're being given as communication is communicated by your own nature. Your nature communicates this, but G_d had to guide you to the way, deen al fitraa, the religion of original nature.

How Man Strayed From His Original Nature

So, the question is asked, "How did man stray so far away from his original nature?" There was a big jinn who offered his assistance to King Solomon, on him be peace, and King Solomon refused to accept the help that he offered. He was not

THE TREASURE UNDER THE WALL: Thursdays with the Imam

comfortable with it. He had moral problems with it. There is no jinn mentioned anywhere bigger than Satan, himself. He is the biggest of all the jinn, and the answer is given in Scripture to the question of how man strayed from his original nature. Satan seduced the original man out of his original nature, and he hasn't stopped working. When he approached the man, he was nothing but a snake crawling on his belly, and he did not have anything to lift him up. But he said, "Once I get this man, through this man I am going to be lifted up to the heavens".

The Satan, the big jinn, he has now gotten into the people. He is both in jinn and in the people. The Arabic word used for people does not just mean social community, like we think people are. It means this life is motivated by kindness and goodness. So, they promote kindness and goodness among people. That is this Arabic word for people. There are different Arabic words for people such as, "Qom." Qom is the common word for people, or human beings standing erect. So, the Satan, he does not want the bad people. He already has them. He wants G_d's people. Those are the good people, because they are the ones that are in the way of his plan. His plan is to discredit all authority, so that you do not have any authority. He does not even want you to believe in him. He just wants you to believe in nothing, just reject all authority, think you are free, and your own opinion, your own mind, is all you need to rely on.

Satan Corrupts the World Through the Good People

So, through the good people he can corrupt the world. However, if the good people are left to be armed with their natural righteousness, etc., he knows he is not going to be successful. You know the Satan, if you look at his challenge in Scripture and for us in the Qur'an, he says, "This creature You have made is not better than I am, and I am going to prove it. I'm going to defeat him. You're going to help him, but I am going to defeat him". And he says, "Only the ones that have committed themselves to You, those are the only ones I won't get". What it means is this: "Only the ones that have been guided successfully to You and they have come into Your light, have come into divine light". These are the seers. "But those who have not become seers, I'm going to get every one of them". He said, "Only Your divine light can protect them". And look at what he says he is going to do. According to the Qur'an and the Bible, he is going to cause them to give up their righteousness and follow his plan for human life, because when he suggested to Adam, the original human type, how we should think, all of us who bought that thinking or are buying that kind of mental makeup or reasoning, we have now become his children. We're not the children of Adam anymore. We are the children of Satan. And when you look at the conclusion of this world right now, where are people, even our leaders, our government leaders? Look at where mankind is now. Are they where Jesus Christ was trying to get them, Dr. Martin Luther King? No. Are they where Muhammed was trying to bring them? No, they are where Satan said he was going to take them. That is where they are, right where he said he was going to take them. So, what does that say? Only a few will be saved, 144,000 will be the stars. That is not many out of the billions we have, 5 billion or more.

Give Them a Treat

We were told that the Honorable Elijah Mohammed stated that Yakub had to trick his people, and he was suggesting that we have to trick our people. But we should treat them, give them a treat. You see their suffering, their ignorance. You see their personal neglect of their own interest and life, and you then should address that from kindness, from human nature and kindness, and do not put a price on it. If you do that and say, "I will give you this under the condition that you make shahada", that is putting a price on it. G_d never asked anybody to make shahada. He just gave us a beautiful creation, then created us with the intelligence and the good heart to make the best of it, but the Satan would not accept that. So, he had to devise his plan to deny men what G_d intended for them, and that was heaven. G_d never intended hell for him, only heaven. Hell is the condition mainly brought about by Satan. So, that is what I mean by treat. Come to them from kindness and not selfishly or not have any motive other than to contribute to their betterment, not to convert them into your religion or anything else. That is the time we are living in. That will work when nothing else will.

You Cannot Talk to Everybody the Same Way

The way I speak to you in the private sessions we have is not the way I speak at the Jumah, the Sunday address, or the first Sunday address, etc., so that is enough. You don't speak to everybody the way you speak to those who have proven to you that they know what you're all about, and they support your interest. You cannot talk to everybody the way you talk to persons like that. I do not have this conversation for an atheist or rebel who is fighting with the movement of goodness in his nature. He does not want it to reach its fulfillment, and he is fighting it, stunting his spiritual and moral development, intentionally, because he does not want to wake up enough to see more than his heart can stand and say, "Oh, you have to stop this corruption!" He does not want to see too much, because he does not want to come to that position saying, "You have to stop this corruption". So, that kind of person you are not supposed to share with them.

A Drink Mixed With Kafurah

My mother loved camphor. She would use it herself. They used it for soreness or external problems, like in the body, or muscle soreness. I think they used it also for colds. When you had a cold, they would rub a little camphor on your chest. It is mentioned in the Qur'an, camphor, and the word for disbelief is the same. It is from the Arabic word, kafara. It is kafurah (camphor), and it has a cold, chilling effect. It has a low temperature, very, very, low temperature, like spearmint. That is what you will get in the paradise, not on this side. In the paradise, you will get a drink mixed with camphor, kafurah. It means a lot of things that you believed in the world you are going to disbelieve them in paradise. It says He is going to give you a drink that is going to help you out. I am talking about in the religion, now. A lot of things that you took for granted in the religion, when you wake up in paradise, it is going to disappear. Those things are going to disappear. That cool drink in heaven is going to make it disappear.

It Is Best to Read the Revelation Before the Commentary

When reading the Qur'an, if you go right to the commentary, sometimes, the one who is making the commentary, you will go to his prejudice. It is not often. It's very seldom, and very rare that you will come upon the translator's prejudice, but you can come upon it. So, it is always best to read the revelation to the Prophet from Allah, then the commentary if you want to. If you need more support or understanding, go to the commentary. A good translator, it is always good to read the commentary after you have read Qur'an, or if you read a verse that has a little note there for you to consult. Commentary, it is best to consult it, especially when you're in the religion and you don't know it that well. But as I said, you have to be aware that the translator is also putting some of his own prejudices in his commentary. Just like Maulana Muhammad Ali, the Ahmadiyyah translation we have, and some of us still have it, it is alright. He says, *"The guilty blue- eyed."* That is his understanding. So, when he says, "blue eyed", I'm going to start looking for blue-eyed people, and they are not all white folks. There are a lot of people with blues eyes. They are not pure Caucasian. They are not pure whites. If you don't believe it, go to Brazil and see those half breeds down there, with those blue eyes.

So, if he is saying that it is the European or the white race, he is putting the reader in a situation where the reader will pick some of those who are not even in his field of reference, like those who are mixed up, in Brazil. I was in prison with a brother who joined the Nation of Islam in prison. His eyes were blue. His face was brown, and he had blue eyes, and it messed him up. So, he came to me, and I know he came to me because he saw that I didn't just take the teachings on face value or literally, but I saw a rational understanding of it. He befriended me all along, but this time I could tell something was burdening his mind and he looked like he was hurt. So, I just came right to the point. I did not ask him anything. I said, "You know, you have blue eyes. They are pretty blue eyes, and you know what the Nation of Islam teaches about the blue eyes". I said, "That is not understood as it is coming from the Qur'an", and I said, "The Arabic word is, zurqan, and it means the disease of the eye that causes the eye to turn whitish and bluish, glaucoma". I said, "But really, it is not referring to that disease, because that disease wouldn't make a person a devil or wicked person. It just makes them a victim of that disease". I said, "So, the real blue that it is referring to is the sky blue". I said, "I have studied when the Europeans came to America, the native Indians of America and South America called them the Wind G_d and gave them blue eyes". This is true. This is what I have learned from a trip to South America.

Aspiring to Have Dominance

I said, "But now, you know the Qur'an was before that. The Qur'an was before the West coming here, the Spanish people and others coming here discovering this part of the world. The Qur'an was before that". I said, "Who or what it is referring to is those who want to rise high and get a dominance and dominate the world. So, the blue there is the blue of aspiring to have a dominance". It is in the Bible, the prince of darkness, he went up on the air and wanted to rise high even to the throne of G_d. For what? A dominance. So, I told him that which has a lot to it. It is a science that those who have greed for power and dominance, they developed a science to put them in power, to assist them greatly, putting them in power.

The song, "Don't let the stars get in your eyes, don't let the moon catch you crying", that is from the lyrics of the song. Another thing, "You've got airs". It does not mean you have that air out there. It means you feel you are above others. You think you are better than everybody else. So, the language for understanding these expressions in Scripture have been given to the world, and now it is common language for the world. But we associate, when I'm talking to you, if you stop at a certain place with me, you will probably say, "That is leading to an error. It is not consistent. It is not. This is not leading to understanding. It is leading to error." That is because you stopped too soon.

Satan Is the Loneliest Creature In Existence

Blue in our world means sad, like the expression, "I'm blue." Why am I sad though? Because I'm alone. Blue means alone and where does it come from? Where most of our understanding of our spiritual side or emotional nature and everything comes from, the Bible. So, there was a time when the world was needing a deliverer. Just before the New Testament, the expectation was Jesus Christ, but it does not say that right there, and it says that, I think it is the sun, but it might say the moon was the only light in the heavens. Only one light was in the heavens. The Arab poet says the night has a thousand eyes, the day but one. What is that one? The sun. We know the moon sometimes appears in the day, too, but it is so overwhelmed by the bright sunlight, it is faint in the sky. It does not have any authority there. And it says, *"And there was only one light in the heavens."* You don't see the sun until clouds are out of the way. You might get the benefit of the strong light piercing through the clouds, because we know it is day, though the sun can't be seen. It is too cloudy. So, the sunlight when you see it, most likely, you're also going to see through the clouds or there are no clouds, and the sun appears to be the only light in the heavens. That is true.

The sky, when the clouds are rolled back, it appears to be blue. So, going back to what I said, why is blue sad? Because the sun has no company in the heavens, and Adam was alone, and G_d said, *"It is not good that the man be alone."* So, He turned off the lights, put him in a deep sleep and gave him his mate. It was not good that he be alone. So, the loneliest creature in existence is Satan. He makes no friends. He lets nobody into his heart. So, that is the blue-eyed Devil. He is alone, he's sad, but he cannot help it. That is his own decision to impose that existence upon himself. He does not confide in anybody. He does not consult anybody. He does not sit down and say, "Let us work this out together". He plans his plan alone, and carries it out alone, and his eyes are to get as high as he can above man so that he controls what is happening down here. So, he is the blue-eyed Devil, meaning he has supremacy in his appetite. He aspires for supremacy, so, he wants to be high above everything, higher than everybody. And Allah says whoever aspires for dominance or to corruption G_d will be against them. They will not succeed, because in the end they will find G_d is against them. That includes Satan.

Cannot Blame the Devil

I think my father, Elijah Mohammed, recognized that in the final analysis the human person has to be responsible for his own decisions and actions and can't blame anybody. He cannot even blame the Devil. I often heard him say that when we come to Judgment, we're going to accuse Satan, the Devil, that "He made me do this. He made me do that!" He said, "But the Devil is going to say, 'I did not do anything but invite you and you came'." That is what I heard the Honorable Elijah Mohammed say. He was speaking from the Qur'an.

You know, it is in the Bible and in the Qur'an, all through the Qur'an, that the Satan wants dominance, and he aspires to go as high as he thinks he can go, even up to the throne of G_d so that he acts in G_d's stead. That is the Bible. He wants to get up there, so he can act in G_d's stead. So, he wants to put G_d out of your sight, out of your mind, and put himself in your mind. That is what it means, as the one that you should be owing gratitude to and whatever, appreciate him for what he has accomplished. Now when we give the secular world credit for everything, Satan has achieved that in us, through us. He has achieved what he wanted through those people that except the secular world as having authority, and religion as being a mystery or something, just faith.

Our Life On a Path

Now, how should you apply my teaching or see my teachings so that you get the benefit from it? Our life in religion is called our life on a path, *"Fee sabeelillah, on the path of G_d"*. So, our life in religion is called life on a path. If we keep that understanding that Allah revealed in the Qur'an to help us be successful on that path, you should relate it to your need to succeed on the Path of G_d. So, that is the way you should, I would say, understand my language and whatever I give you of guidance or of understanding. See it and ask, "What is its use? What use does it have? What benefit is in it to advance me on the Path of G_d towards the destination." A path leads to a destination. So, don't just think of the path. Think also of the destination, because if you forget the destination, you have already gotten off the path. Just like me on the road trying to get to Little Rock, AR, but I have forgotten that it is a road taking me to Little Rock. I am passing rivers. I am passing the road I'm supposed to take to get to Little Rock. I will end up in California and wonder why I do not see Little Rock.

Two Ways to Lead Somebody In Scripture

There are two ways to lead somebody in Scripture. You go out ahead of them, like Joshua did, or you lead them like a shepherd leads his sheep. The shepherd keeps the sheep before him. He leads from behind. But from behind he signals to the sheep which direction to stay in, or which direction to go in. Now even though he is behind you physically, he is in front of you spiritually, and he has to see where he's directing the sheep to go before the sheep sees. If he doesn't, he's not the leader, he's not the shepherd. Now, the person that is seeking to understand my teaching, my tafsir (commentary on Qur'an), sometimes, they may feel like saying, "I know nothing!" Well, that is a good disposition to take. That is my disposition. That is the disposition I take, "I know nothing", and that is the position the righteous, wise leaders take. They take the same position. "We know nothing. You know, G_d. We know not!" Now, I'm going to give you a little more understanding. When they get in heaven, the Qur'an says they will say, *"This resembles what we saw before."* That is what you should be saying. You should be trying to see the likeness, see in my teaching support for what you used to believe, or what you experienced in your life as a seeker.

A Life Fixed for the Meeting

The Qur'an explains our life on the path as a life fixed for the Meeting. Now you know when we went to the Temple of Islam, we said, "We're going to the meeting". Wasn't that what we said? Later on, "We're going to hear the Honorable Elijah Mohammed" or "We're going to the fountain". But the one that we used the most was, "We're going to the meeting". That was the common expression. That word is very important in Scripture, meeting.

Now, the path has no meaning if you do not understand the meeting. So, where is the path taking us? The path is taking us to the Meeting, and it is described as a meeting with G_d, described as a meeting with our Lord, Rabb, and it is also described as a meeting for Judgment. But judgment means standing up. In the Arabic language, judgment means standing up. And what does the word, judgment, say? Standing up. So, it is a meeting at the Great Standing, when the huge crowds are all going to be standing. Even the rappers are going to be standing. Everybody is going to be standing, and what does standing say? You are going to have to be conscious of your own doings, conscious of your own participation in whatever is going on.

The Great Standing Is Also the Great Meeting

The Great Standing is also the Great Meeting, when everybody has to be standing on their own feet, and you are on your own feet when you are responsible for your own rational and moral balance or for your own rational and spiritual balance. How do I know this? From Scripture, from Qur'an, it is plain, but from the Bible it is in a picture. It says a great one stood and he put one foot on the water and the other on the land, and he was able to measure things. He had intelligent balance, because he was supported not only by reason, but he was supported by spirituality. He was a mighty man, and we all are headed for that meeting, when we have to be supported by our soul or our spirituality, and also by our rational mind and its activity, its role in a material world. So, that is the Meeting.

From a Female Mortal to a Community of People

Now, who gets us to the meeting? Our mate. G_d said that *"He saw that the man was alone, and it was not good that he be alone, so He made for him his mate"*, and his mate is called, in the Bible, mate, but also, helpmeet. So, why did G_d see the man in a bad situation because he didn't have a mate? It is because of responsibility. He needed responsibility to get him where G_d wanted him to go. So, if he is responsible for his wife, his obligation fulfilled for her or in her, will take him where he needs to go on the Path of G_d. But now, he starts out needing a wife, a woman. But as his life multiplies through his wife or with his wife, his life is going to multiply. He is going to have children. They will have children, and after a while it will be so many they will have to have villages, towns, cities, states, and nations. So, look how that wife has grown in her role as a help meet. She is no more an individual, mortal, female; now she is a community. He arrived at a community by engaging her. All that he realized as a result of engaging her is called his wife, or his help meet. So, the help meet moves from a female mortal to a community of people. That is his help meet.

The first help was his wife, mortal flesh, but that help meet is going to become the society that he belongs to. The society that he accepts responsibility for, that is going to become his help meet, and without that he cannot make progress on the Path of G_d. The people came to the Prophet and said, "This man is a holy man, a special man, special believer. All he does is pray and fast." And the Prophet asked, "Who takes care of him? Who provides for him his necessities for life, for living on this earth?" They said, "We do". He said, "You are better than he is!" You are making progress on the sabeelillah, the Path of G_d. He is not. He needs a help meet. He is your baby, and you are taking care of the community.

"Eat of My Flesh and Drink of My Blood"

And "meet" is a play on the word, "meat", because in Scripture, meat means knowledge for succeeding with the human family. Jesus said, *"Eat of my flesh"*, and the Bible says the flesh is the doctrine of the New Testament. That is teaching, education, and the blood is the spirit. He said, *"Eat of my flesh and drink of my blood"*. When I first got that language as a young minister, I said, "This Bible tries to promote cannibalism, eating flesh and drinking blood of human beings". I was young, and I just saw the ridiculous. I did not see the light... So, I had to take the kafurah. Before I could get the real thing, I had to drink the kafurah, and that is what I was drinking when I said, "This book is insane!" Then Allah woke me up in heaven, and I looked at the Qur'an, and I said, "I have to drink another glass of kafurah". We were not seeing it. We were just thinking we were seeing it.

Everything You Need Is Already In You

Allah does not go against His Will, and His Will was to create intelligent life, human beings who could find their way to the light with the utility that He created them with. There is no utility outside of you that is going to bring you to the light. All the utility that you need to come to the light is already in you. That is for yourself as an individual, for your own soul, but also for your family, and for the society. Everything you need is already in you. He created you with it, everything. I'm not saying anything but what is written in the Qur'an. It says, *"Get you down from here."* You were in a situation to miss the Path of G_d, so G_d said, *"Get you down from here into the earth, qubad, all of you together"*. Qubad means a fist, 1, 2, 3, 4, 5, with your five senses. "Get you down into the earth with all your five senses, and you're going to find in the earth everything that you aspire for or aspire to achieve. You're going to find it in the earth. It did not say in the sky. That is the Qur'an. He told you to get down out of the sky. Get down from here into the earth, qubad, with your five senses united. A fist unites the five fingers. They work together as one power.

"Get You Down Into the Earth"

And what did Jesus say? Five loaves of bread and two fish. So, all you need is a total of seven, your five senses, your spiritual life, and your rational life. So, He said, *"Get you down from here, qubad"*. That was Iblis. He was told to get down, too. So, that says that G_d sees him, too, as a rational creature, and you are out of a situation to do your job you want to do. "You are up here with the angels. Get down into earth. You're going to find a big field to work in". Isn't G_d so wonderful? He liberates Satan. He was locked up among the angels, trying to rule the world through the angels and G_d sent him down. *"You go down in the earth"*, the Bible says, *"and bite the dust as a serpent. Crawl on your belly and bite the dust"*. But the Qur'an just says, *"Get you down into the earth, qubad, all of you together"*. Now, we are all together like a fist. G_d did not send any angels down. They are supposed to be up there. It is not like the Bible, where the Devil took a third of the angels down. No, the Qur'an does not say that. It says, *"Get you down, qubad, all together*", not a percentage staying up there. *"Get, all of you, down into the earth"*, the man, his wife, and the seducer, or the enemy, Satan. Those two were deceived in heaven by the Satan. So, it says, *"Get you down into the earth".* That is three of them. *"There you will find what you aspire to".* Everything that your aspirations will call for, that is what it means. You will find it there and there you will live, and you will die. You will be gathered, die, and be resurrected from it, again.

The Condition for You Coming Into Heaven Is Inherent

So, even in the earth we will find life, death, and resurrection, according to that statement. It is clear. There you will experience life, death, and resurrection. And the Bible says, or G_d in the Bible says, *"No one has ascended to heaven except he who was in heaven already".* Now, can't you see clearly now what we are given of the fall? It is clear that the one who has a chance to go to heaven was in heaven before. They were in heaven and G_d sent them down into the earth. So, the one who rises is the one who was in heaven already. Is that clear?

We are to understand that also in this way: the condition for you coming to heaven is inherent. Whatever takes you to heaven is already in your makeup, inborn. You are born with it. It is part of your makeup. It is your property as a creature, as a human being. It is your property that you're born with that takes you to heaven, that utility or whatever we want to call it, that takes you to heaven. So, you had it before you were formed in the earth. Am I clear? If it is inherent, you had it before you were formed in the earth, because all of us are formed in our mothers' stomachs. Somebody told me, trying to be smart, to show that they know something, "Brother Imam, we're not formed in our mother's stomach. We're formed in..." and they gave the scientific language. But I don't care what you are formed in, my mother's stomach grew when my little brother, Akbar, was coming into this world, and I saw her stomach get bigger and bigger to accommodate my brother's body growing in her. So, G_d is not talking to us through the intelligence or the knowledge of a few scientists or people. He's talking to us, addressing, appealing to our commonsense. And our commonsense says children, babies, grow in their mothers and are delivered from their mothers' stomachs. So, that is the language G_d uses.

"Islam Is No Vain Imagination or Superstition!"

If He uses the language that science uses, He will miss most of the people, and some of them can't understand anything else but the baby is growing in mama's stomach. So, no matter what is inside the stomach, the stomach is the outer envelope, and it is definitely in there. It is in a shroud or a seal, the water bag. But the water bag is in the stomach and the stomach expands to accommodate the baby. So, what I understand the two books to be saying is that we shouldn't look outside of human life into some realms of the unknown, like most people are conditioned to do in religion, for a situation to achieve our utmost as human beings with the freedom that G_d created for us. I hope all of that is very clear.

So, that marvelous experience where you are going to be transformed into a higher life and for a higher purpose will not take place if you don't believe that the possibilities are in your mind, in your soul, and in your heart. If you think that something has to come from up there, so it can assist you, you are never going to make it. That is what both the Bible and Qur'an are telling us. As Brother Lewis said, who was out of prison, a victim of drugs. He had a nerve condition in his face, but he was an excellent physics teacher. He said, talking to the teenage students in our high school class, "Brothers, Islam is no vain imagination or superstition! Islam is reality! Now, let's have class, brothers!" That is how he started his physics class. I don't know what influenced him to come to this, but a meeting with my Lord influenced me to come to the same conclusion. Islam is no vain imagination or superstition! Islam is reality! Mr. Fard said, "Islam is mathematics, and mathematics is Islam". He meant mathematics is an exact science and Islam is an exact science. Praise be to Allah!

Chapter 11

The Soul

G_d wants us to be whole, w-h-o-l-e, as it's in the New Testament, whole, a whole person, not a fraction of a person. G_d wants us to be happy or pleased with our life, with ourselves as a whole person, not as a fraction of a person. Many of us may be pleased with our careers or in our professions, but when we look at the family life maybe we will not be pleased. When we look at our own individual life, our own spiritual life, maybe we won't be pleased. When we look at our moral life, maybe we won't be pleased. When we look at our behavioral life, how we behave every day when we're up from the bed, we might not be pleased. Man was pleased when G_d first made him, when G_d created us for the first time. He created us the first time and we were pleased until we came into this world and this world began to influence us.

A Higher Dimension of Reality

The reason why I'm a Muslim is the same reason why you're a Christian, most likely. The reason why I'm a Muslim is the same reason why you want to be right, most likely. G_d made us all and He put in all of us a memory. Dr. C. Eric Lincoln, he said there is a memory gene bank, a genetic memory. We may not remember it up here (in the mind) but it's in our life. It is in the life blood. It is in our genes. It's in our biology. It is in our chemistry. It's in that that wakes us up in the mornings, and that that tells us we need to go to rest at night. It's in that feeling that was with us when we were born, a feeling inside, deep inside ourselves, that continues to be alive. When the conscious dies, it stays alive. It is always alive! When we are sleep, it's alive, always alive. And when we die physically, the learned and faithful people, not only the learned, but the faithful people period, believe that that does not die, but it awaits the time of G_d, G_d's Time for it, and it will be given a new creation, a new reality, another dimension of reality, a higher dimension of reality, a better dimension of reality, heaven, paradise, etc. That's what we believe.

The Original State of Life Is Spirituality

The original state of the life was spirituality that wanted to be at rest. Like water, it will keep moving until it can be at rest. It is a picture of the soul in the right state that will show you your true picture. Water comes from the mountain to find its place of rest, forms a river, and goes down to the ocean. If it rests in a little mud hole, it is going to be terminated by the sun. But if it keeps moving, it will eventually find a body that will allow it to rest (the ocean). It comes into a universal body or soul that is its destiny.

Two Birds: Conscious and Ascendant Spirit

Jesus Christ addressed the sensitivities and sensibilities, and the people became excited after his teaching, not like the old teachings that were flat. *"I'm gone, but I left you eating and drinking, so repeat this in remembrance of me"*. He was talking about the Word of G_d, and you can see why this is so beautiful. There were several demonstrations of him bringing life to the dead, too, and the Qur'an doesn't mention giving life to the dead like that, although it is in the Qur'an acknowledged. It says he did it by permission of G_d. With G_d's permission he had the power to do that. But really, the vivid and pictorial description of what is happening for Jesus with his following is told in the Qur'anic story about him having the power to make a clay bird and then breathe into the clay bird, and it becomes a living bird. The bird has always been a symbol of the soul or the spirit in the human soul.

In ancient times and even now, they believed that when you sleep, the spirit, in the form of a bird, leaves your body and returns to your body. At the time of awakening, for you getting out of your sleep, the bird comes back. And some believe, like in the Qur'an, that there are two birds inside you. One bird leaves, and the other bird stays with you to guard you and be with you during your sleep. But one bird goes away. The bird that stays with you is the bird of your conscious, that knows your life. It is your conscious that is symbolized as a bird. It stays with you and appears in the form of dreams, or whatever. It comes up in your dreams, but it stays with you, and the other bird goes away. That is the bird, the Spirit that G_d created to connect with Him, the Ascendant Spirit, but not necessarily ascending, because if your mind is not for ascension, the bird does not go anywhere except where you are. It stays right in the realm of your reality. Though it left your body, it is still in the realm of your reality. It did not go up into the heavens. It is still down here, but it is separated from your body. This is a belief, and I believe it is true. These ancient people, who came up with these ideas, they fixed them in myth, culture, and history. They had experience over a long period of time and most likely, when we discover something, we will find that there were people who discovered it before us, and they left it in symbols.

Seeing All of the Light

Your conscious is your world and your subconscious or part of your subconscious, belongs to G_d. It is His Sanctuary and He says He would not allow anyone to plow in His Sanctuary. So, when the brain is not ruling us, that bird flies away until we wake up, again, then it comes back. It stays with us until we wake up to it. If we never wake up to it, we die having never found the real way to G_d, the real path to G_d. That is the path of the ascending. So, we never can learn it all or discuss it all. But what I want to tell you is that G_d has connected me with the Eternal Reality. This reality is passing away. The perishable is passing away. G_d has connected me with the Eternal Reality. So, when I speak to you, I see the light, and I have seen all of it, trust me! And I knew it long before. That is what it means when it says he spoke in the cradle; he spoke while yet in the cradle. While I was yet not seeing the end, or seeing all these things, the spirit said, "Say it!" And I said it, "I have it all". I knew it in here (inside me). The spirit in here said, "Tell them." I said, "I know it all. I have command of both books and can prove it." I couldn't prove it, but if you had tested me, G_d was going to back me up. It was G_d who said, "Speak that!" If I had been tested, I would have proved myself. G_d would not have me say something that I could not back up. I felt confident that I could. Knowing the language like I know now, no, I did not.

Islamic Logic Does Not Abort!

Scriptural reasoning is not just a communication. What is the reasoning supporting this communication, giving it a new reality and sending it to the destiny that G_d wants? It's the line of logic that started with the need in man to want to get help from G_d, and it represents that logic, as Allah says in the Qur'an, all the way to the conclusion. The logic has a destiny, a conclusion, like that water that comes from the mountain that won't stop until it makes it to a body (i.e., the sea/ocean) in the universal order and nature; that definition that everybody sees and says, "Yes, that's it. That's what I was feeling, etc." Islamic logic does not abort!

All that we see in the physical world is deception, ghurur. Why? Because the soul is invisible, transparent. Our spiritual life is invisible, transparent. So, we are in these environments, so we can support and express that life. We are not in this environment to become this environment. We are in this environment to find ourselves in our true nature and express it in language that will come to our minds and leave a picture or imprint, a concept.

The Home of Everybody

We can't get a concept without having a concept… so, the whole world is nothing but a reflector (not just the water) reflecting what I am, my life, and what I want to do with my life, the conclusion of my life, because He put everything in a universal scheme. These things evolved and evolved and were not satisfied to be at rest until they could connect with each other, and they all could be at rest. According to Scripture and science they started in chaos, as smoke, in violent commotion, mist, restless. Material bodies were restless, as imagined by scientists and in Scripture, churning, but its nature is to be at rest, so it can't stay that way. So, in religion the whole universe begins from restlessness and separation, and then it started to connect with that that it is to connect to. As more and more matter connected, bodies and systems holding bodies in a discipline formed. This is true in the life, the evolution of human life. His evolution is for the community life that can make it comfortable and at rest. In order to have that destiny he has to connect with other individuals, nations, etc. That's where we are right now, symbolized in the Ka'bah. It represents all people, a house under G_d, built by Abraham, the father, leader, and Isma'il, the son, follower. He is called the father of all people. *"Bunia lin nas, built for all people".* Muslims should understand that G_d wants us to come to a perception of a home that is the home of everybody, not just one people. And to reach that destination you have to form connections, and that is what the Ka'bah represents.

Establishing Myself In My Best Condition

So, what is the purpose of going up from the foot and finishing in the head? Man's evolution is not to just have a body, but he needs government, and his evolving is to find that government that has responded and been accepted by the whole body, and the foot and the rest of the body are pleased with the crown. So, man's destiny is government that will please the whole body… *"And you are members in my body".* When you have that kind of authority the body responds, *"I hear and obey".* G_d is telling us if we put the right head on the body, it will not have petty problems. When the head says it's time, they say, *"To hear is to obey".* But when we establish authority pleasing to G_d, when we get there, we will see that we please G_d and ourselves, our own soul. Establishing myself in my best condition is my destiny, not just about pleasing G_d, and I can't do it without G_d's help.

So, if we understand Scripture, it is saying G_d is really outside our reality and He's trying to help us see that when He created us, He was finished. But we don't follow the pattern of creation, and when we get away from it, we have to cry out to G_d, and He has to put us back on the pattern that He created us for. We want to meet G_d, however, we in the creation are not big enough for the challenge that He made us for. But we have no reference to go to for help, except His creation, and it is not big enough to save you from G_d's creation. However, when we find G_d, then we find the spirit and determination to keep going to our destiny. And when we get there, we think we are going to find G_d.

Soul and Mind Are Different

The soul is an entity all to itself and it is sensitive to everything that's happening that puts you in danger or makes you feel comfortable and safe. It registers what is good for you and what is bad for you, everything, not just moral issues, but everything that is good for you or bad for you. The soul is sensitive to that. It registers that. It is the thing that monitors life for the mortal creature, and the spirit is a direction in that life. When that life finds a direction, it wants to take you there. It wants to take you to excellence. It wants to take you to some place in this society. You want to leave this society to find your life in another society. What is working for you to get you to turn from that and go to that may be rational, but it is also spiritual, and you can't do it without spirit. You have to have a spirit for it before you can think about it. First, you have a spirit for it. So, spirit means moving. Soul is stationary, and it is just feeling and responding to what is happening. But it occupies a space as big as the universe. The soul can sense for you an interest on the moon, or an interest any place near or far away.

"Our Lord do not charge us with or punish us if we should forget or make a mistake". The mind forgets. The mind makes mistakes. The soul records, perfectly, everything that happens. But the soul and the mind are different. So, you see how it starts? *"I hear and I obey"*. We hear and we obey. That's perfect obedience, right? We hear and immediately obey, perfect obedience, and then the soul, the self, is not burdened except by what it has the capacity to bear. That's the soul.

Everything That Registers On the Mind Goes to the Soul

And then the soul is recording very accurately everything that we're doing, good or bad. Everything that we're registering on our mind goes to the soul and will never be erased unless G_d erases it. You have no power to erase it yourself. Is there any proof of this in psychology? Yes. They can bring up what happened to you when you were in your mother's stomach. Well, they claim that. They claim they can bring up memory from you when you were in your mother's stomach, not even born yet. You weren't talking, but they know by the responses that this is a response from the fetus, not from a born child. So, that means whatever happened in the fetus was recorded in your soul, and they were able to find some evidence of that. So, the mind is subject to forget. Because of the imperfection of the mind, it's subject to make mistakes, so again, we pray for the soul.

No Other Religion Has the Clarity of Islam

G_d does not burden anyone except with what it has the capacity to bear. But now the mind, we're pleading for the mind, now. These are believers pleading for the mind. *"And do not make us carry or bear a burden as that that You placed on those before us."* This is a particular burden, isn't it? This is a particular burden. It's not an ordinary burden, a particular burden. This is a burden that we see in religions that are not having the clarity that Islam has, and that's all religions other than Islam. No religion has the clarity that Islam has. It is the last of the great revealed religions, and it is the clearest, the clearest of the revealed religions. All the other religions are filled with a lot of mystery, too much mystery, too much esotericism, secret language, language known only by the few who are blessed to get insight. They're filled with that and that's what makes them a great burden on the average adherent or believer or follower of those faiths.

So, here we are praying that G_d will not burden us with the burden that was placed upon those before us. We're praying because, "G_d, we have recognized the clarity in Islam. We have recognized the ease with which we can walk the path of Islam, (siraatal mustaqeem), and we're grateful to G_d for making this religion so plain and so easy for us to follow and live, and we ask Him that He will never place a burden on us like He placed on those before us."

G_d Made You As a Spirit

I live in my own body. It is here to express me. My hand is not doing anything on its own unless it's doing it for me. The life inside this body uses this body for expression, and G_d made you as a spirit. As a spirit, your life goes beyond the boundaries of your flesh, not just, "Oh, you're talking about feeling?" No, you! What are you essentially? You are body, mind, and spirit. Your spirit goes outside of you. We're not only talking about a spirit in some separate entity, or context, separate from your body, and your mind. I'm talking about your mind that is a composite. Your spirit contains your flesh interest, mind interests, and your spirit's interest, all in one entity, a spiritual entity.

So, when you feel bad, your spirit may want to come away from what you are feeling that's out there, or then your spirit may be feeling bad because of something inside you, and it wants to go away from this stuff in here, out there. And your spirit, when it goes out there, your mind goes with it and your material interest goes with it. Your whole life has mobility outside of your limited biological framework. That's what man has to understand about his identity. Don't identify man with his physical form, or picture, only, that man was just put there so that would be a protection for his life. His expression goes beyond his flesh. His interests go beyond his flesh. He lives in a bigger dimension than the biological dimension.

If you just live in your biological dimension, you're not human. That's what makes you human. You must live in a dimension bigger than your biological or flesh form. You get a wife, your interest goes to her and you're living mentally, materially, spiritually, with her in every way. If you are not living with her, materially, why did you bring her a box of candy, tonight, to go to bed with her and get what you want? You brought some chocolates to get some cookies. I know that your life that's shared with her is more than spirit. It's spirit. It's mental. It's material. It's everything.

Allah Created Us for Community

So, here the G_d, the Great Architect of the universe, has designed a human creature, a biological flesh and blood creature, who actually is not contained in his own body, and he must have a bigger body to contain him. So, he wants, all the time, to get more and more living space so he can have bodies, structures, to put his life in, and to see his life having bigger and better expression. Ummah, community, that's what G_d wanted us to have. He created us for community. We must have community life in our charge so that Brother John, Brother Abdullah, and Sister Maryam can have expression. The soul can become defective, distorted, warped, ill-formed. If the wrong thing gets in the soul, it can be destroyed by the world. But if we can keep the soul pure, unadulterated, in the human form that G_d made for it, this soul will keep signaling to our mind, our intellect, our duties, our responsibilities, and will keep pressuring us until we fulfill our part of the bargain with G_d, a commercial bargain that you'll be so pleased with, fulfill your obligation to G_d.

Substrata Expression

We're living as conscious beings and G_d created us before we even became conscious of ourselves, and on that level out of the need to have language (I'm giving some language), let us say that's substrata expression. So, here is our soul before we're even conscious of ourselves. We're on an existence we may call a substrata level of expression, where expression is not controlled by me, like I'm in my sleep. I'm not in control of what I'm doing. And then G_d wants us to come out of that substrata level into a conscious level of expression.

Shahada: 1st Level of Consciousness

What do we say? "Ash hadu an laa ilaaha illallah. I witness there is but one G_d". Testimony, that's the first level of consciousness in Divine Reality, to recognize that there is G_d. In that substrata existence, or expression, we're really like sleepwalkers. We have life, we're going about, but our whole life is like a life of sleep, until we awake to the reality that there's a G_d over us responsible for us existing.

Salat: 2nd Level of Consciousness

Then we go to level 2 of our expression, and that's salat. If we find the G_d, we find the Will of G_d. We find G_d. With G_d is also His Will, His Word for your expression and what is that? What is our prayer? Our prayer is the whole Qur'an. Our expression is our prayer, and our prayer is the Qur'an, the whole Qur'an.

Zakat: 3rd Level of Consciousness

Zakat. What is Zakat"? Growth, money, wealth, useful things that people need in their life for real existence in a material world. How is prayer going bring us to zakat? Testimony brings you to the Qur'an. When you come to see the Qur'an as your prayer, you will then see how the Qur'an will bring us to have material growth, so that we will be able to afford to give support to all the needs in society. We can't take them to Hajj, because we have a big malik over there. I don't know about a big azeez, but he's definitely a malik. Our prayer takes us to be in a position where we can support the institution of salat. We've got to stop looking to people who should be on zakat, for zakat. We're men. Why can't we produce wealth and take care of our needy people? Why do we have to get the needy people to take care of us?

Saum: 4th Level of Consciousness

After zakat, restraint. Once G_d has blessed you to accumulate wealth and then you become charitable, you're giving to others, your charity reaches your ego and devilish intellect as an instrument for enslaving people and building a kingdom for yourself. So, you'll be tempted. The urge in humans is first, especially, when you're called to goodness. The good urge is first, but after people enjoy the luxuries, the luxuries sometimes lull them to sleep. The consciousness, the moral alertness, go to sleep and they are not as morally alert as they were before enjoying the material benefits. Then the tendency comes that you will become a devil in your power or in your authority, and you will start to use your knowledge that you were using for G_d for self-promotion. And you will be able to take advantage of the charitable nature in people to increase wealth for yourself, for your own scheme; and you will use your charity to buy power for yourself. Governments, their charity is destroyed, killed, by their scheme to use their wealth to buy more power and image for themselves. On the Day of Judgment, they have no credit with G_d.

Hajj: 5th Level of Consciousness

All of these are conscious strata. The 5th one is the unity of mankind's expression (Hajj)/Pilgrimage), demonstrating to the world that Muslims acknowledge and promote the unity of all people. There's no superiority for black or white. G_d says He found you on the pit of the brink of fire, and in so doing we became brothers.

Islam Is Built Upon Five

When the Prophet said the religion (Islam) is structured, or built upon five, he was doing commentary on what Allah says in Qur'an, that it is the religion of origin, the origin upon which mankind was formed, was established, Deen al Fitra, the religion of origin. *"Fitraatul ladhee", the origin of which, or upon which, "Fataran naasa", He fashioned humans as society.* "An nas", means humans in a group or society. *"The origin upon which human society was fashioned".* So, when the Prophet said, "Islam, it is built or structured upon five", he was doing commentary, really, on that which I just read.

G_d blessed him with the insight to see that the society was organized and structured upon respect for the five human senses, beginning with feeling, but all five of them. And then we have the religion giving us five to acknowledge five. But the five that we are given are in a different language. The first is to witness that there is but one G_d. That is feeling. The sense of feel will guide us, eventually, to the belief that there is one G_d, if we keep our feelings pure, innocent, like Jesus Christ and like others, too. But he is more typical of that, and he spoke while was in the cradle. It means he spoke before he got learning into his head. He spoke before he was taught anything by anybody. And he knew his calling before anybody came to him, talked to him, or taught him anything.

The Child of the Water

That is the child of the water. It says when his mother was carrying him (this is the Bible) and when John's mother was carrying him, it says they were quickened in the womb. One sent signals to the other and caused him to quicken while he was yet in the womb, had not been born yet. What the Bible is saying is that the nature of these two are similar and that is what Muhammed was guided to understand when he put them on one level. In the second level of the Ascension (Miraj), John and Christ Jesus are on the same level. It does not mean that one was more important to the cause or the purpose for which they were being elevated. Jesus Christ is more important, but they were on the same level, meaning the same level in the Ascension from dead matter to purpose, to the highest level, Abraham.

So, they are ascending, and the first level of Adam is the material level or clay, and the second level is the spiritual level given as water. So, when Christ was conceived, it quickened John or caused John to quiver or shake in the womb of his mother. And you know water, like I always say, is so sensitive that if you touch it the ripples just go until they disappear from our eyes. They go as far as they can go, ripple out, going all out, like air waves. Anyway, the origin is this symbolic water nature. That is the original, the first place. It (Qur'an) says, *"And He began the creation of man from water"*, but it also, says, *"from clay, teen"*, and if you understand, it is talking about the same thing. One is talking about the spiritual nature, water, and the clay is talking about the nature of obedience in the material body. So, they both are talking about the same thing, and that is the nature that responds to influences.

Water responds to influence, and it conforms to its container. If the container is square, the water is square. You get a round container the water is round. If there is a groove, water will fill the groove. So, it conforms to the container, and clay responds to impressions, physical impressions. You touch it, your fingerprint is on it. So, if you want to mold it into a particular shape you can do it, and then you heat it in an oven, dry it out, and it will hold the shape you gave it. All of this has meaning for Scripture. So, it says Prophet Muhammed said, "Islam was built on five." He was coming from his knowledge of what G_d says in the Qur'an about Islam is the religion of origin, the origin upon which G_d fashioned human society, meaning human society formed naturally. And what was the main factor for the way it happened? Five senses, the commonsense of mankind.

Possessors of the First Door

So, Al-Islam is a commonsense based religion. It respects human nature in its origin, and it respects the five senses. And when Allah says in the Qur'an, *"Oh, you men of the first door (uulul al baab)"*, meaning possessors of the first door... Uulu means, first, speaking of the many. Al baab means the door. It is saying the same thing that the revolutionary guy said when he was trying to organize the people who came to settle in the new world against Britain, against the kingdom when he was trying to organize them. What was his name? Thomas Paine. He called them to their common senses. That is how it started, didn't it? He appealed to their common senses, and they started coming together. The writers of the Constitution followed Thomas Paine. He was the mu'adhdhan, calling them to respect their five senses.

No Exaggeration for the Founding Fathers

They saw the concepts and when they saw the concepts and the Will or Purpose of the Divine Word, they understood the language. They understood what Christ Jesus meant. They understood his concept and they understood what he meant for society as a savior, and obviously they understood Muhammed as well. They understood him as a concept in the Plan of G_d for human life, the best of the human condition, that concept, that excellence. They understood that and they understood where he was to take life or take the people. And that's how they were able to plan the future, the Constitution, the forming of our government, and the direction that it should follow in forever, in terms of wisdom, morals and ethics. They obviously had all that, so they are Founding Fathers! That's no exaggeration for them! They are the Founding Fathers!

So, you see, you can look right into the forming of this great country's ideology. You can look and see how it started, and how it came together and see that they, too, came together upon respect for their five senses. So, Prophet Muhammed, G_d revealed to him to have the first one as La ilaaha illallaah. It did not say, "Muhammed, the Messenger of Allah. At that time, he did not include himself. To witness that G_d is one, that is what he said, and then he said to pray. Now you should not establish prayer until you know who you are praying to. So, once you really meet with the real G_d, then you can pray, correctly.

"He Creates You Under Three Veils of Darkness"

So, 333. How many thirds does it take to make a whole? If you have one third, one third, and one third you've got a whole, don't you? And three 3's, if you add them, you've got nine. And that's a whole, too. In nine months, a full life comes. To me, that is a great sign! And my birthday is October the 30th, 1933, 333. They all go together, and it says, *"He creates you under three veils of darkness"*, three veils of darkness, the darkness of the body, the flesh, the material, the darkness of the mind, and the darkness of the spirit. But when He delivers the three together in nine months they are pure and innocent, and they are ready to be formed as He wants them to be formed, if the world doesn't block it. Well, they can block it, but if Allah intends it, the life will escape the block. It will be liberated despite the block. So, the three that are given as a sign are three saying, "Body, mind, and soul (spirit) have been liberated and you're on the right track!" My area code is 333. Yes, so G_d is present as He always has been, and all we have to do is just have a little faith, and we can see His Presence working with us in our lives.

Ascend In Your Own Soul to the Heights of Your Innocence

Three is very important! How many chapters are there in the Qur'an? One hundred and fourteen. Now you all aren't attuned to the kind of stuff I'm going to do right here! If you add one and four you get five. One and four is five and three fives are fifteen. But look at this, also. How many juz' are in the Qur'an, sections, juz'? Thirty. That's very important, very important, because Samson complained that they took his thirty changes of garments, and he was a strong man, wasn't he? His life is all about power, his tremendous power, his superpower that he had. He represents the potential and the potency of the human soul, and it can't get what G_d intends for it until it first becomes innocent or purifies itself. And when it purifies itself, the number for that purity is thirty that represents that purity.

And the way to that purity is to first ascend in your own soul to the heights of your innocence. You ascend up to a certain height and you're still carrying some guilt. You finally get to the seventh level, and you carry no more guilt! And Abraham said, *"Surely I turn myself to You, my whole self"*. He surrendered himself entirely to G_d, and G_d made him a leader of all people, all the nations and called him His friend! It's so beautiful! And then the soul comes back down, and it has earned G_d's Favor, and G_d is going to bless it to complete its purity, not only for the soul, but for the conscious. That's what the thirty means, it has entered the conscious. Three isn't just in the soul. Thirty means it has entered the conscious. And then G_d told him, "Now, you have to work on earth with people! Your soul has been completed!" So, he (Muhammed, the Prophet) went to Madinah and established the ummah.

There Is a Logic for the Order of Islam's Principles of Practice

The answer is in what Allah told the angels. He said, *"Make sajda to Adam"*, and where did He get Adam from? From the earth. He was formed in the earth. So, to make sajda to him you have to be formed, too, again, in the earth, not upstairs. We're reciting the Qur'an all the time. The Qur'an reconciles us with our original nature, and creation and brings us up as a community to develop this earth like Adam did. So, our prayer is an institution.

Our first principle of practice as Muslims is to witness that there is but one G_d, then to pray, and then the next is to give in charity. If you pray you are getting help from G_d, and it is not to help just you. You have to give. You have to share with others. He is the G_d of everybody. Do you see the logic, how it follows? There is a logic for Islam's principles of practice being in the order Prophet Muhammed gave them. The fourth one is fasting, to check bad tendencies in your behavior, to practice, to have an exercise called, fasting, to strengthen your will power and to draw you closer to G_d, the Source of strength.

After you fast and restrain yourself, the last one is you are to join your brothers in making the journey to Mecca to perform the Hajj, Pilgrimage. That brings you to community. Now, if people do not restrain themselves, they cannot support community, Markham, IL, the United States, etc. They have to be able to restrain themselves. There is a law, a certain limit that you have to respect when you want to do your own thing. And if you can respect these limits, then you can become part of the society, be a part of the town, or the community, or this nation. You can become a support for this nation because you respect those limits. You're not going to live as though you have no one to answer to. You are ready for society when you have learned to successfully manage yourself.

The Best Charity

So, we celebrate fasting in the month of Ramadan. There is a holiday celebrating it. It is a victory. I am celebrating my successful management of myself for thirty days as G_d has instructed me with His Word through Muhammed, the Prophet. So, it is a logic. It all goes together. It is not just five. You can't take one of those other ones and put it in the fifth place. No, that is a logic. You first witness G_d in your own life. "Yes, I know there is G_d," and knowing there is G_d makes you turn to that G_d. You know that G_d as Akbar, or Al-Akbar. So, you turn to that G_d for help, and then when you turn to Him, you feel grateful for Him helping you. You want to share it with your brothers and sisters. You want to help somebody else. You want somebody else to benefit as you have benefited. So, you say, "I'm going to give this." And the best gift is not the clothing or something. It is to give them what G_d communicated to your soul and your intelligence. Share that with them. That is the best charity. That is the blood of Jesus Christ, symbolized as the blood of Jesus Christ in the Bible, not Qur'an. But the Qur'an has an indirect reference to it, when Allah says, *"Your blood sacrifices do not reach Me, only your taqwa. They don't come up to Me"*.

Blood Is the Life of the Body

Where should they go? They should go where the Bible says go. The blood sacrifice should go to the people, and that is what Abraham did, didn't he? He thought that he was to sacrifice his son, and when he knew that he was not, then G_d told him to slay a lamb, and he slew it on the altar. And he prepared it for the feast, and they all ate it. They ate the meat. Now, you know the Jews were not supposed to eat blood. It was forbidden to be taken inside, like our halal, no blood. The Jews, in the Torah, the original law of the Jews, they could not take blood. They could not eat blood. The blood had to be drained out from the animal. Now, here comes the New Testament and the blood is what you give. So, don't we have to understand that blood? This is not the blood of just any animal. This is not the blood of just any lamb, or sheep. This is the blood of a lamb without spot or blemish, and this is not blood per se, or blood literally. No, the Bible tells you what this blood is. The wine is commemorating the blood. So, he told them, in the Last Supper, to drink the wine in remembrance of him shedding his blood.

Now, the blood is no more blood then. It is now wine. What did the Jews say the blood was? The Jews said blood is the life of the body. This is in the Bible. We have to apply that. It is not a contradiction. It looks like a contradiction that they are taking blood. We have to trace the language and see where the language takes us, okay? So, the first language is blood in the physical body, and the Bible said that is the life of the body. Now when they said it back then they had a reference to a higher ideology, not just physical blood, but it had not been brought out. So, it has to be brought out, eventually. It has to be taught. The Bible is revealing itself from Genesis to Revelation. So, what was revealed earlier in language is revealed later in another language to advance revelation or the light. So really, the first meaning of blood is saying that it is the life of the body.

Charity of the Word

So, what is the life of the human body? It is not the animal life. The life of the human body is intelligence. Now why is blood identified as the life of the body, and as the intelligence of that body? The heart is an organ pumping the blood and it pumps the blood to all parts of the body, and if it fails to get to any part of the body that part is going to die. So, it is to charity of the Word. The Word is pumped by the heart and the heart is supposed to belong to G_d, number one. So, the heart is pumping in obedience to G_d and the heart is pumping life to every part of the body. I said that the Old Testament, when it said blood is the life of the body, it was referring to a higher idea, not to physical blood, and I think I explained that. Now, it comes out in the New Testament with Jesus Christ. It says, *"Take this in remembrance of me"*, and it was a wine. And they know that is supposed to represent his blood, the blood of Jesus Christ. And the Bible says, *"And the wine is the spirit of the New Testament"*. So, if the wine is the spirit of the New Testament, then the blood, too, is the spirit of the New Testament, and tears are salty and sweet, but blood is only sweet. That is complete charity.

"Put Your Bread On the Water and It Will Come Back to You"

It says the wine is the spirit of the New Testament, and it says the bread is the doctrine. And the Bible says, *"Put your bread on the water and it will come back to you."* It means trust it to the people. Trust it to the faith of the people. Trust it to these spiritual people that you don't want to trust with your intelligence, because they are not educated like you. You can't take it and put it in their hands. You can't take it and show it to them before their eyes. You have to feed it to their spirit. You have to feed it to their soul. They are spiritual, like water. You have to put it on the water. You have to trust it to faith but trust it! Trust your bread to faith. Trust your education, your knowledge, to the faith of the people. I know you can't give it to them through their intelligence. They are not ready for it. They are not that educated or elevated yet in their intelligence but trust it to their faith. Isn't that beautiful?

Now, there are two things there. It means, you know this is a big job and you need a lot of money. You're wondering how you are going to make it. "These people are poor you sent me to. You sent me to a world of poor people. The rulers are not going to listen to me. They are going execute me. If I let them know exactly what you're telling me to do, they will kill me!" So, it means both. Trust the bread to the water means trust the knowledge to the people you think do not have the intelligence for it. Give it to their faith. You know they believe, and you know they have strong faith, so trust it to them as a body of faith, not as a body of knowledge.

Praise be to Allah! And it will come back to you. It means the students will one day give you back that knowledge, show you that they will get it one day. It will come back to you from your students. It also means don't worry about how you're going to make it materially. That will come back to you, too, the blood of the New Testament, the blood of a lamb without spot or blemish, that is why it is halal.

Washing Five Times In a River

The Prophet said, "If a river or stream of water would pass by and you would wash in that water five times, would there be any impurities left?" His followers said, "No". So, he was telling them, "Don't forget your five senses when you're cleaning yourself in wudu', because three times and there might be some filth left. You will still feel unclean though you did it three times". So, he was telling them, in a wise way, "Respect your five senses", because here is a stream that comes, and you wash in it five times and no more impurities are left. It doesn't mean five times, literally. It means we're washing using our five senses, and they understood him. He was speaking to the wise. They said, "No impurities would be left, if we use our five senses".

Rituals Preserve the Knowledge In the Culture

Another support for us not stopping with three is if we don't think the hands are clean, it says Allah gives without counting. This is the Qur'an. So, your ritual is not the highest. But why should we stick with three? Because it is a ritual, and the ritual preserves the knowledge in the culture. And what is that knowledge? Matters are judged by intention and before you make your wudu', you make your intentions. That is first, and intention is proof of the spirit. Intention is the essence of the spirit. So, that three is in Christianity. It is the spirit, father, son, and Holy Ghost. They sprinkle you with water. They want you to come into the spirit. This is the life, giving you the essence of life, or with the beginning of life, water for your spirituality, hoping that you will be touched spiritually, by it, and the spiritual life has the purpose and an aim. It's going to fulfill the intention that G_d clocked into the creature when He made it. So, it is the three.

Now, you know, we were told the story of the Jews, that they had to have ten to have congregational worship, at least ten. But for us, it was reduced to three through Muhammed. If you have three persons, we can have salat, congregational prayer, Jumah, with only three persons. What does it say about us, and why is it said of us in the Qur'an?

Ten Means Conscious With Your Intelligent Mind

The ten is required by the Jews, and only three required by us. So, what does the ten mean? Ten means you are conscious with your intelligent mind. So, that is what the Jews have to have in that faith, or that situation, in order for them to begin teaching you, or having congregational worship. But in Al-Islam, you only have to have three. So, what is this? Three is your developmental nature and how you turn out based upon the purity of your intentions. If your intentions are pure, your intentions will last. Do you see the baby finger? That is where you start dhikr. The other fingers are bigger, but you don't start dhikr with the bigger thing. You start with the smallest thing, with your baby finger, as we call it.

So, dhikr with the baby finger is just like saying the Christians see the world created anew with the lamb without spot or blemish. The little finger is a little lamb without spot, or blemish. It does not help you write. You wrote and did that stuff with your mind, and it was there but not used. So, you start with the baby, original sense, and it is not enough to be used in the building of the world. So, you start with that, in the essence of human nature, creation, the essence that G_d created to take us where we have to go. Matters are judged by intention. Now, when we start our dhikr, we start with the little finger. We start in the base of him and when we come to the top of him, as far as we can go with him, he will take us to the base of the next one. Then the next one, you go up on it from the base and you see the lines are straight, going up on the two parts. When you get to the third, they are in a circle. That means spiritual freedom, you are liberated. So, you go with this little original one until he is liberated, and then you start at the base of the other one and go up with his life. You took his life over to this one, into his base, and you take it up until he is liberated. And you keep freeing them with that little baby, and that little baby, eventually, brings you to the one in his base and stop, and that is 100 times. Stop on this one, that's its conscious.

You Have to Be Transformed From the Original Baby Life

So, you stop on the conscious, in the base of conscious. That means he went into the subconscious, didn't he? His purity went into the subconscious, and you do not have to do it anymore, you are through with it. You did it a hundred times and somebody died. The original thinking died. Allah gives without counting. So now, forget about all this counting and just go with the transition. You have to be transformed from the original purity, baby life. You have to transfer the essence into the other life to transform it, and it will transform these lives, if you put that pure essence in there, and eventually, it will bring the whole mind to die to what it believed before. And once it dies, you do not have to go any further. It is in a new mind, a new life. It is transformed, and it is in the subconscious. You do not have to worry about it. Do not try to force it into the conscious. Just keep working on that essence, keep recognizing that essence, that it is the essence that should be at the base of all the other living parts of my life, or living branches of my life. It should be what is in the base of it. And once you go until the mind dies to its original thinking, that is enough. It is in the subconscious. We should be satisfied with it. I'm a living proof of that. I preached to you, and I used symbolic language and everything until I got the purity, the essence of human life into your spirit, into the deep. And once it was in your spirit, you were free. You were transformed.

Slay Your Own Selves

It says that the Jews were told to die, so that you may live. They were just so fixed to their way of thinking that they wouldn't even listen to Moses. And in another place, they were told, *"Slay your own souls, so that you may live"*. This is in Qur'an. But it did not mean, physically, but saying, nafs, means self, too. So, if you don't know the guidance in the Scripture, you will make the mistake of thinking they meant slay your people physically. That is not what it meant.

It meant you were to slay your own selves. It meant slay your own souls, and it means slay the feelings that you are in. Soul is a spiritual body and to understand it, it registers your feelings more than anything else. So, it means slay your feelings. You have feelings for your riches. You have feelings for your parents. You have feelings for your teacher of old and that is where your feelings are. You have to kill those feelings and come into a new feeling; get rid of those feelings.

Why Elijah Mohammed Followed Mr. Fard Away From Christianity

The route that we were put on didn't start with Muslims acknowledging the religion, or acknowledging Allah, and the Qur'an. It started with the first soul on this continent that found itself at a loss to understand the circumstances that it was put in. And it started reaching outwardly without even Scripture to guide it to the name of G_d or anything. It started reaching outwardly, crying to the distances, "I know there is a just G_d! I know there is justice somewhere out there!" That is where it started, and that is still in us, if we awaken in that particular spirit and mind to understand Allah is with us, and we have awakened in that particular spirit and mind to understand.

That is why Elijah Mohammed followed Mr. Fard away from Christian society and Christianity, and that is why his son, too, kept the same spirit and the same determination to understand why I am in these circumstances, and got the help of Scripture, mainly Qur'an. I was not in the Bible. I started off in Qur'an, and when I said we share the same existence, our existence can't be understood unless we understand what we have experienced as a people, and more importantly, as a spirituality, as a sensitivity, as a soul of that people. We all share one sensitivity. We all share one spirituality that was formed by circumstances that we were touched by more than anybody else. So, that made us a product or design after the influences, or the circumstances in our history. That forming of us is more important than Wallace D. Mohammed, or these different individuals. We only have big meaning once we put ourselves in that group experience and group history for the soul, mainly, because many times the mind couldn't walk the path, couldn't even know what was happening, couldn't travel. It was at a standstill.

The Soul Is Never at a Standstill

However, the soul is never at a standstill. It is always sensing and wanting to understand what it is sensing. That is our true life and that is the life that we don't have alone. We have it only as a people. Remember when I said that to get in heaven you can't go in by yourself? You have to go in as a community, a community of survivors of slavery. If we forget that, to me, we lose sight on what's real in our life, and where we should be going. So, en sha Allah, we will see each other, again, soon. I thank Allah for us.

Chapter 12

Connecting Back to Our Own

Why is the sun setting in the evening? Because the earth is going eastward and when it goes that way it turns away from the sun. When it turns away from the sun, it appears to us that the sun is setting. But the earth is turning eastwards away from the sun. It never changes its movement. The movement is always eastward. But they say, "Go West young man, go West." I say keep going East and you'll be in the West before you know it, because the earth is a sphere, a ball.

The Sun Going to Rise From the West

The Prophet Abraham, our father Abraham, peace be on him, challenged the Pharaoh, the oppressor. The oppressor said, *"I give life, and I give death"* and Abraham said, *"Allah brings the sun from the East, can you bring it from the West?"* Now that was a criticism. He actually was criticizing the service that the Pharaoh was doing for the people, saying *"Allah brings the sun from the East, can you bring it from the West?"* And it said, *"And the rejecters of faith were confounded"*. They did not understand what he was talking about. They were so ignorant in the knowledge of Scripture.

There is a saying of Muhammed, the Prophet, that the sun is going to rise from the West. This is his teaching on the end of the world, the conclusion of things for mankind on this planet earth. Right now, is the time, and that time he lived in was the same, too. It was a time when the matters, the great issues before the world at that time were all concluded. When the Qur'an came by the coming of Prophet Muhammed, light appeared in every area that was dark, and the conclusion of things came. Everything was concluded.

Someone to Revive It

Prophet Muhammed, peace be upon him (pbuh), said there will come a reviver. At the head of everyone hundred years there will be someone coming, and you shouldn't look on the calendar. A hundred years is told in the meaning of hundred in Arabic. One hundred is, "miat", and the same letters, but just pronounced differently because of the way the vowels are to be indicated, "mait", death. "Maitun", is a dead thing. So, here is the same word with a slight accent change. It is not a hundred years, it is death. So, it means, "Every time my community dies there will be someone to revive it." Mr. Fard understood how to make that happen

Praise be to Allah! And it will come back to you. It means the students will one day give you back that knowledge, show you that they will get it one day. It will come back to you from your students. It also means don't worry about how you're going to make it materially. That will come back to you, too, the blood of the New Testament, the blood of a lamb without spot or blemish, that is why it is halal.

Washing Five Times In a River

The Prophet said, "If a river or stream of water would pass by and you would wash in that water five times, would there be any impurities left?" His followers said, "No". So, he was telling them, "Don't forget your five senses when you're cleaning yourself in wudu', because three times and there might be some filth left. You will still feel unclean though you did it three times". So, he was telling them, in a wise way, "Respect your five senses", because here is a stream that comes, and you wash in it five times and no more impurities are left. It doesn't mean five times, literally. It means we're washing using our five senses, and they understood him. He was speaking to the wise. They said, "No impurities would be left, if we use our five senses".

Rituals Preserve the Knowledge In the Culture

Another support for us not stopping with three is if we don't think the hands are clean, it says Allah gives without counting. This is the Qur'an. So, your ritual is not the highest. But why should we stick with three? Because it is a ritual, and the ritual preserves the knowledge in the culture. And what is that knowledge? Matters are judged by intention and before you make your wudu', you make your intentions. That is first, and intention is proof of the spirit. Intention is the essence of the spirit. So, that three is in Christianity. It is the spirit, father, son, and Holy Ghost. They sprinkle you with water. They want you to come into the spirit. This is the life, giving you the essence of life, or with the beginning of life, water for your spirituality, hoping that you will be touched spiritually, by it, and the spiritual life has the purpose and an aim. It's going to fulfill the intention that G_d clocked into the creature when He made it. So, it is the three.

Now, you know, we were told the story of the Jews, that they had to have ten to have congregational worship, at least ten. But for us, it was reduced to three through Muhammed. If you have three persons, we can have salat, congregational prayer, Jumah, with only three persons. What does it say about us, and why is it said of us in the Qur'an?

Charity of the Word

So, what is the life of the human body? It is not the animal life. The life of the human body is intelligence. Now why is blood identified as the life of the body, and as the intelligence of that body? The heart is an organ pumping the blood and it pumps the blood to all parts of the body, and if it fails to get to any part of the body that part is going to die. So, it is to charity of the Word. The Word is pumped by the heart and the heart is supposed to belong to G_d, number one. So, the heart is pumping in obedience to G_d and the heart is pumping life to every part of the body. I said that the Old Testament, when it said blood is the life of the body, it was referring to a higher idea, not to physical blood, and I think I explained that. Now, it comes out in the New Testament with Jesus Christ. It says, *"Take this in remembrance of me"*, and it was a wine. And they know that is supposed to represent his blood, the blood of Jesus Christ. And the Bible says, *"And the wine is the spirit of the New Testament"*. So, if the wine is the spirit of the New Testament, then the blood, too, is the spirit of the New Testament, and tears are salty and sweet, but blood is only sweet. That is complete charity.

"Put Your Bread On the Water and It Will Come Back to You"

It says the wine is the spirit of the New Testament, and it says the bread is the doctrine. And the Bible says, *"Put your bread on the water and it will come back to you."* It means trust it to the people. Trust it to the faith of the people. Trust it to these spiritual people that you don't want to trust with your intelligence, because they are not educated like you. You can't take it and put it in their hands. You can't take it and show it to them before their eyes. You have to feed it to their spirit. You have to feed it to their soul. They are spiritual, like water. You have to put it on the water. You have to trust it to faith but trust it! Trust your bread to faith. Trust your education, your knowledge, to the faith of the people. I know you can't give it to them through their intelligence. They are not ready for it. They are not that educated or elevated yet in their intelligence but trust it to their faith. Isn't that beautiful?

Now, there are two things there. It means, you know this is a big job and you need a lot of money. You're wondering how you are going to make it. "These people are poor you sent me to. You sent me to a world of poor people. The rulers are not going to listen to me. They are going execute me. If I let them know exactly what you're telling me to do, they will kill me!" So, it means both. Trust the bread to the water means trust the knowledge to the people you think do not have the intelligence for it. Give it to their faith. You know they believe, and you know they have strong faith, so trust it to them as a body of faith, not as a body of knowledge.

if G_d had not accepted it as our fate that would put us in a situation to come out of it as a reborn people, and Scripture speaks of it: *"See how the gross metal is put into the refiner's fire and how the impurities are made to separate from the purity of the metal and are better and more durable, and pure substance is created, because it had to be put into the fire?"*

Plantation life, life in America up until the 1960's, was hell fire. It was a fiery furnace fired up by the demons, warp-minded white people, who had lost their sense of what Christ really was to them, and they did this to us. They put us in the fiery furnace, but it didn't burn out anything but our impurity. The pure at heart have survived, and it only burned out our impurities. Now we are ready as a new people to serve our G_d, and to lead humanity back to humanity.

G_d has prepared us to use us in this conclusion of things for man on the earth. Yes, this is the Day of Religion, the conclusion of things. He has prepared us to use us in this day of the conclusion of things, so that we would be a witness to them that G_d is G_d, and there is but one G_d, the One Who created man and everything; and that no matter what happens for His human product in the world, He has power to re-establish them as He intended for them to be established.

Racism Not a Big Issue Anymore

G_d is in charge. Someone said, "Oh, you'd better be careful, whitey might reverse it and have us in slavery, again". I'm not worried about whitey. G_d is in charge! G_d has always been in charge, and your calendar is long. G_d's calendar is short. It seems like it was just last week that we had ugly racism glaring at us, staring us in the face in the South and in the North. I experienced it, also, in Chicago. It seems like it was just yesterday, almost. It is gone. Oh, I hear you, "No, it's not gone!" Well, why don't you get rid of it, you're free? If it isn't gone, you get rid of it. You're free. You need me, call me. I'll help you get rid of it. I'll do my part, maybe more than my part. I'll do some of your part, too, because I know you're much weaker than I am, if you think racism is still such a big issue.

The Germ of the True Human Being's Essence

The need for us to be responsible for ourselves, our families, our houses, our apartments, our neighborhoods, our children, our block, and the trouble on our block, that's the bigger issue right now, buddy! Praise be to Allah! So, all the troubles for the innocent are nothing but trials and tests in a refiner's fire to drive out from us the impurities, so that we will become a pure people. Like refined iron in America and in the world, because he knew, if it was successful in America, it would also take care of the need in the whole world for revival and direction back to the living words of the Qur'an, and Prophet Muhammed. It is true. It is real.

The Slaves Were Muslims

We have recent publications by beautiful authors letting us know that all of us didn't come over here as animists, or worshipers of the spirits of our ancestors, or worshipers of idols, in Africa; and all of us didn't come over here as Christians. In fact, Christian America never wanted to believe that they were bringing Christians from Africa and putting them in bondage here. They didn't want to believe that. So, they didn't want to accept that the slave traders would bring Christians from Africa here. So, if they didn't like that, and didn't want to enslave Christians, then who are we the children of? We're the children of idol worshipers, animists, parent spirit worshipers, or we're the children of Muslims, one or the others. So, these new books document that many Muslims were brought to America in slave ships.

A Natural Urge to Be Reconnected

So, there it is, whether you want it or not, whether you like it or not. You may not want to be a Muslim, but many of you who are not Muslim you have a natural hunger and urge in your soul and in your spirit to be reconnected with what you were cut off from. Dr. C. Eric Lincoln was a great African American theologian. He said, in his studies, that he believed strongly that there is an Islamic, genetic, memory in black people. That means you don't remember it, but your genes, your flesh, your body, remember it. Your body still remembers that you were once Muslim. Your human body with the genes from your fathers in it still remembers that you are Muslim, and that's why you have an interest in Al-Islam. That's why you have an interest in Islam, many of you, not all of you, and that's why you're happy when you become Muslim, and you can't wait until you learn Al-Islam. You don't mind. Inside your body the genes are shouting, "I'm back again where I was before, in Al-Islam!" Your mind can't shout because you don't now Al-Islam yet, but I have learned Al-Islam, and I shout with my whole being, flesh, mind, soul, and spirit.

The Will of G_d That We Be Brought Here

What I want to say is this. Many people have been the victims of inhuman, demonic, horrible, oppressors, and as a student of the Ways of G_d and man I am convinced that it was the Will of G_d that we be put on slave ships and brought to this country, this continent. I'm convinced it was the Will of G_d. They could not have done it

Chapter 12

Connecting Back to Our Own

Why is the sun setting in the evening? Because the earth is going eastward and when it goes that way it turns away from the sun. When it turns away from the sun, it appears to us that the sun is setting. But the earth is turning eastwards away from the sun. It never changes its movement. The movement is always eastward. But they say, "Go West young man, go West." I say keep going East and you'll be in the West before you know it, because the earth is a sphere, a ball.

The Sun Going to Rise From the West

The Prophet Abraham, our father Abraham, peace be on him, challenged the Pharaoh, the oppressor. The oppressor said, *"I give life, and I give death"* and Abraham said, *"Allah brings the sun from the East, can you bring it from the West?"* Now that was a criticism. He actually was criticizing the service that the Pharaoh was doing for the people, saying *"Allah brings the sun from the East, can you bring it from the West?"* And it said, *"And the rejecters of faith were confounded"*. They did not understand what he was talking about. They were so ignorant in the knowledge of Scripture.

There is a saying of Muhammed, the Prophet, that the sun is going to rise from the West. This is his teaching on the end of the world, the conclusion of things for mankind on this planet earth. Right now, is the time, and that time he lived in was the same, too. It was a time when the matters, the great issues before the world at that time were all concluded. When the Qur'an came by the coming of Prophet Muhammed, light appeared in every area that was dark, and the conclusion of things came. Everything was concluded.

Someone to Revive It

Prophet Muhammed, peace be upon him (pbuh), said there will come a reviver. At the head of everyone hundred years there will be someone coming, and you shouldn't look on the calendar. A hundred years is told in the meaning of hundred in Arabic. One hundred is, "miat", and the same letters, but just pronounced differently because of the way the vowels are to be indicated, "mait", death. "Maitun", is a dead thing. So, here is the same word with a slight accent change. It is not a hundred years, it is death. So, it means, "Every time my community dies there will be someone to revive it." Mr. Fard understood how to make that happen

That is why Elijah Mohammed followed Mr. Fard away from Christian society and Christianity, and that is why his son, too, kept the same spirit and the same determination to understand why I am in these circumstances, and got the help of Scripture, mainly Qur'an. I was not in the Bible. I started off in Qur'an, and when I said we share the same existence, our existence can't be understood unless we understand what we have experienced as a people, and more importantly, as a spirituality, as a sensitivity, as a soul of that people. We all share one sensitivity. We all share one spirituality that was formed by circumstances that we were touched by more than anybody else. So, that made us a product or design after the influences, or the circumstances in our history. That forming of us is more important than Wallace D. Mohammed, or these different individuals. We only have big meaning once we put ourselves in that group experience and group history for the soul, mainly, because many times the mind couldn't walk the path, couldn't even know what was happening, couldn't travel. It was at a standstill.

The Soul Is Never at a Standstill

However, the soul is never at a standstill. It is always sensing and wanting to understand what it is sensing. That is our true life and that is the life that we don't have alone. We have it only as a people. Remember when I said that to get in heaven you can't go in by yourself? You have to go in as a community, a community of survivors of slavery. If we forget that, to me, we lose sight on what's real in our life, and where we should be going. So, en sha Allah, we will see each other, again, soon. I thank Allah for us.

once it dies, you do not have to go any further. It is in a new mind, a new life. It is transformed, and it is in the subconscious. You do not have to worry about it. Do not try to force it into the conscious. Just keep working on that essence, keep recognizing that essence, that it is the essence that should be at the base of all the other living parts of my life, or living branches of my life. It should be what is in the base of it. And once you go until the mind dies to its original thinking, that is enough. It is in the subconscious. We should be satisfied with it. I'm a living proof of that. I preached to you, and I used symbolic language and everything until I got the purity, the essence of human life into your spirit, into the deep. And once it was in your spirit, you were free. You were transformed.

Slay Your Own Selves

It says that the Jews were told to die, so that you may live. They were just so fixed to their way of thinking that they wouldn't even listen to Moses. And in another place, they were told, *"Slay your own souls, so that you may live"*. This is in Qur'an. But it did not mean, physically, but saying, nafs, means self, too. So, if you don't know the guidance in the Scripture, you will make the mistake of thinking they meant slay your people physically. That is not what it meant.

It meant you were to slay your own selves. It meant slay your own souls, and it means slay the feelings that you are in. Soul is a spiritual body and to understand it, it registers your feelings more than anything else. So, it means slay your feelings. You have feelings for your riches. You have feelings for your parents. You have feelings for your teacher of old and that is where your feelings are. You have to kill those feelings and come into a new feeling; get rid of those feelings.

Why Elijah Mohammed Followed Mr. Fard Away From Christianity

The route that we were put on didn't start with Muslims acknowledging the religion, or acknowledging Allah, and the Qur'an. It started with the first soul on this continent that found itself at a loss to understand the circumstances that it was put in. And it started reaching outwardly without even Scripture to guide it to the name of G_d or anything. It started reaching outwardly, crying to the distances, "I know there is a just G_d! I know there is justice somewhere out there!" That is where it started, and that is still in us, if we awaken in that particular spirit and mind to understand Allah is with us, and we have awakened in that particular spirit and mind to understand.

Ten Means Conscious With Your Intelligent Mind

The ten is required by the Jews, and only three required by us. So, what does the ten mean? Ten means you are conscious with your intelligent mind. So, that is what the Jews have to have in that faith, or that situation, in order for them to begin teaching you, or having congregational worship. But in Al-Islam, you only have to have three. So, what is this? Three is your developmental nature and how you turn out based upon the purity of your intentions. If your intentions are pure, your intentions will last. Do you see the baby finger? That is where you start dhikr. The other fingers are bigger, but you don't start dhikr with the bigger thing. You start with the smallest thing, with your baby finger, as we call it.

So, dhikr with the baby finger is just like saying the Christians see the world created anew with the lamb without spot or blemish. The little finger is a little lamb without spot, or blemish. It does not help you write. You wrote and did that stuff with your mind, and it was there but not used. So, you start with the baby, original sense, and it is not enough to be used in the building of the world. So, you start with that, in the essence of human nature, creation, the essence that G_d created to take us where we have to go. Matters are judged by intention. Now, when we start our dhikr, we start with the little finger. We start in the base of him and when we come to the top of him, as far as we can go with him, he will take us to the base of the next one. Then the next one, you go up on it from the base and you see the lines are straight, going up on the two parts. When you get to the third, they are in a circle. That means spiritual freedom, you are liberated. So, you go with this little original one until he is liberated, and then you start at the base of the other one and go up with his life. You took his life over to this one, into his base, and you take it up until he is liberated. And you keep freeing them with that little baby, and that little baby, eventually, brings you to the one in his base and stop, and that is 100 times. Stop on this one, that's its conscious.

You Have to Be Transformed From the Original Baby Life

So, you stop on the conscious, in the base of conscious. That means he went into the subconscious, didn't he? His purity went into the subconscious, and you do not have to do it anymore, you are through with it. You did it a hundred times and somebody died. The original thinking died. Allah gives without counting. So now, forget about all this counting and just go with the transition. You have to be transformed from the original purity, baby life. You have to transfer the essence into the other life to transform it, and it will transform these lives, if you put that pure essence in there, and eventually, it will bring the whole mind to die to what it believed before. And

and steel, it becomes harder. It becomes more resistant to rain and rust. It becomes harder and more durable and long lasting. So, you should be a very special people. The man who taught my father, he said, "I can sit on top of the world!" He wasn't talking about what he saw then. He was talking about what G_d had blessed him to envision that would come out of us in the future when America would open up, and we would have a chance to really establish our life ourselves. He said, "I can sit on top of the world", a future picture he saw, "and I can tell anyone that the most beautiful nation is in the wilderness of North America".

He was talking about The Nation of Islam and the members that he had brought together under the Honorable Elijah Mohammed, my father, with no more than three years elementary education from Georgia, a man that didn't know anything. He didn't know anything but just existing in America and trying to fight for his life like an animal, like a nice animal, like a deer, or a nice rabbit. That's all he knew, and a man came and put something in his head. He put a germ in his head that just fed his brain and his life. It was really nothing but the seed, or the germ of the true human being's essence. He put back into the man the human essence that he had lost, that one that had been taken away from him. He put back into that man that human essence that G_d made, and it just erupted in him. It just stretched him out. It just made him see farther and made him more determined not to be treated like he was less than a human being.

A Brand-New People On This Earth

You were important when you didn't know what you were. G_d knew what you were. You were important when you didn't know what religion yours should be. G_d knew what you were. You were His human vessel that He created, and the world had defiled that human vessel. He knew that in time you would throw out, you would puke up what defiled you, and your human essence would begin to manifest and burst forward in you to make you the great giant that G_d created you to be. And it has happened in America! It has happened in the greatest and most powerful country on earth. There has been a new birth. Those who are with me from my father, you are not the same black man. You are not the same black woman. You are a brand-new people on this earth!

You have a brand-new spirit. You have a brand-new will. You have a brand-new intelligence. You have a brand-new mind, and if you think like I tell you to think, buddy, respecting G_d's Word and Muhammed, the model human, you will have brand-new thoughts.! And when you have brand new thoughts, you will be walking behind me and working with me, and I won't feel your weight anymore. You'll be standing on your own two feet.

Attracted to Communism

So, accept the ugly past as G_d's Will, a condition to forge you into the wonderful, bright, and brilliant creature that G_d has made, the new African American in a new Africa on these shores. Isn't that wonderful? Yes, it is! If my father had not presented Al-Islam the way he presented it to us, I would not be a Muslim, because when I got older and started studying on my own, I was attracted to communism. Malcolm, he told me the same thing, that he was attracted to it while he was in prison. I was attracted to communism because I couldn't understand everything I was taught. There were too many questions unanswered. I mean serious questions. There was a conflict for reality. G_d made me to be free as a rational, thinking human being. My father and mother never worked against that development in me. They encouraged me to think, to use my own good senses.

African Americans Are the Worst Off of All American Citizens

I don't know anything that burdens the African American soul more than church religion, and that is what holds them. That is what held them up to now, and those who are still held in bad, human conditions, they are still in the Church, except for a very few. Even those who leave the Church, they don't leave the intelligence of Christian life. They just leave that which turns their intelligence off. The worst off of all the citizens of this country are those who were brought up without knowledge, and left with a belief that Jesus Christ, the physical concept that they see that was introduced to them, is a person, and is G_d. African Americans, they are the worst off of all the citizens in the United States of America. They are the ones who are so far from the light of intelligence that you don't see any evidence of it being in them at all. They actually are seriously mentally retarded. I'm not joking!

When you see them and they talk to you, their minds are so empty of anything that you can respect that much that it almost makes you want to cry, even in their face, or turn and go somewhere and cry. And some of them are not immoral. They have decency. They respect you saying, "Hi, Mr. Mohammed!" If they accidently throw something on your car, they say, "I'm sorry, I didn't mean to do that!" And they will start trying to wipe it off. But they have no spirit to engage you in an intelligent conversation. Some of them work, too. They will go out and work, but they don't have jobs that require much intelligence. They can only hold jobs that require hardly little, or no intelligence. They will go to work, come back, eat, and laugh with each other, go to bed, get up and repeat it, and go back to work. But on the weekend, they will go see a Tarzan movie, and if you tell them that is not real, they will say, "It is real!" They actually think what they see in a movie, on the screen, is actually happening, or is real. I have been in the movie with them. I know it. I've been in the movie with them and heard them argue with each other. The more intelligent, or more educated one was telling the less schooled one, "Man, that is not happening! That is not real! He did not die! He did not get killed!" I heard this myself and, believe me, as advanced as this world is right now, I guarantee you, you can ask the people in the audience, mostly African Americans, but a few other races, too, "Can that really happen? They can't do that. That is not real." They might not say anything. They may just remain silent and just look at you as if to say, "I don't understand what you're talking about! Where in the hell are you coming from?" That is reality. Yes, it is.

I tell you how you can see the effect of unreal things occurring on these people whose minds are not developed by learning or knowledge. You see the behavior on the screen, how it suggests that you won't die if you jump off this high building, or you can get shot, and you can get right back up and keep going. Then you look at the violence in the public life of the people and see how they just invite death. Psychologically, it has been planted in them to think without thinking or to feel without thinking that I can be shot and still live. I can be thrown off the seventh-floor window, roof or ledge, and get off the ground and keep going.

What I'm saying is that what appears to be a desire just to kill themselves is more than that. It is that plus or coupled with influences that have reached their mind and have made them tend to take risks, risk life with a picture in mind of them surviving, escaping it, getting back up and keep running or walking, get shot, get knocked down and appear in another movie. They say, "I saw that guy get killed. There he is again." This is all fiction, but the ignorant, they can't separate fiction from reality all the time. A guy in a movie gets shot by ten or twelve men with automatic weapons. He looks like a sieve, and he keeps coming. So, when the police say, "Stop", their mind goes back to the movie subconsciously, and they think they can keep walking against a barrage of bullets, and the proof is they do it. They threaten the police, keep disrespecting them, and keep threatening the police, and they are shooting, and they are still coming.

Religion Responsible for Lifting Human Life

So, if we can give people religion that respects their intelligence, it will lift the value and worth of human beings in society high enough for Hollywood and the police department, law enforcement and everything to have a high appreciation and respect for human life. It has to come from religion, just like religion has been responsible for not only lifting human life up, but responsible also, for fixing certain people who have no self-assertiveness enough to meet the challenges of life. It has fixed it, so they can be satisfied with a religion of make believe, and that keeps them from advancing their life and intelligence, So, en sha Allah (G_d willing), we're going to defeat it. Yes, we are. We are defeating it. It is slow, but we're defeating it.

There are other people who feel the same as we feel, but most of them don't have faith in the value of the common person created by G_d like we do. Even those who know that language, most of them don't have faith in the common person that we have. The people are not performing beneath the standards for human beings and intelligence because they are really ignorant. A few of them are ignorant, retarded. A few of them are impaired, I mean physically, or have psychological problems, and are not really in a situation or in a condition to be lifted up in life. The great many, the big numbers among these people that are really dropouts who not only dropped out of school, but dropped out of human life, are victims of a make-believe world, and starting right in the Church. And if ever reality can be shown to them, they will come into a new mind, a new interest, and a new determination to work for their elevation in society. I know that.

The Need for An Intelligentsia

In response to my being the best living example among us of Muhammed, the Prophet's example, I have to say that I try to conform to what Allah wants from us in the Qur'an, and in the life example of Muhammed, the Prophet. I try my best to conform to that, but I don't compare to the Prophet. And I can't conclude that if the Muslims got together and took shuraa and chose a leader, it would be me. I can't come to that conclusion. It is not for me to come to a conclusion like that. I'm open to accepting a qualified person upon the character and knowledge of Al-Islam, and I can just be a member of that body, intelligentsia. However, when I spoke about the need for an intelligentsia in a large gathering of Muslims, I don't think they understood me. I don't think the host people understood what I was recommending.

When I was recommending an intelligentsia, in the Qur'an, Allah says people have their own life, their own ways, their own laws, etc., then as He says to us, we should represent the highest standards for society and should be in the forefront of the effort to increase G_d's favor or to invite mankind, people, to G_d's favor, and to serve the best interest of society under G_d's Authority. He invites us to do that. Qur'an says, promoting fair dealing and justice, etc. But then He says,

"Let there arise or come out of you a group". The word is, "ummah". So, it's another community. It is a society out of a society. Let a society be formed of the society and let them be foremost, who will not fear the criticism of those who look or tend to criticize, look for fault. They will not be fearing them. They will not be trying to conform to their expectations, what the world expects of them in their own identity. They will be doing what they know G_d wants them to do and braving the wrath of the society, not fearing their criticism, etc. So, that is a special group.

There is nothing in the Qur'an that says form an ulemah, but it is natural that an ulemah be formed. It just means scholars. That is all it is. It comes from the Arabic word, "Aleem" which means, to be learned. So, the members of the ulemah are expected to be learned people, in the Qur'an, and the life of Muhammed, and I use the term, expression that is in English, "intelligentsia". The essence of aleem or ulemah is, "'ilm", and it is knowledge and science. So, I am using the expression, the term, intelligentsia, but for me the term is, ulemah. It means an organization of scholars. But to say, "ulemah", to an English-speaking audience of Christians, or a mixed audience, you will lose most of the people. But if you say, "intelligentsia", you will reach all of them.

An intelligentsia means a select group, a select group of learned people who are qualified by their intelligence and their learning to preside over matters of importance in a particular focus, or any particular area of life, and what we're talking about is the community life, the whole life. As African Americans, we had an intelligentsia until recently in our history. They did not organize as such, but they all knew each other. They respected each other. They supported each other, and most of them were very good friends and they lived in the same town, like W.E.B. Du Bois, Carter G. Woodson, Booker T. Washington, and many others, and some women. We had a leadership body, and they represented the better minds and the more intelligent of our people. So, to me, that was an intelligentsia, and they were guardians of the African American, black people's life. I mentioned the term, "wali" and it means, a patron, protector, who serves and guards your interest. So, I mentioned it, that we should have that group, an intelligentsia, and they should be the wali of the brothers and sisters of the community, their fellow Muslims. The audience responded, and I mean the immigrant Muslims, non-African Americans, responded very, very, warmly to that.

Used As a Battering Ram

In the movie, *Wanted,* a special group set him up to kill his own father, thinking his own father was the enemy, and they told him in the movie, "He wasn't trying to kill you, but just trying to reach you. If he was trying to kill you, you would have been dead." It is similar to the movie, *Hancock*. *Wanted*, is the one with the highly respected African American actor, Morgan Freeman. If you didn't see that one, you are going to have to see that one, too. All of them are about the same thing, where the African American is the hero. They are always addressing the same thing, what has manifested for the plan to use the African American people, or the African American family tree, to open up the world. I told you in the past and I'm telling you, again, they used us as a battering ram. In Mediaeval times and ancient times, too, they would break down big doors and walls with heavy logs, rams. They called them, "battering rams", and the ram is the male of the sheep, isn't it? So, take a sheepish people, who have all that potential for developing the world and house that potential, so it cannot realize its freedom in the world.

So, what do you do? You build up more and more pressure. Scripture says, *"I will tread the winepress alone."* When you put wine in bottles it becomes stronger and stronger over the years, and if you don't put a good top on it, it will blow the top off. It might even break the bottle. So, that is what they did for our soul. They took our soul away from where G_d wanted it and that is where it can find all its expression in this world that supports industry, that G_d plants in the soul, that He deposited into the soul of Adam, for all of us... as the future plan for man's destiny; all in him as a seed or potential, a capacity and a potential, not just a potential, because before he separated from his counterpart, Eve, he was both capacity and potential. But when the two separated, the capacity separated from the potential, then the man became the potential, and the woman became the capacity. And isn't city life where we find most of our development? Capacity is in the city where the people converge and concentrate.

How Man Lost Himself

The two got separated because Satan made the world more important than the developer that G_d created. The man, he's supposed to be the developer. Satan made the world more attractive and more important to that man than the Plan, or G_d's Will for him. He made the world, itself, more attractive. So, when the world captures your imagination and captures your interest, then you are separated from your own self. But if you are, first, seeking to know self, that is the first curiosity. Man wants to know, what am I? Why am I here? Why do I have this life and nature? Why do I have all these questions? Why do I have this curiosity? Why am I different from the rest of the life? So, the first interest for man's curiosity is himself, and he first discovers himself after he partly discovers other things. He has an interest in other things, and they take him only so far. The more he gives himself to those things outside of himself, the more he's pressured and burdened to look at himself and see what his role should be out here, his role in this reality.

So, when the world occupies your time and mind, your curiosity, it takes you away from that need to know yourself, and your role in the material world. That is how man lost himself. And Abraham says, *"Surely, I have been wrong. I have been oppressing my own self, and I confess my faults."* It really means, "Oppressing". In Arabic, it is, "thalamtu". It means "I turn to G_d, *guide me because I don't know how to get there. Guide me to the best of morals, for none can guide to the best of morals but You"*. Praise be to Allah! What a wonderful Scripture! So, that is how he got separated. G_d showed the angel, Jibril, His creation and the angel said, "How can anyone go wrong in such a creation?" Then, He showed him what the Devil had planned for the creation. He put his allurements, his attractions, all over G_d's work. So, the angel said, "G_d, how can anyone go straight in such a creation?"

"Why Have You Struck Me These Three Times?"

In the Bible, Baal was riding the donkey until the donkey saw an angel with a flaming sword, or a messenger with a flaming sword, with the Word of G_d that's like a flaming sword, a sword that lights up. It doesn't only cut, but it lights. It's a light, also. It cuts and slays, but it's a light also. That's the Word of G_d. The ministers used to preach this. I heard my father preach this subject from the rostrum. The donkey saw this angel holding the flaming sword in the pathway, in the way that it was traveling with its master on its back. So, the donkey said to its master, *"Why have you struck me these three times?"* It says it spoke with a man's voice, not a donkey anymore. The donkey spoke with a man's voice, and he said, *"Why have you struck me these three times?"*

Now that's answered in Bilal. Bilal was a slave to his master, and he was refusing to obey his master. That's asking his master, "Why have you struck me these three times? Why have you put my whole future in slavery, my flesh, my mind, and my spirit?" So, his way was just to protest slavery and for doing that his master put him in the hot sun, and Jesus was put in the heat, too, wasn't he? So, they put him in the hot sun and then put a heavy stone on his back, and they thought that that would make him break and decide to give up his interest in Prophet Muhammed's call to Islam. But when he couldn't speak, he just held out one finger. He was so miserable he couldn't even speak. He just held out that one finger, telling the one who insists he believe in more than one G_d, that he still believed in one G_d. He said, "Ahad, only One". And finally, one from the Muslim side, a friend of Prophet

Muhammed, Abu Bakr, came and paid his ransom, which shows that the master's interest was in money. The reason why he had a slave as a slave was because a slave was giving him money. So, when the money came in a big enough amount, he gave up that slave. After all, he had lost him anyway.

Bilal Is the Answer

So, actually Bilal is the answer. Prophet Muhammed knew this. He is the answer to the Scripture that portrays the poor and ignorant people as a donkey, and that one day the donkey will speak with a man's voice. So, the call to Islam doesn't accept that the people be ruled through their spirit, or by psychology, but that they be free to be educated, that education is the answer. The Prophet was asked to tell them, "What will be some signs?" One of the signs that the Prophet mentioned is that a handmaid of the mistress, the head of the house, the woman who is over the house, will give birth to her child. That refers to Sarah who thought she was too old to give birth, so she asked Abraham to take Hagar, so he could have continuation of his family line.

Now the Prophet, with this saying of his, is saying the same thing is going to happen at the end of the world. At the time, Sarah was the respected and accepted woman over the people. Her husband was the man, she was the woman, and she was worried about her house. It means her people. "Now, I am already old, my husband needs to have children, and I'm beyond childbearing". So, she told him to take Hagar for his wife. He did it and from Hagar came Isma'il, and Abraham and Isma'il built the house for all mankind (the Ka'bah). So, from the rejected and the subjugated girl came hope for mankind through Hagar. In the end of time, he says that a sign of it will be that the servant girl will give birth for her mistress. The same thing will happen again, that the new world leadership will come out of a people that was subjected and rejected.

Bilal Near the Prophet All the Time

The Prophet knew that G_d gave him exactly how the world was going to end, and he knew that the same ones who were mistreating Bilal in his face would do worse in the future; and in time, G_d was going to come to the aid of Bilal as he had already come to the aid of Bilal and made him his companion nearby him all the time. Abu Bakr, none of them were nearby Prophet Muhammed all the time. Who was by him all the time? Bilal. And who did he use to call the morning prayer after people had been in the darkness all night? Bilal. He was his custodian. He performed many personal things for the Prophet. He trusted personal interest more to him (Bilal) than anybody else. When he was on his death bed who was there? Was it Abu Bakr that he told to go get me some cold water from the deepest pool you can find? No, it was Bilal. All this is pointing to the future. And the other thing that he said was, the slave girl would give birth to a child for the mistress. That means for the one who is the boss for the established order of society, it would be the one rejected and subjected that will be the one who would save the future for all of them. Giving birth to her child means saving the future for her and all of them. This child is a new mind, not the old mind of the world. It is not going to come from those who have been responsible and holding the reins. It is going to come from the one who was thought unfit for that. That is the end of time right now. That is what is happening right now. Look at Obama.

We All Are Bilal

When they spoke down to Bilal in the presence of the Prophet, thinking he is a black and inferior, the Prophet said, "We all our Bilal!" That nature that you are criticizing in him, yes, he is spiritual. He is not as rational as we are. He's not devoted to the rational like we are. He loves the spiritual, but we all are Bilal. That is a property of human creation or of human nature, and it is not just in blacks. It is in all of us. And the proof of it is you can go to some white, religious orders or establishments, especially of poor people, and they have so much pain on them there's not too much they can express from the rational mind. Their soul is what is bothered. The world burdens and tortures their soul. So, the message comes to them of joy from G_d, that He is a G_d of justice. He loves me, and He wants me to have His Mercy and His Communication, His Revelation. He wants me to have a good life and has promised me paradise, and down here, I cannot even move into certain areas and not be stoned or killed. I am not just talking about the early times. Right now, maybe it will happen.

A person like that, they are more expressive outwardly, because their soul is so burdened, and when relief comes to them for their soul, they are so happy that there is at least G_d, Who is not seeing me like this ugly world is seeing me. So, that brings them great joy. The Prophet knew all of that and he said, "We all are Bilal."

Competing With Rich People In the Building of Skyscrapers

The other thing he said was a sign of the end of time will be that the poor people will be competing with the rich people in the building of skyscrapers, tall buildings, and it is to be understood literally, and by reference or interpretation. So, us competing with the builders or the rich, in the construction of sky towers or skyscrapers is to be taken literally, to actually mean those people who were poor and thought to be fixed in that condition or in the cycle of poverty, they will be seen coming out of that, investing in society and in great constructions. So, the man, Adam, is our father. He is a concept for our reference, "Did I have any worth in the past?" G_d says He made your father, who is the father of all mankind, to be a khalifah, that is, to be a person who accepts responsibility to take care of the environment even though it be as big as the whole world. And He told that man, our father, that He created everything for it to yield its benefits to mankind.

So, in that understanding, that light comes into the good man who has been denied and made to believe that is not for you. That kind of responsibility is not for you, forget it. The fujur is going to bring about a kind of fajr (dawn) inside his soul, and he is going to be inspired or motivated to accept responsibility for the whole environment, the world, for all the people. And the world is crying now to any man: "Will you come forward and address this serious condition we have in this world?"

Ham Was Egypt

Noah had three sons. Ham was Egypt, and Ham was the one that showed ignorance. He wasn't uneducated, but his character was that of nafsal la amara, the compulsive self, or impulsive self. So, the impulsive self couldn't handle human conditions intelligently, laughing at the condition of the person rather than responding to the need in that person. The other two brothers responded to the need in the person. That was their father, Noah. But Ham did not. The Bible says he laughed, and the curse fell on the children of Ham. That only means that if that disposition, silly disposition, gets into people, it's going to be passed on to their children. Isn't that what happened? The way the poor, ignorant people behave when they have children, their children come up behaving just like them, until one rebels, and sees a way out of it, or sees that it's wrong. His character is too strong to take it, and he leaves it. He departs from his parents or his society, and it happened. But in most cases, it's passed on down from parent to children like that.

Canaan Is the Dogs

That is why they say that African Americans, blacks, are the children of Ham. What they were saying is the curse is on African Americans, blacks, that came upon Ham. It wasn't going to hit them right away or directly, but that disposition in them would carry on and get worse and worse. In those who come after them, it will get worse and worse, meaning it will grow. If you accept that kind of disposition in yourself, it's going to grow. You are going to pass it on to your children, and in your children it's going to become worse, and that will be a curse on the children of Ham. But look at who they call the children of Ham, not Egyptians. They call the children of Ham, the Canaanites, and the Church used to sing about Canaan Land, didn't it? And you know who Canaan is? Canaan is translated, "A dog, the dogs, canine".

A Scheme to Pass Behavior Down to the Lower Class People

Yes, Canaan Land, the children of Canaan. So, the Egyptians were highly educated, and they were the most advanced of all the nations in the time that the Bible is addressing. But the tendency to find fun in things is in all people. So, they pointed this out and said that Ham has this tendency. And you know Africans are jolly people, you know, most of them, and it's going to pass on down to a people lesser in progress, or in development as a people. It's going to pass on down to them. Now, you know what that tells me? It tells me that they were going to see that it's passed on down to them. It's a scheme to pass this behavior down to the lower-class people, who actually have a territory that they call Canaan Land.

Marked Early for Enslavement

In Arabic, it's called, Kana'aan, but it's Canaan, the same Canaan, and it would be passed down to them and would mark them. You see how early they marked black folks, African, black folks for enslavement? So, they said, "It won't hit you, directly. It's going to hit these. They're more vulnerable, so it's going to hit them. They are not scientific-minded or science-minded, like you are. It's going to hit them, and they're going to become the hewers of wood and totters of water for their two brothers". Ham is semitic and of the other two, Shem, is semitic, and other one is the white man, Jephat. They give the highest place to the white man, Jephat. The white man didn't do that. The Jew is lifting the white man, so he can knock him down, later. This is Jafar, in Arabic. It's, Jephat, in the Bible, but it's three of them. One is Ham, that's Africa, representing the semitic African, like Ethiopia, that is still identified as semitic. Shem is semitic, and then the other one that is given most credit to, I think he's Jafar, and he's white. He's the white man. He's of the white race. So, those are the three races that they saw back them, one black, one brown, and one white. And the white one, the Prophet called red. He didn't call him white. So, the Prophet called you by the way you were affected by the sun. If the sun makes you black, you're black. If the sun makes you red, you're red. And if the sun doesn't change you, you're white. And the white person, the sun doesn't change them, it just messes the skin up, might destroy the skin, but they are still white. So, he called them red, the red man. And the Arabs, lately, just here recently in our history in maybe the last thirty or forty years, they don't translate the red as red man. They translate it as white. But when the Prophet said, "There is no superiority of a black over a white", he didn't say, white. The word wasn't white. In Arabic, the white is red. The Prophet said, "There is no superiority of a black over a red, nor a red over a black. The only superiority is in obedience to G_d".

Racists Are Peckerwoods

Instead of being sincere about giving the people the right information they would have worked it out and they would have explained it the way I just explained it, that he identified people according to how the sun affected them, their color, their pigmentation. What do we call the white people down South? Rednecks, we called them rednecks. Another name reached us in the North, too, from the South, peckerwoods. He (the woodpecker) puts holes in the trees. He damages the tree to have a house. Yes, one bird makes a nest, and the other one makes a hole in the tree. That's something to think about. Peckerwoods, I never thought about it before. They fear more than other birds. That's for protection. They put holes in the tree for protection. So, it's difficult. He's more moved by protection than by comfort for his babies. The one that builds a nest is motivated by a desire to have the baby in a comfortable place. The one that makes a hole in the wood wants to make sure that the cat or the rat, or another, bigger bird won't get in there and bother them. So, he's moved by fear, motivated by fear, and the other one is motivated by love. So, I agree, they're peckerwoods, racist peckerwoods.

Not Black Enough

Our people were smart, very smart, and intelligent. There were intelligent ones, always, among them and they would pass knowledge on to the rest of them. And now we have those that want to pass their emotions on to the rest of us, not knowledge. They want us to be of their emotionality, and they hate you if you are not. That's the black leadership right now. It dislikes those who are not inclined to support their life by emotional excitement, emotional pleasures. If you are not inclined to do that, they don't want to identify with you. So, when the leaders from among our people, mainly men, say, "Obama is not black enough", they don't mean not black in pigmentation. They mean that he is not spiritual enough. He is not of our spirit, which is a pity. It's a pity that so many of them are messed up and straying and can't get the life of their following together, can't lift their following up, because they play on the buttons of emotions and think that's the way that Christianity should be supported.

"The Time Is Out!"

They don't want to come out of the water. They have to stay where they are, and they think that's protecting the black church. But that day is over, time is out. As the Honorable Elijah Mohammed used to say, "The time is out!" Obama is too strong. The position that the people who are supporting him are in is just too strong an influence for a man that we identify with without us being affected or influenced by him. His power, his recognition, is going to be stronger than the spirit of the Church, or the spirit of the black Church. It's going to be stronger than that. Most of the men have left the black Church anyway. Most of what they have is women, not even very many children. So, it's not going to last. They are going to have to change, be converted to a different perception of what is the life of Christ Jesus in the Church, or they're going to be like the dust, carried away with the wind. They aren't going to be able to stay established, that's what I mean. They won't be able to stay established. Most of them are going to go the way of the people who are out of step with the times. And the time here, the time I'm talking about is a time that brings about a change from disestablishment to establishment, because the old way has brought about disestablishment.

Now a new way that's on time for G_d's Plan for mankind, all people, it's going to be too strong of an influence coming from Obama to people who identify with him, racially. It's going to be too strong as an influence for the Church to survive. The Church is not going to be able to survive. The intelligent ones who have tried to reach the intelligence and have tried to prepare people to survive in an intelligent world, they'll stay. They won't be affected. They'll be affected only in a good way, positive way. They'll be strengthened, really, by Obama's rise. But those who play on the emotions of their following to keep them and to get them to do things that they want them to do, they are losing and they're going to lose big now. They are going to lose very big. That's my belief. And they can't stop it. They can't escape it.

A People Being Born On the Continent of North America

We are a people who are being born on the continent of North America, the United States. We lost our life as a people. Even if we became good Christians, we still lost our life as a people, because our lifeline goes back to Africa, and slavery severed or cut off that lifeline, slavery on the plantations of the South in the United States. It identified and labeled us as not fully human and treated us like that for all of those years of slavery and after, until we won help enough from the good people of the United States of America to have laws change and attitudes change in the government. We were a people cut off and rejected. They did not accept us into their social societies, and they did not accept us to socialize with them in the public of the United States. If they saw you doing that, they would want to hang around and catch you by yourself and kill you. This is the reality. This is a real history and look how times have changed. Look how Allah has rewarded us and given us back our life and given us back our respect in the society that labeled us, identified us as not human. I don't know if you registered the gravity of that, the importance of that like you should. I don't think most of you do. Because if you did, you would not be the same old Negroes in your kitchens and in your bathrooms, and out on the streets. You would be a new people. You are supposed to be a new people. That is supposed to inspire you and make you change your way of thinking. It is supposed to give you a new heart.

A New Life In the Spirit of African Americans

You are supposed to be like Barak Obama. That is how you are supposed to be. You are supposed to be the character, the dignified man and woman that we see in the human, Barak Obama. Didn't he get the right name? Barak means blessed. He's truly a blessed man and now he has blessed the spirit of African Americans. He blessed our spirit. We will never be the same again. Those who are wasting their lives and just being foolish in the streets having nothing to inspire them or to get their respect enough to lift them up from indecent behavior and self-destruction, Obama, one man, his acceptance by the big white people in these United States is affecting the spirit of black America in a way that is going to sober it up and make it more moral, more decent. That is going to happen. They can't resist it. That is Allah's way. Allah says, *"Your death and resurrection is as the death and resurrection of one soul."* All you need is one person with enough influence, and if you have them in your environment and you do not have direction for your life, that one person will bring the majority of the people down. Just one image, one example, can bring the whole people down, and Allah says, by the same logic, one standing up in the right character, having the right life can lift the whole people up, and that is what we have in Obama. To me, he is much more than a candidate for the president of the United States. He is new life in the spirit of black America. Praise

Very Powerful Antennas

I have been very close to President Bill Clinton. I was on a twenty-one-person committee representing an effort for us to connect with and promote peace, connect with the people of the world who want peace, and promote peace in the world. We were serving the State Department, but directly under President Bill Clinton. So, I had a chance to be with the Secretary of State and to hear from the President and meet the President on more than one occasion. I know he is a great man, and he did a great job as President of the United States… I tell you I have strong, very powerful antennas. You do not know it, but I'm telling you Allah has blessed me with sensitivities and sensibilities that can find things far, far, away, and out of sight. It is just my nature. It is natural for me, and I do not pry. That is the one who gets the blessing. The one who is not prying into people's private lives and their private affairs and wants to see what people are not showing. I do not have that nature, and Allah has blessed me with powerful antennas. Those who know me and are around me all the time, they will tell you I have been favoring Obama before Obama was campaigning. I suspected that powerful white folks in the United States were looking at him for the future, and they were.

I have been with him for a long, long time, and who would not be with a decent man like that, except people under fear? Some of our people are afraid to vote for a man whom they think may get into that high office. They think they will be voting for him to get him killed. They really believe, "They are not going to let him be president. They will kill him!" But that office is too important, and freedom is too important for us to fear death and hold our support back from an African American man because we do not want to get him killed. No, Allah has power over life and death. Nobody can kill anybody unless Allah permits it.

We Don't Believe the White Man Will Accept Us

So, you are not supposed to hold back because of fear saying, "We do not want that!" That is why so many of us have not progressed as we should, because we do not believe that the white man will accept us if we progress. We believe he is going to block us, stop us. That is the trick that the devilish ones among them work on us saying, "Do you want to be popular? Do you want to get somewhere? Your talent that G_d has given you is entertaining people. Sing, dance, that is what you should do. Stay out of these serious matters. That is not for you." That is how they worked on us for generations to get us to accept that kind of mindset. And most of us have not accepted it, but many of us have. The white man used to say, "Stay in your place!"

Leave It With the Generations

Look, he is not saying it anymore, but we are saying it, that "Imam Warithu Deen had better stay in his place! The white man is not going to let him do what he is trying to do! He should know that!" But one thing you have here is no quitter! I'll keep working until I die, and it looks like the Lord is giving me an extension of years. I feel so good! I feel like I'm forty or younger! And I know I am not, but in spirit that is the way I feel. I am blessed with the life that I need for my role in your life, and I'm blessed with hope for many more years. I'm telling you I'm so blessed with knowledge and understanding that really, I can't see me being cut off by death, sickness, or something. No, Allah blessed me with this and did not bless me with it to die with it. He blessed me with it to give it out, to leave it with the generations that come behind us. That is why He blessed to me. I know that. G_d is Intelligent. He is the Most Intelligent. None can ever have His Wisdom and His Intelligence. No, He is too much above us. We can never get His Wisdom and His Intelligence, only in small measures... and I respect that G_d will not do something foolish. He doesn't do foolish things. He only does things that make good sense and reflect supreme knowledge and intelligence. I know that.

The New Resurrection

I'm going to share this with you, too, because I know what is going on. G_d has blessed me to know what is going on. Some are thinking, "Why is the Imam celebrating, observing Savior's Day?" I have been celebrating it since it started. You just could not see what was happening. I have been celebrating it since day one in 1975 when I became your leader. I had been working for it two or three years or more before I got the opportunity to speak to you. I mean working day and night. If Shirley was here, she would tell you she would go to bed and tell me, "Wallace, you should go to bed. It is late!" She would get up in the morning and I'm still there at the table working with my books, papers, all over the table. She would say, "You're still here? You did not get any sleep!" I was working and Allah blessed me to find and understand the light that I needed for this job. You did not know it, but I was working back then. You may ask, "Why did you go against your father's teachings?" That is working. That was a work that I had to do. "Why did you dismantle the FOI (Fruit of Islam, the training program for men in the Nation of Islam) and the MGT (Muslim Girl Training, a training program for women in the Nation of Islam) and change the teachings of the Nation of Islam?" I did it because that is what I was to do. Scripture says, *"Destroy this temple and I'll build it up in three days."* That is the temple of the old language. It was not brought here to stay. It was put here to perish and be done away with one day. But in it was guidance for the searcher. In it was guidance to the new life and the new day, to the resurrection. Inside the dead body was guidance and light for the new day, the new resurrection.

Mr. Fard Left Hints and Signals In His Teachings

Mr. Fard left those hints and signals in his teaching to help the one he named before I was out of my mother's body. I was still in my mother's body, and he named me and told my mother, "You be sure and give him my name." The name I have, Mr. Fard said that was his name, and we have cards where he wrote nothing but, "Wallace" and some of them sent it to my father and my uncle. Some do not want to hear these things. They are so bent upon keeping their same locked up brains, minds, that they do not want to hear things that they believe might open up their mind to accept what I say. That is their fault. That is not my fault. I will just step over that grave and go to the next one and see if there's anybody in the next one who wants to wake up.

So, he gave me his name. Even before I was born, he wrote it with chalk on the wall where the door would open wide, and if you push the door all the way to the wall, you could not see my name. I did not know this. My sister, my mother, and others, those who knew this, had to tell me this. I got this from them. I was a baby. I was not even born, in fact, when he first wrote the name. When you closed the door then you would see my name. Once you were inside and closed the door then you would see my name on the wall. "Wallace D", that is what he put on the wall. I can wear you out. I have more than the patience of Job. He told my father, "Promise me that when the child is born that you will raise him to help us in this work". Now, they would tell me this, that my purpose in life is to help the Honorable Elijah Mohammed and his teacher. Telling me I'm going to help them conditioned me to have no fear to question them.

He gave me his name, and he said that I am going to help them. You need help? I have the right to question you. Is that right or wrong? Does that make sense? It should make sense to you. Telling me that and leaving that with me for my young years and my growing up, it was to condition me to feel equal with them, although I humbled myself. I never tried to stand up to be an equal to either one of them. But fear was not in me. A lack of confidence would never touch me, and Mr. Fard did that. He conditioned me to have that kind of faith, not to fear to pry into any darkness, that is, darkness in the knowledge or darkness in the language of the teachers, not to fear to pry into it. So, he conditioned me to succeed and my father, also. My mother, she would just encourage me.

So, how could I be different? How could I have done something different? Should I have been like all the other ministers? How can I be like them when they were not told that their purpose in life is to help the Honorable Elijah Mohammed and his teacher? His teacher we were taught was G_d in the flesh. And he did not say, "Just help, just be a servant. Help us do this work." So, that is a big job. I saw my father with it, and he was having a time trying to do that job. And I'm supposed to be their helper? For most of my life it escaped me. G_d knows it. My own soul rejected it. I enjoyed my life as a child. I enjoyed my life as a teenager. I enjoyed my life as a young man and only when I saw corruption setting in the Nation of Islam's leadership, only at that time did it wake up in me that, "You're calling us to help." And I began to do that. So, thank Allah.

The Excellent Model for Human Beings to Follow

One of the things that Mr. Fard promised us was that if we qualified, we would get a trip to the holy city, Mecca, to see Brother Muhammed, and this is to see the uswa hasana of Muhammed, the Prophet. His uswa hasana, his excellent human model, is supposed to be in all of us. But in most of us it's sleeping. It has not been awakened. But what was in Prophet Muhammed as human essence upon which evolves that uswa hasana, that excellent model for human beings to follow, is in all of us.

Jesus Christ is a model of it, too and he said, *"I and you and you in me"*. And he said, *"I in the father"*, but you don't know anything about that, so, why should I even mention it? So, when you hear, *"I in the father"*, you think he means, "I in G_d". No, *"I in my father"*. Who was his father? Adam. "I, in my father, who was created by G_d, not by man". And then later he said, *"I in you and you in me"*. He called the people who followed him or identified with him members in his own body, and his body was described or identified as the temple, the same language Mr. Fard used for our places of worship. So, his body is a single figure, a single concept, but his body is also a plural body, because it represents many as well as one. The Bible says, "G_d made Adam and completed him as a creation, and He named them Adam". After using it in the singular, the Bible's same language uses it in the plural. *"He named them Adam and in the day that He created them."*

Prophet Muhammed Saw Black People In the Future

Regarding the black people of Africa, I think Prophet Muhammed saw that the last days would be the days when the world would have to accept that they have oppressed human souls with no justice. There was no justification for it, and the prejudice was there at that time over fourteen centuries ago. The attitude of the white one was to think he was better than the black one. Racism is very old. I think it started in Asia with the Dravidic Scriptures of the Asian people, and in their

Scriptures they describe people as children of the light and children of the dark. What they meant was they were innocent. They were talking about the spirit of darkness and spiritual light, or the Plan of G_d that He blessed some to see, that is the light. They are in the light. Then the Plan of G_d that most of the people are ignorant of, they are in the dark. So, that is what the Dravidic Scriptures were all about, and Genesis is the same. *"In the beginning there was darkness and G_d brought about light out of darkness".* That's what they are talking about. But a person that wants to make money thinks, "These dumb suckers here, black fools, they are the children of darkness. G_d meant for them to be put aside or used."

Zionists Want Dominance In the World

So, they get that attitude, and they are already weak. They are deceived. Money makes you deceived. So, they are already situated to be deceivers, and it just made it easier for them, and they brought in racism. And I think nobody used it better than the ungodly Jews that used it to divide the world. They divided the world to make the world racist. I am talking about the Zionist Jews who want power, and maybe Zionist is not the best word. The Jews who want dominance, want to be the ruler of the world. They think G_d favored them to be the rulers of the world. Those Jews are the ones who gave everybody racism, fun for fun sake, indecency, sexual corruption, and stuff to destroy them.

Not to Think of Ourselves As Black In Skin Color

I knew that we were not to think of ourselves as black in skin color to know ourselves in history, and especially scriptural history. We think of ourselves as victims of the world, who were taken from their land, uprooted from their cultural life, and had no tradition that they could identify with, and no special religious leaders to save us and identify for us what is really our blackness. You know, when I mentioned that the Holy Spirit, in the Bible, came to Mary (it is not in the Qur'an) where it said it overshadowed Mary, and I asked what color the shadow was, they were slow to respond. I pressed them a little bit. They said black. Black is for spiritual life. That is why the high ups in religion wear black, to say, "My life is spiritual". That is in Christianity and Al-Islam, not just one religion. And in a lot of other religions, they wear black as special. Buddha, himself, he was on his journey for enlightenment when he found it. He gave it to his disciples. When he was on his journey for enlightenment, he ran into darkness, and he said, "This is not ordinary darkness. This darkness is my mother." The insight into nature, its hidden laws and whatever, when he saw that, he said he saw his mother. Now when he saw enlightenment, the light, he said, "Now, I know how to pave the way". So, the science is darkness. It is always hidden. Can you put molecular theory in the light for us? You always have to have faith in it. But that same light that G_d blessed the saintly person to find, if he remains patient, it is the light also of this world. It is not true that one light is for one world, and another light is for another world. It is also a light for this world, and that is why we wear a black tuxedo, formal clothes for special occasions. So, the secular world has their high dress and value as black, and the priest society's color is black; and even Satan, it says he wears black, but when you pull his cape up, he is all red under there.

Mr. Fard Loved Jesus Christ

My father said Mr. Fard told him that Jesus was not even a major Prophet, that he was a religious enthusiast. He said that is what Mr. Fard told him, and I believe it. I believe that Mr. Fard told him that. But knowing Mr. Fard as I know him, if he told him that, he told him that to try to free him from Jesus Christ. He knew that he had won their hearts, and if he put Jesus down, they would also put him down. He saw Jesus in their hearts as a problem for Islam, because the Church had Jesus as G_d, the son of G_d, and G_d. So, I believe that Mr. Fard really told him that. But I know Mr. Fard loved Jesus Christ and knew him just as what the Qur'an says he was, a Messenger, a Prophet, a Spirit and a Word from G_d. I know he believed that. But he was a man inspired by Sufism, to use strategies and signs rather than straight talk, to bring a people from a situation that seems almost impossible, and put them on the Path of G_d. I don't believe he was a Sufi, himself, but I know he read up on the Sufis. He knew their philosophies and strategies, and I do believe that he applied them. And not only do I know that, I know, also, that the Honorable Elijah Mohammed said that Mr. Fard told him, "If you're looking for me, I'm in Zechariah", the book in the Bible called Zechariah. "I'm in Zechariah". He said that more than once. The last time I heard it was after I had been accepted back, and it was at his (the Honorable Elijah Mohammed) dinner table. He said Mr. Fard said, "I'm in Zechariah".

Hints That Are Not Spoken

So, later, I had a hunch, something pushing me like a hunch. I said, "He said Zechariah, then I'd better read that. Something must be there". So, I read it, and I had read it before, but never with looking for something that would help me understand Mr. Fard better... So, I read it, and you know the same thing in the Qur'an is in the Bible, that he was not to use his own thinking in taking care of Mary. And a sign of how he was going to take care of Mary, and be successful in taking care of Mary, was that he should fast, and while fasting he should not speak to anybody, *"Il-la ramzah"*. That's the Qur'an, and it means, *"Except by signs"*. But there are different signs, you know. Ramzah is a sign. So, it means hints that are not spoken. He gives hints without speaking, or the speaking, itself is speaking to something else, and you have to be turned on to the kind of thinking that is desired in this situation to know that he's speaking of her, but that is not the reality. That's signaling us to another reality. When you take that language as signals, or signs, it signals you to go to another reality, not the reality you're looking at here.

Mary: The Innocent Congregation of Jesus Christ

Mary, peace be on her, she is representing as a figure, the innocence in the Church, or the innocence in the congregation of Jesus Christ. Now mind you, she gives birth to him, so she was before him. That's a pure order of religious people that had nothing but good intentions, and they were very righteous people, devoted to serving G_d and finding what He wanted for them on this planet earth. They wanted to know, "Where do You want us to go, G_d?"

So, Mary represents that, and in Catholicism isn't Mary the Church? She's the Church. She's the Church of Jesus Christ, although Mary is the mother of Jesus Christ, but she is also the Church. And when Jesus is on the cross, leaving her, passing away, he says, *"Behold your mother!"* She was in the crowd. He was saying, "Don't look at me anymore, I'm gone. Behold your mother." And when Jesus left what did he leave with them except the congregation, the Church? And they call it Mary. The Church is Mary. The Church is Jesus Christ, yes, but also, the Church is Mary, and these Catholics with us, the Focolare, they really know, identify Mary as the Church, the Church as Mary.

The Essenes

So, really, it's the congregation, the congregation of the righteous, devoted believers… When you have people, righteous people devoted to G_d, you can't take them away from that devotion. So, the people remained in that devotion. Before Christianity, they were in this devotion, and they are distinguished from the Jews, because they were of this mindset. Most of the Jews were trying to figure out how to get the world, but these people were not of that kind of spirit. They were pious worshippers of G_d. So, Jews have always had among them that kind of people, people who were spiritual more than material, and they were devoted to serving G_d's Will on this earth and trying to find out, "What does He want for mankind on this earth?" That was their search.

So, Mary, the mother of Jesus Christ, is that people. There's evidence in research, by archeologists and others, who were trying to find more reality to support the beginning of Jesus Christ and his following, and they came up with the name, Essenes. And they believe that the people who originally formed to support the leadership of Jesus Christ were Essenes, were people called Essenes. Now, I don't know if they were called Essenes or not, but I like the language, because essence says, "inherent quality, inherent life". That's what essence says, before it is decorated, before it becomes what we see in the world. So, if that's what he was from, then he was from original creation, and both the Qur'an and the Bible trace the beginning of Jesus back to original creation.

A Spirit and Word of G_d In the World

The Bible says that he was of Joseph and this parent and that parent, going on back to Adam, and it says, *"Adam, who was created by G_d"*, and the Christian Church says that Jesus Christ is the second Adam. So, his origin is traced back to Adam, who was not created by the world or by man, but was created by G_d. So, this is the Jesus. This is the Mary and the Jesus, then Mary is the pure following, unadulterated. I don't have to say more. I think you know the rest.

Okay, the pure following, unadulterated, have not been touched by men of this world, and they were praying for G_d to show them the way, and their prayers blessed them with Jesus Christ. G_d answered their prayers with the blessing of Jesus Christ, a man who was not moved or motivated by the world, but only by his pure excellence and he became a Spirit and Word of G_d in the world. Yes, that's Jesus Christ. I could get on T.V. and preach this and I would have a big following. If you all could support me and get me a channel… I guarantee I could get a big, big following, but I can't do that! G_d has another work assignment for me. But I guarantee you, it would be a big following. People from on high would come and join us.

Matter Births the Mind

You know, Jesus Christ saw himself in Adam, and I see myself in Adam, not in Jesus Christ. I see myself in Adam, and I see myself in Muhammed, because Allah created Muhammed. This isn't the Muhammed that was born of flesh and blood from his mother, Amina. This is the Muhammed that Allah created. Allah created Muhammed and He can create whatever He wills. Whenever He wants a son, He just has to go to the men or the women He created for a son. So, I believe that is what is described as him (Jesus Christ) speaking in the cradle. Not that I am Jesus

Christ, but what describes him is this that I have experienced, and the wise before me experienced it, and they called it, "Speaking." He spoke while he was yet in the cradle. And Mary, whenever she was asked a question, she could not answer, and she pointed to the child in the cradle. That is the virgin mother nature. It is part of my existence, but it cannot speak for me. I have to speak with my own human intelligence and voice. It is wonderful!

It takes the mystery out of it and that is what G_d wants to do. G_d never wanted to burden us. The intelligence, He made it to see, and if we keep it in the dark, that is not G_d's Will. The first time, He puts it in the dark, Himself. He brings the mind under the matter, and matter births the mind, and then mind rules the matter, later. What we should remember is to not ever see ourselves as big and important in life. We are nothing in the light of G_d. What we should remember is that none of this could happen without G_d preparing us for it or creating us for it. So, whenever we realize that, we have the power or capacity for something supernatural, or above normal. That is what I mean by supernatural, above the norm. We should always be very submissive, and as soon as we, ourselves, come in the picture, we should say, "I am nothing but a speck of dust. My Lord has brought me up". And He will continue to, as the Bible says, *"Dwell with you."*

A Second Chance for Adam to Be Redeemed

It is clear to those Allah blesses to seek an understanding that the figure of Adam was lost to the suggestions of the serpent, or the Satan, the Devil. Satan took the first man out of his original life or picture, and Jesus Christ comes back, in the Bible. I'm not giving you anything from myself. Everything I say comes from the Scripture, one or the other, some Scripture, most likely from the Qur'an, or the Bible. So, Jesus comes back, according to the Bible, as the second Adam. It is a second chance for Adam to redeem himself, to be redeemed. So, the innocence and the holding to the purity that G_d wanted for human essence and human life is seen in the figure we call, Christ Jesus. So, in his figure his father is redeemed. The first Adam is redeemed by the second Adam, who is called the Word and Spirit from G_d. And Allah says in the Qur'an, *"Adam met a Word from his Lord, and he repented"*. And Allah accepted his repentance. Is that clear enough for you? Do you want me to put the bulb on your eyes? You can't see if I put it on your eyes. It will blind you. Praise be to Allah! We don't guess, we know. Allah has blessed us to know. There is no guessing here, no guessing, no doubt. Scripture says, *"And he will gather you for a day in which there will be no doubt."* That day is here now.

THE TREASURE UNDER THE WALL: Thursdays with the Imam

The Body Snatchers

Many of you follow these sheiks because they are just not black, African Americans. That is the only reason I know. They sure do not seem to be saying anything that is all that exciting to me. I don't find anything new, nothing exciting in what they are saying, but you follow them. So, to me, it must be because they are just not African American, not blacks from Africa. They can be from Africa as long as they don't speak like us. You just have to know that he is not an American born Negro, or a black. You are so impressed with them. I don't know how to help you, really, because there is no one in your body except somebody else, so how can I help you? There is nobody in that body except somebody else. How am I going to help them? I'm glad the body snatchers never got me. Allah didn't raise me up in the house of my mother and father for some body snatcher to get me. No indeed!

All of Us Could Be Muhammed

"You will get a free trip to the holy city, Mecca, to see Brother Muhammed!" Those are the words of Mr. W. D. Fard, or Mr. W. F. Muhammad. He is known by a few other names. So, he promised us a trip to the holy city, Mecca. And he did not say Brother Muhammed is himself, or is his G_d. What does the name, Muhammed, mean? One worthy of praise. And what in the human being's makeup is worthy of praise? His sincerity, his honesty, his decency, and his service in the society of men under Allah. Any and all of us could be Muhammed, couldn't we, Muhammed in that particular human type that Allah patterned all of us on when He created us? But we cannot find that pattern. We can't express our life from that pattern. Some of us won't even accept that pattern, though it is presented to us as clear as the daylight. But it is in all of us. You are actually promised by Mr. Fard that you will get a trip to Mecca, and if you go as a sincere soul, Allah will awaken the essence, the sunnah, the uswa of Muhammed in you. We are obligated to follow Muhammed. Allah says whatever He gives you take it. Whatever He forbids you leave it. Do not take it. Allah says, *"Obey Allah and obey His Messenger"*.

The Leader Is Given Authority From the People

So, it is very clear what we should be doing. But look, there are other keys for us in the Qur'an. Allah says, *"Obey His Messenger and those charged with authority"*. You can charge a bad person with authority, right? But as long as you charge him with authority you are supposed to obey him. But if you see him going astray, you are supposed to then take his authority from him. The same people who give authority to that person or that leader should take him down from that authority, deny that authority once he proves himself to be a wrongdoer, or one working against the purpose for which he was given that office.

Here is another key that Allah gives us: "Follow the Prophet and those first followers, those first leaders, companions, in the following of Muhammed, the Prophet". Follow them how? Allah does not say just follow them and that is it. No, He said follow them upon their excellence. If they don't have any excellence to convince you, you are not supposed to follow them at all, and you are not just supposed to follow a companion, the companions, Ali, Abu Bakr, or Umar. Allah did not make them gods, angels. They are human. So, He says, *"And follow them upon their excellence"*, because they have some defects, human faults. Don't follow them blindly, but follow them because of their excellence, or upon their excellence follow them. When we give a leader authority, we vote for him, we elect him or accept him as our leader and he starts showing more corruption than excellence, we are obligated to take that authority from him. And if he is too big and powerful for you to deal with him, Allah tells us how to do that through Muhammed, the Prophet. Resist wrong with your actions, and if you can't find the wherewithal to do that, you are afraid you'll lose your life and you want to stay around to see your children grow up, Allah respects that; then resist it with your mouth. Speak out against it. And if you still can't find the wherewithal, sometimes, your mouth will get you killed just as quickly as your hand. If you can't find the wherewithal, resist it in your heart. Don't be for it. Privately, secretly, be against it. Allah says that is the weakest form of faith. But still, He accepts that as your effort to promote what is right or to support and promote what is right. He will accept that.

Follow Them Upon Their Excellence

Follow them upon their excellence. Just don't follow men, blindly. You don't have to wonder about the Prophet's excellence. Allah did not say it of anybody else, not even of Abu Bakr, Umar, Ali, or any of them, only of Muhammed, peace be upon him. He said, *"We have seen him,"* meaning the heavens, G_d and His angels, *"that he is firmly established on a mighty plane of human character."* That is what Allah says about him. He, again, says of Muhammed, the Prophet, of his type, his model, *"Certainly, you have in Muhammed a most excellent model of human life for any who believe in G_d and the Last Day."* That means for any person who believes there is a G_d above Who you have to answer to. That is what it means by the Last Day. The Last Day means "that you have to answer to". You believe in the G_d that you have to answer to. It says "Anybody," it did not say Muslims. That means Christians and anybody who believes in G_d, being accountable to Him and the Last

Day, Christians, Muslims, Jews, or others. G_d says here is the excellent human model for you in Muhammed.

Prophet Muhammed Is Our Brother

I've been to the Hajj more than once and I remember the great thrill I got, the great energy that I got when I traveled in a big number of over three hundred of us. I thank Allah that He did reward me. I saw Brother Muhammed, and I still see him! And I have seen him plainer and plainer as the years passed. Is he our brother, or our father? Adam and Abraham are our fathers; peace be upon the two of them. But Allah says of Muhammed, *"He is not the father of any of your men."* Don't get spooked up after he is gone and make him something that he is not. He is your brother. He is our brother. Mr. Fard knew that, and he was so wise. He knew how to tell us these things and get it past the ears of the so-called righteous Muslim of the world, because he knew that most of those persons are crazier than hell! They have righteousness, but no intelligence, and that tells me that something is wrong with what they have been getting as teaching.

To Last for As Long as the Earth Supports Human Life

Mr. Fard was very sharp, very intelligent. Allah had to bless him with his strategy. He could not have gotten that without Allah's Help. He blessed him with his strategy, and he was able to tell us things, and he knew that if we remained faithful and true that in time our minds would become more open, our hearts would become pure, and we would be able to see into his plan for our future, get the best out of it; and be very successful now and for generations to come, until the earth is not bearing human life anymore. You may not value it, but what I give you is to last for as long as the earth supports human life. Allahu Akbar!

Look at another eye opener that he left with us. He said, "For the neatest and best worker who solves this problem his reward will be a Holy Qur'an Sharrief". Now, here is a man who really gave us a language from himself that looks like it is trying to destroy any hopes of us accepting the Qur'an, because it's saying in its basic teaching what is contrary to the basic, fundamental, teachings of the Qur'an: "G_d is a man, incarnate". The place for that is more in the Gospel, New Testament, than it is in a Muslim's life. There is no place in the Muslim's life for that kind of teaching, that G_d is in the flesh. He gave it to us, but he pointed to the Qur'an.

Sight Has to Begin Inside

Now isn't that something? The man was so wise in the strategies of the saints, and Jesus Christ is the best example of the saints. He came upon a blind man (this is in the New Testament), and what did he do to that blind man? The man is blind. He put mud on the blind man's eyes. He put mud on the blind man's eyes, and the man got his sight back. Sometimes, you have to have your vision blocked, so you can't see long enough to be weaned off of what was holding you that was in the way of your mind coming to the light. If he keeps you blind long enough, the sight will come back, and when it comes back, it is from the inside, not out there, because you don't know how to perceive these things out there. That is your problem. That is why you are blind. So, the sight has to begin inside, in your heart, in your soul, in your spirit. Your sight has to begin inside, and with the sight blocked from seeing outside, don't tell me you were seeing outside. When the Honorable Elijah Mohammed brought you in, you stopped seeing outside. All you could see was inside the Temple. You could not see outside of the Temple. Peace to you all!

Nothing That Happens Is Accidental

People want to know how we came into Al-Islam and what that experience has meant for us. Nothing that happens is accidental in my life. I'm convinced of that. Your name is Morocco (Khalid). In Islam, you are the West, Al Maghrib. Your name is Ronald. It means one who is royal, and your last name, Shaheed, means a witness. Now, you can't go along with everything I do, but you sure are a witness. And you are Al Ghani, which means we've got wealth. So, we've got wealth. We have the destiny, maghrib, and we've got a witness, and that is three, isn't it? We don't even know where we're going and what's happening in our own life, sometimes, but G_d knows.

No One Can Be Named Without G_d's Approval

Some people will call it superstition. Another strong belief I have, strong theory I have is that no one can be named without G_d's approval. No matter what language you're talking about, that is His creation. If somebody is named Black Bitch, that is their name. Now, I was named Wallace. I looked up my name thoroughly. It means, a stranger. Mr. Fard had the same name. He was a stranger among the people of this world, and he named me after him, Wallace. When he wrote on a postcard or something he never put Wali on it. It was always Wallace or W. D. Fard, never W. F. So, I looked up my name and it goes back to the small country of Wales, because that country is small. It is a derivative of Wales, the name itself, Wallace. Because it is small, they gave the meaning, stranger, because if you come out of Wales, it is so small nobody knows you. But I also know I have to look up Arabic, because Mr. Fard, he speaks double. I have to go to Arabic and see if there is any name that sounds like Wallace in Arabic, and I found it. It means one who deceives. Didn't he deceive us? But he deceived us as a friend, and that is what I did, too. I deceived those who voted me into power in 1975, but I deceived them as a friend. That is G_d. What I'm giving you is the sign of G_d's doings. He is Eternal and He knows everything past, present, future. He is aware of everything going on at this particular, split second, and He is as present as we are here, more present, because He has the power to be more present than we are. If you can believe like I believe, He will dwell with you forever.

The Lotus Boy

I'm going to surprise you. You haven't seen the best of W. D. yet. I'm writing a book right now, and I'm speaking through a figure like a fictional figure. I call him, The Lotus Boy, and I'm speaking through him to our folks. The Lotus Boy is talking to the black man. It's Volume II of *"As the Light Shineth from the East"*. A shepherd discovers this little boy, the Lotus Boy, and he lives with the shepherd until he is 12 years old and then goes off on his own and he preaches to our people. I said to myself, "This is the way to slip into their minds. They do not want to hear anything directly from us, but maybe the Lotus Boy can talk to them, and they will listen". It is going to be graphic. It came to my mind because there is an area that Lotus used to grow in, mostly the Northeast, but almost directly North, but favoring the East. I saw on a program that they had on TV about Chicago, that lotus actually used to grow in the water, but they dumped so much filth in there, they stopped growing. Then the water cleared up, because they stopped them from dumping in that area. So, the water cleared up and now lotus is growing in the area, again.

The Black Man Is the Lotus Supported by Water

I picked the lotus because it is supported by water. It is not rooted in the ground. That is the black man. His roots are in his feelings, sentiments, not in the rational. The earth is rational, but we have some beautiful people floating on the waters. The lotus produces a beautiful plant and a beautiful flower, and it is amazing how it can survive on the water like that and form a community. They grow as many. They grow together but they need to be called from the water to land, and that is what the Lotus Boy is going to say after he is rescued by a shepherd and brought into the shepherd's family, and he experiences living on the land. Now, he's going to go talk to black people. We already have the drawing. It looks beautiful. My wife, Khadijah, did the drawing for me. As soon as I can free myself up more, I hope to finish it.

Many Ways to Reach Human Hearts

Allah has opened up things to us, so we can become very, very, productive in many, many ways, especially culture, regular literature, but also fictional literature. We can become very productive. That's what others did, so why shouldn't we? They came into knowledge, and they made their contribution to the world and profited and are still profiting much from contributing their knowledge to the world. So, there are so many ways, now, you can reach human hearts, souls, and minds, to bring about positive change and reform without coming directly from Scripture to try to convert people. In this time, that is not the way. Try to find a way to treat the condition rather than teach the condition. We have the knowledge to treat the condition. Let us do it. They do not have any ears for teaching. They are all deaf and dumb. The world has them turned off. They are not interested in what you have to say. You going to teach them about Scripture? They do not want that. The only people who want that are those who are already devoted to Scripture.

What About That Blind Man?

Well, what about that blind man? Prophet Muhammed, big people had attracted him, but he knew they were not directly accepting right guidance. They were not having their life directed correctly, but he knew that they were not ignorant, and they were not blind. It didn't say the people he was going to were blind. They were informed, rich people. What is the difference between the people he was attracted to and the people that he did not have time for? Some could see and this one could not see. So, the blind man is not really blind. He just cannot see the way. He cannot see how to make it in the world. So, he was going to those big shots who knew how to make it in the world. "And you want them to become Muslim, to be rightly guided? Well, who are you going past to get to them? They are all in your way. They are everywhere. What about those you are walking past to get to these special people you want to convert because you think they will turn your mission into success right away?" So, (in the Qur'an) he was rebuked by G_d for making the wrong decision. His heart was right. He wanted to bring big results to Al-Islam quickly, but it was not just.

So, we have that blind man all around us. Blind people are all around us. So, let us be like Christ Jesus. Treat the condition. He did not teach the blind man. He took mud and put some spit into it and rubbed it on his eyes, and let it sit there a while, and the blind man said, "I can see!" So, insha Allah, G_d has blessed us to come to the right strategy. We have the strategy. We have the medicine. It is going to take us a little time, but I believe in a little while things are going to open more and more.

We Are All Together As Victims of Poverty and Ignorance

We are all together as victims of poverty and ignorance. All of us need to benefit. We're not looking at Christians and Muslims. I do not see that. I just see people who need to change their life for the better and stop being only consumers, non-producers as a people. We have very productive individuals, males, and females, but as a people we are still consumers and not producers. Back in the days before the time when the change came in, the '70s, before we went kind of wild, we were people who had a spirit to better the conditions of our people, and we lost that. But we can get it back and help those who are devoted to succeeding in life, not failing. If we help them, African American Christians, and African American Muslims, share with them our vision, share with them the opportunities that are opened up to us right now, this can change overnight. It can change very quickly where our people will be productive, and our leadership will be morally conscious and devoted to the betterment of the whole as well as succeeding privately or individually. That can happen overnight, and en sha Allah (if it's G_d's Will), that is what I want to see, and I believe I'm going to live to see it.

It is not going to be easy because our people are so selfish and so jealous. They will cut their own throats rather than staying alive by helping another black person get up. It is pitiful, but that is a certain percentage. You have a bigger percentage who will support you if they know you're going right. We will get them, en sha Allah. And those who are already with us we will help their situation when they see us doing things in a big way, unselfishly, to change these neighborhoods from being neighborhoods supported by everybody but us. The neighborhood supported by our businessman, when they see that, I think they are going to look for some ties with us.

Chapter 13

The Ka'bah

Prophet Muhammed actually began the Ascension (Miraj) from the Ka'bah in Mecca, the holy precincts. Right at the Ka'bah, that is where he ascended, straight from the Ka'bah. I understand that to mean that the Prophet was attracted to the Ka'bah because he understood the Ka'bah meant the heart of mankind, the heart of the human people, the human race. It was symbolic of the heart of the human people as though the human people were one body, and they had one heart feeding all of them. So, he saw the Ka'bah as a representation of that, and he understood that you had to ascend if you were going to progress or rise and graduate from one stage of human nature or life to another. You had to first be in the original, or the first state, and that is the excellence of human nature. That is the heart. By the way, the Bible says they looked for Jesus Christ here and there, but where is he going to be? In the heart of the earth, that is where he has to come back from. The same for Muhammed, he had to ascend from that. So, he ascends and goes up to the seventh level to Abraham and then he makes the migration. They call it the travel from the Ka'bah to Jerusalem, to the farthest mosque, and the farthest mosque is called Al Aqsa. The meaning is that he was in his pure human spirit and nature, and it says G_d took him up into the heavens, meaning up into the levels for the ascension of the human spirit.

The Last Stage for Achievement In Society Is Political Order

He took him up the levels of heaven and he passed by all these Prophets and got up to Abraham. What does Abraham represent? He represents the connection, the idea of oneness, the unification that connects the mind and soul with all humanity. That is why the Prophet Abraham is called a leader, a father, or leader for all nations and all people. He comes to that level. He begins travel and it is to Jerusalem, the farthest mosque. That mosque had not been established, but Jerusalem had been established. We can't say it was to King Solomon's temple, or something like that, but what it represents, the farthest mosque, is the progress for Muslims under Muhammed, the Prophet. There was no mosque there. It was the temple of Jerusalem at that time. He progressed to that point, because it represented the last stage in achievement for society.

The last stage for achievement in society is political order. He was taken from a human foundation to a political order, and once he got to the political order, he understood how to raise his people up from just human nature and spirit to political ascension. It didn't say he came down. It took him up and he traveled to that place. It did not say he came down there. So, he had political ascension. A political ascension is above spiritual ascension though it is not given that way, because when you go up, when you ascend upward, you can't go any farther than your natural life and spirit permits you to go, and you have to come down to build society. Going up just gives you insight, vision, and understanding, and when he went up to that level, obviously, he wasn't satisfied. That is why G_d caused him to travel, whereas others went up to those levels and they were satisfied. They stopped on those levels, and they never established the Kingdom of G_d.

Do It for Humanity

So, he had to travel to fulfill the need in his soul. So, when he traveled, he went to the kingdom of the Jews. G_d showed him, "This is what I want you to do, but do it for humanity". Then he had the political vision, and he came down, went to Madinah, and he did it. Praise be to Allah! You come down to establish the kingdom. Scripture says, *"Thy Kingdom come, Thy will be done on earth, as it is in heaven."* So, how is it in heaven? One family in unity and in peace. That is how it appears.

Abraham and his son built the house (the Ka'bah), and Allah says of the house that they built that it is the, *"Awwal bait, the most ancient of houses, the first of the houses".* It is called, *"Al baitu ateeq."* That means the most ancient house and it is called the first of the houses constructed for the worship of G_d. Now really, if we are talking about a physical occurrence, we know that is not the first of the houses built. But if we are talking about the true house with the construction that says this house is for the worship of the true and only G_d, the Ka'bah, built by Abraham and his son is the first one. Many houses were built, but they did not receive guidance. They didn't call on the true G_d. Abraham identified the true G_d, so when he was building that house, he was doing it with a knowledge of the true G_d, and the true G_d is the G_d of everything. The true G_d is the G_d of the universe and also the Lord of the universe, the Lord of all the worlds.

Create Means G_d Brought Matter Into Existence

So, he is the One Who evolved creation, itself. The word, evolved, is different from the word, created. Created means He brought it into existence. Evolved means that he progressed it from a beginning that was simple to its big, huge, complex form that we see now. And we are told that the heavenly space, or the universal, ethereal space, is said to have been smoke, not real smoke, but appearing as smoke, or as dust in confusion, not dust rested; dust in confusion, shaken all about, stirred up, or as smoke in confusion, the same thing as stirred up, going everywhere. And you have seen smoke like that. Some smoke rises straight up. Some goes out and looks like it is just all confused, and that is because of the way the fire is going on. So, it can give a violent motion and some of them translate it, "In violent motion, or commotion." It is a picture of the beginning of the creation in space. No star had formed, nothing orderly had happened. It was in disarrangement. It was in disorder and G_d brought it to order, and He evolved life on earth from nothing to something. So, this is what we mean when we say Allah is the Lord of the worlds. We are talking about that process.

When we say Allah is the Lord of mankind, we are talking about a process beginning with man as empty headed, nonscientific, uneducated, and Allah revealed to one of them who presented himself in form, in the natural body. This is not a revealed person, not a person who received revelation, like Muhammed before revelation. He took a person like that, and He communicated to that person and made him a leader for the beginning of civilization, to start civilization on this planet earth. Abraham built the house with a knowledge of the oneness of G_d.

Built for All people

You look at a little simple house. It is simple, but very deep. It is simple, but complex at the same time. It represents humanity. It represents the beginning of human society in its best construction. Allah says of the house that in it are many blessings. It is a blessed house. What you should understand is that the very house itself exudes or extends, imparts, messages to the true thinker, the one who is thinking for G_d's Way. It imparts messages. It is full of blessings, a house built for all people; not for one people, for all people; not for one nation, for all nations.

G_d made Abraham the leader for all the nations, and the Bible says He made him a father, and we call him father also. In the Bible, G_d actually says that *"I changed your name from Abram to Abraham, and you will be a father to the many"*. This means he is a leader to all the nations. It is in the Bible. It is the same message in the Bible and in the Qur'an of him being the leader for all the nations and all people. Now that is saying something, too, to us. He never said that of Adam, why? Because Adam had not ascended enough to have enough knowledge of G_d's creation. He is the beginning of the rise of the mind, intellect, and heart that G_d wants for the people or wants in the leader for the people. He is the beginning. He is the first. In fact, he was so new, and his thinking was so new and fresh and young that the Satan was able to deceive him out of his mind that G_d created him in. But he met a Word from his Lord, and he repented his wrong and G_d, Allah, accepted him.

The House a Metaphor of the Word of G_d

The expression, "Qawaaid bait", gives us knowledge, not just imagination, and when Abraham was building the house the term for how he was constructing it is, "Qawaaid". The word that is used is the word for grammatical construction. So, the house is a physical picture, but the real meaning is not physical. The house represents language that Allah communicated to Abraham. So, the house is a metaphor of the Word of G_d: *"In the beginning, there was the Word."* So, the house is a metaphor, a physical picture that you should not take as a physical house, but you should think on it, dhikr. You should meditate on it. You should reflect on it. You should think deep into it. Now what does it looks like? It looks like a little small cubicle, and if it is the first house, why is it so small? Because it is the first house. It is saying, "This is your beginning. You have a big house now. You have mansions, but your beginning was from a little, small, simple house, a small, simple structure, no furniture in it. How do I know? The rulers of Saudi Arabia took me and a few who were with me inside the Ka'bah and asked us if we wanted to pray in there. Do you know what I told them? "I don't feel right praying inside the Ka'bah. Prayers are to be done outside."

It is not a real house. It is a sign that is imparting messages to the real thinker who G_d has blessed to be a thinker. So, it is speaking of our beginning as a social body... You know, "house", in Arabic, "bait", is feminine, not masculine in grammar. We know angels and the world, and this is where Islamic knowledge parts, separates from the world. The world has given angels feminine pictures or images, and children images, baby images, as well as men, like Jibril. But with the revelation of Qur'an and Muhammed's teachings to us based upon the Qur'an, he gave us the teachings that are given in the Qur'an that the angels should not be called by female names. Their work is the work that is more representative of male nature and action than female nature and action.

Ka'bah a Sign of How to Structure and Serve

The story and picture of Abraham and his son constructing the house should also be seen by us as what we need in us in order to be successful in structuring society and serving human society in the best way. We need people who are spiritually pure, spiritually balanced, to work with us who are doing the rational or material work.

We need their input and their authority as well as that of the people who are more inclined or more orientated as industrialists, or builders. The building has to include them both... Every people have their own qiblah. That is in the Qur'an.

It is said that one of the great khalifahs kissed the black stone. This is after the passing of the Prophet. He said, "If I hadn't seen the Messenger of G_d doing this I would not do this." Understand that the persons in the immediate association of Muhammed, the Prophet, were men who were called the Hunafaa. They did not believe in superstitions. They only believed in what they could understand with their normal, rational minds. But they also believed that the human being's creation (they did not call it creation but the human's form among living things) was the most excellent of forms. Any thinking person can come to that conclusion. You know, we can do more with our minds than any other living thing. So, we are the best and the highest of all living things on the earth. That was their belief and the logic for their discipline is just that. "Since I am the best, then I should respect my form over all other living forms. I shouldn't behave like a dog. I am a higher creation than a dog, or a higher form than a dog". So, these were the Hunafaa.

They were very intelligent people. So, the companion of the Prophet saw himself above kissing the stone and he said, "I wouldn't do it, if the Prophet, himself, had not done it". But now, if he was not from the Arab people and he had been from Christianity, or another part of the world where Christians had been established, he would not have had any trouble kissing the black stone, if he accepted the Prophet, the Qur'an, and his leadership. These were Arabs who had not been Christians. The Christians were converted, too. They were there, too, making pilgrimage. No Christians were having a problem like that because the Bible says, *"And the rejected stone became the corner in the house.*

Now, if you understand building construction, masonry, which means buildings, what we call now the developer, the one who puts the house up, if you understand what the corner is, especially for back then, you form a right angle. That is the key. You form one right angle on the ground or dig a trench right angle, and once you do that you make a straight line from one side of that right angle to where you want it to go, or as far as you want it to go. You make it as long or as big as you want it, and you stop. You take the other side of the angle, and you stop. Now you have half of the square. So, once you get the corner you can get the whole square building, and the Ka'bah is square. So, once you get one corner right all you have to do is line the other ones up with it. The other three sides are lined up with it, and you have a perfect square for building the house.

The Black Stone Represents the Original Nature of Mankind

So, the one corner is very important. The corner that you start with is very important. And the stone that fell represents the original nature of mankind that fell from heaven, not physically speaking, but ideally speaking. It is an idea that you are not developing a physical structure. Once you get the corner lined up you've got it. The stone is black, but it was not always black. It was shining white in the sky. It burned out, and when it cooled it was black. What is this blackness? This blackness must be understood when we study the human heart. If you kill a person and take the heart out and let it cool off, in time, it will turn black. The blood turns black. So, really, the Ka'bah, that corner, represents the human heart and it is good. The heart made a mistake thinking it can go up above mortal life, or flesh, carnal nature, go above it and become saintly, angelic, or divine. It made a mistake. So, that passion for divinity has to burn out, and that mind that thinks you are something special, not human like other humans, has to die. All that message is in a star, a lit body falling from the sky down here, and cooling off.

So, when we look at it now, it represents the heart, and it did not have a silver ring around it, but the custodians of the Ka'bah put a silver ring around it. You who made the Hajj and kissed the black stone, or just passed by, maybe you didn't have a chance to kiss it because, sometimes, they rush you and you can't get to it. If you saw it, you saw a corner with a stone in there with a silver ring around it. Why did they add the silver ring to it? They added the silver ring to say, "This is not just any heart. This is not a symbol, or a sign of just any human heart. This is a sign of a human heart that was blessed with purity." The white metal represents purity, and the ring is around it to say this was the pure heart of Adam before he was deceived by Satan. So, it represents our first father, and he is the human concept that represents shared identity. All of us have this identity that is social, the social nature. The heart is symbolic, too, of the social nature. We love each other. Our heart registers each other. It tells us that our society of Muslims is ordered, really, for humanity, the same thing. It is ordered upon the social nature.

Human Nature Is What We All Have In Common

When you look at the American flag and you see the red stripes, that is the social nature. And the white stripes that is the conscience of the people. The conscience should be clear, pure, and your passions should be social passions. Your love for people and your spirit for people should be coming from your heart. So, there are red lines, white lines. Then you go up to the sky and there is the dark blue of night, and stars are in that dark blue area. The same way you read this you have to read these signs in the Qur'an, too. You have to read the Ka'bah the same way. You know their red doesn't represent just red. What value would a flag have to us if the red streak is just a red streak saying, "Oh, it is pretty"? And some of us are so ignorant that that is the only way we see it saying, "We've got a pretty flag, red, white and blue, with some pretty stars in it." The Bible says, *"The rejected stone became the corner"*. What was rejected? The common nature that Adam represents, the common human identity and nature was rejected. We all are identifying commonly, altogether, and there is a name for our nature among living things. What is the name for our nature? Human nature, not dog nature, not reptile nature, not elephant nature; human nature, that is what we all have in common, and nothing else has that but we humans.

Did Abraham Build the Ka'bah?

Allah says in Qur'an, *"Righteousness is not in turning your face East or West"*, and it says, *"Whichever way you turn your face there you find the Presence of G_d"*, described as wajhullah. That means His Presence. Literally, it says the Face of Allah, but it means His Presence. The Prophet turned from Jerusalem to the Ka'bah… as though turning from the sight of King Solomon's kingdom to the sight of the Ka'bah built by Abraham. Do you think Abraham actually built that? I'm not going to say that. I'm just going to leave it on your mind. Abraham is the one who orientated the intelligence towards the commonality of mankind, and that is what the Ka'bah stands for. It says Abraham and his son built the Ka'bah and that is good enough for me, but I think anybody could have built it. It looks like a very simple thing to do. It is not complicated masonry.

The Ka'bah Looks Like a Coffin

It looks like a coffin to me. The companions of the Prophet were mostly Hunafaa. They never worshiped idols. His companions were those who did not worship idols. To my knowledge, he never had an associate, a companion, that was an idol worshiper. He had friends who worshiped idols, but they were not in his company or were his companions. They were not to be kept in the company of his companions. His companions were all those men who never worshiped idols. They were called, the Hunafaa, meaning they believed in the natural excellence of human life, man. They believed that nature evolved life to be excellent, and that is true, it does. So, when it (Qur'an) says, *"The religion of the original nature or origin, the pattern upon which He patterned civilization, or mankind"*, it is saying that man or human society, has firstly evolved naturally upon a natural basis, and then G_d complements or completes the rise of man as a civilized order by revealing religion to him, giving guidance in the form of revealed knowledge, religion. The religion is described as *"The religion of Abraham, the upright in his nature"*, and Muhammed, the Prophet, along with the other Hunafaa, although he was the most excellent of them, even the pagans acknowledged that he was the best of their citizens or their men. So, it says *"The religion or the order of Abraham, the upright in his nature"*. That is why Christianity, Judaism, and Al-Islam believe in the inherent excellence of man, of human nature or human life, and that rights are inherent. They are due the person because of created human value, or natural human value.

Chapter 14

Ramadan and the Night of Power

Lailatul Qadr is translated, the Night of Power. Qadr is translated, "power", which is a good translation, because power is a general description. Actually, qadr, is more than just power, but it's a good description, because whoever translated it and said, power, they did not say anything wrong; whereas, if you tried to be specific and describe the nature of that power and how it operates, you could make a mistake, and it would be better if you did not translate it. But you know there are two words that are very similar, in Arabic, in the Qur'an, for this power that Allah has to manifest, or He has to, Himself, enliven or energize. Actually, He doesn't energize it. He has already created it as energy. So, He wouldn't have to energize it. He has to signal its mission, what mission it's going to have, what it's going to do.

So, for the Qur'an, G_d has to make it manifest. The two words are qadar and qadr, qa-da-ru and the other one is qad-ru. If the possessive case is affecting it, it is qad-ri. Usually, it's qad-ri, when it is found in the Qur'an, because it is in an expression that is the possessive case, like, "ki-ta-bul laahi, the book belongs to G_d". So, the last letter gets the kasra. The book is what is possessed, and G_d is the Possessor, so you have to put it on the end of G_d. So, if man is being carried by the qadr, or he belongs to the qadr, the qadr is holding him and he's not holding the qadr, then it's qadri, or qadr. So, to the best of my ability, I'm going to give you the English for both of them.

You Have to Discover the Artist Who Designed Creation

Qadar is a regulation. Its main function is to regulate, whereas qadr is a potential, the energy source. You know, psychology even says that man's psyche has an energy source. According to Freud, it is regulated by sex energy, which is for your reproduction, or it's the creation, the source of energy for creation, producing you all over, again. But I'm using creation, too, because in the higher picture for revelation where we are animated and all our properties or operatives are also animated, the process is like the process of creation. We're talking about a creation process for man, for the world. G_d brings it about. G_d is doing this. That's why we say, "creation", because G_d is doing it; otherwise, we would say, "formation", i.e., the formation of the stars, the formation of this, the formation of that, not the creation of the stars. The formation takes out the factor operating outside of the creation. Formation says the explanation is always in the creation. The creation says the explanation is not in creation, and you have to discover the Artist Who designed creation, Who existed before creation. That's G_d.

So, to understand these things you cannot do it without knowing what was revealed before Prophet Muhammed came. All these things are in the Bible. The Bible talks about a mysterious figure or preacher dropping the plummet, measuring everything. So, the Bible has a figure, and it appears that this figure was supernatural and so much bigger than all creatures on earth. He stands and looks things over and starts measuring everything, and it says the plummet line is dropped. In masonry, the plummet line gives you the vertical line for the base. And the scale is used a lot in describing the judgment to be weighed in the scale, and if you haven't lived an honorable life you are going to be found wanting. You won't have enough to balance the scale. One side of the scale is going to go down, and if you don't have enough to balance it, you are going down to hell. The other side of the scale can bring that side up. So, you know, in your life it might look like you're going to hell, but before you pass, you maybe can pick up good deeds on the right side of the scales that brought it up to a balance.

Jesus Christ Is Al-Qadaru

So, getting back to the qadar… "Al-qadaru khairihi wal sharrihi minal laah ta'ala", this is what the Prophet gave, peace be upon him. "The qadar that regulates benefits and harm to the individual or to the community or mankind, is from Allah, Most High, minal laahi ta'ala." So, I'm getting ready to tell you right now that Jesus Christ is al-qadaru. Jesus Christ, his identity that captures him in his totality is al-qadaru. You can call him the righteous. You can call him many things, but the one that captures him in his totality is al-qadaru. And don't forget what I just said. "Al-qadaru khairihi wal sharrihi minal laah ta'ala. The qadar that regulates benefits and harm to the individual, to the community, or mankind is from Allah, Most High". So, that's the explanation, really, for Jesus Christ being from G_d. When the Prophet said that he gave them the clear explanation supporting Jesus Christ being from G_d. That's more than saying he's a Word from G_d. That's more than saying he's a Word and Spirit from G_d, because after all he's the balance, isn't he? He's the balance. Even when he died, they had to keep him on the cross, because the cross is balance. He was crucified on the balance. He was not out of the balance. He was crucified on the balance, and they crucified him because he was the balance, and they don't want any balance in society. They reject this balance from G_d.

G_d Only Wants Good for Mankind

Again, his identity is to be understood from the saying of the Prophet, the prayers and the peace be on the Prophet, and upon Jesus Christ be peace, "Al-qadaru khairihi wal sharrihi minal laah ta'ala, the qadaru is from G_d, Most High". So, this is a nature, isn't it? It's the nature that regulates how the world or man or anything is going to be affected in terms of the results or benefits that come to it. If you approach it wrongly, then most than likely you will get the sharr of it, the harm of it. Fire is put here for our benefit, but a stupid person may get burned up, injured, or maybe even killed, or may kill or burn up other people with fire. But it wasn't created for that. It was created for man to get the good benefits, because G_d never wants anything for mankind but good. However, if you approach it wrongly you get the harm, and if you approach it correctly you get the benefits, not the harm. So, that operative in matter is from G_d, Himself, G_d Most High.

Our Own Nature Respects G_d

For the believer in Islam, before he does anything he should say, "Bismillahir rahmanir raheem" and mean it, and it's got to come from his heart and soul. Bismillahir rahmanir raheem, if it comes from your heart and soul, you have Allah protecting you. There's only one chapter of Qur'an that doesn't begin that way and it's the 9th chapter. We're in the wombs of our mothers for an expected nine months, and in the ninth month, not the tenth, delivery, and the baby is too young to say, "Bismillahir Rahmanir Raheem". The baby is just going on its nature. The nature that G_d is creating it in is supporting it.

Now there are some old guys, like me, that are still babies, and our natures are still supporting us. We don't have it up here (in our heads), not yet, and a lot of us die and never get it up there. So, we're the ones that as long as we have good intentions, we're in G_d's Will and in his Spirit, and we are a part of His Revelation. So, it's not given in the beginning. That means no one spoke it outside of the context, or outside of the text or the contents. But when you get into the body of that surah, G_d found a way to give it to Muhammed. So, it's there, and it's serving the purpose that *"Bismillahir rahmanir raheem"*, serves in the whole of the Qur'an for 113 chapters. So, it's inside. What is it saying when G_d put it inside like that? Inside of that one that did not have it reach his conscious; it was inside of his nature. His own nature respects *"Bismillahir rahmanir Raheem"*. Praise be to Allah!

Inscribed In Our Nature

He's not saying it with his mouth, but he's innocent. Inside of his own nature is *"Bismillahir rahmanir raheem"*, just like Allah has inscribed many things upon our nature. They're not in our conscious. They're working in our nature. Everyone is a Muslim, but it is not in his conscious yet when he is born, but it is in his nature. It is beautiful!

"Bismillahir rahmanir raheem", and the 'bi" means when the king says, "In the name of the king", or "In the name of the people", he is saying "Whatever I'm doing is owing to fact that I am authorized by the people", or "This is authorized by the king". So, when we say, *"Bismillahir rahmanir raheem"*, that's exactly what we are saying. Whatever we are engaged in or whatever we are getting into here it is authorized by our Lord, Allah, our G_d, Who is the Merciful Benefactor, the Merciful Redeemer. Now what this is saying is your own nature knows its Benefactor, and if it is going to be redeemed, it knows its Redeemer. It knows the Mercy of its Lord. It doesn't claim anything for itself. It just obeys the Laws and Will of G_d, so, it is already performing as though it is saying, *"Bismillahir rahmanir raheem"*. Now, I feel like doing the buck dance right on top of a table!

Cud Comes From Qadr

Now, the qadr… You know, they say the cow chews the cud. I believe they got "cud" from the Qur'an, from Islam. Cud, for the cow has reference to a second stomach. The cow eats and when it finishes eating, it will chew again what it swallowed. When it does that, it's chewing the cud. I think it is spelled, c-u-d, and I do believe that cud and qadar go together, that the English people when they brought that word into their language, they got it from Islam, from the Qur'an, the qadr, chewing the cud.

Lailatul qadr, not qadar, lailatul qadr, that's the one I'm associating with cud for the cow, lailatul qadri. *"Lailatul qadri, khairum min alfi shahr, is better than a thousand months"*. Then it goes on to describe what happened on that night. I'm going to start with, *"better than a thousand months"*. A thousand months, one of the translators in his commentary says it means it's better than a lifetime, because most people don't live for a thousand months. It's like the life expectancy, longevity expectancy.

Better Than Your Schemes to Contain Man's Behavior

I don't have any problems with that. It's a good translation. But I think when it says it's better than a thousand months, it means it's better than the whole duration of your schemes to contain man's behavior under a cultural system. Three months is a season, and four times three is a year. Now, usually they work just upon a year. These cultures work to hold us for a year to get us in the summer, and put us in the winter, bring us to spring, and then again back to summer. That's how they rotate us to govern us and keep our behavior under them. So now, that's just twelve months. But this says better than a thousand months. In the Arabic language system, this is not ordinary language, but this is an esoteric language system, language that has to be translated in order for you to get the real meaning. In that system, a thousand means when it completes itself, once it completes itself and its full life has been lived.

So, after a thousand it dies, not after twelve. In the Bible, it talks about a year. A year with G_d is not the same as with you. Your year is short. Your year is twelve months and when G_d is talking about a year don't think that means twelve months. Your year is short, that's all it is saying, that a year with G_d is so much longer than a year with man. So, this thousand, even the year, itself, on a higher level of discussion in the sciences or language of revelation, a thousand years would be like a thousand light years. Scientists, they say light years, now. A regular year just won't say it. It's too much to try to say it with just man's year, so they say light years. And all they're doing is using the same strategy as G_d uses when He says His year is so much longer than your year.

Alifa Means Love

You know the cabbage that I eat and enjoy so much, it seeks to come to a head, unless it's a different kind of cabbage. But the cabbage that most people like is the cabbage that comes to a head, purple cabbage, green cabbage, white cabbage. And how does it come to a head? It keeps putting leaf upon leaf, and they hug each other tight, and when they have finished their growth and there is no more wrapping of itself, it's called a full head of cabbage. And you know the name in Arabic is melfuuf. It comes from alifa and alifa means love, too. The verb, alifa, means love and it's just hugging, and when it is complete it is called melfuuf. If you look at melfuuf, the language is traced back to alifa, or to alf, which means a thousand.

This World Reordered by the Language and Spirit of Shaitan

This is beautiful! It's beautiful right now, but this is going to cap it right now, what I'm going to say. What is G_d telling us for? He's saying, "Alifa between you, quluubakum, your hearts". So, what is it saying from Allah in the Qur'an and from the Prophet? It is saying, "This world that has been reordered by the language, by the spirit that Shaitan blew into it, inspired it with. It's the one that gives you four seasons of twelve months, and you live for a short time called a year. Now, even for his scheme you may live for several years, but he is going to keep revolving the seasons until he gets you! "So really, we aren't talking so much about the effect on the people... but it effects the people, too, because every year he's got you. Now, he may not have gotten you to do his biddings, yet, but every year he's got you. He affected your life by rotating the seasons, and he's containing you within his grip by rotating the seasons. But in time, he rotates it so much that he gets practically everybody. Generations die and they escape, but the community of mankind is coming to the year that we're in right now, and hell has prevailed. And as the Bible says, he will get them all, except G_d's elect. So, he doesn't have the good Christians. Good Christians still have their good life. Good Jews have their life. Good Muslims we have our life but look at our publics. Look at our race. I'm talking about the human race. Look at where the human race is on this planet, right now. It's gone! If the public life doesn't reflect man's humanity, or the human race, it's gone. Just because there is a few walking around out there that came from the sanctuary doesn't mean hell is not everywhere. It says the fire is going to be everywhere, but it won't touch those that are saved.

Satan Wants to Regulate Your Life

So, this is the time, and this is the time to understand the things that I am sharing with you. It is saying Satan, Iblis, wants to regulate your life. He regulates your life in your year that he gives you, and the seasons that he gives to you... But look, again, at these four. "*G_d revealed, G_d established from time immemorial that four months are sacred*". What are the four? The month that begins summer, the month that begins winter, the month that begins spring, and the month that begins fall. Do you see how I put them? Spring, fall, spring up, fall down, warm up, freeze up. He said four months were established as sacred from time immemorial. This is the Qur'an, my translation of Qur'an, perfect. That is saying, "You can't use these seasons to corrupt human life! G_d will not authorize that! He does not authorize that, and you know it! From time immemorial you know that!" This is talking to the big bosses.

The Firmest Piece of Boneless Flesh

So, what I'm saying supports what I'm saying, and when He says, "alifa", alf is a thousand. When He says "alifa", isn't the heart real solidified like a cabbage, like a hard-headed cabbage? The heart is the firmest piece of boneless flesh in your body, very firm. Even your muscles, the muscles of your heart are firmer than the muscles of your body. It has very strong muscles, and it's very firm.

The Jews say in the Qur'an, in reply to the Prophet, when he was trying to reach them with communication, *"Our hearts are the wrappings.* We're protected by our hearts, and our hearts hold what is of vital importance to us. We don't need you! You received it upon your heart. We know that. But we already have our hearts, and our hearts are our protection. Our hearts are the wrapping that will protect the constitution of the Jewish people, protect their unity and their integrity!"

G_d Holds Them by Love

So, "You use a hidden strategy. G_d uses the innocent human nature and G_d holds them by love, alifa. G_d holds them by love, and by the nature in them to want to embrace each other and be close". I gave you the cabbage as a symbol, so you can see it. They would not have named it melfuuf, after a thousand, if it wasn't a good metaphor. And the one Mr. Fard told us to eat is the white head cabbage, and the green head cabbage, if it matures really good, it's a white head cabbage. I haven't seen any white leaves on the outside. The white is on the inside. That's what Jacob showed his cows, representing his scholars, his followers. He was teaching the learned, the scholars. The Bible says he did this when they came to the water to drink. The picture that comes to mind is not like a trough, or a bucket. It's natural water in the ground, like a natural water pool. When they came there to drink, he went on the other side and stripped off the outer covering of some plants, the bark. He stripped it off down to the white. But the Bible picture that is given, when he stripped it off, they saw green and white. And you know that's what happens when you strip off a lot of plants from in the bushes or whatever. When you strip it off, or break and tear it, you don't only see the brown, the bark, outer covering or whatever that covering was. Even if it's purple, you see green next to the white.

They Had to Go to Jacob

So, he showed them that and when they saw that and gave birth to children, they came out reign streaked. That's the Bible, reign streaked. It's not talking about rain from the heavens, but the other reign, which means to rule, or govern. Reign over them means you govern or rule them. Reign streaked means they had to go to Jacob, had to come under Jacob's reign, because that's the deal he made with Laban. He made a deal with him that, *"I'll take care of your cows, but if any of them that come out reign streaked, they will be mine, and those that do not come out reign streaked will be yours"*. So, they made the deal, and he showed them the white and the green on the underside, or within the life that was growing up out of the earth. White is symbolic of purity there in that picture, too, the pure nature, the innocence, and green is symbolic of production.

So, Jacob was showing them how innocence, purity, and riches can go up together, and he was telling them that it's a part of nature. G_d has created the life this way to grow in purity, but also in fruitfulness, or wealth, riches. The scholars, the ones that he reached, they became his students, scholars. So, it just shows how a plan to defeat the ungodly world works. And how, eventually (because you know he changed his name to Israel), the religious people under G_d will overcome the leaders of the world, and Jacob wanted to, first, get the learned people working with him.

Qadr Is Potential and Qadar Is Capacity

So, the qadr, like lailatul qadr, is the potential. It's more than the capacity. It's the potential, or we can say the capacity's potential, because capacity brings to mind something tangible. The capacity of a building is two hundred people. The motor's capacity is so much horsepower. It brings to mind performance, amount, measurement. But potential, it just brings to mind something that is not in use. It's there, but it can support this and that. "We have the potential to manage this town ourselves". It hasn't manifested, yet, but once we have what we need to really manage that town, we can use capacity, can't we? So, they are different. And the capacity, itself, has a potential, like the capacity of a pail I'm carrying is two gallons, and if I empty it, I can say the potential is two gallons. The potential goes back to the source before it's expressed or brought out. So, lailatul qadr is not talking about what has manifested, but what can manifest.

From the Essence of the Universe to Muhammed's Five Senses

So, lailatul qadri, not qadar, is talking about the capacity's potential, and the capacity is seen in the Qur'an. It is seen in Muhammed. The capacity is seen in the established ummah. So, the potential for that capacity is coming down in the month of Ramadan. It's just starting, but it's going to manifest Muhammed. It manifested Muhammed, because he has to receive it so he can be more. It's going to manifest

Muhammed and it's going to manifest the established ummah, and it's coming down as fifty thousand years. The community enlightenment based upon the five senses of man is going to have to reach Muhammed as though it takes fifty thousand years. It takes much longer than that, so we should say fifty thousand light years. In the new language now in this world we should say its coming takes fifty thousand light years. And it is coming from the essence of the universe before even the universe had come to its capacity. The universe, itself, was nothing but potential. Yes, it's coming from that distance to reach Muhammed in his five senses. His brain is just not capable of carrying this. "We're going to have to trust it to his heart, and in time it will communicate from his soul to his brain, and they'll get it as slow rain."

"Lailatul qadri khairum min alfi shahr", a thousand years; *"tanazzalul malaa'ikatu, therein descend the angels; war ruuhu feehaa, and the Holy Spirit"*. The angels are not on their own. The Holy Spirit is not on its own. *"Bi idhni rabbihim, with the permission of their Lord; min kulli amr, from every order or command"*, not one, command up here and command down there, command all up here, and all down there. *"Min kulli amr"* what? *"Peace, salaam"*, because this is alfi, *"khairum min alfi shahr."* How can there be anything but peace when the operatives of love and peace are in the whole workings? They are in the center of the workings. Love and peace! Yes, that's the Night of Power!

The last part of that sura says, *"Peace till the rise of morning..."* It says, *"Salaamun hiya, peace it is"*. Hiya means, it is, hattaa, until, and *matla'il fajr, the rising of the dawn"*. So, it's a night. All of this is happening in the night. It means all these things happen without man's conscious. G_d brings about all of this. These are forces that G_d puts inside man. They are inside his creation, not in his conscious. G_d has to eventually bring them to his conscious, but they are not in his conscious, and when it comes to his conscious, the peace is over. *"And they did not differ with each other until the Qur'an was revealed, until the clear evidence came to them"*. Before, they weren't differing and when we come back, then we are drawn together again upon the same beautiful, cosmic, forces that are pictured in that night... by cosmic forces I mean what's happening in the universe, but in the universe as a picture of what's happening inside of us.

You Met In the Night

The cosmic world is always bursting forth with new energy, new lights, new bodies, new systems. This is the nature of the universe. So, if you see us as a microcosm, then this is happening in us, and those are forces that will not let us control them or that will not let us get involved in their nature to change their nature or call upon it at will. It's internal and that internal system is the system that brings us together, not what we got from the world, the conscious, I mean. The Dalai Lama, the Sheik, the Rabbi, and the Buddhist, can sit together at the table and have so much peace, harmony, and love. I know because I have sat at the table with them. I have been in that situation at the table, and you forget that this is a Muslim and somebody a Jew, Hindu, and somebody else. You forget that. All you know is it's a good situation where the company is just wonderful, and you're not conscious of anything but the beauty and warmth of the company. That's because of the night. You met in the night.

However, let us start bringing out the wisdom and the strategies of these religions, and the peace is gone. So, *"Peace it is until the rising of the dawn"*. Do you see what Allah is revealing to Muhammed? Allah is saying to Muhammed, "If you would just communicate with them or engage them on the higher realities that have not been given any name or been touched by man, oh, you can have perfect peace with them! But if you start giving the light that is needed to light their world and what Allah wants for you in the world, oh, the peace is going to leave and you're going to have to fight these people! And your heart is so good and so innocent, I'm going to have to order you to fight. You're going to take them beating you up and throwing stones on you and everything, and I'm going to have to order you to fight, because your heart was made in heaven, and I'm going to have to order you to fight.

So, that's the qadr and al-qadar. I don't know everything about either one of them. But I know one is referring to what we can produce, the capacity for producing. That's al-qadar. Right away it suggests measurements. And al-qadr is our potential, or what they call the intellect's cognition. You know, cognizant means to be aware of something. Cognition means to be aware of something in its potential source.

The Process of Enlightenment That Comes Out of Darkness

Now, I'm going to tell you this and then I'm finished, and you can turn your recorders off. G_d is talking about man's intellect. When He created Adam, He's talking about He created the intellect. He created an intellect to engage His creation and be productive for the best possible life on this earth for man in community or for people in community. So, when G_d is telling us of these mystic happenings, mystical things that are going on and relating it to our needs as people down here to establish an ummah, etc., He is addressing our intellect. So, the qadr and qadar is talking about the intellect and how it happens, and the purpose of it is to bring from your body... you know, I mentioned the feet as being where that sensitivity is before it comes up to head. It's in your spiritual form, in your spiritual body. It's in your spiritual life, and the feet register this before the head does. Wise men with their spiritual sciences, they discovered that, and they used the feet to show this. So, when G_d is saying, *"Hattaa matla'il fajr"*, tamaa, means a well going up and matla, means *"until the rising of the dawn"*.

So, this is all metaphorical, but the life source for enlightenment must come all the way up the body and eventually reach the conscious and then be expressed in the world. So, that's the picture that we're to get. Therefore this, *"Rising of the dawn"* is the process of enlightenment that comes out of darkness. It wasn't in the world at all. Its first appearance is in darkness. It appears in darkness as a faint light, but that light grows and grows and grows to become a very bright light. And when it gets to be its brightest, it's going to leave you, so you can get some rest. But it will be up in the morning!

Chapter 15

The Khalifah

I think it is called the ganglia that comes from the spine to the brain and goes back down, back into the system, the whole body. It comes into the conscious, sometimes, maybe no time. But if it comes into the conscious then the brain sees what it couldn't see before. Some may call it the intuitive insight that goes from the ganglia to the forebrain, the forefront. I forget what that is called up there, the one in the front. Most of the time it comes there, but it doesn't register in the conscious. It goes back and forth. It comes from the ganglia. It goes back from the forebrain, the lobe in the front, back to the back of the brain, the hemisphere in the back, and then down to the ganglia.

The Body Has Inherited the Past

I don't think they know where it comes from, but I think insight brought Muhammed, the Prophet, and his followers and many people over the world to understand what it comes from. It's rested in the body, and the body has inherited the past. Every person that lived before that had anything to do with the person, i.e., the genetic line, everybody in the genetic line of that person, all that information can come to that person, and it's in the body. It's in the genes. It's in the body, and the ganglia is the nerve line connecting to the brain. So, it can come from there up into brain and the brain can release it to the conscious, if the person is conditioned to bring it out, and that's what khalifah is... Khalfan means behind you. If I say, "Huwa khalfan, or khalfani, he is behind me". So, khalifah means that that is behind you, behind you in time, your genetic line, and G_d made the khalifah. G_d made Adam a khalifah, didn't He? It means that He made man to register his past in his conscious, and if he registers his past, eventually, he's going to come back to G_d. He's going to realize that in his past there was nothing that was under his control. "All of this is under the control of my Creator", and he gives the credit to G_d. Then he becomes khalifah if he has the desire to release that, to share that with people, like your Imam, Warith Deen Mohammed. But if he has no interest to give to people, he'll never register it in his conscious. It will never register on his conscious. And even if he has the desire, it's still the Will of G_d. The right things have to happen to bring it to the conscious, and don't think you can do it without G_d's Personal Help. You have to prove yourself, first. When you prove yourself, then G_d's Personal Help will come to you.

Khalifah a Common Possession of All People

So, khalifah is a common possession of all people, Adam. Adam is a part of all people, so, khalifah is a common possession of all people. He said He made you *"Khulifah in the earth"*. That's the plural of khalifah. He made you khalifahs in the earth, and then He says He also made you inheritors in the earth. So, you have the khalifah property in your nature, in your creation, but He also made you inheritors. You can inherit that property. You are the inheritor of that property. So, it's a common nature and common property, and all people have it.

And that's the Christ nature, too. But the Christ nature is above this possession, or form. What I'm talking about is a property of form, a property of the human form. But Jesus Christ is on a level above that in the Ascension. He is on a level above that, with John. And that's to say that on his level, the urge is to express it, whereas, on the Adam level, the urge is just to benefit from it, unconsciously.

The Life and Possibilities of the Common People

And Prophet John, peace be on all of them, he's on the same level with Jesus Christ, because his urge, too, was to express it. But Jesus Christ was raised in a religious environment. John, the Baptist, was a desert man, so, he couldn't speak well, but he was expressing it. "You'd better get right! You'd better get right! The time is at hand!" He knew that much. It is beautiful, and it is saying what is the life and possibilities of the common people, for the common people, everybody. But only a few manage to have it expressed in their nature, or for them.

You know, in Genesis (it's not in the Qur'an) it was a snake. The only living creature outside of Adam and his wife was a snake, to start with. He (G_d) made all the others, but in the garden the scene is Adam, his wife, the trees, and the snake and it was a snake that approached them. And who was the snake? Iblis, Because G_d said to them, *"Get down into the earth"*. The Bible says that the serpent was told to, *"Get down into the earth, in the dust, to crawl on your belly"*. The Qur'an says the same thing, but it's just that he was told to get down into the earth. All of them were told to get down into the earth.

I didn't have any help like many have today, and Allah blessed me to get it. The only help I had was faith in my own intelligence, faith in my rational mind, and faith in Allah, and Allah will not lead anyone astray. Now, Allah is definitely Merciful, and if anyone is led astray, that person will be redeemed by His Mercy. Yes, that's all the help I had. And when you are taught to depend upon your own rational mind, you aren't going to be blindly led. You're not going to be led, blindly, and you're not going to see that that conflicts with reason and not suspect that there is something wrong with it, either hidden singly, or it's just a lie.

The help I'm giving you all is the help that's in the Qur'an. But I'm giving it to you, plainly and consciously, that you have to connect back with real life and real nature, and the nature before man changed it and put his language to it. And that's a good situation to be in in order to come to the right perception, or to get Qur'anic insights.

Ignorance Was Heavier On the People of Muhammed's Day

The world is not as dark, now, as it was back there in Prophet Muhammed's day. It was much darker. Ignorance was heavier on the people in his day than it is nowadays. I was raised in a Christian country, in a Christian environment, in a church environment. I heard preachers preach, and I'm an African American born as the son of a man who had rejected the Church, my father, Elijah Mohammed. So, I'm in that Christian environment and I'm hearing them preaching, but I already had been influenced to suspect that something is wrong with what they were saying. So, my situation was much more, I'm favored much more than Prophet Muhammed was. So, my circumstances favored me coming into the light much more than Prophet Muhammed's circumstances favored him coming into the light. If he had any advantage over me, it was taken away by Mr. Fard when he said that "This whole world is nothing but a lie, and the Bible is a lie. Everything is a lie!"

Prophet Muhammed and the Intellectuals of His Day

Now, Prophet Muhammed was born among people who had irrational faith. Their religion was irrational. They worshipped idols, but he was not of them. He was of a special class and that class was the intellectuals of his day in his tribe (the Quraish) who believed in the excellence of nature. They already believed that, and they were called the Hunafaa, the plural of haneef. Then when Muhammed was shown the path and he knew Abraham, in the Scripture, was shown favor as a father, leader for all the people, he identified their belief, the Hunafaa, as the belief of Abraham. That's the only thing that was missing in the Hunafaa. They didn't have revelation. So, when he got revelation, then he understood that revelation complemented the Hunafaa's identity as a creation, human creation, that it complemented it. So, then he saw that to purify that nature, we need revelation. Though we are striving for excellence to purify it, we need G_d to reveal to us. So, G_d gave him revelation to show him how to purify his nature, but he already believed in the excellence of his nature.

Revelation showed him that really the way to continue the life of the excellence of his nature he needed revelation. He needed G_d to open up the whole world to him. So, when Allah says, in the Qur'an, that it is, *"The deen of origin, deen al-fitrah, His religion of origin, the originality, or the origin that this human society is fashioned upon"*, then Muhammed understood that it was the Hunafaa, that nature that Islam came to complement, and that really, the pattern that Allah had designed the Qur'an to fit is really the Hunafaa, the excellence of man's nature.

An Overriding Aim

Abraham is the father. He's the father because he was before Muhammed, and the first one to question the external reality looking for G_d. He concluded that G_d is none of this, that G_d is the One that designed it. And how did he come by that? He was haneefah. He believed that his creation had an overriding aim. Maybe it would commit an offense here or maybe it would disgrace its value here or there, but it has an overriding aim and it's going to come out in somebody. So, it came out in the Hunafaa, that group that he gravitated toward, or they gravitated towards each other. He believed it originated in nature, that it was nature, that it was the dominant nature. And he believed that everything created had that same nature, but it's not called by that name. Only for humans it is called haneefah, or hunafaa.

Why G_d Revealed to Muhammed, the Prophet

When Muhammed, the Prophet, was asked about his life and how he succeeded without being overcome by sin, he said it was because of the Mercy of Allah. The same goes for everybody else, because of the Mercy of Allah. Now, why does the Mercy of Allah work for him, but it doesn't work for so many others? Because his spirit was always to do the best, to do the correct thing and to be his best in his character and conduct. He was always truthful and trustworthy, so he earned Allah's Mercy, and that Mercy was to free all people, *"rahmatan lil 'aalameen, mercy for all the people"*, because of one person. Didn't the Bible say, if there's just one in the city, He wouldn't destroy it? It says, *"Surely your life and your death are as one soul"*, in the Qur'an. So, because there was one, all of humanity got mercy. So, how is all of humanity going to get mercy without revelation? That's why G_d revealed to him.

Now, that's not the end of this logic, because when they asked him, "What accounts for you being saved from that?", he said, "The Mercy of Allah", the same as for everybody else, the Mercy of Allah. So, what do I see in that? Because he was truthful and trustworthy, in his nature was also Mercy from Allah. Allah knew that this creature that has formed from his mother and his father, this creature wants no evil, wants no wrong. G_d knows in the beginning. G_d says, "Here's a soul that wants nothing but Me. He wants Me. He wants to serve Me. He wants to find Me and serve Me. So, I'm going to make it easy for him. I'm going to be the Protector of his purity." So, Allah protected his purity and put him in circumstances that would aid that. So, Allah was working with him as his Lord and Creator right beside him from the day he was conceived in his mother to the time he died, like two arrows shot out of one bow.

We Don't Need Everybody to Save Mankind

Yes, Allah knows. So, none of us, no one, can be without sin. "They all (I'm talking from the Bible) are sinners." Was Jesus Christ a sinner? But it says all are sinners. Did it say Jesus Christ was a sinner? No, it's speaking of him, that all other than him were sinners. And why was he not a sinner? In the language of the Bible, it was because he was the son of G_d, a Spirit and a Word from G_d. How could he sin? Now, for Muhammed, I already explained to you how he couldn't sin. So, we all are human with these human limitations, and without the intervention of G_d, Himself, we all would be lost. Yes, we don't need everybody to save society. All we need is one soul. One soul started it, and one soul can redeem it, or bring about redemption, earn redemption.

Logic That Evolves Naturally

Anything that we endeavor to do to present something, be it our life, our works, our organization, whatever it is, our first major concern is to do this in agreement with the Word of G_d, the Qur'an, and with the life of Muhammed, the Prophet. That's first. Once you are cleared under those two authorities you are clear. For the Qur'anic term, "uulul al baab", baab means the door, but when you put it in that language, it doesn't mean door. It means more than door. The term, uulu, means first and the term al baab means, the door, the first door, or the first of the doors, the door in the singular, but you could say the first of the doors, or the first door, the men of the first door. It means men of moral logic, men of the logic governing how we should behave. That is the first door, men who are devoted to the reasoning and the logic that governs how human beings are to behave. I said moral, but it's a little bit more than just moral, and that is a logic that evolves naturally, and it was the first exercise of reasoning for human beings.

The first thing they wanted to deal with was human behavior, because if human beings don't accept some discipline for their behavior, if they cannot discipline themselves, how can they then perform in any field of discipline? So, it is the first door, men of the first door. It also means possessors. The term, uulu, could mean possessor. They are owners, possessors of the door and by a certain reasoning owners of the door. They are the first at the door and because they are first at the door, they are owners of the door. This is philosophical language and reasoning that supports life and nature. That is what it is, the reasoning that wants to serve the upliftment of nature and life, men of logic, loosely speaking.

Possessors of the First Door

Al-Islam is a commonsense-based religion. It respects human nature in its origin, and it respects the five senses. And when Allah says in the Qur'an, *"Oh you men of the first door"*, meaning, *"Possessors of the first door"*, uulu means, first, speaking of the many. "Al baab" means, "The door". It is saying the same thing that the revolutionary guy said when he was trying to organize the people who came to settle in the new world against Britain, against the kingdom. When he, Thomas Paine, was trying to organize them, he called them to their common senses. That is how it started. He appealed to their common senses, and they started coming together. The writers of the Constitution followed Thomas Paine. He was the mu'adhdhan calling them to respect their five senses.

So, you can look right into the forming of this great country's ideology. You can look and see how it started and how it came together, and see that they, too, came together upon respect for their five senses. So, Prophet Muhammed, G_d revealed to him to have the first one as La ilaaha illallaah. It did not say, "Muhammed, the Messenger of Allah". At that time, he did not include himself. "To witness that G_d is one", that is what he said. And then he said, "to pray". Now, you should not establish prayer until you know who you are praying to. So, once you really meet with the real G_d, then you can pray correctly.

"Uulul Al Baab"

G_d has put His Signs in His Works. You have heard the expression, "He tried to bend the truth." You can't bend light. So, the people of first knowledge, pronounced, in the Qur'anic Arabic, *"uulul al baab"*, not only in the Qur'an, in the world, that is the knowledge born in man upon his observations of the objective world. That is his first knowledge. So, the people of first knowledge, they apply it. Their instruction was to apply it, not just have it. Do not hoard it and feel some kind of security, because you have it, and others do not have it. Apply it, use it in the world.

So, what we call the exact sciences or the scientific world, is the world that got the light and applied it. They are using it and benefitting the world of man, society, with what they have. They make it work in the world, and they are so advanced over the spiritual world that they have lost patience with the spiritual world, and some of them have separated perception from spiritual matters or from G_d. They say, "You can only perceive what is possible for you in this material world. Forget about this that these other guys are busy with. We are supposed to be the leaders in the world, not leaders in some hidden zones above the people's heads, the sky!" They have divided the world into spiritual and material, secular and religious, and it looks like they are the bad guys. The worst of guys is the one who aspired to rise up upon the air or the breath of the earth and set himself up in heaven in G_d's stead. He wants to get up there and take the position that the people see as the Seat of G_d. He wants to get up there, take that seat, and show himself as G_d.

The Creation Was One Continuous Whole

So, first, we want to look at the concept of tauheed with reference to the wholeness of matter or creation. G_d says in the holy book, His Book, the Qur'an, *"Do they not see that the creation was one continuous whole before it was separated as sky and earth?"* You know the belief on this earth was that the earth was the center of the universe and the astronomers who studied it as objectively as they possibly could, they finally concluded that it's not the center at all, but the small earth belongs to the family of the sun. The sun is the center, because all the other bodies are rotating around the sun, or evolving around the sun, going around the sun. And some other ideas, or myths believed that this was really an alienated body beyond the bodies of the heavens, and this is the black hole, the black planet, the alienated one, the one in trouble. Finally, they gave that description to Pluto, because it's too far out. But mind you, when you're studying that astronomy, too, there's some Pluto in all earthlings. So, tauheed is the term for the unity of matter and the unity, consistency, of G_d's creation that forces us to His Unity, His Consistency, His Uniqueness as Creator of all that.

Know G_d In His Performance In the Role of G_d

So, it is through the study of what He did that we can be guided or led to what He is, and you know if you say, "Mother", what is the meaning of "Mother"? The female parent, that's a quick answer. But before you really know what a mother is, you have to know a mother's history, what has been her performance in that role, then we truly see her, the meaning of mother. So, for the meaning of G_d, we have to know G_d in G_d's performance in the role of G_d, how G_d has performed in the role of G_d. When we know that, then we truly know G_d. We see the true picture, the whole picture, we know G_d. The meaning is full now, complete now, and what takes us to that conclusion is the study of what He did. And men have been guided by their nature, by the nature of their intellects. They have been guided in the nature of their souls. They have been guided to conclude that this world couldn't have made itself, that G_d did this. G_d did it. "Let us study His Works and see what His Works tell us of Him". So, G_d gives the servant the help. It says, *"Why can't they see that this scheme of matter was once a consistent whole before it was separated into earth and sky", spiritual and material?*

The Men of the First Logic

So, this is a hint, hinting to the thinkers, the men of uulul al baab, the men of the first logic, first reasoning, first possessors of the door, the door to the knowledge. This is a hint to them that G_d is going to stop this separation in man's life, where he thinks he's spiritual on one side and material on the other side, and the two sides are in conflict. No, G_d made the world in agreement, made it in peace, made it to have a harmonious relationship for its different parts, its different sections, and its different systems, like a great symphony of spiritual life. The spiritual life is a part of that great symphony. The material life is a part of that great symphony. All parts of our life are in that great symphony. G_d played music, man, beautiful music!

G_d is saying, "I am One and My creation is a whole, a consistent, harmonious whole. Discord is in your own mind because of ignorance". So, this is the message that must go to the whole world. If this message goes to the world, it's like a body that's been afflicted with a disease, and then a medicine comes to that body to defeat the disease in that body. The sores start going away. The boils of racism disappear to become a healthy humanity.

Chapter 16

The Love of Knowledge

When Allah tells us there are signs in the heavens, and the earth as well and there are signs also, in the human being, in the people, it does not just mean in the physical people. It means in the life and works of the people. There are signs in man's industry, man's language, and everything. So, his world is like G_d's original world, the universe. Man's world expresses his life, his spirit, intelligence, and everything. Man has expressed everything of his life in his culture. I am using culture now as a complete word. I am not talking about entertainment only.

Culture: Everything That Comes From Man As Expressions of His Life

Culture is everything that comes from man as expressions of his life. So, isn't education culture? The academic world is part of the culture of the people of the West or America, whatever. So, culture is also a word that includes all the expressions of man's life as a thinking, intelligent being. Someone may be thinking, "What is the Imam teaching us? I came here to learn Arabic." You came to the wrong place. My students should know they just don't come to learn Arabic. They come to learn life, and I didn't just start being this way. I can't remember a time when I was not this way... The logic is still the same. My interest is still the same: Life, human nature, intelligence, correcting how we think and reason.

Question it. First, you have to question things. Mr. Fard said, "Ask questions, learn all about yourself. Isn't that something? He didn't say learn about the Qur'an, mathematics. No, "Ask questions and learn all about yourself." So, this man was interested in us knowing ourselves, studying ourselves, and that was and still is our greatest need. We just let the world shape us. We do not question our own creation, our own nature, and how we are made. That is the beginning of philosophy. Study your own creation. Study your own self in the role of a living creatures born by creation or supported by matter, the material world. So, when you start thinking that way lights start coming on.

Philosophers Prepared Civilization for Scientific Inquiries

The Qur'an refers to the thinker over and over again, and it identifies man in his beginning or in his natural life as G_d made him, as a thinker. So, when you think of the Qur'an and its reference to the male as a thinker, from now on think of the history of mankind, and the role of the philosophers in bringing civilization and preparing civilization for society, for its scientific inquiries. It was the philosophers who did this. The word, philosopher, what is its meaning, or philosophy? The subject, itself, what does it mean? Philosophy means love of knowledge. You can say the love for ideas that hold knowledge, education, and enlightenment. Man has a natural love for that, not just men, also women, and the Qur'an did not leave that unsaid. In the Qur'an, the comparison is made of females and males showing how the male is a believer, the female is a believer, the males purify themselves, the females purify themselves, etc. And one of the expressions is in Qur'anic Arabic: *"Adh dhaakereenal laaha katheeran wadh dhaakaraate,"* translated, *"The males who think and the females who think."* So, the Qur'an is forward moving. It was ahead of man.

Everything In Existence Is One Word

The focus is everything in existence, and everything in existence is one word, universe, and universe is one verse. So, that should tell us we should be able to read all of it as one and the same reading, or one line, one statement, and the statement should say "G_d did this, not you!" Terms that I will be addressing will be the cosmos, the universe and cosmism, which is the philosophy or the study of everything that is in existence to understand how it came about, how it evolved, grew, and how we were expressed out of this great material source that G_d made; how it even bore human life, and how our life has to evolve to a completion. I will also be addressing the thinking on this existence, on everything that exists to arrive at some kind of conclusion for our thinking, and the conclusion arrived at by Prophet Abraham and many of the early philosophers, Greek, African, and others. Sometimes, we think the only philosophers were Greek. Actually, the Greek philosophers started out almost worshiping the African philosophers.

The Cosmological Argument

The expression is cosmological argument. That is what we're addressing, this reasoning that Abraham came to that resulted in the conclusion that this whole existence, everything, even us included, is tied by one universal logic, the logic of matter itself that holds matter, material things together. He arrived at that logic, and the systems that have formed upon that logic, the system of planets, of life on earth, etc., systems that represent nature, weather changes, all these systems. He concluded that there must be a Cause behind all of this, Allah. He reduced the many gods to One. He said, "No, there are not many gods. There is only One, the Creator". It has to begin with G_d, the Creator, and he called that G_d his Lord, meaning that G_d formed his life and created the necessary help that life needs, so that it would develop from lesser to greater, from inferior to superior.

Utilizing G_d's creation we are told that G_d made everything. Everything in existence has been formed and put in our life or in our existence for us to utilize. Utilize means to make use of it. Man utilizes the power of electricity. He discovered it, Benjamin Franklin, in the sky when the lightening was flashing, and Thomas Edison got the idea to make an electric light and finally was able to do it with a partner working with him, an African American. Thomas Edison found a way to get the energy out of the matter and use the same principle he saw in lightening to make a light bulb, negative and positive clashing, friction to make fire, light.

G_d Made Everything to Be Mated With Human Intelligence

So, everything has been made for us to utilize, the intelligence of man to utilize. When we say mind, man, we're talking about mankind, all people, male and female. I believe the Qur'an addresses modern man's needs to come out of the darkness of ancient man. G_d says to modern man that G_d made everything to be mated with human intelligence. Everything is a mate for human intelligence and when our human intelligence or our rational, intellectual, curiosities engage the external world there is progress for the mind and progress for the human community. That is how it all happened.

So, the lover, the philosopher, who has that nature of the philosophers, for such persons that is so beautiful! It is fine and beautiful how G_d has shown us our own reality, our own nature. The nature of our own soul, the reality for own soul, that is really what you exist for. Your human creation is to measure what your intelligence and your moral life can be comfortable with. "And you have measured up, oh, soul that has been struggling. I see you have measured up to what your own intelligence and you own moral life approves of, and you presented yourself to Me, and I approve of you, too, and I am pleased with you."

A Natural Need In You to Reconnect With Your Creator

G_d is saying that you have a natural need in you to reconnect with your Creator, your G_d. He says, "I don't have to be moving you and pushing you to do this. You found Me. I wasn't looking for you. I just created you to find Me, and you found Me. You presented yourself to Me, and I am approving of you, and I'm pleased with you. You qualified because you were under the pressure of your own values, standards, your own standards. Your own evaluation of your worth is what pressured you and drove you to be the beautiful creature you now are. Your own life was demanding you to make improvements upon it. And now, you have pleased your own soul. Your moral life likes what it is looking at. Your human intelligence likes what it is looking at, and I want you to know that I, too, like what I see in you". That's G_d, and that is what He is saying.

They Make Their Aspirations Their God

G_d is saying, "Look, you don't understand your own struggle. You don't understand your own life. You don't understand your own struggle to accomplish what your own soul demands of you. You don't understand it. You think you are doing this to please Me. You are doing this to please the best in you, the true you, the Muslim you. The man I created, the woman I created, you are doing that to please yourself. It is yourself demanding that of you. I created it, but you are responding to yourself, what yourself is asking of you." Now, all of us don't do that. A lot of us respond to the urges that are taking away and the appetites that take away that beauty, that excellence, as Allah says, *"They follow their own desires"*. "Hawa" is more than desires. It means your own aspirations. Your own spirits, influences, you just follow them, and they make their god. They make their aspirations their god. Those are the ones that are not moved by the excellence of their creation. They are moved by the weakness of their creation, yielding to temptations in the world that feed those weaknesses. So, they debase themselves. They reduce their value. They put themselves in hell, but those who are true to themselves, true to their own souls, they elevate themselves. They graduate their worth, and they are not satisfied until satisfaction is in their souls.

Appetite for Excellence

So, this happiness that we are talking about is happiness that G_d created us with when He created us. He created us with the appetite for this happiness. The intelligent world recognizes that man is a creature motivated by an inherent, inborn, appetite for excellence. Muhammed, the Prophet, said, "G_d has inscribed, the Creator, has inscribed excellence for everything." So, the appetite for excellence is inherent in all life. It is in us.

"I'm pleased with my life!" You hear people say that and they have a right to say that "I'm pleased with my life." I am pleased with mine and many of you you're pleased with yours, because you know you're doing what's best. You know that you are responding to your better nature, your better sensitivities, and better motivations. You know you're responding to that, so you are happy with yourself, and you are already in a small paradise. You've got a small garden already, and G_d is going to enlarge it for you as time marches on. Praise be to Allah!

The Community Soul Is Male and Female

The Qur'an says, *"And the female infant, who was buried alive will be asked what crime she was guilty of?"* The female there is the soul, the human soul that's blocked by the world, a double cross! Whatever is said of the soul, the single soul, is also said of the whole people, the whole of humanity. It is also said of cities, towns, nations, the whole of humanity! So, it is insight on the destiny of the human soul, that the human soul starts with the individual, but that soul's nature incorporates more and more individuals. So, as the groups enlarge, the single soul is still the most important characteristic of that life! And if the world blocks it, it says, *"As you have done to the least of these you have done unto me"*. And in the Qur'an, *"Your death and your resurrection are as the death and resurrection of a single soul"*. So, it is the soul, and it's given in the creation of man, that He created you male and female from one soul, *"Min nafsin wahidah"*. That's it. And then, *"Wa baththa minhumaa, and then He created from that one its mate, zaujahaa"*. It's not feminine! Zaujahaa is masculine! So, really when you read it, it appears that the man was the *"Nafsin waahidah"*, but the man and the woman are the *"Nafsin wahidah"*! They were both in one soul, male, and female, and when it says, *"Wa khalaqa minhaa"*. It's a female entity while it's including male and female characteristics. Then it says, *"Wa khalaqa minhaa zaujahaa."* This is a female entity, but it's made to appear to be Adam, a male entity.

Adam Is a Single Soul and a Composite Figure

But doesn't the Bible say that *"In the day that He created them, He named them Adam"*? He named them Adam, male and female, it goes on to say. So, actually Adam is a single soul and a composite figure, including all people, both genders, male and female. So, it's really the community soul. The community soul is both male and female, and its destiny is to liberate all things that are not liberated or are bound or enslaved. That's it's destiny, to reach its purpose or its destination, the true nature of community, natural, evolved community that G_d intended. Like the United States, following the Constitution, if it follows the Founding Fathers' guidance, then it's this community soul I'm talking about right now! So, if it reaches its destiny, it's going to free all people, both genders, male and female, all groups, black, any color, the poor and the rich, all. Sometimes the rich are enslaved! Yes, so it is the natural community, *"ummatin wahidah"*. It's the natural community, the single community, with the Divine Purpose in it. If it has G_d's Will in it, then it is going to liberate everything enslaved, or everything dealt with unfairly, or unjustly.

Winter Anywhere Is Beautiful

Life is beautiful. Even the worst things we see we don't perceive them correctly, most of us. The environment we live in of people negatively influences the way we see things. So, here you're living in an environment in one area of the world and winter is ugly and cold. In another area of the world, winter is beautiful, cool, or chilly, but beautiful. Winter anywhere is beautiful. All you have to do is look at one snowflake under the microscope, or under a magnifier, and you have enough to warm you up. Look at the beauty in dust that does not show its beauty. You have to look very closely. Allah says, in the Qur'an, He spread the earth out like a carpet. Now, even if you're flying over the sands of Saudi Arabia and you look down, it looks like a carpet. That beautiful sand looks like a carpet and when you're flying over the jungle, if you're high enough, it doesn't look like you're looking down on trees. It looks like you're looking down on a carpet, because they come so much together when you far away until, actually, it looks like its covered with green. That is some deep carpet. Then you have long stretches of grass and because man loves grain, there are long stretches of grass where they grow wheat and other grasses, rye, miles and miles of it. It looks like a beautiful, green carpet. Then the grass is taken and mown, so it really looks like a carpet.

Allah Made Creation In Layers of Beauty

The Lord has made this creation in layers of beauty. In His world, even violence is beautiful. You see the way a hawk or eagle comes swooping down. It is like a theater. You can just watch it. If you don't put your mind on the victim, you will really enjoy it. That is some artful stuff they're doing there. So, Allah has always left something beautiful in whatever He presents. He leaves something beautiful to tell you this is happening, but this is not the general rule, or pattern. What you should be seeing is the beauty that is prevalent in everything, even death. The dead thing looks so restful.

The ice that we don't like that makes the winter cold, they put it in the glass to pour champagne or soft drink over it and look at how pretty it looks. Crystallization, they have exploited it all the way, as much as they could, to make beautiful China, or crystal glassware. The artist, he looks at it very close up, with a magnifying glass, and he finds inspiration in the crystallization, and ends up making a masterpiece of art just copying the crystallization in the material, and colors, too.

Crystals, they form beautiful colors. They all are not clear, not transparent. Some of them are colored and very beautiful. So, you go to the redwood forest in California. They call it the petrified forest, and you find some beautiful pieces of petrified wood where crystals have formed, and colors have formed in such beautiful patterns. Now, look at how they died. They died beautifully, didn't they? So, it is speaking to man's spirit. Don't just look at the outer picture. Look into it. As the Honorable Elijah Mohammed said, "No, brother, you don't have it yet! You have to look deep!" He was right.

Love for the Study of Knowledge

If you don't pair up, you stay ugly. Isn't that true? When you find people who don't want to be with anybody, aren't they ugly? I don't care how beautiful they look in the outer appearance, ugliness inside makes them even appear ugly outside. I was born a philosopher among you. G_d birthed me a philosopher and some of my statements are so philosophically powerful. If you were to give them to somebody else or write it, they would say, "Wow!" I'm telling you what I know. Those who are philosophical in their thoughts, or mental makeup, they would not be able to pull away from me, if I would start talking like I talk. I never thought of myself as a philosopher, but I'm a lover of knowledge. That is what a philosopher is. Philosophy is love for the study of knowledge.

The Likeness of Your Creation Is the Plant

Here comes some more philosophy: *"And the likeness of your creation is the creation of the plant"*, or *"a parable of man's creation is the parable of plant life"*. The Bible and the Holy Qur'an are about sowing seeds. Is it really taking about seeds, or is it talking about people? The seed that is being sown are the seeds of people. You're planting people. You're making a crop of people. You're going to have a harvest of people. So, he is throwing out seeds. Now, when the seeds were thrown, I was not there and one of those seeds produced Elijah Mohammed and Clara Mohammed. And then he goes up animated and he starts throwing seeds, and one of those seeds produced me from Elijah and Clara Mohammed in his tilth. My mother was his tilth. So, he planted it there and I came out, and they named me a new seed, Wallace D. Mohammed. But before I was Wallace D. Mohammed, I was forming in my mother's womb, and I was Elijah and Clara. Does that make sense to you? So, who is this but Elijah and Clara? So, I'm asked, "Do you think he's here?" Yes, he's here, right now, enjoying the progress and everything, because I'm not only a new person. I'm, also, the person I came from in every way, genetically, spiritually, mentally, emotionally. And if you've ever sat and watched my father, this is he. Now, isn't that beautiful how life continues, if G_d blesses the soul that comes peacefully? My father said, "He (Wallace) is different! He always will be different, because when he was conceived, I was in the height of my work with the savior. It went right into him." That is what he said, and he is right. Now, that I look back I have to say that he was right. So, Elijah has not gone anywhere. He is progressing. He has a new life in Wallace.

You Are Moving Into the Future All the Time

The Prophet said, "Marriage is half of your religion." If you don't marry and don't have children, you have no future. Al-Islam is, "Al Awwal, Akhir, the First and the Last", and it orientates us to work for the future. You don't work for the past. You don't work for the present. You work for the future, and it is the bigger reality, because it has the past and the present in it and the present is never with us. It is gone by the time you say it, and that is philosophical. You can speak in the present but can't hear what you said in the present. So, by the time you hear it it's gone. It's in the past and you are moving into the future all the time, just like the earth on its axis always turning towards the sun.

Friday Is the Best Day of the Year

You take fourteen and add another seven to it, what is it? Twenty-one. That is when you're a man. One week a boy, two weeks a youth, three weeks a man, and four weeks you should be ready to lead, be responsible for society. That is 28 days. And Mr. Fard wanted you to have twenty-six, ten in the conscious, ten in the mind, six in the spirit. Your spirit should be for six and Allah created Adam on the sixth day, and once six comes into your conscious you have sixty, six in your conscious. When you're conscious of the purpose that G_d made for you on this earth, then you are sixty. And when you are sixty degrees in your conscious, you're ready to take responsibility for the garden. The garden is the whole, good earth, life.

Prophet Muhammed said that Friday is the best day of the year. It is the day Allah made or created Adam, and He created Adam on a pattern of sixty arm spans. So, that six has to go into the conscious. The science, the understanding, has to dawn in the conscious, then you become sixty degrees in the mind, and you're ready then to accept responsibility for society, for your role, your part, in keeping, preserving, advancing, and progressing the society. Mr. Fard said, "Mathematics is Islam and Islam is mathematics, and we can prove it in no limit of time". He said, "What is one?" One is the first number, or the first figure in counting, in numerals, but what is it for the spiritual philosopher, or scientist in Al-Islam, or in religion? One is a symbol that takes our mind, firstly, to G_d. G_d is one. And what about this one is so suitable for the discussion of G_d, or the theology of G_d? One is infinity. It is eternal and all things are depending on One to have their existence. You cannot have two until you first have a concept of one, and any of the numbers beyond that.

The World That Man Did Not Make

Hear what the bigger world, the world bigger than man or the world that man did not make, hear what it has to say. Natural phenomenon, pictures talk. The sky view, the clouds, the night view, the returning day, the positions of the moon, the positions of the sun, the lower position of the moon, the higher position of the sun, picture views talk. The sun rising to a higher position is defended on more than one account. Firstly, the sun puts light on matters not seen in the dark, and again, the sun fires up production. When the sun is shining on a garden and the sunlight is bright and hot, the production of beans is much greater, not only beans, but other crops as well. The sun lifts the human spirit, and then the sun sets for a well-deserved rest, and what is the picture talk? It is rest. The sun rests upon its labor. The sun has labored from dawn to sunset, and it has fed not only the mouth, but it has fed, also, the spirit and it takes its rest. It fed the body and the spirit, and it takes its rest, a well-deserved rest, I repeat, because all the daylight time it was laboring. This is speaking of the sun with the voice of the poet, with the voice of the philosopher, or with the voice of the singer, who speaks of the sun rolling around in heaven all alone… To go up hill is not easy and to roll downhill too fast is dangerous. The sun has a great message. It goes up and then it goes down. It seems to be rising slowly, and it seems to set fast. Once it gets close to the earth it seems to set fast. That is the time you can speed up a little bit, when the fall is not too long. But it goes down slowly, and when it gets near the earth it quickly goes to its rest.

G_d's Handiwork

There is great guidance that the natural world of natural phenomena imparts to the curious and thinking person who was thinking not on himself, thinking not from the glory of man, but thinking of the wonders of creation. That kind of thinking produced what is called philosophers. It produced what is called seers. It even produced what is called Prophets. In Scriptures, we have Prophets saying that they study G_d's Handiwork. I am using the exact words in Scripture that they used, i.e., handiwork. It means a work that they thought that G_d's controls have brought about, and they said that work, itself, brought them to see G_d.

They believed that this could not have happened in such a marvelous way to speak to the human soul, mind, and spirit, and make the human mind and human life so resourceful and so productive that they said, "This could not have happened without there being an Intelligence bigger than man bringing it about." That is the thinking. I repeat, the philosophers from home, in this world, got the sciences and that is speaking of Prophets who brought the great religions to earth for us.

This World Is Nothing But Deception

Allah says, in the Qur'an, *"This world is nothing but ghurur"*, and it means that which appears to be what it's not, deception. It is decorated with allurements that attract you and are so attractive it blinds you to its defects. The philosophers in Al-Islam, they say all of this (the objective world) is unreal. You get but a few followers. The rest of the people believe it, go wild, and go crazy. All this is unreal. That is not what it means. It is real in the context of man's perception and understanding of himself and his environment. It's real, but if you want to put it in Scripture, it is unreal, because, in the Scripture, a tree is not talking about that tree out there. It is not talking about that moon that you see at night. It is not talking about the sun that you see rising and setting. All these things are nothing but symbols in religious language, symbols that represent something that is in my spiritual world, in my psyche universe. Am I clear? I am clear to myself, but I want to know if I am clear to you. So, we are to understand that G_d created all these physical pictures and objects to communicate to us the makeup of our own soul, spirituality, and psyche. That is His language, this universe. His language is addressing the nature of our souls, our spirituality, our psyche, and our life, if we understand it, because this is the real life, not that out there.

The Higher Level of Islamic Expression

I enjoy expressing these things very much. It is philosophical, but that's the higher level of Islamic expression. Islamic expression is reasoning, insight, and love for knowledge. The love for knowledge, if it is in the philosophical person to please Allah, first, then Allah advances the knowledge of the philosopher. The history of Al-Islam is not just the history of Prophets and Imams. It is the history, also, of philosophical thinkers. In fact, when it says, thinker, it says, "dhakir, think", and that the male is a thinker. It is saying that the philosophers were those who appreciated and loved knowledge, and they were able to lead man to a deeper and richer way of thinking and reasoning. So, Al-Islam has its philosophers, and it has its Islamic philosophy. So, there are many good philosophers. Khalil Jibran, he was poetic, but he was also a philosopher, and many others. Rumi was a philosopher.

"And We Would Not Have Found Our Paths If You Had Not Guided Us"

This world, this reality, is very, very strange. It's not easy to know the real reality, and that's with everything, and it is much bigger than we think it is. But the people of Scripture they knew. They mentioned things like human life and compared it to sand and compared it to dust and different things of the outer world. So, they knew the outer world was designed by G_d to show us our reality, and to even show us that that we can't see of our reality. So, it gave us guidance or light that would bring us to study our reality as a science, as a scientist, scientifically, to look for scientific guidance and answers. *"And we would not have found our paths if You had not guided us" (Qur'an).* So, we couldn't get it, we couldn't find the paths of the sciences. That's what it is talking about, the paths of knowledge, science, astronomy, mathematics, and all these other sciences. "We couldn't have arrived at this if You didn't guide us". And so, the great Seers and Prophets, they saw the need for the mind to meet the matter. Mind and matter must meet and come to a workable relationship where the intelligence, the mind, and heart are working with the matter, the material universe, and they saw that. And when they saw that, they gave credit to Whoever designed this universe for opening up the matter to them, so they would find the paths of the sciences, or the pathways of the sciences.

G_d Is Going to Give You Pure Virgins

We're told in the Qur'an and taught by the Prophet Muhammed, too, that in the next world we shall have mates pure and compatible. They will be mates pure and compatible, of like nature. They will be like our own nature. So, if I'm devoted to solving issues for humanity, I should have a wife like that. It may not be in this world, but the next, at least in the next one. *"And they shall have "huri'ain, and they shall have big, wide eyes, open eyes, bright, big, wide, open eyes"* (Qur'an). That's what comes when you have "Huri, freedom", when the intellect is free. It is not talking about any flesh and blood women. No, it's talking about the interest you'll take and the issues you'll engage, and they will be of your nature. Isn't that wonderful? Isn't that what we want? Yes, but the world denies you a chance. The world doesn't want to see you develop this that you want to develop, or to have children by this interest; then man has to suffer until the day comes, the Hereafter. So, that's what it's talking about. When seventy virgins are mentioned, seven is the figure that's used for the hidden sciences.

Whatever Allah says in Qur'an, it is true to your mind that is uneducated and true to the mind that is educated in the language of revelation. It has to be true in both. So, if G_d says He is going to give you pure virgins, He means that the pure ones will get pure virgins. You probably cannot handle seventy of them, but it says seventy. Now, that is the part you need interpreted, but not the virgins. You are going to get some virgins down here. It (Qur'an) says, *"The virgin man is worthy of the virgin woman, and the virgin woman is worthy of the virgin man"*. But we know on this sensual level, that is the cheapest reward. The more expensive reward is on the level of the translation and interpretation. *"The Hereafter is more valuable, more precious, both in quantity and in quality"*. This is G_d's Word in Qur'an.

Perception From the Sky

He is going to give us from the sky. Will it be these metals that fall from the sky? No. What is He going to give us from the sky? He is going to give us something to govern our appetites. He is going to fulfill our appetites from the earth for us to survive our appetites. Don't you know man has to survive his own appetites? His appetites will kill him, and his appetites will get him killed, because if he wants what I have, I might kill him. You know that many of you. If he wants something without bothering me, he might kill himself consuming too much or consuming the wrong thing. So, it is not talking about the earth giving or fulfilling that, our appetites. What is He going to give us from the sky? He is going to give us perception. Those who are students should write that down. The clear perception that will free the life down on earth is the perception we get from the skies.

The Arab quote says, "The night has a thousand eyes and the day but one". This one is talking about the sun, and the thousand is talking about the stars. Actually, we know it is more than a thousand, but he said that just to make a picture, a comparison. The night has eyes means the night has light, and when you understand those lights, it will open your eyes to a bigger reality. So, it is the heavens that open our eyes to the bigger reality. We will never know this system of matter unless we study the sky, and you cannot see the sky until the sun has gone. The sun sets, darkness prevails, and then we can see on a clear night when there are no clouds in the lower heavens. We can see a big space up there. That right away tells us that space is much bigger than our space down here. Any common person knows that, and so many lights. The farther you look, the deeper you go, you still see signs of more lights behind those lights. They invented the telescope, and it revealed many lights that we couldn't see or reach with our eyes. They made the telescope powerful enough to see beyond what we can see, and even the telescope reaches its end, and it is just like the eye sees. There are more lights behind the lights that it cannot see too well.

We know that we cannot reach the end of the lights. We cannot reach the end of space. Man has progressed to this degree. He has progressed in science and technology, but he cannot give anybody on earth a map of the universe, because he is steadily tuning his glass to see farther and farther away, and every time he gets a high-powered glass to see farther away, he is seeing more stars. He doesn't know the end of it, so he cannot give us a map of this reality. He cannot give us a map of the creation, itself, and some of you want to see the ends of G_d to see where G_d starts and stops. First, see where His world starts and stops that you are living on, living in. You cannot see that, and none of your highest scientists can see that. The United States cannot see that. It cannot give us a map of the universe. It can only give us a map of what is known to them, to science so far. That is a reality that ought to humble you and stop you from asking disrespectful questions of G_d, disrespecting your G_d, asking stupid questions.

Creation Uses the Scientist As a Tool to Express Itself

The philosopher, the thinker, was before the exact sciences, or the true sciences. I don't know why we call them the true sciences. These are not true sciences. He (the scientist) is a true tool of creation and that is all he is. He is a tool of creation. He thinks he is making some creation (invention), and it is using him to express itself and give itself to more people. He is nothing but a tool of creation, and the proof of it is the creation says, "Don't use your brain, just watch me. Just keep digging into me and studying me. Just look at what I have inside of me and share it with others."

So, we should also be identifying with what the West does. If we say we are members in the Abrahamic faith, Abraham was the son of Adam. So, you start with Abraham, the son of Adam, which means we have to be in the Abrahamic faith. We have to accept him, too, as a legitimate creation of G_d. And if we are the children of Abraham, then we should be for enlightenment, education, science, for knowledge and everything, and we should not be cutting out anybody. Abraham was leader for all people, father of all the nations. So, to me that is where the substance is, and we should identify with that substance and not just say we are the children of Abraham, a man of faith and leave it vague. He was more than a man of faith. He was a man of faith and logic. He brought the two to be reconciled.

Everybody Is Born a Muslim

They connect but not directly, because the identity that is given to us as Muslim, according to the Prophet Muhammed, that identity belongs to everybody, because he said everybody is born a Muslim. So, it is not just our identity, because we claim it by faith. It is everybody's nature and everybody's identity. I believe it is introduced in the Qur'an to be introduced to mankind, because after all, he is a mercy to mankind, not just to Muslims. I believe what it is saying is this. Here, you call yourself bashar, which means mortal human being. All these names are good. However, bashar does not say that your nature is an accord with the Will of G_d. But if you are a peacemaker and that is your inherent nature to want peace and make peace, now you are in accord with the Will of G_d. Bashar just refers to skin, that human beings are sensitive creatures. They have feelings of love, rejection, hate and whatever. They register pain, pleasure, kindness, and cruelty. That is all bashar says. Nevertheless, that is the good news bringer. He is a bashir. Why? Because if he does not register anything, he is finished. If he is not alive, he is not human.

So, bashar, means a mortal person that registers pleasure, pain, cruelty, goodness. It means he is a humanly sensitive person. That is how we would say it, and there are different names, but G_d, when He gave us our distinctions, He said, "ins". *"He neither created the jinn or ins, except for His worship"*. Ins is another Arabic term for human. Insaan means a human being, a human person, and that word is akin to, nas, people plural, and the human beings' sociability, or tendency to want to congregate and be with each other, have activities together, and share the burden of society together. It is a very important term for man. The language of the Qur'an refers to the ins, and the jinn. They are called a group, and it says if all the jinn could get together and the men could get together as to separate groups that identifies them as sociable creatures, or gregarious creatures, creatures who want to congregate, want to be with one another, that group together. You know that is the nature, or tendency. It is identifying the tendency in the nature to want to group together.

Jinn and Men Created for Service to G_d's Will and Plan

So, it describes both jinn and men (humans) as being of that nature, tending to want to socialize or group together, and G_d says He did not create that creature for any purpose other than His worship. That means service to His Will and Plan for human life. I understand that to be a projection not just a statement. It means this tendency in you that G_d created you with is going to, eventually, bring you together, and is going to be stronger than any other tendency in your life. G_d had a plan for it to bring you to your judgment, and it is going to eliminate these weaker tendencies that you have that take you away from G_d. That is the way I understand it. When the word, Muslim, is used it should relieve the Muslim who accepts that identity, who feels comfortable with that identity as his own inheritance, or as his own true self or true nature. Mr. Fard asked, "Who is your own self? Your own self is a righteous

Muslim." He did not say a black man. He did not say a member of the human race. He said, "And what is my own self? My own self is a righteous Muslim." So, obviously, he had insight. To me, he must have had that insight.

The Lord of All the Systems of Knowledge

Science gave us the term, human. But science had no real belief in educating the public, mankind or the publics of nations, until they saw what Scripture was saying. So, everything they have that is really important for establishing and progressing society, if you want to understand it, they got direction from Scripture. I am convinced of that. So, human is a man of the soil. Scripture says, *"G_d made Adam from the earth."* Man of the ground, that is what a human is, a man of the earth, and that is Adam. They are therefore saying the same thing Scripture says. You see, the little people come out, then the big people get afraid asking, "Where are they going to take this? We have to prepare the world to protect itself against these newcomers, these young boys taking things out of order, or causing problems for the order that we have established!" So, then they come out and they might like you, but they fear you, too, because they do not know where you may go. They then come out with the light that they did not show before, and if you notice that language that I have used, it is not long before they come out and turn the light on. They see me talking about nature. They hear me, in my language, saying that our schools should include the support we get from the natural creation for education, etc. So, they came out, not so long ago, and said that science and religion are coming together. I said, *"G_d has made everything to broadcast knowledge and mercy".* That is the Qur'an. But I'm saying it and explaining it, too, doing a kind of commentary, tafsir, on it. They get that and they say, "This guy is going to get too much recognition. Let us turn the light on."

They try to keep us from getting the credit, because they know the wise, they are going to respect what we're saying. I spoke over in Malaysia and that is when I first shared it with the public. I had said it among us, but that was the first time that I shared it with the public, my translation, *"Lord of all the worlds"* and at that gathering where they had me speaking to them, I said it is more than Lord of all the worlds. That could just be the one who has the power over all the worlds, but I said, it is Lord of all the systems of knowledge. Many of their scientists were in this audience, and one, he stood up and he said, "Imam Mohammed, I just want to thank you very much for the insight. I never thought of it that way." That is what he told me. You could see the enthusiasm and the appreciation for what I said. You could see it in his face. His face and voice registered that.

Science Borrowed From Religious Language

When they talk about distances in miles, after a while the perceptions of time measurement become burdensome, especially when they're talking about the distances of planets or galaxies from one another. So, to make it easy they say light years. But where do they get that language from, light years? Light is also wisdom and knowledge, so to understand it outside of this science borrowed it from religious language. In fact, they borrowed most of what they have from religious language.

That expression, light years, it helps us understand how to see a year with G_d in comparison with a year with man. Man bases his time measurement on the movement of physical things, objects. The sun is a physical object, and it starts in the morning, dawn, goes and sets, and that is a certain amount of time; and when it comes back and shows again, it is one day, twenty-four hours roughly. So, this is how man measures time, and we survive one winter and now we're ready for spring, and good times and work. Comfortable temperatures are going to end, and we will start winter all over again. That is a year but look at what has happened. These are physical pictures of changes in the man's life, but what about an idea? How long will it take it to materialize, to bring about the changes which that idea has the potency to bring about? That is a light year with G_d.

The light bulb is a perfect picture for explaining how ideas work. One idea lights up the area for you to see other ideas. It depends upon how clear the idea is. If it is too opaque, it is not going to give you much light. It is not going to show you too many things. But the more transparent it is you are now talking about light. People think light is white. No, heated up pieces of substance, certain substances won't even burn white. Only certain substances burn and heat up white, but light is not white. If it was white, you could not see. Pure light is transparent. They also say, and I think Einstein is responsible for this, the whole universe bends. They even say light bends because matter, the whole universe, bends, everything bends. But when you see clouds separate and seem to have small openings after darkness and a heavy rain, you see color bending. That is the rainbow, but you see light going straight. Light does not bend. It goes straight. Have you ever seen the beams coming down through the clouds? They come perfectly straight. They are not bent.

Nothing Has Advanced Man More Than Language

If you understand the Qur'an, it says Jesus Christ is a Word and a Spirit from G_d. So, in other words, he is nothing but language and an influence, and what influences the course of civilization more than language? Just think about it for a minute or so.

Nothing has advanced man in this material world more than language. If you don't have language, you can't advance. The most primitive, backward, societies that exist today, they have the most undeveloped languages. Those languages that have engaged the external reality and man's own reality, those are the languages that have become universal, and they are the languages that carry light, and move man into civilization. So, it is the Word.

Everything That Man Has Achieved In Him Already

Jesus Christ makes it very plain. The Bible says: *"In the beginning was the Word"*. *"Before the foundations of the world I am, I existed"*. That is the Bible. He had to exist, first, to materialize the knowledge, so that we will have foundations for the world. If you could understand it, if you could get this picture and not have it stress you out or confuse you, all that man has achieved in the world or on this earth is nothing but an unfolding of what was in him already, everything. G_d gave man a mental appetite for everything in creation, and then how he engages matter, responds to it, and reproduces it, is what has given us all that we have. So, the advancement of knowledge and science, the evolution of it, or the advancement of it, is focused as a human person.

When we look at the human person we see, by way of interpretation, or translation, the future creation, the world that we see now of man and his productions. We see the whole environment of man, for he is a physical body, but look at where he comes from. Look at where that material body started. It started in something that you can't even see with your physical eyes. The more it grows towards its destination, or its maturity, its fulfillment for its own growth and development, the more complex it gets and the more productive it gets. It starts with a germ you can't even perceive. You cannot see it with your physical eye. As far as your physical eye is concerned, if you question the physical eye and say, "Does he exist, yet?" The physical eye will say, "No, I can't find it anywhere!" But he already exists in a germ and the germ, like a seed, if it is placed in the right environment where it can rest and be comfortable and not disturbed by anything, it starts to grow in that environment, and turns out to be a complete structure, a human person, and delivered from the computer or from the factory there, called the mother, a full person. Then when that full person comes into the world, it starts feeding on everything it can reach, and then a world that had no visibility either starts coming into form.

Philosophy Had to Come Before Science

So actually, the human person was a condition that was to happen before even the world could be formed or have existence. I'm not talking about the world G_d made that was out there long before humans. I'm talking the world that counseled us, the world of man, not the world that G_d made. The world that G_d made is nothing but food for man, and He says He made the world for man. For His human creation He made the whole world, and He didn't create man for any purpose greater than the purpose of His Mercy. What is His Mercy for? His Mercy is to relieve the burden on life. What life? Human life. There is no burden on any other life. Other life is not even aware of burden. Everything that hurts them they think it was necessary. It was expected consequences. But man, questions consequences and asks, "Why did this happen?" And "I believe I can change this". This is philosophy. This is religious or Scriptural philosophy. But philosophy had to come before science. There was no possibility for science to develop before philosophy developed. Man had to first fall in love with the creation, with G_d's Handiworks, and extract from what he was engaging direction for his own intelligence and for his heart; then when he was able to do that, pretty soon, he caused the material world to open up and reveal its hidden nature, or its hidden operations that he didn't see readily. He had to have experiments, etc., to see the inner workings of the material reality.

"G_d Is a Hidden Treasure"

So, if he had not fallen in love with G_d, he would not have fallen in love with knowledge, and if he had not fallen in love with knowledge, he would not have fallen in love with G_d; and if he had not fallen in love with something external, beyond himself, he would never have gotten the pure sciences. This is all truth. And they say, *"We would not have found our paths if You had not directed us to them."* That is in the Qur'an. In Qur'anic Arabic it is: *"Wa qad hadaana subulanaa"*. The philosopher says, "G_d is a Hidden Treasure, and He created man because He wanted to be discovered". Does G_d have an ego like humans, like men, that He wants to be known for His High Value, or Divine Existence? No. Why does He want to be discovered, and why did the philosopher say He was a treasure?

The Human Mind Pictured As Abraham

It is because the human mind, pictured as Abraham, searched the existing world of reality to make sense of it, and concluded that this is one system of logic. It is not in conflict with itself. That tells me that it could not have happened without a purpose and without it being designed that way, because I am a mind, I am human, and this world feeds my mind and has fed my mind and shown me its unity. So, my conclusion is there must be a living Reality behind it that is of a different nature and superior to it that caused it to exist, and He did it all for the human, for His creation, so it would advance and have comforts unimaginable. So, we have the expression, "He created man expressly for His Mercy".

I had this idea, even when I was a young minister. Long before I came to this development I'm in now, I had this mind... and I reflected right away, when I started thinking this way, on the so-called primitive people and how the Indians and some other primitive people have tried to show the evolution of man and put creatures on a totem pole showing a progression for life; that all these lives are in one stream, or in one progression. This is a picture or diagram of something showing man's existence with all these other creatures, and man ascends highest on the pole.

The World Has No Real Purpose Without Man

So, philosophically thinking (and that's my nature to think that way), this is a forward step, or progression that eventually unfolds in the exact sciences. So, I'm a man, and I think, and I have more freedom to think and there are more possibilities for me as a freethinker than it is for any other life that exists. I am made of the world. My living body is made of the world. It came from the world that G_d created, and then my mind is influenced by the world G_d created, and it comes to life and starts to form and grow because of its feeding on the life that G_d created. I eat chicken, and when I eat it, it has a chance to rise high, to the highest possibility for flesh or matter, when it enters my matter. When he becomes a part of my matter, now, he is in a situation that lifts him up to the highest possibility for living things. Can't you see how it is justified that G_d give us these things and that He says He created man for the world and the world for man?

The world has no real purpose without man, and man has no real purpose without the world. So, if we look to make sense of things, we can do it much better than anybody that is trying to do it without the Guidance of G_d. In fact, we are the only ones that can do it. Now, you tell me I eat, and what I eat makes, replenishes, my cells in my body. So, you tell me this body is not chicken? This body is chicken, fish, lamb, vegetables, oxygen, hydrogen, etc. This is everything that comes into my body. So, if G_d crowns the creation with me, everything has been crowned or lifted into the seat, the throne, because of my existence.

If you can't follow that line of reasoning, then look at it this way. They can't appreciate each other, and they can't appreciate their own existence, but G_d has created me to appreciate myself and all of them in a framework. That is wonderful and beautiful! Actually, their reality remains low until man engages them in his thinking. Even if we can't see the material proof that these things have not been put down, but they have been put on earth to be lifted up once they enter man, at least see that by themselves they have no real exciting existence, or glory. But when they come into the life of man and become a part of his world, they are raised up in importance and value. Their meaning becomes so much greater. So, everything is fed into the higher and that is intelligent man, and man is consuming all of them, whether he takes them physically into his body or not. With his intelligence he's consuming all of them. So, that concept becomes much more important once man brings their concepts into his vision, or into his reading of matter and the world, then they become so much more important, but that is real.

Whatever We Consume Becomes a Part of Us

Whatever you consume, if it is consumed by your flesh, it becomes your flesh. The reason why we can't eat pig is because we digest pig with our mind, our intelligence, but we can't eat the flesh. The Muslim can't eat the flesh of the pig, or the hog. That has to do with psychology and moral interest. In the history of his progress as a civilizer, man once ate with little moral discretion. He was hungry, so he killed something and tore the hide off it. They eat it raw. He saw something and he was hungry. If he smelled it and thought it wouldn't kill him, he ate it. That is how he survived. But the moral nature in him grew as he grew. As he interacted with the world, it grew to become so strong that he could not stomach his past behavior. Now, he wants to wash it up. He wants to clean it, and he doesn't even want to eat it raw. He wants to cook it. So, he rises to a level of moral insight, and moral discretion, and he looks at a thing that just arouses disgust in him. The behavior is disgusting. Pig behavior, pig sound, is disgusting, and he says to himself, "If I accept this thing into my life as a support for my life, and I continue to kill and eat it, it is going to affect my moral nature and my human sensitivities. It is going to affect me, psychologically, that I don't like to pass gas in the presence of people eating around me. But this thing passes gas even in the face of the other pig that is eating with it and makes all these nasty sounds. If I eat that thing, it is going to affect me, psychologically." Now, I know there are societies that are really bad, but I think the most shameless society you can find on this planet earth is the American people. You go among those who are less developed, and they don't have these nasty habits, do they?

Jesus Christ Is the Son of Light and Sciences In the World

Those who fixed up the Bible, they had respect for the Word of G_d and for people, human life and conditions, but really, they never said that pig was good to eat. That was the Church interpreting it that way, that Jesus Christ said, *"Behold! I make everything new"*. Making everything new doesn't mean that everything is fit to put in your mouth! A new rat shouldn't be eaten! A new pig is still a pig, but before he was only a pig. Now, if you understand the science of Jesus Christ, how he is the son of light and sciences in the world, now, when he shines on a pig, it is no more a pig, physically. A pig is a pig as a body of knowledge, or science. So, that is the newness of the pig. The intelligence has been advanced, lifted up, and raised so that it doesn't see only a pig. It sees sciences in the skin, hair, bones, life germs of the pig. And then he gets science and finds that this is a pig, but it will heal this disease, or help this condition in man, as medicine from the pig. That is the newness and making everything new. He raises the value of everything previously perceived, because it is no more just a physical animal. It is an embodiment of knowledge and science.

Everything Created to Broadcast Knowledge and Mercy

The Qur'an says, *"Allah caused everything He created to broadcast knowledge or science, and mercy."* Did mercy come to society before science? Only a little bit. But when the knowledge or science came to society, then great relief came to man, just a whole new possibility for life, comfort, freedom from sickness, or diseases, or pain. Transportation, itself, look at how it has reduced the pain that people had to undergo to travel to their relatives who lived thousands of miles away, or less. But with the modern transportation that has all been brought about because of man's brain digesting what it engages, and then reproducing it for the benefit of society, knowledge and mercy, in the whole creation. Everything in it, a speck of dust, no matter how small the material reality is, it all communicates knowledge, or science and mercy.

That is the strongest urge in the soul and intelligence of people. A lot of them don't register it, because they are so taken by other things of less importance in their environmental circumstances. So, they never are really turned on as an intelligent being, or organism, that wants to make sense of things, of what it is exposed to, or what is exposed to it. But for those who find or are situated to start developing that way, the greatest urge in them is to do just that, make sense of things. When babies come here, girls and boys, it is obvious, right away. As soon as they get here, they have an interest in what their eyes have opened upon. The mother will be holding them, and they will be picking the skin, wanting to know what this is, and they don't know that the eye is very sensitive. Sometimes, they will be picking at it and the mother has to pull their hand away, because they are going to stick their hand right under the eyelid where the eye is. They are going to touch that because they want to know.

The First Appetite Is to Eat Mentally

So, the first appetite in human life is not an appetite to fulfill your physical needs, to eat physically. It is the appetite to eat mentally, and that is the meaning of Adam, that He created, the first man. Adam, meaning the first man, was the man that wanted to make sense of the world he was exposed to including himself. So, G_d said, *"He taught him the names of all the things"*, then the Devil came up and offered him an apple. All the animals know to go to the physical things and eat. That is no big deal. But the human is made to go to the physical thing and eat it with his mind, not with his physical mouth, and teeth, etc. Things must make sense to satisfy the human soul.

Chapter 17

The Nation of Islam

I will begin by saying the Nation of Islam was built by the Honorable Elijah Mohammed and its blueprint was given to him from a Muslim from overseas whose name was W. Fard Muhammad, also called W. D. Fard. It is important for us to know that Mr. Fard was interested in all African Americans, and that he came from a people of India, who were also under British rule; and many of the Indians who were under British rule, their skin color was black, not black people as we know, but their skin color was definitely black. They range from white to black, and I mean the whitest of white and blackest of black. The northern Indians are a white color, and they have mixed all together now. The Indians who lived in the hotter zones are black in skin color.

Mr. Fard had dark color. He was not very white-skinned. He was brown-skinned and when he came to America, he experienced some discrimination. I think what he experienced in his own country of India under the British with his people there, and what he saw and experienced when he came to America had something to do with him accepting to assist African American people in the ghetto with their lives. He came to Detroit, Michigan, to the black bottom or the poor area of the African American or black people's community, and he began preaching or teaching of separation from white people and having your own. He told the Honorable Elijah Mohammed and other African Americans who he preached to or spoke with that the African Americans in America, the blacks, had a great past, that they came from an Islamic past and they should return to their religion. So, that gives you an idea of how it all started. It is important also to know that Mr. Fard had all African American's interest at heart. He said that there were approximately seventeen millions of us existing when he came and that was around 1931, and in his esoteric language or preaching, which is a kind of occult language, a secret language, he said that he had 17 million keys to unlock or free black people.

Some Teachings of the Nation of Islam Not Meant to be Followed

What I was told not to do I did not do it, until I found out it was not meant for me to follow it. That was some part of the teachings. It was not meant to be followed the way we thought it was meant to be followed. In fact, it was not meant to be followed at all. It was just something that was given to us to steer us in a certain direction without curiosities. You know, maybe other nationalities, or ethnic groups, weren't left in the dark to search for reality, but we certainly were, when you think how we were separated from Africa, separated from our past life and history, and then raised by people who rejected us as humans. So, we were left with strong curiosities. Why? Why? Why? And Mr. Fard, he had the wisdom to give us something that we would buy, because we were so starved for answers that respected our own picture of ourselves, or our own appreciation for ourselves as humans with value.

So, he had the wisdom to come among us, especially the uneducated ones. He did not go to the educated ones. In fact, he condemned the educated ones. He used to call them the ones who were with the blood suckers of the poor. I think that was kind of harsh and extreme, because he copied the strategy... I wouldn't say the strategy, but he copied the issues. He took from the issues and made it a strategy, the issue of the black man being rejected, and the white man being depicted as a G_d, or the son of G_d. Father Divine, he reacted to that by calling himself divine, father, and divine, and I read his words. He told his congregation, "If you want to see Christ Jesus look at me."

Blacks' Problem Was Confused and Denied Identity

So, Mr. Fard knew the issue was confused identity and denied identity. The real identity that G_d wants us to have, we were denied that. That is the human identity in its excellence, not three fifths of a human, the whole human. He had the wisdom to take these things, i.e., Dubois' emphasis on getting inside, asserting your rights to be included, to be a part of this nation with rights. He was the one who paved the way for the NAACP (W.E. B. Dubois). A lot of people don't know that now. So, Mr. Fard, without going back to them (the educated African Americans), condemned them, because he didn't want anybody coming in and confusing what he had set up for the ignorant African Americans. He had set up a plan to guide us where we could get our answers, get the answers we wanted, and educated African Americans would laugh and ridicule a lot of the things that were in that plan, that strategy, like the so-called teachings of the history of the black man dating back 25,000 years, and all of that being renewed every 25,000 years. The educated would say, "All this is made up stuff!" So, he did not want them coming in there.

They Appreciated Themselves As Decent, Intelligent Human Beings

So, a man who never read anything else, any other story of how creation started, he was not taught, he was ignorant. So, he buys it right off, and he's not going to argue with the man that said, "You're beautiful and you're powerful." The other man said,

"You're ugly, akin to the monkey and the ape, and you're weak and sinful." He was happy to hear that one who said, "No" to that kind of stuff and said, "Yes" to the appreciation that they really already had. They appreciated themselves as human beings and as intelligent, decent, forward moving human beings in their minds and intellect. They were already that, even though still slaves. Frederick Douglass is the truth, and he is just one. And if the one who founded the A.M.E. African Methodist Episcopal Church, Richard Allen, came out of slavery and founded a church, he couldn't have been culturally deprived. Though he was a slave, he had something. He was studying something, if it wasn't any more than the white man that gave him education. That man wasn't stupid. He was educated. So, Mr. Fard, knowing all that said, "All I have to do is put the best of what I see in them and their history, put the essence of it in my work and direct the spirit of these people to want to remove darkness wherever it is in their way". That is what he did, and he was successful.

The Honorable Elijah Mohammed Had Interest In All Black People

When I was questioned by some investigators from the intelligence department here in the United States just before the passing of the Honorable Elijah Mohammed, during the time I was put out of the community, they investigated me and told me, "We know that your father, Elijah Mohammed, does not only help Muslims. We know that he helps other black people as well. He has even given charity to some black Christians." This is what I was told by them, but I know from my own experience with the Honorable Elijah Mohammed, as his son and a minister preaching for the Nation of Islam under his leadership, he also had the interest of all black people, not just those who were Muslim. What I mean by that is this: He did not see Muslims only benefitting from his teaching. He saw all black people benefitting from his teaching.

That brings me to the direction that I have taken as the leader upon the passing of the Honorable Elijah Mohammed, in February of 1975. The Honorable Elijah Mohammed had set up an organization or had been successful at establishing an organization that included religion, preaching, schools, education, and strong, great, emphasis on building business for African American people. His economic blueprint, called by different names, had farmland and businesses, and the cities that he hoped would be supported by farmland, such as grocery stores selling meats and whatever. So, the Honorable Elijah Mohammed's vision was not small in any way. His vision was community vision, and community vision is what Al-Islam is all about. Al-Islam addresses us as community and asks us to accept responsibility for community life. So, the Honorable Elijah Mohammed was really Islamic in his programs and in his designing of his programs. Al-Islam requires that Muslims belong to community life and that they are about establishing their own identity as a community. So, that has been the direction that I have followed.

Encouraged to Be a Free Thinker

Also, it might be said that I have differed so much with the Honorable Elijah Mohammed's teachings and with his programs that I have been charged as the one who did away with or destroyed his programs. Well, that is not correct. But I am the one who changed the thinking of his following and thank G_d for the help that I received to do that. You may be surprised to know that the biggest help I got to do that came from the Honorable Elijah Mohammed. He always encouraged me to be a man of Scripture and not the Bible, but the Qur'an. He always encouraged me to be a free thinker. He did not hold me to the thinking of the Nation of Islam. He told his followers, especially his leaders, "He is not going to preach like the rest of you. He is going to be different. He is going to use the Qur'an." So, the Honorable Elijah Mohammed prepared his leaders to accept me in my different posture that I took. I took a different posture or stand from the Nation of Islam in that I came to establish Islam as given in the Qur'an.

This then was not easy to understand, the movement from Mr. Fard and the Honorable Elijah Mohammed to my leadership, if you do not see it as a strategy. Mr. Fard planned to introduce the Qur'an and real Islam in America, but he knew blacks were militant and angry with whites. So, he sought the angry, dissatisfied ones and they were receptive and received his teachings. Consequently, he planted among them the Qur'an. However, he did not encourage the Honorable Elijah Mohammed, his ministers, or leaders to preach it, but told them that it was the pure, holy book, the book without defect or errors. He pointed to that book only in that way. He did not point to his esoteric teachings. He never gave his esoteric teachings the kind of sacred respect he gave the Qur'an.

"Take Good Care of the New Arrival"

So, in time, he prayed and hoped that I would be the one he said would become an assistant to my father and help do the work. He hoped. At that time, I was just in my mother as a fetus. He left right after I was born, in the early part 1933. I was in my mother's womb. On October 30, of 1933 I was delivered, I was born. Mr. Fard was still in touch with the Honorable Elijah Mohammed and my mother and the small community that he started, and he sent my mother a message saying, "Take good care of the new arrival", meaning me. Then he was gone.

Coming back to the present time, I definitely have always had an interest in all African American people, in human beings, period, but mostly in African American people. What should be expected of me other than that? It should be expected of me that I would have the interest of all African American people at heart. We have a spiritual life together as well as a racial life together. Racially, we know we're tied together, because we all came from Africa, originally, and we're called black people. We have a history coming from slavery to the present time, liberated, or a free people who have been included in the American citizenry and in the American society, American life. You know we said in one convention, "We cannot stop now!" That is what I just said. With the light on, we have to build the leadership for Islam in America, but we're doing it for the whole world.

The Liberator Fortunate to Be Put In Favorable Circumstances

During the course of my leadership, I met with more than one president of the United States and other national and international leaders. Again, the doings of G_d in the religious experience of a people who were searching for themselves, wanted to discover where they should be in the world under G_d. People who are searching for their destiny under G_d, if they have had a liberator, I don't want to point to myself in this way, but I have to. If they have had a liberator, he has been fortunate to be put in circumstances where that liberator talks to the top ruler in the land. Joseph, of the Bible, and Yusuf, the same Joseph of the Qur'an, Moses, Muhammed, peace be upon them, you name them, Jesus Christ, etc., anyone who was important for G_d for leading people's lives, they had to meet with the top rulers, because G_d knows the little boy needs to meet with the big men, so he can see what it is to them.

Accepted In the Vatican

Now, my meeting with Pope John Paul II, I thought it was possible, but really, I thought I would be rejected. My thoughts of me being rejected were much stronger than my thoughts that I would be welcomed to the Vatican and be in the presence of the Pope, John Paul II. But I said to myself, "I heard that Reverend Jessie Jackson was the guest of the Vatican once". On the strength of him accepting my friend, the Reverend Jessie Jackson, I said, "I'm going to make a try", and I did. So, I expressed my desire to make a visit there and someone may say, and I can understand the question being asked, "Why would the son of Elijah Mohammed and a Muslim want to go to the Holy Seat, Rome, Italy, the Vatican, and be a guest or a visitor visiting the Pope of Catholicism, of the Catholic Church, or the Catholic world under the Roman Catholic Church?" So, I knew it would be looked at as strange and people would wonder why, but do you know what I said to myself? "If the Honorable Elijah

Mohammed's son is accepted in the Vatican to have an audience with the Pope, the head of the Catholic Church, that is going to make news everywhere, and it is going to say he is different. He does not dislike nor have anything against Christians. He visited the Pope." And it turned out to be much more in it for me than what I thought would be in it for me. It became much more than I expected, but just that alone was enough for me.

I said, "If I could just have it hit the news that I visited the Pope and made the visit there as a Muslim who came in friendship to speak with the Pope and have an audience with the Pope, if it is known, it is going to free my community to move throughout the United States and be more accepted by Christians." It is important. This is a Christian country. It is extremely important that we go in friendship and move friendly through these United States with our Christian brothers and sisters. I know some of our brothers, they openly will befriend us, and they have done that since the time of the Honorable Elijah Mohammed, in the time of Malcolm X, and even more from the Christian Church leadership. One grew up and came up with us. He's been helped by the civil rights movement and asked, "Why did he go to the Vatican?" Well, if there is any question in the minds of our people whether I prefer Catholicism over Protestantism or not, I have to admit the decision could crucify me, because I have one arm going out to one, and the other arm going out to the other. I'll be stretched forever, and the center will never change. The center is the qiblah. The center is Abraham and the house he built. The center is Muhammed and his community. The center is Islam. I don't want to be crucified. I love all good people, and I am no more interested in Catholicism than I am in Protestantism, when it comes to supporting what is right and good.

The Temple of Islam Was a Concept

Mr. Fard said that "In 1929, twenty-three scientists met in the root of civilization concerning the lost found nation and they must return to their own. So, they sent a messenger to teach them of their own." Now, who was that? That was Mr. Fard. The Temple of Islam is really a concept, and it became real and alive for us. So, he gave a concept to us that we brought to life. But with him it does not mean anything like that. He did not mean a physical wall. The temple is all inside the mind, training for the soul, to discipline the soul, the marching and everything, the original salute. As soon as you came in, you were supposed to salute that flag on that board. The original salute, that is not a salute. Salute is a gesture of respect, isn't it? The original respect that you originally had in your nature you have to bring it back out. It is beautiful when you understand it. It is all in the abstract. The concrete is not to be seen as concrete. It is supposed to be seen in the abstract. It is a teaching. Everything is a teaching.

Temple means it is not going to be around here always. When you wake up you are going to leave this. This is just time, tempo, temporary. Christ Jesus, what did he say? *"Destroy this house and I'll put it back together in three days"*. This is just something that you are going to have to destroy, because when you catch on to what is going on, you are going to do away with it. It is going to be too small for your intellect.

Mr. W. D. Fard Started In Homes

Now, he couldn't have put all that together by himself. He said that is what happened, and I believe it. They met overseas and you know the record says when he first began preaching in Detroit, he first started in homes, and do you know how he got in the homes? He was selling silk, yard goods on the street, carrying it on his arm and they did that in Detroit. Even now, I think some Arabs still do it. There is a big Arab population in Detroit, especially Yemenites. He would put the yard goods on his arm and the women would ask him questions about the material. So, he said, "This material is the kind of material you wore, what your people wore before you were brought to America. Most of you come from royal families. You wore silk and long dresses." That is how he got their attention and when he got their attention, he finally asked one of them, "Do you have a home" and they said, "Yes". He asked, "Would you like to hear more of this?" They said, "Yes". I'm telling the story that was told to me. He asked, "Would you like to hear more of this about your people who came from the holy land?" They said, "Yes, we would like to hear more".

So, finally, some Christian sister invited him to come into her home and have meetings, and he had meetings in that home until he collected enough followers and collected enough charity to rent a facility. I understand it was the same way it happened here (in Chicago). Nobody would let them in but the Shriners, Masons. So, they rented from the Masons and Shriners' facilities, and they started. And I was told that he would come on himself and he would speak, first. Then after he would speak for a little while, he would introduce a Japanese man. This was told to me, by one of the pioneer brothers, Edward Ali. He was a captain way back then in those days. He met Mr. Fard and got his name from Mr. Fard. He said he would introduce that Japanese man, and he would just tell them that they need to get on to their own kind right away, because the world is going to change. The end of time is coming.

When the Japanese man finished, then he (Mr. Fard) would come on and would preach. After about a year and a half, he started using my father, and he (Elijah Mohammed) would give the main part of the lecture, not him. He started out, himself, following the Japanese man. He would preach for hours, but he started having my father teach for hours, and he would just introduce him saying, "Hear Elijah." He would not say, "Here". He said, "Hear, hear Elijah!" And he would just greet them and tell them, "Hear Elijah". They say the last time he spoke, it was in Milwaukee and Chicago, and he spoke for a long time, saying, "You won't be seeing me anymore, and when he finished, he said, "Hear Elijah", and left.

Mr. Fard Was Raised As An Ahmadiyyah

I know he didn't have the ability to do all that and I'm sure Muhammed Abdullah was that man, but I don't think he had the ability to put all that together. He had the mind to do it. He most likely, was the one presiding over the meetings. He had the mind to do it, but I'm sure he got help from different ones who were headed into esoteric metaphysics. I think they helped him and I'm sure he had others who had other skills, political, psychology, and different things. I really believe they met and planned how they were going to do this. But I think the main idea of setting up a temple and accusing the white man of being the main trouble for everybody everywhere, the Devil, I think that was him. I believe that was straight from him. He was raised as an Ahmadiyyah, but he turned on them and set up his own thing. In the Fiji Islands, he set up a school, and he taught on his own. He did not make them Ahmadiyyah. He said, "No", and they called him, Master Gee, like we call him, Master Fard. Gee means honorable, reverential. They are not Ahmadiyyah you meet. They have a different mind, but they are his staunch followers. They love that man. They are very strong followers of his. He took me to visit them. He took me there. He took me to the Fiji Islands and introduced me to them, and them to me. They are much like the Nation of Islam followers, very devoted to him, like we were to the Honorable Elijah Mohammed. I plan to go back there. I really want to go back there.

"Like a Pearl That Is Down In the Mud"

The men and women of Fiji, they are big-limbed, strong-bodied. It is really something. I am sure that he did meet with persons, and just like he said, he came to the United States on July the 4th 1930. It is symbolic, 1929 is symbolic. It meant that he came to give us, have us come into independence. That is all it means, because July 4th is Independence Day. So, 1929 means one short of thirty. It did not reach purity yet, but he's going to clean us up. That is what he had in mind, saying,

"I'm going to clean these people up and they are going to be very valuable". He told the Honorable Elijah Mohammed, "They are like a pearl that is down in the mud. All you have to do is pick it up and wash it off".

I am sure that Mr. Fard left Europe and was here for a few years earlier than 1930. And I'm sure that he studied the ghetto in Detroit, and he studied what black leaders were saying. He knew what they were saying, he took it all in, and he tried to incorporate something from each of them. He took the ones who were looking at G_d and divinity, and that was Father Divine. He looked at him and studied his followers to see what they were and how they were having problems with Jesus Christ as a white man, because he (Father Divine) changed it from Jesus Christ is a white man. He said, "If you want to see Jesus look at me". That is what he is recorded to have said. And he was a heavy, strong, black-skinned man. I know he (Mr. Fard) studied W. E. B. Dubois, Booker T. Washington, and he studied the Jamaican, Marcus Garvey. Those are the main ones he studied and especially, Noble Drew Ali. He put the fez on the Fruit of Islam, just like Noble Drew Ali, the same fez. He added the drills of Booker T. Washington, because at Tuskegee, he had drills for all the boys. I think the girls drilled, too. Booker T. Washington explained why he had the drill. It made it easy to discipline them, his students, for work. You know they did vocational work. They built the facilities and everything of bricks that they made themselves.

The Asiatic Black Man

Obviously, Muhammad Abdullah, called Master Fard, he studied all of that, and Noble Drew Ali identified with Islam in Asia. He said we were not Africans; we were Asiatics. So, Mr. Fard used the same thing, the Asiatic black man. Let me tell you something about the word, Asia. In Arabic, it means foundation, "Asia", and a form of the word is in the Qur'an, but it is in there as a word that means foundation, not in there as a country. Asaasa, is from Asia. Asia is Aseya, in Arabic, and asaasa, means structure, foundation. But if you want to stretch your mind a little bit more, Asia is the biggest continent, isn't it? It is possible that man, a long time ago, knew Asia as the biggest continent and instead of the planet being called earth (it is from European language) they probably called the ground, Aseyah, which means foundation. The Qur'an says, *"The foundation that was built upon regardfulness"*. That is in the Qur'an. All these things they are mysteries, or just unknown, but G_d has taken me by a route that I know I am right. I do not want you to believe things that I know you have no basis for, no reference, but what I tell you is true.

Mr. WD-40

They have an oil, now. It is it called, WD-40. They did not name that oil for me. They named it for Mr. Fard, WD-40. WD-40, it is a hint for Fard. They have to express and communicate what has happened, but not to us, to themselves. They have to leave it in the language of themselves where they will be able to get it. If you ask them, they will say "Yes, we finally put Mr. Fard in history. He is a new oil. W. D. Fard, the new oil". Oil means essence. What kind of essence is in this particular language that I am using right now? It means the pure wisdom that reduces friction, and it goes smoothly. It quiets it down, too. It makes no noise. I couldn't die knowing these things. It is impossible for me to let myself die and leave the world. What do I have this for? Am I going to die with it? That is insane. Even though you can't even follow me, I'm going to give it to you anyway.

The Soul Is a Recording Camera

I do not say it to you like this until I know it is right, until I am convinced myself without any doubt, then I speak it. So, it is a mystery. We will never know everything, but to me it is real. It is as rational and real as anything, because I know I am made of the same material that the world is made, and I know my soul is a camera as well as an ear. It hears and then it takes pictures, and I know G_d has made this soul very special. Somebody in my family said, "We know he could not know that about the Qur'an. That old man he was hanging around told him." That old man's eyes lit up when I told him a few things, Muhammed Abdullah. I'm telling you this because I believe you know I am not important. I do not want to be seen. If I thought you wanted to worship me, I would not tell you these things.

Imam Muhammad Abdullah

I wish I had time to do a lot of things that I love to do in the way of compiling literature for Islamic knowledge and Islamic study in the future, en sha Allah (G_d Willing), for presently and in the future, but I don't have any presently. I have one book. It is good I think for teaching beginners how to make the phonetic sounds and how to quickly learn how to recognize the characters, the letters, the Qur'anic Arabic characters, make the sounds correctly, and practice the script, the writing. The book was compiled by my old friend, who passed away several years ago now, Imam Muhammed Abdullah, who was the head of the Islamic Center in San Francisco when I met him, and he was associated with the Ahmadiyyah movement. He, himself, never liked to be called an Ahmadiyyah, but he was born among Ahmadiyyahs. He was raised by them and then went his own way later. He was a friend of my father before he was my friend, a very good friend of my father. When I first met him, he was bringing my father something. My father was sickly at that time with bronchitis and when I first met this man, Muhammed Abdullah, an old man, he was sitting at my father's table when I came from Philadelphia. I was a minister in Philadelphia at the time, and I came to make the regular reports to my father, and this time when I came, he was at the table. My father always had some guests. He hardly ever ate without some guests being at the table. So, I saw him there and he made a point of speaking to me.

Now, I had heard about him. He was in Philadelphia. He had a paper that he had produced. I think it was called, *The Muslim Herald*. He wanted the Philadelphia Mosque to take some of his newspapers. So, he was there. My father said, "Son, the brother came, and he brought me some dried red salmon for my bronchitis condition". He said it would help", and that was that. But later, we got to be good friends and when I, myself, left Oakland, CA (I was the imam there for about three years), I asked him to be the imam there, and the people knew him. They all knew him and most of them had great respect for Muhammad Abdullah, so he became the imam of one of our masjids. An immigrant Muslim became the imam one of our masjids, the Oakland, California Masjid, and later, I think he was voted out. I am not sure whether he was voted out, or he resigned. I think he was voted out. Really, the imam who is there now, he was a about nineteen years old. He was young. I thought he was younger than that when I first saw him in Oakland. He became a student of mine. I mean a devoted student of mine and he learned the language. He could speak it well. He could explain to others, and he became very popular within a few years. You all know him, Imam Shuaibe of Oakland, California. Muhammad Abdullah, he put a book together that was intended for students to learn the vocabulary of Qur'an, but only in practicing the script and it is not to teach us meanings, or to teach translation, not that at all. And I believe it is on tape, too, and these tapes will help.

Imam W. Deen Mohammed's Dream

I had a dream (I don't ever recall dreaming about it before) of my Arabic teacher and Darnell Karim, his sister, Zahirah, and my youngest brother, Akbar. In fact, there were several of us. We are missing maybe two thirds of them. They just got wasted and separated from the Nation of Islam, and from us. Dr. Jamil Diab, I dreamed about him, and when I dreamed about him, I dreamed about my father, too. He was in the dream… I was dreaming of what my father said about Jamil Diab. He said, "He looks like our savior. You see him and look at him, especially when he holds his head down." That is what I was dreaming. I was seeing that in the dream.

You know how dreams are. They are not always in line with reality. I opened my wallet up in the dream, and I pulled out the picture of Muhammed Abdullah when he was younger, and I've seen the picture of him when he was younger, Mr. Fard's picture that was also in the Detroit newspaper when they had a conflict with the law, the police department.

Professor Jamil Diab, it looked like him. I'm looking at this picture and I'm saying to myself, in the dream, "That sure looks like Dr. Jamil Diab", and I'm saying, "Could he have been the son of Mr. Fard?" Because when my father advertised in the paper, he came and got the job, so you never know. I just wanted to share that. He (The Honorable Elijah Mohammed) told us Mr. Fard looked just like Jamil Diab, and that is right. He looks just like Jamil Diab. When he holds his head down, they look just alike, the same expression, the same everything, even the same shape of the head. We met his father as an old man, Jamil Diab's father. He had his father to come visit us.

So, you never know. I know if I made an investment in America, in the black community like Mr. Fard did, I would be in touch with my investment and I believe he did. I believe he had his own way of staying in touch. My father described him to a tee to us. Around the table he said, sometimes, Mr. Fard would be laughing, and he would turn red in the face. And then, here comes this old man, and I am seeing everything that my father was saying. He was sitting at the table, that is, Muhammad Abdullah, and I'm seeing all this behavior. My father said he had really quick eyes. His eyes would dart around.

"That Old Man Is Not Our Savior!"

I am seeing this man doing the same thing, his eyes darting around. I didn't ask anybody a thing. I didn't ask anybody any question. I am just there at the table and observing what is going on and wondering, "Who is this man, here, who is supposed to be your friend, who is bringing you something for your bronchitis? My father had asthmatic bronchitis. He brought him some dried, red salmon fish and he told him to eat that. It would be good for his bronchitis. I didn't ask any questions. After the guest left and I'm getting ready to leave, my mother and father were together and my father said, "Son, that old man is not our savior!" And my mother said, "No, he is not our savior!" Now, I am suspicious! "I did not ask you who he was!"

He spoke to me directly at the table. He said, "I hear your father has sent you to Philadelphia." I said, "Yes". He said, "I will be coming there, soon, from San Francisco and I'm starting a newspaper there, *The Muslim Herald*. I'd like to talk to you about it when I get there." I said, "Certainly". He did come later. It was not long that he came and visited me and did the same thing in my kitchen that my mother told me Mr. Fard did in her kitchen. He came in and just took over the kitchen and cooked. But he asked, "Have you ever had Pakistani, Indian food?" I said, "Yes, I like it". He said, "Would you like for me to cook some?" I said, "If you want to, yes, sure".

Only Saw Mr. Fard for Three Years

He cooked. My wife was Shirley then, and we turned the kitchen over to him. He said, "First, let's go out and shop." We went to get groceries, to get the things that he needed, came back there, and he cooked. The same thing that Mr. Fard did in my mother's kitchen this man did in our kitchen. I'm convinced as to who he was, so, I said to myself, "You see me thirty years later, you probably won't recognize me. You would be saying, "I don't know that old man", especially, somebody you did not see, except for three years. The whole time they saw him was three years, and they were not seeing him every day of those three years. You see somebody only for a few years, you knew them, and you see them, occasionally, and they could come back thirty or forty years later, and you wouldn't know them, especially when you don't want to know them. You're not ready to turn everything over to them saying, "We have too much here. We don't know you". He wasn't the type of man to push himself on anybody, or anything. If they didn't invite him, he wouldn't come. He told me once, "I was leaving, going back to San Francisco, and your father gave me two hundred dollars. You don't have any money, and I was leaving you, going back, and you gave me two hundred dollars." I'm too generous. Sometimes, I run out, and I have to go back to the same people I gave money to and ask for some back. We should know about these people who put us on this road, as much as we can about them. The knowledge of them should not die with us. We should pass it on to others, so it lives and stays with us, always.

"The Temple Is Not Fit to Pray In"

The Honorable Elijah Mohammed said on Stony Island, "The Temple is not fit to pray in". Now, why doesn't Farrakhan teach that? That place he is in, the Honorable Elijah Mohammed said that it is not fit to pray in, and he was talking about the vessels who were in there. They were defiled. He mentioned the sisters, some of them, "All wrapped up in filth." I'm telling you Allah protected me, because if it wasn't for His Protection, I think that kind of stuff that was going on in the Nation of Islam would have broken my mind... They dropped that load on me, and these are my father's followers, even if I don't care about them, individually. So, I think that thing was planted in me, "You are going to help your father and Mr. Fard". Maybe that is what was working behind my mind to make me strong and stand up against that kind of stuff. It was terrible, drugs, etc. The FBI told me that they were known as the Black Mafia, they said, in Philadelphia, Kansas City, and Detroit. I brought it to them because this was alarming.

"He is not the one!"

Believers wrote me and didn't mention any names. They wrote me several letters telling me what they knew was going on, i.e., torture of prostitutes because they did not pay the temple or mosque off, drug addicts giving big money, so they could continue to do drug business in the area where the Muslims were. They called it the Black Mafia. Then I learned from the staff in Chicago about the captain, what she was into, and believe me, Farrakhan knows about that. If he was any kind of decent person, he would have supported me all the way, wouldn't he? No, he tried to knock me down to make people think, "He is not the one! The Messenger wanted me! I'm his spokesman!" He did not change that, and you know, he intentionally didn't come to the Honorable Elijah Mohammed's funeral, claiming that he was afraid somebody was going to kill him if he came. I don't care what somebody told me they were going to do. I would be at my father's funeral. I know I cannot say for sure, but with my mind that I've always had, there is no way a leader like the Honorable Elijah Mohammed could be buried or have his service and I would not be there. If he was not my father, no kin at all, no blood relationship, I would have to be there. And if somebody told me they were going to kill me, I would say, "You are just going to have to kill me!" So, that guy was no good from the beginning. Farrakhan. He is no good! You see how he deceives us all the time, saying that he is going to do this and that? After you give him what he wants at that time, what he is asking for, when that is over, he goes right back to the same old Farrakhan. I heard his paper came out, and it is the same way, nothing changed, and he told me, he called me to a meeting at his house in Michigan and told me that he's changing all of that.

I'll never see him, again. He can call me. I will never answer his call, again. I don't even want to talk to any of his people again, unless they are calling me to let me know, "We want to join you and become members with your people and follow you". That is the only way I'll talk to him and that includes my half-brothers, all of them, because if they put up with something and they know what he said to me, if they put up with a liar and show businessman like that, then I don't want to talk to any of them. I don't want to talk to anybody from that group at all. If he passes and they show themselves to be decent and honest leaders, I will congratulate them and embrace them. But time will have to show us that.

I never turned him (Minister Farrakhan) down, even when I knew that he was not going to change that much. It is the end of it, now. I am through with it. There is nothing more that he can get from me. I am not going to attack him, because it would do nothing but hurt those who are with him. But I am just not going to give him any support, no friendship, nothing. I do not wish any bad luck for him. I wish nothing but good luck for him. He can be saved, Allah knows, and Allah knows my heart. He can be saved. I want him saved, but it is hopeless. I am convinced it is hopeless. That man would deceive G_d, Himself. If G_d would show Himself and prove, "I'm G_d", he would not believe it. He would try to deceive G_d saying, "Just let me get these bills off me for this building. Let us get this tax problem out of the way, G_d, and I will never worship anybody but You". And as soon as G_d does that for him, he would be right in the same thing, again. He is hopeless! We pray Allah for the good ones among his following, but those who are like him, we pray that all of them just be forgotten. We do not want them in our memory or anything, have no thoughts of them at all. We just have our thoughts only for those who are innocent and need help, that they keep coming to the truth, and a few of them have.

They Always Come In When the United States Is In Trouble

I will tell you who did see what was going on and favored it, the intelligence department in this government. But the religious, secret orders, they didn't think so. It was really a nightmare for them! I think they were blinded by their own scheme. I'm sure they thought Mr. Fard was going to be successful in creating a new leadership for the African American people, and that leadership would be against the United States, help divide the African American people and force, bring about, a situation that would open the way for Israel, the wise, Jewish Zionists, to come in and negotiate with the United States government. This is a trick, another scheme. You see, they always come in when the United States is in trouble to say, "We know this religion! We know Islam! We know where they're coming from. If you give us this and that, we will make sure these boys don't give you any trouble!" Then they will come in and talk to the leader and will show the leader something that he didn't have, would even tell him how he was made, tell him how the Nation of Islam was formed and everything.

Qur'an, Jewish Wisdom, Taught to Mr. Fard

The Ahmadiyyahs, they did not form on their own. The Jews influenced their direction, and Muhammed Abdullah, who I know as Mr. Fard, he told me, "The Jews have been living in Asia for a long time. They are also in China, but when you go over there and see them, they look just like everybody else. They have blended in, married into the Chinese people", he told me, "Hundreds of years ago." And when the Muslims came over, the Jews were coming over at the same time. Muslims came over about eight hundred years after the Prophet's passing. Muslims started coming to Asia in big numbers and Muhammed Abdullah said the Jews were over there at the same time. I have a strong suspicion that Muhammed Abdullah was not a pure Indian, but a mixture of some white and Indian, and I believe he had some Jews in his family.

You see, that is what they do. They don't trust just anybody with that knowledge. I do believe (I never told you, but I hinted it) the Jewish wisdom was blended with some other ideologies, including Qur'an, and taught to Mr. Fard when he was young. He was raised in that knowledge, and he was able to see connections for Hinduism, his religion, the religion of his people before they became Muslims. Hinduism, Islam, Christianity, and Judaism, I do believe he had all of it, and I believe the Jews are the ones who influenced the Ahmadiyyahs. In fact, I heard that the Jews also influenced Ghulam Ahmad. He was a Qadiyyain.

"Who Made the Devil?"

It all goes back to Jacob. Mr. Fard said, "Who made the Devil?" Yakub, but he said he was black. He didn't mean black-skinned. He didn't say black, nappy headed. He just said black. He meant that he was a man of nature. Black means two things, importantly, in mythology and in religion. It means the absence of knowledge, ignorance. But the absence of knowledge doesn't necessarily have to be ignorance. It could be innocence, too. So, the same condition that they describe as ignorant in this world, those people who know the sciences don't see that as ignorant. They see it as innocent. So, black is your innocence, and the people identify black with faith. Knowledge is light, faith is darkness. But faith is not the darkness of ignorance. It is the darkness of just what it says, faith. You trust without evidence. You trust without seeing. So, that is obedience to whatever you're following. You trust in it without seeing, faith in the unseen. But actually, the Arabic language is, "Bil ghaib". It means that you are keeping the trust and the faith, and knowledge is absent. "Bil ghaib" means with the awareness that there is no proof. "I do not have any evidence. The evidence is absent. I do not have it with me", but you keep going. You keep trusting, keep following the discipline. So, that is black.

The black stone is black, but up in the sky it was white. *"Lucifer, that bright star in the morning, why has thou fallen?"* So, it was bright in the heavens. It was bright, white light, but it fell to the earth, and it is black. So, it gave up thinking it knew everything and became faithful and followed, "Bil Ghaib, without proof". In the absence of knowledge, it still held the discipline. That's the human intellect thinking it knew everything, up in the heavens. He was situated then for G_d to bless him and establish him in Laban and Leah's world.

Scripture About the Dawning of the Human Potential

So, all these things are tied together, and all of them speak to the future, not to the past. The Scripture is all about the evolution or the dawning of the human potential. So, it starts in the darkness and eventually it lights the whole world, because it is the potential for fulfilling man's aspirations on this earth, in society. The potential is always in the human being for that. G_d did it. Scripture is all about addressing that. *"Darkness prevailed everywhere, and the Spirit moved on the face of the water and G_d said, 'Let there be light'."* The Spirit moved on the face, the surface of the water, not in the depths. Darkness was upon the deep, upon the potential. The potential had not been revealed. Deep, means in the core, the potential. *"Darkness was upon the deep and the Spirit moved along the face of the water and G_d said, 'Let there be light'."* G_d said, "When My creature tries to see, though he's just skimming the water, I'm going to open up the depths!" Isn't that wonderful?

Esau and Jacob Reconciled

So, at the end of that, Esau runs into Jacob, and he lined up all the sheep and he's asking him, "What do you need?" That is speaking to the hidden order of rule for Jacob that is speaking to them, telling them this plan that I'm giving you now. This is the enlightened one telling the rulers, because he was working for the rule to make it bigger and greater: "This plan that I'm giving you will, eventually, bring you the material world. Then those who we have wronged, when they see we have it, they are going to come to us and apologize and wish us well, and they are even going to share what they have with us. But we're going to turn it down, because we're going up to the heaven. We're going to rule from above their heads. We won't need it. We're going to have it all!"

Prophet Muhammed Did Not Interfere With the Schemes

Prophet Muhammed saw all of that. Allah blessed him to see all that. He was such a genuine and wise human being. He had such faith in the power of righteousness and the innocence of human beings that even with the Devil scheming, plotting, and had done it before his time, had everything rigged and set up to bring the people down to defeat the cause of G_d, he had such faith in G_d and mankind that he wouldn't confront them. He was wise, not only good, but his goodness is what made him that wise. He couldn't be that wise without that goodness, that purity of heart. He didn't confront them. He had no clashes with them. It says, in the Qur'an, G_d revealed it, *"Our contention is not with you"*, the people of the book. He avoided bringing a clash with them like what happened in the Crusades. He avoided that by going around the trouble spots and not addressing them or not alarming the Christian or Jewish rule.

But certain things he outright condemned. G_d revealed to him to outright condemn certain things and make it clear that there was no way to negotiate it. This is the way of G_d and that remains, and there is no way for us to meet eye to eye or agree on the belief that a man, Jesus Christ, is the son of G_d. He would not negotiate that, but short of that, he did. They were wise enough to know. Those who really knew Scripture, knew Prophet Muhammed was not condemning Christianity. He was condemning those who failed to see correctly in Christianity. So, even the Christian order saw that he was not really condemning the Christian Church, or the Christian people as such, but he was condemning their misperception of Jesus Christ and his mother, Mary, that they didn't perceive them correctly. They could see his moral excellence, his human excellence, and his noble work. They could see all that, so they didn't want to do battle with a man like that.

Jesus Christ Is the New Testament

And who knows, perhaps, they even thought, "Muhammed, if he lives, maybe he will come to our side. He doesn't see our side, yet!" But he did. When you see their side, they don't believe like the common people believe, the high ups in Christianity. They know that Jesus Christ is not flesh. Jesus Christ is Scripture. He is the Word of G_d. He is the New Testament. He is the Gospel. They know that. And he is the teacher of the Gospel. He is the Gospel and the spirit, meaning the leader of the Gospel. So, he's the teacher of the Gospel, and the Gospel is his life or his body. The Qur'an addresses that when it says he was a Spirit and Word from G_d.

They looked at that and said, "Muhammed is right. Christ is G_d's Word and a Spirit from G_d". But who can see that, except those high in understanding? The masses can't see that. What the masses take is the flesh. They say, "So, as much as Muhammed wants us to change, we can't do that! We will lose our masses." Jesus, in the Gospel, he took his disciples up to show them something. So, he took them up in the mountain and they followed him and here is what they say they saw in the Bible. I'm sure you've read it, some of you who read the Bible like I have.

They saw the light of Elijah, the light of Moses, and the light of Jesus Christ. There were three lights, and they became one.

So, what is Jesus teaching his followers by that? He's teaching them how to rightly identify him, not in the flesh. "I'm going to take you up to see me. I'm not flesh. You have to go up to see me, I'm light." And the light of Moses was a great light. It was the light of how to govern, how to rule, and then the light of Elijah was the light of how to fight, defend, to battle. Elijah did battle with Ahab. He challenged them like Moses. Moses challenged the Egyptian rule, but he's mainly to be seen as a law giver, one who established government. He is the one who represents the light, the science of how to establish government. Elijah is the science how to heal the people. Elijah was a healer of the widow's son. He raised him from the dead. It doesn't mean physical dead. Elijah was the medicine man. He was a healer. Moses is the government light and Jesus Christ is the moral light, innocence, moral innocence, pure light. So, when they come together, then you see Jesus. So, Jesus was empowered with the science of government, the science of psychology, how to heal the masses, how to heal the public, the people, and his own moral excellence, his moral innocence. They all came together.

World of Jewry Not Supporting Zionism

I'm happy to know that the world of Jewry is not supporting Zionism. They have a website. You should see it, sometimes. I don't know the number. You just look on the website for the world Jews' position on Israel. They say, now, what I said as a minister many years ago. They say that there is no support in the Torah for the establishment of Israel, and they say Israel is not a piece of geography. Israel is a concept, an ideology, and I said it before them. I said, "No, it is not a piece of land. It is portable." You can take it anywhere. You can live it any place and that is what their people are saying. They live in the United States and anywhere they want to. They say if Israel is successful that will make a lot of Jews think they have to go to that place to establish their life, and they don't want that.

The Cedars of Lebanon

Lebanon is very important to the Zionists, those who want to eventually be seen as the sons of G_d given the power to rule the world. You know how they talk about the cedars of Lebanon in the Bible. So, you know, they use language. They are masters of playing on language. The cedars are great trees, and they make great, beautiful furniture out of cedar trees. They are tall, beautiful, green trees. They teach their people this… so their children and their children's children have been drawn to Lebanon and admire what Lebanon has. If they have beautiful cedars, they want to see what else they have beautiful to get their coming generations to have interest in that land, to say, "We're the children of G_d. We're the only rightful children of G_d. We should have those beautiful cedars and everything else over there."

There are those who wonder about how I see these things happening and I don't talk about them. The Honorable Elijah Mohammed said there is coming a time when they are going to be in so much trouble that you will have to be careful of what you say. You will get yourself killed. I guess that kind of reasoning just stuck with me.

Worse Than Sodom and Gomorrah

Regarding the history of the time of Sodom and Gomorrah, according to Scripture, things in society are much worse today. And I think it was Christ Jesus who said he would wipe the dust from his feet, and he said it would be worse, didn't he? He said it would be worse than Sodom and Gomorrah. Well, that's what has happened to this society, today. The dust has gone from his feet. It means the poor, you know. That was the dust, the poor, the poor people, meaning, "I'll disown your poor and if I do that, your society will be worse, today, than Sodom and Gomorrah". And he hasn't disowned the poor, but the general population has disowned Jesus Christ. He's no authority in their lives, so we're experiencing this, right now. The situation is worse than Sodom and Gomorrah when it comes to, especially, social corruption. It's worse than Sodom and Gomorrah were then, and it's because the poor are not connected with Jesus Christ.

Feet mean the poor people and dust is another sign of poverty, or abandonment. And I think in our time there's more abandonment than it is poverty. Abandonment, the leaders have abandoned their interest and responsibility to keep the poor morally upright and in line with Christ Jesus's nature. So, that was the prophecy that was expected to be fulfilled in time, that the society would grow more and more in numbers and the leadership weak as it was it their time. With more burden on it, it is going to get weaker, so a prediction could be made, and it was made. Now, we are experiencing just what he pointed to.

Prophecy Points to the Future

Everything has to live within plans. Everything is supported by a plan, and plans are not left to the ignorant people. Plans must be left with the heads of people, not the feet. So, if they don't stay with the plan, hell is going to break loose, in time and eventually, it brings down the people and the Bible warns us, too. It says they put the precious metal in the head and the cheap things in the feet. So, if the feet give way, what can that heavy head do but fall to the ground? They can't support it. So, those are pictures of this time, not pictures of the times before. They're really a picture of this time. It was seen in small degrees compared to how it's seen now. Prophecy points to the future, you know. So, it anticipates what's going to develop and then it warns the people against the bad development that they are headed towards, if they don't become conscious of the trends and work against the trends that will destabilize society or bring about its ruin. And the Qur'an says the mountains are put up as pegs, so the earth wouldn't shake with you. Stability, governments represent stability, and it has to be enforced from the top because down there can't support it.

The Poverty of the Society

The same lack of moral future, the same lack of a priority for moral interests that brings about the corruption of the social life of the people, that same lack of interest is what brings the people to be less responsible for their own circumstances, immediate circumstances, less responsible for their own immediate circumstances; and causes the political leaders to ask for more government involvement, more government assistance. So, the same thing that's contributing to the demoralization of the society is also contributing to the poverty of the society, and consequently, more government spending.

More Than Fifty Percent of Our Preachers Are Pimps

And you know more than fifty percent of our preachers are pimps, and more than fifty percent are fishing. They just need to pull a con, a famous con, like I could overnight. I could just be one with the authority to take care of business. I could be harder on them than you are on flies. I wouldn't give them any more warning than it takes me to get to them. That's all the warning I would give… and look, you don't have to have a Jesus card to do that… Society is killing them off like flies, already. You know that there is nothing being done, already. They talk about it for a while, but they are just going to pass right over it. They are going to keep dying of violence, drugs, and social diseases. That's the law of G_d's justice, you know, and if they don't wake up and turn around maybe they should be eliminated, and I'm a compassionate man. I think you all know that. But my compassion shouldn't be misplaced. Look how they are hurting good people and look how they are causing good people to go bankrupt. And society is just penalizing all of us, right? So, what does this mean? It's not our fault. We're paying for their faults.

Chapter 18

Interfaith Dialogue

We have to make progress and to make progress we have to be the beautiful people that G_d made us to be. The picture of Muslims is a beautiful picture of human beings, and we have Christians, Jews, and others in America and all around the world who are trying to live their religion and be in that beautiful picture as human beings. We have plenty of friends. Do not look at the few bad people that misuse the name of the religion or misrepresent their religion. Think about the many who are sincere, honest, and loving G_d and loving people.

Dr. Robert Shuler and Reverend Billy Graham

Dr. Robert Shuler was a man that I was attracted to a long time before I met him. In fact, I was a minister for the Honorable Elijah Mohammed when I first noticed him on the television, and I said, "I don't have any problems with this evangelist". I said, "He's not like the rest of the evangelists". Billy Graham was another one that I respected and liked, and Malcolm X really liked Billy Graham. In fact, if you ever saw Malcolm a lot and saw the way he preached, his style, you would have seen that he had been influenced by Billy Graham. They both had similar stature, tall, bony faces, and he (Malcolm X) told me that he liked the way Billy Graham made his delivery. Dr. Shuler, I admired him, too. I said, "This man has studied psychology." I said, "He's coming from psychology, not just from Scripture." So, I got to meet him, and I said, "Dr. Shuler, I want to share something with you. I used to watch you", and I told him how I liked him and everything. I said, "I knew that you were different. You were making everybody comfortable in your audience, even me, the son of Elijah Mohammed, and I said to myself, 'That man must have studied psychology'." He said, "Yes, I did. I got my degree in psychology." And most good preachers, they have studied psychology, and even bad preachers. Religion was the first to give us psychology. It branched out of religion. Religion was the first to give us psychology and many other sciences.

Visit With Pope John Paul II In the Vatican

The benefit I wanted from my visit with Pope John Paul II in the Vatican wasn't for the community, directly, it was for myself, directly, and I knew the Muslim community behind my leadership would get many benefits from it when they (the public) are hearing the news that the son of Elijah Mohammed was received at the Vatican by Pope John Paul II, and was on the list of speakers who addressed the

485

gathering that was there, where the Pope was hosting religious leaders and some other Muslims, too, from around the world and the audience was a big Catholic audience of over 150,000 people or more. They say it was like 200,000.

A Relationship of Catholics and Muslims Who Were Once Black Muslims

So, I knew that effect would do what I wanted it to do, and that is say that "We have overlooked these people. We have underestimated their importance in religion. The Pope would not be receiving this man if there was not something very special about him and his organization, or his people that he leads." I knew that would happen and the religious leadership, right away, I knew the immigrant Muslims would not like that. They have never commented on that directly to me, not a one of them, because that was a surprise. It was like the atomic bomb being dropped on Hiroshima and Nagasaki. They did not expect that. They said, "Good G_d Almighty, the Imam was holding an atomic bomb trump card. He dropped it on us!" So, no matter what they say, they can't kill the effect of that around the world. They can say that "They are an off brand. The Nation of Islam, it never was on the right way, and he brought it to the right way. But they are a little, small group there in the United States." They cannot say that now!

The time it takes, the travel and resources, etc., it takes to participate in interfaith dialogue, is not easy, but when you look at the big picture then you say that is a small price to pay for the result that will reach innocent people who are not scheming, who do not have designs on you. They are just people who believe, and they are so impressed that this kind of relationship is formed for Catholics and Muslims who were once Black Muslims and separatists. That is powerful. I have had leaders come to me and tell me that, "We heard about your relationship with Chiara Lubich" and they are letting me know that is really touching and "It is really something of great importance for us. It has great significance among us." That is what I felt coming from those leaders.

Rev. Jay Rock of the Presbyterian Church USA, he expressed that to me, and he is just one of several males and females, more females than males. But on the stage of world peace, religious tolerance, and cooperation, people like that have come to me, more females than males, but males, too, and they have been touched by the news of Chiara Lubich and myself joining to promote the principal of love and one family for man. And long after we are gone, believe me, they will be writing about it. I mean very important people are going to be writing about it.

Chiara Lubich, the Wonderful Saint of the Focolare Movement

We are very happy to have the company and friendship of a great international movement (the Focolare) founded by its leader Chiara Lubich, the lady that I believe to be a servant of G_d, and an inspired servant of G_d, inspired by G_d. Chiara, experienced as a child, as a young lady, a teenager about 17 years old, the horrors of World War II, with bombs falling all around. So, she decided to give her mind to Jesus Christ, peace be on him, as a servant, as a Catholic, as the person working hard to bring people to love one another, to call people back to Christ's love.

I think we are the first ones (Muslims) I have heard of embracing a group of Catholics in this fashion, and only Chiara Lubich was able to do that. She pulled people from other religions. She was a wonderful saint, and I do believe she was a saint. As a young, innocent, girl, she was just registering saying, "Look, these bombs are killing us, and they are dropped by Christians on us." That is who was dropping them. Christians were dropping them on Christians, and then I bet she said to herself in her own soul and heart, "We are not really demonstrating the message and love that Christ brought into the world." And she decided to form that organization and got the Pope's blessings on it, and he named it, "Fireplace". That is what the Focolore is. That is what they explained to us. I guess he was saying "The fireplace warms you up, but if the fire gets out of control, it burns the house up. I do not know which one you are. I would just like for you to accept this name, Fireplace." The Pope was something else.

Progress of the Original Family Life

I became acquainted with Chiara by reading her book on her life, and I fell in love with her soul and her mind. Consequently, we formed a friendship, and that friendship now is a friendship for myself and those who are associated with me in the following and herself, and those associated with her in her following. What is being done by G_d through man, but also through the forces of nature is the progress of the original family life. G_d is evolving the single-family life for the whole of mankind, and the single home life for the whole of mankind. So, here is the core of man in his original social nature and spiritual nature growing, influencing, as it grows, until it fuses into all the children of mankind and brings them into accord with the single soul of mankind, of all people. Do you know we are many souls, just as many as there are humans? But we're also a single soul, as it was in the beginning. And G_d says, "*As it was in the beginning so shall it be in the end.*" We are different souls, but at the same time, we are one soul. And it's that one soul that's going to make a home for all of us. Each one of us separately cannot make a home for all of us. But all of us in our collective life, in that one spiritual life that we call human life, in that one soul, we can. When we conform to it and we become reconciled with it again and conform to its hungers and its thirst, we can have this earth as one home, accommodating all of us as one family.

Where We're Going

That's the destiny. That's where we're going. The great lady, Chiara Lubich, she sees that with the light of her own Bible, the New Testament, the teachings of Jesus Christ, peace be upon him. And we see it with the light of Qur'an and the works of Muhammed, the Prophet, to show us how to live our religion. We see it, too. We're in harmony with her aspirations for humanity and she's in harmony with our aspirations for humanity. And there are many up in the heavens with controls down here working for the same thing, and we're not going to fail. No, this is G_d's Movement, and you can't reverse G_d's Movement. We are not going to fail!"

Dialogue With the Presbyterian Church USA

Imam W. Deen Mohammed met with Presbyterian Church USA National Leaders to discuss the initiation of a 4-year dialogue, on September 6, 2007, in Homewood, IL: Present: Imam W. Deen Mohammed (IWDM), Rev. Robina Winbush (RW), Rev. Jay Rock (JR), Imam Ronald B. Shaheed (RS).

JR: You want to say a word about the Committee on Ecumenical Relations? You might be able to explain it more succinctly than I can.

RW: We have a national committee that oversees or gives guidance to both our ecumenical work and to our interfaith work, and they have really expressed a keen interest more so in the interfaith work than necessarily the ecumenical work. And so, we always have a theological, even Bible study reflection, a panel, and this time they wanted to focus on what does it mean to be good neighbors, for us as Christians, what does it mean to be good neighbors with our interfaith partners?

IWDM: I like that.

Opening the Door to Deeper Understanding

RW: And so, they worked with Jay in terms of putting a panel together and I think the panel will have three persons, from the Jewish community, the Islamic, and Hindu communities. So, it will be for us a learning opportunity, but hopefully, you know, opening of the door to continue in some deeper understanding and relationships.

IWDM: Well, I'm glad you all included me, because that's where my focus is and my interest, for us living together in the world, particularly in the United States, and that's been my mindset for many, many years. I didn't just come into this. I think it started when I started thinking where I would take my life in the Nation of Islam, the same as Farrakhan. Well, not quite the same. He changed it some after my father, but pretty much the same, and I wasn't comfortable with contradictions I was looking at, even as a child. So, my mind was already on humanity, on human beings. I knew I was a human being, and I was wondering why we had to be so different and so much opposed to what we believed, and that worked in me. My father, I think he awakened that in me. I was a boy sitting on the seats in the Temple. We didn't have pews. He would begin speaking to new members, new people who were visiting, etc., "Islam is freedom, justice and equality!" He said that consistently for many years until he changed the spirit and direction. "Islam is freedom, justice and equality!" He said that because black people were denied that in the United States, and he knew that that would catch them. It caught me, even as a child.

RW: And not just simply because you were his son?

IWDM: No, no. I never thought about any importance. G_d really favored me. He blessed me not to have any interest in importance for myself, not as a child, not now. And I pray to G_d that I never become like that. So, I don't look at myself as myself. I don't! I say, "That's Imam W. Deen Mohammed". There's a Wallace in here, too.

JR: That's a nice distinction. It will keep you healthy... One of the reasons that this is such a blessing for me, at least, but I think for both of us to sit here with you is that we had a very active connection dealing with racism between African American Muslims and African American Christians. Robina was right in the middle of putting that together within the Bay area, and I don't know whether you've heard about it, but it was really so significant, and we haven't done enough with it in terms of continuing that healing process. Robina, you probably recall more about it than I do.

IWDM: I didn't hear about it, but if there's any material on it, condensed or summarized, I would really be happy to see it.

JR: I will make a note and get it to you.

RW: Imam Faheem Shu'aib, he was the leader in that in the early 90's. We had a Christian pastor, two in the Bay area. Eugene Farlow, who was pastor of Sojourner Truth Presbyterian Church, and Dr. Will Hertzfeld, who was pastor of Bethlehem Lutheran Church, and the two of them, along with Imam Shu'aib, really pulled together a dialogue between African American Christians and Muslims in the Bay area... One of the things I was struck by was that the Muslims in that dialogue understood Christianity much better than the Christians understood Islam; and on some levels, it is difficult for us as Christians to sometimes articulate the essence of what we believe, but it was an important time for us. We ended up with a publication in one of our magazines on the dialogue and I think that's what Jay can get you. We ended up dealing with issues related to how we can work together in community development. We ended up looking at how we understood Scripture and how we each approached Scripture. There was one particular panel that I participated in related to women in both of our traditions, and I think the other thing that was significant, at least for me, was an opportunity to share with Muslims sisters and brothers many of whom who had left Christianity in the early 60's, what were the correctives that some of us had done within Christianity for the very reasons that they left, and a little bit for us, around the work that had been done by James Cohn and others in liberation theology.

So, that was a good time for us. I'm not sure where the energy is to continue that, or how we might even broaden that. The other issue that came out (which was a beautiful moment between Rev. Farlow and Imam Shu'aib) was around conversion and the loved ones and what that meant for us, because it was difficult for our sisters and brothers to understand, sometimes, why Christians got locked up or had issues around conversion, and on the other hand, why as Christians we were called, much of what you said, to embrace a love ethic across the board for folks that we may or may not be so inclined to do. But it was a good beginning for us.

IWDM: Very interesting. Shu'aib, I remember him. I don't think he was more than about 19 or 20, maybe, and I went to Oakland to be the Resident Imam. Yes, I was their Resident Imam, a long time ago, and I was imam for about three years there, and I noticed how curious he was to know, to understand everything; not just to hear things, but to understand what he was hearing, and we got to be very close friends. I think of him as a son, almost.

RW: He is my cousin's imam and so he has been dear to the family.

IWDM: He's your cousin?

RW: No, he is my cousin's imam. My cousin and his family are in the masjid in Oakland, CA, and he's become just a good friend of the family…

IWDM: He has a very active mind.

JR: I serve right now as the person in charge of interfaith connections for our Church, and I've been watching with a great deal of interest what you have done with the Focolare, and the way in which that relationship has grown. And now Ronald tells me there's going to be an exploration of how to make it or take it a little deeper, maybe this next week.

IWDM: Yes, they're going to be in Rome, right?

RS: Yes sir.

JR: And so, I've been watching all of that and I've been thinking a lot about how we could develop a similar kind of relationship between our Presbyterian Church and your movement.

IWDM: I see no problem for that.

JR: Good. You know I haven't tried to make picture… Actually, it has felt to me like it would be improper of me to try to figure out what an agenda would be, how to start, or how to look at it. So, I'm really grateful for this meeting, because if we're to do such a thing I would hope that we would imagine it together. And from the very beginning, I don't want to bring any agenda to this. I don't want to close anything off.

Nature Lovers In Prophet Muhammed's Immediate Circle

IWDM: I believe that our Prophet, Muhammed, peace be on him, was in a situation that didn't permit him to disclose what is the real, I would say, theme, overriding theme, for the Qur'an and for his own mission, because he was talking to persons who had been idol worshippers and a few who had been nature lovers, and those nature lovers were in his immediate circle. They were his companions. They're called in the Qur'an (I'll try to put the idea in English, in the common language) those who were upright in their nature. That's what the meaning is, those who were upright in their nature, and their name is in the Qur'an, the Hunafaa.

JR: Say that again.

IWDM: The Hunafaa, and when the Prophet got revelation and got connected with Scripture, he was told by G_d, by revelation, that Abraham was the first of the Hunafaa, those upright in their nature. So, what I have come to see and very clearly for me, is that that hunafaa nature and the Prophet's main focus on humanity, helping humanity, is in the Bible. It's in the Gospel. It comes to light in the Gospel. And when he (Muhammed) said, "The world or the people will come to see myself and Christ together", I think that's what he was addressing, that he was all about uprightness, the inherent goodness in human nature that G_d put there. So, without quoting the Bible, or tying this with the Bible by giving references from the Bible, which can be problems for us, I just share that idea with Christians, and I think that's where we should begin, us, for my association, not for the general Muslim community, the general Muslim population. But for us, those persons in my association, I think that's where we should begin. If you feel comfortable with that, that's where I am.

JR: I'm very moved by that.

Discovering the Purity of Human Nature

IWDM: And I think when you say, "Christ within", you're saying the same thing we're saying when we say, "the uswaa of Muhammed within", which means his model, his human model. We're to emulate his human model.

JR: It's not quite the same as talking about righteousness, is it?

IWDM: No, it's talking about discovering the purity of human nature that G_d put in us, that purity, and living it to the best of your ability for you. I'm speaking to you, now. Jesus Christ is put in the nativity scene, with animals, right? So, it's something he had in common even with animals. That's what we're talking about, what G_d preserved in human beings, in nature, and in creatures, all creatures.

JR: What the Bible maybe talks about, maybe that's what it means when it says, "Created in the image of G_d".

IWDM: We don't say that what you're saying, but I understand it.

Science and Religion Coming Together

RW: I was reading *Romans* this morning. It was talking about all creation is longing for this restoration to the Spirit of G_d, and coming to life again, but a sense that it's just not for humanity. All creation is waiting for this restoration.

IWDM: I like the idea that's out now about science and religion coming together. Darwin and other thinkers in science, they have their theories, and they come from religious communities, and I think they just wanted to avoid trouble. But I think a lot of those ideas that are truly good for the world are in science but were found in religion before they were given to us in science, because, actually, it's clear in the Qur'an that G_d created everything to evolve from simple to complex, from corrupt to pure, or from corruption to purity.

JR: So, that readiness is built right into creation, built right into the nature of it?

IWDM: Oh yeah, the Prophet said, "Everything that exists G_d has inscribed upon its nature excellence". G_d has inscribed into the nature excellence, and in science every living thing is selected, and the species has evolved because of selecting the better and rejecting the worse; environmental situations, but also, the choice of climate, in eating, and everything. And because of the creatures being selective they have evolved, including human beings. This is science. I love science, religiously, and I think that's why the Muslims made so much progress under Muhammed, the Prophet, not spiritual progress, community progress. It was because they understood the connection with nature, the natural environment.

JR: And the Muslim world never seemed to teach a kind of dualism that Christianity fell into for a while, where the material was suspect to be rejected, and the spiritual was to be embraced. So, we had all these centuries when the Church was pushing science as far to the margins as possible, and in the Muslim world, the academies and the libraries were lively and the interaction between science and religion was maintained. Thank G_d for all of us, historically, all the things that would have been lost if that had not been true.

IWDM: You know, I've come to believe that the Christians had to protect themselves from powerful governments, that if they knew what the Christians were all about, persecution would have been much worse, more killing of the faithful. They didn't want to do things that would excite the barbaric rule, so they hid themselves. But sometimes you can hide things so thoroughly you can't find them, yourself, down the road.

Muslim and Christian Worlds Having An Awakening

RW: And worse yet, you forget that it ever existed.

IWDM: So, we all have an awakening. The Muslim world is having an awakening, and the Christian world is having an awakening. This is a good time. I call it the Day of Religion, this time we're living in, because never in the history of religion did, we all come together, until now. I never heard of Mecca inviting Jews...

JR: We're coming together in ways that were unheard of before.

IWDM: Yes, there were some incidents, or some local occurrences, where nice persons met from Islam and Christianity, and they developed a good relationship and became friends and admirers. But never did the leadership work for dialogue with the other religions until now. And the things that we see manifesting in what is called, the popular culture, or the corrupt life, all abound in prophecy, and what we are seeing is just what we call, al akhira. In Christianity, I believe it would be eschatological manifestation. These conclusions couldn't happen until we became connected all around the world. Once mankind becomes connected all around the world, then we're going to see the end that the Bible points to, and the Qur'an points to.

JR: The restoration.

IWDM: Yes.

JR: Well, I am very blessed myself to have leadership like Robina, who is our Associate Stated Clerk, and Cliff Kirkpatrick who is our Stated Clerk, the head of our Church, and also, Linda Valentine, who is from Chicago here, who is now our Executive Director, all of whom are solidly behind interfaith dialogue and wanting to do just this kind of reaching out that you were just talking about.

IWDM: I believe it's a great time, but it's not our doing. It's G_d's doing.

G_d's Plan Overrides Our Plans

RW: We have for fifteen years I guess, looked for ways to reach out and open up this relationship, again. I really do see this in the fullness of G_d's Design, that this is the season, both with Jay formally on staff and with my being in this situation just opening the doors. I know that Jay and Ronald met at Collegeville (St. John's University of Minnesota), which is a place where I sit on the board, now. I was there for other consultations and just fell in love with the place, because it opens up people meeting and talking, not in the abstract, but in the first person, about what it means to live out our faith in a different context... I was in a consultation with Evangelicals and Catholics, but the opportunity to move beyond our own self-imposed and self-limiting worlds to engage others is a gift, and the world is so in desperate need of a witness of that being a possibility.

IWDM: Yes.

JR: Do you believe in chance, Imam Mohammed? Do you believe that anything happens by chance?

IWDM: No and yes.

JR: I mean you could say that Ronald and I met by chance at a discussion at the Collegeville Institute, talking about what it means to be faithful to our different faiths. You could say that was by chance, but it doesn't feel very much like chance.

IWDM: I believe in G_d's Plan nothing happens by chance. G_d's Plan overrides our plans and engulfs our plans, but we don't know that most of us. So, in our plans, yes, things happen by chance. That's why I said no and yes.

RW: We have this phrase, sometimes, in preaching circles. It will say, "There is no such thing as coincidence. There's only G_d's Incidence".

IWDM: Yes, we say it, too. It's worded a little bit different, but we say that, too, and that's true. I believe like you believe, nothing happens by chance. "Illa mashaa Allah, nothing occurs except as G_d has willed it". If G_d has willed it, it happens. It's in G_d Will.

JR: So, what do you suppose would be the way? I don't know much about how you started out with the Focolare Movement, and whether that's the right model for us…

IWDM: It may not be.

JR: It may not be, but it would be interesting to talk a little bit, if we can, while we're here, about what your thoughts are about how we might begin to get acquainted and bring our people together.

IWDM: Imam Ronald B. Shaheed, he can help me with this. But for myself, really, the relationship that we have was with me being interested in Chiara Lubich, the founder of the Focolare Movement. The Focolare people approached us, first of all. They heard about my leadership, and they were interested in meeting me. So, when I met with them, I thought their headquarters was in Chicago. So, I met with them, and they introduced their leader to me by way of a publication, and right away I was excited. I said, "I'd like to meet her". I said, "Obviously, she's a spiritually blessed woman", and they said, "Would you like to have her book?" So, they gave me her book, written by her, how she came to be the person she is, the leader that she is.

It said that bombs were falling all around them during World War II, and she was wondering why Christians were bombing Christians. What was wrong? So, she decided at the age or 18 or 19 to start a movement, and Jesus said, *"I leave you one commandment"*, and she said she would take that one commandment, only. And she thought that commandment was universal in its appeal, and it would attract non-Catholics and non-Christians, as well. So now, today, she has an international movement, as you know, that's got Muslims in it, too. They're Focolare, also. So that's what attracted me to her. So, I read her book and the more I read the more I was convinced that G_d had chosen her. That's how it started. So, I finally met her in Rome, and I told Chiara Lubich, I said, "Your commandment is also a commandment with us. So, we have no problem identifying with what the Focolare are all about and working with you." I said, "I want more than just interfaith relations." I said, "I want something to happen that will permit us to work together to promote good in the world".

JR: It's not just about making a relationship. It's for a purpose.

IWDM: Yes, exactly, that we can join with each other in serving G_d's Purpose. So, she accepted that. Much later, she told me she went to the Pope, John Paul II, and she asked the Pope. She said she told him of what my interest was and expressed her interest, and she asked for the Pope's blessing on our relationship and the Pope said, "You have it!" I'm quoting her, now. He said, "You have it!" But we are still trying to develop that one thing, or several things that we can work together on to advance G_d's Purpose and G_d's Will in the world for mankind.

JR: It takes a while to discern what that is.

IWDM: Yes.

Chapter 19
The Treasure Under the Wall

(This last chapter contains excerpts from our final two meeting with Imam W. Deen Mohammed. The following is excerpted from our next to last meeting, August 14, 2008)

Jonah and the Whale

I said you, my three brothers, are the friends that ride around in a big whale (black car). It was the big whale that swallowed up Jonah. Let me tell you something about that whale now, what most people wouldn't get from that story. That whale was better than Jonah. That is why it puked him out. Something bad on your stomach you throw up. First of all, the ship was better than Jonah, so the captain said, "Throw this man off into the water. He's the problem". And then the big fish got him and held him until he prayed to G_d. When he prayed to G_d, the fish could not stomach him. And the one who prays to G_d in bad circumstances, is that one put in good light in the Qur'an, or in bad light? In the Qur'an, Jonah and all the Prophets, peace be on them, are put in a good light. Jonah is not put in a bad light in the Qur'an. It just says a big fish swallowed him, and it does not say that he prayed in the big fish. That is in the Bible. Again, in the Qur'an it does not mention that he was on the ship first, in the cargo. It just mentions that he met with a bad fate out at sea, and the big fish swallowed him and took him to land, which is all positive. But then sleeping on the cargo is negative, so he deserved being thrown out by the captain of the ship.

"I Have a Three-Day Journey"

So, the big fish, the waters are raging because there was a storm and that put the ship in bad trouble. But the cause of the storm was Jonah, because of Jonah being thrown off the ship. The reason for the whale swallowing Jonah up was Jonah. But the whale did not even like the mission that G_d gave it. It swallowed him but could not stomach him. It headed straight for the shore with him and puked him out on the shore. That is all a negative picture. So, what the Qur'an is saying by not having those negative scenes is that this is not the description of the behavior or the spirit of a Prophet. This is the picture of his negligent, rebellious people. And this is the fate that they got into and the consequences for them were bad. You know, it is the Bible that says, *"I have a three-day journey"*, not the Qur'an? The Qur'an says he was puked out upon the seashore, and on it G_d had mercy on him and caused a gourd plant to grow up over his body to shade him from the burning sun. So, he was not left to trial.

Shall I continue? What the Qur'an gives is the positive picture, because it is only the positive picture that is acceptable to be given the name of Prophet. As I was saying, even the mentioning of a three-day journey after he was saved from the raging waters and the belly of the whale, the mentioning of a three-day journey says, "My troubles are not over yet. My destiny is a three-day journey and really, I set it back myself, and I am just free now to get back on the mission that I ignored and got myself into all of that trouble."

So, the journey is a three-day journey. But see, in the Qur'an, the Qur'an situates the Prophet, Jonah, on the seashore in a picture where he was rescued by G_d. And G_d's Mercy was still with him when he was puked up upon the shore. G_d's Mercy was still with him, because G_d caused a gourd plant to grow over his body and shade his head from the burning sun. So, it is all positive, and I think I have clearly explained it now.

A Good Fate or a Bad Fate?

So, when I said your car was the whale someone would hear it and say, "Oh, he said that this car is the whale that swallowed Jonah, and that was a bad fate." Maybe it was a bad fate. It's a bad fate if you look at the consequences for a people who were rebellious. But if you look at the consequences for a Prophet who was thrown off course, then it is not a bad fate. It was a good fate. It was a good fate that the whale swallowed him, and it does not even charge him with being infested with commercial greed where his comfort is just being with the wealth and resting on it. That means depending on it and getting his rest and his comfort by sleeping on a pile of money he's got.

So, what the Qur'an is saying is, "No, this is not the description of a Prophet. This is a description of the greedy people that the Prophet was trying to lead to the right way". There's a difference. So, the whale, now, this vehicle (black car) is the whale, and the whale can't make it outside of water. So, you all have certain sensitivities that you share together and you're in the same boat, so to speak. But this time it is not manmade, it is G_d made. The whale is G_d made. The boat was manmade, and it went from manmade to a G_d made vehicle.

(We travelled with Imam Mohammed to eat lunch at an Applebees Restaurant near his home)

A Journey for Your Purpose

So, you all have a destiny. It is three days long and not necessarily a journey for each of you, individually, but it is a journey for your purpose. And just like the whale (black car) has arrived at *Applebees* and the destiny was *Applebees*, one day, if you all stay with me, we're going to arrive at the destiny, and it's going to be much bigger than *Applebees*, just keep supporting faith in G_d.

Really, what I was saying is, have you ever heard of a boat in the sky in poetry or anything? And in the Qur'an, there is water that is in the sky, the upper water and lower water. It came from mythology. These objects in space swimming along, that is the Qur'an: *"See how they hang in space without support?"* So, it is a sign from G_d of faith. What does it say? Faith could move mountains. If you had as much faith as a mustard seed, you could do those mighty things. So, the conclusion that the saints came to was that really, faith is what upholds everything, and that is true. They are not talking about a world of aliens. They're talking about a world of humans. No matter what we're talking about up there or down here, we're talking about that which humans live in. So, it is supported by faith. No matter how far science goes it has a limit to how far it can go explaining reality. You know, Jesus Christ walked on the water as one of his miracles, and the head of the Catholic Church, Peter, he tried and he sank like a stone, and that's what Peter means, stone.

The Sheep Know the Voice of the Shepherd

Just like the Qur'an and Bible are different, the Bible pictures are true, but they are not true the way most people understand it, because people see it as the picture of a Prophet and actually the Prophet is used as a figure to represent his people. So, instead of saying people of Moses, the Bible will give a mythological picture or fictional picture, and it will call it, Moses. But actually, things that are attributed to Moses, if they are out of character for the good person, that's not Moses. It's the mythological Prophet. So, this is so you know the difference, and the real Prophet and people who were seen in transmission in his body, they were embodied in him.

You know, the car has headlights in the dark. The light goes ahead of the car. The light helps you know how to guide the car to stay on the road and out of trouble. Just like those lights go ahead of the vehicle, in olden days the shepherd, the sheep went ahead of him, and he would be driving the sheep, and there would always be a sheep in the lead, and that sheep knows. The Bible says, *"The sheep knows the shepherd's voice"*. The shepherd is behind the sheep driving the sheep. It is kind of like a back wheel drive on a vehicle. That is a picture of me and all of you. Actually, the vision is in the rear and the people are in front. They're signaled to go out front and they are all searching through the darkness. But the stimulus is in the rear.

Three Lights Agreeing in One

When Jesus showed his disciples himself, he didn't show them his physical picture. He showed them light, and he didn't show them just his light. He showed them his light agreeing in two other lights; three lights agreeing in one and that was the light of himself, the light of Moses and Elijah. The light of those three is called The Transfiguration. So, he gave me the help that I need for you all. He (Morocco) said, "Well, how should we see you?" That's how you should see me. So, Moses means spiritual, and Jesus means spiritual, and Elijah, too, means spiritual. They all were spiritual. Moses was spiritual, but his people were hard core rational. If they couldn't make sense out of it with their own reasoning, they rejected it.

So, here you have a light inspired by a spirit, a fire inspired by the spirit, and the same thing with Jesus Christ. Jesus Christ, he's a word. So, you have the light of the word, the light that reason supports and the light of law, Moses, and you have in Elijah, the light of faith, a strong man of faith. So, you have three lights in one and they all depend on the spirit to burn like a flame in the air. They are all spiritually rooted. They are forces in the person's spirit.

Imam W. Deen Mohammed Has Three Lights

And that's what I see here, and my word that fills me is the Word of G_d, Qur'an, and my reasoning that I hold so faithfully to, and I want to say so finely, so pointedly to, is my faith in what appeals to my rational mind. I don't like to feel that I don't have support in my rational mind for what I'm holding on to, faith. And also, my spirit is one for understanding and finding that in Scripture which is coming from sentiment and coming from reason, like Elijah. And if he was blessed to come from his sentiments to command himself for what is right, he had to have a feel for what is right; and he not only had to have a feel for what is right, he had an appreciation for wisdom, Elijah, and the two made him a healer. He was a healer. And his drive was really the drive to relieve misery, to heal people, and to defend those who were victims of power, to address those powers and defend those people against those powers, Elijah. I believe it was Elijah that rebuked the queen, the female leader of his time. I can't think of the name of the wicked woman that was ruling…

Jezebel Sheared the Sheep and Stole the Wool

Jezebel, I think that was her name. Right now, I can't find the word meaning for the connection, but I know exactly what she was. She was the one who exploited the innocence of the following, the religious following, or the one who sheared the sheep and stole the wool, and Elijah was opposed to her capitalizing on innocent people. So, he attacked her openly and that brought her wrath down. If you understand the message of Jesus Christ in the Gospel, that is the kind of man he was. You have to put all those together to really understand what kind of man, leader, he was, what kind of leader he was. His leadership wasn't just in one picture. His leadership is a man who was created of Scripture, itself. Scripture created him. The Word of G_d created him. He is the Word of G_d depicted in the picture of him as a type, a leadership type, and that doesn't fully describe him.

The Oppressive Cultural Language Is Everywhere

He's also a man like Moses who wants to lead people out of Egypt. If we understand, out of Egypt is true, but the Qur'an alludes to the correct way to understand Egypt, saying, *"If that is what you want, these pot herbs, go to any Egypt."* Egypt must be universal then. So, he's leading them out of the world of darkness, confusion, and oppression. He's leading them out of the world. He's a liberator, Moses. He's leading the people out of one reality, out of one environmental language, into a new environmental language that gives them freedom, freedom from the old oppressive, environmental language; and that language is not confined to any nation by name like Egypt, or ancient Egypt. No, it's all over. It's everywhere. The oppressive language is everywhere, but with Pharaoh it was condensed, a strong concentration of it. You're oppressed by the cultural language. So, naturally Elijah, he was known as a healer and Jesus Christ's mission was also to heal the sick and the wounded, and to raise the dead, too. So, wasn't it Elijah who went to rescue the widow's son, and the widow thought the son was dead? So, when he got there, he said, *"He's not dead. He is only sleeping"*. If he was sleeping why couldn't his mother wake him up? The mother should know how to wake him up, if anybody knows how to awake him. So, that was a sleep that resembles death convincingly, but in reality, the person was not dead. They were only as Mr. Fard said, "Dead mentally". Since man is mind, if you're mentally dead, you are dead. So, by him associating himself with Elijah, the Prophet, the events in the history of life of the people was just that, that he was able to revive the widow's son who was thought to be really dead but was not. His potential or his life that G_d gave him to stand him up and help him go forward to the destiny was arrested in him, and it had to be freed. Jesus Christ and Elijah had the keys to unlock, as Mr. Fard would say, "the rusty locks", so that the people would have their life and freedom to live that life that G_d planned and preferred for them.

In the Bible, it also said a certain woman. It's more than one, but here it is again, the proper place to put it. Now, she put yeast and three measures of meal into something. Do you know how it reads? *"A certain woman"*, that means that woman to a very special group to understand what's being revealed or what's being said. It is very important for understanding what is being said. *"As it was in the day of Noah, so shall it be in the day of the coming of the son of man"* and Jonah said, *"I have a three-day journey"*.

Going Directly to G_d's Purpose

So, the three-day journey and the three measures of meal mentioned in the Bible are addressing the same need for development in the human being to bring them to the mental awakening that G_d wants for us to go to in human reality. You must progress through and beyond your mortal protection or your mortal picture of your reality, this physical flesh, this body, to see the purpose in your mind, to see how the purpose moves in your mind to make you perform correctly and incorrectly and miss the Path of G_d or get the Path of G_d; and get enough progress or develop through your mind, your rational faculties, or your natural abilities. You must progress beyond that, through that, but beyond that to be sparked by the Spirit of G_d. And the Spirit of G_d lights up in you and you make those sacrifices. In time, the Spirit of G_d is going to light up in you. And when it lights up in you, then you are no more depending solely on your mind and external reality. You have G_d's Will and Spirit inside of your life and it is a stream, and it is going directly to G_d's Purpose.

The Highest Level for Human Development

So, now in your spirit you're going like you were going by habit in the world. You're in the world under habit. The habit of thinking a certain way, a habit of feeling a certain way, etc. Now, spirit has replaced habit for you, and it is just your nature to go in the direction that you're going in and your nature is patient. It is the nature created by G_d. It is very patient. It won't even move until it knows that G_d has ordered this action or ordered you to move. So, it stops automatically. The person stops and says, "That's wrong", or "It is necessary as long as G_d wills". He is just happy to go and happy to stop, and he can't be satisfied until he has pleased his G_d, and he knows that.

So, he is traveling now by spirit, not by physical momentum nor physical movements, and not by rational movement, but by spirit he's traveling. That is the highest level for human development, that we accept the Will of G_d so completely for ourselves, that it becomes our new life. It becomes our new happiness and we're so happy just to be in that state, so we don't question. It is just automatic. It's like taking a rest and laying on the street without a mattress or something. So, stopping on the road is automatic, and we're just as pleased to stop and stay there as we are to take a rest at night in the bed, and when G_d replenishes us, and we wake up,

Prophets Were Plural Figures While Being Single Figures

So, it says a certain woman and there was a woman. It didn't say the mother of Jesus Christ. It says the dragon sent out a flood of water to overtake the woman, and the woman was told to, *"Flee to Egypt with your child"*. That certain woman in the Bible is that woman who was told to, *"Flee to Egypt with your child."* So, the woman flees to Egypt, and she learns a strategy for protecting the innocent so that they live to see the fulfillment of G_d's Promise. She learns that strategy and she puts the strategy into the doctrine, and that strategy becomes the spirit of the doctrine, like yeast from the stomach of an animal. Most yeast comes from the stomach of an animal. You can get it from other places, but yeast in the Bible is forbidden. So, it says they were told not to put yeast in bread, the Jews.

So, a lot of things that were not permissible in the Old Testament are permissible in the New Testament and that is one of them, using yeast in bread. They were told not to put yeast in bread, only to have flat, un-leavened bread. So, this is the certain woman that did that. And here Mary is not an individual just as Jesus was not always an individual. He was the congregation, Moses, too, all of them. They were plural figures while being single figures at the same time. So, this is not Mary, the single person. This is Mary, the Church, Mary, the Christian leadership, and you put the yeast and three measures of meal. Now what does the word, meal, imply? Meal is what we take as a dinner, sustenance, but mill is also a place for grinding wheat. So, in this case, that is what meal is. So, the woman put yeast in three measures of meal. This is not grinding wheat. This is the intelligence trying to break down complicated ideas to make sense of them, wanting to get to the essence.

Then G_d Comes to You

So, three measures. The first measure is the activity of the mind engaging the mortal body. As I said, you have to not just experience that stage, but you have to complete that stage. So, when it completes it, it goes now to the rational mind, and you have to stay there until it completes whatever it can do there. And if it's stimulated and inflated (because yeast inflates the dough), it's stimulated and inflated by the power of this new doctrine that is a potent agent inside of the thinking, and it has to complete its work in the mind and the mind says, "I have gone as far as I can go". Then you rest, and you don't give up faith, and then G_d comes to you. He puts His Spirit into it. So, the third rising is resurrection from the dead.

And isn't that what yeast does? A good bakery, they are not satisfied to have it rise once, are they? It rises once, then they beat it down and it has to rise up again, at least twice. Now, this is my cup of tea! As David said, *"He anoints my head with oil, and it runs over."* So, I get more than I can use. I have more than enough for the job. I only need a cup full, but my G_d is so generous, my cup runs over! And in the Qur'an, it says *"He gives without counting"*, that which has the power to stimulate our thinking like yeast effects the dough to make it lighter by volume, so it is easier to chew. You derive more pleasure and comfort when eating a nice, soft, piece of bread than snatching on a tough piece of bread. The pleasure is more. So, this is the difference between the old law in Scripture and the new liberation Scripture that liberates you from that condition that makes you accept the oppressive people of law. So, it is talking about relief, freedom, liberation.

The Creation Is G_d's Pure Act

So, if G_d's Spirit comes into us, it gives us new life. It invigorates us, but this is a plan for bringing the people to be liberated. It is a scheme that goes back to Egypt. How did the Egyptian dynasty manage to survive so long and keep the people under them so long? They had a powerful scheme, a powerful strategy, a methodology that works in the life of the people without their direct knowledge of it. So, a language environment was created to give birth to their thinking, support their thinking and feed their thinking, a picture language that had its beginning not in the creation of G_d like it should. Our pictures that come to our mind or our imagination that form pictures should be forming pictures that are given to us in G_d's world; not affected by man or not altered by man, but the natural world, and those pictures speak to us directly from G_d. It would be speaking to us directly from G_d because the creation is G_d's pure act.

This new thing in Scripture that is given in language like yeast, meal, mill, woman told to flee to Egypt with her child, all points to the language environment of what we call, now, the pagan world. So, that is why it is given so secretly, because most believers, it was thought that they would be turned off or they would reject support from a world order that was condemned by G_d, the world of the pagans. So, it is of paganism, all this importance of mortal flesh, the mortal flesh picture, and it was used by Egyptian dynasties, and they survived for thousands of years.

The Language of Paganism a Hidden Strategy

When the serpent approached the man in the garden and he addressed the man's interest in the tree of life, it was said, *"Eat of this tree. You won't die. Your eyes will come open and you will become as angels and gods."* One of the names of the tree is the Tree of Eternal Life. So, what the Bible is saying is that the Egyptians were known for their survival over many, many, generations, one dynasty behind another, for thousands of years. So, we go to where the achievement in this particular knowledge strategy is superior. So, woman, "Flee to Egypt with your child." From what? From the dragon who wants to drown you and your child. He has a flood of water coming out of his mouth and that flood is a flood of what? False accusations, accusing her of bad intentions. She was only a good and innocent person. So, "Go to Egypt and disguise your true life under the guise of paganism, and that will hide it from the dragon." When the dragon sees it, he will be satisfied, because it is not showing the Way of G_d. His language is the way of paganism. So, when the dragon sees that he will take for granted that this woman has now bought or chosen paganism.

So, what appears to be paganism, if the people hold on to their faith, that language environment, there is going to be a time when I will say, "No more". There is going to be a time when I am going to say, "Stop, that is enough!" I do know and understand, but I feel I want to do that for you. I accepted this. The language that appears to be paganism is really a mask or cover for a hidden strategy. It increases their spirit and gives them more ease for their mind ... It gives them more ease in understanding and digesting the ideas that they are to master.

G_d's Own Spirit As An Agent In the Thinking

In time, that which is superfluous or of lesser importance, it is going to shed it and shed it. It will shed it first, by trying to understand why it is in this physical picture, mortal flesh, and then when you digest the flesh, and you find the agent or the help, nutrient, or whatever you want to call it, for rational activity, then the rational mind starts all over again with the concept. And like I said, then the rational mind completes its ability, and it gives up, but it does not give up faith that the truth is here, the truth is in this. So, eventually, G_d comes into that person, rewarding their faith with His Own Presence and with His Own Spirit as an Agent in their thinking. So, really that which appears pagan is not there for paganism, it is there to strip paganism of its clothing, so that you don't see the clothing anymore, but you see the reality that the clothing has been shrouding.

False Charges Made Against the Innocent Human Being

And you notice in the picture language of Jesus's trial, crucifixion and burial that they actually didn't say when we came there. His robe was gone, why? Because that wasn't important for the discovery at the site of his grave where he was put away. So, that was taken out of the picture, so it wouldn't have any presence at the site for the resurrection. So, he had already been stripped of his garments. The presentable clothing had already been taken off of him, and he was just left with a little something to cover his private parts. But where the attention is to go, they have already prepared the reader not to look for the body to be covered, but the head is covered. So, his thinking was wrapped. Intelligence was covered, wrapped up. They said, "We know he's resurrected, because his head wrap is left here, and he is gone."

So, you come right back to Mr. Fard, the mentally enslaved, the mentally dead, and you know the word, "wrap", has a lot of meanings. You rap (knock) at the door, right? And you say who is rapping at the door? And a man convicted before the judge, what does he have? He has a rap. You look at that kind of language, then you can see what it means when they say, "He is not here, his wrap is here." He has gone freely from his charges. The world charged him and wrapped his head up with charges. When they complete something, they say, "That's a wrap!" So, they may have thought it was a wrap, thought it was all over, but the man is free, gone, and left the wrap back there at the site of his death or his being put away. The wrap is also referring to the false charges made against the innocent. They say that "He was just another one of those saintly looking religious leaders that go with their heads all wrapped up."

The Righteous Teacher Gave Out Talents

One water comes down on an area of land and though the same land receives the same level of water, or the same number of inches or whatever, in measurement, some come up inferior, some come up superior. This is the Qur'an. So, the same is given to everybody, but in the Bible, it says the righteous teacher gave out talents.

To some he gave five, to some he gave three, and he gave one. Some he gave two and those who received the least buried the talent. But the one he gave only two when he came back to inspect them, they had caused it to multiply. That is saying the same thing. Every time we speak, we breathe. There is no way to say any word without air coming out. So, the same life breath that is given to everybody is going to affect them differently. They are going to respond to it differently. Those who have faith in their own intelligence, five senses, they want to hide it so that nobody sees it but them. That is burying it. You're not sharing it with the people, so it lives among the people. Those who accept this upon their spirit or upon their desire to go forward with their life, they will get benefits, but those who take it into their rational minds to see it and then reflect on it, they are the ones who are going to multiply. So, that's the reality.

The angel that appeared while the Prophet was teaching the believers was Jibril, so the report says. They wanted to know who this man was sitting among us looking different in clothing that was the whitest of the white and blackest of the black, asking you those questions. The Prophet replied that that was Jibril, the angel Gabriel. He came to teach you your religion. Now what is this saying by metaphor or language that needs translation? That this outer appearance we observed was the purest of the pure, whitest of the white and the blackest of the black and the most original of the original, or the strongest in faith. G_d created the darkness. Really, to get the benefit from this report we have to get the whole language, all of it. Don't leave out any of it. He asked Muhammed, the Prophet, "What is Islam?" Then after asking it secondly, maybe just as importantly, he asked "What is the Judgment, the conclusion of all of this. What is the end of the world?" And Jibril could only point to signs, right? So, he pointed him to certain signs and one of them is the female who is the mistress, the servant girl, her maid, will deliver a child for her mistress.

Our Faith Tells Us This Is the Time

Now, how is her mistress' house preserved for the future? From the one who she had regarded as her slave, the maiden has a child for her mistress, not for the slave. She delivers this child for her mistress, meaning for the ruling order she bears a child, a sign of the conclusion of the great issues of Scripture. And another sign is that poor people will be competing with rich and mighty people in the construction of skyscrapers. This is an allusion to a time that is coming, when the mountain shall be moved, sent away as a mirage, and the land shall be leveled. It means material support, economics, shall be just. It shall be leveled, so that it is fair for all people.

We are there now; there is no doubt about it. The maid has already given birth to a child in the house of the big lady, to extend the life of the house of the big lady and all that she rules over. So, these are signs that point to this time that we're in right now. The Prophet gave us guidance that will serve us in that time when it comes, in the time of conclusion of the great issues in Scripture. When it comes, Gabriel's language we can turn to and rely upon that language to know for sure to have our faith strengthened in the circumstances that we find ourselves in. That's the conclusion of these matters. In the time of the conclusion, we have great help to support our faith that this is, for sure, the time!

Nobody To Talk To

You know, most of our family members don't see all that's happening. You all don't see that I like your company so much because I don't have anybody to talk to at home. That's G_d's Way, you can't change it. They haven't earned it. They can't have it no matter how good and innocent they are in our eyes. How do you earn rewards from G_d? Faith. G_d rewards your faith. He doesn't reward you because of your mind, your wealth, or popularity among people, good deeds and all that, but because of your faith. This person's faith has been strong and continuous. He has not deserted and turned his back on faith, and he is firstly and lastly a servant of faith, in faith and of faith. Those are the ones He rewards.

So, we can have all the other merits to our account. But our faith has not been strong and continuous, consistent, though one time you're walking among heathens, but you're still upon the same logic. G_d knows "He was among them, but he was walking to Me". G_d takes the burden off of us. He won't let us stay out. *"There shall be no fear for them and no grief"*, but it really means no burden of grief. It doesn't mean they won't be afraid. They are human. They have the nature, so they will fear certain things. It is of the mortal nature to fear bad consequences to your life, future, or your loved ones. It says they will only have a touch, taste of death. Well, this doesn't mean physically dying only. It means if death of doubt comes to them it will just be a touch and it will go away, and the person will keep living. Touch means you experience it with your feelings and with your conscious. So, they will have a touch of that. It doesn't mean they won't fear something, or they won't have that particular nature in them. They will still have that nature in them, but it will never become a burden, because as soon as they realize it, they turn to their Lord and He makes it light for them. They will have neither burden of fear nor grief and sometimes it will be someone close to you that is so burdened by fear they burden your life with it or so burdened by regret and grief that they burden your life with it. But if you are constantly on the path towards Allah, it is made light for you. Allah reduces it by degrees, and pretty soon they're wondering why you are not suffering and now they hate you. "What kind of mind do you have that you are not suffering with me? You're not responding to this the way I'm responding to it." No doubt, I had it happen to me. They will say that to you.

Let me tell you, I said this when I became the leader in 1975. The strongest, bravest person on earth is the person who stands upon faith in Allah, faith in G_d. Nobody can be braver than that person. Nobody can be stronger than that person, and his bravery is not ego-based. It is based in his loyalty to his G_d. Therefore, he is prepared to face anything that he has to face. He is not stupid. He is not going to ask to be killed. If they try to intimidate me, they're wasting their time. If they think I will be responding to threats, they're wasting their time. I respond alright, to see how I'm going to deal with you… Sometimes, I'm unaware of things that happen in my immediate environment. I could be unaware of it, but if I'm unaware it is because G_d intends that I be unaware, because I have sold my whole life, soul, and purpose on this earth in exchange for my Lord's approval, and He has accepted it.

G_d Protects

No matter how demanding a slave master is over the life of the slave there is a certain amount of freedom that he can't take away from the slave. So, who ordered life like that? The Creator, G_d, Allah, if He ordered that, it means that's what he likes. So, I sold my whole self to Him that I have no authority, no freedom to determine my life, what is going to happen now, or whatever. "I give it all to You". And what did He take? He took no more than what was easy for me and still allowed me to be free as a normal, natural person. So, there will be people right in my face and I won't be seeing what they're up to. I will be taking them for friends until something happens to manifest what is in them, and then I see them. So, I don't see everything. Only Allah sees everything. Allah only, because by nature I don't want to see fault in people. That is not my nature to want to catch a person wrong. That is far from my nature. I want to catch you right, not wrong. If he's got Satan working on him, that's his job not mine.

Whale Symbolic of Big, Powerful, Spiritual Organizations

So, don't get rid of the big fish (the black car we travel in to visit Imam Mohammed on Thursdays). No, if you get rid of that big fish, you might lose one of your companions in the fish. You are better off than Jonah. He didn't have any companions. So please, I'd like to have another ride on the whale (black car). The whale does stand also for wealth among the life of the water in that religious, spiritual body. So, though it is in the water it is... on the land. That is why Jesus Christ said *"Come, let me lead you so that you will become fishers of men."* You're still going to be addressing the same life in the water. These fish are really going to be men, and the water is the spirituality, or the spiritual pride.

So, we should understand the whale that swallowed Jonah. He's the biggest of the spiritual organizations, bodies, or institutions that swallow up people, and we should also associate it with these strong, big, powerful, spiritual orders of wealth, and that is in Scripture. I don't go there for myself, but I go there because it came to my mind right away. It says when you fish look in his mouth and you'll find a piece of money. And it so happened that the Catholic order became the richest of all religious orders, still might be. I know at one time they were the richest of all religious orders on this planet earth. No religion was so organized and had so much wealth as the Catholic Church. They might still be number one. I think they are. I can't think of anybody who could challenge them.

Can a Man Inherit Another Man's Mind and Purpose?

So, the same water that was supporting the boat was the natural habitat for the big fish, wasn't it? Mr. Fard said, "Do not let me catch any of you overweight in regards to living the life and weighing properly." So, he knew the dangers in the road, and he did his best to point them out to us. Do you believe a man can inherit another man's mind and purpose? Mr. Fard planned that I inherit his mind and purpose, and it has happened. And if he was living, he would say, "Follow him, not me!" Why? Because he would see himself reborn in a time of freedom for more opportunity and more understanding. He would actually make sajdah... I'm telling you. I did not say that to lift myself above him but to point to an extension. G_d created generations to produce bigger communities. With increase in numbers there also should be increase in productivity. That is how G_d wants it. So, if G_d extends another man's thinking that He chooses to protect and He allows all of it to be implanted in another one, it is to increase. It not to give the same measure. That is the reality. The man (Mr. Fard) is bigger now than he ever was, but in my works. Thank Allah!

I think that Mr. Fard intentionally wanted to present the picture of a seed that came from him and was planted in my father, and then my father gave birth to me. So, it is one, two, three, and you notice the picture that my father had taken (i.e., the Honorable Elijah Mohammed sitting with Imam W. Deen Mohammed standing next to him with the Qur'an in one hand and the other on the Honorable Elijah Mohammed's shoulder, and Mr. Fard's picture is on the wall), it shows three. He wasn't there, but his picture is shown. His picture is above ours. He's above us. My father is sitting on the throne, my arm or hand is on his shoulder, and the other hand is holding the big Qur'an, meaning that my ascent is from my father's leadership. Upon his leadership is my ascent and my life is not his life. My life is what I'm holding (the Qur'an).

The Heart Remembers the Life

It might be different than the way I see it. I say it exactly the way I see that picture. Mr. Fard's picture is all about the Qur'an. You look at the man, he's looking at the Qur'an. So, the point is not Mr. Fard. The point is the Qur'an. That is what he is saying with his picture that he's letting them see. He's saying, "The importance is not me. It is the Qur'an". And my father is the one who was left in charge, with authority and my right hand is upon his shoulder, meaning my authority is supported by his balance. The shoulder is the balance, like the old scale. So, my authority is consciously in his balance, but subconsciously in the Qur'an. The Qur'an is in my left hand, meaning my natural behavior holds the Qur'an. *"And He revealed it upon his heart"*. The brain is the right, the heart is the left, awareness and memory. The heart symbolically represents the memory. The heart doesn't lead the body. The mind leads the body, but the heart remembers the life. It says, "You're getting ready to get in trouble once again, or you're doing the right thing now. This is wonderful!" That is the heart and mind, because the heart is going on the right and memory is not going on events taking place and decisions, that is for the mind. But the mind that is ignorant or disrespectful of the heart, it ignores or forgets to consult the heart.

They say the first sign of life in a living body, human being's fetus, embryo, or whatever, is the beating of the heart. That is the first sign of life. The Bible says, *"The first shall be last and the last shall be first."* So, your heart is first. It is the first sign of life in the human being. Now it is the first, but it is going to be the last. So, the heart is going to be the last. The mind is going to mess up the world and burden the world so much until in the end of the world, it's going to be the innocent heart that is going to receive the light and take the burden off of the world. *"He revealed it upon his heart"* And if we understand it correctly, Jesus is the heart. Scripture says, *"Behold, I come quickly!"* The mind comes gradually. Praise be to Allah!

Jesus Born of the Heart

Some symbols they show where they have Jesus Christ, and they have the heart projected out of his body. When it says he's born of a woman that's what it means. He's born of the heart, not like Adam is born of the brain. It is a beautiful reality when we get into the reality of Scripture. Now we know the Qur'an, itself, one of its names is Al Bayyan, and it means the clear evidence; and it says that, *"They shall see it with clear vision"*, with a vision or perception by the eye that will not leave any room for any doubt, pronounced in Qur'anic Arabic, *"Ainal yaqeen"*, a clear vision that's so certain, precise, so perfect that they will not have any doubt about what they're seeing.

Sitting at the Table of the Lord, Himself

This is happening right now, and I tell you it's amazing to me where we came from. Now, we're the ones sitting at the table of the Lord, Himself. He has prepared the table and the feast, and there are no big shots at the table. All these guys from the ghetto have been transformed new creatures with the heavenly light on high. It's amazing, it's true, it's justified, and it's the rational conclusion to come to. If it was somebody else who didn't come through what we came through, they would not be justified to be there like we're justified. So, justice supports us to be at the table. Truth and mercy, kindness from Allah justifies us being at this table. That is what sustains me, because I'm not the kind of guy that wants this kind of pressure or this high, special gift that Allah has prepared and given to us. I'm not the kind of person to feel comfortable with it. Every time I feel that somebody else should be there and maybe I shouldn't look at myself, the logic comes back, "Well, who else, if not you? Look at those people who were given five talents, those who were given three and look at what you have done who were given only two, the ability to see and think about what you're looking at, see and reflect. And you, because of your strong faith in a just and righteous G_d, you have stayed the course and grown stronger in faith year behind year. So, who else?" Nobody else!

The wonders for the end of time or the Last Day is that the hand maiden will give birth for her mistress of the house, the master's wife. So, who are we going to look for if not ourselves? That is the hardest thing in the end of time, for the victims of the world to accept as their reward, the place Allah has put us in. Most of them, when they hear me talk, their mind just locks, and they are afraid to think into this big dimension that I'm in. They can't believe it. It is not in them to believe it. "No, this can't happen to us, not this much!" But as long as we talk about how much we've been mistreated and put down, they are ready to shout all day and all night saying, "Yes, that is the truth, brother!" But what about this new reality we're in? This is the truth more than what you're agreeing with. There's a lot of exaggeration in what you're agreeing with.

I have sometimes thought that there are those who don't want me to live very long. They can't accept that, can't believe that I might be around here another fifty years or more. It's too much for their little, small minds. They don't have the patience to really try to connect logic to logic, go back and see how we got where we are now, put logic to logic. If you will do that, you'll accept the conclusion that we have as a reality for our existence, purpose, and future, right now. All you have to do is go back, see what our circumstances were and see how we turned to G_d, that we didn't even know the Bible's G_d, because they wouldn't let us read the Bible. So, we didn't know. We had no way of knowing who G_d was, but we knew there was justice somewhere, and that this world was designed by a just G_d, and He is the G_d of justice, and He doesn't approve of what has been done to us. That is what the slaves went on. And from that point, that circumstance, they got help. The more they protested, the more they resisted their mistreatment, the more they got help from white people and others, and finally a strong abolitionist movement was successful in getting slavery to be abolished, and we didn't stop there as a free people. We leaned upon our faith in G_d, and we knew that our need was to be educated, because we were denied education. So, we turned to education for a way to improve our life and qualify to meet the challenges of the white man's world. And we came all that way and received leader after leader that emphasized the need to qualify to be more competitive in this advanced world we live in, to have knowledge but also industry or jobs, employment, to increase our material strength in this world of the white man.

We continued that and our parents who didn't have any of these things would try to put their children in situations where they would be able to accomplish much more than they did and have much more to offer their children than those parents had to offer their children to do better. So, when you trace all that down to the present time and see how we lost that kind of help or thrust in our life given to us and encouraged by our parents, and we see some of us who didn't lose it in the Church, in the neighborhood, in the work force, and are still pushing forward trying to make it, haven't given up, still believe in a just G_d and growing in the system in spite of the bad look on the public scene; when they look at all of that, they then look at the kind of language that my father brought and how his son came out of that language. He is now in the circle of the greatest chiefs on this planet earth in religion, but also in government. If they follow the logic, it points to a conclusion, and that is that the spirit of these people who are helped by G_d and those who stay in the spirit that G_d blessed them with, they are the ones, now, who not only present themselves as downtrodden or their underclass race, but they're presenting themselves with a hope for themselves and America, and the world.

That is the reality today. If that's not enough to make them believe, they are not supposed to believe. They're supposed to be counted out. I don't worry about them, not at all. I love them and I'm going to keep doing my best to reach them, but their deaf ears don't bother me at all. I know I'm clear. The only thing that would make me feel thoroughly uncomfortable is if I would think these big crowds that are going the way of hell may overcrowd hell and may have to be pushed up to me somewhere. But the Scripture says hell will speak out and say, *"Are there anymore?"* So, we don't have to worry about that, do we?... It's my pleasure always to share my concerns, feelings, in Scripture, and understanding that Allah has blessed us with.

Jonah Ignored His Destiny

Actually, America is a spiritual public. You know that. We are a people based in faith. We are spiritual and the spiritual establishment they could not stomach Jonah. They ignored his destiny, and you know that is the reality today. Really, the establishment, they accept that we give up our future and let the commercial world feed on us. They accept that, but do you think they like it? Do you think they are happy with that? No, they don't like that at all. They don't appreciate our people who go after the perishable things in the world and don't make a really serious effort to elevate their souls, their inherent worth. So, when they see Obama and people like us who meet the challenge of this world and hold on to the mission to elevate the human worth, to lift the human person up as G_d wanted us to be lifted, when they see us struggling to do that and not giving up, they appreciate and value us so much. We are a big source of happiness and joy in their private lives, and I'm sure a lot of them are making it public knowledge or conversation when they meet each other, and I think that is what the Scripture is saying.

The biggest life in the water does not really like that people give up their destiny and care nothing about their purpose on earth or their purpose in life and just live for those things that are transitory, perishing, and all of the time going away. That is what keeps a lot of our people down. They think, "Oh, the world is against us, it is not ever going to be for us. The establishment, they do not care about us." But the reality is that they are hurt that you care nothing about your own life in humanity and give yourself away so cheaply. If you would just change the way you treat your own self, you'd find that they will be happy to welcome you into their situation, into their system. So, to me that is the message of Jonah being swallowed up by the whale and the whale could not even stomach him. "This guy is ignoring his mission! I do not want him in me!" He started repenting inside the whale and the whale said, "Hell, is that what you were guilty of? I can't stomach you! You've got to get out on your own! This is no free ride!"

The Gourd Plant Over Jonah's Head

Concerning the gourd, in the Qur'an, that Allah caused to grow over Jonah's head to shield him from the sun, his mental progression that is needed for the improvement of his life and the deliverance, eventually, of his life before G_d, Himself, is in the beginning starting out in its first stage where he is completely ignorant; and you know when you come suddenly out of darkness into light it hurts your eyes. You have to kind of cover your eyes, sometimes, because you have been for too long in the dark and in such thick, dense darkness that the light hurts your eyes. And when it says to cover his head, it means burning his mind. Now this is not the eyes out here, it is the mind's eye. It is under so much heat from the light of day and heat means, sometimes, pressure. Under a lot of heat means pressure coming from something. Here is this uneducated mind in the knowledge of the world system and how it exists and works. It is so much for him until G_d had to cause a gourd plant to grow up. Now a gourd plant is a plant that has a lot of seeds, but a lot of emptiness. It does not have much meat. You can take the meat out and it is loose and hollow. It is light and there's mostly seed in it. You take the meat out and you do not have much left, a big a hole.

Well, that is how an ignorant mind is. It is like a big, empty, gourd and it was once full of seeds before you emptied it, full of thoughts and ideas undeveloped, so many undeveloped seeds, so many undeveloped thoughts and ideas. So, you have more curiosity than anything else. Take the curiosity out and the head is empty. It has not put together much at all. But from that state of emptiness and ignorance, meaning empty-headed and full of curiosities, from that state G_d causes life to grow. And the life that grows from that gourd seed, it gives you shade that relieves your mind, gives it some relief while it is bombarded by so much knowledge and understanding that is in the light of the world. Do you know that song (*A Lovely Day*), "When I wake up in the morning, love, and the sunlight hurts my eyes... then I look at you and the world's alright with me"?

That gourd we're talking about gave shade, brought comfort to Jonah's mind, meaning even though you're just beginning to try to survive the light of the world, and your head is empty or you're ignorant in the knowledge of the world, but your head is filled with ideas that want to be developed, filled with thoughts that are curious. Curious thoughts, though that is your beginning, that alone will work to give you some understanding of what your circumstances are, how you are situated in this world filled with light or knowledge, a whole world filled with light and knowledge and a great system that challenges you so much until it just puts you at a standstill to go forward in it. But your effort is there even though you are in that situation where your head is empty except for curiosities, undeveloped seeds that don't help except for curiosity. Your effort to survive in those circumstances will produce, start some kind of logic to grow inside of your life to support your life.

So, this gourd plant, it gives some kind of logic, and its logic is to pull up on something, because it is too flimsy. It does not have enough strength by itself, so it pulls up on your body that G_d created. You did not design your body. So, that life that comes out of the earth is weak, empty, and not showing much promise, except as a lot of questions unanswered. But if you will let that life live in you and let it form a logic growing out of the earth, taking roots in the earth, and then growing up and using your own life as its support, now isn't that what we did when we didn't have any knowledge of the world? Didn't we use our own life as our support? We said, "I know this body is just like his! I know I'm a man just like he is! He called me a boy!" Now, that is that gourd plant, that logic is growing up on that body!

(The following is excerpted from our last meeting with Imam W. Deen Mohammed, August 21, 2008):

Faith and Patience

We have to have faith and patience. You have to have faith and are at least righteous or do good deeds. But actually, the word is, righteous. In Arabic, it is, "saalehaat." Amelu means works and saalehaat means righteous. But then times get difficult, and things try you. *"Wa tawaasau bil haq, and they give mutual support for truth"*, not just by yourself. *"Wa tawaasau"* means you're working in association with others to promote truth, and the word for truth is, "Sidq", and another word. In the common, spoken language of Arabic, "Haq" is not really truth. It is reality. It is much stronger than truth, because truth may be in your opinion, or may be as you view the situation. That's the truth. But "haq", means universal truth supports it, reality supports it. Then patience in Qur'anic Arabic, it is pronounced, *"Wa tawaasau bis sabr."* Don't try to take the burden on by yourself. Again, it is, *"Wa tawaasau,* work with other people, in association with other people".

If you look at the four, *"Except those who have faith and righteous deeds"*, so far, it is addressing the individual. Though the individual is identified with the believers, it is really addressing the individual. So, faith is an individual, or personal matter. That's your faith, and your deeds are an individual matter. We don't go to G_d in twos, or in a group to answer for our deeds. Individually, you will come up before Him, bare and alone, stripped of all pretenses. That is what it means, bare and alone, by yourself. You have to answer for yourself. But the second two address the person who is going to work for or live for this in association with others. We don't find reality by ourselves, on our own. We find reality by interacting with others and having experience in a broad field, and then once that is found, you should identify with those people who support truth and reality and be patient. Only in Allah's good time will He cause truth to prevail. So, we might be working hard for it, but it might not be the time for Allah. For Allah, it might not be this time. We have to wait until He blesses us with His Help, though we promote it.

Look at how much truth and reality has been advanced by philosophers, scientists, over all these generations and centuries, a few thousands of years. Maybe more than that, but at least for 2, 3, 4 or 5 thousand years it has been going on. But look how slow truth was coming to be accepted. It is only now it looks like to me. It is only now that it looks like the time for truth to be really accepted. It is now. I'm not talking about truth of the Qur'an, or truth that the Qur'an brought. We know many Muslims accepted it. The truth that Jesus Christ brought many Christians accepted it. But our publics are still divided when it comes to supporting whether it is truth and reality.

One Day the Gates of Abundance Will Be Opened

But it is okay in the work area for industry. It is okay for certain restricted disciplines, like the disciplines of science that respect reality. But when it comes to applying it, politically, no. Look how much truth and reality is violated by these campaigns and the people who so-call analyze the campaign, and what they're saying and doing. Look how much they violate truth and reality working on the prejudices of the people, but that is where truth and reality is supposed to come home. It comes home in the life of the human society, because that is where Satan exploits the interest of society and tempts that interest to follow his advice, because it seems to promise little and give them a lot. Where G_d promises us a lot and we're not patient and you say, "He's giving me little". He promises you a lot, but you may get only a little, and you might have to get it and be satisfied with that, be patient with that, generation after generation. However, He promises that one day the gates of abundance will be opened if you have patience, if you would just be patient.

"Is It Not for the Creator to Both Create and Command?"

The Bible has a picture of Job, and it means job. It is not spelled, J-o-b-e. It is spelled, J-o-b that is pronounced job, not Jobe, and it says job, not Jobe. But that is the way they designed the language to open your eyes, if you are thinking and make connections. So actually, there is no person sitting, being tried. That is the activity that earns income, benefits and comforts, and no matter who the people are or the person, they have to understand that won't come to you on your time, or when you think it should. The Lord Who created the whole material world, He's the One Who oversees it. *"Is it not for the Creator to both create and command?"* That is the Qur'an.

The Bible says Job was a man of conscience, so he could not accept to get money any kind of way. He had to get it and feel morally comfortable with how he got it. His friends were getting it. So, obviously, what it is saying is that this man suffers because he just won't do anything to get over. Even his own wife told him, "Why don't you curse that G_d and go on and die? If He cared, you would be better off!"

Stages of Development Tied to Patience

But the stages of development, how you will succeed in the world are tied to how you will succeed with your own development, and they both require faith in G_d, commitment to truth and decency, and then the will to suffer bad situations and not be tempted to relieve the situation by doing wrong. No, you have to have patience. There is no time limit on how long you have to be patient. G_d knows best!

"The patience of Job", especially church people and older people, I used to hear that language when I was a child, from them. They used to say, "He's got the patience of Job!" Job, faith, and patience, go together in the Bible and Qur'an, faith and belief, or faith and good deeds. You see, that is what goes before patience. Why should I be bothered that much with patience, if I don't care how I behave or conduct myself, or what kind of moral choices I make? I'm not even interested in moral choices. So, patience is not something that concerns me.

When Moses went up in the mountain, it is both in the Qur'an and the Bible, the Bible before the Qur'an, but the Qur'an did not ignore it, or the revelation to the Prophet did not leave it out. The people of Moses came from a land that had big achievements in the visible world. Their achievements were visible, that is, their achievements were physical, and material, not just spiritual. They were spiritual, too, if we understand it, very strong spiritual achievements they had managed, the ancient Egyptians under that particular pharaoh, in the time of that one, and other pharaohs, too.

The people of Moses were used to just seeing things where nobody had to have a plan to get bread. Egypt had plenty of bread. Nobody had a plan to have comforts. Egypt had plenty of comforts. But here you are leaving Egypt, going out on your own, and it is going to require faith, good deeds and patience, and a commitment to truth and reality. While Moses was up there (on the mountain), they lost faith in him, lost patience. They couldn't keep patience. He was up in the mountain seeking G_d for light and understanding for them that would benefit the society, but they couldn't have patience with him.

"We Want It Quick!"

So, they showed haste. "We want it quick! He's up there. He's a holy man! We don't have time for that kind of leader! Aaron, you know how to direct this thing. Build, make for us a golden calf. We want a society of wisdom. We don't need this special guidance that he's looking for. We want a society of wisdom like Egypt has. So, make us a society of wisdom and do it quickly", because the golden calf was a young calf. That language says it was very youthful and quick. In Arabic, it is, "Ajlan" from, "Ajala", from which we get the words, "To hasten, go fast". It did not say, "golden cow". It said a golden calf. A calf is a baby, young, ready to rip and run. So, it is not talking about what you know. What do we have? What kind of society have we been brought to? This was not like this, always, or when I was a boy. Now, we have a very fast-paced society, don't we? And we have fast food. Everything is fast. They want it just like that, and we have more corruption than we ever dreamed could come into our lives.

Pictures of What Is Going to Happen

So, these things are not pictures of something back there. They are pictures of what is going to happen as man multiplies and grows in wealth and comforts. Therefore, it is future oriented. The language is future-oriented, although that back there was nothing like what the language points to, because all the time that is going on, G_d's Promise is with the people. Actually, the Promise He made the first time was with the first man, Adam, when He told him, "All this is for you. I made it to yield its benefits to you." When He told Adam that, it was the first promise, then came His Promise to Abraham, because man went out on his own and made the world so difficult for a righteous person to live in.

Muhammed and Moses Couldn't Read Language of Secret Religion

So then, He makes His promise to Abraham, the second father, before He revealed to Moses. Moses is doing his part of the book, his Scripture. He's living his part of the Scripture. His people, they are living that part of the Scripture, but at the same time, the promise is still hanging over their heads, G_d's Promise. They wanted to get out of Egypt and have independence, so they could live like the Egyptians lived. So, "We're not interested in this conversation that you want to have with your G_d! We know how to get over! We want to get over like Egypt got over. Aaron, can you help us?" And he could. That is why G_d gave Moses, Aaron, because he could read the wisdom of the Pharaoh, or of ancient Egypt. That is why G_d gave him to Moses as an assistant, or as a helper, so that when he had to deal, or meet the challenge of Pharaoh's high priests, and those who were high in the secret, or hidden knowledge (that is what it is), he had Aaron to help him. Like Prophet Muhammed, Moses couldn't read Scripture. He could not read the language of secret religion, or the wisdom.

So, they said, *"Make us a golden calf!"* Now, if they asked that question, they knew the wisdom existed. They were not an ignorant society for they knew that he was the most advanced in that skill. That is why they asked him to do it. Then what he says to them, in reply, exactly what I just said. He said, "Give me your earrings," meaning "give me the wisdom that you hear that rings a bell for you." You have a lot of wisdom here in this gathering, or in this community of faithless Jews." They were a people of no faith. They did not have faith. Do you see any time that they leaned back on their faith? When? They never leaned back on their faith. All the crisis in their life and you never hear, in the Scripture, that the Jews cried out upon their faith.

(After some time, rather than preparing a meal for us, Imam Mohammed thought it would be best to treat us to a meal at one of his favorite restaurants near his home. When we settled in at the restaurant, he shared these reflections with us):

Satan Is the Movement for World Dominance

The scheme of Satan is nothing but world dominance. He is the movement for world dominance. The scheme of Satan is to separate the people from a sense of natural growth into excellence, because people who believe that they have a very strong and deep respect for human life, and the work of Satan cannot succeed with you having that kind of respect. He wants to exploit human life, even corrupt human life if it will assist him rising into a position of dominance. So, when Satan says, *"Since You have embarrassed me like this, putting this mud man, mortal, above me, I'm going at him from the left, right, front, and from the rear"*. That is a cross.

Secularism Masters Man's Essential Nature

Now, what does that cross say? It says a lot of things. It says right off, "I'm going to block him. I'm going to fix him so he can't go East, West, North or South". He won't be able to move. It will hold him at a standstill. But what it also says is, "I'm going to master his essential nature!" That is universal, East, West, North, South. That is what secularism does. It takes away the universal and presents human beings not in connection with human beings rising to civilization, and not in connection with their inherent essence that is universal. So, the people are taken from the knowledge of their best teachers, philosophers, and educators, and put under a new knowledge or new schooling, or education, that does no more than take G_d out of education. But it also takes the human person, as a focus for the unity of mankind and as a focus for human beings' common excellence away, so the human being can be led in directions that human persons with that knowledge would not be open to be led that way. And that is what it is designed to do, to cause you to discard belief that G_d designed the natural pattern of human life. When you remove G_d as the explanation, what do you have left? Only your teachers who claim that they are the ones who discovered all these things, the knowledge and whatever, which is true. But they could not do it without following the pattern that G_d created.

Sin Didn't Exist Until Satan Exposed Man to His Capacity to Sin

The soul has the capacity for taqwa, respect for things that the intelligence recognizes as being due respect, taqwa and fujur. Taqwa, is the tendency on the part of the soul to promote respect for that which intelligence recognizes as a value and is due respect. The fujur, the other half, is the tendency in the soul to question things, and it's the tendency in the soul to also cause the soul to be seen as having a capacity for injury, or harm. So, it has a capacity for respect and the highest respect is what we give G_d, the Creator in religion, reverence for G_d. In Al-Islam, as you know, there is no such thing as original sin, meaning we don't believe that human life comes here corrupt or sinful. New life, the innocent baby, can be displeased and can even be angered, and then it wants to hurt, and it might even strike out against its own mother, hit her. That is evidence of the tendency in the soul, the newborn, to express rejection and express a desire to hurt or harm. But that is not saying that the child is evil. The child just has a capacity and a tendency to express disapproval, and if hurt, to want to also hurt or do harm.

And if Allah blesses us to understand the Qur'an that addresses the innocence of human life, it explains evil as something that Satan, himself, opens to people or man. *"Don't let him seduce you out of your original goodness, righteousness or innocence as he did your parents."* He appealed to their desire and to their logic, their reasoning, and influenced them to accept his reasoning. And the effect of that on his victim is described in these words: *"And he showed them their sin"*. So, they had no knowledge of a capacity in them to commit sin until the Devil, Satan, influenced them to follow his reasoning. When they followed his reasoning, then he exposed them to their capacity to sin, to do wrong, to become corrupt. His power over you is only the power to invite you.

So, their sin was that they were weak for Satan's suggestions. There was a weakness in them for Satan's suggestions, and that is explained as a tendency to go the way of harm, or to put ourselves in harm's way, a tendency, not a predisposition. So, sin in Adam is seen as a slip from the original nature, that an appeal can be made to the human person promising him that "You're going to have more comforts in your life, more relief in your life, and you're going to have more freedom to become greater, richer, more productive, more knowledgeable, wiser, etc." This is because it is also the nature of the human person to want to be free from misery, or to have a more comfortable life. The opening is there for Satan, if he can get past the rational and moral defenses, to appeal directly to his pleasure principle. That is what Satan is skillful in doing. So, it says Adam had no intent to go wrong. He slipped from his natural disposition.

Adam and Eve All In One Personage As Tendencies

It's quite different from the Bible. It suggests the woman, his wife, his mate, as the doorway through which Satan was able to reach the heart of the man, Adam, which has some truth to it, because the woman there is not a person. We're discussing knowledge, principles, tendencies, etc., in nature. It is not talking about the woman as a separate person, because after all, they are all in one entity and G_d caused them to separate, and they became male and female. Actually, it is talking about your sentiments, your skin, your feelings, etc. So, he did not go directly to Adam's intelligence. He did not speak to his rational mind, because if he had, he would not have ever gotten in. He spoke to the joint. Believe me, though it appears to be clean language, the focus for bringing man down, or the focus on his weak points, or his vulnerability is his sex urges. That is a powerful appetite! So, the first thing he wanted was the man's heart, and when he gets that he reduces him down to his hard. It is also pronounced, heart. We don't articulate it that well. It is not normal to articulate it so well. Both words sound the same. So, he appeared to the woman. He did not appear to the man, did he? He appeared to the woman as a snake. Now, what looks like a snake in the structure of the man? Adam had no homosexual tendency yet, so that was for a female, not for him. "I want your love, so make it to become as cold as I am", as cold as a serpent.

The responsibility of these intelligent people who say they are our leaders is to promote understanding of the nature, natural urges, and how to get control. That is their responsibility. Mr. Fard said, "What is the duty of a civilized person? To teach the uncivilized."

Man Grows More and More Into Human Form

There have been many leaders like me in the past. The world wasn't ready to support their growth like it is ready to support my growth. Man grows more and more into human form to deal with problems, but also, the world grows. The world is growing, too, in response to his growth, but also, in response to restraints on that growth. So, the world is growing, too, to accommodate what G_d put in man to solve problems and bring the world together at one time in the history, or in the future. So, in the time of the great leaders and our Prophet included, the world had grown very little, but the Prophet had grown a lot. So, they recognized him in small measures, small dimensions, and when he was gone, their light started going out.

The Christ Formula

Jesus said, *'Give me your tired, your weary, your worn-out people that you can't use.* You cannot use them, so why don't you give them to me, and I will take them out of your hair. They will not be troubling you anymore." And that is what Mr. Fard said to the United States government. "Give me these people who are dissatisfied with you and not content to be American, black citizens. They are defying that. They want to be their own, independent people, so let me take them out of your hair." He did not design any new plan for himself, or anything. He saw the plan in the Bible, Christ Jesus... You see, he understood Christ Jesus in the Bible, and he understood what it meant. He understood the formula. It is a formula for bringing about a certain effect. Convert people and eventually bring them back to their originality, that is the plan. But Christianity is so complicated that most Christians cannot get the benefit. However, Mr. Fard proved that it works, because he produced me. He set the stage to produce me, and this is real. So, it is a formula.

The Christ formula existed even before Christ. It is no new thing, but the New Testament introduces it anew. However, it was not just in the Bible. It was in different parts of the world. They have this secret knowledge of how to put or make sure that the child is born in a sincere, obedient environment to G_d, whatever they call the G_d, and then condition his mind to be independent, so that he thinks independently and give him support from the members, whatever the congregation is, give him support from the best of the members to be independent. And as he grows older, this influence takes him over. Eventually, he comes to realize that he cannot fulfill his soul's needs without following that pattern that they set for him or living in that pattern and proceeding with his life upon that pattern. So, it works. Where the other members are accepting things on face value he is not. He is conditioned not to accept things on face value.

I Am "Wall Ace"

They were trying to produce a leader who would be of and in purity, and it works, but it does not work all the time. That is why Jesus is named, Esaa, from the Arabic verb, asaa, meaning "perhaps, maybe" and it said his name is, Esaa, which alludes to "perhaps'". It does not happen all the time. That is why in the story of Zachariah and Mary, they threw lots, first, didn't they? It means it was chance, and then they gave the child (Mary) into the charge of Zachariah. Zachariah is a play on purity, put him in the charge of purity, so she would not be defiled. 'Esaa is the letters ain, seen, and then the letter ya. 'Asaa is the letters ain, seen, and ya, but you pronounce it, asaa, the same letters; and if you put the kasrah under the letter, 'ain, it becomes, 'Esaa. That is his name.

So, the root meaning hasn't changed. The nature is in all of us, but how it is brought out, the formula for bringing it out works most of the time, but not all the time. That is why he (Mr. Fard) named me, Wallace. Wallace means a stranger. I traced it back to its origin. Wallace, also means, a deceiver. He did that just in case I didn't come right, I would be a deceiver, either way he is naming me. If I am a deceiver, the name still is good for me, because I am a deceiver.

I did not let them know where I was going when I accepted to be the leader, on February 26, 1975. I couldn't let them know where I was going. They would not have go with me. I gave them all a lot of language to hold them. I knew Mr. Fard had that knowledge, so I had to give them a language that would hold them. So, I had to wean them off one trick with another trick. So, I was, Wallace, wasn't I? I am Wallace. But right now, I am "Wall Ace".

They Buried the Treasure Under the Wall

They buried the treasure (for the orphans) under the wall, and I am the "Wall Ace". Now, Mr. Fard couldn't do that, but G_d could do it! My father, he was talking to me one day about Mr. Fard naming me and he said, "He did not call you like we call you, Wallace". When he said it, it didn't sound like that. It sounded more like Waris." The name, Warithudeen, I accepted it after Mr. Muhammed Abdullah, my old friend who passed, told me, "Your name is not Wallace". Now, he is telling me what Mr. Fard named me. He said, "He did not name you, Wallace. He named you, Waris. Now, in Pakistan, the letter 'Th' is 'S', so, he named you Waris.'" As soon as he said it, I remembered what my father said and I said, "My father probably forgot the "R". He said Walis and Mr. Fard was probably saying, "Waris". That is how it came about. I respect him so much until when he named me that, I accepted it. When he told me that was my name, I accepted it, so I started using Warithudeen. All of us are Warith. G_d said He made us Warithun, the plural of Warith. He made us to be inheritors on the earth. So, we are all supposed to inherit the Christ nature. We are all supposed to inherit the original Muslim nature. The original Muslim nature and Christ nature are the same. The Christ nature, in Qur'an, is the original, Muslim nature, and in the Bible, it is the Christ nature. One refers to purity, Christos, and the Muslim nature refers to purity, too, by explanation. But it just says, peaceful nature. Muslim means of peaceful nature, and what does the Bible say about the peacemaker?"

Everything Is by Inheritance

Giving the picture of the genesis of man, in the Qur'an, G_d says, *"Surely I am forming in the earth a khalifah"*, meaning coming from one to the next. Khalifah, he is an inheritance, he, himself. He inherits directly from G_d by nature of his hunger for G_d and understanding. His own nature gets from G_d what G_d wants to communicate to him. Then when he gets it, Qur'an says, *"Tell Me your names, if you know."* They (the angels) couldn't tell Him. They said, "We don't know. We can't do this, only You, G_d". Then He told Adam, *"Tell them their names"* and when Adam performed that responsibility that G_d put on him, the angels made sajdah to Adam, not the human. Now, from that point on everything is by inheritance. Continuing that process is by inheritance, because nobody short of the destiny has enough knowledge to bring it on without the process of inheritance.

The Name Wallace ("Wall Ace") Not Accidental

So, He (G_d) has made you khalifahs in the earth, plural, not one, inheritors in the earth. You have heard of the orphans as inheritors of what is under a wall, and in the Qur'an, the wise man came to the wall. He recognized that the inheritance was under that wall, so he would not tear it down. My name is Wallace ("Wall Ace") and that was not accidental.

The inheritance was supposed to be for the ones who didn't have parents to take care of them and oversee their life, and to see that they had what G_d established to be given to all human beings. There was nobody to take care of that for them, so they are orphans. That's the Prophet and that's us (African Americans) as a people.

Allah Expanded the Prophet's Breast

Allah expanded the Prophet's breast, opened up his breast, the chest area, expanded it so that there would be more room there for the whole of mankind. It means his heart. He expanded his breast, so there would be enough room for the whole of mankind inside his heart, or inside his breast, and relieve from him the burden which weighed down the khalifah. His back is symbolic of the khalifah in him, which weighed down his back. Now, usually men carry burdens, heavy things, upon their back. So, that is to give the picture of a poor person who's regarded or treated as a burden bearer. The world has weighed him down.

So, the world has weighed him down and what burdens his back, also, specifically for him in his life as a person in the history is the strain on his mind to bring the message to his people in Arabia, and also to the world, of the liberation of mankind; not one people, not one man, but the whole of humanity. So, he's carrying the weight of that desire to bring liberation to the whole of the people on this earth, because they all were slaves to their masters, to their personal interest, slaves to ideologies. But once the universal message comes that has as its recipient the soul of mankind, all the people, then he knew that the world would be a much better world, and the world would be on its way to the destiny.

The Full Light For All Mankind

Therefore, G_d had to first, open his heart, expand the room in his heart to accommodate all people. That shows a progression for the Prophet. It means he was so sincere and wanted to help people. First, he saw the misery of the Arabs, and that's what sent him up the mountain to the cave to call on a Higher Reality. Now, to go further, He has to open up his heart to the whole of mankind, not just the Arabs, not just to the suffering people. So, when that was done, the burden was taken off his back, and he was found an orphan.

The Qur'an says, *"Didn't We find you an orphan straying"*, worrying, about the Arabs, and didn't We find you straying, thinking the Jewish accomplishments for the religious community in Jerusalem was where you should begin? You should begin at the site of the Ka'bah, the symbol that represents the full light for all mankind. Your nature is cheated, so didn't We find you groping, and We said, *'Now We're going to turn you to a Qiblah that will please you'?"* Well, that need in his soul is typical of the need in the human soul, period!

Not Awakened to Their Created Purpose

Chapter seven of the Qur'an says that the Prophet released them from the yokes, and it didn't name any particular people, did it? It didn't say Arabs, blacks. That's because the whole of mankind is treated as slaves, and who enslaves them? Their own souls enslave them, because their own souls have not been awakened to the purpose for which G_d created them on the planet earth. The Christ principle is human innocence, and that is what you need to receive the Light of G_d for all mankind, for no particular people. The opening chapter in the Qur'an addresses the mentality that focuses on itself and excludes the rest of mankind. It says, *"In the Name of G_d, Allah, the G_d, the Gracious, the Compassionate, or the Merciful Benefactor, the Merciful Redeemer"*. Then it says, *"The praise is due to G_d, the Lord of all the worlds"*, not the Lord of Israel. The Bible is filled with "the Lord of Israel, Lord of Israel". The Lord of all the worlds, that is sent to the man whose heart is open to the whole of mankind, and it is said of Jesus Christ in the New Testament, *"In my father's house are many mansions."* Just add to that, *"And He found you drooping, an orphan, with your back burdened, weighed down, and He opened your chest to receive the whole of humanity"*, not the children of Israel, who are going to be called the chosen and the only begotten, and the rest are going to be called Gentiles and adopted children. This is a new language. The real Lord is the Lord of all people, not just one people.

One Day the Treasure Is Going to Be Found Under the Wall

So, Prophet Muhammed, himself, was found an orphan. In the early days of this country's industrial development, in their homes, Christians used wallpaper, especially those who could afford it. The wallpaper is the language of Christianity, which shows that they had some understanding that the wall that protects and holds in, the same wall separates and keeps out. One day the treasure is going to be found under those walls, and then the separation will be just, and the enclosures will be just. The connections will be everywhere. People will be connected all over the world though living in their separate habitats. That's the time right now. You can see it as plain as day.

Epilogue

The Treasure Is Still There

So, for most Thursdays, for nearly four years, we sat in the quiet of Imam W. Deen Mohammed's home, notebooks in hand, digital recorders on, hearts open, ears straining to catch not just his words, but the pauses between them—the spaces where his spirit spoke just as clearly. These conversations were never hurried. They unfolded in a purposeful manner: deliberate, layered, intimate. And though his passing has left his home silent and empty, those Thursdays still live with me. I often find myself reflecting on the hurried car trips that we made from Wisconsin to the south suburbs of Chicago to confer with him. It's not habit. It's memory pulling at the sleeve of the present. People ask me what he was like in those moments, away from the microphones, the gatherings, the public expectations. My answer is simple: he was consistent. The same man you heard at the podium was the man who sat across from us sharing his commentary, Scriptural insights, and also his friendship. He was always thinking—always seeing deeper than most. But what stood out most was how often he chose humility over spectacle, substance over shine.

One Thursday (as I mentioned earlier), he shared with us a passage from our holy book, the Qur'an—one you may already know. It's about the Prophet Moses, who vows to travel far and wide searching for *"the junction of the two seas"* (the treasure), who finally meets a wise man who helps him to discover it buried beneath a crumbling wall, an inheritance for two orphaned boys who lived in the town that had just rejected them. In explaining to us who these two orphaned boys were the Imam said, "That's the Prophet and that's us. That is us as a people." So, we've got treasure—deep treasure—but most of us don't know it, or don't know where to dig. That's how the title of this book came to me. "The Treasure Under the Wall" is more than a metaphor. It's a map. The wisdom the Imam shared wasn't for us alone. It belongs to you too—to all who are searching, who feel a stirring in their soul that there's more to faith, more to life, more to understand. He never claimed to be the treasure, but he knew its value.

This book isn't a monument to Imam W. Deen Mohammed—it's a window into a way of seeing, a way of being. I hope you felt that as you turned these pages. I hope, like me, you found yourself nodding, pausing, maybe even whispering "yes" under your breath when something clicked inside you. But most of all, I hope this isn't the end. I hope you return to the conversations. I hope you gather with others and ask the same questions we (Morocco, Al-Ghani and I) asked on those Thursdays. I hope you become curious enough, patient enough, brave enough to start digging for the treasure under the wall. And remember, Imam W. Deen Mohammed is the "Wall Ace"! Thanks for sitting with us!

Ronald B. Shaheed

Index

Culture, 12, 64, 73, 87, 133, 158, 173, 180, 198, 202 262, 264, 299, 303-5, 309, 312, 317-8, 328, 334, 338-9, 347, 364, 378, 413, 427, 442, 494

Dawn, 183, 318, 394, 431-3, 449, 450, 457

Dawning, 117-8, 199, 480,

Day of Judgment, 371

Day of Religion, 384, 494

Delilah (see Samson), 248-9, 250

Desert, 81,83-4, 103, 111, 140, 173, 226, 284, 325, 435

Destiny, 22, 79, 85-7, 109, 113,165, 167-8, 170-1, 175, 182, 185, 222-3, 270, 330, 339, 344, 347, 364-7, 390, 411, 446, 448, 488, 498-9, 502, 514, 525-6

Dhikr, 47, 81, 225, 379, 418

Diabetes, 325

Donkey, 42, 82-3, 85, 160, 246, 326, 391-2

Door, 8, 34, 58, 67, 108, 175, 178, 251, 266, 304, 323, 325, 344, 373, 401, 438-9, 441, 488-9, 506

Dream/s, 22, 30, 291, 364, 475

Dunya/Dunyaa, 241-2

Dust, 96, 142, 153, 230, 268, 274, 313, 360, 397, 407, 416, 435, 447, 452, 462, 483

Eden, 206

Encrypt, 326-7

Enlightenment, 87, 109, 158, 180-1, 184, 196, 250-1, 270, 291, 299, 322, 403, 431-3, 443, 454

Feet, 94, 140, 142, 179, 193, 201, 210, 227, 230, 274, 318, 338, 342, 358, 386, 433, 483-4

Feathers, 84, 227, 241-2

Fig, 81, 131, 183-4, 226, 334-5

Figment, 184, 226, 334-5

Fifth Column, 304

Finger/s, 81, 133, 225, 333-4, 360, 379, 391

Five Senses, 63, 110, 230-1, 304, 360, 372-3, 378, 430-1, 439, 507

Foundation, 127, 142, 166, 227, 260, 415, 472

Frankenstein, 302-3, 305, 307, 309, 310-1

Ganglia, 197, 283, 345, 434

Garden (Jannah), 62, 84, 120-1, 123-4, 171, 197, 204, 247, 268, 291-2, 325, 330, 335, 383, 435, 446, 449, 450, 505

Genes, 37, 282-3, 314, 363, 383, 434

Genesis, 31, 37-8, 73, 120, 138, 173, 178, 198, 237, 264, 312, 376, 403, 435, 525

Genetic, 282-5, 363, 383, 434

Gog, 307-8

Golden Calf, 200-1, 519, 520

Golden Fleece, 148

Pillar/s, 122, 165

Plant/s, 26, 69, 99, 190, 221-5, 230, 243, 258, 295, 335, 351, 390, 412, 448, 498, 515-6

Plantation/s, 12, 13, 73-4, 88, 384, 397

Principle/s, 121-2, 161-2, 210, 289, 375, 444, 522, 527

Prometheus, 262, 320

Psyche, 22, 94, 179, 256, 423, 443, 451

Psychology, 52, 65, 255, 314-5, 325-6, 367, 392, 423 461, 471, 482, 485

Qiblah, 419, 469, 527

Quraish, 161, 181, 436

Race, 45, 65, 96, 165, 208, 214, 268, 286, 336, 354, 376, 387, 395, 406, 415, 428, 456, 513

Racism, 29, 171, 214, 384, 399, 402-2, 441, 489

Rain, 17, 140, 232, 308, 315, 385, 429, 431, 457

Ramadan, 23, 122, 290, 375, 423, 430

Rapper/s, 107, 328-9, 358, 300

Resurrection, 48, 148, 205, 278, 361 398, 400, 446, 504, 506

Rich Man, 321 324-5

Ritual/s, 103, 177, 111, 341, 378, 388

Ritualism,311

Rod,197,202

Ruh, 257, 290

Sabeelillah (The Path of G_d), 149, 357, 359

Saints, 50, 149, 184, 350, 411, 499

Salt, 186, 208, 324

Salt Water, 324

Scholar/s, 77, 104, 129, 135, 168, 199, 210, 218, 243, 248, 256, 268, 389, 429, 430

Scriptural Reasoning, 113, 365

Seal/s, 115-6, 329, 361

Sealed, 126

Secular, 148, 150, 220-1, 232-3, 241, 357, 404, 440

Secularism, 149, 332, 521

Seers, 42, 140, 258, 342, 352, 450, 452

Seven, 9, 18, 63, 67, 89, 116, 238, 244, 248-9, 301, 360, 449, 452, 527

www.ingramcontent.com/pod-product-compliance
Lightning Source LLC
Chambersburg PA
CBHW050226270326
41914CB00003BA/588